Dictionary of
World Monasticism

Also by Steven Olderr and from McFarland

Symbolism: A Comprehensive Dictionary, 2d ed. (2012)

The Pan American Games / Los Juegos Panamericanos: A Statistical History, 1951–1999, bilingual edition / *Una Historia Estadística, 1951–1999, edición bilingüe* (2003; paperback 2009)

Reverse Symbolism Dictionary: Symbols Listed by Subject (1992; paperback 2005)

Dictionary of World Monasticism

STEVEN OLDERR

McFarland & Company, Inc., Publishers
Jefferson, North Carolina

ISBN (print) 978-1-4766-8309-6
ISBN (ebook) 978-1-4766-4087-7

Library of Congress and British Library
cataloguing data are available

Library of Congress Control Number 2020028164

Printed in the United States of America

McFarland & Company, Inc., Publishers
Box 611, Jefferson, North Carolina 28640
www.mcfarlandpub.com

For my brothers and sisters
in the Companions of St. Luke

CONTENTS

Preface

When I began my personal monastic journey 15 years ago, I was amazed to discover how much had been written about monastic life. The roots of monasticism may go back as far as 1700 BCE to ascetic practices in India, and it seems people have been scribbling about it ever since. Naturally enough, during all that time it developed its own distinct vocabulary.

Early in my formation I sought a dictionary of monastic terms only to discover that there were none. I started collecting terms to make a brief glossary for my own use and those of my Benedictine community and soon discovered why there were no existing dictionaries. Occasionally an author may include a brief glossary, but usually not. A word may be defined in the text or it may not be. Some words are in standard dictionaries, but when they are, they are not covered in any great depth. Much of what I wanted to know had to be pried out.

For example, St. Benedict famously defines four kinds of monks: cenobites, anchorites/hermits, sarabaites, and gyrovagues. Sarabaites are those monks without formation or an abbot, but you would not know that John Cassian and St. Jerome called sarabaites *remoboths* unless you read St. Jerome's *Letter 22*, or John Cassian's *Institutes*. Or that the Anglo-Saxons called sarabaites *sylfdemas* unless you read St. Aethelwold's translation of the *Rule of St. Benedict* from Latin into Anglo-Saxon together with the translation of Aethelwold's work into modern English by Jacob Riyeff. Four sources for one simple concept. The idea of doing an accompanying bibliography quickly was discarded.

Further, I found that for all the differences between Christianity, Buddhism, Hinduism, and other religions, there are many similarities in monastic practice and outlook. In many respects monasticism is as much about the human soul as it is a specific religion. Accordingly, I expanded my research beyond just Christian monasticism and sought to fill in gaps, and the result, some years later, is before you.

For the purposes of this dictionary, the concept of monasticism is given wide latitude. While many Christians would say celibacy is an absolute requirement, that has not always been the case. There were married Desert Fathers and monastics of the Celtic Church. In some Buddhist sects marriage is still permitted. Nestorian monks were for a time required to be married. To be picky, even the term *monastic* may be called into question. Its Greek root is *monos*, meaning single or alone. If we cleave to the original use, then one could argue that only anchorites and hermits should rightly be called monastics. This dictionary casts a wider net.

Some criteria that were used for inclusion herein:

- Vows
- Rules of life
- Organized formation

- Poverty
- Obedience—this is, both obeying and listening
- Celibacy
- Sanction of an established religion
- Discipline
- Monastic lifestyle (*conversatio morum suorum*)
- Historical interest

Not every entry in this work meets all these criteria, but all entries meet some of them. When there was a doubt, it was included in the interest of usefulness.

The Dictionary

~A~

A.A. The post-nominal initials of the Augustinians of the Assumption

abba An Aramaic word for "father," used for an abbot or spiritual father; used in the *Apophthegmata Patrum* as a title of respect for Desert Fathers

abbacy The dignity, estate, or jurisdiction of an abbot

abbas laicus *see* **lay abbot**

abbas miles *see* **lay abbot**

abbatia nullius dioecesis *see* **territorial abbey**

abbatial Of, like, or relating to an abbey, abbot, or abbess

abbatocomes *see* **lay abbot**

Abbaye Saint-Pierre de Solesmes *see* **Solesmes Abbey**

abbe; abbé From the Aramaic word *abba*. The name was originally used for commendatory abbots (abbés commendataires) authorized by a concordat between Pope Leo X and Francis I of France in the early 16th century, which gave the kings of France the right to nominate 255 of them. Since the mid–16th century, the title abbé has been used for all lower ranking clergymen in France and other French speaking areas. • *See also* **commendatory abbot**

abbess; mother superior; reverend mother; magistra; khenmo (Tibetan); upadhyayani (Tibetan) The female head of a monastic community • *See also* **prioress**

abbey A complex of buildings used by members of a Christian religious community under the direction of an abbot or abbess • *See also* **monastery; territorial abbey**

abbey lubber A term of contempt for an able-bodied idler who lived off the charity of religious houses; sometimes applied to monastics themselves

abbey nullius *see* **territorial abbey**

abbey town; nun town; temple town A town that grew up around an abbey, nunnery, or temple, housing those lay people who worked for the monastic house. At first, monastic superiors might exercise a great deal of control over abbey towns, caring for roads and bridges, controlling trade, courts of justice, and appointing civic officials. Gradually, however, the towns would gain autonomy.

abbeystead The site of the abbey; an estate owned by an abbey

abbot; fangzhang (Chinese); zhuchi (Chinese); khenpo (Tibetan); chuji (Korean) The male head of an abbey or monastic community; one of a class of bishops whose sees were formerly abbeys. In some Buddhist traditions, the abbot is usually chosen by a vote of the monastics in a monastery; in others, Thailand for example, the abbot is chosen by the lay community. • *See also* **commendatory abbot; prior; territorial abbot**

abbot general The head of the Order of Canons Regular of Prémontré

abbot nullius *see* **territorial abbot**

abbot nullius dioeceseos *see* **territorial abbot**

Abbot of Russia A nickname of St. Sergius of Radonezh

abbot president The head of the English Benedictine Congregation

abbot primate An official who is the coordinator of Roman Catholic Benedictine communities but has little authority to manage their affairs. The office was established by the pope in 1893.

Abelard, Peter (1079–1142) French Benedictine monk, abbot, scholastic philosopher, theologian, and logician. While a brilliant teacher and academic, he had a difficult personality and a checkered career. In 1115 or 1116, he became the tutor of Héloïse d'Argenteuil, the niece of the secular canon Fulbert, began an affair with her and she became pregnant. In an effort to protect his career prospects, he married her secretly, but in his anger, Fulbert publicly disclosed it. Abélard sent her away to the convent at Argenteuil in order to protect her from her uncle. Fulbert then arranged for a band of men to break into Abélard's room one night and castrate him. At this point, Abélard became a monk at the monastery of St. Denis, near Paris and made Héloïse take vows as a nun even though she felt she had no calling to the religious life.

In the Abbey of St. Denis, Abélard returned to his difficult ways, picked quarrels, was criticized for some of his teachings, and was asked to leave. In 1125, he was elected abbot of St. Gildas de Rhuys, near Vannes, but the monks complained of his strictness and tried to poison him.

He then returned to teaching and writing and again gained wide public popularity, but again ran afoul of the authorities, notably St. Bernard of Clairvaux, and was excommunicated in 1141 by Pope Innocent II. Perpetual silence was imposed upon him and his books were ordered to be burned, but eventually a reconciliation was arranged with Bernard and the sentence of excommunication lifted. Abélard was placed under the aegis of Cluny where he was respected as a scholar.

He died and was buried at the priory of St. Marcel, near Chalon-sur-Saône, but his remains were secretly taken away and given to Héloïse, who in time herself came to rest beside them in 1163. Their remains were moved several times and are since 1817 are thought to be in the famous Père Lachaise Cemetery in eastern Paris where they are popular attraction.

Abhishiktananda *see* **Le Saux, Henri**

Abrikosova, Anna Ivanovna; Sienskaya, Ekaterina (1882–1936) Russian Roman Catholic religious sister, abbess, and translator. Born to a wealthy Russian Orthodox family, she family, she attended Cambridge University for three years then returned to Russia and married. During the next decade she travelled extensively with her husband and gained an interest in Roman Catholicism. In 1908, she converted and was received into the Roman Church, although for canonical reasons, she was considered a member of the Greek Catholic Church. In 1909, her husband also converted. In 1910, they returned to Russia and joined a group of Dominican tertiaries. In 1917, her husband was ordained a priest in the Greek Catholic Church, which according to canon law, allowed her to take monastic vows, and she joined the Dominican Order and then established the first community of Dominican Third Order Regulars in Russia.

After the Russian Revolution that same year, her convent was put under surveillance. Because of her work with the Papal Aid Mission to Russia, she was arrested and imprisoned in solitary confinement from 1924 to 1932. After her release for illness, she re-established relations with the remaining sisters of her order and was arrested again in 1933 and charged with "papal theocracy," plotting to assassinate Stalin, overthrow the Communists, re-establish the Romanov royal family, and restore capitalism as well. Re-imprisoned, she died of bone cancer.

absconce A lantern used in monasteries at night offices

acarya; precept master A senior Buddhist monastic who guides a novice in *Vinaya* (the collected rules for monks and nuns)

accedie *see* **acedia**

accidie *see* **acedia**

accusations That time at chapter meetings in which faults of discipline were revealed either by oneself or by others

acedia; accidie; accedie; akedia (Greek) A state of spiritual listlessness or torpor. It can lead to a state of being unable to perform one's duties in life. Its spiritual overtones make it related to but arguably distinct from depression. Acedia is not solely confined to monastics, but was originally noted as a problem among them, particularly those who maintained a solitary life.

acharya The leader of a Jain monastic order; in Zen Buddhist monasteries, a polite form of address for a monk with at least 5 years of training

Acoemetae *see* **Acoemeti**

Acoemeti; Acoemetae; Akoimetoi Fifth century Basilian monks founded by the monk Alexander the Acoemete in 425. They maintained continual choir services by dividing the communities into choirs, which relieved each other by turn in the church. The alternating three choirs were grouped by liturgical language: Greek, Latin, and probably Syriac. At one time they were quite influential and had monasteries with hundreds of members, but their influence gradually declined after 534.

Act for the Dissolution of the Greater Monasteries *see* **Dissolution of the Greater Monasteries Act**

Act for the Dissolution of the Lesser Monasteries *see* **Dissolution of Lesser Monasteries Act**

Act of Supremacy, 1534 Through this act, King Henry VIII declared himself head of the Church in England and members of religious orders were required to take the Oath of Supremacy to acknowledge Henry's status and to pledge their allegiance to him. Anyone who resisted him was deemed guilty of treason, but there was not a great deal of resistance to this in the English monastic community; they were, after all, Englishmen, and shared the common prejudice of their contemporaries against the politics being played out in Rome where the pope was a virtual prisoner of Charles V, the Holy Roman Emperor and nephew of Catherine of Aragon whom Henry was seeking to divorce for failing to produce an heir.

active community *see* **apostolic community**

active/contemplative community *see* **apostolic/contemplative**

ad succurrendum A benefactor of a monastery who, in old age or illness, joined that house as a full member to be cared for until death

adelphaton An annuity administered by monasteries which provided elderly laity with an allotment of food and other necessities in exchange for an initial cash payment or donation of property

administrator *see* **commendator**

advocate; advocatus ecclesiae In the Middle Ages, a lay person, generally of noble birth, whose duty it was, under given conditions, to represent a particular church or monastery, and to defend its rights against force. This position was sometimes abused as the protector asked for what today would be termed "protection money."

advocatus ecclesiae *see* **advocate**

Aelred of Rievaulx, St. (ca. 1109–1167) English Cistercian monk, abbot of Rievaulx, and writer. In 1142, Aelred was novice master at Rievaulx. In 1143, he became the first abbot of a new daughter house of Rievaulx at Revesby in Lincolnshire. In 1147, he was elected abbot of Rievaulx itself, a position he held until his death. Under his administration, the abbey expanded greatly. In addition to his work as a monk and abbot, Aelred was deeply involved in political affairs. Known for his historical writing, he also wrote several influential books on spirituality, among them *Speculum Caritatis* (*The Mirror of Charity*) and *De Spiritali Amicitia* (*On Spiritual Friendship*).

affirmation *see* **ordination**

agapetae Nuns in the early Church who lived celibately in the same house with monks

agapetai Monks in the early Church who lived celibately in the same house with nuns

Agrypnia In the Greek Orthodox Church, an all night vigil performed on Saturday nights and the eves of major feasts

Agwin of Clysma; Mar Agwin; Saint Eugenios (d. 363) Founder of the first cenobitic monastery in Asia on Mt. Izla in Mesopotamia. Originally from the monastery of Pachomius in Egypt, he left with 70 followers about 350 to found the first cenobitic monastery in Asia on Mt. Izla in Mesopotamia, and which is now part of Turkey. From this monastery the cenobitic tradition spread to Persia, Armenia, Georgia, India, and China.

A.H.C. The post-nominal initials for associates of the Order of the Holy Cross

ahimsa Non-violence, a basic tenet of Hindu monasticism

Aidan of Lindisfarne, St. (d. 651) An Irish monk, bishop, abbot, and missionary known for his asceticism, patience, and for restoring Christianity to Northumbria. He traveled continually preaching to both the nobility and the disenfranchised. He founded many churches, schools, and monasteries, including Lindisfarne Priory which also served as a cathedral.

ajahn A title of address for Buddhist monks who have passed ten annual rain retreats (Vassa). The term is customarily used to address Thai Buddhist forest tradition monks.

ajirogasa Large hats woven of bamboo and worn by Japanese Zen Buddhist monks when begging or on a pilgrimage

akedia ***see*** **acedia**

Akhara A paramilitary group of Hindu warrior monks from the 12th to 19th century • *See also* **Hindu warrior monks**

Akoimetoi ***see*** **Acoemeti**

akrodha Not to become angry even if you are abused by others—a basic tenet of Hindu monasticism

Albert Avogadro ***see*** **Rule *of St. Albert***

Albert of Cologne ***see*** **Albert the Great**

Albert the Great, St. (1193?–1280); Albert of Cologne; Albertus Magnus A German Dominican friar and bishop. He became a priest, and then joined the Dominican Order in 1223 or 1229. He taught in Cologne, Regensburg, Freiburg, Strasbourg, and Hildesheim. He then held the seat of the Chair of Theology at the College of St. James at the University of Paris where Thomas Aquinas studied under him.

In 1254 Albert was made provincial of the Dominican Order. In 1260 he was named the bishop of Regensburg, but he resigned after three years. While the bishop, he refused to ride a horse as was customary and his parishioners affectionately referred to him as "Boots the Bishop." He became known as a mediator in conflicts, and also founded Cologne's first university there.

With his wide-ranging intellect and curiosity Albert became a scientist, philosopher, theologian, and diplomat. He is even credited with the discovery of the element arsenic. His writings were collected in 1899 and comprised 38 volumes. He digested, interpreted, and systematized the whole of Aristotle's works. Most modern knowledge of Aristotle was preserved and presented by Albert.

During his lifetime he was called both "Doctor Universalis" and "Doctor Expertus," and has been called the greatest German philosopher and theologian of the Middle Ages. The Roman Catholic Church has since named him a Doctor of the Church.

Albertus Magnus ***see*** **Albert the Great**

Alcuin of York (ca. 735–804) English Catholic scholar, clergyman, abbot, poet, mathematician, theologian, and teacher from York, Northumbria. Alcuin wrote many theological and dogmatic treatises, as well as a few grammatical works, and a number of poems. He was made abbot of Tours in 796, where he remained until his death. He was considered "the most learned man anywhere to be found," and was also among the most important architects of the Carolingian Renaissance. Among his pupils were many of the dominant intellectuals of the Carolingian era. He is even credited with inventing the first known question mark, though it didn't resemble the modern symbol.

Aleppians *see* **Mariamite Maronite Order**

alien priory Usually a small religious foundation in England dependent on a French foreign mother house. The term was applied also to any property owned by a foreign monastery whether there was actually a priory on it or not. The precedent for seizing or dissolving them went back at least to 912 but increased greatly after the Norman Conquest. Off and on during the 12th and 13th centuries when England was at war with France, the French alien priories would be seized, but then returned when peace resumed. In 1414 all of the alien priories were seized for the last time and the revenues taken into the hands of King Henry V, however, in most cases the property was transferred to English monasteries.

almoner; elemosinarius A monastic in charge of distributing alms to the poor

almonry; domus elemonaria The place from which alms were dispensed to the poor

almshouse; bedehouse; beadhouse A house for a semi-monastic community living under a modified rule usually with the requirement of praying for the repose of the soul of the founder in return for room and board

ama *see* **bhikkhuni**

amaniko *see* **cassock vest**

ambulatory An aisle around the cloister in a monastery

amma An Aramaic word for "mother" used for an abbess or spiritual mother; commonly used in the *Apophthegmata Patrum* as a title of respect for a Desert Mother

Ammon, St. *see* **Amun, St.**

Ammonas *see* **Amun, St.**

Ammonius the Hermit *see* **Amun, St.**

Amoun *see* **Amun, St.**

ampelikos In the Eastern Church, the monastic in charge of a monastery's vineyards

Amun, St.; Ammon; Ammonas; Ammonias the Hermit; Amoun (fl. 4th century CE) 4th-century ascetic and Christian monk. Forced into a marriage at age 20, he convinced his wife to take a vow of chastity along with him. He lived with her for 18 years then she moved away and founded a convent in her own house. He moved to the Nitrian Desert and is said to have joined with Saint Anthony the Great to form Kellia.

an; hoan; soan A hermitage or small hall built on the premises of the graveyard of the founder or an eminent monk of a Japanese Zen Buddhist temple; a small hall before it is elevated to the rank of a temple; a small hall belonging to a large temple

anagarika; anagārika A person who has given up all, or most, of their worldly possessions and responsibilities to commit full-time to Buddhist practice. It is a midway status between a monastic and layperson where one takes on the Eight Precepts for the entire anagārika period, which could be for life. Anagārikas usually wear white clothes or robes, depending on the tradition they follow. Some traditions have special ordination ceremonies for anagārikas, while others simply take the Eight Precepts with a special intention.

In monastic settings, anagārikas are needed because the rules restrict monks and nuns from many tasks, including the use of money, driving, cooking, digging, and cutting plants. Anagārikas differ from laity by their commitment to Buddhism and to the Precepts. There is usually a notable difference in their manner, appearance and attire. In most cases, they are full-time residents at the monastery where they were ordained. Anagārikas often have the intention of becoming a full monastic at a later point. In some monasteries a period as an anagārika, often one year, is required in order to take novice ordination. The main difference between the Eight Precepts of an anagārika and the Ten Precepts of a novice monk is the rule of not handling money.

analavos The distinctive scapular of the great schema, worn by both schema monks and schema nuns in the Orthodox Church. Traditionally made of either leather or wool, it covers the shoulders and then comes down in the front and back, forming a cross. The Greek form does not have a hood; the Slavic form has a hood and lappets. The analavos is held in place by a cord called a polystavrion. • *See also* **great schema**

Ananda Marga monasticism A socio-spiritual quasimonastic organization and movement founded in India in 1955 by Prabhat Ranjan Sarkar to promote personal development, social service, and the transformation of society. Ananda Marga has both monks and nuns. They are engaged in direct services to society, so they have no permanent retreat. They have to follow strict celibacy, poverty, and many other rules of conduct.

anchorage ***see*** **anchorhold**

anchoress A female anchorite

anchoret ***see*** **anchorite**

anchorhold; anchorage The cell of an anchorite. These tended to be built against the wall of a church. Most anchorholds were small, perhaps no more than 3.7 to 4.6 m (12 to 15 ft.) square, with two or three windows. Viewing the altar, hearing Mass, and receiving the Eucharist was possible through one small, shuttered window in the common wall facing the sanctuary, called a "hagioscope" or "squint." Another window might be used to receive food, water, and visitors. A third window was sometimes used to provide outside light. Anchorites were supposed to remain in their cell in all eventualities. Some were even burned in their cells, which they refused to leave even when pirates or other attackers were looting and burning their towns.

In legend, there were Tibetan monks in cells with no windows in complete darkness, with only a single stone in the wall that could be removed once a day to provide bread and water, and to remove a chamber pot, but there is no solid proof of this. • *See also* **burying ceremony; hermitage**

anchorite; anchoret; anchoress (female); eremite; westensetla (Anglo-Saxon) One who lives the life of a religious recluse. Sometimes popularly used as a synonym for hermit, but by the early 13th century, anchorites were technically considered distinct from hermits. The hermit vocation permitted a change of location, whereas the anchorites were bound to one place of enclosure, generally a cell connected to a church. Some anchorites could move between their cell and the church, while others were immured, that is, sealed into a small walled cell to spend their life there in prayer and meditation. In Germanic-speaking areas, from at least the 10th century, it was customary for the bishop to say the Office of the Dead as the immured anchorite entered his cell. This signified the anchorite's death to the world and rebirth to a spiritual life of solitary communion with God and the angels.

Anchorites generally ate frugal meals and spent their days both in contemplative prayer and intercessions, but they did not necessarily live in poverty. In medieval times some had guest rooms, servants, and even a private chaplain. There was no one set rule that anchorites had to follow, nor did an anchorite have to be a member of a formal religious order, although many of them adapted a monastic rule or had one written for them. There are, however, two notable rules: *De Institutione Inclusarum* written in around 1160–1162, by St. Aelred of Rievaulx for his sister, and the better known early 13th century *Ancrene Wisse*.

The earliest recorded Christian anchorites lived in the 3rd century. From the 12th to the 16th centuries, female anchorites consistently outnumbered their male equivalents, sometimes by as many as four to one in the 13th century, dropping eventually to two to one in the 15th century. • *See also* **hermit**

anchoritic; anchoretic; eremitic; eremitical Of, like, suitable for, or relating to an anchorite; after the manner of an anchorite

anchoritism; anchoretish Of, like, or relating to an anchorite or anchoritism; the practice or mode of life of an anchorite

ancilla Latin for female slave. In medieval times, nuns would sometimes refer to themselves as ancillae.

Ancrene Riwle **see** ***Ancrene Wisse***

Ancrene Wisse; Ancrene Riwle; Guide for Anchoresses; Rule for a Recluse An anonymous eight-part monastic rule for anchoresses written in vernacular English sometime between 1190 and 1220, for three sisters who chose to enter the contemplative life. It was the longest and most complete of the anchoretic rules at the time and had a widespread influence in its day.

It is estimated that the daily set of devotions detailed in *Ancrene Wisse* would take about four hours, on top of which anchoresses would listen to services in the church, and engage in their own private prayers and devotional reading.

angelica vestis A monastic garment that members of the laity in Europe might formerly wear a little before their death so that monastics would pray for them

Angelines *see* **Company of St. Ursula**

Anglican monasticism British religious communities were dissolved by King Henry VIII when he separated the Church of England from papal primacy in 1534. Semi-monastic groups, such as Little Gidding, existed by 1626, but it wasn't until between 1841 that formal religious orders were begun. They included the Community of St. Mary the Virgin at Wantage and the Society of St. Margaret at East Grinstead, both of which were for women. Religious orders for men appeared later, beginning in 1866 with the Society of St. John the Evangelist (Cowley Fathers). In

North America, the founding of Anglican religious orders began in 1842 with the Nashotah Community (for men) in Wisconsin, followed in 1845 by the Sisterhood of the Holy Communion in New York. In recent decades, there has been a remarkable growth of religious orders in other parts of the Anglican Communion, most notably in Tanzania, South Africa, the Solomon Islands, Vanuatu, and Papua New Guinea. There are currently about 2,400 monastics in the Anglican communion, about 55 percent of whom are women and 45 percent of whom are men.

Religious communities in the Anglican Communion tend to be Benedictine as Benedictinism had a profound influence on the Church of England dating from St. Augustine of Canterbury in 595. Anglican Benedictine abbots are invited guests of the Benedictine abbot primate in Rome at abbatial gatherings at Sant'Anselmo. Cistercian and Carmelite communities have been founded but have generally not been enduring. There are also Anglican Augustinian and Franciscan communities.

There is no single central authority for all religious orders, and many member churches of the Anglican Communion have their own internal structures for recognizing and regulating religious orders. Some central functions are performed by the Anglican Religious Communities Department at Church House, Westminster. This department publishes the bi-annual *Anglican Religious Life,* a world directory of religious orders, and also maintains an official Anglican Communion website for religious orders. *Anglican Religious Life* defines four categories of community within the Anglican Communion.

1. *Traditional Celibate Religious Orders and Communities*: Orders and communities in which members take a vow of celibacy (among other vows) and follow a common rule of life. They may be enclosed and contemplative or open and engaged in apostolic works.
2. *Dispersed Communities*: These are orders or communities whose members, while taking vows (including celibacy), do not live together in community. In most cases the members are self-supporting and live alone, but follow the same rule of life, and meet together frequently in assemblies often known as "chapter meetings." In some cases some members may share a common life in very small groups of two or three.
3. *Acknowledged Communities:* These communities live a traditional Christian life, including the taking of vows, but the traditional vows are adapted or changed. In many cases these communities admit both single and married persons as members, requiring celibacy on the part of those who are single and unfailing commitment to their spouse on the part of married members. They also amend the vow of poverty, allowing personal possessions, but requiring high standards of tithing to the community and the wider church. These communities often have residential elements, but not full residential community life, as this would be incompatible with the elements of married family life.
4. *Other Communities:* This group contains communities which are

ecumenical (including Anglicans) or that belong to non–Anglican churches which have entered into relationships of full communion with Anglican churches (particularly, but not only, certain Lutheran churches).

ango; seichū The 90 day summer and winter training seasons in a Japanese Zen Buddhist monastery, with their origins in the rainy season meditation retreats (Vassa) at the time of the Buddha. They involve concentrated practice without leaving the monastic enclosure, except for necessary temple business.

angya Traditionally, a pilgrimage Japanese Zen Buddhist prospective monastics made from monastery to monastery seeking a master. Considered an aspect of the early monk's training, in ancient times angya sometimes lasted for many years. In modern times the term refers to seeking admittance into a monastery for the first time.

angyaso An itinerant Zen Buddhist monk

anja A Japanese Zen Buddhist abbot's assistant

anju A Japanese Zen Buddhist hermit or monk of temporary habitation; a Zen Buddhist novice who lives in a small temple; a Zen Buddhist nun who lives in a hermitage

Anselm of Aosta *see* Anselm of Canterbury

Anselm of Bec *see* Anselm of Canterbury

Anselm of Canterbury, St. (ca. 1033–1109); Anselm of Aosta; Anselm of Bec A French Benedictine monk, abbot, philosopher, and theologian of the Catholic Church, who held the office of Archbishop of Canterbury from 1093 to 1109.

Anselm entered the abbey of Bec as a novice in at the age of 27. Three years later, in 1063, he became the claustral prior. In 1078, he was elected abbot. Under his direction, Bec became a noted center of learning in Europe, attracting students from France, Italy, and elsewhere. Anselm became noted both for his intellect and his kindly method of discipline, but also for his strong defense of the abbey's independence from lay and archiepiscopal control.

William II, King of England nominated Anselm to be the new Archbishop of Canterbury in 1093 and the clerics gathered at the court to acclaim him, forced the crozier into his hands, and bodily carried him to a nearby church. Anselm tried to refuse on the grounds of age and ill-health but eventually relented when King William agreed to the agenda of the Gregorian Reform, to return seized church lands, and to recognize Pope Urban II. Despite all this, Anselm was exiled from England twice.

Beginning at Bec, Anselm composed dialogues and treatises with a rational and philosophical approach, sometimes causing him to be credited as the founder of Scholasticism. Although not recognized in his own time, Anselm is now known as the originator of the ontological argument for the existence of God and of the satisfaction theory of atonement. He was proclaimed a Doctor of the Church in 1720.

antaravsaka *see* antarvasa

antarvasa; antarvāsa; antaravāsaka The inner robe covering the lower body of fully ordained Buddhist monks and nuns. It is the undergarment that flows underneath the other layers of clothing. It has a high top and almost entirely covers the torso. In representations of the Buddha, the bottom of the antarvasa usually protrudes, and appears in the rough shape of a triangle. The garment is essentially a skirt, which was common as ancient menswear. When needed, its height could be adjusted so it did not hang to the ankles. • *See also* **kasaya**

anteri *see* **inner cassock**

Anthony of Egypt *see* **Anthony the Great**

Anthony of the Desert *see* **Anthony the Great**

Anthony of Thebes *see* **Anthony the Great**

Anthony the Abbot *see* **Anthony the Great**

Anthony the Anchorite *see* **Anthony the Great**

Anthony the Great, St. (ca. 251–356); Antony the Great; Anthony of Egypt; Anthony the Abbot; Anthony of the Desert; Anthony the Anchorite; Anthony of Thebes Egyptian Christian hermit, he had been sometimes regarded as the "Founder of Christian Monasticism," and the "Father of Monks," but neither of these contentions is true. He became the first of the Desert Fathers, however, when he moved to the Nitrian Desert around 270, and the biography of Anthony's life by Athanasius of Alexandria helped to spread the concept of Christian monasticism, particularly in Western Europe via its Latin translations.

Anthony spent many years in the desert in isolation and is famous for battling the demons of acedia (boredom, laziness), and fornication (the temptation to have sex). At one point he lived strictly enclosed as an anchorite for 20 years in an abandoned Roman fort as an anchorite. While in the fort he only communicated with the outside world by a crevice through which food would be passed and he would say a few words. Anthony would prepare a quantity of bread that would sustain him for six months. He did not allow anyone to enter his cell; whoever came to him stood outside and listened to his advice. He did not emerge until villagers broke down his door.

antiphonary, antiphoner A book containing the chants for the Daily Office

Antonian Order of St. Ormizda of the Chaldeans An Eastern Catholic, Chaldean Rite monastic order for men founded in 1808. Its headquarters is in Baghdad. In 2012, it had 6 houses with 40 members, including 21 priests.

Antonians A congregation of Orthodox Armenians founded during the 17th century by Abram Atar Poresigh. The monastery of the Most Holy Saviour was founded at Mt. Lebanon to supply missioners. A second foundation was made on Mount Lebanon and a third in Rome (1753). Some members of this congregation took a prominent part in the Armenian Schism (1870–1880).

Antonin Maronite Order *see* **Lebanese Antonin Order**

Antonines *see* **Order of St. Anthony**

Antonins *see* **Lebanese Antonin Order**

Antony the Great *see* **Anthony the Great**

apegha A monk in the Armenian Apostolic Church. Because all monks in the church are also priests, an apegha is the equivalent of a hieromonk in the rest of the Orthodox Church.

apeuelogia In the Orthodox Church, the punishment of not receiving the abbot's blessing

aphoriosmos In the Orthodox Church, the punishment of solitary confinement and excommunication from the daily office and the sacraments

aphypnistes The monk in a Greek Orthodox monastery who duty it is to waken the other monks for Orthros (Lauds)

Apodeipnon The name for Compline in the Orthodox Church

Apophthegmata Patrum; Sayings of the Desert Fathers A collection of sayings and wisdom stories of the Desert Fathers and Desert Mothers from the end of the 4th century into the 5th century. Beginning as an oral tradition in the Coptic language, they were only later written down in Greek and Ethiopic. They have since been translated into many languages and have exerted an influence on monasticism that continues to this day.

The sayings describe the spiritual practices and experiences of early Christian hermits living in the desert of Egypt. They are typically in the form of a conversation between a younger monk and his spiritual father, or as advice given to visitors. An example is: "Abba Theophilus, the archbishop, came to Scetis one day. The brethren who were assembled said to Abba Pambo, 'Say something to the Archbishop, so that he may be edified.' The old man said to them, 'If he is not edified by my silence, he will not be edified by my speech.'" • *See also **Ethiopic Collectio Monastica***

apostasia a religione *see* **apostates**

apostasy; derainment Leaving a religious order after taking solemn vows

apostatae *see* **apostates**

apostates; apostatae; fugitive religious; fugitivi; vagabundi; vagantes; apostasia a religione Those who leave a monastic community after making a solemn profession. In the eyes of the church it was apostasy; in the eyes of civil law, it was a breach of contract. Either way, it was once considered a heinous crime. In the Middle Ages, it is estimated that 4 to 5 percent of religious became apostates. The figure is much higher in modern times.

Apostle of Northumbria A nickname of St. Aidan of Lindisfarne

Apostle of the Germans A nickname of St. Boniface

Apostoli *see* **Apostolic Brethren**

Apostolic Brethren; Apostolics; Apostolici; Apostoli; Pseudo-Apostles A Christian sect of penitents founded in northern Italy about 1260 by the Italian mendicant monk Gerard Segarelli. He was of low birth and without education and when he applied for membership in the Franciscan Order at Parma he was rejected. He then resolved to devote himself to the restoration of what he conceived to be the apostolic manner of life. About 1280, he was thrown into prison by the Bishop of Parma, and then was banished from the diocese in 1286.

At Parma in 1294 four members of the sect were burned, and Segarelli was condemned to perpetual imprisonment. In 1300 he was made to confess a relapse into heresies which he had abjured, and was burned.

A man of greater gifts then took the lead of the sect. This was Dolcino, the son of a priest in the diocese of Novara, and a member of the order since 1291. He was an eloquent, enthusiastic utterer of apocalyptic prophecies. As the head of the group, who were in daily expectation of seeing the judgment of God on the Church, he maintained in a guerrilla warfare campaign against the Crusaders who had been summoned to put him down. Finally the remnant of his forces were captured by the bishop of Vercelli. About 150 persons in all, including Dolcino himself and his "spiritual sister," Margareta, both of whom, refusing to recant, were burned at the stake in 1307. This was really the end of the sect's history. Later, in the middle of the century, traces of their activity were found, especially in Spain, France, and northern Italy but these were only isolated survivals.

The Apostolic Brethren did not have a fully developed theory, but based their belief on the Acts of the Apostles. All who believed had all things in common. They sold their possessions and goods, and distributed them to all, according as anyone had need. They lived a simple life of fasting and prayer; often they worked to earn enough to eat, otherwise living off charity, preaching, and always invoking penitence. When the order was prohibited, however, the refusal to submit to ecclesiastical authority stamped its members as heretics.

Apostolic Clerks *see* **Theatines**

apostolic community; active community A monastic community called to minister primarily outside their community, often in education, health care, and pastoral work. Members of apostolic communities may or may not live together.

apostolic/contemplative community; active/contemplative community A monastic community that is both apostolic and contemplative. They pursue outside ministries, but live together and make a point of praying together every day.

Apostolici *see* **Apostolic Brethren**

Apostolics *see* **Apostolic Brethren**

apostolnik; epimandylion A cloth veil worn by Orthodox and Eastern Catholic nuns that, except for the face, completely covers the head, neck, and shoulders. It is similar to the hijab worn by Muslim women, and is usually black, but sometimes white. It is sometimes worn with a skufia (soft-sided brimless hat). The nun typically receives the apostolnik when she becomes a novice. While it is usually replaced with the epanokalimavkion (a cloth veil, usually black, which is worn with a kamilavkion) when the nun becomes a rassophore (one rank above a novice). Many nuns will continue to wear the apostolnik for the sake of convenience, much as a monk will continue to wear a skufia instead of a klobuk (a stiff hat with a veil) when not attending the divine liturgy.

In some practices, a novice nun will wear a black scarf covering her head and tied under her chin. She will then receive the apostolnik at her tonsure. In this practice, the epanokalimavkion may be reserved for the abbess and for nuns of the great schema.

apothekarios In the Eastern Church, the monastic in charge of a monastery's warehouse

appamattakavissaajaka In a Theravedin Buddhist monastery, an official in charge of trifles such as scissors, sandals, and other utensils used by the monks

appropriation In medieval England, the formal transfer to a monastic house of the tithes and other endowments of a parish church, usually in return for the promise to provide a vicar from the proceeds, but any excess funds could be used as the monastery pleased • *see also* **impropriation**

arama; ārāma Permanent housing for Buddhist monastics that is more comfortable than an avasa (temporary house). Generally this property is financed by the wealthy.

aramika A lay attendant in a Theravedin Buddhist monastery

aramkiapesaka In a Theravedin Buddhist monastery, a monastic in charge of supervising aramikas (lay monastics)

archabbey A chief Roman Catholic Benedictine abbey, so designated by a pope. There are only eleven in the world, two of which are in the United States.

archabbot The abbot of an archabbey

archimandrite In the Orthodox or Eastern Catholic Church, originally the title of an abbot of an important monastery or one whom a bishop appointed to supervise several other hegumens (abbots) or monasteries; later also an honorific granted on clergy in gratitude for exemplary service; after 1874, the head of a monastery of the first or second class

archivist The keeper of deeds, charters, licenses, and records of the monastery. Usually this job was conflated with that of the librarian.

archontares A monastic in charge of official visitor's quarters in an Orthodox monastery

armarium *see* **library**

armarius *see* **librarian**

Armenian monasticism The Armenian Apostolic Church is Eastern Orthodox. In modern times, Armenian monks are also priests. They have a novitiate of eight years. Upon ordination, they are given a veghar, a conical head covering symbolizing the renunciation of worldly things. A monk is called a apegha (equivalent to a hieromonk). Those who receive advanced studies receive the rank of vardapet (equivalent to a hegumen) and carry the staff of an abbot. The rank of dzayraguyn vardapet (equivalent to an archimandrite) can be granted after successfully and defending a doctoral thesis. Armenian bishops are elected only from those who are vardapet or above.

There are now three monastic brotherhoods in the Armenian Apostolic Church: the Brotherhood of the Mother See of Holy Etchmiadzin, the Brotherhood of St. James at the Armenian Patriarchate of Jerusalem, and the Brotherhood of the Holy See of Cilicia. Armenian monks become members of the brotherhood in which they are ordained in.

The Mekhitarists are an Armenian Benedictine congregation in communion with the Roman Catholic Church. • *See also* **Mekhitarists**

arra Money paid in advance by medieval merchants for the wool produced by monastery flocks. It was profitable for merchants because they got a discounted price, but could lead monasteries into debt if sheep died from disease, and the Cistercian Order prohibited the practice.

arsenas A storehouse in an Athonite monastery

aryika A solemnly professed Jain or Hindu nun

Asanga; Asaṅga (fl. 4th century CE) A Mahāyāna Buddhist who was a major exponent of the Yogacara tradition in India, also called Vijñānavāda. Traditionally, he and his half-brother Vasubandhu are regarded as the founders of this school. The two half-brothers were also major exponents of Abhidharma teachings. Asaṅga was initially a Mahīśāsaka monk, but soon turned toward the Mahāyāna teachings. Asaṅga wrote many of the key Yogācāra treatises such as the *Yogācārabhūmi-śāstra*, the *Mahāyānasaṃgraha* and the *Abhidharma-samuccaya* as well as other works, although there are discrepancies between the Chinese and Tibetan traditions concerning which works are attributed to him and which to Maitreya.

ashram A spiritual hermitage or a monastery in Indian religions. An ashram would traditionally, be located far from human habitation, in forests or mountainous regions, amidst refreshing natural surroundings conducive to spiritual instruction and meditation. In contemporary times ashrams are not necessarily located in rural isolation.

Asketikon; Rule of St. Basil Although often referred to as the *Rule of St. Basil*, it is not like Western monastic rules, but rather a collection of St. Basil's responses to questions about the ascetic life. There were two such collections, the *Greater Asketikon* and the *Lesser Asketikon*. The *Asketikon* is the basis for most Eastern Orthodox and some Greek Catholic communities. St. Basil make poverty, obedience, renunciation, and self-abnegation the foundation of the monastic life.

aspirant Someone who lives with a community for a short period of time to see if they are attracted to and comfortable with the life. When an aspirant has been accepted, they become a postulant.

Assumptionists ***see*** **Augustinians of the Assumption; Religious of the Assumption**

Athonite Of, like, or relating to Mt. Athos; a monk of Mt. Athos

Athonite gerontikon A saying or apothegm of a monastic elder from Mount Athos

Athos, Mount; Holy Mountain A mountain and peninsula of 335.6 square kilometers (129.58 square miles) in northeastern Greece that is home to 20 Eastern Orthodox monasteries. Seventeen of the monasteries are predominately Greek, one is Serbian, one is Russian, and one is Bulgarian. There have been monks on Mt. Athos since at least 800. The peak population was reached in 1902 when there were 7,000 monks. Today there are 2,000.

No women are permitted in the territory, although in the 14th century, the Serbian Emperor Dušan the Mighty brought his wife, Helena of Bulgaria there for protection from the plague, but she did not touch the ground during her entire visit. Female animals such as chickens, cows, ewes, nanny-goats, mares, and sows are also barred, but not female cats, insects, or songbirds.

auditorium ***see*** **parlor**

Augmentation Court A court instituted by King Henry VIII of England to augment the revenues of the crown by the suppression of monasteries

Augustine of Canterbury, St. (d. 604) Benedictine monk who was the prior of St. Andrew's monastery in Rome when Pope Gregory the Great chose him in 595 to lead a mission to Britain to Christianize King Ethelbert and his Kingdom of Kent from Anglo-Saxon paganism. Ethelbert's seat of government was in Canterbury, and Canterbury is the seat of the Church of England to this day. Shortly after his arrival, Augustine founded the Monastery of Saints Peter and Paul immediately outside the city walls. In 597, Augustine became the first archbishop of Canterbury. Augustine's mission left an indelible Benedictine stamp on the Church of England and the Anglican Communion.

Augustine of Hippo, St. (354–430) An Algerian raised as a Christian who left the Church to follow the Manichaean religion and as a youth lived a hedonistic lifestyle for a time, associating with young men who boasted of their sexual exploits. Later, he traveled to Rome, studied under St. Ambrose and in 386 converted to Christianity, was baptized, and tonsured as a monk.

Back in Africa he gave away his wealth to the poor, keeping only his house which he used as a monastery for himself and some friends. In 391 Valerian, Bishop of Hippo, ordained St. Augustine a priest, and in 395, appointed him bishop coadjutor of the See of Hippo. After the death of Bishop Valerian, St. Augustine took his place. Augustine's large contribution of writings covered diverse fields including theology, philosophy, and sociology which influenced virtually all of Western philosophy and theology. His most important contribution to monasticism is the *Rule of St. Augustine* which is widely used to this day.

Augustinians Those orders and groups which follow the *Rule of St. Augustine* • *see also* **Augustinians of the Assumption; Canonesses of St. Augustine of the Mercy of Jesus; Order of St. Augustine; Order of St. Jerome; Ursulines**

Augustinians of the Assumption A congregation of Roman Catholic priests and brothers that is active in nearly 30 countries. It was founded in Nîmes, France, by Fr. Emmanuel d'Alzon in 1845. The current rule of life draws its inspiration from the *Rule of St. Augustine.*

The congregation is involved in education, the press, ecumenism, pilgrimages, and the missions. They are one of the largest Catholic publishing houses in the world publishing more than 100 magazines in 15 languages. They also run pilgrimages to the Holy Land and Lourdes which are attended by thousands of pilgrims. Members of the congregation used the post-nominal initials A.A.

Aum Shinrikyo A Japanese-based new religion—some would say a doomsday cult—founded by Shoko Asahara in Japan in 1984. The belief system draws upon idiosyncratic interpretations of early Indian and Tibetan Buddhism, Hinduism, and millennialist ideas from yoga, Nostradamus, and the Christian book of Revelation. They claimed they would restore original Buddhism. It was also thought that by killing someone they could prevent them from bad karma and thus save them when the world ended. By 1995, it had 10,000 members, of whom 1,200 considered themselves monks and nuns. These lived rigorous ascetic common lives in barracks.

When the movement stalled, the leadership became convinced an apocalypse was at hand and turned to violence to hasten it. This resulted in an infamous nerve gas attack on a Tokyo subway in 1995. Although the leadership was jailed and sentenced to death, in 2011 about a thousand so-called monks and nuns remained. In 2017, the organization was still under police surveillance.

Austin Canons ***see*** **Canons Regular of St. Augustine**

Austin Friars ***see*** **Order of St. Augustine**

avasa; avāsā Temporary and more spartan housing for Buddhist monastics as opposed to an arama. Generally an avāsā had individual cells.

avowess ***see*** **vowess**

Ayres, Anne (1816–1896) Episcopalian nun and the founder of the first Episcopalian religious order for women. Born in London, she emigrated to the United States in 1836. In 1845, influenced by an Episcopal priest, she elected to follow a religious life. She organized other teachers at her church's school and established the Sisterhood of the Holy Communion of which she was the superior. The priest of her church gave her private vows. The sisters in the community did not wear religious habits because of Protestant prejudice against religious orders in those days. Members renewed their vows every three years. In 1852, the House of Bishops formally recognized the new order. In 1853, the order began providing nursing care. In 1863, five members left and formed what became the Community of St. Mary. In 1870, Ayres help found St. Johnland, a Christian community that provided refuge for the needy, the aged, and the handicapped. The Sisterhood remained active until 1940. St. Johnland is still active under a board of directors and now concentrates on services for the elderly.

ayya Noble lady, a form of address to a Buddhist nun

~B~

Bacon, Roger (**ca. 1220–ca. 1292**) An English Franciscan friar, scientist, alchemist, astrologist, grammarian, educator, writer, and philosopher. He is sometimes credited as being one of the earliest European advocates of the modern scientific method inspired by Aristotle and by the Arab scientist Alhazen. Bacon was given the nickname "Doctor Mirabilis," but although he was a brilliant scholar, taught at both Oxford and the University of Paris, and was part of important educational reforms, there is no evidence that he ever earned a doctorate. In 1256 or 1257, he became a friar in the Franciscan Order in either Paris or Oxford. In 1277, Bacon was imprisoned, or at least placed under house arrest, for a time because some of his writings were contrary to current beliefs. It may be that a somewhat combative personality contributed to this.

bagenares In the Eastern Church, the monastic in charge of wine or the wine-cellar

Bahaism The Baha'i faith specifically forbids the practice of monasticism.

Bahtawiyan Ethiopian Christian monks who live a completely isolated life in a cell. They do not know or communicate with each other. They own only their own clothing, a water jar, and a plate. They devote each day to prayer and hundreds of prostrations. Food delivery from monasteries or from nearby villages can be spotty and a Bahtawiyan can go for days without food. Their isolation is so complete that sometimes the only way to tell that one has died is if food left at a previous time remains sitting on their doorstep.

bailiwick An administrative unit of the English province of the Knights Templars that comprised a region, county, or group of villages

Bairagis ***see*** **Hindu warrior monks**

Baizhang Huaihai (720–814 CE) Chinese Chan (Zen) Buddhist monk during the Tang Dynasty. According to legend, Baizhang established the *Pure Rules of Baizhang,* for use in the Ta-chih Shou-sheng Ch'an-ssu Monastery which he founded. The rules are still used today in some Chan monasteries. His monastery contained a monk's hall, an innovation which became typical for Chan monasteries.

bakehouse; pristrinum In Western monasteries, the kitchen where bread was prepared for the community and also for distribution to the poor. Singing bread, that is, the unleavened bread for the Eucharist, was prepared in a separate place under the direction of the sacristan.

Baker, Augustine (1575–1641); Baker, Austin English Roman Catholic Benedictine monk, priest, mystic, and ascetic writer. He was educated at Oxford where he lost his faith in the existence of God, but after some years and a close brush with death regained his faith and became a Roman Catholic. In 1605 he joined the Benedictine Order. He was an early member of the English Benedictine Congregation that was newly restored to England after the Reformation. He was also a prolific writer of mystical treatises which have the reputation of being diffuse and unstructured. He died from the bubonic plague in London at the age of 65.

Baker, Austin ***see*** **Baker, Augustine**

Baladites ***see*** **Lebanese Maronite Order**

balcanifer The standard-bearer of the Knights Templar

balcanum The standard of the Knights Templar

banchung A young Tibetan Buddhist monk

bandeau A thin headband traditionally worn—until recently—underneath and supporting the veil by many Roman Catholic nuns, together with the wimple (which covers the cheeks and neck) and the white coif (hat) to which it would be attached

bangan An old Tibetan Buddhist monk

bangjang The quarters of a Zen Buddhist abbot

Barah Panthi An oversight organization for Nath monastics

barb; barbe A tall pleated collar formerly worn by medieval widows and nuns

barbati Christian mendicants and lay brethren who had beards as opposed to most monks who did not

barbati fratres ***see*** **fratres barbati**

barbe *see* **barb**

barber surgeon A monk who shaved faces and heads and performed light surgery

bard A professional poet supported by a patron. In the later Middles Ages, in an immodest manner hardly befitting the monastic life, a number of bards resided in Cistercian monasteries where they wrote poems celebrating the achievements of the abbots.

bardocucullus A short hooded cloak originally worn by Gallic peasants, and later adopted by Romans and some monastics

Barefoot Carmelites *see* **Order of Discalced Carmelites**

barefoot friars *see* **discalced**

Barettini *see* **Humiliati**

Basil of Caesarea *see* **Basil the Great**

Basil the Great, St. (ca. 330–379); Basil of Caesarea Greek Bishop of Caesarea, theologian, and monk known as the "Father of Eastern Monasticism." His *Asketikon* (*Rule of St. Basil*) is the basis for most Eastern Orthodox and some Greek Catholic communities. Along with Pachomius he is considered a founder of communal monasticism in Orthodox Christianity.

By 358 he, his brother Peter, and a group of disciples founded a monastic settlement on his family's estate near the confluence of the Iris and Lycos Rivers. His widowed mother Emmelia, sister Macrina, and several other women also took part in the community. Some authorities think it may have actually been Macrina who founded the community. Basil was noted for the moderation of austerities previously common in monastic life and he also created a proper balance between work and prayer. His influence particularly on Orthodox monasticism has been incalculable.

Basilian Chouerite Order of St. John the Baptist; Ordo Basilianus Sancti Iohannis Baptistae; Ordre Basilien Chouerite de St. Jean Baptiste A religious order of the Melkite Greek Catholic Church. It was founded in 1696 by monks looking for a better place to more closely follow the *Asketikon* (*Rule of St. Basil*). They settled in 1710 in the village of Choueir in Mount Lebanon using the church of St. John the Baptist. It is still their motherhouse. They use the post-nominal initials B.C.

They are one of the two main religious orders of the Melkite Catholic Church. The other order is the Basilian Order of the Most Holy Saviour. The Basilian Chouerite Order is more contemplative, while the Basilian Order of the Most Holy Saviour has a more missionary focus. Attempts to unite these two orders in the 18th century failed.

Up to the first half of the 19th century, these two religious orders ran a large number of parishes and provided most of the bishops of the Church. With the increasing importance of the celibate diocesan priests since the patriarchate of Maximos III Mazloum, the religious orders lost some of their importance.

Basilian Chouerite Sisters A religious order of the Melkite Greek Catholic Church and considered the female branch of the Basilian Chouerite Order. It was founded in 1737. Their first house was the Monastery of the Annunciation at Zouk Mikael.

Basilian Fathers ***see*** **Congregation of St. Basil**

Basilian monks Monks who follow the precepts set down by St. Basil the Great in his *Asketikon* (*Rule of St. Basil*). In the Eastern Orthodox Church, monks do not generally call themselves "Basilians," while the Greek Catholics do. Thus the expression "Basilian monk" almost always refers to religious of those Eastern Catholic Churches that follow the Byzantine Rite.

Basilian Order of St. Josaphat ***see*** **Order of St. Basil the Great**

Basilian Order of the Most Holy Saviour; Ordo Basilianus Sanctissimi Salvatoris; Ordre Basilien Salvatorien; Basilian Salvatorian Order; Salvatorian Fathers An Eastern Catholic religious order of the Melkite Greek Catholic Church founded in 1683 by Euthymios Saifi, Bishop of Saida, with the aim of supporting pastoral and missionary activities. Their specific rules were formally drafted and approved only in 1934.

The order soon became one of the two main religious orders of the Melkite Catholic Church. The other order was the Basilian Chouerite Order. The Basilian Order of the Most Holy Saviour traditionally has a more missionary focus, while the Basilian Chouerite Order emphasizes contemplation. Attempts to unite these two orders in the 18th century failed.

Up to the first half of the 19th century, these two religious orders ran a large number of parishes and provided most of the bishops of the Church. With the increasing importance of the celibate diocesan priests since the patriarchate of Maximos III Mazloum, the religious orders lost some of their importance.

In the 19th century some difficulties arose due to the lack of respect for their vows of poverty and conflict between the order's Damascene and Lebanese wings. Reforms in the early 20th century resolved the issues.

As of 2005, the order had 18 monasteries and 114 monks, of which 97 are priests. In 2012, it had 11 houses left and 92 members, of which 87 were priests.

Basilian Salvatorian Order ***see*** **Basilian Order of the Most Holy Saviour**

bathhouse; balnearium In the Western Church, monastic bathing facilities. In medieval times they were not a common feature of monasteries because of the difficulty of pumping the water and then heating it.

battan In Japanese Zen Buddhism, a lower ranking unsui (postulant or novice)

bearded brothers ***see*** **fratres barbati; barbati**

beards ***see*** **rasura**

Beatrice of Silva, St. ***see*** **Order of the Immaculate Conception**

Beauduin, Lambert (1873–1960) A Roman Catholic Benedictine Belgian monk professed in 1907, who founded the monastery now known as Chevetogne Abbey in 1925. He was noted as a liturgist and ecumenist. He expressed a wish for the Anglicans to be "united to Rome not absorbed," which resulted in his expulsion from the abbey in 1928, and a condemnation by Rome in 1930. He was not able to rejoin his community until 1950.

Bede, St. (ca. 673–735); Bede the Venerable; Venerable Bede A prolific and brilliant English Benedictine monk, scholar, ecumenist, translator, teacher, and writer. At the age of seven, Bede was sent as an oblate to the monastery of Monkwearmouth. About 692, he was ordained a deacon, and about 702, he became a priest.

Due to his book *The Ecclesiastical History of the English People* he has been called "The Father of English History." He also wrote Biblical commentaries, worked on dating Easter, and established the custom of dating forward from the birth of Christ. He is considered to be one of the greatest scholars of his time and wrote over 60 books in his life. He died on the Feast of the Ascension, on the floor of his cell. It is said that he was singing "Glory be to the Father and to the Son and to the Holy Spirit" at the time.

In 1899, he was declared a Doctor of the Church. He is the only native of Great Britain to achieve this designation.

Bede the Venerable *see* **Bede, St.**

Beghards; Beguini (Latin); Begardi (Latin); Beggarden (German); Bégards (French) A quasimonastic community of Roman Catholic laymen living in imitation of the Beguines. They were founded about 1220 in Belgium. The Beghards did not take vows or affiliate with an approved order but were nominally called to a life of chastity, penance, and good works. Many were weavers and textile workers, but the group had the reputation—rightly or wrongly—of being itinerants and vagrants and were attacked by the Church. Still, they lasted until the end of the 18th century.

beguinage A collection of small houses occupied by a community of Beguines

beguinal Of, like, or relating to the Beguines or beguinages

Beguines; Beguinae (Italian); Begijnen (Dutch); Beginenen (German); Béguines (French) Pinzochera (Italian) A quasimonastic community of Roman Catholic women founded in Belgium about 1200. They did not take vows or affiliate with an approved order but were called to a life of chastity, poverty, and good works. The communities lived by a rule, pledged obedience to the superior, and lived in beguinages, but were not cloistered. They had a somewhat better reputation than their brother Beghards, but were still attacked by the Church as heretics. Nevertheless, some groups lasted until the mid–20th century.

Benai Qeima *see* **Members of the Covenant**

Benat Qeima *see* **Members of the Covenant**

Benedict of Aniane, St. (ca. 750–821) Frankish Benedictine monk, scholar, monastic reformer, and promoter of the *Rule of St. Benedict.* Originally a courtier of Charlemagne, he left to become a monk and around 780 founded a community based on Eastern asceticism but this failed. In 782, he founded another monastery based on the *Rule of St. Benedict,* which was so successful that he was able to form or reform a number of other monasteries and gave him a great deal of influence over all the monasteries of Charlemagne's empire.

In 817, he was head of a council of abbots that created the *Codex Regularum,* a set of regulations binding on all their houses. Not long after, he compiled the *Concordia Regularum,* in which sections of the *Rule of St. Benedict* are given with parallel passages from the other rules.

Although both these codes fell into disuse shortly after his death, they had a lasting effect on Western monasticism.

Benedict of Nursia, St. (ca. 480–ca. 547) An Italian Catholic monk and abbot called the "Father of Western Christian Monasticism." While his importance to Western monasticism can scarcely be underestimated, but he was not widely known in his own day and there is little known about his life. He was the son of a Roman noble of Nursia (the modern Norcia), in Umbria. By tradition he is thought to be a twin with his sister St. Scholastica.

Benedict was sent to Rome to study, but being dissatisfied by life there, he left about 500 and settled near Subiaco where he became a monk. He spent three years as a hermit then was asked to be the abbot of a nearby abbey, but unruly monks tried to poison him, then a jealous priest tried to seduce him with prostitutes and he left.

Benedict founded 12 communities for monks at Subiaco before moving to Monte Cassino where he founded the abbey where he eventually died of a fever. Benedict's main achievement is the *Rule of St. Benedict,* containing precepts for his monks. He is venerated in Eastern Orthodox Churches, the Roman Catholic Church, the Oriental Orthodox Churches, the Anglican Communion, and Old Catholic Churches. • *See also* **Order of St. Benedict; *Rule of St. Benedict***

Benedictine Of, like, or relating to St. Benedict, the *Rule of St. Benedict,* or the Order of St. Benedict; living under the *Rule of St. Benedict;* any religious, monastic community, or religious order that follows the *Rule of St. Benedict,* including the Cluniacs, Cistercians, Trappists, and others.

Benedictine Camaldolese *see* Camaldolese Order

Benedictine centuries The years 550 to 1150 when Benedictine monasteries made great contributions in Europe to religion, economics, education, and government

Benedictine Confederation of the Order of St. Benedict; Confœderatio Benedictina Ordinis Sancti Benedicti An loose international union of most Roman Catholic men's congregations of the Order of St. Benedict. It was established by Pope Leo XIII in 1893. Despite the union, however, the congregations maintain their own autonomy. The Congress of Abbots elects the abbot primate, but he lacks direct jurisdiction over the congregations. The headquarters are at Sant'Anselmo in Rome, which is the seat of the abbot primate. There are Protestant—predominantly Anglican—Benedictine groups that maintain friendly relations with the Confederation, although they are not formally linked with it or its congregations.

Throughout the Benedictine world independence and autonomy among individual communities are highly valued; too much so for Pope Pius XI, who complained that the Benedictine Order was "an order without order."

Women's Benedictine congregations are represented by the Communio Internationalis Benedictarium. • *See also* **Communio Internationalis Benedictarium**

Benedictine Reform *see* Cluniac Reform; English Benedictine Reform

Benedictines *see* Order of St. Benedict

benefactor A donor who supports a monastic community with financial or other aid

benji Leaving a Zen Buddhist monastery for a day or so on private business

Benson, Charles Chapman *see* **Society of St John the Evangelist**

beopdang *see* **Dharma hall**

Bernard of Clairvaux, St. (1090–1153) A French monk, abbot, theologian, and diplomat of the Roman Catholic Church. In 1115, while a monk at the abbey of Cîteaux, Bernard was sent with a band of 12 others to found a new abbey at Clairvaux, of which he was later named abbot. Clairvaux grew rapidly under his leadership. His reforms of Benedictine monasticism caused the formation of the Cistercian Order. He was a champion of contemplative prayer and lectio divina. In 1130, schism broke out in the church with the election of two competing popes and Bernard played a major role in healing it. He earned the nickname the "Mellifluous Doctor" for his eloquence.

He was a prolific writer and his theology and Mariology are of major importance, particularly within the Cistercian and Trappist orders. Bernard was influential in the founding of 163 monasteries in different parts of Europe and also in the establishment of canon law. Cistercians honor him as the founder of the order. In 1830 he was named a Doctor of the Church.

Unfortunately, late in his career the pope asked him to preach and gain support for the Second Crusade, but when it ultimately failed, Bernard was unfairly saddled with the blame.

Berno, Abbot *see* **Cluniac Order**

Beta Israel A sect of Ethiopian Jews out of contact with mainstream Judaism until the later part of the 20th century. Beta Israel is unique in Judaism in having had a relatively well-developed monastic tradition based in part on Christian monasticism. Beta Israel monasticism played a key role in developing and sustaining the Beth Israel sect. Tradition recognizes Abba Sabra, who lived during the 15th century, as the founder of their monastic movement. He was either a Christian monk who converted to the Beta Israel religion or a Beta Israel who decided to withdraw from the world and become a monk. There is also mention in a 15th or 16th Christian hagiography of a Christian monk by the name of Qozmos, who, following a dispute with his abbot, joined a group of people who followed Beta Israel. With the 20th century mass migrations to Israel, Beth Israel has virtually disappeared.

Bethlehem Brothers *see* **Order of Bethlehemite Brothers**

Bethlehemite Brothers *see* **Order of Bethlehemite Brothers**

bhandagarika In a Theravedin Buddhist monastery, an official in charge of the storeroom

bhante Venerable sir—a term often used when addressing a Buddhist monk

bhattuddesaka An official in charge of distributing soft food in a Theravedin Buddhist monastery

bhikkhu (Pali); bhikṣu (Sanskrit); gelong (Tibetan) A fully ordained Buddhist monk

bhikkhuni; bhikkhunī (Pali); bhikṣuṇī (Sanskrit); bǐqiūní (Chinese); bikuni (Japanese); ama (Japanese); biguni

(Korean); tì-khâu-ni (Vietnamese); gelongma (Tibetan) A fully ordained Buddhist nun. In Buddhism, women are as capable of reaching nirvana as men. According to Buddhist scriptures, the order of bhikkhunis was first created by the Buddha five years after he created the order of monks at the specific request of his aunt and foster-mother Mahapajapati Gotami, who became the first ordained bhikkhuni. Bhikkhunis are required to take extra vows, the Eight Garudhammas. Nuns at the time of the Buddha had equal rights and an equal share in everything. They are subordinate in the sense of being younger sisters to older brothers, not in the sense of being slaves to masters. Until recently, the lineages of female monastics only remained in Mahayana Buddhism and thus are prevalent in countries such as Korea, Vietnam, China, and Taiwan, but a few women have taken the full monastic vows in the Theravada and Vajraana schools in modern times. A woman is to be ordained, according to the traditional *Vinaya*, by both a monk and a nun.

bhikkuhunovaadaka In a Theravedin Buddhist monastery, a teacher of nuns

bhiksha Food obtained by Hindu monastics asking for alms. Usually, bhiksha is the meal served to a monk who visits a devout Hindu household. Occasionally, bhiksha has also referred to donations of gold, cattle, and even land, given to Brahmins in exchange for ritual services.

bhiksuni ***see*** **bhikkhuni**

bibliotheca ***see*** **library**

biguni ***see*** **bhikkhuni**

bikuni ***see*** **bhikkhuni**

bilo ***see*** **semantron**

biqiuní ***see*** **bhikkhuni**

Black Book A book containing details of the alleged enormities practiced in the English monasteries and religious houses, compiled by in the reign of Henry VIII, to hasten their dissolution

Black Canons ***see*** **Canons Regular of St. Augustine**

black fast A severe fast, with only one meal permitted, and that not until after sunset. No meat, dairy, eggs, or alcohol could be consumed. During Holy Week only bread, salt, herbs, and water was permitted. Formerly practiced by the faithful in the Roman Catholic Church, Anglican Communion, it is now confined only to some monastic communities and the Eastern Church.

Black Friars ***see*** **Order of Preachers**

Black Monks ***see*** **Order of St. Benedict**

Black Nuns ***see*** **Order of St. Benedict**

bleeding ***see*** **bloodletting**

Blessing of the Water A Cistercian ceremony on Sundays before Terce and the major Mass. The Mass-servers, monks, and novices filed in front of the celebrant who stood on the presbytery step and sprinkled them with newly blessed Holy Water. The 12th century customary of the order states that the sacristan should take some of the Holy Water to a stoop where the guests and familiars were, and then do the same for the lay-brothers; this suggests that the lay-brothers remained in their own area.

bloodletting; bleeding; phlebotomy; seynies; seyny Bloodletting was a supposed preventative and restorative treatment frequently administered during the Middle Ages. It was thought to restore balance to the body, to sharpen the senses and clear the brain; it was also believed to produce a musical voice, to promote longevity, and quench sexual desire. It became a ritualized part of some monastic communities: Cistercians were bled four times a year, Carthusians five, Canons Regular of St. Augustine every seven weeks, etc.

The time of bloodletting was known as the time of lessening or tempora minutionis. The person who performed the operation was known as the minutor. Those who were bled were called minuti or sanguinati, excused from night offices and other demands of the rule, allowed to recuperate in the infirmary, to speak, and to be given food normally granted only to the sick. In time it was all abused and bloodletting became a kind of holiday. There was to be no bloodletting at harvest, when everyone was needed to help in the fields or at feasts when the entire community was expected to participate in all the services. • *See also* **infirmarian**

Blue Friars *see* **Friars of the Sack**

Bodhidharma (ca. 470–543); Daruma (Japan) A Buddhist monk traditionally credited as the transmitter of Chan (Zen) Buddhism to China, and regarded as its first Chinese patriarch. According to legend, he trained with the monks of Shaolin Monastery and that led to the creation of Shaolin kung fu.

Bodhidharma is thought to be either a "Persian Central Asian" or a "South Indian." In Buddhist art, he is represented as an ill-tempered, non–Chinese person with a bushy beard. He is sometimes referred to as a "blue-eyed barbarian."

Failing to gain a following in south China, he went to the Shaolin Monastery but after failing there he is said to have retreated to a nearby cave, where he faced a wall for nine years and did not speak. In legend, he is then said to have fallen asleep after seven years, and then cut off his eyelids to prevent it happening again. His eyelids are then said to have become the first tea plants, which thereafter would provide a stimulant to help keep students of Chan awake during zazen (meditation).

Bojo Jinul (1158–1210); Jinul; Chinul A Korean Seon (Zen) Buddhist monk who began his studies at 15, and was ordained as a monk in 1173 at age 24. In 1182, he qualified for a higher position, but turned it down and traveled and studied instead. He then worked to establish a new Seon movement of disciplined believers with a balance of chanting, lectures, and meditation and this became the Jogye Order. In 1209, he finished his most famous work, *Excerpts from the Dharma Collection and Special Practice Record with Personal Notes*, which is an extensive exploration of Chan Buddhism in China.

Bon monasticism Established in Tibet in the late 10th century. Although similar to Tibetan Buddhism in many respects, there is controversy whether it is a school of Buddhism or a separate sect altogether. Bon is also practiced in Bhutan. Bon monastics undergo a very rigorous nine year training period of up to 17 hours a day. When Tibet was annexed to China in 1951 there were more than 300 Bon monasteries. Presently there are about 264 active Bon monasteries, nunneries, and hermitages.

Bonaventure, St. (1221–1274) An Italian Franciscan friar, scholastic theologian, philosopher, and prolific writer. He is known as the "Seraphic Doctor."

He entered the Franciscan Order in 1243. In 1253 he held the Franciscan chair at the University of Paris. He was elected Minister General of the Franciscan Order and directed them on a moderate path. After helping Gregory X to be elected pope, Bonaventure was named Cardinal Bishop of Albano.

At the Second Council of Lyon in 1274, after significant contributions leading to the union of the Greek and Latin churches, he died suddenly and in suspicious circumstances.

He was canonized in 1482 and declared a Doctor of the Church in 1588.

Boni Homines *see* **Grandmontines**

Boniface, St. (ca. 675–754) Anglo-Saxon Benedictine monk and missionary who brought Christianity to the Germanic parts of the Frankish Empire during the 8th century. He was made the archbishop of Mainz by Pope Gregory III and was martyred in Frisia in 754, along with 52 others. He is known as the "Apostle of the Germans." Through his efforts to reorganize and regulate the church of the Franks he helped shape Western Christianity. He is regarded as a unifier of Europe, and is considered as a Germanic national hero.

Bonshommes *see* **Grandmontines**

bonze A Buddhist priest, monk, or nun. Now an obsolete term, it was sometimes formerly used in the West.

bonzery A Buddhist monastery. Now an obsolete term, it was sometimes formerly used in the West.

book of hours Most often, an abbreviated form of the breviary that also contained the Daily Office. Other elements that might be included were church calendars, a litany of the saints, the Hours of the Cross, Gospel excerpts, some psalms, etc. They were first developed for lay people who wanted to have monastic elements in their devotional life. Many editions were plain, but those produced for the wealthy could have elaborate artwork and fine calligraphy.

Book of the First Monks; Decem Libri–Liber de Institutione Primorum Monacharum A medieval Catholic book that is supposed to embody the spirituality of the Prophet Elijah, who is honored as inspiration of the order. It has influenced many Carmelite saints. In medieval times the book was thought to have pre-dated the Carmelite *Rule of St. Albert*, but there is no evidence of this being the case.

Book of the History of the Fathers and of Their Words **see** ***Ethiopic Collectio Monastica***

Boots the Bishop A nickname of St. Albert the Great

bottlery The wine storage area of a monastery

bozu Strictly speaking, a resident priest of a Japanese Zen Buddhist temple, but popularly, any Buddhist priest or monk

bracinium *see* **brew house**

brebion A list of possessions, lands belonging to a monastery or church; a list of donors to be commemorated

Brethren of the Common Life; Fratres Vitae Communis; Broeders des Gemeenen Levens (Dutch) A Dutch quasimonastic Roman Catholic pietist community founded in the Netherlands in the 14th century by Gerard Groote.

While they did not take solemn vows, like traditional monastics, they lived together, gave up worldly goods, and lived chaste lives. Like Benedictines, they strove for a balance of work and prayer, and took meals in together accompanied by the reading aloud of Scripture. Notably, a community of the Brethren in Herford converted to Lutheranism in 1532 and were threatened with expulsion, but Martin Luther wrote in defense of them and they were allowed to stay in the Brethren until the house finally folded in 1841.

Brethren of the Holy Cross *see* **Canons Regular of the Order of the Holy Cross; Crutched Friars**

breviary A book used in the Western Church that contains all the liturgical texts for the Daily Office, consisting of psalms, Scripture lessons, writings of the Church Fathers, as well as hymns and prayers

breviator Sometimes a monastic scribe—usually the precentor—responsible for drawing up the mortuary roll of members of the community who had died; more often, a salaried lay messenger on the almoner's staff who carried the mortuary roll around to other monasteries so that they might pray for the deceased. In the latter sense, the person was also called a rotularius.

brewhouse; bracinium A common feature of monasteries in the Middle Ages since it was safer to drink beer than water. At first a sub-cellarer was generally in charge of the brewhouse, but in the later Middle Ages, it was generally a paid staff position.

Bridget of Sweden, St. *see* **Order of the Most Holy Savior**

Bridgettines *see* **Order of the Most Holy Savior**

brief *see* **rotulus**

Brigid of Ireland *see* **Brigid of Kildare**

Brigid of Kildare, St. (ca. 451–525); Brigid of Ireland Irish nun and one of Ireland's patron saints, along with Patrick and Columba. Information is sketchy, but she is reputed to have been an abbess and founder of several monasteries of nuns, including that of Kildare in Ireland, which was famous and revered. For centuries, Kildare was ruled by a double line of abbot-bishops and of abbesses, the abbess of Kildare being regarded as superior general of the monasteries in Ireland. Her successors have always been accorded episcopal honor. Brigid's oratory at Kildare became a center of religion and learning, and developed into a cathedral city. She is noted for her kindness to the poor and sometimes called the "Mary of the Gaels." Brigid, with an initial group of seven companions, is credited with organizing communal consecrated religious life for women in Ireland. One of her notable miracles was reputed to be turning water into beer.

Broeders des Gemeenen Levens *see* **Brethren of the Common Life**

brooms *see* **ogho; picchi; rajoharan**

brother; fra A man in a religious community. Often the term father is used for a man who is ordained, but sometimes all men in a community or order are called brother as an expression of equality and community. In the Eastern Church monks are generally called father, but in some places may address one another as brother. Novices are most often referred to as brother, although in some places, for example, on Mount Athos, novices are addressed as father.

Brothers and Sisters of Penance *see* **Third Order Secular of St. Francis**

Brothers Hospitallers of St. John of God *see* **Hospitaller Order of the Brothers of St. John of God**

Brothers of Mercy *see* **Hospitaller Order of the Brothers of St. John of God**

Brothers of Penitence *see* **Friars of the Sack**

Brothers of Saint Mary of Mount Carmel *see* **Carmelites**

Brothers of the Poor Life *see* **Spiritual Franciscans**

Bruno of Cologne, St. (ca. 1030–1101) A German monk ordained as a priest around 1055. Educated at Rheims in France, he gained fame as an educator, writer, philosopher, and theologian. Pope Urban II and many abbots and prelates were his pupils in their youth.

In 1075, Bruno was appointed chancellor of the Roman Catholic Archdiocese of Rheims, which involved him in the daily administration of the diocese. On the verge of being made bishop himself, he withdrew to live as a hermit under the direction Robert of Molesme, but soon found that this was not his vocation. He and his companions then built an oratory with small individual cells at a distance from each other where they lived isolated and in poverty, entirely occupied in prayer and study. He was then called to Rome but wisely kept himself apart from church politics and rivalries. There was an effort to install him as Archbishop of Reggio in Calabria, but he deferred and returned in 1091 to his solitary life near companions in isolated cabins. It was apparently never his intention to form a separate order, but the two monasteries he founded turned into the Carthusian Order

Buddhadasa Bhikkhu (1906–1993); Phra Dharmakosacarya; Nguam Phanit Thai Buddhist monk, scholar, philosopher, and reformer. Although he was qualified as a Buddhist monk and never renounced his vows, he came to consider all faiths essentially as one and was able to explain Buddhist beliefs through Taoism, Hinduism, Confucianism, Jainism and even science. He famously said, "There is no Buddhism; there is no Christianity; there is no Islam. How can they be the same or in conflict when they don't even exist?"

Buddhist monasticism Buddhist monasticism was instituted by Gautama Buddha between the 4th and 5th centuries BCE, and is central to Buddhism. It was inspired by earlier groups of wandering ascetics, although Buddhist monastics primarily live in monasteries. Monks are called bhikkhus and nuns are called bhikkhunis. They are considered to be vital for the preservation and spread of Buddhism.

While monastics are expected to live simple lives and concentrate on meditation, study, and morality, there is no central control so there is a wide variation in practice and philosophy. Traditionally, Buddhist monastics wear robes, but the color of varies by community: saffron is characteristic for Theravada groups; blue, gray, or brown for Mahayana Sangha members in Vietnam, maroon in Tibetan Buddhism, gray in Korea, and black in Japan. Monks usually wear a skirt, shirt vest, and an outer robe, which may be insulated for cold weather wear. Nuns wear the same, but add a bodice and an outer skirt. Both monks and nuns shave their heads. In Thailand, monks also shave their eyebrows.

In some traditions it is possible to keep a relationship with their original families. While celibacy is generally of primary importance in monastic discipline, there are some sects in Japan and Korea where members are permitted to be married.

Some Buddhist monastics eat only one meal a day, others eat more. Vegetarianism is often practiced, but meat is not generally forbidden unless an animal is killed specifically for their benefit.

In distinction from Christian monastics, most Buddhist monastics, while respecting their seniors, do not take vows of obedience. Abbesses and abbots tend to be more like administrators rather than rulers, but respect is still given to senior members.

Monastics make their decisions collectively through regular gatherings of the community. Abbots and abbesses are generally elected by a vote of members in the community, although sometimes, as in Thailand, they are elected by the lay community.

budo The stupas of Zen Buddhist monastics

budo sawaong A Zen Buddhist temple whose abbacy can only be assumed by the Dharma descendants of the previous abbot

bursar; hordarian; terrar The treasurer of a monastery • *See also* **docheiarios**

bursary; spendement The treasury of a monastery

burying ceremony A ceremony a prospective anchorite could undergo before being walled up in a small cell attached to a church. The cell would have windows built into it for receiving food and other necessary items, for communicating with servants and supplicants, and for observing Mass and receiving Communion, but there would be no doors. • *See also* **anchorhold; anchorite**

Bussho Dento Kokushi *see* **Dogen Zenji**

Butler, Cuthbert (1858–1934) Irish Benedictine monk of Downside Abbey in England, who became known as a monastic reformer and writer on mysticism and ecclesiastical historian and writer. From 1906 to 1922, he was the abbot of Downside Abbey. He played an active role in the reform movement of the English Benedictine Congregation that restored normal Benedictine government within English Roman Catholic monasteries.

Butler, William John *see* **Community of St. Mary the Virgin**

buttery An annex to the kitchen from which food and drink was served to the frater

~C~

Caesarius of Arles, St. (468/470–542) French Cistercian who was the foremost ecclesiastic of his generation in Merovingian Gaul and considered to be of the last generation of church leaders of Gaul that worked to promote large-scale ascetic elements into the Western Christian tradition. His practices were so strict his health suffered and he went to Arles and the community there helped him recover. It was here he was made a bishop in 502. His *Regula Virginum* (*Rule for Virgins*), was produced in 512, and is the first western rule written exclusively for women. He also founded a monastery in Arles.

caitaya A meeting hall used for worship and teaching by Buddhist monastics

Cajetan, St. *see* **Theatines**

calced Religious orders that wear shoes, as opposed to discalced that do not

caldarium A large cauldron for boiling water. There were usually three in a monastery: one for cooking beans, one for vegetables, and one for hot wash water.

calefactorium *see* **warming house**

calefactory *see* **warming house**

caloyer A monk of the Greek church; a cenobite, anchorite, or recluse of the *Aeskiton* (*Rule of St. Basil*), especially, one on or near Mt. Athos

Camaldolese Of, like, or relating to the Camaldolese Order

Camaldolese Hermits of Monte Corona *see* **Camaldolese Order**

Camaldolese Order; Ordo Camaldulensium The Camaldolese were established through the efforts of the Italian monk St. Romuald (ca. 950–ca. 1025/27). His reform sought to renew and integrate the eremitical tradition of monastic life with that of the cenobium. Around 1012 Romuald founded the Sacred Hermitage of Camaldoli in the Tuscan hills. There monks lived in individual cells, but also observed a common life, worshiping daily in the church and breaking bread in the dining hall. Here the distinctive white habit first appeared. Also at Camaldoli are first found in combination the cenobite and hermit branches that are now so marked a feature of the order. The order was approved by Pope Alexander II, in 1072. It should be noted that St. Romuald never thought of himself as anything but a part of the Benedictine tradition, and the order continues to think of itself that way. Although heavily influenced by the *Rule of St. Benedict*, the Camaldolese way of life is more ascetic. St. Romuald himself left no written rule. Never numerous, most, but not all, Camaldolese communities are in Italy. Soon after the various communities established by St. Romuald began to develop, communities of nuns desired to share in this reform and by 1068, had their own "Little Rule."

There are two Camaldolese congregations: The Benedictine Camaldolese are headquartered at Camaldoli (known as the Holy Hermitage) and maintain a mix of monasteries and hermitages of men. The Benedictine Camaldolese may use either O. Camald., or O.S.B. Cam. for post-nominal initials.

The other congregation, known as the Camaldolese Hermits of Monte Corona, was established by the Renaissance reformer, Paolo Giustiniani. This group lives solely in hermitages, usually with a very small number of monks comprising the community. Unlike the other congregation, it is not a member of the larger Benedictine Confederation. The Camaldolese Hermits use the post-nominal initials Er. Cam.

camera A specialized farm or holding belonging to a military order, but without a resident preceptor

camerarius *see* **chamberlain**

Candidus et Canonicus Ordo Praemonstratensis *see* **Order of Canons Regular of Prémontré**

Cannon, Harriet Starr (1823–1896) American Episcopalian nun and superior who founded what is now the Community of St. Mary, one of the first orders of Augustinian nuns in the Anglican Communion. She was confirmed in 1844, although she was not particularly religious as a girl. As a young woman she taught music but when her younger sister died in 1855 she was moved to become a deaconess in the Sisterhood of the Holy Communion and worked with the poor in New York City. In 1863 a conflict with the Sisterhood of the Holy Communion led Ayers and four others to found what is now the Community of St. Mary to work with homeless, women, and children and is still functioning. • *See also* **Community of St. Mary**

canonesses Members of a religious community of Christian women living a simple life. The name corresponds to the male equivalent, canon. As with the canons, there are two types: canonesses regular, who follow a monastic rule, and secular canonesses, who do not follow a monastic rule.

Towards the close of the 8th century, the title of canoness is found for the first time among communities of women who lived a common life and took vows of chastity and obedience. They cared for church vestments, and taught the young, particularly the daughters of the nobility. Their superiors were known as abbesses. • *See also* **canonesses regular**

Canonesses of St. Augustine of the Mercy of Jesus; Hospital Sisters; Hermit Sisters of St. Augustine A Roman Catholic order of canonesses who care for the sick and needy and lead a semi-contemplative life. They originated as a confraternity of French lay women in the 13th century to assist the Augustinian friars who cared for the poor and the sick at the fishing port of Dieppe. In time, they were formed into a religious congregation with both lay sisters and canonesses.

The lay sisters were employed at the manual tasks of the community, did not have to say the Daily Office and did not care for the sick. The canonesses said the Daily Office and cared for the sick and the poor.

The religious habit of the canoness is a white tunic girdled by a leather cincture. On their head they wear a black veil for the professed—with a white veil for the novices—formerly attached to a coif and bandeau. To this was added a starched guimpe (a high necked undergarment) covering the neck and chest, and for choir duties, a rochet, all covered by a black cape, before the simplification of the habit in the 20th century. The order expanded first in France and then worldwide, notably in Europe and South Africa.

canonesses regular Communities of women in the Western Church who took the name and the rule of life laid down for the various congregations of canons regular. As regards origin and antiquity the same is to be said of orders of women both in general and in particular as of orders of men. St. Basil in both of his rules addresses both men and women. St. Augustine of Hippo drew up the first general rule for communities of women in the year 423. The occupations of the canonesses consist of recitation of the Daily Office, the care of the church vestments, and the education of the young The canonesses regular, for the most part, follow the *Rule of St. Augustine*. Their superiors are known as abbesses.

Canonical Hours *see* **Daily Office**

Canonici Regulares Ordinis S. Augustini Congregationis *see* **Canons Regular of St. Augustine**

Canonici Regulares Ordinis S. Crucis *see* **Canons Regular of the Order of the Holy Cross**

Canonici Regulares Sancti Antonii *see* **Order of St. Anthony**

Canonici Regulares Sanctissimae Crucis a Stella Rubea *see* **Knights of the Cross with the Red Star**

canonry The office of a canon; canons considered as a group

canons Members of a religious community of clerics in the Western Church living a simple life. There are two type of canons: canons regular, which live together and follow a monastic rule, and secular canons, which do not follow a monastic rule or live together. The title of canon is sometimes given as an honorific to a dean or senior cleric in which case it has nothing to do with monasticism.

Canons of St. Ambrose *see* **Canons Regular of the Lateran**

Canons of St. Mary of Reno *see* **Canons Regular of the Lateran**

Canons of the Order of St. Benedict An quasimonastic organization of lay and clerical non-residential communities of men and women of the Anglican Church of Canada and the Episcopal Church of the United States similar to the Christian Communities of the Episcopal Church. While most canons live under the *Rule of St. Augustine,* these live under the *Rule of St. Benedict,* and they do not live in a cathedral. One may become an aspirant as a solitary but may not take vows until a local community is formed. These local communities meet together on a frequent basis. Members may either be professed or oblates. The head of a local community is called a prior and each community is independent, although there is also a prior general. Members use the post-nominal initials O.S.B. Cn. • *see also* **Christian Community**

canons regular Communities of clergy in the Western Church who live together and follow a monastic rule. Usually they follow the *Rule of St. Augustine*—in which case they are thus Canons Regular of St. Augustine. Distinct from monks, the purpose of a canon is to engage in public ministry of liturgy and sacraments for those who visit their churches. Canons take vows of chastity, poverty, and obedience, though this is a later development. The first communities of canons regular took vows of common property and stability. In modern times, the vow of stability is sometimes omitted. By the 12th century canons regular were common Western Europe. Usually they were not connected with one another. Ministries were varied, but it was common to find them in cathedrals.

Canons Regular of Fregionaia *see* **Canons Regular of the Lateran**

Canons Regular of St. Anthony of Vienne *see* **Order of St. Anthony**

Canons Regular of St. Augustine; Augustinian Canons Regular; Canonici

Regulares Ordinis S. Augustini Congregationis; Black Canons (UK); Austin Canons (UK) A Roman Catholic religious order for clerics who follow the *Rule of St. Augustine* and that had its genesis in the middle of the 11th century. While monasticism was primarily lay in its early days, the canons are clerics with pastoral duties who have added religious vows. The order grew and flourished until the Protestant Reformation and the French Revolution. Modern emphasis has been on mission, educational, and hospital work. They use the post-nominal initials C.R.S.A.

The Canons usually wear a rochet over a cassock or tunic although there is some same variation in different congregations. Some Canons wear white tunics and scapulars. The Austrian congregation wears a sarozium (a narrow band of white cloth) which hangs down both front and back over a cassock for their weekday wear. For solemn occasions, they wear the rochet under a violet mozzetta (shoulder cape).

The order is not one legal body, but a union of various independent congregations. Their houses are called abbeys. The superiors of larger houses are abbots while smaller houses are priors or provosts.

Canons Regular of St. Augustine of the Congregation of the Most Holy Savior at the Lateran *see* **Canons Regular of the Lateran**

Canons Regular of Santa Maria in Portu *see* **Canons Regular of the Lateran**

Canons Regular of the Holy Cross of Coimbra; Ordo Canonicorum Regularium Sanctae Crucis An order of Roman Catholic canons regular founded in Portugal in 1131. Enjoying widespread support and royal patronage the order flourished. They were entrusted with the mission of the re-evangelization of the territories freed from the Moors.

In time, however, internal dissension and conflicts with bishops took a toll. While attempts at reform were made in the 15th and early 16th centuries, the order became decadent and suppression began in the 18th century. It was finally dissolved by the Portuguese government in 1834.

In 1977, a movement called the Work of the Holy Angels was begun to restore the order. Members of the order use the post-nominal initials O.R.C.

Canons Regular of the Lateran; Canons Regular of St. Augustine of the Congregation of the Most Holy Savior at the Lateran; Congregatio Sanctissimi Salvatoris Lateranensis An order of priests and brothers Roman Catholic canons regular descended from the 12th century Canons Regular of Santa Maria in Portu, on the Isle of Corizo near Ravenna. Due mainly to commendatory abbots there was only the prior and one canon left by 1419 when a union was effected with the Canons Regular of Fregionaia, and in 1449 the Canons Regular of the Holy Cross of Mortara was added, but decline was still an issue until 1431 when Pope Eugene IV asked them to serve at the Basilica of St. John Lateran in Rome and they assumed the present name.

The Canons wear a white cassock, sash, shoulder cape (mozzetta) and skull cap (zucchetto) that matches what the pope wears. They have provinces in Europe and North and South America use the post-nominal initials C.R.L.

Canons Regular of the Order of the Holy Cross; Canonici Regulares Ordinis S. Crucis; Crosiers; Brethren of the Holy Cross A Roman Catholic order of priests and brothers granted full and final papal approval in 1248. The order grew to about 90 houses but many were suppressed during the Protestant Reformation and the French Revolution. By 1840, only five members remained, but they were able to rebuild and now have an international presence. Members follow the *Rule of St. Augustine*, live and worship together, and perform such ministries as preaching, teaching, spiritual direction, and prison ministry.

The religious houses are called priories, the superiors are called priors. The order has provinces that are headed by priors provincial. The order is headed by a master general.

Formation consists of a year of postulancy, a year of novitiate, and three years of temporary vows, before solemn profession may be given. Members use the post-nominal initials O.S.C.

cantor; cantrix (female); provisor; custos A singer who sets the pitch, leads the singing, and sings solo in appropriate spots. In larger communities, they are appointed for a week at a time.

cantrix *see* **cantor**

capella ante portas A chapel at the gate of a religious house for use by visitors so that the monastics' chapel would be undisturbed by outsiders. The Cistercian Rule specifically required these.

capicerius In the Western Church, an assistant to the sacristan who is in charge of church vestments, altar cloths, and clothes for the monks

capitular Of or relating to a monastic chapter; an act passed in a chapter; a member of a chapter

capitular definitor *see* **definitor**

capitularly In the manner or form of an ecclesiastical chapter

capitulary A capitular; the body of laws or statutes of a monastic chapter, or of an ecclesiastical council

capitulum The short reading from the rule of a monastic community, which was read at chapter

capoch *see* **cowl**

cappa A cloak or cape worn over a habit, as by the Dominicans

capuccio *see* **capuche**

capuce *see* **capuche**

capuche; capuce; capuccio A large hood or cowl, as worn by Capuchins, Society of St. Augustine friars and Camaldolese monks

Capuchin Poor Clares; Sisters of Suffering Cloistered nuns of the Order of St. Clare, who form the female branch of the Capuchin Order. They were founded in 1538 in Naples by Maria Launtina Longo. She and the other nuns of that community embraced the then-new Capuchin reform movement, and so austere was the life that they were called "Sisters of Suffering." They live according to the same rules and regulations as the Capuchin friars, and are members of the friars' provinces. They use the post-nominal initials O.S.C. Cap.

Capuchiness A member of the Capuchin Poor Clares

Capuchins *see* **Friars Minor Capuchin**

caputium *see* **cowl**

Carmelite Order of the Ancient Observance *see* **Order of Discalced Carmelites**

Carmelites In the late 12th century a group of European Christian pilgrims came to live as hermits on Mount Carmel in Palestine in the tradition of Elijah the prophet and with a special devotion to the Blessed Virgin Mary. They became known as the Brothers of Saint Mary of Mount Carmel. Somewhere between 1206 and 1214 the hermits asked St. Albert, the patriarch of Jerusalem and papal legate to create a rule for them. The *Rule of St. Albert* consists of 16 articles and demands strict obedience to the prior and abstinent from meat.

About 1235 they were forced by the Saracens to abandon Mt. Carmel and most members went back to Europe where they flourished. In 1452, an order of cloistered nuns was formed. In the 15th and 16th centuries, there was some relaxation of discipline in various communities and various reforms were introduced. The most notable of which was that of St. Teresa of Avila and St. John of the Cross. In 1592, their reform became the separate Order of Discalced Carmelites.

Before the French Revolution, the Carmelites had 13,000 members, but by the beginning of the 20th century it was reduced to 727 religious. In 2001, it had over 2,000 friars, 700 nuns, and over 25,000 third orders members. • *See also* **Order of Discalced Carmelites; Order of the Brothers of the Blessed Virgin Mary of Mount Carmel; Secular Order of Discalced Carmelites; Third Order of Our Lady of Mount Carmel**

carrels Divisions of a chamber or cloister walk into individual study areas

Carta Caritatis **see** ***Charter of Charity***

Carthusians; Ordo Cartusiensis; Order of St. Bruno A Roman Catholic religious order of enclosed monks and nuns founded by St. Bruno in 1084 that combines both eremitical and cenobitic life in a building called a charterhouse. The charterhouse is generally a small community of hermits based on the model of the 4th century lavras of Palestine with separate cells for each hermit. The focus of Carthusian life is contemplation. To this end there is an emphasis on solitude and silence. The monks' community is headed by a prior and populated by choir monks (who are referred to as hermits) and lay brothers. The hermits all eventually become priests.

The hermit usually only leaves his cell only for three daily prayer services in the chapel, including the community Eucharist. Once a week, the members take a long walk in the countryside during which they may speak. On Sundays and solemn feast days a community meal is taken in silence. Twice a year there is a community recreation day, and the members may also receive an annual visit from immediate family members.

About 40 percent of a Carthusian men's community is composed of lay brothers who do the majority of the labor. Carthusian nuns live a life similar to the monks, but with some differences. Choir nuns tend to lead somewhat less anchoretic lives, while still maintaining a strong commitment to solitude and silence. There are currently 25 active charterhouses on three continents.

Postulancy is 6 to 12 months, the novitiate is two years, and simple vows are for three years. Carthusians use the post-nominal initials O. Cart.

cartulary A keeper of monastic records; a register containing copies of the deeds or charters relating to the lands, churches, and other properties of a monastery; a book of collected documents usually dealing with legal and economic transactions of a monastery

Casel, Odo (1886–1948) German Benedictine priest, liturgist, and theologian. He became a monk in 1905, was professed in 1907, and ordained a priest in 1911. He earned doctoral degrees in both theology and philology, was a prolific writer, and a proponent of Mystical Body theology. His groundbreaking theological reform work sometimes brought him into conflict with the church hierarchy and the theological establishment.

Cassian, St. John ***see*** **John Cassian, St.**

Cassinese Congregation ***see*** **Subiaco Cassinese Congregation**

Cassino, Monte The Italian Roman Catholic monastery first established by St. Benedict in 529. It is about 130 kilometers (81 miles) southeast of Rome. Once established at Monte Cassino, Benedict never left. It was here that he wrote the *Rule of St. Benedict* that became the founding principle for Western monasticism. Unfortunately, its prominent site has always made it an object of strategic importance. It was sacked or destroyed a number of times, starting with the Lombards in 580. Another notable sacking was by Napoleon's troops in 1799. The worst was in 1944 where a major battle was fought and the Allies destroyed it in the mistaken belief that German troops had taken up positions there. As it turned out, the Germans only moved in after the bombing. The abbey was rebuilt after the war and reconsecrated in 1964.

Cassiodorus (ca. 485–ca. 585); Flavius Magnus Aurelius Cassiodorus Senator A Roman statesman, monk, and writer serving in the administration of Theoderic the Great, king of the Ostrogoths. Senator was part of his surname, not his rank.

In 537 or 538, he left Italy for Constantinople where he remained for almost two decades, concentrating on religious questions. Upon retirement, he founded the monastery of Vivarium on the shores of the Ionian Sea. It seems to have been governed by Cassiodorus' work *Institutiones* which was composed from the 530s into the 550s. Cassiodorus spent much of time in Christian education and instituted a course of study at the vivarium that stressed reading and meditation, beginning with the Psalms. Cassiodorus also promoted a more organized and professional system of copying manuscripts which became normative for monasteries and contributed greatly to the preservation of ancient texts.

In spite of his contributions to literature and monastic education, Cassiodorus was not highly acclaimed after his lifetime and medieval scholars sometimes made mistakes for his name, residence, profession, and even his religion.

cassock ***see*** **inner cassock; outer cassock**

cassock coat In the Eastern Church, a garment with the same cut as an outer cassock, but of slightly larger and of heavier material that may be worn on cold days over the outer cassock or in lieu of it. It may or may not have a fur-lined collar.

cassock vest; kontorasson; amaniko; gileko In the Eastern Church, a closely fitted collarless vest, usually falling slightly below the waist. It is sometimes worn over the inner cassock in lieu of the outer cassock.

caterer Usually a paid servant who served under the kitchener. The caterer supervised the cooks, oversaw meal service, and was sometimes also responsible for bulk purchases of food.

cathedral monastery; cathedral priory A monastic community attached to the church holding the diocesan's throne. The bishop was usually styled as the abbot, but the community was headed by a prior and the bishop had no voice in the chapter.

cathedral priory ***see*** **cathedral monastery**

Catherine of Bologna, St. (1413–1463) Italian Poor Clare nun, mystic, writer, teacher, and artist. In 1426, she left the court and joined a lay community of Beguines which later converted to a house of Observant Poor Clares in 1431. In 1456, she became abbess of a new convent, Corpus Domini in Bologna, and remained as such until her death.

Catherine's major religious work is *Seven Spiritual Weapons Necessary for Spiritual Warfare* (*Le Sette Armi Spirituali*). Probably first written in 1438, she kept the book hidden until she neared death. It was important in late medieval mysticism. She also wrote lauds, short religious treatises, letters, and poetry and illuminated books. She was canonized, in 1712 and is a patron saint of artists, although paintings previously attributed to her are now thought to be by someone else.

Catubhummika Mahasatipaṭṭhana Nikaya ***see*** **Hngettwin Nikaya**

Celestines; Hermits of St. Damiano; Morronites A Roman Catholic monastic order founded in in Italy as the Hermits of St. Damiano, by Pietro da Morrone in 1244. About 1254, the founder gave the order a rule based on his own severe practices. In 1264 the order was approved as a branch of the Benedictines by Pope Urban IV. It followed the *Rule of St. Benedict*, but the founder supplemented it with additional severities and privations. Notably, they said matins at 2 a.m., and only the sick were given meat. In 1294, Pietro was elected as Pope Celestine V, and the order adopted the name of Celestines. Members of the order wore a white woolen cassock with a black hood and looked very much like that of the Cistercians. They used the post-nominal initials O.S.B. Cel. The order became extinct in the 18th century.

celibacy While celibacy is the norm for monastics of all stripes, there are some Buddhist sects where members are permitted to be married. This was also the case with early Celtic monastics until they came under the authority of Rome. Members of the present-day quasimonastic Christian Communities of the American Episcopal Church have exactly the same rules as traditional monastic communities with the sole exception that members must be chaste, as opposed to celibate.

Among Buddhist monastics, it is allowed in some places but not in others. Men in Thailand typically ordain only before being married. Men in Laos, Myanmar (Burma), and Thailand could traditionally return to the monastery from time to time after being married, provided that they secured permission from their wives. In Japan, starting in the 9th century, they began a new form of ordination based on the bodhisattva vow that allowed marriage. Monks of some traditions of Tibetan Buddhism, like the Nyingmapa, can marry, while other Tibetan traditions, like the Kagyupa, cannot. The same is true for Korean, Chinese, and Taiwanese Buddhists: some can marry, and some cannot.

In the 5th century CE, Nestorian monks were required to be married and this lasted a number of centuries.

In New Monastic communities, marriage is sometimes allowed.

Celibacy is common among Hindu and Jain monastics, but some sects experiment with consensual Tantric sex as a part of their practice. Sex is viewed by them as transcendence from a personal, intimate act to something impersonal and ascetic.

cell; monasterium; parivena (Buddhism); drashag (Tibetan) The individual room of a monastic where one can pray and work in solitude, as well as read and rest; also, the hut of an anchorite

cellar; cellarium The great storehouse of a monastery

cellarer; cellaress (female); procurator; manciple; econome (Eastern Church); oikonomos (Eastern Church) A steward of a monastery who has charge of procuring and keeping the provisions and equipment, and as such, one of the most important positions in a monastery

cellaress *see* **cellarer**

cellarium *see* **cellar**

Cells *see* **Kellia**

cena *see* **supper**

cenobite; mynstermon (Anglo-Saxon) A person living a monastic community, under a rule and a superior—as opposed to an eremite (one living alone). The organized version of Christian cenobitic monasticism is commonly thought to have started in Egypt in the 4th century. Christian monks of previous centuries were usually hermits, especially in the Middle East. While there had been previous cenobitic communities in Christianity, St. Pachomius is generally credited with organizing cenobitism as we know it today. His cenobitic monasteries are thought to have been modeled after the barracks he lived in while serving in the Roman army.

cenobitic Of or relating to a cenobite or cenobitism

cenobitism The state of being a cenobite; the belief or practice of a cenobite

cenobium *see* **monastery**

census Monetary tribute paid by some monasteries to Rome; monetary tribute paid to Cluny by its dependent houses

C.F.R. The post-nominal initials of the Community of the Franciscan Friars of the Renewal

chamberlain; camerarius; vestiarius A monastic in charge of providing clothing, beds, tools, wood for the calefactory, and other items for the community.
• *See also* **docheiarios**

chanter; chantress (female) A monastic official in charge of choral service and production of books

chantress *see* **chanter**

chaplain Sometimes a personal assistant to the superior of a large house who functioned much like a business manager

Chapman, John (1865–1933) English Benedictine monk, abbot, writer, patristics and New Testament scholar. He was ordained as a deacon in the Church of England in 1889 but was troubled and left his curacy. In 1891 he entered the Roman Catholic Jesuit novitiate but felt that was not his vocation and entered the Benedictine Maredsous Abbey in Belgium. He professed solemn vows in 1895 and was ordained a priest in 1895.

In 1914, at the outbreak of World War I, Chapman first became a professor of theology at Downside Abbey, joining the many monks who had fled Maredsous to England. In early 1915, he became army chaplain to the British forces. From 1919 to 1922 he spent most of his time in Rome working on the revision of the Vulgate translation of the Bible. In 1929 he was elected abbot of Downside Abbey.

A brilliant scholar, Chapman read both Greek and Latin with facility, but also read and wrote French, Italian, and German with ease. His writings have had a lasting value, particularly his *Spiritual Letters*. An oft quoted statement of his was: "Pray as you can, not as you cannot, but whatever you do, don't stop praying."

chapter The assembly of a monastic community at which a chapter of their rule is read and business is transacted

chapter house; synodikon (Eastern Church) A room in a monastery in which chapter is held

chapter of faults An assembly of a monastic community at which community members confess their external faults and ask the forgiveness of other members.

charism A particular gift of God that identifies or is characteristic of a monastic community

charistikarioi; charistikarios The beneficiary of a charistike, who held administrative power over the monastery's estates and gained financially from his position

charistikarios *see* **charistikarioi**

charistike; charistikion A feudal institution of the Middle Byzantine Period of the Eastern Roman Empire in which the financial management of a failing monastery was given to a layman for life or several generations. The practice of granting charistikia probably began in the late 9th century. It became widespread in the 11th and 12th centuries, but mostly disappeared by the 13th century. The original idea for charistikia came from the founders of monasteries and was supposed to put the monasteries on a firm financial footing, but in practice it was widely abused by the landed gentry who would often take monastic revenues for themselves.

charistikion *see* **charistike**

Chariton the Confessor, St. (fl. 3rd century CE**)** Christian monk and ascetic from Asia Minor. Nearly martyred during the persecution of Christians under the Emperor Aurelian, he was released from prison in 275 then abducted by bandits on a pilgrimage to Jerusalem. When freed from them he became a hermit in the Pharan Valley and established a church and monastic community that was one of the first lavras. He later established lavras near Jericho and in the Hasmonean Valley. He is credited with establishing by example some of the main traits of Christian monastic life including silence, solitude, manual work, and prayer at fixed hours.

Charter of Charity; Carta Caritatis A document that sets out the constitutional framework of the Cistercian Order and defines the familial arrangement of the houses. It was first compiled about 1114 but has since been revised and updated.

charterhouse A Carthusian monastic building providing extreme privacy in the cells. Each hermit has his own cell traditionally consisting of a single room used for storage of wood for a stove and a workshop for required manual labor. A second floor is used for sleeping, study, and prayer. Each cell also has a walled garden. Next to the door is a small revolving compartment, called a turn, so that meals and other items may be passed in and out of the cell without the hermit having to meet the bearer. Most meals are provided in this manner and the hermit eats in solitude. • *See also* **turning window**

chartreuse A liqueur made by French Carthusian monks since 1737. According to legend, it is based on a recipe given to them by François Annibal d'Estrées, a French marshal of artillery, in 1605. The formula is said to include 130 herbs, plants and flowers and secret ingredients combined in a wine alcohol base.

Chatsumarn Kabilsingh ***see*** **Dhammananda Bhikkhuni**

chaturmas The four-month monsoon period in India during which Jain monastics stay in one place to reduce the risk of accidentally killing insects and other small forms of life which thrive during the rains

checker; chequer; saccarium A monastic counting house where accounts were tallied, payments made, etc. It is usually controlled by the cellarer.

Cheonggyu ***see*** **Pure Rules**

chequer ***see*** **checker**

chernichki In Russia, Orthodox semi-monastic lay women who wore black clothing and followed monastic lifestyle but did not enter a monastic community

chi phram In Thailand, a temporary maechi (quasimonastic woman). They typically do not shave their heads. • *See also* **maechi**

Chih-i ***see*** **Zhiyi**

child oblate; puer oblatus A child vowed and given by their parents to the monastic life, in houses under the *Rule of St. Benedict* up to 656 when the Tenth Council of Toledo forbade their acceptance before the age of ten and granted them free permission to leave the monastery when they reached the age of puberty if they so desired.

Chinul ***see*** **Bojo Jinul**

Chishin ***see*** **Ippen Shonin**

Chittister, Joan (1936–) American Roman Catholic Benedictine nun, prioress, theologian, author, and speaker. She was the prioress of the Benedictine Sisters of Erie, Pennsylvania, for 12 years. She has been president of the Federation of St. Scholastica, a federation of 20 Monasteries of Benedictine Women, the Leadership Conference of Women Religious, and co-chair of the Global Peace Initiative of Women. In 2001, the Vatican's Congregation for Institutes of Consecrated Life and Societies of Apostolic Life asked that she not speak at the Women's Ordination Worldwide conference in Dublin, but she did anyway. Holder of a PhD and formerly a research associate of St. Edmund's College at

Cambridge University, she is author of over 50 books and 700 articles.

Choboq Ar-Rayès, Rafqa Pietra; St. Rafka, St. Rebecca Lebanese Maronite nun. At age her stepmother wanted her to marry her stepbrother, and her maternal aunt wanted her to marry her cousin and she fled to the Convent of Our Lady of Liberation to avoid either. In 1855, she became a novice with the Daughters of Mary of the Immaculate Conception. She became a teaching sister and took her vows in 1862. In 1871, her religious institute merged with another to form the Order of the Sacred Hearts of Jesus and Mary. At this time, Rafka chose to become cloistered and joined what is now the Lebanese Maronite Order of St. Anthony. She made her solemn vows in 1873. Life was very rigid and ascetic there.

In 1885, she prayed that she had never been sick and felt abandoned by God. She developed a pain in one eye that night and it was removed without anesthetic at her request. The pain then moved to the other eye and that too was removed. Both eye sockets continued to hemorrhage several times a week for 30 years and she was in continual pain, but she to participate in choral prayer and knit stockings for the other sisters and to spin cotton and wool. In 1907, she became paralyzed. She was canonized by Pope John Paul II in 2001.

choir; quire The chapel within the monastic enclosure where the sisters or monks gather for Mass, the Daily Office, and other prayers throughout the day

choir monastics; choir religious; choir monks; choir nuns Originally, monastics devoted to constant liturgical prayer in the choir of the church. This was made possible by using lay monastics to do most of the chores. The terms are now used for monastics who are professed and are full members of their communities, as opposed to novices, oblates, and lay monastics

choir monks *see* **choir monastics**

choir nuns *see* **choir monastics**

choir office A service, typically one of the Daily Offices, sung or said in the choir space of the chancel

choir religious *see* **choir monastics**

choir stalls; stalls; quire stalls (UK) Specialized church seating provided for those monastics and others who were required to be seated for a long time in church. Originally just plain benches, over the years, abbreviated wooden screens were added to the sides and front to minimize drafts. Sometimes canopies were added. Misericords were added to provide support when prolonged periods of standing were required, and ledges were added in front of the stalls to hold service books.

Christian Community In the Episcopal Church of the United States, a quasimonastic order of Christians in communion with the See of Canterbury (Church of England), who voluntarily commit themselves for life, or a term of years, in obedience to their rule and constitution. The only canonical difference between a monastic order and a Christian Community in the Episcopal Church canon law is that the members of monastic communities must be celibate, while those in a Christian Community are required only to be chaste. • *See also* **Canons of the Order of St. Benedict; Secular Institute**

Chrodegang, St. *see* ***Rule of St. Chrodegang***

Chrysostom, St. *see* **John Chrysostom**

Chu Hung *see* **Zhu Hong**

chuji *see* **abbot**

C.I.B. Abbreviation of Communio Internationalis Benedictinarum

cincture The rope or a belt worn with the monastic habit

cinctured Having or wearing a cincture

circaria *see* **circary**

circary; circaria A geographic unit of administration in the Premonstratensian Order. There are seven circaries within the order.

circas *see* **circator**

circator; circatore; circas; custodes ordinis In large monasteries in former times a third, fourth, or even fifth prior whose duty it was to make the rounds of the monastery to see whether anything was amiss and whether the members were working as assigned. He had no authority to correct or punish the brethren, but was to report to the claustral prior whatever he found amiss or contrary to the rules. • *See also* **epistemonarches; warden of the order**

circatore *see* **circator**

circumcelliones *see* **gyrovagues**

Cistercians of the Common Observance; Cistercians of the Original Observance; Ordo Cisterciensis; Bernardines; White Monks; White Nuns A Roman Catholic order derived from the Benedictines as a separate and reformed community in 1098 at Cîteaux, France, led by Robert, Abbot of Molesme. They are governed by a form of the *Rule of St. Benedict.* Lay brothers were used to do farming, allowing choir monks more isolation from the world. The lay brothers had an abbreviated rule known as the *Uses.* At one time there were as many lay brothers as monks, but that number gradually decreased over time.

During the 12th century, the Cistercians grew more powerful and influential than the Cluniac Order. The first Cistercian monastery for women was established at Tart-l'Abbaye near Dijon in France, in the year 1125, by Benedictine nuns. At their height in the 15th century, the Cistercians had 750 communities. In time, the order grew extremely wealthy and the initial rigors were increasingly relaxed. From the 15th century onward, the order struggled and the Trappists broke away as a reform movement. Today, Cistercians are known as following the Common Observance, while Trappists are known as following the Strict Observance. The Cistercians of the Common Observance had 30 monasteries and 800 choir monks in 2017. The members use the post-nominal initials O. Cist. • *See also* **Order of Cistercians of the Strict Observance**

Cistercians of the Original Observance *see* **Cistercians of the Common Observance**

Citeaux Abbey; Abbaye de Cîteaux A Roman Catholic abbey located near Dijon, France. Founded in 1098 by Robert of Molesme. Largely through the activities of the St. Bernard of Clairvaux the abbey became the headquarters and mother house of the Cistercian order, with abbeys scattered all over Europe.

Only a part of a Gothic cloister and some 18th century buildings remain of after the destruction of the French Revolution. In 1898, the remains of the abbey were bought back and occupied again by the Cistercians. It is now occupied by about 35 members of the Trappists.

civarabhajaka An official in charge of distributing robes in a Theravedin Buddhist monastery

civaranidahaka An official in charge of storing robes in a Theravedin Buddhist monastery

civarappatigahaka An official in charge of receiving robes in a Theravedin Buddhist monastery

Clairvaux Abbey A Cistercian monastery in northeastern France. The abbey was fortified with a strong wall furnished at intervals with watchtowers and other defenses. The wall was entirely surrounded by a moat. The original building, founded in 1115 by St. Bernard, is now in ruins; the present structure dates from 1708. The grounds are now occupied and used by a high-security prison.

clapper A noisemaker consisting of two pieces of flat wood attached to a handle, used in monasteries instead of a bell at certain times

Clare of Assisi, St. (1194–1253) Italian abbess and founder of the Poor Clares. Little is known of Clare's childhood, although legend has it that she came from a fairly well-to-do family in Assisi.

At the age of 18, inspired by the preaching of St. Francis of Assisi, she ran away from home to join his community of friars at the Portiuncula, some way outside the town. According to legend, her family wanted to take her back by force, but Clare's dedication to holiness and poverty inspired the friars to accept her resolution. She was given the habit of a nun and transferred to Benedictine monasteries, first at Bastia and then at Sant'Angelo di Panzo, for her monastic formation.

In 1212, with the assistance of St. Francis, she became the founder of the Poor Clares, a Franciscan order of women. By 1216 Francis was able to offer Clare and her companions a monastery adjoining the chapel of San Damiano where she became abbess.

claswyr Hereditary groups of non-celibate quasimonastic canons that ran the ancient churches of Wales just before the Anglo-Norman Conquest

claustral; cloistral Of, like, relating to, or confined in, a cloister

claustral oblate *see* **conventual oblate**

claustral prior; prior claustralis; claustral prioress A monastic next in rank to the superior in a monastery. Called a dean in a few communities. The claustral prior has no ordinary jurisdiction by virtue of his office, since he performs the duties of his office entirely according to the will and under the direction of the abbot. His jurisdiction is, therefore, a delegated one and extends just as far as the abbot desires, or the constitutions of the congregation prescribe. He is appointed by the abbot, generally after a consultation in chapter with the professed monks of the monastery, and may be removed by him at any time. In some monasteries, the claustral prior is a monastic subordinate to either the third prior or third prioress, or the subprior or subprioress, and charged with ensuring that religious do not loiter in inappropriate places.

claustral prioress *see* **claustral prior**

Clerici Regulari a Mater Dei *see* **Clerics Regular of the Mother of God**

clerics regular; clerks regular Clergy in the Western Church who belong to a clerical religious order of clergy, but are not canons regular. They differ from canons regular in that they do not stay in cathedrals or collegiate churches but devote themselves to parochial care instead of the corporate Daily Offices. Clerics regular are quasimonastic and distinguished from the monks in that they are devoted to ministry as opposed to worship and are recognizably clerical in dress.

In the 4th century, St. Augustine of Hippo established a community of priests leading a religious life, and drew up a rule for them. He is commonly thought of as the founder of both clerics regular and canons regular.

Early on, there was no practical distinction between clerks regular and canons regular. The present distinction between the two did not arise until the 16th century.

The first order of clerics regular to be founded was the Congregation of Clerks Regular of the Divine Providence, better known as Theatines established at Rome in 1524. No new orders of clerics regular have been added since the end of the 17th century.

Clerics Regular of the Mother of God; Clerici Regulari a Mater Dei A Roman Catholic religious order of priests, dedicated to education and pastoral care. It was founded by St. John Leonardi in 1574 to spread devotion to the Blessed Virgin Mary, to promote the Forty Hours devotion, and to encourage frequent reception of the Blessed Sacrament. Its members use the suffix of O.M.D. The superior general is called the rector general.

clerk of the works *see* **matricularius**

clerks regular *see* **clerics regular**

Climacus, St. John *see* **John Climacus**

cloistered Dwelling in cloisters

cloistered communities; enclosed communities Christian religious communities with a strict separation from the affairs of the external world. Enforced in the past with a largely uniform severity, at least in the case of women, it is now practiced with a wider variety of custom according to the nature and charism of the community in question. The stated purpose for such enclosure is to prevent distraction from prayer and the religious life. Depending upon the reason and the length of time, the proper authority (usually the superior gets approval from the local bishop or the Holy See) can allow enclosed men or women to leave the enclosure "for a grave cause and with the consent of the superior." In the Roman Catholic Church, this matter is regulated within the framework of canon law.

cloisterer One belonging to, or living in, a cloister

cloistering; enclosure The barring of the laity from the monastery; the barring of monastics from exiting the monastery

cloisters Covered passages or ambulatories around a court, especially that of a monastery; a monastic establishment; a place for retirement from the world for religious duties; the buildings making up a monastic complex; the monastic life in general

cloistral *see* **claustral**

close The enclosed area of a monastery or cathedral

clothing day The day on which a new member of a community makes a commitment and is given the habit of the order

Cluniac Of or related to the reformed branch of the Benedictine Order founded in 912 at Cluny in France; a monastic of the Cluniac Order

Cluniac Order A reformed branch of the Benedictine Order founded in 910 when William I, Duke of Aquitaine had acquired a piece of land in Burgundy and asked Abbot Berno of Baume Abbey (Jura, France) to preside. Berno had established both St. Peter's Monastery at Gigny and Baume Abbey on the *Rule of St. Benedict* as interpreted by Benedict of Aniane, who had sought to restore the primitive strictness of the monastic observance wherever it had been relaxed. In contrast to the balance or labor and worship envisioned by St. Benedict, Cluniacs spent most of their time in worship and used servants to do manual labor.

Cluny developed a highly centralized form of government entirely foreign to the Benedictine tradition. While most Benedictine monasteries remained autonomous and associated with each other only informally, Cluny created a large, federated order in which the administrators of subsidiary houses served as deputies of the abbot of Cluny and answered to him. Cluniac daughter houses, being directly under the supervision of the abbot of Cluny were styled priories, not abbeys. Many other Benedictine monasteries, even those of earlier formation, came to regard Cluny as their guide. When in 1016 Pope Benedict VIII decreed that the privileges of Cluny be extended to subordinate houses, there was further incentive for Benedictine communities to join the Cluniac Order.

The customs of Cluny represented a shift from the earlier ideal of a Benedictine monastery as an agriculturally self-sufficient unit. As perhaps the wealthiest monastic house of the Western world, Cluny hired managers and workers to do the traditional labor of monks. The Cluniac monks devoted themselves to almost constant prayer, thus elevating their position into a profession.

Despite the monastic ideal of a frugal life, the order was known for its splendor, its lengthy and embellished liturgy, its richly decorated churches, and its great wealth. Cluny Abbey commissioned candelabras of solid silver and gold chalices made with precious gems for use at the abbey Masses. Instead of being limited to the traditional fare of broth and porridge, the monks ate very well, enjoying roasted chickens, wines from their vineyards, and cheeses made by their employees. The monks wore the finest linen religious habits and silk vestments at Mass.

Run by a feudal system, the abbot of Cluny retained authority over the daughter houses the order founded. During its height (ca. 950–ca. 1130), the movement was one of the largest religious forces in Europe and by the 12th century the Congregation of Cluny included more than a thousand monasteries. The 11th century saw the introduction of female religious into the order, but men always outnumbered women and their foundations were wealthier.

Near the end of 12th century, the

order began to suffer from poor management and discipline. To zealous reformers, Cluny was too opulent, and the suspicion of decadence hung over its members. The order was suppressed in France in 1790. Over time, the Cluniac Order merged into the existing Benedictine Order, and no longer exists as a separate order.

Cluniac Reform; Benedictine Reform A movement in medieval Benedictinism to restore traditional monastic life. It began in the Benedictine Order at Cluny Abbey largely though by St. Odo (ca. 878–942) and spread throughout Europe.

In the early 10th century, Western monasticism experienced a decline due to unstable political and social conditions and secular interference from wealthy nobles and landowners and the reforms sought to insulate the monasteries from this. • *see also* **English Benedictine Reform**

Cluny Abbey The mother house of the Cluniac congregations that was founded in Burgundy in 910 by William of Aquitaine.

There were three successive churches conventionally called Cluny I, II, and III. The construction of Cluny II, ca. 955–981, led the tendency for Burgundian churches to be stone-vaulted. Cluny III was the largest church building in Europe until the 16th century when St. Peter's in Rome was rebuilt.

The Cluny library was one of the richest and most important in France and Europe, but was sacked by the Huguenots in 1562 and the holdings dispersed or destroyed. Some of the remains are now held by the Bibliothèque Nationale de France at Paris. The British Museum holds some 60 or so charters originating from Cluny.

In 1790 during the French Revolution, the abbey was sacked and mostly destroyed. It was used as a quarry until 1823. Today, little more than one of the original eight towers remains of the whole monastery. In total the surviving parts amount to about 10 percent of the original floor space.

coarb; comharba In medieval Ireland and Scotland, a lucrative monastic office transmitted by natural or nepotic descent within ecclesiastical families, as successors to the patron saint or founder of a monastery

coenobite ***see*** **cenobite**

coif A tight fitting cap worn under the veil by nuns

Colettans A branch of Roman Catholic Franciscan friars following the spirit of St. Colette's reform that was established and approved under the leadership of Henry de Beaume. They were connected to the monasteries of the Colettine nuns. By 1448, there were 13 friaries of this branch. Along with other smaller reforms, they were merged by the Rome into the Observant branch of the Franciscan friars in 1517.

Colette, St. ***see*** **Colettine Poor Clares**

Colettine Poor Clares A reform branch of the Poor Clares. In 1408, the French saint Colette established her first community in a semi-derelict monastery Besançon. Before her death in 1447, she established a total of 18 communities. They follow the interpretation of the *Rule of St. Clare* written by Colette in 1410. She prescribed extreme poverty, going barefoot, and the observance of perpetual fasting and abstinence. The Colettines follow their own constitutions approved in 1448 by Pope Nicholas V, in 1458 by Pope Pius II, and in 1482 by Pope Sixtus IV. The community still exists and includes both cloistered nuns and extern sisters.

collation A daily reading from the *Lives of the Fathers* or John Cassian's *Collationes Patrum* (*Conferences*) which usually took place in the north claustral walk and before Compline; a light repast or luncheon, called a disklysmos in the Eastern Church—first applied to the refreshment on fast days that accompanied the reading of the collation in monasteries

Columba, St. (521–597) Irish abbot and missionary credited with spreading Christianity in what is today Scotland. Columba studied under some of Ireland's most prominent church figures and founded several monasteries in the country. Around 563 he and 12 companions founded Iona Abbey which became an important regional religious and political center. Columba is credited as being a leading figure in the revitalization of monasticism. He wrote a great deal but did not leave a written rule. The *Rule of St. Columba* is attributed to him, but was set down much later.

Columban, St. *see* **Columbanus, St.**

Columbanus, St. (543–615); Columban An Irish missionary notable for founding a number of monasteries from around 590 in the Frankish and Lombard kingdoms. Modern scholars, however, sometimes question whether his missionary work was prompted by religious motives or political ones. Columbanus also produced the *Rule of St. Columbanus.* • *See also* ***Rule of St. Columbanus***

comharba *see* **coarb**

commandery A monastic house of the military Order of Hospitallers

commendam In the late Middle Ages, the practice of granting the headship of a monastic house as a perquisite to a secular priest or bishop

commendator; administrator A non-member of the community employed to take care of its business affairs. They had no spiritual authority. They were common in nunneries or enclosed communities and could be laymen or religious.

commendatory abbot; abbé commendataire (France) A non-monastic ecclesiastic or layman, who held an abbey in commendam, drawing its revenues but not usually exercising any authority over its inner monastic discipline. The system often resulted in the decline of a monastery.

A commendatory abbot who was a layman rather than an ecclesiastic could more accurately be called a lay abbot, secular abbot, abbas laicus, abbas miles, or abbatocomes.

At first, this practice was used only for vacant abbeys or those temporarily without a superior. In the 8th century, however, Anglo-Saxon and Frankish kings assumed the right to appoint commendatory abbots over functioning monasteries as a reward for military service or other service to the kings. Later, French kings did the same and results were similarly harmful. An agreement between Pope Leo X and Francis I of France in the early 16th century gave the kings of France the right to nominate 255 commendatory abbots (abbés commendataires).

In spite of various efforts to reform

the system of commendatory abbots, it continued to plague the monastic orders until the French Revolution and the general secularization of monasteries in the beginning of the 18th century. After that time commendatory abbots became rare, but a few continued to exist among cardinals and Pope Pius X himself was commendatory abbot of the Benedictine monastery at Subiaco near Rome.

commensalis The son of gentry or nobles placed in a monastery in the 15th and 16th century for education

commissariat Among Roman Catholic religious orders—most commonly Franciscans—a semi-autonomous division of the order that is less viable than a full province.

commissary The superior of a commissariat

commissi Formerly, among the Cassinese Benedictines, those who made simple vows and dressed like monastics but without the scapular

common house *see* **parlor**

Common Observance *see* **Cistercians**

Communio Internationalis Benedictinarum; C.I.B. Communities of Benedictine nuns and religious sisters in 61 congregations and federations associated with the Benedictine Confederation of the Order of St. Benedict, although they do not have full membership.

communion window A small opening in the choir grate in some nunneries used for receiving Communion as well as for the reception of the veil at a nun's solemn profession • *see also* **hagioscope**

Community of St. Mary The oldest American Episcopal women's order still in existence. It was founded by Harriet Star Cannon and four other nuns originally who left the Sisterhood of the Holy Communion in 1863 and was at first called the Sisters of St. Catherine, then in 1865 the Sisterhood of St. Mary. Mother Cannon became the superior. Its prime work was at first to serve the homeless, women, and orphans. They later expanded to run girl's schools and hospitals. At first working in New York, they expanded to Tennessee, Wisconsin, and Connecticut. Since 2002, they have also been working in Malawi and the Philippines. The nuns follow a modified *Rule of St. Benedict,* and use the post-nominal initials C.S.M.

In 2008, the Community merged with the American branch of the Sisters of Charity but the Community has maintained its modified Benedictine rule while the Sisters use a rule modeled on the principles of St. Vincent DePaul. • *See also* **Sisters of Charity**

Community of St. Mary the Virgin An Anglican religious order for women founded in Wantage, England, in 1848 by Fr. William John Butler and Mother Harriet. Mother Harriet became the first superior, and Fr. Butler became the warden. It was one of the first Anglican monastic communities formed since the dissolution of the Monasteries by Henry VIII in the 16th century and also one of the oldest still surviving. It grew over the years and provided services for schools, old age homes, mothers and babies, offenders, addicts, and people with learning disabilities. Branch houses were started elsewhere in the United Kingdom and in India and South Africa. As the number of members has decreased in current times, the community has concentrated more on retreats and ministry in parishes and schools. In 2013 the mother superior and eleven sisters joined the Roman Catholic Anglican ordinariate for Great Britain. Members of the Community use the post-nominal initials C.S.M.V.

Community of St. Michael and All Angels A South African religious order of nuns in South Africa founded in 1874 by Allen Webb, the Bishop of Bloemfontein in 1874 to set up schools for girls. Their first school St. Michael's still exists and is one of the leading schools in South Africa. In 1877 they also opened St. George's Cottage Hospital, the first hospital in the Orange Free State. As of 2018, only one sister remained in the order. Members use the post-nominal initials CSM and AA.

Community of the Franciscan Friars of the Renewal A Capuchin religious institute of the Roman Catholic Latin Church founded in New York in 1987 to follow what is perceived to be a more authentic Capuchin way of life and to strive for renewal within the Roman Catholic Church. The friars are noted for their devotion to the pope and serve the local bishop where needed. Members wear a hooded gray habit, sandals, and often, a beard. Postulancy is 10 months, the novitiate a year, and solemn vows are given after five years. Newly professed members must live in a friary for at least a year. Members use the post-nominal initials C.F.R.

Company of St. Ursula; Secular Institute of St. Angela Merici; Angelines; Federated Ursulines A semi-monastic organization of consecrated women in the Roman Catholic Church founded in 1535 in Brescia, Italy, by St. Angela Merici. They are dedicated to the service of God and part of the Ursuline family. They live independently and are responsible for their own well-being. They meet regularly for conferences and prayer and have a rule of life, but do not wear habits or take vows.

In the 16th century, they were forced into an enclosed religious order called the Order of St. Ursula, but this was suppressed by Napoleon in 1810.

In 1958, the semi-monastic community was revived as Secular Institute of St. Angela Merici and now exists in 23 countries. • *See also* **Order of St. Ursula**

Compline; Apodeipnon (Orthodox) The final Office of the day in the Christian tradition of canonical hours. The English word *Compline* is derived from the Latin *completorium*, as Compline is the completion of the working day. The word was first used in this sense about the beginning of the 6th century by St. Benedict in the *Rule of St. Benedict*. Compline tends to be a contemplative Office that emphasizes spiritual peace. In many monasteries it is the custom to begin the "great silence" after Compline, during which the whole community, including guests, observes silence throughout the night until the morning service the next day. It is one of the Minor Hours.

computation The periodic, formal accounting by a monastery's leaders

Conceptionists ***see*** **Order of the Immaculate Conception**

confederation An agreement between monastic houses to offer prayers for each other's deceased members

confession temple ***see*** **tungshag hakang**

confraternity; societa An agreement between a religious house and a layperson that designates the latter a confrater or honorary member; an agreement between two monasteries to provide mutual spiritual support

confraters Clerics or laity who have entered into an agreement with a monastic community stating that in return for donations, they are to be considered honorary members. This is usually a less formal arrangement than that of oblates.

Congregatio pro Institutis Vitae Consecratae et Societatibus Vitae Apostolicae *see* Congregation for Institutes of Consecrated Life and Societies of Apostolic Life

Congregatio Sanctissimi Salvatoris *see* Canons Regular of the Lateran

congregation A company of religious persons forming a subdivision of a monastic order

Congregation for Institutes of Consecrated Life and Societies of Apostolic Life; Congregatio pro Institutis Vitae Consecratae et Societatibus Vitae Apostolicae The Roman Catholic congregation responsible for everything which concerns institutes of consecrated life and societies of apostolic life. Founded in 1586, as the Sacred Congregation for Consultations about Regulars. In 1908 it became the Congregation for Religious. In 1967, it became the Congregation for Religious and Secular Institutes. In 1988, it was given its current name, the Congregation for Institutes of Consecrated Life and Societies of Apostolic Life.

Congregation for Religious *see* Congregation for Institutes of Consecrated Life and Societies of Apostolic Life

Congregation for Religious and Secular Institutes *see* Congregation for Institutes of Consecrated Life and Societies of Apostolic Life

Congregation of Clerics Regular of the Divine Providence *see* Theatines

Congregation of Fiore; Fiorensians A reform order devolved from the Cistercians. It was founded in Calabria in 1188 by the Cistercian monk Joachim of Fiore (ca. 1135–1202). It grew to 40 houses, but many of these eventually returned to the Cistercian Order. Joachim was condemned by the Cistercians in 1192.

Congregation of Notre-Dame des Feuillants *see* Feuillants

Congregation of St. Anthony A defunct Augustinian congregation founded in Flanders in 1615 that operated under the *Rule of St. Augustine*. Their only monastery was called Castelletum.

Congregation of St. Basil; Basilian Fathers; Teaching Priests of the Arche A Roman Catholic apostolic community of priests, students for the priesthood, and lay associates founded in 1822. Members profess simple vows and work primarily in education and evangelization. Suppressed in France in 1903 by the French government, the Congregation today operates in Canada, the United States, Mexico, and Colombia.

Congregation of St. Maur; Maurists A French Benedictine reform congregation of established in 1621 noted their scholarship. In their time they had about 220 writers and over 700 published works. Most of the non–Cluniac Benedictine monasteries of France joined the new congregation, which grew to almost 200 houses. The headquarters and residence of the superior-general was Saint-Germain-des-Prés, in Paris.

During the end of 18th century to laxity crept in and even some freethinking. During the French Revolution the congregation was largely scattered, but the superior-general and 40 of his monks were hanged.

Congregation of Savigny *see* **Savignac Order**

Congregation of the Most Holy Savior *see* **Canons Regular of the Lateran**

consecrated virgin A Roman Catholic woman who vows to live in perpetual virginity as an exclusive bride of Christ. They do not necessarily belong to a religious community, but may continue to be a part of their local parish, performing works of penance and mercy. Such a life was mentioned in the New Testament. The first consecrated virgin is considered to be the Blessed Virgin Mary, who was consecrated by the Holy Spirit during the Annunciation. In 2014, there were estimated to be about 300 consecrated virgins in the United States among the 6,000 to 7,000 worldwide.

Constitutiones Hirsaugienses *see* **William of Hirsau**

Constitutions of Theodore *see* **Theodore the Studite, St.**

consuetudenary *see* **customary**

consultive definitor *see* **definitor**

contemplative community A community devoted primarily to contemplative life, as opposed to an active ministry in hospitals, schools, and the like

contemporary religious order *see* **New Monasticism**

contemptus mundi Literally, "disdain for the world." In the 13th to 15th centuries, a prevalent attitude in monastic communities of strong disdain for delight in the physical existence

continual prayer *see* **perpetual prayer**

convent Originally a monastic house occupied by monastics of either sex; now used to primarily to designate a nunnery, that is, a house occupied by a community of nuns. In the Eastern Church however, religious houses are called monasteries.

conventical prior *see* **conventual prior**

conventual Of or relating to a nunnery; monastic; one who lives in a convent; a monk or nun; a recluse

conventual builders *see* **fratres barbati**

conventual church; minster A church attached or belonging to a nunnery or monastery

Conventual Franciscans *see* **Order of Friars Minor Conventual**

conventual oblate; claustral oblate; regular oblate; intern oblate An oblate who lives in a monastic community. Typically, this involves a year's probation before acceptance by the superior. They partake of community life and wear a distinct habit, but are not considered monks or nuns. They may leave at any time or be sent away by the superior's decision.

conventual prior; conventual prioress; conventical prior; prior conventualis An independent superior of a priory. Among Benedictines communities are considered priories until they qualify to be abbeys. Among the Camaldolese and Carthusians, conventual priors are the norm and there are no abbots, but there are abbesses in major communities of Camaldolese nuns. Among Dominican and Carmelite nuns, however, all superiors are called conventual prioresses.

conventual priory An autonomous house which has no abbot or abbess, either because the canonically required number of 12 monks has not yet been reached, or for some other reason

conventualis A term indicating that a monastery had at least 12 members, which was considered the necessary number for success

Conventuals *see* **Order of Friars Minor Conventual**

conversae *see* **conversi**

conversatio morum suorum A controversial phrase in the *Rule of St. Benedict*, RB 58:17. St. Benedict says, "When admitted to profession, they shall make a promise in the presence of all, before God and the saints, of stability, conversatio morum suorum, and obedience." The word *conversatio* did not carry over into later Latin and confused scribes. Thinking it was a mistake, they rendered it as *conversio*, that is, "conversion" or "conversion of life." This error was not discovered until 1912, but correcting it still remains tough sledding. While it is difficult to translate into English, most scholars now believe that *conversatio morum suorum* means essentially the monastic lifestyle and all that it entails. As such, it subsumes stability, and obedience, and even, for that matter, conversion. Much nitpicking still ensues, but to think of it as meaning only conversion is to needlessly limit the fullness of the *Rule*.

conversi (men); conversae (women) Adult converts to the monastic life, as opposed to *nutriti* or *nutritae* (those raised in a monastery from childhood). The term was also sometimes applied to lay monastics.

conversion of life *see* **conversatio morum suorum; metanoia**

conversus *see* **conversi**

Coptic monasticism Christian monasticism developed among the Copts in the 3rd century deserts of Egypt. St. Anthony the Great is notable among the pioneers, but was not the first monk as is sometimes claimed. St. Pachomius, a Copt from Upper Egypt, established cenobitic monasticism essentially as we know it today. It is estimated that in 345 there were 3,000 monasteries in Egypt. Within a generation, it is estimated there were 7,000 including those in Palestine, Syria, and North Africa. There are currently 33 Coptic monasteries in Egypt with about 1,000 monks and 300 nuns. The largest monasteries, and most famous, are at Scetis, about 60 miles northwest of Cairo. They are the only four of the ancient fortified self-sufficient monasteries which have survived out of the many that were in Scetis.

The Coptic Orthodox Church was founded through the influence of monastics and the tradition is now that all Coptic bishops are chosen from monastics.

In the Coptic Church there are only two degrees of professed monks, one corresponding to the rassophore combined with the stavrophore and the other corresponding to the great schema. There is nothing equivalent to separate stavrophore status in the Coptic tradition. The two rites of rassophore and stavrophore are usually held one immediately following the other, as a single service.

coquinarius *see* **kitchener**

Cordelier A Franciscan Observant—so called in France because of the knotted cord worn by all Franciscans

cordon The cord worn by a Franciscan friar

corrector The religious superior of a house of the Order of Minims; among the Grandmontines, the choir monk who had charge of spiritual matters in a priory

corrodian A lay person who had obtained the right to board and lodging in a monastery, usually by payment at an earlier date; a lay servant of a monastic community who has entered into an agreement with the community agreeing that in return for their services, they will be taken care of in old age

corrody An allowance of meat, drink, or clothing granted to a lay person by a monastery, often at the request of the king or patron of the house, who billeted retired servants and retainers on the monastic establishment in this way; the stipend given to an individual by the community either in return for gifts received or as a reward for previous services

council *see* **executive council**

Council of Major Superiors of Women Religious A Roman Catholic association of major superiors of religious institutes for women in the United States. It was established in 1992 in reaction to the perceived liberality of the Leadership Council of Women Religious. It seeks to cooperate more fully with the pope, the U.S. Conference of Catholic Bishops, and to support religious life. • *See also* **Leadership Council of Women Religious**

cowl; capoch; caputium; hood Strictly speaking, the hooded portion of a monastic scapular, although the term cowl came to sometimes mean the cowl and scapular together. The hood originally was worn simply to give greater warmth to those who regularly spent long hours in unheated and drafty churches.

Cowley Fathers *see* **Society of St. John the Evangelist**

C.R. The post-nominal initials of the Theatines

crosier *see* **crozier**

Crosiers *see* **Canons Regular of the Order of the Holy Cross**

Crossed Friars *see* **Crutched Friars**

crossfigill An ascetic exercise practiced by Celtic monks, which involved standing in prayer for long periods with the arms outstretched in the form of a cross

Crouched Friars *see* **Crutched Friars**

crozier; crosier; pastoral staff A symbol of the pastoral authority of a bishop or a monastic superior. Originally a walking stick, it later acquired the symbolism of a shepherd's crook. Its use dates from the 7th century. In the Eastern Orthodox Church the staff is surmounted by a cross between two serpents.

Croziers *see* **Crutched Friars**

Crucigeri cum Rubea Stella *see* **Knights of the Cross with the Red Star**

Crucigeri Stellati *see* **Knights of the Cross with the Red Star**

Crutched Friars; Crossed Friars; Crouched Friars; Croziers; Brethren of the Holy Cross; Fratres Cruciferi A Roman Catholic Order which according to legend was founded by St. Cletus in the 1st century, and to have been reconstituted by St. Cyriacus, in the 4th century, but there is little record of them before 1100. Although called friars, they are not actually considered a mendicant group and were much involved in the running of hospitals. At first they wore black or brown habits, but later they wore a blue habit with a red cross upon it. At one time they had 208 monasteries in Italy, with others in England and Ireland. Those in England and Ireland were dissolved by King Henry VIII in 1539. In time corruptions were allowed to creep in, and from that and other causes their numbers dwindled down to no more than 50 houses in 1656, when, unable to reform itself, the order was suppressed by Pope Alexander VII.

C.S.M. The post-nominal initials for members of the Community of St. Mary

C.S.M. and A.A. The post-nominal initials for members of the Community of St. Michael and All Angels

C.S.M.V. The post-nominal initials for members of the Community of St. Mary the Virgin

Ctistae *see* **Ktistai**

cuculla A long, closed, hooded monastic garment with wide sleeves that may be worn by Roman Catholic and Anglican monastics. Originally worn merely for warmth in unheated churches, they are now used primarily for formal occasions. In Benedictine communities it is black with 73 pleats in the back, representing the 73 chapters in the *Rule of Benedict*, and may be worn as a death shroud.

Culdean Of, like, or related to the Culdees

Culdees; Céilí Dé (Irish); Kaledei A quasimonastic ascetic group that lived in various parts of Scotland, Ireland, England, and Wales in the 8th to 14th centuries. They first arose as anchorites in Ireland in the 8th century, but gradually formed eremitic communities and were attached to cathedral or collegiate churches. They lived in monastic fashion and had abbots, but did not take monastic vows. As such, they fell in between monastics and secular canons. There is a lack of clarity about the manner of their lives due to variations in different communities. Some communities had hereditary leaders, and some of the members may have been married. There were some Culdee missions that were established in France and Germany, but these disappeared. In the British Isles, the Culdees were gradually absorbed during the 14th century. Some Culdees became Augustinians, and some became canons regular. • *See also* ***Rule of Ceili De***

cura monialium The overseeing of and priestly support of a nunnery by male clergy

curia The outer courtyard of a religious house containing the brewhouse, granary, guest-house, stew-pond, etc., where much of the needed physical work of the monastery could take place, while still keeping peace in the cloister, church, and dorter.

curiosis The lay monk who had charge of temporal matters in a Grandmontine priory

curtal friar *see* **porter**

Cusack, Margaret Anna (1829–1899); Cusack, Mary Frances Irish nun of shifting religious associations, Irish nationalist, social reformer, and author of many books, pamphlets, and poems. As a girl she was an Anglican, as a young woman she was aligned with the evangelical Plymouth Brethren. After the death of her fiancé she was motivated by the Oxford Movement to become an Anglican nun. Disappointed at not being sent as a nurse to the Crimean War, she became a Roman Catholic and joined the Poor Clares and became a teacher in Ireland. Her controversial opinions sometimes put her in physical danger, but when her superiors tried to move her for her safety, she went off on her own. Often at odds with her superiors, she was also known for her temper and sometimes physically attacked sisters who displeased her. After she claimed to have seen an apparition of the Blessed Virgin Mary at Knock in Ireland in the 1870s, she became even more difficult to deal with. At odds with her superiors, she received permission from the pope to found the Sisters of St. Joseph of Peace to care for friendless girls. The order now has houses in the United Kingdom, Canada, Haiti, Ireland, and the United States. Unfortunately, while opening a house in New Jersey she again ran afoul of the Church hierarchy when she wrote a pamphlet criticizing the archbishop about social issues. When she tried and failed to halt publication, she resigned as head of her order and returned to the Anglican Communion and wrote anti–Roman Catholic books.

custodes *see* **custos**

custodes ordinis *see* **circator**

custodian; warden The head of a custody in the Franciscan Order

custody A subdivision of a province in the Franciscan Order

customal *see* **customary**

customary; consuetudinary; costumal A document setting out the customs regulating the daily organization of the monastery, compiled to supplement the constitution and the general prescription of the rule

custos The precise meaning of this term varies among branches of the Franciscans—it may be used for a cantor, the caretaker of a monastery, a religious superior, or some other sort of official

custos custodum; discretus discretorum A representative of a Franciscan province at a general chapter held to elect a minister general

custos general In the Capuchin Order, a member elected every three years at the provincial chapters. He has the right to vote at the election of the minister general should a general chapter be held during his term of office. In addition, he has the obligation of presenting to the general chapter an official report on the state of his province.

custos provinciae In the Order of Friars Minor, a member elected every three years at the provincial chapter. Besides having a voice in all capitular acts of his province he takes part in the general chapter, should his minister provincial be impeded.

custos provincial In the Capuchin Order, a member elected every three years at the provincial chapters. He has no voice in the general chapter and his rights and duties are much restricted and unimportant.

custos regimens In the Order of Friars Minor, a friar who rules over a custody, or sub-province. He possesses ordinary jurisdiction and has all the rights and privileges of a minister provincial.

Cuthbert, St. (ca. 634–687) A Christian monk, priest, missionary, bishop, and hermit in the Kingdom of Northumbria. He decided to become a monk after seeing a vision in 651. He was made prior of Melrose Abbey about 662 and prior of Lindifarne Abbey about 665.

Although an ascetic, Cuthbert was known for his kindness and generosity. His gifts of healing and insight gained him the nickname "Wonder Worker of Britain." In 676, he retired to Inner Farne Island where he lived a life of great austerity. Eventually he confined himself to his cell and opened his window only to give his blessing.

In 684, he was elected Bishop of Lindisfarne but by 686 returned to his island cell where he died in 687, after a painful illness.

~D~

Daily Office; Divine Office; Canonical Hours; Opus Dei; Liturgy of the Hours; Hours A daily cycle of Christian worship typically including prayers, psalms, and Scripture readings and often other elements such as hymns, that are repeated at set times. The Eucharist is not included in the Offices. Recitation of the Daily Office is not confined to monasticism, but it a crucial part of monastic life and derives from ancient Jewish practice.

Historically, the Daily Office comprised the seven daytime Offices of Lauds, Prime, Terce, Sext, None, Vespers, Compline, and the night office of Matins (Vigils). Some communities still observe all of these for their Daily Office, while some have reduced it to Lauds (Morning Prayer), Sext, Vespers, and Compline. Oblates may be required to only to say Lauds and Vespers. Lauds and Vespers are considered Major Hours because they are longer. All others are considered Minor or Little Hours. The names and applications of the Daily Office Hours have sometimes changed in history and it can get confusing. • *See also* **Compline; Lauds; Matins; None; Prime; Sext; Terce; Vespers; Vigils**

Western Church	Orthodox Church	Time	Notes
Lauds	Orthros	Sunrise	Formerly called Matins, Nocturnes
Prime	First Hour	6 a.m.	
Terce	Third Hour	9 a.m.	
Sext, Diurnam, Noon Prayer	Sixth Hour	Noon	
None	Ninth Hour	3 p.m.	
Vespers, Evening Prayer, Evensong		Sunset	
Compline	Apodeipnon	7 p.m.	
Vigils	Mesonyktikon	Midnight	

daishu Japanese Zen Buddhist monks residing in the zendō (meditation hall)

dalai lama A title given to the monk who is the spiritual leader of Tibetan Buddhists. He is considered to be the successor in a line of incarnations of Avalokiteśvara, a bodhisattva of compassion. The dalai lama is a symbol of the Tibetan state and represents Buddhist values, but has no formal authority in any of the various Tibetan Buddhist schools. China has occupied Tibet since 1951 and claims the right to name the next dalai lama, but this is rejected by most Tibetans. In 2018, Tenzin Gyatso, the Dalai Lama said that he may choose not to be reincarnated at all, or to be reincarnated as a woman.

dame A title sometimes used in Benedictine communities for a professed nun

Damian, Peter *see* **Peter Damian, St.**

Daniel, Metropolitan of Moscow (ca. 1492–1547) Russian monk, writer, and abbot. He was metropolitan of Moscow from 1522 to 1539 and supportive of an alliance with the princely authority.

He became a monk at the Joseph-Volokolamsk Monastery. In 1515, he was elected hegumen (abbot) of the monastery. In 1525, as a metropolitan, he ignored church canons and helped imprison Vasili Shemyachich, Prince of Seversk. He also allowed the divorce between Vasili III, Prince of Muscovy and his childless wife Solomonia Saburova, which was unpopular with the people. He solemnly blessed Ivan IV (Ivan the Terrible) and was the author of a number of works condemning heretics in Russia. In the conflict between the Shuisky family and Prince Ivan Belsky in 1538, Daniel supported Prince Ivan for which he was defrocked a year later by the Shuiskys. He died in the Joseph-Volokolamsk Monastery, where he was imprisoned.

dansa chenpo An abbot-ruler in Tibetan Buddhism

Daruma *see* **Bodhidharma**

dasa In a Theravedin Buddhist monastic monastery, a slave who served the monastery

dasa sil mata *see* **maechi**

Dashanami Sampradaya Wandering Hindu monastics of "single-staff renunciation" (Ēkadaṇḍisannyāsi) generally associated with the Advaita Vedanta tradition. Their practices differ from Shaiva Trishuldhari and Vaishnava Tridandi monastics. Any Hindu can seek Sannyāsa as a renunciate in the Dasanāmi tradition. They first appeared in the 2nd century.

daughter house A monastic community that was founded by members of another house—the term can imply a subordinate position with respect to the mother house.

Daughters of St. Mary; Deir Banat Maryam A Egyptian community of Coptic nuns based founded in 1965 to serve the poor, the elderly, orphans, the mentally and physically handicapped, and the elderly. They interact with the secular world, unlike other Coptic nuns, who usually are cloistered in nunneries. The sisters of St. Mary dress in gray, and although called nuns are technically deaconesses. They are addressed as tasooni, which means sister in Coptic.

Daughters of the Covenant *see* **Members of the Covenant**

David, St. (fl. 5th or 6th century) Legendary Welsh saint, ascetic, monk, and bishop, said to have founded 12 or 13 monasteries. The monastic rule of David demanded that monks had to pull the plough themselves without draft animals, drink only water, eat only bread with salt and herbs, and spend the evenings in prayer, reading, and writing. No personal possessions were allowed. Widely venerated in the Middle Ages, St. David is the patron saint of Wales and honored in both the Western and Eastern churches.

Day Hours Terce, Sext, and None of the Daily Office

day room *see* **parlor**

day stairs The stairway in a monastery giving access to the dormitory by a claustral walkway

Dayananda, Swami *see* **Griffiths, Bede**

deace *see* **third prior**

dean A monastic in charge of ten others, a grange, or assigned a specific responsibility in a monastery

decana A vice-abbess

de Chantal, Jane Frances *see* **Order of the Visitation of Holy Mary**

dedication The holy person to which a monastic community is dedicated. Often communities, especially the many dedicated to the Virgin Mary, are referred to by other names, but the dedication is noted in the foundation document and usually other official documents.

deece *see* **third prior**

definitor In Roman Catholic monastic life, a member of the governing council of some monastic orders chosen to aid superiors in the government of the order. The office originated in the 11th and 12th centuries in an effort to ameliorate the excessive authoritarianism of the Cluniac structure, and it was adopted and developed further by the mendicant orders during the 13th century.

Consultive definitors are those relating to the permanent council of the superior. They serve only as a consensual or advisory body to the general or provincial superior, who, according to the constitutions, must obtain their consent or advice for the validity of his administrative acts.

Capitular definitors have a voice in the affairs of a chapter, general or provincial, and who are also electors in an elective chapter. Capitular definitors as a body, the definitorium, usually enjoy complete general or provincial authority while a chapter remains in session.

In the Cistercian Order, the abbot general is assisted by a council of five definitors. In the Franciscan Observants, the definitor is the third highest office of the order, below the minister general and procurator general. In the Camaldolese Order, definitor may be given as the personal title of a prior. In the Dominican Order a provincial definitor serves under the prior provincial.

The title definitor general is used by the Discalced Carmelites, the Friars Minor, and the Capuchins and is usually someone elected by the general chapter of their orders for a specified period of time.

definitor general *see* **definitor**

definitorium Capitular definitors as a body

defrock *see* **uncowl**

deice *see* **third prior**

Deir Banat Maryam *see* **Daughters of St. Mary**

de la Barrière, Jean *see* **Feuillants**

demesne Land owned and administered directly by a monastery

Dengyo Daishi *see* **Saicho**

denization The process by which an English alien priory was detached from their mother house in France. It involved gaining a royal charter, replacing the superior and sometimes the whole community with English monastics, and sometimes paying a fee to the king.

densu A Japanese Zen Buddhist monk in charge of waking the others monks in the morning, leading the sutra (aphorism or teaching), chanting, and other ceremonies, and of cleaning the ritual halls

Deo gratias Latin for "thanks be to God." The traditional greeting of the porter given to a visitor of a Benedictine monastery

deposition The removing of a superior from a monastic community. It is a difficult process. Sometimes it can be initiated by the local bishop, but in exempt communities of the Roman Catholic Church it has to be started by the head of the order or the pope.

derainment *see* **apostasy**

de Rancé, Armand Jean le Bouthillier (1626–1700) Founder of the Trappists, first abbot of La Trappe, and scholar. Son of a wealthy family, when he was ten years old he was made the commendatory abbot La Trappe and two other abbeys, prior of two priories, and canon of Notre-Dame de Paris. A brilliant scholar, he published a translation of Anacreon with Greek notes when he was only 12. He was ordained a priest in 1651 by his uncle Victor Le Bouthillier, the Archbishop of Tours. When his father died in 1652 Armand became very wealthy in his own right and his uncle the archbishop made him an archdeacon. After 1660, however, he disposed of all his possessions, except for the Abbey of La Trappe, which he visited for the first time in 1662. He retired to his abbey, of which he became the regular abbot in 1664. His prescribed a rigidly ascetic regime featuring penitence, manual labor, silence, world isolation, and limited study. Nevertheless, he continued to write spiritual works. He resigned his abbacy in 1695, owing to declining health.

Desert Fathers Early Christian hermits, ascetics, and monks who lived mainly in the deserts of Egypt, Syria, and Palestine in the 3rd and 4th centuries. Eventually there were thousands of monks in the desert and lesser numbers of women. The Desert Fathers and Mothers had a major influence on the development of Christianity. The desert monastic communities that grew out of the informal gathering of hermit monks became the model for Christian monasticism. All of the monastic revivals of the Middle Ages looked to the desert for inspiration and guidance. Much of Eastern Christian spirituality, including the Hesychast movement, had its roots in the practices of the Desert Fathers.

Three main types of monasticism developed in Egypt around the Desert Fathers. One was the austere life of the hermit, as practiced by St. Anthony and his followers in lower Egypt. Another was the cenobitic life—communities of monks and nuns in upper Egypt formed by Pachomius. The third was a semi-hermitic lifestyle seen mostly in Nitria, Kellia, and Scetis, west of the Nile, begun by St. Amun. The latter were small groups (two to six) of monastics with a common spiritual elder. These separate groups would join together in larger gatherings to worship on Saturdays and Sundays. This third form of monasticism was responsible for most of the sayings that were compiled as the *Apophthegmata Patrum* (*Sayings of the Desert Fathers*).

Desert Mothers Female Christian ascetics living in the desert of Egypt, Palestine, and Syria in the 4th and 5th centuries. They typically lived in the monastic communities that began forming during that time, though sometimes they lived as hermits. The Desert Fathers are much more well-known because there were more of them. It also has to be remembered that women had very little freedom at the time, and that in any event, the desert was a dangerous place. Nevertheless Palladius mentions 2,975 women living in the desert. Many desert women had leadership roles within the Christian community. Theodora of Alexandria originally went to the desert disguised as a man and joined a community of monks. The Desert Mothers were known as ammas (spiritual mothers) due to the respect they earned as spiritual teachers and directors.

Dhammananda Bhikkhuni (1944–); Chatsumarn Kabilsingh Thai Theravedan Buddhist nun, abbess, teacher, social activist, and author of over 100 books. In 2003 she was ordained as a bhikkhuni (Buddhist nun) in Sri Lanka. She is abbess of Songdhammakalyani Monastery, the only temple in Thailand where there are bhikkhunis. She was married and has three sons. Her mother Voramai Kabilsingh was ordained as bhikkhuni in Taiwan in 1971 and was the first modern Thai bhikkhuni. • *See also* **Voramai Kabilsingh**

Dhammarakhita Samaneri (1946–); Varangghana Vanavichayen Thai Theravedan Buddhist bhikkuni (nun). In 2002, she became the first bhikkuni to be ordained in Thailand, at least in modern times. Prior to being ordained, she was a maechi for 9 years. She is the mother of two children but had to divorce her husband because maechis and monastics are required to be celibate.

Dharma hall; beopdang The building in a Zen Buddhist temple complex where the abbot gives teachings on behalf of the Buddha

Dharmaguptaka Vinaya* *see* *Vinaya

Dharmapala (1864–1933); Dharmapāla Sri Lankan Buddhist monk, reformer, revivalist, missionary, and writer. He was the first global Buddhist missionary and one of the founding contributors of non-violent Sinhalese Buddhist nationalism and Buddhism. He was also a pioneer in the revival of Buddhism in India after it had been virtually extinct there for several centuries. At the latter stages of his life, he entered the order of Buddhist monks as Venerable Sri Devamitta Dharmapāla.

Dhuni A sacred fire tended by Nath monks when they are not traveling

dhutanga A group of 13 ascetic practices most commonly observed by the practitioners of the Forest Tradition of Theravada Buddhism. All forest monks will observe at least one of the dhutanga austerities to deepen the practice of meditation, assist in holiness, and help develop detachment from the body and material things including the body.

The practices are:

1. Wearing patched-up robes (pamsukulikanga)
2. Wearing only three robes (tecivarikanga)
3. Going for alms (pindapatikanga)
4. Not omitting any house while soliciting alms (sapadanikanga)
5. Eating at one sitting (ekasanikanga)
6. Eating only from the alms-bowl (pattapindikanga)
7. Refusing all further food (khalu-paccha-bhattikanga)
8. Living in the forest (araññikanga)
9. Living under a tree (rukkha-mulikanga)
10. Living in the open air (abbhokasikanga)
11. Living in a cemetery (susanikanga)
12. Being satisfied with whatever dwelling (yatha-santhatikanga)
13. Never lying down (nesajjikanga)

diakonetes *see* **lay monastics**

diakonia In the Greek Orthodox Church, a service or ministry performed by a monastic

Digambara One of the two Jain monastic orders. Digambaras take 28 vows: five mahāvratas (great vows); five samitis (regulations); the five-fold control of the senses (pañcendriya nirodha); six şadāvaśyakas (essential duties), and seven niyamas (restrictions). In the Digambara tradition, an ascetic rises from kshullak (one who uses two pieces of cloth) through ailak (one who uses one piece of cloth) to muni (solemnly professed). Observing complete abstinence, male Digambara monks wear no clothing and wear their hair in thick dreadlocks called jata. A monk may be called a nirgrantha, which means without bounds in Sanskrit. The aryikas (nuns) wear plain, seamless white saris. Digambara monks and nuns carry a broom-like object, called a picchi made from fallen peacock feathers to sweep the ground ahead of them or before sitting down to avoid inadvertently crushing small insects. They also carry a water pot called a kamandalu, and scriptures, called shastras. The Bhattaraka of the Digambara Terapanth do not wander; they usually live in temples and perform daily rituals. In 2009, there were only 100 Digambara sādhvīs (nuns).

discalced A term applied to those religious congregations whose members go entirely barefoot or wear sandals, with or without other covering for the feet. The custom was introduced into the West by St. Francis of Assisi for men and by St. Clare of Assisi for women.

Discalced Augustinians *see* **Order of Discalced Augustinians**

Discalced Carmelites *see* **Order of Discalced Carmelites**

Discalced Mercedarians; Ordo Frati Excalceatorum de B.M.V. de Mercede A Roman Catholic mendicant order, which developed in the 17th century from the Mercedarian Order. After an initial period of growth, the order was suppressed in the late 18th century. Their revival did not begin for nearly a century. As of 2008, the order consisted of 11 monasteries, with 47 friars, 38 of whom were priests. They operate in Spain and the Dominican Republic.

The goals of the order is instruction for the preservation of the Catholic faith. The friars commit themselves to pastoral care, as well as giving to spiritual direction to nuns of enclosed religious orders. Additionally they work with prisoners and the sick. They follow the *Rule of St. Augustine* and use the post-nominal initials O.M.D.

discarius A paid servant in larger monastic houses of the Western Church who served as a waiter, server, washed dishes, dumped garbage, and so forth

discipline A short whip or strap with which monastics could beat themselves in pursuit of mortification

discretus discretorum *see* **custos custodum**

Dissolution of Lesser Monasteries Act; Act for the Dissolution of the Lesser Monasteries An act passed by the English Parliament in 1535 of Parliament that was the beginning of the legal process by which King Henry VIII set about the dissolution of the monasteries in England. The act applied only to houses with an annual income of less than £200.

dissolution of monasteries In the late medieval period there was widespread dissatisfaction and envy among secular and religious leaders with Roman Catholic monasticism. Secular leaders wanted their wealth. Many bishops believed monastic wealth would be better spent on educating priests to serve the public rather than on monks performing the Daily Office. Nevertheless, monastics usually enjoyed a great deal of public support.

Dissolution of monasteries is most famous in England in the 1530s and 1540s where it took place under Henry VIII, but in fact it also occurred in Scotland, Denmark, Switzerland, France, Germany, and Sweden as well—some of it before the English dissolution, and some after.

In the 11th and 12th century founders often endowed monasteries with both the income from landed estates, and income from tithes from parish churches under the founder's patronage. As a result, English monasteries in the 16th century controlled appointment to about two-fifths of all parish benefices, disposed of about half of all ecclesiastical income, and owned about a quarter of the nation's landed wealth. There was a medieval proverb in England that said if the Abbot of Glastonbury married the Abbess of Shaftesbury, their heir would have more land than the King of England. One adult man in 50 was in a religious order.

The dissolution of monasteries in England, Ireland, and Wales under Henry VIII was revolutionary in the society because it disbanded all monastic houses, took their income, sold off their property, and either dismissed or reassigned their members. The original purpose was to increase the income of the crown, but in fact most of the money went to fund Henry's military campaigns in the 1540s.

Dissolution of the Greater Monasteries Act; Act for the Dissolution of the Greater Monasteries An act passed by the English Parliament in 1539 that provided for the for the dissolution of 552 monasteries remaining after the Dissolution of the Lesser Monasteries Act of 1535

diurnal A prayer book containing the monastic Daily Office, except for Matins

Diurnum *see* **Noon Prayer**

Divine Office *see* **Daily Office**

Dix, Gregory (1901–1952) English liturgist, Anglican Benedictine monk, priest, prior, and liturgist at Nashdom Abbey. He was ordained a deacon in 1924 and a priest in 1925. He became a Benedictine novice in 1925 and was sent to the Gold Coast in Africa but his health broke down in 1929 and he returned to Nashdom as a conventual oblate to recover. He did not make his final profession until 1940. During World War II he served as a parish priest, but returned to Nashdom afterward and became the prior in 1948. Dix's work as a liturgist, notably *The Shape of the Liturgy,* has had a profound influence on the Anglican Communion.

doan; dōan The person sounding the bell that marks the beginning and end of zazen (meditation) in a Japanese Zen Buddhist monastery

docheiarios In the Greek Orthodox Church, the monastic in charge of the treasury, or the clothing and footwear • *see also* **kellarios**

Doctor Expertus A nickname of St. Albert the Great

Doctor Mirabilis A nickname of Roger Bacon

Doctor of the Assumption A nickname of St. John of Damascus

Doctor Universalis A nickname of St. Albert the Great

doge Monks who start their careers in a Japanese Zen Buddhist monastery during the same ango (training session)

Dogen Kigen *see* **Dogen Zenji**

Dogen Zenji (1200–1253); Dōgen Kigen; Eihei Dōgen; Kōso Jōyō Daishi; Busshō Dentō Kokushi A Japanese Zen Buddhist monk, writer, poet, philosopher, and founder of the Sōtō school of Zen. He was originally ordained as a monk in the Tendai School in Kyoto, but became dissatisfied with it and went to China for five years to study what he felt was a more authentic Buddhism. Upon returning to Japan, he promoted the practice of zazen (meditation). He eventually broke relations the Tendai School, and left Kyoto for the mountainous countryside where he founded the monastery Eihei-ji, which remains the head temple of the Sōtō school to this day.

dokusan Sanzen (formal meditation study) on an individual, voluntary basis with the rōshi (monastic master) in a Japanese Zen Buddhist monastery. Most sanzen at Rinzai monasteries is dokusan. • *See also* **sosan**

Dolcino of Novara *see* **Dulcians**

dom An abbreviation of the Latin word *dominus,* which means master. Not in wide use, it is predominately employed by professed Benedictine monks.

domestic bell A small bell used inside some monasteries to call individuals who have special duties or offices; it is also used for some of the Daily Office when the tower bells cannot be rung or may not be heard throughout the monastery where the members are working

Dominic, St. (ca. 1170–1221) A Castilian nobleman who became a Roman Catholic priest in 1194, and joined the Canons Regular in the Cathedral of Osma. Working to convert the Cathars in the sought of France, he came to believe that only preachers who displayed real sanctity, humility, and asceticism could win over Cathar believers and that the preachers Church of the time did not generally have those virtues. In 1215, gathered six followers in a house in Toulouse and formed a new type of community between secular clergy and traditional monasticism to provide both education and spiritual care to the growing cities of the era. The community followed monastic rules of prayer and penance. In 1217, it was recognized as The Order of Preachers, which became popularly became known as the Dominicans.

Dominic followed severe practices, abstaining from meat, fasting, silence, poor accommodations, mean clothes, and never sleeping in a bed. When travelling he would sometimes go barefoot over thorns and sharp stones. He died of a fever at the age of 51, exhausted with work and austerities. He was canonized in 1234.

Although some Dominicans took part in the Inquisition, it should be noted that the Inquisition was not instituted until ten years after Dominic's death. The notion of his involvement seems to have been spread knowingly as a political ruse to discredit him.

Notably, the spread of the rosary, a Marian devotion, is attributed to the preaching of St. Dominic.

Dominicans ***see*** **Order of Preachers**

domus Converso rum The housing for conversi

domus fenstrae Latin for "the house of windows." A building in a Gilbertine double monastery that stood between the male and female houses, that kept the sexes separate but allowed them to communicate.

domus necessarium ***see*** **rere-dorter**

donai In Japanese Zen Buddhism, monks living in the zendō (meditation hall)

donati ***see*** **lay monastic**

donchee ***see*** **maechi**

dormitorium ***see*** **dorter**

dormitory ***see*** **dorter**

dorter; dormitorium; dormitory A hall where the community members slept in common—in the later Middle Ages some dormitories were partitioned into cubicles to provide privacy

dosan; eka A group of monks who all trained under the same rōshi (monastic master) in a Japanese Zen Buddhist monastery

doso; hall monk A lower-ranking or undistinguished monk in the Japanese Tendai school of Buddhism

double monastery; double house; mixed house A combined monastery for men and women but separated by sex—ruled by either an abbot or an abbess

dovecot; plumbarium A place in a monastic house to keep doves and pigeons to provide a ready source of food during the winter. It was usually located among the buildings of the curia (outer courtyard) or in the eaves of major buildings.

dowry A gift of land or an entrance fee often required by a nunnery for accepting a new member. Canon law forbade the exaction of dowry, but permitted voluntary gifts. In the case of men's houses, it was normal practice for a postulant to bring an endowment with him.

drashag ***see*** **cell**

dresser window The serving window between the monastery kitchen and the frater. There was a table or dresser on each side of the window. The caterer in the kitchen would put the food from the kitchen on one side and the discarius would take it off the other side.

drying room A place sometimes found in the southeast corner of a monastery cloister. It is thought to have been for the use of the lay monastics that would get wet working in the fields.

Dunstan, St. ***see*** **English Benedictine reform; Westminster Abbey**

dzayraguyn vardapet An archimandrite (abbot) in the Armenian Apostolic Church

~E~

Early Mass; Morrow Mass; Missa Familiaris The Mass that followed Prime, chiefly for the benefit of servants, outside workers, and lay monastics

Eastern Christian monasticism Christian monasticism began in the 3rd century and ever since has had an important place in the life of the Church. The founder is considered to be St. Anthony the Great (251–356). He was a hermit who retreated to the Egyptian desert to seek God and other hermits in his vicinity, but they all lived solitary lives.

In time, monks began to form closer communities. St. Pachomius (ca. 292–348) is regarded as the founder of cenobitic monasticism, in which monastics live together under the direction of an abbot. The first such monastery was in Tabennisi, Egypt.

A third type of monastic institution, the skete, was inadvertently founded by St. Macarius (300–391) when he went to the desert as a hermit and other monks gathered around his dwelling. A skete has individual monastic dwellings surrounding a common church. Each monk lives by himself, or with one or two others. The community only comes together on Sundays and feast days.

All subsequent Christian monasticism was built on this threefold foundation.

The monastics of Armenia, Chaldea, and of the Syrian countries in general were influenced by neither the ecclesiastical nor imperial authority of Byzantium, and continued those observances which were known among them from the time of St. Anthony.

About 350 Mar Awgin founded the first cenobitic monastery of Mesopotamia on Mt. Izla above the city of Nisibis and monastic communities began to thrive. Under pressure from their Zoroastrian rulers, the Synod of Beth Lapat in 484 declared that the teaching of Nestorius was to be the official doctrine of the Assyrian Church of the East, and decreed that all monks and nuns should marry. This severely weakened the church and spiritual life declined. Some opponents to this decision left altogether and joined the newly established Monophysite church. This decision was reversed in 553, and in 571 Abraham the Great of Kashkar founded a new monastery on Mt. Izla with strict rules. The third abbot of this monastery was his student Babai the Great (551–628). Babai finally drove out the married monks from Mt. Izla, and as visitor of the monasteries of the north ensured that the monastic ideal was taken seriously throughout northern Mesopotamia.

Monks in the Eastern Orthodox monks are called Father as are priests and deacons, but in some places they may address one another as Brother. Novices are most often referred to as Brother, although in some places, for example, on Mount Athos, novices are addressed as Father. Among the Greeks, old monks are often called Elder (Gheronda) out of respect for their dedication. In the Slavic tradition, the title of Elder (Starets) is normally reserved for those who are of an advanced spiritual life, and who serve as guides for others.

Nuns who have been tonsured to the stavrophore or higher are addressed as Mother. Novice and rassophore nuns are addressed as Sister. Nuns live identical ascetic lives to their male counterparts and are their communities are called monasteries. • *See also* **Armenian monasticism; Coptic monasticism; Ethiopian monasticism**

ecclesiarch ***see*** **sacristan**

ecclesiastikos In a Greek Orthodox katholikon, a monk who functions more or less as a sexton, ringing bills, sounding the sematrons, lighting candles, cleaning, etc.

Eckhart, Meister (ca. 1260–ca. 1328); Eckhart von Hochheim German Dominican friar, priest, theologian, philosopher, teacher, writer, and mystic. He joined the Dominicans when he was about 18. In 1294, he was made prior at Erfurt and provincial of Thuringia. From 1303 to 1311 he was provincial for Saxony and had responsibility for 47 monasteries and also founded three nunneries. Complaints made against him at the general chapter in 1306, but came to nothing and in 1307 he was made vicar-general of Bohemia with full power to set the demoralized monasteries there in order.

He was widely read and admired despite sometimes annoying traditionalists and in later life was accused of heresy and brought up before the local Franciscan-led Inquisition, and tried as a heretic by Pope John XXII. Eckhart died before a verdict could be rendered. From the 16th to 19th centuries he was largely ignored. Since the 19th century, however, he has received renewed attention and has acquired a status as a great mystic within contemporary popular spirituality.

Eckhart von Hochheim ***see*** **Eckhart, Meister**

econome ***see*** **cellarer**

economus; oeconomus In the Western Church, the bursar or finance officer of a monastery; in Byzantine monasticism, a chief steward or treasurer

Eight Precepts The precepts for those devout Buddhists who wish to practice Buddhism more strictly than through adherence to the five precepts. The Eight Precepts focus both on avoiding morally bad behavior, as do the Five Precepts alone, and on leading a more ascetic life.

1. I undertake to abstain from causing harm and taking life (both human and non-human).
2. I undertake to abstain from eating at the wrong time (the right time is after sunrise, before noon).
3. I undertake to abstain from luxurious places for sitting or sleeping, and overindulging in sleep.

4. I undertake to abstain from sexual activity.
5. I undertake to abstain from singing, dancing, playing music, attending entertainment performances, wearing perfume, and using cosmetics and garlands (decorative accessories).
6. I undertake to abstain from taking what is not given (for example stealing, or from displacements that may cause misunderstandings).
7. I undertake to abstain from using intoxicating drinks and drugs, which lead to carelessness.
8. I undertake to abstain from wrong speech: telling lies, deceiving others, manipulating others, using hurtful words.

Eihei Dogen *see* **Dogen Zenji**

Eisai (1114–1215); Yosai Japanese Buddhist monk and priest, credited with bringing both the Rinzai school of Zen Buddhism and green tea from China to Japan. He was ordained as a monk in the Tendai sect. In 1168 he went to Mt. Tiantai in China, where he learned about the Chan (Zen) school of Chinese Buddhism.

He was certified as a Zen teacher and returned to Japan in 1191, bringing with him Zen scriptures and tea seeds. He then founded the Hōon Temple in Kyūshū. It was Japan's first Zen temple. His efforts to teach Zen were met with opposition from the traditional Buddhist schools of the time and he moved to Kamakura in 1199, where his teachings met with greater support. Eisai never renounced his status as a Tendai monk, and until the end of his life continued to engage in Tendai practices. Though he is credited with transmission of the Rinzai line to Japan, it remained for later teachers to establish a distinctly Japanese Zen culture.

eka *see* **dosan**

Ekadandisannyasi *see* **Dashanami Sampradaya**

ekklesiarches In the Greek Orthodox Church, the monastic in charge of a monastery church, chapel, or oratory

ekklesiatikos In the Greek Orthodox Church, a literate monastic who was involved in liturgical offices

elachary A Jain senior monk

elder; gheronda (Greek monks); gerontas (Greek monks); gerontissa (Greek nuns); starets (Slavic) In the Greek Church, old monks are often called Elder (Gheronda) out of respect for their dedication. In the Slavic tradition, the title of Elder (Starets) is normally reserved for those who are of an advanced spiritual life, and who serve as guides for others.

elect In Manichaeism, those who lived apart from the auditors (laity) to concentrate on reducing the material influences of the world. They did this through strict celibacy, poverty, teaching, and preaching, therefore, the elect were probably at least quasimonastic.

eleutheron, idiodespoton A Byzantine monastery not under patriarchal or imperial control

Elisabeth of Schonau, St. (ca. 1129–1164) German Benedictine nun and visionary who transcended the conventional gender roles of her time.

She was educated at the double monastery of Schönau in Nassau and made her profession as a Benedictine in 1147.

From 1147 to 1152 suffered recurrent disease, anxiety, and depression as a result of her strict asceticism. St. Hildegard of Bingen admonished Elisabeth in letters to be prudent in the ascetic life.

In 1152, she began to experience visions of Christ, the Virgin Mary, an angel, or the special saint of the day would appear to her and instruct her. She also saw realistic visions of the Passion, Resurrection, and Ascension, or other scenes of the Old and New Testaments. On the advice of Abbot Hildelin, she set down other visions on wax tablets for her brother Egbert, a cleric at Bonn who edited them and had them published in three books under her name. When Egbert tried to exert authority over her work, she successfully resisted him.

Due to her visions, she became a well-known person and was consulted by bishops and abbots. In 1157 she became abbess of the nuns at Schönau under the supervision of Abbot Hildelin.

embrimia A simple woven stool sometimes used in their cells by the Desert Fathers and Mothers as a prayer stool. It could also be used as a pillow at night.

emptiness monks *see* **Komuso**

emptor The purchasing agent of the kitchener. He was a paid servant and responsible for the wise and prompt purchase of kitchen stores.

enclosed communities *see* **cloistered communities**

enclosure *see* **cloistering**

encowl To make a monk of

English Benedictine Congregation A group uniting autonomous English Roman Catholic Benedictine monastic communities. It was formed in 1216, but destroyed at the Dissolution of the Monasteries in 1535–1540. The present English Benedictine Congregation was revived from 1607 to 1633 when numbers of Englishmen and Welshmen that had become monks in continental European monasteries and were coming to England as missioners. The Congregation is headed by an Abbot President who serves a four-year term. In addition to the United Kingdom, it now also has houses in the United States, Africa, and South America.

English Benedictine Reform The monastic reform of the English church in the south and in the Midlands during the late 10th century when most monasteries had secular clergy who were sometimes married. Inspired by continental reforms, the reformers tried to install instead celibate contemplative monks who followed the *Rule of St. Benedict* and thus reverse the decline monasticism had been experiencing. Among the clerical leaders of the movement were Dunstan, Archbishop of Canterbury, Ethelwold, Bishop of Winchester, and Oswald, Archbishop of York. The reform movement gained strength under King Edgar (959–975), who supported the reforms, but it declined near the end of the 10th century when the leadership died off. • *See also* **Benedictine Reform**

enkleistos A Byzantine monk or nun who confined themselves in a cell

enkleistra The cell occupied by an enkleistos

Ennin (793 or 794–864 CE); Jikaku Daishi (Japan) Japanese Tendai Buddhist abbot and priest who was ordained at the age of 14. In 838, he went to China where he studied and lived through the Great Anti-Buddhist Persecution of 842–846. He was deported back to Japan to Japan in 847.

In 854, he became the abbot of the Tendai sect at Enryakuji, where he built buildings to store the sutras and religious instruments he brought back from China. His dedication to expanding the monastic complex and its courses of study gave a prominence to the Tendai school in Japan. While his chief contribution was to strengthen the Tendai Tantric Buddhist tradition, the Pure Land recitation practices (nembutsu) that he introduced also helped to lay a foundation for the independent Pure Land movements of the subsequent Kamakura period (1185–1333). He wrote more than 100 books.

enpatsu Begging done at a long distance from a Japanese Zen Buddhist monastery, usually lasting a full day or longer

enzu The vegetable garden in a Japanese Zen Buddhist monastery vegetable garden; also the gardener

epanokalimafko ***see*** **epanokalimavkion**

epanokalimavkion; epanokalimafko; epanokamelavkion A cloth veil worn by Eastern Orthodox Christian monastics who are rassophore (one rank above a novice) or above, including bishops. It is worn with a kamilavkion (a stiff fez-like hat). The epanokalimavkion attaches or is laid over the front of the kamilavkion and extends over the top to hang down the back, with lappets hanging down on each side. In some traditions, the lappets hanging over the shoulders, but nuns bring them together and fasten them behind the apostolnik (veil). In the Russian tradition, the kamilavkion covered by its epanokalimavkion is called a klobuk.

epanokamelavkion ***see*** **epanokalimavkion**

ephoros The guardian or protector of a Byzantine monastery; the lay administrator of a Byzantine monastery

epistemonarches In a Byzantine monastery, the monk in charge of discipline • *see also* **circator; warden of the order**

epiteretes In a Byzantine monastery, an overseer

E.R. Cam. The post-nominal initials of the Camaldolese Hermits of Monte Corona. • *See also* **Camaldolese Order**

eremite ***see*** **anchorite**

eremitic ***see*** **anchoretic**

eremitical ***see*** **anchoretic**

esorason ***see*** **inner cassock**

Essaioi ***see*** **Essenes**

Essenes; Isiyim (Ancient Hebrew); Essēnoi (Greek); Essaioi (Greek); Ossaioi (Greek) A Jewish sect of Second Temple Judaism that flourished from the 2nd century BCE to 100 CE which some scholars claim seceded from the Zadokite priests. The Essenes lived in various cities but congregated in communities dedicated to asceticism, voluntary poverty, daily ritual bathing, and abstinence from worldly pleasures, including, for some groups, marriage. Many separate but related religious groups of that era shared similar practices and beliefs, but all are referred to as Essenes. They became widely known with the discovery of the Dead Sea Scrolls at the abandoned settlement at Qumran in Israel. Judaism does not encourage the monastic ideal of celibacy and poverty, and many writers are reluctant to call the Essenes monastics, yet they shared many of the traits of other monastics, ancient and modern, so were at least quasimonastics.

Essenoi *see* **Essenes**

Ethelwold of Winchester, St. *see* **English Benedictine reform; *Regularis Concordia***

Ethiopian monasticism Ethiopia was one of the first nations to accept Christianity, officially converting to it in 341. From that time it was subject to the Patriarch of Alexandria, gaining its independence only in 1959. The church is officially known as the Ethiopian Orthodox Tewahedo Church. In 480 the Nine Saints came from the Mediterranean world to establish Ethiopian monasticism which has continued to flourish despite wars and persecutions. Ancient and inaccessible monasteries are still occupied to this day throughout the Christian regions of the country. • *See also* **Bahtawlyan; Beth Israel; *Ethiopic Collectio Monastica*; Gahusan**

Ethiopic Collectio Monastica; Ethiopic Paternicon; Wisdom of the Elders of Ethiopia; Book of the History of the Fathers and of Their Words; Gannat A book of 68 chapters and with sayings of the Desert Fathers, most of which have no parallel in the *Apophthegmata Patrum (Sayings of the Desert Fathers)*. It was probably written by a 5th century monk who either lived with the Desert Fathers at Scetis, or knew the monks who lived there. • *See also* ***Apophthegmata Patrum***

Ethiopic Paternicon **see** ***Ethiopic Collectio Monastica***

Eugenios, Saint *see* **Agwin of Clysma**

Evagrius Ponticus (345–399) Middle Eastern Christian monk, archdeacon, ascetic, teacher, and writer. He was one of the most influential theologians in the late 4th century church, and was well known as a thinker, polished speaker, and gifted writer.

In Constantinople he became infatuated with a married woman and to avoid temptation, fled to a monastery in Jerusalem where he became gravely ill and did not recover until he confessed his sin. He became a monk in 383 and joined a cenobitic community in Nitria in Lower Egypt in around 385, but later moved to Kellia where he studied under Macarius of Alexandria and Macarius the Great.

Most Egyptian monks of that time were illiterate and Evagrius is thought to be a pioneer in recording and systematizing the sayings and teachings of the Desert Fathers.

In 375, he developed a comprehensive list of Eight Evil Thoughts, or Eight Terrible Temptations, from which all sinful behavior springs. In 590, Pope Gregory I, (Gregory The Great) revised this list to form the more commonly known Seven Deadly Sins.

The influence of Evagrius is less than it might have been had he not been caught up in the speculations of Origen on the nature of God and Christ which were declared heretical by the Second Council of Constantinople in 553. Although Evagrius is not mentioned by name in the Council's 15 anathematisms, in the eyes of most contemporaries, the Council did indeed condemn the teachings of Evagrius, together with Origen and Didymus the Blind.

Evening Prayer *see* **Vespers**

exarch In the Eastern Church, the superior over several monasteries; in the modern Greek church, a deputy of the patriarch, who visits the clergy, investigates ecclesiastical cases, etc.

exclaustration A release from religious vows to return to the secular world

excommunication In the *Rule of St. Benedict,* this is not being thrown out of the Church, but more like being sent to Coventry. If, however, you believe that the opposite of poverty is community—as Benedict does—it is a severe enough punishment. The aim is never meant to drive transgressors out, but rather to encourage them to amend and come back in. Witness RB 27, which is devoted entirely to caring for the excommunicated.

exeant *see* **exeat**

exeat; exeant A permit for temporary absence from a monastery

executive council A small consultative and deliberative body of a monastic community that assists the superior with matters that do not require the attention of the whole chapter

exemption The status held by some Roman Catholic monasteries exempting them from the jurisdiction of the local bishop and instead putting them under the jurisdiction of the pope

exennia In the Middle Ages, small tokens of affection supplied to monastics by the cellarer four times a year that could be sent to friends and relatives; also gifts of produce from a monastery's estates given to the archbishop at Christmas and Easter

exorason *see* **outer cassock**

extern sacristan The monastic responsible for the upkeep and maintenance of the monastery buildings and grounds

extern sisters *see* **lay monastics**

extra-claustral buildings Those in the curia (outer courtyard) of a monastery, as opposed to those in the cloister

~F~

fakir An Asian religious ascetic or begging monk

Falconieri, St. Juliana Founder of the Nuns of Third Order of Servites

familia *see* **familiars**

familiars; familia Laity who were nonresident and received the spiritual benefits of the abbey such as prayers and Masses; laity who resided within the abbey distinct from the monks and lay brothers—they might include men who were not fit to carry out the lay brothers' duties, those who died before taking their vows, or lay brothers who had misbehaved and were thus demoted

fangzhang *see* **abbot**

farmery *see* **infirmary**

Fatebenefratelli *see* **Hospitaller Order of the Brothers of St. John of God**

father In Western Christianity, the term father is reserved for priests.

In Eastern Christianity, a monk, priest, or deacon is called Father, but when conversing among themselves, monks in some places may address one another as Brother. Novices are most often referred to as Brother, although in some places, for example, on Mount Athos, novices are addressed as Father.

father abbot The abbot of an abbey that had established a new Cistercian foundation (daughter-house); in a nunnery, the abbot appointed as the nuns' mentor, who oversaw their spiritual care and might offer guidance in other matters

father immediate The abbot of the Cistercian mother-house

Father of Eastern Monasticism A nickname of St. Basil the Great

Father of English History A nickname of St. Bede the Venerable

Father of Monks A title sometimes mistakenly gives to St. Anthony the Great. He is very important in the history of monasticism, but there were many other monks who preceded him both in Christianity and in other religions.

Father of Scholasticism A nickname of St. Anselm of Canterbury

Father of Western Christian Monasticism A nickname of St. Benedict of Nursia

Federated Ursulines *see* **Company of St. Ursula**

Felix of Valois, St. *see* **Order of the Most Holy Trinity**

fenestra parvula A small window through which nuns and canons of a Gilbertine double house communicated, made confessions, etc.; a small window through which nuns could speak to their families. • *See also* **communion window; hagioscope; parlor window**

feretrar *see* **warden of the shrine**

fermerer *see* **infirmarian**

fermery *see* **infirmary**

Feuillantine A female member of the Feuillants

Feuillants; Congregation of Notre-Dame des Feuillants (France); Bernardoni (Italy); Reformed Bernardines A reform Cistercian order founded in 1577 at Les Feuillants Abbey. Les Feuillants was originally a Cistercian abbey in 1145 near Toulouse. In 1562 Jean de la Barrière (1544–1600) became its commendatory abbot. He went to Paris to continue his studies and in 1573, having decided to introduce a reform into his abbey, became a novice there himself, made his solemn profession, and was later ordained a priest. He then tried to reform the abbey but the 12 monks there resisted and tried to poison him. In 1577, Barrière reaffirmed his intention of reform and seven monks left.

The reform was exceedingly rigid and renounced wine, fish, eggs, butter, salt, and all seasoning. They ate only bread, herbs cooked in water, and oatmeal. Tables were abolished and the monks ate kneeling on the floor. They went barefoot in the monastery, slept on the ground or on bare planks, with a stone for a pillow, and slept for only four hours a night. In addition, silence and manual labor were prized. Despite, this austere regime, the community grew with the admission of fervent postulants.

The order also had women religious, known as the Feuillantines. They were established in 1588 and had two houses in France.

In 1791, the order had 24 abbeys and 162 members. The French congregation was suppressed in 1791 during the French Revolution, and the Italian congregation rejoined the Cistercians.

filatio The Latin word for the obedience required of a monastic

filiation A system of monastic organization developed by the Cistercians that made each monastery responsible for supervising its daughter foundations; also a group of abbeys linked in this way to a common mother-house

Fiorensians *see* **Congregation of Fiore**

First Hour *see* **Prime**

first order Within the Roman Catholic Church a religious institute for men

first vows *see* **simple vows**

Five Bhikkhus The first five of Buddha's monastics: Ajnata-Kaundinya, Asvajit, Bhadrika, Dasabala-Kasyapa, and Mahanama-Kulika

forest monks *see* **Forest Tradition**

Forest Tradition; Kammaṭṭhāna Forest Tradition A practice in the family of Theravada Buddhist monasticism. It emphasizes that the mind precedes the world, and seeks to attain awakening through meditation proficiency and elimination of unwholesome conduct.

The forest tradition originated in Thailand about 1900 with the Dhammayut monks Mun Bhuridatto and Sao Kantasilo who wandered the countryside seeking out the classical Buddhism still practiced there. The tradition is known for scrupulous adherence to the *Vinaya*, the Buddhist monastic code. At the same time, the tradition is known for an anti-textual stance, as it is believed that cleansing of the mind should come through application of Buddhist principles rather than rote memorization. The founders notably did not write down their teaching, preferring to teach orally. In the late 20th century, however, adherents wrote detailed texts and the Forest Tradition spread to Thai cities and then to the West.

Forest Tradition monks are celibate, do not handle money, and emphasize meditation. They also commonly engage in a practice known as tudong in which they wander on foot through the countryside either on pilgrimage or in search of solitary retreat places in nature. During such wanderings, the monks sleep wherever is available and eat only what is offered by lay people along the way. They inhabit remote wilderness and forest dwellings as spiritual practice training grounds.

In Thailand, Maha Nikaya and Dhammayuttika Nikaya are the two major monastic orders that have forest traditions. Sri Lanka has the Galduwa Forest Tradition. The Taungpulu Forest Tradition is in Myanmar (Burma), and there is also a Lao Forest Tradition in Laos. • *See also* **dhutanga**

formation guide *see* **formation master**

formation master; formation mistress; formation guide A senior monastic appointed by the superior to oversee the formation of a postulant, novice, or junior monastic

formation mistress *see* **formation master**

fornication When spoken of by the Desert Fathers and Mothers in the *Apophthegmata Patrum*, this refers to the temptation to have sex, not actually having it

Founder of Christian Monasticism A title sometimes mistakenly given to St. Anthony the Great. He was very important in the history and development of Christian monasticism, but there were many Christian monastics that preceded him.

Four Pillars of Dominican Life Community, common prayer, study, and service

Francis de Sales, St. *see* **Order of the Visitation of Holy Mary**

Francis of Assisi, St. (1181 or 1182–1226) Italian Roman Catholic deacon, and preacher. He founded the men's Order of Friars Minor, the women's Order of St. Clare, the Third Order of St. Francis, and the Custody of the Holy Land. Francis is one of the most venerated Christian religious figures in history.

He was born in Assisi in a well-to-do family and lived a carefree life as a young man. Around 1202 he was taken captive in a military expedition and spent a year as a prisoner. In 1205, Francis was ready to enlist in the military again but a vision caused him to become disenamored of the worldly life. He later had another vision of Christ telling him to repair his house, which he took to mean the run-down church in San Damiano where he was praying. Francis stole some cloth from his father and sold it but the priest refused to accept the money. When his father found him, he was beaten, bound, and locked in a small storeroom until his mother freed him.

Afterwards Francis worked in the kitchen in a monastery and begged for stones to repair San Damiano and then rebuilt it himself. He also nursed lepers. Within a year gained 11 followers and they preached in the district of Umbria. In 1209 he composed a simple rule for his followers (friars), the *Regula Primitiva* (*Primitive Rule*), which came from verses in the Bible. In 1210 Pope Innocent III gave Francis permission to found the Order of Friars Minor. Francis was canonized in 1228.

Francis of Paola, St. (1416–1507) Italian friar and the founder of the Roman Catholic Order of Minims. He was educated by Franciscans, and at 13 he entered a friary for a year to fulfill the vow made by his parents. In the following year he went on a pilgrimage to Assisi, Rome, and other places holy places. Upon his return he went to live in solitude in a cave on his father's property for six years. In 1435 he was joined by two companions, and the following year they founded the Hermits of St. Francis of Assisi, which would later be renamed Order of Minims.

Francis was canonized in 1519.

Franciscan Clarist Order *see* **Poor Clares**

Franciscans The original order of Franciscans, the Friars Minor, was an ascetic mendicant community of men founded by St. Francis of Assisi in 1209. Mainly because of disagreements over the strictness of adherence to the *Rule of St. Francis*, the order produced a confusing array of controversies, communities, and sects, all sometimes referred to as Franciscan, although the Order of Friars Minor is considered the original order. • *See also* **Colettans; Colettine Poor Clares; Order of Friars Minor; Order of Friars Minor Conventual; Spiritual Franciscans; Third Order Regular of St. Francis; Third Order Secular of St. Francis**

frater *see* **refectory**

frateries *see* **nikayas**

fraticelli Literally, "little brethren," a name which St. Francis of Assisi gave to his followers early in the 13th century. Later, in the century the name degenerated when it was used by the Spiritual Franciscans.

Fraticelli *see* **Spiritual Franciscans**

Fraticelli de Paupere Vita *see* **Spiritual Franciscans**

fratres barbati; barbati fratres; bearded brothers; conventual builders In the Roman Catholic Church, craftsmen admitted to monastic communities beginning about the middle of the 9th century, whose social grade was more elevated than the ordinary workmen and were freeborn. They were a type of lay brother and wore a monastic kind of dress, could leave their profession whenever they chose, and could return to civil life if they wished to. The fratres barbati incurred the anger of their coreligionists by their haughty deportment, sumptuous garb, liberty of movement, and refusal to shave their long, flowing beards. In the middle of the 13th century, Abbot William of Prémontré attempted to enforce the rule of shaving the beard, but the fratres refused and threatened to burn down every cloister and cathedral in the country. The abbot then withdrew the demand. Gradually, however, the fratres barbati ceased to exist.

Fratres Conventuales *see* **Order of Friars Minor Conventual**

Fratres Cruciferi *see* **Crutched Friars**

Fratres Minores Conventuales *see* **Order of Friars Minor Conventual**

Fratres Saccati *see* **Friars of the Sack**

Fratres Vitae Communis *see* **Brethren of the Common Life**

friar A brother or member of a mendicant order such as Franciscans, Augustinians, Dominicans, or Carmelites; a popular name for the mendicant orders which emerged in the 13th century as distinct from a monastic attached to a monastery. They were committed to poverty—communal as well as individual—and thus relied on begging for their daily subsistence. In contrast to monks, friars were not bound by vows of stability and moved around towns, preaching and caring for the sick.

Friars de Domina *see* **Friars of the Blessed Mary**

Friars Minor Conventual *see* **Order of Friars Minor Conventual**

Friars of Our Lady *see* **Friars of the Blessed Mary**

Friars of St. Mary of Vauvert *see* **Friars of the Blessed Mary**

Friars of the Blessed Mary; Pied Friars; Friars of our Lady; Friars De Domina; Friars of St. Mary of Vauvert; Friars of the Mother of Christ A small mendicant order founded in Marseilles in the middle of the 13th century. They were called "pied" because of their brown and white habit. They were suppressed by the Council of Lyon in 1274 and the members made to join one of the major orders.

Friars of the Mother of Christ *see* **Friars of the Blessed Mary**

Friars of the Penance of Jesus Christ *see* **Friars of the Sack**

Friars of the Sack; Friars of the Penance of Jesus Christ; Blue Friars; Brothers of Penitence; Order of the Penance of Jesus Christ; Fratres Saccati A mendicant order that came into being in Spain sometime in the 13th century. Their rule was based on the *Rule of St. Augustine*. They spread rapidly and by 1257, were established in England, where they became the largest of the lesser groups of friars in England. For a time, they rivaled the Augustinians, nevertheless, the order was dissolved for what now seems to be no good reason by the Second Council of Lyon in 1274, and they were gradually absorbed into other orders, chiefly the Augustinians and Dominicans.

Friars of the Strict Observance *see* **Order of Friars Minor**

Friars Preacher *see* **Order of Preachers**

friary A monastery of friars; the institution or practices of friars; the community of friars

fuga mundi; flight from the world A concept for the early Christian hermits who sought to isolate themselves from the lay world about them. Early cenobites tried to adhere to this concept as well but over the years have moved away from it to a greater or lesser degree.

fugitive religious *see* **apostates**

fugitivi *see* **apostates**

Fujii, Nichidatsu (1885–1985) A Japanese Buddhist monk, founder of the Nipponzan-Myōhōji order of Buddhism, and peace activist. He is known for building Peace Pagodas around the world. The first were built in 1947 in the Japanese cities of Hiroshima and Nagasaki where the atomic bombs killed over 150,000 people in World War II.

He was ordained a monk at 19 in the ascetic and intellectual Hōon-ji tradition. He began missionary work in Manchuria in 1917 and worked in India in the 1930s. During World War II he declared himself a pacifist and actively promoted pacifism in Japan. Although this was illegal at the time, he was never imprisoned. During the Cold War period, he preached nonviolence and did hunger strikes for peace.

fukuten The assistant to the head cook in a Japanese Zen Buddhist monastery

fusu; fūsu In a Japanese Zen Buddhist monastery, the officer in charge of financial affairs. In the Rinzai and Obaku sects, the shika (hostler) is often appointed as the fūsu and also assists the chief priest and supervises the monks.

fuzui The fūsu's assistant in a Japanese Zen Buddhist monastery

~G~

gahapati *see* **householder**

gahattha *see* **householder**

Gahusan Ethiopian Christian monastics that live in complete isolation in forests. They try to avoid people and are seen only occasionally by hunters and herdsmen. They live by eating wild plants. Sometimes human bones are found with Christian artifacts and it is assumed they are Gahusan monks that died either of natural causes or from being attacked and eaten by a predator.

galilee A porch or waiting room, usually at the west end of an abbey church in England, where the monks collected on returning from processions, where bodies were laid previous to interment, and where women were allowed to see the monks to whom they were related, or to hear divine services

Gampopa (1079–1153); Sönam Rinchen A Tibetan Buddhist physician and monk. Originally he was married and had two children, but the plague killed them all. He then renounced his layperson's status and became a monk in 1104 at the age of 25. He was famous for clarity of perception and his knowledge of both Kadam and Mahamudra methods. He subsequently became the founder of the Dagpo Kagayu school of Tibetan Buddhism.

ganini aryika A senior Jain nun

ganini aryika pramukha A Jain nun who is the head of a monastic order

Gannat *see* ***Ethiopic Collectio Monastica***

garth An open central space in a monastery, normally a quadrilateral, enclosed by a cloister

Gaston of Valloire *see* **Order of St. Anthony**

gatekeeper *see* **porter**

geku *see* **zealator**

gelong *see* **bhikkhu**

gelongma *see* **bhikkhuni**

general The title of the head of the Order of the Service of Mary

general chapter An annual general meeting attended by the heads of houses. The Cistercians were the first to make this an integral part of the order's administration; it was soon taken on by other orders and in 1215 Pope Innocent III made it mandatory.

general superior *see* **superior general**

German Order *see* **Order of Brothers of the German House of St. Mary in Jerusalem**

gerontas *see* **elder**

gerontikon In the Eastern Church, a saying or apothegm of a monastic elder

gerontissa *see* **elder**

getsul *see* **samanera**

getsulma *see* **samaeri**

gheronda *see* **elder**

gidan In Japanese Zen Buddhism, the "ball of doubt" that prompts a monk's drive to practice and attain enlightenment

gihin *see* **householder**

Gilbertines A monastic order founded in 1131 by St. Gilbert in Sempringham, England. The order began for contemplative nuns and was based on the Cistercian Rule. Then lay sisters were accepted to serve them. There followed lay brothers to work the fields. In 1148, canons that lived according to variant *Rule of St. Augustine* were added to serve the communities as priests and administrators. Each establishment was a double house with a single church that had a wall down the dividing the men from the women.

The Gilbertine nuns wore a black tunic, scapular, and veil. The lay sisters wore a black tunic but no scapular. The lay brothers wore a dark tunic.

Although very popular for several centuries, by the end of the 15th century, the order was impoverished. The Gilbertines were the only completely English monastic order and it came to an end with the Act for the Dissolution of the Lesser Monasteries. In 1538, the 26 houses then existing surrendered without a fight and the monks and nuns in them were given lifetime pensions.

gileko *see* **cassock vest**

Gioacchino da Fiore *see* **Joachim of Fiore**

Giovanni Pietro Carafa *see* **Theatines**

goannai In a Japanese Zen Buddhist monastery, to forcibly take a monk to sanzen (meditation) in order to help him resolve his kōan

godo; godō In a Japanese Zen Buddhist Sōtō zendō, (meditation hall) the monk in charge of the zendō, second to the rōshi (monastic master). The godō uses the kyōsaku (encouragement stick) to deliver sharp blows upon the shoulders of monks found dozing off or loose in their form.

goenpa A Bhutanese Buddhist monastery

going forth *see* **pabbajja**

gomai A kind of takuhatsu (begging round) in which individual monks go to designated households once a month to receive rice set aside by the family for the monastic community

Gosains *see* **Hindu warrior monks**

gozan bungaku Japanese Zen Buddhist literature of the Five Mountains. The term Five Mountains refers to the principal Zen monastic centers of the Rinzai sect in Kamakura, Japan and to an additional five in Kyoto. It also refers to the five Zen monastic centers in China in Hangzhou and Ningpo that inspired the religious and cultural organization in Japan.

Gozzolini, St. Sylvester *see* **Sylvestrine Congregation**

granarias *see* **granatorius**

granator *see* **granatorius**

granatorius; granarias; granator A cellarer's assistant to who had charge of a monastery bakery and grain supply

grand master The title of the heads of the military orders such as the of Hospitallers or the Knights Templar

grand mistress The head of a Beguine complex

Grandmontines; Order of Grandmont; Boni Homines; Bonshommes An austere contemplative order with a rule of silence that began when St. Stephen of Muret founded a hermitage in 1078 near Limoges in France. Apparently he had no intention of founding an order, but between 1140 and 1150 the prior Stephen Liciac formed a formal order and the *Rule of Grandmont* was created. It is also called the *Rule of St. Stephen*, and is based on the homilies St. Stephen gave. Ironically, St. Stephen himself said, "The only rule is the Gospel of Christ."

Daughter houses, called "cells," were never to exceed 13 people, and consisted of three or four choir monks and the rest lay brethren who had equal voting rights. The cells were headed by a choir monk called a corrector, and a lay monk called a curiosis, who dealt with temporal matters. Although Stephen Liciac expressly forbade admission of nuns, there were eventually four communities of them. The order grew rapidly but began deteriorating by 1185 when lay monks began asserting their authority over the choir monks. Eventually, with papal intervention in the 14th century, the order became cenobitic, the prior of the order made an abbot, and the lay monks lost their power. From 1471 until 1579 commendatory abbots were assigned, which didn't help matters. In the 17th century a group known as the Strict Observance of the Order of Grandmont also existed, but it never had more than eight houses. The troubles continued, however, and in 1787, both branches were suppressed.

grange A form of manor used by certain monastic orders to farm outlying lands—they were generally managed by a monastic dean and worked by lay brothers

Great Lavra *see* **Mar Saba**

great schema; megaloschemos (Greek); schima (Church Slavonic) A ranking given to monks and nuns in the Orthodox Church whose superiors feel they have reached a high level of spiritual excellence. In some traditions it is never given; in other traditions it is given only on the deathbed; on Mt. Athos, it is common for it to be given only three years after entry into monastic life. In the Russian tradition and some others, when a bearer of some monastic title acquires the great schema, their title incorporates the word "schema," so a hieromonk (priest monk) would become a hieroschemamonk, a hegumen (abbot) would become a schema-hegumen, etc.

great silence; greater silence; night silence The time of strict silence prescribed from after Compline in the evening until after Lauds or Morning Prayer the next morning

greater prior *see* **prior major**

greater silence *see* **great silence**

Greco-Buddhist monks Greeks were exposed to Buddhism when Alexander the Great invaded Asia Minor and central Asia in 332 BCE and later invaded India in 326 BCE. The active interaction between Greece and Buddhism did not end until the 5th century CE. There were Greek Buddhist monks as early as 260 BCE during the reign of Emperor Ashoka.

Gregory the Great, St. (ca. 540–604) Italian monk who is best known as a highly successful and venerated pope, although his roots were in monasticism. After the death of his father, Gregory converted his family villa into a monastery.

Pope Pelagius II ordained Gregory a deacon and solicited his help in trying to heal the schism of the Three Chapters in northern Italy. Gregory had a deep respect for the monastic life. He viewed being a monk as the "ardent quest for the vision of our Creator." Although Gregory was resolved to retire into the monastic lifestyle of contemplation, he was unwillingly forced back into a world that he no longer wanted to be a part of. He frequently complained of the burden of office and the loss of the life of prayer he had enjoyed as a monk. When elected pope in 590, he wrote letters disavowing any ambition to be pope and praising the monastic life. Still, he went on to become one of the greatest popes of the Roman Church.

Grey Friars *see* **Order of Friars Minor Conventual**

Grey Monks *see* **Order of Tiron**

grhapati; grhin; grihastha *see* **householder**

Griffiths, Bede (1906–1993); Dayananda, Swami English Roman Catholic Benedictine monk and priest who lived in ashrams in southern India and became a noted yogi and a leading thinker in the development of the dialogue between

Christianity and Hinduism. He was part of the Christian Ashram Movement.

After college, he sought ordination in the Church of England but had a crisis of faith and joined the Roman Catholic Church. He was received into Prinknash Abbey as a postulant in 1932 and received solemn profession in 1937. In 1940, he was ordained as a priest.

In 1955, he left England with a plan to establish a Benedictine Abbey in India, but his abbot made him give up his vows before permission was granted. In 1958, he joined with Father Francis Acharya, a Belgian Trappist monk, to establish Kristiya Sannyāsa Samaj, Kurisumala Ashram (Mountain of the Cross), a Syriac Rite monastery of the Syro-Malankara Catholic Church in Kerala and sought to develop a form of monastic life based in the Indian tradition. He took the saffron monastic habit and took the Sanskrit name "Dayananda."

He wrote 12 books on Hindu–Christian dialogue. Griffiths still desired to reconnect himself with the Benedictine order and sought a congregation which would accept him in the way of life he had developed. He was welcomed by the Camaldolese monks, and he and the ashram became a part of their congregation.

Groote, Gerard *see* **Brethren of the Common Life**

grwa phrug A Tibetan Buddhist child monk

grwa tshogs A congregation of Tibetan Buddhist monks

Gualbert, John *see* **Gualberto, Giovanni**

Gualberto, Giovanni (ca. 985–1073), St.; Gualberto, John Italian Roman Catholic abbot and the founder of the Vallombrosan Congregation. Gualberto originally took pleasure in vanities and romantic intrigues and at one point set off to kill the man who slew his brother Ugo. When he found the culprit in Florence, however, he had a conversion experience and offered the man forgiveness and friendship.

Soon thereafter Gualberto became a Benedictine monk at San Miniato where he opposed the simoniacal actions of which both his abbot Oberto and the Bishop of Florence Pietro Mezzabarba were guilty. Unwilling to compromise with them he left to lead a more perfect life far from those impurities. He spent some time with Camaldolese monks, but then started his own monastery at Vallombrosa. He often fasted and imposed other strict penances on himself, and he became noted for his compassion to the poor and the ill. He was canonized in 1193. • *See also* **Vallombrosan Congregation**

Gualberto Visdomini *see* **Vallombrosan Congregation**

guardian The superior of a Franciscan friary

guardian of the cloister A minor official with varying duties, sometimes functioning as a porter, sometimes more as a circator, keeping order in the cloister

Gueranger, Prosper Louis Pascal (1805–1875) French Benedictine monk and priest, who served for nearly 40 years as the abbot of Solesmes Abbey (which he founded in the abandoned Priory of Solesmes). He was the founder of the French Benedictine Congregation (now the Solesmes Congregation), which reestablished monastic life in France after it had been wiped out by the French

Revolution. He revived the Benedictine Order in France.

With private donations he was able to buy the derelict Priory of Solesmes in 1832 and in 1837 it was made an abbey and Guéranger took his vows as a Benedictine, was made its abbot and superior general of the head of the French Benedictine Congregation.

guesthouse; hospice; hospitium A hostel attached to a nunnery or monastery that usually provides a chapel to pray in, a refectory to eat in, and a dormitory to sleep in. Often guesthouses were in the curia (outer courtyard) of the monastery, but sometimes they were separate and more or less independent. They were often located on some difficult road or pass, as in the Alps. They are supervised by a hostler.

guestmaster *see* **hostler**

guestmistress *see* **hostler**

Guide for Anchoresses **see** ***Ancrene Wisse***

Guigo I (1083–1136) French Carthusian monk and prior. He entered the Grande Chartreuse monastery in 1106. In 1109, at age 26, he was elected the 5th prior of the monastery and maintained the position until his death in 1136. During his priorate the monastery grew and he composed the first customary. He was noted for his considerable learning, eloquence, and great memory.

Guigo II (fl. 12th century) Carthusian monk, writer, and 9th prior of the Grande Chartreuse monastery, from 1174 to 1180. He may have died in 1188 or 1193. His most famous book is *Scala Claustralium* (*The Ladder of Monks*), which has also been called *Scala Paradisi* (*The Ladder of Paradise*) and the *Epistola de Vita Contemplativa* (*Letter on the Contemplative Life*). Drawing from Jacob's vision in Genesis 28:12 of angels ascending and descending a ladder to God. Guigo named the four steps of this "ladder" of Lectio Divina prayer, a practice which continues to this day in contemporary Benedictine ritual meditation, with the Latin terms *lectio, meditatio, oratio*, and *contemplatio*.

guimpe A high-necked undergarment formerly much worn as part of the habit by nuns of the Western Church to cover the neck and shoulders

guru A Hindu, Jain, or Buddhist spiritual teacher. One need not be a monastic to be a guru, but many gurus are monastics. Sikhs also have gurus, but monasticism is expressly forbidden in Sikhism.

guruma *see* **maechi**

Gutoku *see* **Shinran**

Gyatso, Tenzin *see* **Tenzin Gyatso**

gyodo Sutra (aphorism or teaching) chanting during Japanese Zen Buddhist ceremonies, in which the monastics chant while walking in line inside the ceremony hall

gyrovagi *see* **gyrovagues**

gyrovagues; gyrovagi; circumcelliones; widscrithul (Anglo-Saxon) Wandering or itinerant monks without fixed residence or leadership, who went from place to place taking advantage of the charity and the hospitality of others. The Council of Chalcedon (451) and Second Council of Nicaea (787) prohibited this practice. Augustine called them circumcelliones (literally, those who prowl around the barns) and attributed the selling of fake relics as their innovation.

They were almost universally denounced and eventually faded into obscurity.

~H~

habit The customary clothing of a monastic. While there are many variations in the habits of Western monastics, the habits for both monks and nuns of the Eastern Church are largely the same with only certain slight regional variations.

hagioscope; squint; leper window; lychnoscope A small splayed window through a wall of a church in an oblique direction to enable one or more worshippers not in the church to view the altar, hear Mass, and receive the Eucharist. Originally developed for lepers, they later came to be used for anchorites so they did not have to leave their cells and for nuns so they did not have to leave their cloisters. • *See also* **communion window; fenestra parvula; parlor window**

Haid, Leo (1849–1924) American Benedictine abbot and Roman Catholic bishop. He made his first profession as a monk in 1869, and was ordained a priest in 1872. In 1885 he became the first abbot of Mary Help of Christians Abbey in North Carolina, and in 1886 founded a seminary there. In 1888 he was appointed Vicar Apostolic of North Carolina and was ordained as a bishop, becoming the first American abbot-bishop.

Hakuin Ekaku (1686–1768) Japanese Zen Buddhist monk, priest, and teacher. He is regarded as the reviver of the Rinzai school from a period of stagnation and as one of the most influential figures in all of Japanese Zen Buddhism.

He entered monastic life at 15 and struggled for a time until he learned visualization and breathing techniques. At age 31 Hakuin returned to Shoin-ji, the temple where he had been ordained and became the head priest for the next 50 years. Here he attracted hundreds of students and made the temple a center of Zen teaching.

Halabites *see* **Mariamite Maronite Order**

halios In the Eastern Church, the monastic in charge of fish supplies

hall monk *see* **doso**

han In a Japanese Zen Buddhist monastery, a thick rectangular wooden board measuring about 45 × 30 × 8 cm hung in front of the zendō (meditation hall) and struck with a wooden mallet three times a day—at dawn, at dusk, and before going to bed • *see also* **kaihan**

Harding, Stephen *see* **Usages**

Harriet, Mother *see* **Community of St. Mary the Virgin**

hashin kyuji In a Japanese Zen Buddhist monastery, the days before sesshin (the intensive meditation retreat) during which the unsui (postulants) can rest, repair clothes, and treat illnesses

he shang *see* **osho**

hebdomadarian *see* **hebdomadary**

hebdomadary; hebdomadarian The monastic whose duty for the week it is to begin and end the Daily Office and the solemn *Salve*, and to lead the prayers at the graces before and after meals

hegumen; hegumenos; igumen; hegumenia (female); ihumenia (female) The head of a monastery in the Eastern Church. After 1874, the abbot a monastery of the third or lowest class. • *See also* **kathegumen; pro-hegumen; protohegumen**

hegumenate The part of an Eastern Orthodox monastery reserved for the hegumen

hegumene The head of a community of nuns in the Eastern Church

hegumenia *see* **hegumen**

hegumenos *see* **hegumen**

helle *see* **prisons**

Heloise (ca. 1100–1164) French nun, abbess, writer, and scholar. As a girl, she was the ward of an uncle, a secular canon in Paris named Fulbert. In 1115 or 1116, Fulbert hired the canon Peter Abélard as her tutor. They had an affair and Héloïse became pregnant and gave birth to a boy. To placate Fulbert, Abélard agreed to marry Héloïse if the marriage should be kept secret so as not to damage Abélard's career. Héloïse returned to Paris and the couple were secretly married. Filbert reneged, however, and began to spread news of the marriage. Fearing for her safety, Abélard sent Héloïse to the convent of Argenteuil, where she became a nun at Abélard's insistence and much against her own wishes. She eventually became prioress there. In 1129, she became abbess at the Oratory of the Paraclete, near Nogent-sur-Seine in Champagne.

Héloïse's letters constitute one of the earliest, most radical of feminist philosophies. She disdained marriage and feminine life, saying, "I preferred love to wedlock, freedom to a bond." She later said, "What man, bent on sacred or philosophical thoughts, could endure the crying of children? And what woman will be able to bear the constant filth and squalor of babies?" She goes so far as to define marriage as the ultimate form of prostitution.

When Abélard died he was buried at St. Marcel, but his remains were soon carried off secretly and given over to the loving care of Héloïse, who in time herself came to rest beside them in 1163. Their remains were moved several times but since 1817 are thought to be in the Père Lachaise Cemetery in eastern Paris where they are popular attraction.

hemina The amount of wine allowed each monk in the *Rule of St. Benedict*. It is estimated to be about ten fluid ounces or 0.75 of a liter.

herb garden; herbarium A small garden of herbs. These were almost always found in monasteries since herbs were necessary for medicines, air fresheners, and cooking.

herbarium *see* **herb garden**

hermit; eremite; recluse; solitary; westensetla (Anglo-Saxon) One who renounces the world and goes into seclusion, usually for religious reasons. In the Christian tradition, hermits preceded cenobites. The Egyptian Paul of Thebes (fl. 3rd century) was the first known Christian hermit. His disciple Anthony the Great (fl. 4th century) is the best known of all the very early Christian hermits because of his biography written by Athanasius of Alexandria. In the Middle Ages Carmelite hermits liked to claim that they were following in the footsteps of the Jewish hermits organized by Elijah.

Christian hermits in the past lived in isolated hermitages in the desert or forest and were sometimes so sought out for counsel that they had no physical solitude at all. In the Egyptian desert, hermits often wove baskets to support themselves. In medieval times hermits in or near cities might earn a living as a gate keeper or ferryman.

From the Middle Ages to modern times eremitical monasticism has also been practiced within the context of religious institutes in the Roman Catholic Church. The Carthusians and Camaldolese arrange their monasteries as clusters of hermitages where the monks spend most of their time gathering only briefly for communal prayer and only occasionally for community meals and recreation.

Cistercian, Trappist, and Carmelite orders are predominately cenobitic, but allow certain monks and nuns after a certain period of time to live in a hermitage on monastery grounds.

By the early 13th century anchorites have been considered technically different hermits in that anchorites vow to stay in a single location, whereas hermits are free to change their locations. • *See also* **anchorites; Order of Watchers; poustinik**

Hermit Sisters of St. Augustine *see* **Canonesses of St. Augustine of the Mercy of Jesus**

hermitage; hermitary A hermitage is the dwelling place of a hermit. While hermitages can be anywhere from an isolated cave to an apartment in high rise, they are usually near to a monastery or at least a church. Typically, hermitages are simple with one room for worship, sleeping, and cooking. Sometimes there is also a workroom.

Christian monasticism began around 300 CE with the first Desert Fathers living in hermitages in Egypt's Nitrian Desert. Their piety attracted others who lived nearby in their own hermitages but close enough for contact. These formed the first cenobitic communities called were called sketes and in time it proved convenient to cooperate closely and the first cenobitic communities were formed. • *See also* **anchorhold; hesychasterion; kathisma**

hermitary *see* **hermitage**

Hermits of St. Augustine *see* **Order of St. Augustine**

Hermits of St. Damiano *see* **Celestines**

Hermits of St. Francis of Assisi *see* **Order of Minims**

Hermits of St. Jerome *see* **Order of St. Jerome**

Hermits of the Order of the Minims *see* **Order of Minims**

Hesperinon *see* **Vespers**

hesychasm; hesychia A mystical approach to prayer and meditation that developed late in 4th century Egypt among the Desert Fathers and Mothers. The practices of hesychasm include contemplative prayer, quiet sitting, and recitation of the Jesus Prayer. While originating with hermits, it is not merely separation from noise and speaking with other people, but the possession of interior quiet and peace. Thus it is possible to use the term of those who are not solitaries. It means more specifically guarding the mind, constant remembrance of God, and the possession of inner prayer. Still an active practice, it is especially popular in monastic circles of the Eastern Church, but also practiced by the laity. The *Philokalia* is the foundational text on hesychasm. Nikodemos, in his introduction, described the collected texts as "a mystical school of inward prayer" which could be used to cultivate the inner life and to "attain the measure of the stature of the fullness of Christ." • *See also* ***Philokalia***

hesychast One who practices hesychasm

hesychasterion In the Orthodox Church, a small cell or hermitage where intensive hesychasm is practiced, distinct from the cenobitic hesychastic life of a monastery. Legally and canonically, a hesychasterion is a hermitage established with the blessing of the diocesan bishop but owned by the monastic of the hermitage, as distinct from a monastery, which is owned by the bishop.

hesychia ***see*** **hesychasm**

hierodeacon An Orthodox or Eastern Catholic monk who has been ordained a deacon

hieromonachos ***see*** **hieromonk**

hieromonk; hieromonachos An Orthodox or Eastern Catholic monk who has been ordained to the priesthood

Hieronymites ***see*** **Order of St. Jerome**

hieroschemamonk In the Eastern Orthodox Church, a schema monk who is also a priest

Hilarion, St. (291–371) A desert hermit who is considered to be the founder of Palestinian monasticism. He converted to Christianity about the age of 15 and lived in a hut that resembled a tomb. He never washed his clothes, shaved his hair only once a year, and ate one meal a day, frequently only of bread and water. Legend has it, he was once visited by robbers but they left him alone because he did not fear death and had nothing worth stealing anyway. After 22 years in the Syrian desert he became so famous that frequent visitors drove him to move several times and he finally died in Cyprus.

Hilda of Whitby, St. (ca. 614–680) English nun and abbess. She was baptized at age 13, and became a nun in the Celtic tradition at age 33. She became the second abbess of Hartlepool Abbey, then in 657 became the founding abbess of the double monastery of Whitby Abbey in 657. Hilda was a skilled administrator and teacher, and so known for her wisdom that kings and princes sought her advice. Whitby Abbey was held in such esteem that King Oswiu of Northumberland chose it for the Synod of Whitby, the first synod of the Church in his kingdom.

Hildebrand of Sovana ***see*** **Gregory VII (ca. 1015–1085)**

Hildegard of Bingen, St. (ca. 1098–1179); Hildegard von Bingen German Benedictine abbess, writer, composer, philosopher, mystic, visionary, and polymath. She is considered to be the founder of scientific natural history in Germany. She became a nun at age 14 at the Duisberg Abbey and in 1136, was elected as magistra (superior) of the nuns there. In 1150 she founded St. Rupertsberg convent in 1150, and in 1165, a second convent at Eibingen.

Hildegard's works include three great volumes of visionary theology, liturgical musical compositions, the musical morality play *Ordo Virtutum*, nearly 400 letters, two volumes on natural medicine and cures, and even invented the *Lingua Ignota* language with its own alphabet.

Despite her regular belittling of herself as an unlearned women she has drawn great interest from feminist scholars. It seems her self-denigration lent authority to her visions of the divine and gave her authority to speak at a time when it was not generally permitted for women. She particularly criticized simony and other corrupt practices in the Church.

In 2012, she was named a Doctor of the Church.

Hildegard von Bingen *see* **Hildegard of Bingen**

Hindu monasticism A Hindu monk is called a sannyāsī, sādhu, or swāmi. A Hindu nun is called a sannyāsini, sādhvi, or swāmini. The goal of the Hindu monasticism is moksha (liberation). Exactly what that means varies from tradition to tradition. Hinduism has no formal demands or requirements on the lifestyle or spiritual discipline, method or deity—it is left to the choice and preferences of the individual. This freedom has led to diversity and significant differences in the lifestyle and goals of those who adopt Sannyāsa (renunciation of material desires). There are, however, some common themes. Adherents commit themselves to a life of simplicity, celibacy, detachment from worldly pursuits, and the contemplation of God. Other behavioral characteristics, in addition to renunciation, include: ahimsa (non-violence), akrodha (not become angry even if you are abused by others), disarmament (no weapons), amati (poverty), self-restraint, truthfulness, sarvabhutahita (kindness to all creatures), honesty, non-possessiveness, and shaucha (purity of body speech and mind).

Some Hindu monastic orders require this behavior in form of a vow before a renunciate can enter the order. Some monastics live in monasteries, while others wander from place to place, trusting in God alone to provide for their physical needs. They may have a walking stick, a book, a vessel for food and drink, and often wear yellow, saffron, orange, or ocher colored clothes. They may have long hair and appear disheveled, and are usually vegetarians.

Some minor Upanishads (sacred texts) as well as some monastic orders consider women, children, students, fallen men (those with a criminal record), and others as not qualified for Sannyāsa (renunciation of worldly desires); while other texts place no restrictions. Most Hindu monastics adopt celibacy, however there are exceptions, such as the Saiva Tantra school of asceticism where ritual sex is considered part of liberation process. Sex is viewed by them as transcendence from a personal, intimate act to something impersonal and ascetic.

Hindu warrior monks; Gosains; Bairagis In India, in the 12th century Hindu-Muslim conflicts provoked establishment of a military order of Hindu ascetics in India to counter Muslim oppression. These warrior monks formed paramilitary groups called akharas.

The Nath Siddhas may have been the earliest of the akharas. In some cases, these akharas cooperated with Muslim fakirs who were Sufi and also persecuted. The warrior became a political force during the early years of the British Raj and some of them played a key role in helping British establish themselves in India. Nevertheless, their influence declined as the British established themselves more firmly in the 19th century. • *See also* **Naga Sadhus**

Hirsau Reforms *see* **William of Hirsau**

Hngettwin Nikaya; Catubhummika Mahāsatipaṭṭhana Nikāya A small Buddhist monastic order in Burma [Myanmar]. It was founded in the mid–19th century and has about 1,000 monks. It is very austere and orthodox. Members worship and venerate Buddha but not his image.

hoan *see* **an**

hojo The abbot's room in a Japanese Zen Buddhist monastery

Holy Lavra of Saint Sabbas *see* **Mar Saba**

Holy Man of Renunciation A nickname of Ippen Shonin

Holy Mountain *see* **Athos, Mount**

Honen (1133–1212); Hōnen Japanese Tendai monk, priest, religious reformer, and founder of Japanese Pure Land Buddhism. He became a monk at age nine and studied for 12 years at Mount Hiei near Kyoto.

Seeking a way of salvation for all people through Buddhism, Hōnen gained a following among fortune-tellers, robbers, prostitutes, samurai, and others often ignored by Buddhists of the day. He paid particular attention to women, who were often held to be inherently spiritually defiled because of menstruation. His teachings were controversial and in 1207 Emperor Tsuchimikado exiled Hōnen and his followers. The ban was not lifted until 1211, and Hōnen was permitted to return to Kyoto where he died the following year.

hood *see* **cowl**

horarium The daily schedule by which a monastery lives, including, of course, the Daily Offices

hordarian *see* **bursar**

horo One's career as a Japanese Zen Buddhist monastic

horologion In the Eastern Church, a liturgical book containing the ordinary elements of the schedule of daily prayer for monks

hospice *see* **guesthouse**

Hospital Brothers of St. Anthony *see* **Order of St. Anthony**

Hospital Sisters *see* **Canonesses of St. Augustine of the Mercy of Jesus**

Hospitaller Order of the Brothers of St. John of God; Ordo Hospitalarius S. Ioannis de Deo; Brothers Hospitallers of St. John of God; Fatebenefratelli; Brothers of Mercy; Merciful Brothers A Roman Catholic order of men founded in 1572 by St. John of God. The order carries out a wide range of health and social service activities in 389 centers and services in 46 countries. In 2014, the membership of the order was 1,099. The co-workers who partner with the Brothers in their activities number approximately 40,000. Their mission is caring for the sick and preparing those with special needs to receive the sacraments.

The members are primarily brothers, but priests may be received. Besides taking the usual three monastic vows of poverty, chastity, and obedience, members take a fourth vow of serving the sick. The novitiate lasts two years, and after three years of simple vows, solemn profession may be made. The head of the order is called the prior general. Members of the order use the post-nominal initials O.H.

Hospitallers *see* **Knights Hospitaller**

Hospitallers of the Observance A women's order formed from the wives of the first Humiliati. under the direction of Clara Blassoni. They devoted themselves to the care of the lepers in a neighboring hospital. They grew until the suppression of the male branch of the order, although the women's branch was not suppressed. The nuns recited the Daily Office, fasted rigorously and engaged in other severe penitential practices, such as the self-inflicted whipping. Their habit was a white robe and scapular over an ash gray tunic with a white or black veil. Lay sisters wore gray. The community lasted until the early 20th century.

hospitarius *see* **hostler**

hospitium *see* **guesthouse**

hosteler *see* **hostler**

hostillar *see* **hostler**

hostler; hosteler; hospitarius; hostillar; guestmaster; guestmistress The monastic official charged with providing for the needs of guests. This is an important position and requires patience, kindness, competence, and good judgment.

Hours *see* **Daily Office**

householder; gihin (Pali); gahattha (Pali); gahapati (Pali); grhin (Sanskrit); grihastha (Sanskrit); grhapati (Sanskrit); khyim-pa (Tibetan) In the Buddhist, Hindu, and Jain religions, a semi-monastic layperson who devoutly follows the precepts of their religion; in contemporary usage, it can also mean an ordinary lay person of the faith

Hrabanus *see* **Rabanus Maurus Magnentius**

Hrothswitha of Gandersheim (ca. 932–1000); Roswitha German Benedictine nun, dramatist, and poet who lived at Gandersheim Abbey in Lower Saxony. She was known for her great learning. She was well aware that her sex made her less likely to be taken seriously in her time, and accepted the common view of the time that women were not as suited to writing as men, but argued that she was a divinely inspired exception.

Huaihai *see* **Baizhang Huaihai**

Hubbard, L. Ron *see* **Scientology monasticism**

Hugues de Payens *see* ***Specific Behavior for the Templar Order***

Huineng (638–713 CE); Dajian A Chinese Chan (Zen) Buddhist monk of the Southern School, traditionally viewed as the 6th and last Patriarch of Chan Buddhism. According to legend, his father died when he was young and his family was poor so Huineng never learned to read and write, but attained an awakening when he heard the Diamond Sutra and went to the monastery of the Fifth Patriarch, Daman Hongren.

Doctrinally the Southern School of Chan Buddhism is associated with the teaching that enlightenment is sudden, while the Northern School is associated with the teaching that enlightenment is gradual. This may be an exaggeration, since both schools were derived from the same tradition, and the so-called

Southern School incorporated many teachings of the more influential Northern School. Eventually both schools died out, but all later Chan schools traced their origin to Huineng, and "sudden enlightenment" became a standard doctrine of Chan.

According to modern historiography, Huineng was a marginal and obscure historical figure and some researchers speculate that his story was created around the middle of the 8th century.

Huiyuan (334–416 CE) A prominent Chinese Buddhist monk who founded the Pure Land School and played an important role in adapting Buddhism to Chinese culture. He had been trained in Taoism and Confucianism before his conversion at age 21 to Buddhism by the monk Dao An. In 402 he organized a sect known as Pure Land Buddhism and is now considered its first patriarch.

In 404 he wrote *On Why Monks Do Not Bow Down Before Kings,* asserting the political independence of Buddhist clergy from royalty but at the same time seeking to convince Confucian government officials that Buddhism was not subversive.

He spent the last 30 years of his life in seclusion at the Tonglin Temple which he founded on Mount Lushan. It is claimed that he never came down from the mountain during that time.

Hume, Basil (1923–1999) English Roman Catholic Benedictine monk, abbot, priest, and bishop.

At age 18, Hume considered joining the Dominicans but instead entered the novitiate of the Benedictine monastery at Ampleforth Abbey in 1941. He was solemnly professed in 1945. He was ordained a priest in 1950 and returned to Ampleforth to teach before becoming the abbot of in 1963.

In 1976, he was appointed Archbishop of Westminster, but always considered himself a Benedictine monk first and interpreted his duties as those of a Benedictine abbot. Hume belongs to the very short list of Benedictine cardinals in the history of the Catholic Church.

Humiliati; Barettini A semi-monastic Italian religious order of men formed in the 12th century. Their origin is obscure, but one story is that they were Italian noblemen taken prisoner by the Emperor Henry V (1081–1125) after a rebellion and taken to Germany where they adopted a penitential garb of gray and performed acts of charity and mortification, and eventually were allowed to return to Lombardy. They wore beret-shaped headgear, hence the name Barettini. At first they had no rule, but it is thought they later adopted a modified *Rule of St. Benedict.*

They grew rapidly for a time, but eventually they grew wealthy and became lax. When St. Charles of Borromeo, then archbishop of Milan, tried to reform them, a few Humiliati attempted to murder Charles. The conspirators were then executed and the order suppressed. There was also a women's order called Hospitallers of the Observance that was founded from the Humiliati and it lasted into the 20th century.

Humilitas *see* **Humility, St.**

Humility, St. (ca. 1226–1310); Humilitas An Italian woman usually regarded as the founder of the Vallombrosan nuns. She was married at 15 to a nobleman and had two children, both of whom died as infants. In 1250, her husband became a monk after recovering from a near fatal illness. She became a nun in the same double monastery of canons. Later she became an anchoress in a cell attached to the Vallombrosan church of St. Apollinaris in Faenza, where she lived for 12 years. She then founded a convent outside Faenza and became its abbess. In 1282, she founded a second convent at Florence, where she died in 1310. She left a number of mystical writings. She was canonized in 1720. • *See also* **Vallombrosan Congregation**

Huntington, James *see* **Order of the Holy Cross**

hyaku-nichi kaihogyo *see* **kaihogyo**

hyoseki A senior Japanese Zen Buddhist monastic who serves as one of the temple officers

hypertimos The honorary title of a Byzantine metropolitan

hyphantes In the Eastern Church, a monastic in charge of weaving

~I~

idiodespoton *see* **eleutheron**

idiorhythmia *see* **idiorhythmism**

idiorhythmism; idiorhythmia A practice in the Byzantine Church permitting monks to acquire property by working, to sleep and eat in their own cells, and to be governed by an elected body rather than by a superior

iera kinotis A synod of representatives from the 20 monasteries on Mt. Athos that supervises the internal affairs of the monastic republic

Ignatius of Jesus, Father *see* **Lyne, Joseph Leycester**

igumen *see* **hegumen**

ihumenia *see* **hegumen**

Ildebrando di Soana *see* **Gregory VII**

immixtio manuum Latin for the "mixing of hands." The ceremony in which a monastic kneels, places their hands between the superior's and pledges obedience

imposed guest; katapemptos (Greek) A guest sent to the monastery by an outside authority

impropriation The income from the endowment of a parish given to a layman in return for which a priest was supplied to the parish. It was technically a form of simony and was open to abuse. With the closing of monasteries many appropriations became impropriations and by 1603, about a third of English benefices were in lay hands. • *See also* **appropriation**

infirmarer *see* **infirmarian**

infirmarian; infirmarer; infirmarius; master of farmery; fermerer A monastic who takes care of the sick or aged in a monastery; also the monastic responsible for the periodic bloodletting common in medieval times. • *See also* **bloodletting**

infirmarius *see* **infirmarian**

infirmary; farmery; fermery A part of a monastery, commonly situated to the east of the main complex, with its own dormitory, chapel, kitchen, and refectory, which housed monastics who were sick or who were too old and infirm to take part in the normal monastic round of duties

inji *see* **jisha**

inner cassock; inner rason; esórason (Greek); anteri (Greek); zostiko (Greek); podryásnik (Church Slavonic); pidryasnyk (Ukrainian); podriasnik (Russian) In the Eastern Church, the equivalent of the tunic of the Western Church. It is worn by all monks and nuns. The Russian or Slavic style is double-breasted, closely fitted through the torso and flaring out to the skirt, with a high collar buttoned off-center, and may be cinctured with either a leather or wide cloth belt. The Greek version is somewhat fuller, gathered at the waist with a narrow cloth belt, and with a high collar buttoned in the front.

inner enclosure *see* **enclosure**

inner parlor *see* **parlor**

inner rason *see* **inner cassock**

ino Formerly, the Japanese Zen Buddhist monastic in charge of supervising the work duty; at present, the monastic who leads chanting during a service

inryo In a Japanese Zen Buddhist monastery, the living quarters of the rōshi (monastic master)

institutes of consecrated life Institutes in the Roman Catholic Church whose members vow poverty, chastity, and obedience. The most common are religious institutes, who members live a life in common as brothers or sisters, and have some separation from the world. There are also secular institutes, whose members live in the world and who work for the sanctification of the world from within. Either type needs the approval of the diocesan bishop. • *See also* **Congregation for Institutes of Consecrated Life and Societies of Apostolic Life**

Institutione Inclusarum de Institutione Inclusarum A rule for anchoresses written about 1164 by St. Aelred of Rievaulx for his sister. Historically, it was wrongly attributed to St. Augustine. It is strongly influenced by the *Rule of St. Benedict* and the Cistercian Constitutions, and to a lesser extent to Guigo the First's *Consuetudines.*

intentionarius The monastic who prepares the intentions to be used by the priests at Mass

intern oblate *see* **conventual oblate**

Iona Abbey Founded by St. Columba in 563, Iona is one of the oldest Christian centers in Western Europe and was hugely successful at first. It is located on the Isle of Iona, off the west coast of Scotland. Unfortunately, it was in harm's way and frequently attacked by Vikings, and the monks were sometimes slaughtered. The final Viking slaughter in 825 resulted in the destruction of the abbey. In 1203, construction began on a Benedictine monastery and an Augustinian nunnery. They were both abandoned after the Scottish Reformation in the mid–16th century. In 1938, the abbey was rebuilt and is now used by the Iona Community, a non-monastic Christian community of men and women.

Ippen Shonin (1239–1289); Zuien An itinerant Japanese monk and preacher who founded the Ji-shū branch of Pure Land Buddhism. He was originally named Chishin. He first studied Tendai, but when his father died, he returned to secular life, got married and became head of the household. During a pilgrimage to the Kumano Shrines, the kami (divine beings) enshrined there revealed to Ippen that enlightenment was determined by Amida (a celestial Buddha) and that Ippen should devote himself to preaching the importance of nembutsu (chanting Amida's name).

He then traveled about with a band of followers proselytizing with their ecstatic nembutsu dance, and won a wide following among common people. Ippen's insistence on constant traveling and giving up of family and possessions led to his nicknames: "Traveling Saint" and "Holy Man of Renunciation." An English translation of his writings is *No Abode: The Record of Ippen*. After Ippen's death many of his disciples committed suicide in the hope of being reborn in the Pure Land, and this may explain the limited spread of the Ji-shū branch.

Isaac of Nineveh, St. (ca. 613–ca. 700); Isaac the Syrian A Christian monk, bishop, ascetic, writer, and theologian. He was born in Eastern Arabia. He entered a monastery when very young and devoted himself to asceticism and study.

He is noted for his spiritual homilies on inner life, for his ascetic texts, and for his devotion to the Holy Spirit. He avoided the controversial theological topics of his day so his standing has not suffered as some others have. His influence is particularly strong in the Eastern Church.

He was ordained Bishop of Nineveh in the middle of the 7th century but resigned after only five months and became a hermit eating only three loaves of bread a week together with some raw vegetables. Blindness forced him to retire to the Shabar monastery in Mesopotamia, where he died.

Isaac the Syrian *see* **Isaac of Nineveh**

Isiyim *see* **Essenes**

iskeem A leather belt that a monk of the Eastern Church fastens round his waist when he lives in solitude

Islam Islam forbids the practice of monasticism.

~J~

Jacobins *see* **Order of Preachers**

Jain monasticism In Jainism, monasticism is encouraged and respected. Monks and nuns are celibate and live extremely austere and ascetic lifestyles broadly structured by three ideological formulas: the Five Great Vows (Mahavrata), the Eight Matrices of Doctrine (Pravacana-Matrka), and the Six Obligatory Actions (Avasyaka). The first two are restrictions, and the third is positively framed in what the monk is encouraged to do daily. They do not have a home or possessions, avoid services such as telephones and electricity, and engage in activities such as meditation, seeking knowledge, and acquiring self-discipline. They do not use vehicles and always travel barefoot from one place to another, irrespective of the distance. They rise before dawn, most around 5:00 a.m., but some as early as 2:00 a.m. Defecation takes place in the open where feces will not harm living creatures; urination is into a shallow pan, which is emptied onto a dry patch of ground. They wander from place to place except during the months of chaturmas (monsoon season). They do not prepare food and live only on what people offer them.

Jain monastics should not be confused with priests. Some sects of Jainism often employ a priest, who need not be a Jain, to perform special daily rituals and other priestly duties at the temple.

A Jain monk is called a sādhu; a Jain nun is called a sādhvī. The sādhus and sādhvīs are intertwined with the Jain lay society, perform Murtipuja (Jain idol worship), lead festive rituals, and are organized in a strongly hierarchical monastic structure. The head of a monastic order is called an acharya if a monk, and a ganini aryika pramukha if a nun. A senior monk is called an elachary or a ganini aryika if a nun. A professed monk is called a muni, and a professed nun is called an aryika. A junior monk is called a kshullak, and a junior nun is called a kshullika.

The Jain community is divided into two major denominations, Digambara and Śvētāmbara. • *See also* **Digambara; sadhu; sadhvi; Svetambara**

jata Thick dreadlocks worn by Digambara Jain monastics

Jerome, St. (ca. 345–420) Christian priest, confessor, monk, abbot, theologian, writer, and historian who was born in Dalmatia. He converted to Christianity sometime between 360–366. About 373 he became seriously ill in Antioch, Syria, had a vision, and thereafter devoted himself to God. He lived for a time in the desert then returned to Antioch where he was ordained as a priest, apparently unwillingly. Between 382 and 385, he lived in Rome as secretary to Pope Damasus I and began his revision of the Latin Bible which he later became the Latin Vulgate.

His criticism of the secular clergy caused them to force him out of Rome after the death of Pope Damasus in 384. In 385, he went to Jerusalem and became the founding abbot of a monastery where he spent the rest of his life writing.

He is recognized as a saint by the Roman Catholic Church, the Eastern Orthodox Church, the Lutheran Church, and the Anglican Communion. He is also considered a Doctor of the Church.

Jeronymites *see* **Order of St. Jerome**

Jesuit's drops *see* **friar's balsam**

Jewish monasticism *see* **Judaism**

jihatsu The set of eating utensils for the personal use of Japanese Zen Buddhist monks in the Rinzai-shū and Ōbaku-shū sects. A set consists of three black plastic nesting bowls, two chopsticks, a wooden spoon, a small rubber spatula, a gray napkin, and a wiping cloth, all of which are wrapped tidily in a gray cloth with a topknot resembling a lotus blossom. • *See also* **oryoki**

Jikaku Daishi *see* **Ennin**

jikido; jikidō In a Japanese Zen Buddhist monastery, an assistant whose job it is to run the zendō (meditation hall) according to the rules prescribed by the teacher, and maintain the zendō's schedule. The jikido signals the start and end of sitting periods by striking the han (block of wood). He also embodies and exemplifies practice as the functioning of no-self—the forgotten self—that responds to each thing in turn, performs each function in turn without a thought of right or wrong or "how am I doing or how do I look doing it?" In a Japanese Zen Buddhist Rinzai monastery, a jikido is the room where meals are eaten.

jikijitsu In a Japanese Zen Buddhist Rinzai zendō (meditation hall), the monk in charge of meditation in the zendō, second to the rōshi (monastic master). This is approximately equivalent to the godō in a Sōtō monastery.

jingren Taoist monastic servants

jinju; jinjū The sanitation steward at a Japanese Zen Buddhist monastery, responsible for keeping the toilets clean

Jinul ***see*** **Bojo Jinul**

jisha The abbot's attendant and monk in charge of caring for the monks of the zendō (meditation hall) of a Japanese Zen Buddhist monastery. The jisha prepares for and greets all guests, tends to the needs of the students, takes care of the sick, and organizes the cleaning of the monastery. He is also the abbot's attendant during a sesshin (meditation retreat). In the Rinzai school of Zen Buddhism, the term inji or sanno is used for the same position.

Joachim of Fiore (ca. 1135–1202); Gioacchino da Fiore An Italian Cistercian monk, priest, theologian, and the founder of the monastic order of San Giovanni in Fiore (Fiorensians). Later followers, inspired by his works in eschatology and historicist theories, are called Joachimites.

About 1159 he went on pilgrimage to the Holy Land and had a conversion experience that turned him away from his successful worldly life. Returning to Italy, he lived as a hermit for several years, the joined the Cistercians as a lay brother of Sambucina Abbey where he engaged in preaching. About 1168 he became a priest at the Corazzo Abbey and devoted himself to biblical study, especially Revelation. To his dismay he was made abbot of Corazzo Abbey about 1177.

In 1182 Joachim appealed to Pope Lucius III and was relieved of his abbacy and allowed to return to his writing and study. Joachim retired first to the hermitage of Pietralata, then founded the Abbey of Fiore which became the center of a new and stricter branch of the Cistercian order, the Congregation of Fiore. Although approved by Church authorities in his day, his writings became controversial, especially when spurious works began to circulate in his name. His views also inspired several subsequent movements: the Amalricians, the Dulcinians, and the Brethren of the Free Spirit, all of which were later declared heretical, although Joachim himself was never declared a heretic. • *See also* **Congregation of Fiore**

Joachimites; Joachites A 13th century millenarian offshoot of the Franciscans that based their beliefs on the writings of Joachim of Fiore (ca. 1135–1202). They believed a new age would be brought in by a virtuous Franciscan leader whom they considered to be Pope Celestine V. They considered his resignation, and subsequent death in 1296 in the dungeons of the next pope as an augur of the coming of the Anti-Christ. The Joachimites believed the new age would be egalitarian and have a monastic nature.

Joachites ***see*** **Joachimites**

John Cassian, St. (ca. 360–ca. 435) A monk, deacon, mystic, hermit, theologian, and writer born in Scythia Minor or Gaul who is venerated for bringing the ideals of monasticism to the Western Church. He traveled extensively in Palestine and Egypt visiting early monastic foundations.

About 415, he founded the Abbey of St. Victor near Marseilles that was for both men and women. About 420 he produced two notable books. *Institutes of the Cenobia (De institutis coenobiorum)* had a direct influence on organization of monasteries described in the *Rule of St. Benedict*. Benedict also recommended that selections of the *Conferences of the Desert Fathers (Collationes patrum in scetica eremo)* be read to Benedictine monks. As such, these books had a great influence on the Benedictines, Cistercians, and Trappists that continues to this day.

John Chrysostom, St. (ca. 349–407) Syrian priest, bishop, monastic who was baptized in 368 or 373. Such was his zeal that he spent six years as a hermit continually studying and praying. For two years he spent most of his time standing and scarcely sleeping while memorizing Bible passages. This permanently damaged his stomach and kidneys and forced him to return to Antioch where he was ordained as a deacon in 381, and a priest in 386. He became very popular because of his eloquent preaching and his care for the poor. In 397, he was appointed Archbishop of Constantinople. During his time as archbishop he adamantly refused to host lavish social gatherings, which made him popular with the common people, but unpopular with wealthy citizens and the clergy. His reforms of the clergy were also unpopular. The Patriarch of Alexandria and the wife of the emperor conspired to have John deposed and banished, but popular uproar caused him to be brought back. Later, John was exiled once again possibly because of an alleged connection with Arianism. He died in exile.

The Eastern Orthodox, together with the Byzantine Catholics, hold him in special regard as one of the Three Holy Hierarchs (alongside Basil the Great and Gregory of Nazianzus). In the Roman Catholic Church he is recognized as a Doctor of the Church.

John Climacus, St. (fl. 6th-7th centuries); John of the Ladder A Christian monk of the monastery on Mount Sinai (now called St. Catherine's Monastery). Solid information about his life is scanty, but he is thought to have come to the monastery and become a novice when about 16 and was taught by the elder monk Martyrius. After the death of Martyrius, John withdrew to a hermitage at the foot of the mountain and lived in isolation for about 20 years, constantly studying and very learned. When he was about 75, the monks of Sinai elected him their igumen (abbot).

John is famous today for his classic work, *The Ladder of Divine Ascent*, which describes how to raise one's soul and body to God through the acquisition of ascetic virtues. Climacus uses the analogy of Jacob's Ladder as the framework for his spiritual teaching. It also describes the now common ascetic practice of carrying a small notebook to record one's thoughts during contemplation. Originally written simply for the monks of a neighboring monastery, the *Ladder* swiftly became one of the most widely read and much-beloved books of Byzantine spirituality.

He is honored as a saint in both the Eastern and Western Church.

John Damascene *see* **John of Damascus, St.**

John de Matha, St. *see* **Order of the Most Holy Trinity**

John of Damascus, St. (ca. 675–749); John Damascene Syrian monk, priest, and writer born and raised in Damascus. He was a polymath and learned in theology, philosophy, and music. It is believed that John became a monk at Mar Saba about 706 and that he was ordained as a priest in 735.

He wrote works expounding the Christian faith, and composed hymns which are still used both liturgically in Eastern Christian practice throughout the world as well as in western Lutheranism at Easter. He is one of the Fathers of the Eastern Orthodox Church and is best known for his strong defense of icons. He is often referred to as the "Doctor of the Assumption" due to his writings on the Assumption of Mary.

The Roman Catholic Church regards him as a Doctor of the Church.

John of God, St. *see* **Hospitaller Order of the Brothers of St. John of God**

John of the Cross, St. (1542–1591) A Spanish Carmelite friar, priest, prior, mystic, writer, and major figure of the Counter-Reformation. He was born into a converso (descendants of Jewish converts to Christianity) family in Fontiveros, near Ávila. In 1563 he entered the Carmelite Order, and in 1564 professed his religious vows.

In 1567, he met the charismatic Carmelite nun Teresa of Jesus and began working with her to restore the purity of the order by encouraging adherence to the strict *Primitive Rule* of 1209. Part of this rule forbade the wearing of shoes, and for this reason followers of the *Primitive Rule* became known as Discalced Carmelites, which differentiated them from the non-reformed friars and nuns. They opened a number of discalced houses, but by 1575 tensions arose between the two branches and John was ordered to leave Ávila. John refused on the basis that his reform work had been approved by the Spanish nuncio, a higher authority than these superiors. In 1577, a group of Carmelites opposed to reform kidnapped John and made him a prisoner in a monastery in Toledo where he was kept under brutal conditions, which included public lashing. In 1578, he managed to escape and continue his reform work.

In 1580, Pope Gregory XIII separated the Calced and Discalced Carmelites. In 1585, John was elected provincial vicar of Andalusia, but because of a disagreement with his superiors he was removed from his post and sent by 1591 to an isolated monastery in Andalusia where he died of erysipelas.

He was canonized in 1726. In 1926, he was declared a Doctor of the Church.

John of the Ladder *see* **John Climacus**

joju The administrative section of a Japanese Zen Buddhist monastery, as opposed to the zendō (meditation hall)

jokei A junior officer in a Japanese Zen Buddhist monastery. In most Rinzai monasteries there are two.

josaku A day of rest in a Japanese Zen Buddhist monastery

Joseph of Volokolamsk, St. (1439 or 1440–1515); Joseph Volotsky Russian Orthodox monk, theologian, and leader of the "possessor" monastic movement which defended monastic ownership of land. He became a monk at the Borovsk Monastery in 1459. He later became the abbot and tried to introduce stricter rules but the monks rejected them and he had to leave. Disappointed with what he considered lax morals at other monasteries, he founded his own near Volokolamsk in 1479. Joseph's charter demanded absolute obedience to the abbot and a monk's life was strictly controlled.

During the synod of 1503, Joseph and his supporters (Josephites, Josephinians) managed to defeat the proposal to eliminate of monastic ownership of land. Joseph was also a supporter of Russia's grand princes, who were increasingly referred to as tsars. He said that the tsar was a "man in essence, but his power is that of God" and that he was God's deputy on Earth. Joseph is also known to have been a staunch opponent of the heretical Sect of Skhariya the Jew which was spreading in Russia at that time. Ironically, during the synod of 1504, he demanded that all heretics be executed by the state.

He was canonized by the Russian Orthodox Church in 1591.

Joseph Volotsky *see* **Joseph of Volokalamsk**

Josephinians *see* **Joseph of Volokolamsk**

Josephite monasticism A Russian Orthodox style of monasticism inspired by St. Joseph of Volokolamsk, which emphasized choir services in a manner similar to that of Cluny.

Josephites *see* **Joseph of Volokolamsk**

jubilarian One who celebrates 50 years as a monastic

Judaism Judaism does not encourage the monastic ideal of celibacy and poverty. To the contrary—all of the Torah's Commandments are a means of sanctifying the physical world. Historically, however, there were both Jewish monastic and quasimonastic groups • *see also* **Beta Israel; Essenes; Nazirites; Therapeutae**

Julian of Norwich (ca. 1342–ca. 1413) An English mystic and anchoress. The origin of her name is uncertain. It may be from the Church of St. Julian in Norwich, to which her cell was attached, or it could have been her original given name, as Julian was a common name for women in the Middle Ages. Her book, *The Revelations of Divine Love,* also known as the *Book of Showings,* written around 1395, is the first book in the English language known to have been written by a woman. She is also the first theologian to have written in English. She may have been from a wealthy family residing in or near Norwich, at the time the second largest city in England. At least one source considered it likely that she received her early education with the Benedictine nuns at nearby Carrow.

junior A monastic under temporary vows, still under the direction of a formation master, who continues their study of monasticism and theology and works in community enterprises. After three years the junior decides whether they want to make lifetime vows or ask to extend their temporary vows. The solemnly professed members then decide by vote whether to accept the junior into solemn vows.

juniorate The stage of monastic formation between the novitiate and final or solemn monastic profession. Also the body of juniors within a community.

~K~

kaapiya-karaka One who accepts gifts on behalf of a Buddhist monastic who cannot accept them directly

kafu The customs and atmosphere of a Japanese Zen Buddhist monastery

kaichin Bedtime at a Japanese Zen Buddhist monastery, marked by a short sutra (aphorism or teaching), chanting, and the unrolling of the kashiwabuton (futon)

kaihan Striking of the han (wooden board) in a Japanese Zen Buddhist monastery to announce various ceremonial times • *see also* **han**

kaihogyo An exhausting ascetic practice performed by Japanese Tendai Buddhist monks that involves marathons around Mount Hiei while offering prayers at shrines and other sacred places. Practitioners are popularly known as "marathon monks." The practice is believed to have been initiated by the monk Sōō Oshō (831–918 CE). In Tendai Buddhism it is believed that through service and devotion enlightenment can be attained in the current life. Kaihōgyō is seen as the ultimate expression of this.

There are two kaihōgyō practices: that of 100 days (hyaku-nichi kaihōgyō) and that of 1,000 days (sennichi kaihōgyō). The 1,000-day challenge is one of the most demanding challenges in the world. Only 46 men have completed it 1885. Of these, three have done it twice. The 1,000 day kaihōgyō takes seven years to complete.

Year 1 30 (40) km per day for 100 days.
Year 2 30 (40) km per day for 100 days
Year 3 30 (40) km per day for 100 days
Year 4 30 (40) km per day for 200 days
Year 5 30 (40) km per day for 200 days
Year 6 60 km per day for 100 days
Year 7 84 km per day for 100 days, followed by 30 (40) km per day for 100 days.
(The numbers in parentheses indicate the distance of the Imuro Valley course, which is longer.)

The 100 day challenge requires the monks to travel 30–40 kilometers a day for 100 days, and constitutes the first year of the 1,000 day challenge.

For the 1,000 day challenge no withdrawal is permitted after completion of the first year and those failing to complete the 1,000 day were traditionally required to kill themselves although this practiced ceased by the 20th century.

During the fifth year of the challenge, monks must go for seven and a half days without food, water, or rest of any kind. In the seventh year the monks must run the equivalent of two Olympic marathons per day.

All abbots at Mt. Hiei monastery must complete the 100 day challenge, but no other monks are required to complete either challenge.

kaijo Morning wake-up at a Japanese Zen Buddhist monastery

kaisando; kaisandō The founder's hall in a traditional Japanese Zen Buddhist monastery. The size may range from a single room to its own building.

kaiyoku Bath time in a Japanese Zen Buddhist monastery. In traditional practice, this was about every five days or on dates with the number four or nine in them.

kalimavkion; kalymafki; kalymmavchi; kamilavka The stiffened hat of Eastern Orthodox and Eastern Catholic monastics. It is something like a fez, only black and with straight sides, and covered with a veil called an epanokalimavkion. In the Greek Church it is normally worn only by monks, but in the Russian Church it is worn by both monks and nuns. In the Russian tradition, a kamilavkion covered by its epanokalimavkion is called by the collective term klobuk.

kalymafki *see* **kalimavkion**

kalymmavchi *see* **kalimavkion**

kamandalu A water pot carried by Digambara Jain monks and nuns

kamilavka *see* **kalimavkion**

kammatthana; kammaṭṭhāna Literally, "basis of work" or "place of work"—the word refers to the occupation of a meditating Buddhist monastic: namely, the contemplation of certain meditation themes by which the forces of defilement (kilesa), craving (taṇhā), and ignorance (avijjā) may be uprooted from the mind. Although every meditator may be said to engage in kammaṭṭhāna, the term is most often used to identify the Forest Tradition lineage.

Kammatthana Forest Tradition of Thailand *see* **Forest Tradition**

kanban bukuro The bag used by Japanese Zen Buddhist monks while begging. The name of the temple is usually written on the front of the bag.

kancho; kanchō The head abbot in a Japanese Zen Buddhist monastery

kandelarios The monk who tends the candles in a Eastern Orthodox monastery church

kanonarches In the Eastern Church, the precentor, or monastic officer in charge of the choir

kansho; kanshō In a Japanese Zen Buddhist monastery, the small hanging bell rung by the monks to signal entrance to the master's room during dokusan (voluntary meditation)

Kapalika; Kāpālika A legendary ascetic quasimonastic non–Puranic Shaivism order that existed in India. It was said they carried a skull-topped trident (khatvanga) and used an empty skull for a begging bowl. They were also reputed to smear their bodies with cremation ashes and perform rituals with blood, meat, alcohol, and sexual fluids.

karmapa A Tibetan Buddhist monk that is the head of the Karma Kagyu, the largest sub-school of the Kagyu. Düsum Khyenpa (1110–1193), was the first karmapa. The traditional home of the karmapa was the Tsurphu Monastery in Tibet, but in exile it is the Rumtek Monastery in Sikkim, India. Because of a controversy within the Karma Kagyu school over the recognition process, the identity of the current 17th karmapa is disputed.

kasava *see* **kasaya**

kasaya; kāṣāya (Sanskrit); kasāva (Pali); kesa (Japanese); gasa (Korean); jiāshā

(Chinese); cà-sa (Vietnamese) The robes of fully ordained Buddhist monks and nuns, originally named after a brown or saffron dye, although colors may now vary by country or sect. A kasaya typically consists of three parts: the antarvasa (inner robe), the uttarasanga (middle robe), and the samghati (outer robe). • *See also* **antarvarsa; samghati; uttarasanga**

kashaku; kato To formally enter a Japanese Zen Buddhist monastery for training

kashiwabuton A large square-shaped futon used for sleeping in a Japanese Zen Buddhist monastery. It is folded in half, and the unsui (postulant) sleeps inside. In the morning, it is rolled up and stored for the day.

katapemptos *see* **imposed guest**

kathegumen; katheoumenos In the Eastern Church, a hegumen (abbot) who had been previously ordained

katheoumenos *see* **kathegumen**

Kathina A Buddhist festival which marks the end of Vassa, the three-month rainy season retreat for Theravada Buddhists in Bangladesh, Cambodia, Laos, Myanmar (Burma), Sri Lanka, India, and Thailand. It beings after the full moon of the 11th month in the Lunar calendar (usually October). It is a time of giving, for the laity to express gratitude to Buddhist monks. • *See also* **Vassa**

kathisma A hermitage for a solitary on Mt. Athos

kathismata In Eastern Orthodox monasteries, a row of individual choir stalls with full backs. They have hinged seats that flip up so monastics can stand, and often the seats have misericords on the underside so the monastics can rest while standing.

katholikon In the Eastern Church, the principal church of a monastery

kato *see* **kashahu**

Keating, Thomas (1923–) Trappist monk, abbot, and priest who became a monk in 1944. He became the abbot of St. Benedict's Monastery, Snowmass, Colorado, in 1958. In 1961 he was elected abbot of St. Joseph's Abbey, Spencer, Massachusetts. While there he helped develop centering prayer, a contemporary method of contemplative prayer.

In 1981 he retired as abbot and returned to St. Benedict's Monastery where he established ten-day intensive centering prayer retreats. In 1984, he cofounded Contemplative Outreach, Ltd., an international, ecumenical spiritual network teaching centering prayer and lectio divina.

keisaku *see* **kyosaku**

kellarios; kellarites In the Eastern Church, the cellarer, the monastic in charge of a monastery's cellar • *see also* **docheiarios**

kellarites *see* **kellarios**

kellia The plural of kellion

Kellia; Cells A 4th century Egyptian Christian monastic community covering over 125 square kilometers in the Nitrian Desert. It was one of three centers of monastic activity in the region, along with Nitria and Scetis.

Founded in 338 by St. Amun and St. Anthony the Great, it was laid out for cenobitic life in a semi-eremitic monastery. It was for monks experienced in desert living. Most cells were cells far enough apart so they would not normally see or hear others. Some cells had two or three monks living together, and there were some larger cells where older monks lived together. All would come together on weekends for a common meal and to attend church, but otherwise lived alone. In the 5th and 6th centuries they numbered in the thousands, but the population dropped off in the 7th and 8th centuries because of doctrinal disputes in Egypt and raids from nomads. It was abandoned in the 9th century.

kellion In the Eastern Church, a small religious house housing not more than three monks and three lay brothers; in modern Greek Orthodox usage, a cell within a convent; a Byzantine monastic cell in the vicinity of a cenobitic monastery occupied by a kelliotes

kelliotes A Byzantine monk living alone or with a companion in the vicinity of a cenobitic monastery that would be visited for worship and weekly supplies

kenchen A Tibetan Buddhist senior abbot

kentan In a Japanese Zen Buddhist monastery, the formal checking of the sitting monks in the zendō (meditation hall) by the rōshi (monastic master) or the jikijitsu (assistant to the rōshi).

kesa *see* **kasaya**

kesa bunko In Japanese Zen Buddhism, the luggage bundle carried by unsui (postulants) during their angya (search for a monastery), containing their kasaya (robe), razor, jihatsu (bowls), sutra (aphorism or teaching) book, and rain poncho

khajjabhajaka An official in charge of the distribution of hard food in a Theravedin Buddhist monastery

khatvanga A skull-topped trident said to have been carried by Kāpālikas • *see also* **Kapalikas**

khenchung A Tibetan Buddhist junior abbot

khenmo *see* **abbess**

khenpo *see* **abbot**

khenrab A Tibetan Buddhist scholar abbot

khyim-pa *see* **householder**

kiku The Japanese Zen Buddhist monastic regulations

kilrosi In the Orthodox Church, an octagonal flat topped lectern used in the choir of monasteries

King's Book **see** ***Valor Ecclesiasticus***

kitan ryushaku The ending of the training period when a Japanese Zen Buddhist monastic notifies the monastery whether they will be staying for the next training period or leaving to continue their angya • *see also* **angya**

kitchener; coquinarius; kitchenmaster The monastic in charge of a monastery kitchen and the cooking

kitchenmaster *see* **kitchener**

klepalo *see* **semantron**

klobuk A collective term used in the Russian tradition to designate a kamilavkion (a stiffened fez-like hat) covered by its epanokalimavkion (a cloth veil, usually black, which is worn with a kamilavkion)

Knights Hospitaller; Hospitallers; Knights of St. John; Order of Knights

of the Hospital of St. John of Jerusalem; Order of St. John; Order of Hospitallers; Sovereign Military Order of Malta A Roman Catholic monastic military order founded in Jerusalem the 11th century. Their major work at that time was protecting Christian pilgrims to the Holy Land. After the fall of Jerusalem, they moved to the island of Rhodes, then Malta. They defended Christian lands against Muslim forces and even protected Christian shipping at sea, but despite their vows of poverty, elements of the order were involved in profiting from privateering and increasingly the order fell out of favor, losing support and power. In the 19th century they turned increasingly to religious and humanitarian causes. Now headquartered in Rome, the Hospitallers are formally known as the Sovereign Military Order of Malta.

Knights of St. John *see* **Knights Hospitaller**

Knights of St. Julian *see* **Order of Alcántara**

Knights of the Cross with the Red Star; Military Order of the Crusaders of the Red Star; Ordo Militaris Crucigerorum cum Rubea Stella; Canonici Regulares Sanctissimae Crucis a Stella Rubea; Crucigeri cum Rubea Stella; Crucigeri Stellati; Stelliferi A monastic military order begun in 1233 in Bohemia by Franciscan tertiaries under the direction of St. Agnes of Bohemia. It was the only religious order founded in Bohemia and the only male monastic community founded by a woman. In 1238 they were formally acknowledged as an order under the *Rule of St. Augustine*. It was devoted mainly to offering medical care at first, but soon priests were added and the care of souls also became an important mission.

In the Hussite Wars, the order declined almost to the point of dissolution, but it recovered, only to be suppressed after the Czechoslovakian coup d'état of 1948. After the Velvet Revolution of 1990, the order was revived.

Members use the post-nominal initials O.M.C.R.S.

Knights Templar; Templars; Poor Knights of Christ; Poor Fellow-Soldiers of Christ and of the Temple of Solomon; Order of Solomon's Temple A Roman Catholic monastic military order founded in 1119 that was active until 1312 when it was disbanded. As fighting monks they served in the Holy Land guarding the pilgrim routes to Jerusalem and protecting the crusader states. They took vows of chastity and obedience and lived under a rule that was compiled by the Cistercian, St. Bernard of Clairvaux. While the Templars became prosperous through generous benefaction from home and their victories in the East, their reputation suffered a blow following the fall of Acre in 1291 and was undermined further when their financial practices came into question and King Philip IV of France—who was heavily indebted to them—sought to gain control of their wealth, burned many at the stake, and eventually got Pope Clement V to disband them in 1312.

Knowles, M. David (1896–1974) English Benedictine monk, Roman Catholic priest, and noted historian. In 1923 he became a member of the monastic community at Downside abbey.

Ironically, while teaching there he became involved in resisting the demands of teaching on the contemplative monastic life and was transferred to Ealing Abbey, another teaching establishment.

In 1944 he was appointed to the University of Cambridge and in 1954, he became the Regius Professor of Modern History until he retired in 1963. He served as president of the Royal Historical Society from 1957 to 1961. While pursuing his academic career he was exclaustrated from Downside Abbey and released from his vows. Before his death in 1974 from a heart attack, however, he was readmitted to the order.

Kobo-Daishi *see* **Kukai**

koinobion In the Eastern Church, a monastery for monks or nun emphasizing a communal lifestyle, including attendance at church services and meals in the refectory

kokuho An announcement by the head monk to the community in a Japanese Zen Buddhist monastery, usually setting out the schedule for that day

kolonsowa A hood usually embroidered with crosses that is worn on the head by Syrian and Coptic monks. It is believed that an angel of the Lord had passed on the kolonsowa and monastic habit to St. Anthony the Great. Other Orthodox monks also wear a hood like a kolonsowa, but usually with no embroidered crosses.

Komuso; Komusō A "monk of emptiness," a member of the Japanese Zen Buddhist semi-monastic Fuke sect that were half-monks and half-laymen, neither shaving their heads, nor wearing ordinary monk's robes. They begged for alms and played the shakuhachi, a bamboo flute, while begging for alms. They were identified by a tengai (straw basket hat).

komvoshinion (Greek); tchotki (Russian) A prayer cord used by Orthodox monks and some lay people. Commonly it has 100 knots with a woven cross attached.

kontorasson *see* **cassock vest**

koromo A robe worn by ordained Japanese Zen Buddhist monks

korwat The standards and rules of a Thai Buddhist monastery

Koso Joyo Daishi *see* **Dogen Zenji**

kotai The changing of monastic duties at the end of the training period in a Japanese Zen Buddhist monastery

kotan A senior Japanese Zen Buddhist monk

kotsu In Sanbō Kyōdan and some other schools of Japanese Zen Buddhism, the ceremonial scepter of a rōshi (monastic master)

koukoulion; kukol (Church Slavonic) In the Eastern Church, a headdress worn by monks and nuns of the highest degree. One type is a stiff rounded cap to which is attached an epanokalimavkion (a cloth veil, usually black, which is worn with a kamilavkion). In the Slavic tradition it is a pointed hood and two long lappets covering the back and breast. In the Greek Church the koukuolion is of a distinctive thimble shape, the veil of which is usually embroidered with crosses.

koun ryusui *see* **unsui**

koza A lecture by the rōshi (monastic master) to the monks in a Japanese Zen Buddhist monastery

Kozłowska, Feliksa Magdalena (1862–1921); Sr. Maria Franciszka; Mateczka

A Polish Christian nun, mystic, and visionary. In 1883 she entered Roman Catholic Congregation of the Franciscan Suffering whose purpose was to care for the sick. In 1887 she and five other Franciscan women entered into communal living in the town of Plock. In 1893, she began having religious visions that instructed her to form a new clerical order to promote the adoration of the Blessed Sacrament and the Blessed Virgin Mary, which became known as Marivitism. In 1903 her group, led by Fr. Jan Maria Michal Kowalski attempted to gain canonical status in the Roman Church but it was rejected by the pope in 1904 and the Congregation of the Roman and Universal Inquisition said her visions were hallucinations. In 1906, the pope criticized the Mariavites for treating Kowalska as a living saint equal to the Blessed Virgin and excommunicated her and all the members for being heretical. On the other hand, the Russian government, which controlled Poland at the time, recognized the Mariavites in an effort to weaken the Roman Catholic Church in Poland. In 1909, she and her followers became part of the Old Catholic Church and by 1917 her group had about 160,000 members. The movement collapsed after Russia lost control of Poland.

krestonets *see* **stavrophore**

kshullak A junior Jain monk

kshullika A junior Jain nun

Ktistai; Ctistae A quasimonastic group of Mysian men in ancient Thracian culture that avoided consuming any living thing, and therefore lived on such foodstuffs as milk and honey. They led celibate lives, never marrying, and dedicated their lives to the gods.

kufu; kufū To maintain one's practice during stillness and movement. In a Japanese Zen Buddhist monastery it means something like something like "creative inventiveness" during work.

Kukai (774–835); Kūkai; Kōbō-Daishi Japanese Buddhist monk, civil servant, scholar, poet, engineer, artist, and writer of over 50 religious works, who founded the Shingon or "True Word" school of Buddhism. He is also credited with inventing kana which in combination with Chinese characters is still used to write Japanese. He is revered as an important Buddhist saint.

Kumbh Mela A mass-gathering of Hindu monastics from all parts of India that takes place every three years at one of four points along sacred rivers in India, including the holy River Ganges. Sādhus (Hindu monastics) of all sects join in this reunion. Millions of non-sādhu pilgrims also attend the festivals, and the Kumbh Mela is the largest gathering of human beings for a single religious purpose on the planet. At the festival, sādhus appear in large numbers, including those who are smeared with ashes and completely naked and dash into the chilly waters at the break of dawn.

Kunga Gyeltsen (1182–1251) A Tibetan Buddhist monk, spiritual leader, scholar, and the fourth of the Five Sakya Forefathers. He is commonly known Sakya Pandita and is said to have been an emanation of Manjusri, the embodiment of the wisdom of all the Buddhas. He was professed as a monk in 1208. He became the dansa chenpo (abbot-ruler) of Sakya in 1216. He had a profound influence on Tibetan Buddhism and his works are still studied to this day.

kuri The kitchen in a Japanese Zen Buddhist monastery, or, more generally, the living quarters

kushalaka A waist cloth sometimes worn with the kāṣāya by Buddhist monks and nuns

kuti; kuṭī (Pali, Thai) A hut or small dwelling place for a Buddhist monastic

kyosaku; kyōsaku; keisaku (Rinzai) In Sōtō Japanese Zen Buddhist monasteries, an "encouragement stick" used to strike the shoulders during zazen (meditation), to help overcome fatigue or reach satori (sudden enlightenment). It is called a keisaku in Rinzai monasteries. Monks will sometimes ask to be struck with the stick as an aid.

kyozo The sutra (aphorism or teaching) library of a Japanese Zen Buddhist monastery

kyriakon In the Eastern Church, the principle church of a skete

~L~

lagan A senior Tibetan Buddhist monk

lama A title for a teacher of Tibetan Buddhism. The name is similar to the Sanskrit term guru. Historically, the term was used for venerated spiritual masters or heads of monasteries. Today the title can be used as an honorific title conferred on a monk or nun. It is also used in the Mongolian Buddhist tradition.

Lament, Bolesława Maria (1862–1946) A Polish Roman Catholic religious sister, prioress, and founded of the Missionary Sisters of the Holy Family. Trained as a seamstress, in 1884, she joined the Congregation of the Family of Mary but left in 1893 just prior to her solemn profession. Moving to Warsaw, she became the director of a homeless shelter. In 1900, the death of her seminarian brother prompted her to return to religious life and she joined the Third Order of St. Francis. In 1905 she founded the Missionary Sisters of the Holy Family in Russia. She served as superior general until 1935 and was beatified in 1991. • *See also* **Missionary Sisters of the Holy Family**

Lanfranc (ca. 1005–1089) Italian Benedictine monk, abbot, archbishop, scholar, writer, and teacher. Born in Pavia, Italy, he became a highly successful teacher in France, then in 1042 became a monk at Bec Abbey and later its prior. In 1066, he became the first abbot of the Abbey of Saint-Étienne at Caen in Normandy. When the See of Rouen fell vacant in 1067, the electors wanted Lanfranc to fill the position, but he declined. Then in 1070 he became Archbishop of Canterbury and worked to institute reforms such as clerical celibacy.

laosynaktes A Byzantine monastic official in charge of maintaining order in the church

larderer An official in charge of the larder, subordinate to the kitchener. It was his job to keep the kitchen supplied with meat, fish, and poultry, which also involved the killing and skinning.

Latin Rule **see** ***Specific Behavior for the Templar Order***

Lauds A Daily Office that takes place in the early morning hours. The name is derived from the Laudate Psalms (148, 149, 150), which in former versions of the Lauds of the Roman Rite occurred every day, and in all of which the word "laudate" is repeated frequently.

At first, Lauds designated only the end of Matins, that is to say, these three psalms. Little by little the title Lauds was applied to the whole office, and supplanted the name "Matins." In the later Middle Ages Matins and Lauds were collectively referred to as Vigils.

Lauds is the Office of daybreak, and hence its symbolism is of Christ's resurrection. The office of Lauds reminds the Christian that the first act of the day should be prayer and that one's thoughts should be of God before facing the cares of the day.

laura A lane or path connecting the cells to the main complex of a lavra, but the term is sometimes confused with the lavra itself

laus perennis *see* **perpetual prayer**

lavatorium *see* **laver**

laver; lavatorium A place at the entrance of a medieval refectory for the washing of hands. It was usually a trough with running water.

lavra A semi-eremitic monastic community of the Eastern Orthodox and Eastern Christian tradition that was comprised of a group of scattered hermit's cells associated with a central complex where the monastics assembled on weekends for the Eucharist and a communal meal. One of the first lavras was developed by Chariton the Confessor in the Judean Desert in 275, but the term became increasingly used for large, usually rural, monasteries. A laura—a term sometimes confused with lavra—is a lane or path connecting the cells to the main complex of a lavra.

lavritic Of, like, or relating to a lavra

lay abbot, abbas laicus; abbas miles; abbatocomes A commendatory abbot who was a layman rather than an ecclesiastic

lay brothers *see* **lay monastics**

Lay Carmelites *see* **Third Order of Our Lady of Mount Carmel**

lay monastics; lay brothers; lay sisters; extern sisters diakonetes (Greek Orthodox Church) Originally, members of a monastic community who were not priests. Later applied to monastics who took vows of poverty, chastity, and obedience but were only expected to recite a shortened form of the Daily Office and were employed in manual labor thus freeing the choir monastics from labor and interaction with the outside world. Lay monasticism may now also refer to those who are fully vowed members of a traditional monastic community, such as oblates. It may also include the Christian Communities of the American Episcopal Church n which members have rules similar to traditional monastic communities with the exception that they are only called to be chaste as opposed to celibate.

lay sisters *see* **lay monastics**

Leadership Conference of Women Religious An association of the leaders of congregations of Roman Catholic women religious in the United States. Founded in 1956, it had over 80 percent of American women religious in their membership. Some members broke away in 1992 and formed the Council of Major Superiors of Women Religious because of what was perceived as a deviation away from the official positions of the Church. The Council of Major Superiors has since been attracting twice the number of new members under 30 as has the Leadership Council.

In 2012, the Vatican initiated an investigation of the Leadership Conference and this embittered many American Catholics against what they perceived as heavy-handed tactics by Rome against the sisters. In 2015 a meeting of the minds was reached.

leaning staff In the 11th and 12th centuries, it was forbidden to sit down in church, but ill or elderly monastics were permitted to use a staff to lean on • *see also* **reclinatoria**

Lebanese Antonin Order; Antonin Maronite Order; Antonins; Mar Chaya Monks A monastic order of the Levantine Catholic Maronite Church founded in 1700 when it split with the Lebanese Maronite Order. It is headquartered in the Mar Chaya monastery in Lebanon.

Lebanese Maronite Order; Baladites; Valadites; Ordre Libanais Maronite A monastic order of monks and nuns of the Catholic Maronite Church. It was founded in 1694 in the Monastery of Mart Moura, in Lebanon. Members use the post-nominal initials O.L.M.

Two other orders have split off from it—the Mariamite Maronite Order and the Lebanese Antonin Order.

LeClercq, Jean (1911–1993) French Benedictine monk and scholar. He entered Clervaux Abbey in Luxembourg in 1928, and was professed in 1930. He studied theology at Sant'Anselmo from 1933 to 1937. He spent most of the war years at Abbaye de la Source in Paris. In 1946, he began his prolific publishing career in earnest with three books and 20 articles. His total literary output was over 40 books and 1,000 articles. Although best known for his classic study of Medieval monasticism *The Love of Learning and the Desire for God: A Study of Monastic Culture,* he wrote on a wide variety of monastic topics throughout his productive career.

lectio divina Meditative reading of Scripture and other holy works through which the monastic seeks to achieve communion with God rather than scholarly knowledge. It was not originally a monastic invention, but became associated with monasticism in the 6th century through the *Rule of St. Benedict* and its influence in the Benedictine, Cistercian, and Carthusian orders.

During the 12th century, the Carthusian monk Guigo II described it as a four step process of reading (lectio), meditation (meditatio), praying (oratio), and contemplation (contemplatio). That is, first a passage of Scripture is read, then its meaning is reflected upon. This is followed by prayer and contemplation on the Word of God.

St. Clare of Assisi outlined the Franciscan model which was gazing on the Cross (intueri), consideration of the reading (considerare), contemplation (contemplari), and imitation (imitare).

lecture hall *see* **Dharma hall**

legenda Readings from the lives of the saints, especially those used in the second nocturne of Matins on saint's days

Lent *see* **monastic Lent**

Leonardi, St. Giovanni *see* **Clerics Regular of the Mother of God**

leper window *see* **hagioscope**

leprosarium A hospital for the care of lepers. The staff and patients of those run by monastic communities lived a semi-monastic life, even if not monastics themselves.

LeSaux, Henri (1910–1973); Abhishiktananda French Benedictine monk born in Brittany who was active in the Hindu-Christian monastic dialogue. At the age of 19 he was admitted as a postulant to the Benedictine monastery at Sainte-Anne de Kergonan where he spent another 19 years—with a short break between the years 1939 and 1941 when he was required to participate in the World War II as a sergeant of the French Army.

He felt a call to India as early as 1934 in his quest for a more contemplative life than was present in the Western Church. Finally, in 1949 he was able to travel there and in 1950, he and the French priest Jules Monchanin established the Saccidananda Ashram (Shantivanam) on the banks of the holy river Kaveri (Cauvery). Its aim was to enable monks of different traditions to live together in contemplation. Its routine was morning, noon, and evening prayer together with study.

In 1968 he left the Saccidananda Ashram and passed it on to Bede Griffiths. He then settled in at Gyansu where he could spend more time in solitude.

lesser schema ***see*** **stavrophore**

lesser silence ***see*** **little silence**

libellikon A reduced land tax paid by Byzantine monasteries to which the state ceded lands whose tax-paying owners had disappeared

libellos A document assigning to a Byzantine monastery property in a village commune on which taxes had ceased to be paid

liber vitae A monastery book usually kept near the altar listing those who were benefactors or had a special claim to the intercessory prayers of the community

librarian; armarius; bibliophylax (Eastern Church); bibliothekarios (Eastern Church) Originally, the monastic in charge of the books in the armarium, book cupboard; the monastic in charge of the library; the monastic responsible for providing materials for the scriptorium; the monastic responsible for what was read by the community either privately or publicly (as in the frater). Often this position was conflated with that of the precentor and archivist.

library; bibliotheca; armarium The *Rule of St. Benedict* written in the 6th century specifically mentions that a book from the library shall be given to each monk to read during Lent (RB 48:14), but monastic libraries were already extant in the 4th century. By the Middle Ages, every monastery in western Europe had a library of some sort. A French monk in 1170 said, "Claustrum sine armario, castrum sine armamentario," that is, "A monastery without a library is a fort without an armory."

The Cluny Abbey library was one of the richest and most important in France and Europe. It was a storehouse of numerous very valuable manuscripts. During the religious conflicts of 1562, the Huguenots sacked the abbey, destroying or dispersing many of the manuscripts. Of those that were left, some were burned in 1790 by a rioting mob during the French Revolution. The French Government worked to relocate such treasures, including those that ended up in private hands. They are now held by the Bibliothèque Nationale de France at Paris. The British Museum holds some 60 or so charters originating from Cluny.

The first monastic library in England was probably established at Canterbury when Pope Gregory the Great gave Augustine of Canterbury nine books to assist with his mission.

Eastern Church monasteries had libraries as well. In fact, the world's oldest continually operating library is at St. Catherine's Monastery in Egypt, and it possesses the second largest collection of early codices and manuscripts in the world, outnumbered only by the Vatican Library. It contains Greek, Arabic, Armenian, Coptic, Hebrew, Georgian, Aramaic, and Caucasian Albanian texts.

Although the libraries were for the education of the monastics, many classical documents were copied and thus preserved for later generations.

Originally, an armarium was a bookcase near the entrance of a monastery, later the term was also applied to a more formal monastery library.

licentiate A friar in former times authorized to receive confessions and grant absolution in all places, independently of the local clergy

Liciac, Stephen *see* **Grandmontines**

life vows *see* **solemn vows**

limitation A certain precinct within which friars were allowed to beg, or exercise their functions; it was also the time during which they were permitted to exercise their functions in such a district

limiter; limitour A friar licensed to beg within certain bounds, or whose duty was limited to a certain district

limitour *see* **limiter**

liti The outermost part of an Eastern Orthodox monastic church used for the celebration of the Minor Hours

Little Flower of Jesus A nickname of St. Thérèse of Lisieux

Little Gidding A small semi-monastic Anglican religious community in England established in 1626 by Nicholas Ferrar, two of his siblings and their extended families. It was founded around strict adherence to Christian worship in accordance the *Book of Common Prayer* and the High Church (Catholic) heritage of the Church of England. Ferrar was ordained a deacon in 1627. Although derided by the Puritans as a "Protestant nunnery," contrary to popular belief the Puritans never physically attacked the community. Nicholas Ferrar died in 1627, but the community survived under the leadership of John Ferrer and did not collapse until he died in 1657. The community was never a formal religious community, took no vows, and had no rule of life, but they said the Daily Office and performed works of charity. It is seen today as an experiment in family monastic living.

little habit The dress of rassophore (one rank above a novice) monastics in the Orthodox Church

Little Hours *see* **Minor Hours**

little schema *see* **stavrophore**

little silence; lesser silence; simple silence The silence that should be kept during working hours in monastic communities. It is generally less absolute than the great silence of the night hours. Its purpose is to help community members keep internal peace while performing their daily tasks.

Liturgy of the Hours *see* **Daily Office**

Lives of the Fathers; Lives of the Desert Fathers; Vitae Patrum Hagiographical stories about the Desert Fathers and Desert Mothers. Most of the original narratives are from the 3rd and 4th centuries and originally written in Greek. The 6th century *Rule of St. Benedict* recommends the *Lives of the Fathers* for spiritual reading.

In the 13th century, a version printed in Latin was popular and many changes were made in the stories. In the early 14th century, the Italian Dominican friar Domenico Cavalca did a very popular version that also made many changes in the stories. Another influential edition was published in 1615 by the Jesuit priest Heriert Rosweyde who studied the previous versions and noted changes that had occurred over time.

locutorium *see* **parlor**

locutory *see* **parlor**

lodge The chamber of a monastic superior

Longo, Maria *see* **Capuchin Poor Clares**

luang phi Literally "venerable elder." It is used as a reverential term for a younger, freshly ordained Thai Buddhist monk.

luang por; luang pho Literally, "venerable father." It is used as a term of respect for senior Thai Buddhist city tradition monks—that is those who have passed ten rain retreats (Vassa).

luang pu Literally, "venerable grandfather." It is used fas a term of respect for Thai Buddhist monks even more senior than luang por.

luang ta Literally, "venerable uncle." It is used as a reverential term for an elderly Thai Buddhist monk without titles.

Luther, Martin (1483–1546) A German Augustinian monk, priest, hymnodist, and professor of theology. As a monk, he was dedicated to his order, and devoted himself to fasting, pilgrimage, long hours in prayer, and frequent confession. He was made provincial vicar of Saxony and Thuringia in 1515 and supervised 11 monasteries.

In time, however, Luther came to reject several teachings and practices of the Roman Catholic Church, especially indulgences. He published *Ninety-Five Theses* in 1517. When he refused to renounce his writings he was excommunicated in 1521.

His translation of the Bible into the German vernacular made it more accessible to the laity and had a great effect on both the Church and German culture.

In 1523, he married Katharina von Bora, a former nun, which set the practice of allowing Protestant clergy to marry. He and his wife moved into a former monastery.

Lutheran monasticism Although Martin Luther criticized monasticism neither he nor the Lutheran Church ever prohibited it. Several Benedictine houses joined the Lutheran movement in the 16th century, and there were some Lutheran semi-monastic Brethren of the Common Life communities, but in time they all disappeared. In the mid–19th century some quasimonastic women's groups arose that were close enough to traditional Roman Catholic orders that critics called them "Lutheran nuns." In 1956, the Fellowship of St. Augustine was formed in the U.S.

It was not until 1960 in Sweden, however, that a true Lutheran monastic community. Franciscan in nature at first, by 1970 it had become Benedictine. In 1967, a small Benedictine group was formed in Germany. All these groups are very small, but continued to function in 2018.

lychnoscope *see* **hagioscope**

Lyne, Joseph Leycester (1837–1908); Ignatius of Jesus, Father An eccentric English Anglican deacon, nominal Benedictine monk who tried unsuccessfully to revive monasticism in the Church of England. He was ordained to the diaconate in 1860. As a curate in Plymouth he started the Society of the Love of Jesus. It was for men and boys and he was the superior and grew to 40 members. Unfortunately, the experiment was cut short by his illness. When he recovered, he became a curate in London in 1861 and assumed a Benedictine habit. When the vicar of the church objected to the habit, Lyne resigned. In 1862 he began calling himself Father Ignatius and issued a pamphlet promoting a revival of monasticism in the Church of England and formed a small community in Suffolk despite Protestant opposition. The Bishop of Norwich then refused him a license to preach. In 1866 he was dispossessed of his religious house because of a flaw in the title deed. In 1867 founded an enclosed religious community for women, but they eventually joined the Roman Catholic Church. From 1866 to 1868, he preached in London but then the bishop suspended him. In 1869, he built Llanthony Abbey in Wales and constituted himself as the abbot, but the community was not popular and he again ran into trouble with the local bishop. In 1877, his father repudiated both him and his practices. Unable to preach in churches, he traveled about and appeared in lecture halls. In 1890 and 1891 he even lectured in Canada and the U.S. but was not popular because of his obsession with heresy. All this time, he was unable to be ordained as a priest by the Church of England, but in 1898 he was ordained by In 1898 Lyne was finally ordained as a priest by Joseph René Vilatte, a sort of wandering bishop associated with a number of different religions includes the Episcopal Church of the United States, the Roman Catholic Church, the Old Catholic Church, and the Christian Catholic Church. At various times it was reported that Lyne was a Druid, a member of the Ancient British Church, a Zionist, a British Israelite, and a believer in the flat earth theory. Because he was a controversial character and associated with the High Church movement before it became acceptable to the establishment, it is hard to tell how much of the claimed associations are true.

lynghouse *see* **prisons**

~M~

Macarius of Egypt, St. (ca. 300–391); Macarius the Elder; Macarius the Great Egyptian Christian monk, and hermit. Before he became a monk, he was a smuggler of saltpeter in the Nitrian Desert. After the death of his parents, however, he gave his money to the poor and became a disciple of an elder in the desert. Ten years later he was ordained a priest.

According to legend, at one point a pregnant woman accused him of having defiled her. Macarius did not attempt to defend himself, and accepted the accusation in silence. However, she did not manage to give birth until she confessed Macarius's innocence. A multitude of people then came asking for his forgiveness, but he fled to Scetis to escape the attention.

When he began to attract followers there, St. Anthony inspired him to become a teacher and to found a monastic community. The community was a skete, which allowed monks to live for the mostly separated from one another, but to come together when needed for worship on the weekends and in times of trouble.

Macarius the Elder *see* **Macarius of Egypt**

Macarius the Great *see* **Macarius of Egypt**

Macrina the Younger, St. (ca. 330–379) Early Christian nun who was born at Caesarea, Cappadocia. Her grandmother was St. Macrina the Elder. St. Basil the Great and St. Gregory of Nyssa were her brothers. When her fiancé died before the wedding she did not believe it was appropriate to marry another man, saw Christ as her eternal bridegroom and became a nun.

She had a profound influence upon her brothers with her adherence to an ascetic ideal. She devoted herself to the study of Scripture and other sacred writings and turned the family estate into a monastery and nunnery. Macrina's example influenced her brother Gregory of Nyssa who declared that virginity showed the "radiant purity of God."

mae chee *see* **maechi**

mae jis *see* **maechi**

maechi (Thailand); mae chee (Thailand); mae jis (Thailand); dasa sil mata (Sri Lanka); donchee (Cambodia); thilashin (Myanmar, Nepal); guruma (Nepal, Laos), sayalay (Myanmar); siladhara (England); ten precept mother A Buddhist quasimonastic woman in countries where nuns are generally not accepted who has dedicated her life to religion, vowing celibacy, living an ascetic life, and holding the Eight Precepts or even the Ten Precepts (instead of lay Buddhists' Five Precepts). They occupy a position somewhere between that of an ordinary lay follower and an ordained monastic and similar to that of the novice. Permanent maechis shave their heads. Temporary maechis, who typically do not shave their heads, are called chi phram.

Maechis are not recognized as monastics by the Thai government and are not eligible for monastic benefits but they are denied the rights of other lay citizens. In the 20th century there were some improvements but the situation remained unacceptable according to modern standards of human rights.

Most maechis live on the premises of a temple but receive little support beyond lodging and meals. They typically work as servants or other staff. Those maechis living in their own communities generally have better conditions.

Theravada maechis wear white or pink robes.

Mael Ruain, St. (d. 792); Máel Ruain Irish abbot-bishop of the monastery of Tallaght. He is thought to be a leader of the monastic movement known as the Céli Dé (Culdees). He is not to be confused with the later namesake Máel

Ruain, Bishop of Lusca (County Dublin). The *Rule of Céli Dé,* used by the Culdees is thought either to have been written by him or his disciple Óengus the Culdee (fl. 9th century). • *See also* ***Rule of Ceili De***

mageiras In the Eastern Church, a monastic in charge of the kitchen and preparation of food at a monastery

magistra ***see*** **abbess**

magna fenestra versatilis ***see*** **turning window**

magoulikion; phakiolion; skepe A Byzantine nun's head covering

Maha Dwara Nikaya; Maha Dwaya Nikāya; Mahādvāra Nikāya A Buddhist monastic order of Burma [Myanmar] with 3,000 to 4,000 monks, primarily in Lower Myanmar. It is very conservative in its approach to Vinaya regulations. It was founded in 1855 in a dispute with the Thudhamma Nikaya. In 1900, the Anaukchaung Dwara separated from the Maha Dwara Nikaya, and in 1908 the Mula Dwara also separated from them.

Maha Dwaya Nikaya ***see*** **Maha Dwara Nikaya**

Mahadvara Nikaya ***see*** **Maha Dwara Nikaya**

mahant A Hindu title that literally means a chief priest of a temple or the head of a monastery

Mahapajapati Gotami; Mahāpajāpatī Gotamī (Pali); Mahāprajāpatī Gautamī (Sanskrit) In Buddhist tradition, the first bhikkhuni (Buddhist nun), ordained by the Buddha himself.

Mahāpajāpatī was both the Buddha's maternal aunt and adoptive mother, raising him after her sister Maya, the Buddha's birth mother, died. When her husband King Suddhodhana, died, Mahāpajāpatī sought to become a nun. The Buddha at first refused, but she cut off her hair and donned monastic robes anyway. Ananda, one of the principal disciples of the Buddha, then took up her case and asked the Buddha, "Lord, are women capable of realizing the various stages of sainthood as nuns?" "They are, Ananda," replied the Buddha. Ananda then said, "If that is so, Lord, then it would be good if women could be ordained as nuns." The Buddha then said, "If, Ananda, Mahāpajāpatī Gotamī would accept the Eight Conditions it would be regarded that she has been ordained already as a nun."

Mahāpajāpatī then agreed to accept the Eight Garudhammas and was accorded the status of the first bhikkhuni. Subsequent women had to undergo full ordination to become nuns.

Mahasthabir Nikaya A nominal Bengali anti-reformist order of Bengali Buddhist monks formed to counter the Sangharaja Nikaya formed by Saramitra Mahasthabir in 1864. The Mahasthabir Nikaya was formed by Radha Charan Mahasthabir, a Bengali monk who ironically, had originally invited Saramitra Mahasthabir in 1856. It should be noted that Rahan Charan and his followers were not opposed to the reforms of the Sangharaja Nikaya but objected to a Bengali order being under the influence of a foreigner. The practical differences between the two orders are minimal.

mahathera; mahāthera Great elder—an honorific title automatically conferred upon a Buddhist monk of at least 20 years standing

mahavihara A monastic complex of viharas (Buddhist monasteries), in the manner of Mt. Athos in Greece

Main, John (1926–1982) English Roman Catholic Benedictine monk and priest and promoter of contemplative prayer in the Western Church.

Born in London, he joined the Canons Regular of the Lateran in the 1940s and studied at the diocesan seminary but began to doubt his vocation to the priesthood and left his order to study law at Trinity College where he graduated in 1954. He then joined the British Colonial Service and was assigned to Kuala Lumpur in Malaya, where he met Swami Satyananda, who taught him meditation using a mantra as the means to arrive at meditative stillness.

In 1959 he decided to join the Benedictines at Ealing Abbey in London and was ordained a priest in 1963. In the early 1970s while headmaster at St. Anselm's School in Washington, D.C., he discovered the parallels between the writing of John Cassian and the meditation he had learned in Kuala Lampur. In 1974, he returned to Ealing Abbey and began Christian meditation groups there. He was assisted in this work by Laurence Freeman, also a monk of Ealing Abbey.

majjhima A Thai Buddhist monk of 5 to 10 years standing

Major Hours Morning Prayer and Vespers, the longest Hours of the Daily Office. All other Hours are considered Minor or Little Hours.

major superior A monastic who has the ultimate authority of a given order or congregation or one of its designated sub-divisions. They may have the title of abbot, abbess, prior, prioress, superior general, provincial superior, etc. • *See also* **superior general**

manciple ***see*** **cellarer**

mandias ***see*** **mantle**

mandorasson ***see*** **outer cassock**

mandriarch The founder or leader of a monastic order

mandyas ***see*** **mantle**

Manichaeism A dualistic religion originating in Persia in the 3rd century CE. Its prophet was Mani. It grew rapidly into the 7th century, but gradually faded away in the 14th century. It had a monastic component, but little is known about it. A Manichaean monastery was called a manistan and was modeled after Buddhist monasteries. St. Augustine of Hippo was a Manichaean for about ten years before converting to Christianity shortly after the Roman Emperor Theodosius I had issued a decree of death for all Manichaean monks in 382 and shortly before he declared Christianity to be the only legitimate religion for the Roman Empire in 391.

manistan A Manichaean monastery. They were modeled after Buddhist monasteries.

Mantellatae ***see*** **Nuns of the Third Order of Servites**

mantiya ***see*** **mantle**

mantle; mandias (Greek); mandyas (Greek); mantíya (Church Slavonic) A long, full cape, extending to the floor and joined at the neck which Eastern Orthodox and Eastern Catholic monks and nuns wear over the other parts of the habit. It is worn in processions and while attending certain church services, such as Vespers or Matins, but not at the Eucharist. The mantle is not worn by rassophores (the rank between novice and stavrophore). In Greek practice it is used less commonly by those of the lesser schema (stavrophores). In other traditions it is worn by those of both the lesser and greater schemas (a high honorific rank). In the Russian tradition, the mantle usually has 33 pleats symbolizing the years of Christ's earthly life. When a monk or nun dies, they are vested in their religious habit. A strip of cloth is torn from the bottom of their mantle and is used to bind their body three times: around the chest, around the waist, and around the feet. The mantle worn by an archimandrite (senior abbot) is joined in front at the bottom as well as at the neck, and has large rectangular pieces of red or green cloth sewn onto the corners—two at the neck and two at the feet. The tablets at the neck are embroidered with crosses. When an archimandrite dies, his mantle is laid on his coffin in place of a funeral pall.

Mar Chaya Monks *see* **Lebanese Antonin Order**

Mar Saba; Holy Lavra of Saint Sabbas; Great Lavra A Greek Orthodox monastery overlooking the Kidron Valley halfway between Jerusalem and the Dead Sea. About 473, the monk St. Sabbas moved to a cave in the area causing the Great Lavra to spring up. In 483 or 484, the monastery was founded with St. Sabbas as abbot. It is one of the oldest inhabited monasteries in the world and considered the mother of Orthodox monasteries. It was the home of St. John of Damascus and his grave is located there. The *Jerusalem Typikon* was developed there which became standard in the Orthodox Church and the Eastern Catholic Church worship. In a modified form, it is still used today. Legend has it that Mar Saba will host the last Eucharist on earth before the Parousia. The monks of Mar Saba and those of subsidiary houses are known as Sabaites. • *See also* **Sabbas the Sanctified, St.**

marathon monks *see* **kaihogyo**

Mariamite Maronite Order; Aleppians; Halabites; Ordo Maronita Mariamita; Ordo Maronita Beatae Mariae Virginis Aleppians A monastic order of the Levantine Catholic Maronite Church that split from the Lebanese Maronite Order in 1770. It is headquartered in Aleppo, Syria.

Marie, Mother *see* **Presbyterian Church monasticism**

Marmion, Columba (1858–1923) Irish Roman Catholic Benedictine monk, priest, abbot, teacher, and writer. He was born in Dublin, entered the seminary at the age of 16, completed his studies in Rome, and was ordained there in 1881. On his journey back to Ireland, he passed through Maredsous, Belgium, saw the Benedictine abbey there and wished to join but his archbishop refused and he became a curate in Ireland, and then a professor of metaphysics at Holy Cross College.

In 1886, he was finally allowed to join the Benedictines in Maredsous. He made his solemn profession in 1891, and in 1899, helped found the Abbey of Mont César, Louvain, Belgium, and became its first prior in addition to being the director of studies for young monks, a professor of theology, and a spiritual director of Carmelite nuns.

In 1909, he was elected abbot of

Maredsous. Under his leadership the monastery gained great influence and an increase in vocations.

marriage *see* **celibacy**

martha *see* **mistress**

Martin of Tours, St. (ca. 316 or 336–397) Christian monk and bishop who born in what is now Hungary. He spent most of his childhood in Pavia, Italy, and lived most of his adult life in France. At the age of ten he attended the Christian Church against the wishes of his parents, and became a catechumen. Conscripted as a soldier into the Roman army at age 15, he found the duty incompatible with the Christian faith he had adopted and became an early conscientious objector. Martin declared his vocation and went to Tours, where he became a disciple of Hilary of Poitiers, taking sides against the Arians he was scourged and exiled, and took refuge as a hermit. When he was able to return to Tours he established a hermitage that became the Benedictine Ligugé Abbey, the oldest monastery known in Europe.

In 371 Martin was made Bishop of Tours apparently by tricking him. In 372 he withdrew to the Abbey of Marmoutier, which he founded to live again as a monk even though he remained the bishop and continued to set up monastic communities.

martyrdom According to a classification system arising in 8th century Ireland and which then spread throughout Christendom, there were three types of martyrs. Red martyrs were those who died for Christ, and not necessarily monastics. White martyrs were those who gave up titles, possessions, and previous relationships for God. The term was associated mostly with monastic life. Green martyrs were devout non-monastics who lived ascetic and penitential lives, seeking to do God's will. The classification system is somewhat loose. The Blessed Virgin Mary has been called a white martyr, and St. Columba a red martyr because he was willing to die for Christ, even though he wound up dying a natural death.

martyrology A list of Christian martyrs, read at Prime; the death dates of people to be remembered in monastics' daily prayers

Mary of the Gaels A nickname of St. Brigid of Kildare

master general The superior general of certain religious orders and congregations including the Canons Regular of the Order of the Holy Cross, Dominican Order, Order of Friars Minor Conventual, Order of the Blessed Virgin Mary of Mercy, Order of St. Lazarus, and the Trinitarian Order • *see also* **superior general**

master of children; mistress of children A monastic in charge of child novices and/or school children. The office may be merged with the novice master or novice mistress.

master of work *see* **matricularius**

matha A monastic or similar religious establishment in Hinduism and Jainism

Mathurins *see* **Order of the Most Holy Trinity**

Matins; Night Office; Orthros (Orthodox) The first and longest Office of the day, sung during the night sometime between midnight and 2 a.m. Commonly called Nocturnes in medieval texts, this office is now known as Lauds. In the later Middle Ages Matins and Lauds were collectively referred to as Vigils.

matricularius; master of work; maître d'oeuvre; clerk of the works A literate monastic or cleric who supervised construction on behalf of a monastery or church. The position arose in the 13th century. As workmen became more literate, the position was transferred to laymen.

Maturins ***see*** **Order of the Most Holy Trinity**

Maurists ***see*** **Congregation of St. Maur**

Maximos the Greek ***see*** **Maximus the Greek**

Maximos the Hagiorite ***see*** **Maximus the Greek**

Maximus the Greek, St. (1475–1556); Maximos the Greek; Maximos the Hagiorite; Maximus the Philosopher Greek monk, writer, scholar, and translator active in Russia. Maximus was greatly influenced by the preaching of the fiery Dominican priest and reformer Girolamo Savonarola and became a Dominican friar.

About 1504, he left the Dominican monastery of St. Mark and went to the Greek Orthodox Monastery of Vatopedi and Mt. Athos where he took his monastic vows in 1507. In 1515, he was sent to Russia at the request of Grand Prince Vaili III to translate religious texts even though he had no knowledge of Church Slavonic. After he translated the Psalter he requested to return to Greece but was refused so he continued his translation work and became active in church reform which made him some enemies, particularly among those who favored the right of monasteries to own land. In 1525, a synod in accused him of nonconformism and heresy and he was then exiled to the Joseph-Volokolamsk Monastery and placed in a dungeon without the right to receive communion or correspond. After annoying his captors, he was tried at a synod in 1531 where the exhausted monk confessed to some mistakes in translation and excessive wine drinking. The synod maintained the ban on receiving communion but let him out of the dungeon and exiled him to the Otroch Monastery in Tver.

Efforts to free him by the patriarchs of Antioch, Constantinople, and Jerusalem all failed because Russian authorities feared he would expose church abuses. In 1551 or 1553, he was transferred to the Troitse-Sergiyeva Lavra where he remained until his death.

He left many translations and original writings in Russian Church Slavonic and did much to interpret and explain Church practice and teachings, and is now considered a saint by the Eastern Orthodox Church.

Maximus the Philosopher ***see*** **Maximus the Greek**

Mechitarists ***see*** **Mekhitarists**

mediocre Formerly, a young monastic who was excused from performing a portion of a monastic's duties

megaloschemos ***see*** **great schema**

Mekhitar of Sebaste Founder of the Mekhitarists

Mekhitarists; Mechitarists A congregation of monks of the Armenian Catholic Church. It was founded in 1717 by Abbot Mekhitar of Sebaste. They originally used the a rule attributed to St. Anthony, but they now use a modified *Rule of St. Benedict.*

They are noted for their scholarly publications on the Armenian language and of Armenian versions of ancient Greek documents and also do missionary work. The congregation was divided into two branches for a long time, with one mother house in Venice and another one in Vienna. In 2000 they were united into one institute.

The novitiate is two years. Their habits and hoods are black and all members have beards. Abbots are elected for life.

Mellifluous Doctor A nickname for St. Bernard of Clairvaux, who was noted for his eloquence

melote; pera A cloak made of sheepskin used by the Desert Fathers and Mothers. It could also be used as a blanket and as a bindle to carry their few possessions.

Members of the Covenant; Sons of the Covenant; Benai Qeima (men); Daughters of the Covenant; Benat Qeima (women) A 4th century monastic group of men and women in Syriac Christianity, before the rise of the Egyptian or Hellenistic monasticism. They committed themselves to sexual abstinence, asceticism, and the service of the church, but lived among the common people. The Members of the Covenant understood themselves to be what we might think of today as deacons and servants of the clergy and assumed a responsibility for serving as teachers, arbitrators, providing hospitality, serving the poor, caring for lepers, etc. They usually lived together or with their family members, although there are instances of the Daughters of the Covenant having nunneries and other communal organizations with which they could live and study God's Word together. Still, they were readily accessible to ordinary people. They did not view their ascetic lifestyle as radically unobtainable for the average Christian of the day, and instead of an unimaginable leap of faith separated by monastic discipline and judgment, they encouraged a faith-building understanding of discipleship that viewed the Christian faith as a journey in which we all find ourselves. Because of this, they felt a sense of duty to come alongside those they could mentor and guide to the next step in their faith, hoping to see those on earlier steps to grow as well. During the 4th century, however, a major shift occurred in the church in Syria and the Roman model of monasticism came more into practice.

mendicant A begging friar; a member of impoverished religious order; a reliance on charity or begging for subsistence

Mendicant Century The 13th century, sometimes so called because it saw the founding and flowering of a number mendicant orders, including the Franciscans in 1209, the Carmelites between 1206 and 1214, the Dominicans in 1215, the Mercedarians in 1218, the Servites in 1233, and the Augustinians in 1254.

mendicant orders Certain monastic orders which are forbidden to acquire landed property and are required to be supported by alms, especially the Franciscans, Dominicans, Carmelites, and Augustinians

mensa That part of a monastic estate allocated to the direct support of the community and to supplying its table food

Mercedarians ***see*** **Order of the Blessed Virgin Mary of Mercy**

Merciful Brothers *see* **Hospitaller Order of the Brothers of St. John of God**

Merici, St Angela *see* **Company of St. Ursula**

Merton, Thomas (1915–1968) American Trappist monk, priest, writer, mystic, and theologian. He was a keen proponent of interfaith understanding. He received a BA, MA, and PhD in English from Columbia University. He was the author of more than 70 books, the best known of which was his autobiography *The Seven-Storey Mountain*. He was highly influential and brought many people to monasticism.

Not particularly religious in his earlier life, he converted to Catholicism in 1938. In 1941, he entered the Abbey of Gethsemani in Kentucky. In 1947 he was solemnly professed as a monk, and in 1949, he was ordained as a priest. In 1965 he moved into a hermitage on the Gethsemani grounds. Merton died 1968 where he was accidentally electrocuted in a Bangkok hotel when he touched an electric fan while stepping out of a bath. He was in Bangkok attending an interfaith conference between Christian and non–Christian monks.

Mesonyktikon The Orthodox name for Vigils, the midnight Daily Office

metanoia Basically, a fundamental change in thinking that leads to a fundamental change in behavior and/or way of living, but in more recent writings it can have the meaning of conversion of life, particularly the conversion involved in monastic life

Meteora A mountain formation in central Greece first inhabited by Orthodox hermits in the 9th century, then by monastic communities in the 11th century. At its peak, there were 24 monasteries, in 2019 only six remain, four for men and two for women. The first woman to visit Meteora was Queen Marie of Romania in 1921.

Methodist monasticism There have been a few new monastic experiments in the United Methodist Church dating from at least the 1970s. The only monastic establishment of note is the St. Brigid of Kildare monastery in St. Joseph, Minnesota. It is a Benedictine double house founded in 1999 by Mary Ewing Stamps. In 2012, it had 16 members, apparently all oblates. The Order of Saint Luke is a dispersed religious order within the Methodist Church.

metochion In the Eastern Church, a small monastery subordinate to a larger independent establishment and under the jurisdiction of the latter's hegumen (abbot)

Michaelites *see* **Spiritual Franciscans**

Milarepa (ca. 1052–ca. 1135 CE) Tibetan Buddhist monk and poet. According to legend, when Milarepa's father died his uncle and aunt took all of the family's wealth and Milarepa studied sorcery to take revenge. At a wedding celebration he sent a giant hailstorm that demolished their house and killed 35 people. When the villagers set off looking for him in anger, he sent another hailstorm that destroyed their crops. Remorseful for his revenge he sought counseling with a lama, then studied on his own for 12 years and attained Vajradhara (complete enlightenment). At the age of 45, he became a teacher and subsisted on nettle tea which caused his skin to turn green and waxy.

Milarepa's life represented the ideal

bodhisattva (one able to reach nirvana) despite oppression, poverty, and difficulty. His life shows that one can reach Buddhist ideals with renunciation, discipline, and perseverance.

military order Originally a Roman Catholic monastic order with military purpose established during the medieval crusades for the protection of Christians in the Holy Land, the Iberian peninsula, and eastern Europe. The attempt was made to combine the military life with monasticism, and members of the orders often took religious vows of poverty, chastity, and obedience. Despite the name, they were not purely military and often cared for the sick and poor. There were nuns as well as monks. The most notable orders were the Knights Templar, Knights Hospitaller, and the Order of Brothers of the German House of St. Mary in Jerusalem (Teutonic Knights). Although the military function is long gone, remnants of military orders survive to the present day as honorary or service organizations.

Military Order of the Crusaders of the Red Star *see* **Knights of the Cross with the Red Star**

Milleret, St. Marie Eugénie *see* **Religious of the Assumption**

Minimi *see* **Order of Minims**

Minims *see* **Order of Minims**

minister general; general minister; minister generalis The term used for the superior general of the different branches of the Order of Friars Minor. It is a term exclusive to them, and comes directly from its founder, St. Francis of Assisi. He chose this term over "superior" out of his vision that the brothers of the order were all to be equal, and that the friar supervising his brothers was to be a servant who cared for (ministered to) them, not one who lorded over them. In the 20th century, the term also came to be used as well by many religious congregations of the Third Order of St. Francis in the effort to follow more closely the spirit of the founder of their order. • *See also* **superior general**

minister generalis *see* **minister general**

minister provincial The head of a Franciscan province

Minor Hours, Little Hours Prime, Terce, Sext, and None—the less elaborate of the services of Daily Office. Morning Prayer and Vespers are considered major hours.

Minoresses *see* **Poor Clares**

Minorites *see* **Order of Friars Minor Conventual**

minuti *see* **bloodletting**

minutor In medieval Western monasteries, the monastic in charge of bloodletting

mircoschema *see* **stavrophore**

misericord; misericordia A small wooden shelf on the underside of the hinged seat of a choir stall to give support monastics who had to stand for a lengthy time; a temporary relaxation of monastic rules; a special apartment in a monastery for the use of monks receiving special indulgences in respect of diet and discipline; the meat kitchen of a monastery where a special diet was prepared for the sick or infirm

misericordia *see* **misericord**

Missa Familiaris *see* **Early Mass**

Missionaries of Charity; Missionariarum a Caritate A Roman Catholic religious order founded in Calcutta, India in 1950 by Mother Teresa. Members of the order take vows of chastity, poverty, obedience, and wholehearted service to the poorest of the poor. By 1996, the organization was operating 517 missions in more than 100 countries. In 2012, the order consisted of over 4,500 religious sisters.

The sisters wear white habits with a white sari but do not get the distinctive three blue stripes until they make their simple profession. Postulancy takes one year, the novitiate is two years, and then there are five years of simple vows before solemn profession. Members of the order don't smoke, drink alcohol, or take an annual vacation, but they may visit their families once every five years. They use the post-nominal initials M.V.

In 1963, the Missionary Brothers of Charity were founded in Australia. In 1979, they added a contemplative branch, and in 1984, the Missionaries of Charity Fathers, a priest branch was founded by Mother Teresa with Fr. Joseph Langford, combining the vocation of the Missionaries of Charity with the ministerial priesthood. As with the sisters, the priests live a very simple lifestyle without television, radios, or items of convenience. They neither smoke nor drink alcohol and they beg for their food.

Missionary Sisters of the Holy Family A Roman Catholic order of religious sisters founded in Russia in 1905 by Boleslawa Lament with the goal of promoting the unity of Eastern Orthodox Christians with the Catholic Church. The sisters accepted all children and youth without regard to their religion or nationality. Through the first 16 years of its founding, the order did not reveal its religious affiliation or wear habits. Their religious activity largely ended after the Russian Revolution of 1917. Some sisters stayed in Lithuania and Byelorussia and continued to work, but those who were discovered were sent to prison or Siberia. In 1922, the bulk or the order moved to Poland and 33 convents were subsequently established. Their work gradually expanded from teaching to include work in nursing homes, orphanages, daycare, homeless shelters for women, soup kitchens, and prisons. As a result of World War II many sisters were scattered, imprisoned, arrested, or forced to work as slave labor and only six convents survived. There was a rebound after the war, but the communist government squashed it. In 1966 and following the order established itself in the United States, Italy, Kenya, Zambia, and Libya. In 1990, they were able to open convents in Russia, Lithuania, Byelorussia. There are now 25 convents in Poland. There are 347 sisters worldwide. • *See also* **Lament, Bolesława Maria**

mistress; martha The head of a convent of Beguines. A grand mistress was the head of a Beguine complex.

mistress of children ***see*** **master of children**

miter Ceremonial headgear worn by bishops and by some privileged abbots. The first miters were modeled close to those worn by Jewish priests. In time, the miters of the Western Church came to resemble the flames that appeared on the heads of the Apostles when they received the Holy Spirit. The miter was not used in the Eastern Church until the fall of Constantinople in 1453. It resembles the closed imperial crown of the Byzantine empire.

mixed house *see* **double monastery**

mixed rule The monastic practice, especially in the 7th century, of a community following observances from several rules, commonly those of St. Benedict and St. Columbanus, rather than any single rule

mixtum In the Western Church, a meager breakfast of bread soaked in wine allowed to the old, infirm, and to novices not used to the long morning fast which did not end until midday

mnemosyna In the Eastern Church, commemorative services celebrated on the anniversary of the death of a donor to a church or monastery

monachae *see* **nuns**

monachise To cause to become a monastic

monachism *see* **monasticism**

monasterial Of, like, or relating to a monastery, or to monastic life

monastery; cenobium; matha (Hinduism); goenpa (Dzongkha); lamasery (Tibet & Mongolia) A house of religious retirement and of seclusion from ordinary temporal concerns. It provides a place for religious activities, work, and housing of the community and provides some degree of separation from secular life. Early monasteries tried to be as self-contained as possible and would incorporate such things as a mill, bakehouse, dovecote, brewery, etc. In the Western Church, a monastery is now generally considered a religious house for men, and religious houses for women are called convents. In the Eastern Church, a religious house for either men or women is called a monastery.

Monastery of St. Anthony A Coptic Orthodox monastery in the Eastern Desert of Egypt, in the Red Sea mountains. It was first established between 298–300 and is considered to be the oldest Christian monastery in the world. At first it consisted of only of a few buildings for communal functions and the monks lived separately. Gradually they adopted a cenobitic way of life which is maintained to this day. It is about 2 kilometers from the cave where St. Anthony the Great once lived as a hermit. The monastery has been devastated and rebuilt several times and occupied by Melkites and even Franciscans. In the 21st century it was been rehabilitated and is now home to about 120 monks. Modern roads have made it possible for several thousand visitors to flock to the monastery on weekends.

Monastery of St. John the Forerunner *see* **Stoudios**

Monastery of Stoudios *see* **Stoudios**

monastic A monk or nun; of or relating to monasteries, or to their occupants, rules, etc.; secluded from temporal concerns and devoted to religion

Monastic Family of Bethlehem, of the Assumption of the Virgin, and of St. Bruno; Monks and Sisters of Bethlehem A Roman Catholic religious order founded in 1951 in France by a group of women after the promulgation of the dogma of the Assumption of the Blessed Virgin Mary into Heaven. The brothers were founded in 1976 in the Chartreuse Mountains. The vocation of the order is listening to the Gospel with the Blessed Virgin Mary in the heart of the Church, in love, in solitude, through liturgical life, study, work, and poverty.

In 2018, the order had more than 600 nuns and about 70 monks. They live in 30 convents of women and four monasteries of brothers located in fifteen different nations. The order also contains lay associates, companions, and friends.

monastic fraternities *see* **nikayas**

monastic Lent In the Western Church, the period from the Feast of the Holy Cross (September 14th) to the end of Lent in the universal Church in the universal Church

Monastic State of the Teutonic Knights; State of the Teutonic Order; Staat des Deutschen Ordens; Deutschordensstaat A crusader state formed by the Teutonic Knights after their conquest of the pagan Prussians in the 13th century. It expanded into parts of what is now Estonia, Latvia, Lithuania, Poland, and Russia. After their defeat on the Battle of Grunwald in 1410, the Teutonic Knights fell into decline, and remaining lands were secularized in 1525 during the Protestant Reformation and absorbed into modern states. Despite the name, the state was never monastic.

monastical In a monastic manner

monasticism; monachism A religious way of life in which one renounces worldly pursuits to devote oneself fully to spiritual work. Monastic life plays a role in many Christian churches, especially in the Roman Catholic, Orthodox, and Anglican traditions. Similar forms of religious life also exist in other faiths, most notably in Buddhism, Hinduism, and Jainism, although the expressions differ considerably.

monasticon A book giving an account of monasteries

Mongkut (1804–1868); Rama IV Siamese Buddhist monk, reformer, and king. Outside Thailand, he is best known as the king in *The King and I.* He was the second son of Prince Isarasundhorn, son of Phutthayotfa Chulalok, the first Chakri king of Siam. In 1824, Mongkut became a Buddhist monk, following a Siamese tradition that men aged 20 should become monks for a time. When his father died could have become the next king, but the nobility instead chose the older and more experienced Prince Jessadabodindra (Nangklao), son of a king's concubine rather than of a queen. Mongkut then remained a monk and devoted himself to monastic reform. In 1836, Mongkut became the first abbot at Wat Bowonniwet. Finally in 1851 left monastic life and became the king where he not only worked to modernize his country, but also continued monastic reform.

It should be noted that after a lifetime of celibacy Mongkut acquired 32 wives, and they gave him 82 children.

monk A man who retires from the ordinary temporal concerns of the world, and devotes himself to religion and is generally bound by vows to a life of chastity, obedience, and poverty

monkery The life of monks; monastic life; monastic usage or customs; a monastery—now usually applied in a pejorative manner for all senses

monkhood The character or condition of a monk; monks, regarded collectively

monkish Like a monk, or relating to monks; monastic, as monkish solitude

Monks and Sisters of Bethlehem *see* **Monastic Family of Bethlehem, of the Assumption of the Virgin, and of St. Bruno**

Monte Cassino *see* **Cassino, Monte**

monydrion In the Eastern Church, a dependency of a larger monastery and that has a lesser status than a metochion (a small monastery)

More, Gertrude (1606–1633) English Roman Catholic nun. After her mother died when she was young she joined the community of Our Lady of Comfort, in Cambrai, France in 1623. Despite not initially feeling called to the religious life she became attracted to it.

After the French Revolution, her community moved back to England in what is now Stanbrook Abbey. Despite her short life, it is felt that together with Dom Augustine Baker, she did much to encourage the revival of Benedictine life in England.

Morning Prayer The Daily Offices of Matins, Lauds, and Prime first combined into a single office by Archbishop Thomas Cranmer in the 1559 *Book of Common Prayer*. It is used instead of these three offices in those communities that use a fourfold Office. The other three offices of a fourfold set are Noon Prayer (Diurnam), Evening Prayer (Vespers), and Compline.

Moronites *see* **Celestines**

Morrow Mass *see* **Early Mass**

mother In Eastern Christianity, a commonly used term of address for nuns who have been tonsured to stavrophore of higher, but note that among themselves, they call each other sister; in Western Christianity a term of address for an abbess or prioress—in Anglican communities, they may be addressed as "reverend mother"

mother general The female head of a religious order in the Western Church.

mother house The monastic house which founded a daughter house

mother prior *see* **prioress**

mother superior *see* **abbess**

Mount Athos *see* **Athos, Mount**

Mula Sangha An ancient Jain monastic order. Today the Digambara Jain tradition is synonymous with Mula Sangha. The oldest known mention of Mula Sangha is from 430 CE. • *See also* **Digambara**

Mulasarvastivada Vinaya **see** ***Vinaya***

Mun Bhuridatta Thera (1870–1949) Thai Buddhist monk of Lao descent who is credited together with Sao Kantasīlo, with establishing the Forest Tradition (Kammaṭṭhāna) that subsequently spread throughout Thailand and to several countries abroad.

Ordained as a monk in 1893, he spent his life dwelling and wandering through Thailand, Myanmar (Burma), and Laos and in meditation. He followed the *Vinaya* (monastic discipline) faithfully, lived from alms, wore ragged robes, wore robes of cast-off rags, and ate only one meal a day. Monks following this tradition are known as forest monks. In spite of his isolated life, he attracted a large following of students.

muni; nirgrantha A Digambara Jain monk

murmuring A term popularized in monastic circles by St. Benedict to designate disaffected muttering or complaint, although the term was previously used in Judaism. This does not apply to occasionally going to the superior and respectfully voicing a concern, rather it is a chronic, usually quiet, veiled, and insidious complaining that undermines morale and instills negative attitudes. It is a form of passive aggression.

mustardarius *see* **salter**

mynstermon *see* **cenobite**

~N~

Naga sadhus; Naga sādhus In the 16th century, Mahhusudana Saraswati of Bengal organized a section of the Naga (naked) tradition of armed Hindu monks in order to protect Hindus from the Mughal rulers. Today Naga sādhus are generally non-violent, though some groups practice the sport of wrestling. • *See also* **Hindu warrior monks**

naginata *see* **sohei**

nakatan In Japanese Zen Buddhism, a middle-ranking unsui (postulant)

nap; siesta Most monastic rules allow a nap time between the noon meal and None. Adults could either read or sleep, but children were mandated to sleep.

narashimono The various sound-producing implements (bells, clappers, gongs) used in a Japanese Zen Buddhist monastery to signal the times for various activities

Nath; Natha A Shaivism sub-tradition within Hinduism that combines elements from Shaivism, Buddhism, and yoga traditions. They formed monastic organizations, itinerant groups that walked great distances to sacred sites and festivals as a part of their spiritual practice. The Naths also have a large settled householder (semi-monastic lay) tradition in parallel to its monastic groups. Gorakhshanatha is traditionally credited with founding the tradition of renunciate ascetics, but the earliest textual references of an organized entity (sampradaya) that have survived into the modern era are from the 17th century. In 2008, there were about 10,000 ascetics (predominantly males) in the Nath ascetic order, distributed in about 500 monasteries across India but mostly in northern and western regions of India. The householder population is much larger.

Most of the monks continually move from one monastery or holy place to another, but gather regularly for festivals such as Navratri, Maha Shivaratri, and Kumbh Mela.

Nath monks wear loin cloths, dhotis (male skirts), and little else. They usually cover themselves with ashes and tie hair in dreadlocks. When not walking, they keep a sacred fire called Dhuni. Both the monks and householders wear a singnad janeu around their necks. This is a small horn, rudraksha bead, and a ring attached to a woolen thread.

The Yogis and Shaiva sampradayas such as the Nath became a warrior ascetic group in the late medieval era, with one group calling itself sastra-dharis (keepers of scriptures) and the other astra-dharis (keepers of weapons). The astra-dharis were particularly notable during the Hindu-Muslim conflicts from the 14th to 18th century.

Nath Siddhas *see* **Hindu warrior monks**

Natha *see* **Nath**

navaka A newly ordained Thai Buddhist monk

navakammika In a Theravedin Buddhist monastery, an official who supervised building projects or restorations

Nazirite A Jew who voluntarily takes a consecration vow to be holy before YHWH (God). The vow are described in Numbers 6:1–21 and require a person to abstain from wine, vinegar, and grapes, to refrain from cutting the hair, and not to become ritually impure by contact with graves or corpses. Nazarite vows may be either temporary or permanent. Permanent Nazirites are allowed to cut their hair once a year if it becomes bothersome. Although Naziritism sometimes comes up in discussions of monasticism it is hard to consider it as even semi-monastic.

necessarium *see* **rere-dorter**

necrology A list kept by a monastery of monastics, donors of lands or money, and the dates of their death. The necrology at Cluny had 48,000 names.

nen *see* **samanera**

neophyte *see* **novice**

Nestorian monasticism The Nestorian Church was a Syrian rite Christian church that believed in the teachings of Nestorius (ca. 351–ca. 451) that the human and spiritual nature of Christ were separate (dyophysite) rather than fused (monophysite) in accordance with the orthodox Byzantine view.

The Nestorian monastics had their roots in Antiochian monasticism. Gradually pushed eastward to Turkey, by the end of the 5th century they were a national church in Persia. This worked well for a time until the Persian Zoroastrian rulers, who placed no value in virginity or celibacy, decreed at the Council of Acacius in 486 that monks could marry, and in some cases could be forced to. In some places it was not uncommon for monks to keep wives and children in their cells, but some monasteries were of such a size and lacked so much communal life that the abbot was unaware of which monks had wives and children.

In the 6th century, reform movements were well underway to return to celibacy. The reforms prompted the greatest growth of Nestorian monasticism and it spread throughout the greater Persian empire, and by the 8th and 9th centuries it reached as far as China. Nestorianism, however, disappeared after the 14th century.

Nestorian monasticism was notable for inspiring a high level of intellectual mysticism. They were also notable for Bible study and for producing a large number of manuscripts. To be admitted to a monastery, a candidate had to be able to read. Besides the obligatory prayer and fasting, monks were expected to study and proselytize. Most of Nestorian monastics were cenobitic, but there were a few who were hermits.

nestyazhateli *see* **non-possessors**

New Monasticism A diverse and ill-defined movement, not confined to a specific religious denomination and including varying expressions of contemplative life. The movement differs from other Christian monastic movements in that traditional monastic vows of celibacy, poverty, and obedience are not normally taken, habits are not worn, and it is acceptable to be married. A Christian Community of the Episcopal Church or a third order group of an established religious order are more traditional and as such should probably not be considered as New Monasticism. The origin of the new monastic movement is difficult to pinpoint but it has been in existence since at least 1968 when Fr. Bede Griffiths, a Roman Catholic Camaldolese monk, oversaw a Christian-Hindu ashram in India.

Most Protestant new monastic communities emphasize the following:

1. Thoughtful, prayerful, and contemplative lives
2. Communal life (expressed in a variety of ways depending on the community)
3. A focus on hospitality
4. Practical engagement with the poor

The "Twelve Marks" of new monasticism detailed in *Schools for Conversion* express the common thread of many new monastic communities.

1. Relocation to the "abandoned places of Empire" (at the margins of society)
2. Sharing economic resources with fellow community members and the needy among us
3. Hospitality to the stranger
4. Lament for racial divisions within the church and our communities combined with the active pursuit of a just reconciliation
5. Humble submission to Christ's body, the Church
6. Intentional formation in the way of Christ and the rule of the community along the lines of the old novitiate
7. Nurturing common life among members of an intentional community
8. Support for celibate singles alongside monogamous married couples and their children
9. Geographical proximity to community members who share a common rule of life
10. Care for the plot of God's earth given to us along with support of our local economies
11. Peacemaking in the midst of violence and conflict resolution within communities along the lines of Matthew 18
12. Commitment to a disciplined contemplative life

The New Monasticism movement differs from other Christian monastic movements in many ways.

1. Traditional monastic vows of celibacy, poverty, and obedience are not normally taken, as with members of traditional monastic orders, such as the Benedictines, Cistercians, Carthusians, and Franciscans.
2. Communities do not always live in a single place, but geographic proximity is emphasized by the movement.
3. The movement allows married couples. Most traditional forms of Christian religious life do not admit married couples. Certain centuries-old Catholic and more recent Anglican groups, known as "third," "secular," or "lay" orders, also admit married individuals who profess the spirituality of the order.
4. Members of the movement do not wear religious habits. This contrasts with the long-established Roman Catholic third orders, whose members may wear some form of

the religious habit of the order with which they are associated.

In McEntee and Bucko's *The New Monasticism: An Interspiritual Manifesto for Contemplative Life,* they describe the "Nine Vows of the New Monastic," which were based on Brother Wayne Teasdale's "Nine Elements of Spiritual Maturity" and developed by the Rev. Diane Berke.

1. I vow to actualize and live according to my full moral and ethical capacity.
2. I vow to live in solidarity with the cosmos and all living beings.
3. I vow to live in deep nonviolence.
4. I vow to live in humility and to remember the many teachers and guides who assisted me on my spiritual path.
5. I vow to embrace a daily spiritual practice.
6. I vow to cultivate mature self-knowledge.
7. I vow to live a life of simplicity.
8. I vow to live a life of selfless service and compassionate action.
9. I vow to be a prophetic voice as I work for justice, compassion and world transformation.

Nguam Phanit ***see*** **Buddhadasa Bhikkhu**

Nguyen Xuan Bao ***see*** **Thich Nhat Hanh**

Nhat Hanh, Thich ***see*** **Thich Nhat Hanh**

Night Hours Compline, Vigils, Lauds, and Prime of the Daily Office

Night Office ***see*** **Matins**

night silence ***see*** **great silence**

night stairs The staircase that linked the dormitory to the choir in the church—it provided a covered access to the church for the night Office of Vigils

nikayas; nikāyas; monastic fraternities; frateries Monastic divisions in the Theravāda Buddhist nations of Southeast Asia that develop due to government patronage, differences in the interpretation of the monastic code, or caste restrictions. Nikāyas are not considered separate sects because they usually follow the same monastic codes.

Nil Sorsky ***see*** **Nilus of Sora, St.**

Nilus of Sora, St. (ca. 1433–1508); Nil Sorsky Russian Orthodox monk, ascetic, advocate of hesychasm, leader of the "Non-Possessors" movement, and helped establish skete monasticism in Russia. He was tonsured as a youth at the Kirillo-Belozersky Monastery. Later he traveled to the Holy Land and Constantinople, and thereafter lived at Mt. Athos for a time. Returning to Russia he found himself so bothered by the interruptions of regular monasteries that about 1473 he founded a skete on the Sora River where he and his disciples could live an obscure and simple life.

At the Synod of 1490, Nilus opposed both the secular persecution and ecclesiastic trial of heretics and apostates, and resolutely opposed their capital punishment. He also fought against monastic landownership rights at the Synod of 1503 in Moscow believing they corrupted monastic ideals.

Ninth Hour ***see*** **None**

nirgrantha; muni A Digambara Jain monk

nissaya-muttaka A Thai Buddhist monk of five years standing

nisshitsu To enter the rōshi's (monastic master's) sanzen (formal meditation study) room in a Japanese Zen Buddhist monastery for meditation instruction

Nitria The earliest of the three major centers of Christian monastic activity in Egypt's Nitrian Desert, the other two being Kellia (the Cells) and Scetis. It was founded in 330 CE by Ammon and attracted thousands of monks. By 390, it evolved from an isolated group of solitary monks into a community with merchants and tourist services. The number of monks declined during the 5th and 6th centuries and around the middle of the 7th century the sire was abandoned.

nitten soji; nitten sōji The daily cleaning done inside and outside a Japanese Zen Buddhist monastery

niwazume; tangaryo; tangazume The period in which a postulant at certain Japanese Zen Buddhist monasteries must sit in the entrance hall (genkan) in a bowing posture, asking for admission—it may be for a period of several days to several weeks depending on local custom and the quality of one's sitting

niya sanjitsu Two nights and three days, the maximum period of time for which a Japanese Zen Buddhist monastic may be absent from the monastery without having to receive permission for zanka (permitted absence)

nocturnes Sections of the Daily Office of Matins. In the monastic office each nocturne consisted of three psalms followed by four lessons; on important festivals Matins comprised three such nocturnes and thus included 12 lessons. In medieval texts Matins is commonly called Nocturnes.

Nolasco, St. Peter *see* Order of the Blessed Virgin Mary of Mercy

None; Ninth Hour (Orthodox) None is pronounced "noan." A fixed time of prayer of the Daily Office of almost all the traditional Christian liturgies. It consists mainly of psalms and is said around 3 p.m. Its name comes from Latin and refers to the ninth hour of the day after dawn.

nonnae *see* nuns

non-possessors; nestyazhateli Those who belonged to a 16th century movement in the Russian Orthodox Church that opposed monastic ownership of land. It was led initially by Nilus of Sora and later on by Maximus the Greek and was opposed to the Josephites led by Joseph of Volokolamsk and later Archbishop Theodosius II of Novgorod. The non-possessors were defeated at the Stoglav Council in 1551.

Noon Prayer; Diurnam The Daily Offices of Terce, Sext, and None combined into a single office. It is used instead of these three offices in those communities that used a fourfold Office. The other three offices of a fourfold set are Morning Prayer, Evening Prayer (Vespers), and Compline. Noon Prayer first appeared in the 1979 American *Book of Common Prayer*.

Norbert, St. *see* Order of Canons Regular of Prémontré

Norbertines *see* Order of Canons Regular of Prémontré

noso; nōsō A patched-robe monk—that is a Japanese Zen Buddhist monk who sews his robe (kasaya) together out of discarded rags

novice; neophyte; poslushnik (Russian) In the Western Church, a monastic who has passed on from postulancy but has not yet taken simple vows. A novice is addressed as brother or sister.

In the Eastern Church there is no formal ceremony for the clothing of a novice; they simply receive permission to wear the clothing of a novice. They may or may not dress in the black inner cassock and wear the skufia (soft monastic hat) depending on the tradition of the local community, and in accordance with the abbot's directives. In some communities, the novice also wears the leather belt. Novices are given a prayer rope and instructed in the use of the Jesus Prayer. When the abbot or abbess deems the novice ready, they is asked if they wish to join the monastery. Some, out of humility, will choose to remain novices all their lives. Every stage of the monastic life must be entered into voluntarily.

novice guardian; novice master; novice mistress The monastic in charge of novices and responsible for overseeing the training and development of novices

novice master ***see*** **novice guardian**

novice mistress ***see*** **novice guardian**

novitiate The time of assessment and training in a religious house before taking the vows—usually this lasts a year; also, the place where novices live or are trained

nun town ***see*** **abbey town**

nunnery ***see*** **convent**

nuns; sisters; sanctimoniales; monachae; nonnae; tasooni (Coptic) Women religious. Technically, in the Roman Catholic Church, nuns are women who live and work primarily in a nunnery or priory as contemplative religious, and sisters are women religious who work outside their community housing in an active ministry, which may be anything from teaching and nursing to pastoral work, social work, or missionary work. In actual practice, neither the women themselves nor anyone else draws too fine a point on it. Most nuns are called sister, and sisters often refer to themselves as nuns.

In the Eastern Church, nuns who have been tonsured to the stavrophore or higher are addressed as Mother. Novice and rassophore nuns are addressed as Sister. Nuns of the Eastern Church live identical ascetic lives to their male counterparts and their communities are called monasteries.

Nuns of the Third Order of Servites; Mantellatae Nuns of the Third Order of Servites, founded in Florence by St. Juliana Falconieri (1270–1341). They are devoted to care of the sick and poor and the education of children. The name comes from the Italian word mantello (cloak) in reference to their distinctive short-sleeved habits. • *See also* **Order of the Service of Mary**

nuntius In Franciscan communities, a person authorized to receive and hold money given to the community

nutritae ***see*** **nutriti**

nutriti (male); nutritae (female) Monastics raised from childhood in a monastery as opposed to adult converts (*conversi* or *conversae*)

~O~

O. Camald.; O.S.B. Cam. The post-nominal initials used by the Camaldolese Order

O. Cart. The post-nominal initials used by Carthusians

O. Cist. The post-nominal initials used by the Order of the Common Observance

O. de M. The post-nominal initials used by the Order of the Blessed Virgin Mary of Mercy

Oath of Supremacy *see* **Act of Supremacy**

obedience (noun) In the Western Church, a small, dependent monastic community that is the offshoot of a larger monastery and is governed by a prior. It is also the written precept of a superior of a religious order or congregation to a subject.

obedience (verb) A basic tenet of Christian monasticism—it means listening as well as following instructions. In modern times, the former meaning has gotten little attention which makes the latter seem all the more unattractive. There is no denying one must follow instructions to have a successful community, but monastic communities are not looking for slaves—rather, they are trying to free the members from the tyranny of their own egos which causes separation from God. It's counter-intuitive and certainly counter-cultural, but as the *Book of Common Prayer* has it, "To serve God is perfect freedom." It may be hard to grasp the truth of this until one actually tries it.

Unlike Christian monastics, in some schools of Buddhist monastics are not required to live a life of obedience to a superior. However, it is expected that monastics will offer respect to senior members. Individual groups of monastics are expected to make decisions collectively through regular gatherings of the community, at which decisions regarding violations of monastic rules and the dispositions of communal property are to be made. Individual relationships of teacher/student, senior/junior, and preceptor/trainee may be observed among groups of monastics, but there are no formal positions, nor is there any authority to give orders or commands invested in senior monks.

obedientiary A monastic in charge of one of the administrative departments of a monastery, such as the cellarer, the sacristan, or the infirmarian. They are charged with managing a subset of the community's holdings.

obedientiary prior One who heads a monastery created as a satellite of an abbey

obedientiary priory; simple priory A dependency of an abbey. When an abbey becomes overlarge, or when there is need of a monastery in a new area, the abbot may appoint a group of monks under a prior to begin a new foundation, which remains a dependency of the mother abbey until such time as it is large and stable enough to become an independent abbey of its own.

obedientiary system A system used by some monastic communities to manage their holdings, including land, appropriated churches, and other property. The holdings are divided among the various obedientiaries, each of whom manages his or her portion. Critics criticize the system for crossing the line between corporate and private monastic property. The Cluniac Order was notable for being organized entirely on this obedientiary system, with a single abbot at the Abbey of Cluny, and with all other houses remaining obedientiary priories.

oblates This term has been used in different ways at different times by different orders and different writers. Originally it was used by St. Benedict to mean children dedicated in their early years to the monastic life forever. This practice was eventually abandoned because the children lacked freedom of choice.

In the Middle Ages, oblates were a class of persons who offered themselves and their property to a monastery in return for living and being cared for by the monastery. They were could also be lay men or lay women pensioned off by royal and other patrons upon monasteries or benefices, where they lived as in an almshouse.

In modern times, most oblates are technically secular oblates, that is either clergy or laity affiliated in prayer with an individual monastery of their choice, who have made a formal private promise (annually renewable or for life) to follow the *Rule of St. Benedict* in their private life at home and at work as closely as their individual circumstances and prior commitments permit. Typically, most monasteries can receive Christians of other religions as oblates. • *See also* **child oblates; confraters; conventual oblates; conversi; fratres barbati; lay monastics**

oblation In modern times, to formally commit oneself as an oblate; in former times, offering oneself or a child to serve as a monk or a nun

Observantines *see* **Order of Friars Minor**

Observants *see* **Order of Friars Minor**

O.C.D. The post-nominal initials of the Order of Discalced Carmelites

O.C.S.O. The post-nominal initials used by the Order of Cistercians of the Strict Observance (Trappists)

oeconomus *see* **economus**

Oengus the Culdee *see* ***Rule of Ceili De***

office hymn A hymn sung as part of the Daily Office. The practice began in the Western Church the 4th century.

officiant One who leads the Daily Office or another church service. The term may indicate a member of the clergy or a lay person.

O.F.M. Cap.; O.M. Cap.; O.S.F.C. The post-nominal initials used by the Friars Minor Capuchin

ogho A small broom made of wool given to Jain Śvētāmbara initiates from their mentor as a symbol of welcome into the monastic order. Later they are given a rajoharan (a broom-like object made from dense, thick thread strands). • *See also* **picchi**

O.H.C. Post-nominal initials for the Order of the Holy Cross

oikonomos *see* **cellarer**

Olivetans; Order of Our Lady of Mount Olivet A small Roman Catholic monastic order founded by Bernardo Tolomei in Italy in 1313. In 1344 they adopted the *Rule of St. Benedict.* Since 1960 they have formed the Olivetan Congregation within the Benedictine Congregation. They have houses in Europe, the U.S., Ghana, South Korea, Israel, Brazil, and Guatemala.

O.M. The post-nominal initials used by the Order of Minims

O.M. Cap.; O.F.M. Cap.; O.S.F.C . The post-nominal initials used by the Friars Minor Capuchin

O.M.C.R.S. The post-nominal initials of the Knights of the Cross with the Red Star

Opus Dei *see* **Daily Office**

Ora et Labora Latin for "pray and work." A Benedictine motto sometimes attributed to St. Benedict, but in fact originated by the 19th century German abbot, Maurus Wolter. It should be noted that in more recent times this motto has sometimes been quoted as "Ora, labora, et leger" (pray, work, and study), but that is not the original saying.

oratory May designate either a monastic church or simply a chapel

order *see* **religious order**

Order of Alcantara; Knights of St. Julian; Orde de Alcántara (Leonese); Orden de Alcántara (Spanish) Originally a military order founded in León, Spain in 1166 to defend against the Muslims. After various changes, it continues to this day, but is no longer a military order.

Order of Aubrac A hospitaller and military order founded in Aubrac, France in the mid–12th century. Its original mission was protecting the hospital for pilgrims going to St. James to Compostela and to Rome. Four satellite hospitals called commanderies were established. The *Rule of St. Augustine* rule was approved for the order by the bishop in 1162. The order had priests, knights, lay brothers, and lay sisters. The Knights Hospitaller failed in several attempts to annex it, and it remained independent and operational until the French Revolution, when it disappeared.

Order of Augustinian Recollects; Augustinian Recollects; Ordo Augustinianorum Recollectorum A mendicant Roman Catholic religious reform order of friars and nuns. It was founded in 16th century Spain as a separate province of the Augustinian friars, under their own vicar general. The reform entailed fidelity to the *Rule of St. Augustine* and emphasized community prayer and simplicity of life.

In 1997, the Recollects had 1,258 members in 201 religious houses, distributed into eight provinces (regions) in four continents, but the strongest were in Spain, the Philippines, and Colombia.

Augustinian Recollects use the post-nominal initials O.A.R.

Order of Bethlehemite Brothers; Ordo Fratrum Bethlemitarum; Bethlehemite Brothers; Bethlehem Brothers; Order of the Brothers of Our Lady of Bethlehem The Bethlehemite Brothers were founded by in Guatemala in 1658 by Peter of St. Joseph Betancur, a native of the Canary Islands. He was a member of the Third Order of St. Francis and wore their habit even after his own order was founded. The order operates under the *Rule of St. Augustine*. They were established to serve the sick, but soon expanded to also care for the poor and prisoners and to pray for souls in purgatory.

In 1688 Brother Anthony of the Cross founded a community of Bethlehemite nuns in Guatemala and a hospital exclusively for women. The nuns were cloistered and observed the same rule as the men. The order operated only in Latin America and was widely admired. It had 33 houses when all religious orders were suppressed in 1820. Later in the 19th century, Blessed Encarnación Rosal revived the female branch of the order, establishing houses in Guatemala, Costa Rica, Colombia, and Ecuador.

The Holy See restored the Bethlehemite Brothers in 1984, but they have only one house and it is located in the Canary Islands. In 2007, the order had 17 members, living in a single community.

Order of Brothers of the German House of St. Mary in Jerusalem; Ordo Fratrum Domus Hospitalis Sanctae Mariae Teutonicorum in Jerusalem; Teutonic Knights; Teutonic Order; German Order A Roman Catholic military order founded about 1190 in Acre, Israel to aid Christians on their pilgrimages to the Holy Land and to establish hospitals. After the loss of the Holy Land to Muslims, the order continued to be militarily active in Europe where it sometimes defended Christians, but sometimes fought against them for political purposes. It was sometimes used by monarchs and sometimes attacked by them.

The order kept its considerable holdings in Roman Catholic areas of Germany until 1809, when Napoleon Bonaparte ordered its dissolution and the order lost its last secular holdings. The order, however, continued to exist as a charitable and ceremonial body until it was outlawed by outlawed by Adolf Hitler in 1938. It was re-established in 1945 and today operates primarily with charitable aims in Central Europe. They use the post-nominal initials O.T.

Order of Calatrava Originally a Roman Catholic military order formed by St. Raymond of Fitero in Spain in 1164 from Cistercian monks who became warriors to fight against Muslim invaders. By the 15th century, the order had gained a great deal of wealth, money, and power, but in the process became increasingly secularized. In 1540, Pope Paul III commuted their vow of celibacy to one of conjugal fidelity. In 1551, members were authorized by Pope Julius III to make free use of their personal property. In 1652 they took a new vow which was that of defending the doctrine of the Immaculate Conception. Most of the political and military power of the order dissipated by the end of the 15th century, but the last dissolution of the order's property did not occur until 1838.

Order of Canons Regular of Prémontré; Candidus et Canonicus Ordo Praemonstratensis; Norbertines; Premonstratensians; Premonstratensian Order; White Canons; White Canonesses An order of canons regular founded at Prémontré, near Laon in Picardy (northern France), by St. Norbert in the year 1120, which combines the regular canonical life with many of the customs and practices of the Cistercians. They follow a form of the *Rule of St. Augustine* influenced by Cistercian ideas. As each abbey or priory is autonomous, practices and apostolates differ; some are contemplative in character while others are highly active in pastoral ministry. Like most orders they were almost completely devastated by the successive onslaughts of the Reformation, French Revolution, and Napoleon, but then they experienced a revival in the 19th century. As of 2005, the number of monasteries had increased to nearly 100 and spread worldwide with about 1,000 men and 200 women as members.

Though technically called canonesses, women in the order are enclosed religious and commonly called Norbertine nuns. In the Middle Ages there were a few double houses where men and women lived in cloisters next to each other and shared the same church.

The head of the order, the abbot general, resides in Rome, and he is assisted in his duties by the definitors (high council). Members of the order use the post-nominal initials O. Praem.

Order of Cistercians of the Strict Observance; Ordo Cisterciensis Strictioris Observantiae; Trappists (men); Trappistines (women) A Roman Catholic order of monks and nuns founded as a reform community of the Cistercians by Armand de Rancé in 1664 at the monastery of La Trappe in Normandy. Extreme austerity characterizes their discipline. They broke away from the Cistercians in 1892, and became an independent order. "Strict observance" refers to their goal of following closely the *Rule of St. Benedict*.

Trappists do not take a vow of silence but generally speak only when necessary. A unique Trappist sign language has developed to render speaking less necessary. Unlike Benedictines and Cistercians, Trappists are vegetarians, but sometimes eat fish.

Following the admonition of the *Rule of St. Benedict* most Trappist monasteries produce goods such as beer, cheese, and even coffins to provide income for the monastery. There are nearly 170 Trappist monasteries and nunneries in the world, which are home to approximately 2,100 Trappist monks and 1,800 Trappistine nuns. The order uses the post-nominal initials O.C.S.O. • *See also* **Cistercians of the Common Observance**

Order of Contemporary Benedictines A semi-monastic religious order inspired by the *Rule of St. Benedict* and operating under the auspices of the Reformed Catholic Church International. Members live and work in the world and minister as they feel called. The guiding principle is to "be in the world, but not of it." The aim is to enable those who cannot live in a traditional monastery to have a contemplative life in service to God and neighbor. Both male and female members are accepted, and one does not need to be celibate. The community is "respectful of the faith and practices of the Roman Catholic Church as well as faith communities of other Christian traditions and world religions." Their post-nominal initials are O.C.B.

Order of Discalced Augustinians; Discalced Augustinians; Ordo Augustiniensium Discalceatorum A Roman Catholic Augustinian order formed in 1588 in Italy as a reform movement of the Order of St. Augustine. They have their own constitutions, differing from those of the other Augustinians. Their fasts are more rigorous and their other ascetic practices stricter. They wear sandals, not shoes. In an effort to preserve their roots in the hermit life, the Discalced Augustinians practice strict silence and have in every province a house dedicated to recollection, situated in some retired place, to which friars striving after greater perfection can retire in order to practice severe penance, living only on water, bread, fruits, olive oil, and wine. In 2012, they had 220 friars, 139 of whom were priests, and they served at 33 parishes in Italy, Brazil, and the Philippines. They use the post-nominal initials O.A.D.

Order of Discalced Carmelites; Ordo Carmelitarum Discalceatorum; Discalced Carmelites; Barefoot Carmelites; Teresians A Roman Catholic mendicant order devoted to the Virgin Mary rooted in the eremitic tradition of the Desert Fathers and Mothers. The order was founded in 1593 through the efforts of St. Teresa of Avila and St. John of the Cross and is a reform of the Order of the Brothers of the Blessed Virgin Mary.

The nuns are cloistered and strictly contemplative. The friars are contemplative as well but also work in parishes and retreat centers. All follow the Rule of St. Albert as interpreted by the constitution of St. Teresa of Avila. Members wear a brown scapular and use the post-nominal initials O.C.D. • *See also* **Carmelites; Order of the Brothers of the Blessed Virgin Mary; Secular Order of Discalced Carmelites**

Order of Friars Minor; Ordo Fratrum Minorum; Friars of the Strict Observance; Observants; Observantines A mendicant Roman Catholic religious order founded by St. Francis of Assisi in 1209. The original *Rule of St. Francis* approved by the Pope disallowed ownership of property, and required members of the order to beg for food while preaching. The austerity was meant to emulate the life and ministry of Jesus Christ. Franciscans traveled and preached in the streets, while boarding in church properties. The extreme poverty required of members was relaxed in the final revision of the rule in 1223. The degree of observance required of members remained a major source of conflict within the order, resulting in numerous secessions. The Order of Friars Minor, in its current form, is the result of an amalgamation of several smaller orders completed in 1897 by Pope Leo XIII. Despite the tensions caused by this forced union the order grew from 1897 to reach a peak of 26,000 members in the 1960s before declining from the 1970s onwards. In 2013 the order had 2,212 communities and 14,123 members, of whom 9,735 were priests. The order is headed by a minister general. Members of the order use the post-nominal initials O.F.M.

Order of Friars Minor Capuchin; Ordo Fratrum Minorum Capuccinorum; Capuchins An order of friars within the Roman Catholic Church that is among the chief offshoots of the Franciscans. The order arose in 1520 when Matteo da Bascio, an Observant Franciscan friar sought a return to the life of solitude and penance practiced by St. Francis. Although opposed by the Observants, by 1529, they had four houses. The eremitical idea was abandoned, but members lived in extreme austerity, simplicity, and poverty. Members could not even wear shoes or touch money.

The movement struggled with scandals at first. Matteo da Bascio returned to the Observants, another founding member who was the vicar general became insubordinate and was expelled, and the third vicar general became a Calvinist pastor and got married. The order was nearly suppressed for heretical tendencies, but eventually won back the trust of the church authorities and by the end of the 16th century the Capuchins had spread all over Europe. By the end of the 18th century there were approximately 31,000 Capuchin friars. As of 2012, there were 10,286 Capuchins in 106 countries. They wear brown tunics with a unique pointed hood. Shoes and sandals are now allowed.

The worldwide head of the order is called the minister general. Members of the order use the post-nominal initials O.F.M. Cap.

Order of Friars Minor Conventual; Friars Minor Conventual; Ordo Fratrum Minorum Conventualium; Conven-

tual Franciscans; Minorites; Grey Friars; Friars of the Community; Fratres Conventuales; Fratres Minores Conventuales; Relaxati A branch of the mendicant community of Franciscans founded by St. Francis of Assisi in 1209. There was a long-simmering debate within the original Franciscan order between the "Observants," that is those who desired the traditional Franciscan life of solitary meditation in rural areas, and the "Conventuals" those who desired to live together in friaries and work among the urban poor. In 1517, the Franciscans were officially split into the Order of Friars Minor Conventual and the Order of Friars Minor.

The Conventuals follow a modification of the *Rule of St. Francis*. The head of the order is called the master-general. In 2013, the Friars Minor Conventual had 667 communities and 4,289 members, 2,921 of whom were priests. Both priests and brothers are called friars. The order uses the post-nominal initials O.F.M. Conv.

Order of Friars Servants of Mary *see* **Order of the Service of Mary**

Order of Grandmont *see* **Grandmontines**

Order of Hermits of St. Augustine *see* **Order of St. Augustine**

Order of Hospitallers *see* **Knights Hospitaller**

Order of Interbeing *see* **Thich Nhat Hanh**

Order of Knights of the Hospital of St. John of Jerusalem *see* **Knights Hospitaller**

Order of Merced *see* **Order of the Blessed Virgin Mary of Mercy**

Order of Minims; Minims; Minimi; Hermits of the Order of the Minims; Hermits of St. Francis of Assisi An austere Roman Catholic order founded as hermits in 1435 in Italy by St. Francis of Paola. When it was approved by Pope Sixtus IV in 1474, the status was changed from hermits to mendicant friars. Contemplative nuns were admitted in 1495. Members take fourfold vows of poverty, chastity, obedience, and "a Lenten way of life." They also promise perpetual abstinence from all meat and dairy products. The order spread throughout Italy, France, Spain, and Germany in the 15th century, however it was suppressed everywhere but in Italy following the French Revolution. In 2010 it had 46 communities with 174 members, 112 of them priests. Minims wear a black tunic with broad sleeves, hood, and a short scapular. A thick black cord worn around the waist has four knots to symbolize the four vows.

The order uses the post-nominal initials O.M. There is now also a third order of lay people. • *See also* **Francis of Paola, St.**

Order of Our Lady of Mount Olivet *see* **Olivetans**

Order of Our Lady of Ransom *see* **Order of the Blessed Virgin Mary of Mercy**

Order of Preachers; Dominicans; Ordo Praedicatorum; Preaching Friars; Friars Preacher; Black Friars; Jacobins (pejorative) An Roman Catholic order of mendicant monastics that began when St. Dominic formed a convent of women in 1206 in Prouille, France. Soon thereafter he established a community of men. The order was recognized by the papacy in 1216. They follow the *Rule of St. Augustine* and observe corporate as well as individual poverty.

Dominicans are active in preaching, and contemplative in study, prayer, and meditation. Scholarship is integral to the Dominican way of life and members were given a theological training to equip them to combat heresy. The Four Pillars of Dominican Life are community, common prayer, study, and service. In 2013 there were 6,058 Dominican friars, including 4,470 priests. There are currently 24,600 sisters belonging to 150 congregations in 109 countries. Some of the nuns are enclosed contemplatives and some are involved in active ministries. The traditional habit of Dominicans is a white habit with a black cappa (cloak). Dominicans use the post-nominal initials O.P.

Order of St. Anthony; Canons Regular of St. Anthony of Vienne; Canonici Regulares Sancti Antonii; Antonines A Roman Catholic congregation founded in France about 1095 by Gaston of Valloire, to care for those afflicted with ergotism.

At first laymen, they received sanction as a monastic order from Pope Honorius III in 1218. In 1248 they adopted the *Rule of St. Augustine.* They were constituted canons regular by Pope Boniface VIII in 1297. The members of the community wore a black habit with the Greek letter Tau (also known as St. Anthony's cross) in blue, and used the post-nominal initials C.R.S. Ant.

At their peak in the 15th century, they had about 370 hospitals in France, Spain, Italy, Flanders, and Germany and also cared for those with the black plague. The order declined when the connection was made between St. Anthony's Fire and the ergot fungus, and the incidence of the affliction fell sharply. In 1777 the congregation, hugely reduced, was canonically united with the Knights of Malta, then disappeared entirely because of the French Revolution and the secularization of 1803.

Order of St. Augustine; Ordo Fratrum Sancti Augustini; Austin Friars (UK); Augustinian Friars; Augustinian Hermits; Order of Hermits of St. Augustine; Hermits of St. Augustine An order of mendicant friars the basis of which came from the Little Union of 1243 when Pope Innocent IV united different groups of Tuscan hermits under the *Rule of St. Augustine*. In 1256 Pope Alexander IV joined together various other hermit groups from around the world in the Grand Union and ultimately joined them to this existing Augustinian Order.

By the 14th century, the order had about 2,000 monasteries and 30,000 members. There are currently about 2,800 friars in the world, and about 1,500 women in enclosed convents. Most of the friars are ordained, but it is not a requirement. The work of the Augustinians includes teaching, scientific study, cure of souls, and missions.

The order has exempt status, which places it under the direct dependence on the pope without interference from local bishops. They wear a black wool habit with long, wide sleeves, a black leather cincture, and a long pointed capuche (hood). In the summer they may wear a white habit. Their post-nominal initials now used are O.S.A., but formerly were O.E.S.A.

Order of St. Basil the Great; Basilian Order of St. Josaphat; Ordo Sancti Basilii Magni A monastic order of the Greek Catholic Church founded in 1631. Its brothers and priests work primarily with Ukrainian Catholics, but are also present in central and Eastern Europe. Its life is based mainly on the *Rule of St. Basil.* In 1772 the order had over 200 monasteries and over 1000 monks, 6 seminaries, 20 schools and colleges and 4 printing houses.

Under Soviet occupation the order was greatly reduced and survived mainly in the Ukrainian diaspora. It was reestablished in central and eastern Europe after the collapse of the Soviet Union. In 2001 there were over 600 monks, 300 of them in Ukraine.

Order of St. Benedict; Ordo Sancti Benedicti; Benedictines; Black Monks (UK); Black Nuns (UK) An order founded by St. Benedict in 529 in Italy that follows the *Rule of St. Benedict.* There is an abbot primate that heads the Benedictine Confederation, but he has no real power over the individual communities. Throughout the Benedictine Confederation and its subdivisions, independence and autonomy among communities are uniquely valued; too highly for Pope Pius XI, who complained that the largely nominal confederation was "an order without order." The basic unit has always been the individual abbey, rather than the Congregation.

By the 9th century, Benedictinism had become the standard form of monastic life in Western Europe. It is still the predominate form of monasticism in the Western Church. Benedictines take vows of obedience, stability, and conversatio morum (roughly translated as "fidelity to the monastic lifestyle.") Benedictines use the post-nominal initials O.S.B.

During the more than 1,500 years of their existence, the Benedictines have had several reform movements to return to a stricter observance of the *Rule of St. Benedict,* at least as they understood it. Examples include the Camaldolese, the Cistercians, the Trappists (a reform of the Cistercians), and the Sylvestrines.

Following the golden rule of "Ora et Labora" (pray and work), Benedictines ideally devote each day to eight hours of prayer, eight hours of sleep, and eight hours of manual work, sacred reading, or works of charity.

Although primarily associated with the Roman Catholic Church, there are also Benedictines in the Anglican Communion, Lutheran, and Eastern Orthodox churches. • *See also* **Benedict of Nursia, St.;** ***Rule of St. Benedict***

Order of St. Benedict (Orthodox) *see* **Orthodox Community of Saint Benedict**

Order of St. Bruno *see* **Carthusians**

Order of St. Clare *see* **Poor Clares**

Order of St. Damiano *see* **Poor Clares**

Order of St. Jerome; Hieronymites; Jeronymites; Order of St. Jerome, Ordo Sancti Hieronymi; Hermits of St. Jerome An enclosed religious order of Roman Catholic hermit monks and nuns founded in Spain and living according to the *Rule of St. Augustine,* though the inspiration and model of their lives is the 5th century hermit and scholar St. Jerome. The men's order was recognized by Pope Gregory XI in 1373; the women's order was recognized in 1375. The men's order was suppressed by the Spanish government in 1873. At that time, there were 48 monasteries with about a thousand monks. The women's order was allowed to continue. In 1925, the pope re-established the men's order, which is now contemplative. As of 2012 one community of monks exists, that of St. Mary of Parral, and 18 monasteries of nuns (17 in Spain and one in India). Their religious habit is a white tunic with a brown, hooded scapular and a brown mantle. For liturgical services, they wear a brown cowl. Hieronymites use the post-nominal initials O.S.H.

Order of St. John *see* **Knights Hospitaller**

Order of St. Lazarus; Order of St. Lazarus of Jerusalem A Roman Catholic hospitaller and military order founded by crusaders around 1119 at a leper hospital in Jerusalem. In 1255, it was canonically recognized under the *Rule of St. Augustine* by Pope Alexander IV. After the fall of the Kingdom of Jerusalem the order split into two main branches, one in Italy and one in France.

In 1572, the branch in Italy was merged with the Order of St. Maurice under the Royal House of Savoy to form the Order of Saints Maurice and Lazarus, which still exists.

In 1609, King Henry IV of France attempted to link its French section to the Order of Our Lady of Mount Carmel to form the Royal Military and Hospitaller Order of Our Lady of Mount Carmel and St. Lazarus of Jerusalem United. This branch went into decline and ceased to perform its original functions after the French Revolution. It ceased exist by 1830.

Order of St. Paul the First Hermit; Ordo Fratrum Sancti Pauli Primi Eremitae; Pauline Order A monastic order of the Roman Catholic Church, formed in Hungary in 1250. The name refers to the hermit St. Paul of Thebes. After several different rules, the *Rule of St. Augustine* was adopted in 1308. The charism of the order is contemplation of God in solitude, the love of liturgical prayer, a poor and industrious life, and apostolic activity, especially preaching the Word of God and the administration of the sacraments.

At one time, the order had 170 houses scattered throughout Hungary, Poland, Germany, Croatia, and Sweden, but many were suppressed in 1783 because of political problems. At the beginning of the 20th century only two Pauline monasteries remained. By 2012, however, the order had 69 homes, monasteries, and parishes in 16 countries with 516 monks.

The original brown habit was replaced by a white one about 1341. Members have the prerogative of wearing a white zucchetto, but many choose not to. A black cloak is worn during the winter. The order uses the post-nominal initials O.S.P.P.E.

Order of St. Ursula A Roman Catholic religious order that sprang from the Company of St. Ursula, a semi-monastic community, founded in 1535 in Italy, by St. Angela Merici for the education of girls and the care of the poor and sick. In 1572 they became an enclosed religious order under the *Rule of St. Augustine,* in place of Merici's rule. The members of the order historically wore a black dress bound by a leather girdle, a black sleeveless cloak, and a close-fitting headdress with a white veil and a longer black veil, but this now varies. They use the post-nominal initials O.S.U. • *See also* **Company of St. Ursula**

Order of Solomon's Temple *see* **Knights Templar**

Order of the Blessed Virgin Mary of Mercy; Mercedarians; Order of Merced; Order of Our Lady of Ransom; Order of the Blessed Virgin Mary of Mercy; Ordo Beatae Mariae de Mercede Redemptionis Captivorum; Royal, Celestial and Military Order of Our Lady of Mercy and the Redemption of the Captives A Roman Catholic mendicant order of friars and nuns founded in 1218 by St. Peter Nolasco in Barcelona for the redemption of impoverished Christian captives who could not afford the ransom to the freed from the Muslims. Uniquely, its members take a fourth vow to die for another who is in danger of losing their faith. Their post-nominal initials are O. de M.

Order of the Brothers of Our Lady of Bethlehem *see* **Order of Bethlehemite Brothers**

Order of the Brothers of the Blessed Virgin Mary of Mount Carmel; White Friars A Roman Catholic religious order originating in the late 12th century when a group of European Christian pilgrims came to live as hermits on Mount Carmel in Palestine in the tradition of Elijah the prophet and with a special devotion to the Blessed Virgin Mary. They became known as the Brothers of Saint Mary of Mount Carmel. Somewhere between 1206 and 1214 the hermits asked St. Albert, the patriarch of Jerusalem and papal legate, to create a rule for them. The *Rule of St. Albert* consists of 16 articles and demands strict obedience to the prior and abstinence from meat. It was modified somewhat in 1247 as the order became more mendicant than eremitic. As with many other religious orders of the time, problems continued to mount, however, and in 1432 the Pope Eugenius IV mitigated both the *Rule of St. Albert* and the 1247 modification.

This created some tensions and reformers—notably St. Teresa of Avila and St. John of the Cross—sought a return to the eremitic tradition and to the more austere regulations and in 1534, the Order of Discalced Carmelites was formed. While at obvious odds over some points at the time, in modern times their differences are not great. • *See also* **Carmelites; Order of Discalced Carmelites**

Order of the Holy Cross An Episcopal Benedictine monastic order for men founded in New York City by Fr. James Huntington in 1884. Today it has houses in West Park, New York, Toronto, and South Africa. They offer retreats, spiritual counseling, parish work, and in South Africa education. Members use the post-nominal initials O.H.C. Associates of the order use the post-nominal initials A.H.C.

Order of the Immaculate Conception; Conceptionists; Ordo Inmaculatae Conceptionis A contemplative religious order of Roman Catholic nuns. Founded in 1484 at Toledo, Spain, by St. Beatrice of Silva. In 1489, they adopted the Cistercian rule. In 1501 they were united with the San Pedro de las Duenas community under the *Rule of St. Clare.* In 1511 they devised their own rule and were recognized as a separate order. Their habit is white with a white scapular and a blue mantle.

Order of the Most Holy Savior; Bridgettines; Bridgettine Order; Ordo Sanctissimi Salvatoris A Roman Catholic monastic order of Augustinian nuns and monks founded by St. Bridget of Sweden in 1344 and dedicated to devotion to the

Passion of Jesus Christ. Each monastery had a small community of monks to act as chaplains, but it was always under the government of an abbess. The nuns were strictly enclosed at first, emphasizing scholarship and study, but the monks were also preachers and itinerant missionaries. At their high point the order had 80 monasteries, but most were destroyed during the Reformation. Although greatly reduced in size, they are still active, especially in India. The nuns wear a distinctive metal crown with five red stones symbolizing the five wounds of Christ. Monks wear a red cross with a Eucharistic host embroidered on the right breast of their cloak. Bridgettines use the post-nominal initials O.Ss.S.

Order of the Most Holy Trinity; Order of the Most Holy Trinity and of the Captives; Ordo Sanctissimae Trinitatis et Captivorum; Redemptionists; Mathurins; Maturins; Red Friars A small Roman Catholic religious order founded in France in 1198, by St. John de Matha and St. Felix of Valois. Its original purpose was ransoming Christian captives from the Muslims, but their ministry also included hospitality, care of the sick and poor, churches, education, etc. Its members have always had a special devotion to the Holy Trinity. Although considerably smaller than it once was, it now engages in evangelizing non–Christians, assisting immigrants, educating the young, and becoming involved in parishes. In 2015, the order had a membership of 525, mostly priests, but also brothers, nuns, sisters, and a third order. They use the post-nominal initials O.SS.T.

Order of the Most Holy Trinity and of the Captives *see* **Order of the Most Holy Trinity**

Order of the Penance of Jesus Christ *see* **Friars of the Sack**

Order of the Service of Mary; Servites; Ordo Servorum Beatae Mariae Virginis; Order of Friars Servants of Mary One of the five original Roman Catholic religious orders, it was founded in 1233 in Florence, Italy by seven wealthy patricians, now all canonized. The order embraces a membership of friars (priests and brothers), contemplative nuns, active sisters, and lay groups. Its objects are the sanctification of its members, preaching the Gospel, and the propagation of devotion to the Blessed Virgin Mary, with special reference to her sorrows. They follow the *Rule of St. Augustine* and use O.S.M. as their post-nominal initials. The head of the order is called a general.

Order of the Visitation of Holy Mary; Vistadines; Visitation Sisters; Visitation Order; Ordo Visitationis Beatissimae Mariae Virginis; Salesian Sisters; The Visitation of Holy Mary An enclosed Roman Catholic women's order founded in France by St. Francis de Sales and St. Jane Frances de Chantal in 1610 on the example of Mary in her journey of mercy to her cousin Elizabeth. The order welcomes those not able to practice austerities required in other orders, whether from age, delicate constitution, or handicap. Instead of chanting the canonical office in the middle of the night the sisters recite the Little Office of the Blessed Virgin at 8:30 in the evening. There is no perpetual abstinence nor prolonged fast. They stress the hidden, inner virtues of humility, obedience, poverty, even-tempered charity, and patience. The motto of the order is "Live Jesus." There are now about 160 convents around the world. Members use the post-nominal initials V.H.M.

Order of Tiron; Tironensian Order; Grey Monks A reformed Roman Catholic Benedictine monastic order for men founded in France in 1106 by Bernard de Ponthieu (also known as Bernard d'Abbeville). The Tironensians emphasized asceticism, strict observance of the *Rule of St. Benedict,* and manual labor. The order grew rapidly, but the houses in Great Britain were closed by Henry VIII in the dissolution of the monasteries, and in 1627, the remaining houses in France were integrated into the new Benedictine Congregation of St. Maur.

Order of Watchers; Ordre des Veilleurs A community of Protestant hermits founded in 1923 by Wilfred Monod. The hermits live in their own preferred church community and pray three times a day. Like the poustiniks in Russia, they are always available to those in need.

ordifex The monastic who prepares the directives for the ordo calendar for the weekly services, and may also assign liturgical ministers

ordination While in Christianity ordination always means elevation to the priesthood, in Buddhist, Hindu, and Jain monasticism it also means the taking of monastic vows.

In Shin Buddhism, ordination is called affirmation rather than ordination, but it serves the same purpose. In Sri Lanka, Thailand, Cambodia, Laos, Taiwan, and Hong Kong it is possible to have temporary ordination during a retreat or a school break. Men in Thailand typically ordained only before being married; men in Laos and Myanmar (Burma) can traditionally return to the monastery from time to time after being married, provided that they secure permission from their wives. Monastics who have taken life vows can renounce them and return to non-monastic life and even take the vows again later. Depending on the tradition, a person can take them up to three times or seven times in one life, although in some traditions women can never retake them.

Ordo Augustinianorum Recollectorum *see* **Order of Augustinian Recollects**

Ordo Augustiniensium Discalceatorum *see* **Order of Discalced Augustinians**

Ordo Basilianus Sancti Iohannis Baptistae *see* **Basilian Chouerite Order of St. John the Baptist**

Ordo Basilianus Sanctissimi Salvatoris *see* **Basilian Order of the Most Holy Saviour**

Ordo Beatae Mariae de Mercede Redemptionis Captivorum *see* **Order of the Blessed Virgin Mary of Mercy**

Ordo Camaldulensium *see* **Camaldolese Order**

Ordo Canonicorum Regularium Sanctae Crucis *see* **Canons Regular of the Holy Cross of Coimbra**

Ordo Carmelitarum Discalceatorum *see* **Order of Discalced Carmelites**

Ordo Carmelitarum Discalceatorum Saecularis *see* **Secular Order of Discalced Carmelites**

Ordo Carmelitarum Discalceatorum Saecularis Ordo Cartusiensis *see* **Carthusians**

Ordo Cartuensis *see* **Order of St. Bruno**

Ordo Cisterciensis *see* **Cistercians of the Common Observance**

Ordo Cisterciensis Strictioris Observantiae *see* **Order of Cistercians of the Strict Observance**

Ordo Franciscanus Saecularis *see* **Third Order Secular of St. Francis**

Ordo Fratrum Bethlemitarum *see* **Order of Bethlehemite Brothers**

Ordo Fratrum Minorum *see* **Order of Friars Minor**

Ordo Fratrum Minorum Capuccinorum *see* **Order Friars Minor Capuchin**

Ordo Fratrum Minorum Conventualium *see* **Order of Friars Minor Conventual**

Ordo Fratrum Sancti Augustini *see* **Order of St. Augustine**

Ordo Fratrum Sancti Pauli Primi Eremitae *see* **Order of St. Paul the First Hermit**

Ordo Hospitalarius S. Ioannis de Deo *see* **Hospitaller Order of the Brothers of St. John of God**

Ordo Inmaculatae Conceptionis *see* **Order of the Immaculate Conception**

Ordo Maronita Beatae Mariae Virginis Aleppians *see* **Mariamite Maronite Order**

Ordo Maronita Mariamita *see* **Mariamite Maronite Order**

Ordo Militaris Crucigerorum cum Rubea Stella *see* **Knights of the Cross with the Red Star**

Ordo Praedicatorum *see* **Dominicans**

Ordo Sancti Basilii Magni *see* **Order of St. Basil the Great**

Ordo Sancti Benedicti *see* **Order of St. Benedict**

Ordo Sancti Hieronymi *see* **Order of St. Jerome**

Ordo Sanctissimae Trinitatis et Captivorum *see* **Order of the Most Holy Trinity**

Ordo Sanctissimi Salvatoris *see* **Order of the Most Holy Savior**

Ordo Servorum Beatae Mariae Virginis *see* **Order of the Service of Mary**

Ordo Visitationis Beatissimae Mariae Virginis *see* **Order of the Visitation of Holy Mary**

Ordre Basilien Chouerite de St. Jean Baptiste *see* **Basilian Chouerite Order of St. John the Baptist**

Ordre Basilien Salvatorien *see* **Basilian Order of the Most Holy Saviour**

Ordre des Veilleurs *see* **Order of Watchers**

Ordre Libanais Maronite *see* **Lebanese Maronite Order**

Orthodox Community of St. Benedict; Order of St. Benedict (Orthodox) An informal group of Orthodox Church monastics who live according to the *Rule of St. Benedict*. There were efforts in the 19th century to restore the Western Rite to the Orthodox Church and this encouraged the reviving of the Benedictine tradition in the 20th century.

Orthros In the Eastern Church, the name for Lauds, the daybreak service

oryoki; ōryōki; patra (Sanskrit) A set of nested bowls and other eating utensils for the personal use of Buddhist monks. The cantaloupe-sized bundle consists of three black plastic nesting bowls, two chopsticks, a wooden spoon, a small rubber spatula, a gray napkin, and a wiping cloth, all of which are wrapped tidily in a gray cloth with a topknot resembling a lotus blossom. The term is mostly used in the Sōtō-shū sect of Japanese Zen Buddhism. Ōryōki also refers to a meditative form of eating using these utensils that originated in Japan and emphasizes mindfulness awareness practice by abiding to a strict order of precise movements. • *See also* **jihatsu**

O.S.A. The post-nominal initials used by the Order of St. Augustine

O.S.B. The post-nominal initials used by the Order of St. Benedict

O.S.B. Cam.; O. Camald. The post-nominal initials used by the Camaldolese

O.S.B. Cel. The post nominal initials used by the Celestines

O.S.B. Cn The post-nominal initials of the Canons of the Order of St. Benedict

O.S.C. The post-nominal initials used by the Order of St. Clare; the post-nominal initials of the Canons Regular of the Order of the Holy Cross

O.S.C. Cap. The post-nominal initials used by the Capuchin Poor Clares

O.S.F.C.; O.M. Cap.; O.F.M. Cap. The post-nominal initials used by the Friars Minor Capuchin

O.S.H. The post-nominal initials of the Order of St. Jerome

oshiku The 14th of each month and the last day of every month, when Japanese Zen Buddhist monks sleep late, shave heads, do a major cleaning, and, during the afternoon, rest

osho; oshō (Japanese), he shang (Chinese) A high-ranking or highly virtuous Buddhist monk

O.S.M. The post-nominal initials used by the Order of the Service of Mary

O.S.P.P.E. The post-nominal initials of the Order of St. Paul the First Hermit

Ossaioi ***see*** **Essenes**

O.Ss.S. The post-nominal initials of the Order of the Most Holy Savior

O.SS.T. The post-nominal initials of the Order of the Most Holy Trinity

ostiarios ***see*** **porter**

O.T. The post-nominal initials of the Order of Brothers of the German House of St. Mary in Jerusalem

outer cassock; rasson (Greek); exorason (Greek); mandorrason (Greek); riasa (Russian); ryasa (Russian, Ukrainian); raso (Byzantine) A voluminous garment worn by worn over the inner cassock by monastics of the Eastern Church as their regular outerwear. The Greek version tends to be somewhat lighter weight and more fully cut than the Russian version. In form the outer cassock is similar to the cuculla of the Western Church.

outer enclosure ***see*** **enclosure**

outer parlor ***see*** **parlor**

~P~

pabbajja; pabbajjā (Pali); pravrajya (Sanskrit); shinbyu (Burmese); shinpyu (Burmese); going forth When a layperson leaves home to live the life of a

Buddhist renunciate among a community of monastics. This generally involves preliminary ordination as a novice. After a period of time, or when the novice reaches 20 years of age, they can be considered for the upasampada (higher ordination) whereby the novice becomes a monk or nun. In some traditional Theravada countries, such as Myanmar (Burma), boys undergo pabbajja at the age of puberty. In Mahayana countries such as China and Japan, the pabbajja is preceded by a probationary period.

pabbijjaniya-kamma The legal act of expulsion from a Buddhist monastic dwelling

Pachomius the Great, St. (292–348) An Egyptian monk considered the founder of Christian cenobitic monasticism. Legend has it that at age 21 he was impressed into the Roman army and Christians brought him food which made deep impression on him. He converted to Christianity in 314. In 317, he set out to lead the life of a hermit near St. Anthony of Egypt. Between 318 and 323 more than 100 monks settled nearby and Pachomius brought them into a formal organization which became the first cenobitic community where they lived together under his leadership. The monks called him *abba*—which means *father* in Hebrew—and this is where the term *abbot* derives from.

St. Athanasius wished to ordain him as a priest in 333, but Pachomius ran away. By the time of his death there were eight monasteries and several hundred monks following his cenobitic model.

padre A Christian priest or monk—used in Italy, Spain, Portugal, and Latin America

Paisius Velichkovsky, St. (1722–1794) A Ukrainian Eastern Orthodox monk, translator, and theologian who helped spread hesychasm in the Slavic world. His father, Ivan, was a priest in the city cathedral. His grandfather was the poet Ivan Velichkovsky. In 1735, he was sent to study at the Kiev Theological Academy.

In 1741, he became a rassophore (one rank above a novice) monk. In 1746, at age 24, he moved to Mount Athos in Greece where he spent the four years in solitary prayer and extreme poverty. In 1750, he was tonsured him as a lesser schema monk. He then gave up the solitary life and became the leader of a hesychastic skete. In 1758 he was ordained a priest. He stayed on Mt. Athos for 17 years and attracted many disciples.

In 1764, at age 42, Prince Grigore III Ghica asked him to come Moldavia to revive monastic life there. Starting with 64 monks his monastery there grew to 700. In 1790 he received the great schema and became an archimandrite (senior abbot) and vicar to the Metropolitan of Moldavia. In 1793, his Slavonic translation of the *Philokalia*, was published in Russia.

Palamas, Gregory, St. (ca. 1296–1357 or 1359) A Byzantine Orthodox monk of Mt. Athos, born in Constantinople, who became a prominent theologian and ecclesiastical figure of the late Byzantine period. His father, Constantine, was a courtier of the Byzantine emperor Andronikos II Palaiologos, but died when Gregory was still young. The emperor himself took part in the raising and education of the fatherless boy and hoped that the gifted Gregory would devote himself to government service, but Gregory, then barely 20 years old, withdrew to Mount Athos in the year 1316, and became a monk and teacher of mental prayer known as "prayer of the heart" or hesychasm.

In 1326, because of the threat of Turkish invasions, he retreated to the defended city of Thessalonika, where he was ordained a priest and ministered to the public and also founded a small community of hermits. He served briefly as the abbot of the Esphigmenou Monastery but was forced to resign in 1335 due to discontent with the austerity of his regime.

Because of a controversy over hesychasm, he was excommunicated and jailed in 1344, but released 1347 and became metropolitan of Thessalonika. The people of Thessalonika did not at first accept him, and it was 1350 before that he was able to assume the episcopal chair.

In 1354, during a voyage to Constantinople, he was imprisoned for a year by Turkish pirates until he was ransomed and returned to Thessalonika for the last three years of his life.

panchen bogd see panchen lama

panchen lama A Tibetan Buddhist monk with authority second only to the dalai lama. Lobsang Chökyi Gyaltsen, in 1645 was the first panchen lama to be accorded this title during his lifetime. The title at that time was panchen bogd. He was the tutor and a close ally of the 5th dalai lama. The panchen lama traditionally lived in Tashilhunpo Monastery in Shigatse. From the name of this monastery, westerners sometimes referred to the panchen lama as the tashi-lama, tesho-lama, or teshu-lama.

The dalai and panchen lamas are closely connected, and the panchen lama is part of the process by which a new dalai lama is chosen. The identity of the current, 11th panchen lama is controversial. Under Chinese official support, Chökyi Gyalpo currently acts as the 11th panchen lama in Tibet, but he has been rejected abroad. The Chinese government has been accused of kidnapping the panchen lama recognized by the Tibetan Government in Exile, Gedhun Choekyi Nyima. China annexed Tibet in 1951, and now claims authority to name both panchen and dalai lamas. This is rejected by most Tibetans.

Paolo Consiglieri *see* **Theatines**

paradise An open space within a monastery or adjoining a church, as the space within a cloister, the open court before a basilica, etc.

parakellarios *see* **subcellarer**

parakellarites *see* **subcellarer**

paraman *see* **paramand**

paramand; paramandyas (Greek); paraman (Church Slavonic) A piece of black cloth, approximately 5 inches square which is attached by ribbons to a wooden cross. It is first given to stavrophores (lesser schema) in the Orthodox Church and they retain it if elevated to great schema monastics. The cloth is embroidered with a cross and the instruments of the Passion. The wooden cross is worn over the chest, then the ribbons pass over and under the arms, symbolic of the yoke of Christ, and hold the cloth centered on the back.

paramandyas *see* **paramand**

parchmenter; percaminarius One who made parchment. Before the 13th century most parchment was made by monasteries, but with the rise of universities the trade moved to the laity.

parlor; locutorium; locutory; auditorium; day room; common house; speke house A room in a monastery where the rule of silence is relaxed to allow necessary conversation as for greeting visitors, meeting with merchants and tradesmen, teaching novices, etc. There may be an outer parlor used for meetings with outsiders, and an inner parlor reserved for members of the community.

parlor window A small window in an anchorite's cell facing outside that was used to speak with visitors • *see also* **communion window; fenestra parvula; hagioscope**

paroikonomos In the Eastern Church, the deputy steward at a monastery

paruchia In the early Celtic Church, the area and the churches over which a monastery had spiritual jurisdiction

Patimokkha; Prātimokṣa (Sanskrit) The basic code of Buddhist monastic discipline contained in the *Vinaya*. The *Vinaya Piṭaka,* written in Pali, has 227 major rules for monks and 311 major rules for nuns. Tibetan Buddhists in Tibet, Bhutan, Mongolia, Nepal, and other places follow the *Mūlasarvāstivāda Vinaya,* which has 253 rules for the monks and 364 for nuns. Buddhists in China, Korea, Taiwan, and Vietnam follow the *Dharmaguptaka Vinaya,* which has 250 rules for monks and 348 for nuns. Saicho, the founder of the Japanese school of Tendai reduced the number of *Vinaya* rules down to about 60 based on the Bodhisattva Precepts.

patisaraniya kamma Legal reconciliation when a Buddhist monk or nun asks forgiveness for a fault

patra *see* **oryoki**

Paul of Thebes, St. (ca. 227–ca. 341); Paul the Anchorite An Egyptian regarded as the first Christian anchorite. At the age of 16, he fled to the desert to avoid persecution and there lived alone in a cave from age 16 to the time of his death at the age of 116. It was said that St. Anthony the Great heard of him and had one visit with him.

Paul the Anchorite *see* **Paul of Thebes**

Pauline Order *see* **Order of St. Paul the First Hermit**

peculiar A English parish church owned by a monastery located outside the diocese where the church was, so it was exempt from the supervision of the local bishop. The concept began in Anglo-Saxon times, but most peculiars were done away with in the 19th century and only a few remain.

peculium A personal allowance for monastics in the Western Church. At first this was only small gifts in cash to be given to the poor, but later it expanded to include spices, medicines, and holiday gifts. While the gift was always small, it tended to have a demoralizing effect and reformers tried to get rid of it, but it did finally not disappear until the 16th century.

penitentiary A small building in a monastery where penitents confessed

pera *see* **melote**

percaminarius *see* **parchmenter**

perpetual adoration In some Roman Catholic orders of nuns the perpetual adoration of the Blessed Sacrament in addition to the usual complete daily liturgical celebration of the Eucharist and

Daily Office. It usually involves having at least two members of the monastic community always being present in prayerful, silent contemplation of the Blessed Sacrament exposed to view in a monstrance on the altar of the principal chapel.

perpetual prayer; continual prayer; laus perrenis The Christian practice of continuous prayer carried out by a group. It was inaugurated by the Eastern Orthodox Archimandrite Alexander (died about 430), the founder of the monastic Acoemetae or "vigil-keepers." It was imported to Western Europe at St. Maurice's Abbey in Switzerland, where it was carried on, day and night, by several choirs, who succeeded each other in the recitation of the Daily Office, so that prayer went on without cessation. The practice has since spread worldwide.

perpetual vows ***see*** **solemn vows**

Peter Damian, St. (ca. 1007–ca. 1072) Reforming Italian Benedictine monk, cardinal, and writer. A brilliant student, he became a respected teacher by the time he was 25. About 1035, however he became a monk at the hermitage of Fonte Avellana and by 1043 became the prior, remaining so until his death. In his zeal for reform, Peter introduced a more severe discipline—including the practice of flagellation—into the house, which, attained celebrity and became a model for other foundations, even the prominent abbey of Monte Cassino. About 1050, during the pontificate of Pope Leo IX, he wrote a scathing treatise on the vices of the clergy, including sexual abuse of minors and actions by church superiors to hide the crimes. When Frédéric, the Abbot of Monte Cassino, was elected pope as Stephen IX, he made Peter Cardinal Bishop of Ostia despite his protestations. As cardinal, Peter continued to work for reform of the Church.

He was named a Doctor of the Church in 1828.

Peter of Alcantara, St. (1499–1562) Spanish Franciscan friar, founder of the Alcantarine Franciscans, and advocate of the Counter-Reformation. He became a Franciscan friar of the Stricter Observance in 1515. At the age of 22, he was sent to found a new community at Badajoz. He was ordained a priest in 1524, and the following year was appointed guardian of the friary of St. Mary of the Angels at Robredillo, Old Castile. In 1538 Peter was made minister provincial of the Franciscan province of St. Gabriel of Estremadura but resigned when his plans to enforce severe rules were opposed. He then retired to a life of eremitical solitude in Portugal.

Returning to Spain in 1553 he founded some Conventual friaries. In 1556 they were made a semi-autonomous body, with Peter as commissary (superior), and in 1561 they were made a religious province under the title of St. Joseph. Undiscouraged by the opposition to the earlier opposition to his reforms at the province of St. Gabriel, Peter again drew up severe regulations, but this time they met with great success in both Spain and Portugal.

Peter was canonized by Pope Clement IX in 1669.

Peter of St. Joseph Betancur ***see*** **Order of Bethlehemite Brothers**

phakiolion ***see*** **magoulikion**

phalabhajaka An official in charge of the distribution of fruit in a Theravedin Buddhist monastery

Philokalia A collection of texts written between the 4th and 15th centuries for the guidance of monks in the practice of hesychasm. The collection was compiled in the 18th century by St. Nikodemos of the Holy Mountain and St. Makarios of Corinth. The book is a principal spiritual text for all the Eastern Orthodox Churches and is thought by some to . have exercised an influence second only to the Bible in the Orthodox Church.

Nikodemos described the collection as "a mystical school of inward prayer" which could be used to cultivate the inner life and to "attain the measure of the stature of the fullness of Christ." • *See also* **hesychasm**

phlebotomy *see* **bloodletting**

phongyibyan; phongyibyan pwe; pongyibyan The ceremonial cremation of high-ranking Burmese Buddhist monks, used especially for those in the Thudhamma Nikaya order.

phra Venerable—used as a prefix to the name of a Thai Buddhist monk

Phra Dharmakosacarya *see* **Buddhadasa Bhikkhu**

picchi A broom-like object, made from fallen peacock feathers carried by Digambara Jain monks and nuns to sweep the ground ahead of them or before sitting down to avoid inadvertently crushing small insects • *see also* **ogho; rajoharan**

pidryasnyk *see* **inner cassock**

Pied Friars *see* **Friars of the Blessed Mary**

Pilgrimage of Grace In the reign of England's Henry VIII, the first suppression of religious houses—those with an annual income under £200—sparked off uprisings in the north known as the Pilgrimage of Grace. Beginning in Lincolnshire the insurgence soon spread to Yorkshire where it was led by a local barrister, Robert Aske, who was later hanged at York for his actions.

A number of monastics joined the rebels, though not all were willing participants. Abbot Sedbar of Jervaulx was literally dragged off to join the insurgents, and then was hanged by the authorities at Tyburn in 1537 for his involvement.

pindapat A Thai Buddhist monk's morning alms round

Pinzochera *see* **Beguine**

Pirmin, St. (ca. 700–753); Pirminius A French monk, missionary, and writer who in 718 was made abbot of Quortolodora Monastery in Antwerp. He then helped rebuild Disentis Abbey in Switzerland. In 724, he founded Mittelzell Abbey at Reichenau Island in Germany and became its abbot. For political reasons he was later banished to Alsace.

Pirmin's missionary work mainly took place in Alsace and the upper area of the Rhine and Danube rivers where he founded or reformed many monasteries. His most important book is *Dicta Abbatis Pirminii, de Singulis Libris Canonicis Scarapsus* (*Words of Abbot Pirminius, Extracts from the Single Canonical Books*), which collects quotations from Church Fathers and scriptures. Written between 710–724, it contains the earliest appearance of the present text of the Apostles' Creed.

Pirminius *see* **Pirmin, St.**

pisalis *see* **warming house**

piscina A fish-pond attached to a monastery; a large wash basin used in monasteries

pittance An extra dish of fish or eggs that is eaten in addition to the standard dishes specified by the rule under which the community lives—usually served once a day at most; also, an extra serving of food, money, or wine, received by each monastic to celebrate a festive occasion

pittancer A monastic official charged with providing pittances to the community

plumbarium ***see*** **dovecot**

podriasnik; podryásnik ***see*** **inner cassock**

podryasnik ***see*** **podriasnik**

polystavrion In the Eastern church, a cord with a number of small crosses plaited into it. It forms a forms a yoke around a monk or nun and serves to hold the analavos (scapular) in place.

Poor Clares; Order of St. Clare; Poor Ladies; Poor Enclosed Nuns; Order of St. Damiano, Minoresses; Franciscan Clarist Order; Second Order of St. Francis; Urbanist Poor Clares A Franciscan contemplative order of women founded by St. Clare, under the guidance of St. Francis of Assisi in 1212. The movement quickly spread, though in a somewhat disorganized fashion.

Ugolino, Cardinal Bishop of Ostia (the future Pope Gregory IX), was given the task of preparing a formal rule. *Ugolino's Rule,* originally based on the *Rule of St. Benedict,* was amended in 1263 to allow for the communal ownership of property and was adopted by a growing number of monasteries across Europe. Communities adopting this less rigorous rule came to be known as the Order of St. Clare (O.S.C.) or the Urbanist Poor Clares.

Clare resisted *Ugolino's Rule,* since it did not closely enough follow the ideal of complete poverty advocated by Francis. In 1253, she managed to obtain a papal bull establishing a rule of her own, more closely following that of the friars, which forbade the possession of property either individually or as a community. Originally applying only to Clare's community at San Damiano, this rule was also adopted by many other monasteries. Communities that followed this stricter rule were fewer in number than the followers of the rule formulated by Cardinal Ugolino, and became known simply as Poor Clares or Primitives. They use the post-nominal initials P.C.

The extreme poverty required of members was relaxed in final revision of the *Rule of St. Clare* in 1253, but the degree of observance required of members remained a major source of conflict within the order, resulting in numerous secessions. Other branches established since that time, which operate under their own unique constitutions, are the Colettine Poor Clares (P.C.C.) founded 1410, the Capuchin Poor Clares (O.S.C. Cap.) founded 1538 and the Poor Clares of Perpetual Adoration (P.C.P.A.) founded in 1854.

As of 2011 there were over 20,000 Poor Clare nuns in over 75 countries throughout the world. They follow several different observances and are organized into federations. • *See also* **Clare of Assisi, St.; *Ugolino's Rule***

Poor Clares of Perpetual Adoration A branch of the Poor Clares founded in France in 1854 by Marie Claire Bouillevaux. It is a contemplative order of nuns in the Franciscan tradition. They are dedicated to the perpetual adoration of the Blessed Sacrament. They use the post-nominal initials P.C.P.A.

Poor Enclosed Nuns *see* **Poor Clares**

Poor Fellow-Soldiers of Christ and of the Temple of Solomon *see* **Knights Templar**

Poor Knights of Christ *see* **Knights Templar**

Poor Ladies *see* **Poor Clares**

Poresigh, Abram Atar *see* **Antonians**

porter; gatekeeper; doorkeeper; ostiarios (Greek Orthodox); pyloros (Greek Orthodox); thyroros (Greek Orthodox) An official who controls entrance by visitors into a religious house. In large houses there might be several porters with a chief porter in charge. It was common to have a kitchen porter since many suppliers had cause to enter and the poor also came begging food. A friar who acts as the porter at the gate of a monastery can be called a curtal friar.

posadha *see* **uposatha**

poslushnik *see* **novice**

possessors In the 16th century Russian Orthodox Church, those who were in favor of monastic landownership. They were led by led by Joseph of Volokolamsk and later by Archbishop Theodosius II of Novgorod and were opposed by the non-possessors. The possessors finally prevailed at the Stoglav Council in 1551. • *See also* **non-possessors**

post-nominal initials Initials indicating the identity of the religious order in the Western Church to which a person belongs—such as O.S.B. for the Order of St. Benedict or O.F.M for the Order of Friars Minor

postulancy; probation The period between a postulant's request to join a community and reception into the novitiate. It is generally a year.

postulant A candidate for admission to a religious order, who had not yet been accepted as a novice

poulter A monastic charged with supplying poultry to the monastery

poustinia A small sparsely furnished hermitage where one goes to pray and fast alone in the presence of God. It usually has a bed, a table and chair, a cross, and a Bible. The word *poustinia* has its origin in the Russian word for desert. One called to live permanently in a poustinia is called a poustinik.

Originally a Russian Orthodox tradition, it was introduced to Western Christians by Catherine Doherty in her book *Poustinia: Christian Spirituality of the East for Western Man,* first published in 1975.

poustinik One called by God to live life in the desert (poustinia), alone with God in the service of humanity through prayer, fasting, and availability to those who might call upon him or her. They were not uncommon in Russia before the Soviet suppression of the Church in the early 20th century.

Historically, one who felt the call to be a poustinik asked for the blessing of their spiritual director, then asked permission of the village elders.

Poustiniks are like hermits in that they live alone and are free to move about outside their dwelling, on the other hand they are like anchorites in that they are wedded to a particular place.

Praeceptor Germaniae A nickname of Rabanus Maurus Magnentius

praepositus ***see*** **provost**

prandium At one time, the main, and usually the first meal of the monastic day, which was generally taken at noon

Pratimoksa ***see*** **Patimokkha**

pratyekabuddha Legendary hermits said to achieve enlightenment on their own, without the use of teachers or guides, according to some Buddhist traditions by contemplating the principle of dependent origination. They are said to arise only in ages where there is no Buddha and the Buddhist teachings are lost.

pravarana (Pali); jishi (Japanese) A Theravada Buddhist ceremony in which monks and nuns at the end of their annual three-month rainy season retreat (Vassa) confess and repent their monastic errors and improper acts

pravrajya ***see*** **pabbajja**

Preaching Friars ***see*** **Dominicans**

precentor A monastic charged with directing choral liturgical celebrations, maintaining the mortuary roll, and with overseeing the library and scriptorium

precept master ***see*** **acarya**

preceptor The resident knight or sergeant in charge of a preceptory of a military order

preceptory A monastery of a military order—used particularly to refer to establishments of the Knights Templar

precinct The space around a monastery enclosed by walls, a ditch, or a bank

prelate Usually, one in charge of a diocese, but occasionally the superior of a monastic community

Premonstratensians ***see*** **Order of Canons Regular of Prémontré**

Presbyterian Church monasticism The Community of the Sisterhood Emmanuel was founded in 1973 in Cameroon by Mother Marie. It has ten solemnly consecrated sisters, four in simple vows and a handful of others in formation. One of their charisms is ecumenism. The Sisterhood Emmanuel remains the only Presbyterian monastery.

president-general The head of the English Benedictine Congregation

Prime; First Hour Pronounced "preem." The Daily Office usually read immediately after Lauds. First established around 382. It is now largely suppressed by the Roman Catholic Church, but still common in the Eastern Church. Prime consists mostly of psalms. A martyrology was traditionally read at Prime.

Primitives ***see*** **Poor Clares**

prior The head of a priory or the second-in command in an abbey. In the *Rule of St. Benedict*, the term appears several times, referring to any superior, whether an abbot, provost, dean, etc. In other old monastic rules the term is used in the same generic sense.

With the Cluniac reforms, the term received a specific meaning; it supplanted the provost or dean (praepositus), spoken of in the *Rule of St. Benedict*. The example of the Cluniac congregations was gradually followed by all Benedictine monasteries, as well as by the

Camaldolese, Vallombrosians, Cistercians, Hirsau congregations, and other offshoots of the Benedictine Order.

The term is also used by various mendicant orders, such as the Carmelites and the Dominicans • *see also* **warden of the order**

prior claustralis *see* **claustral prior**

prior conventualis *see* **conventual prior**

prior general The head of certain orders, such as the Carmelite Order, Camaldolese Order, Carthusian Order, and the Hospitaller Order of the Brothers of St. John of God

prior major; greater prior In the Middle Ages, at Cluny and some other very large monasteries, a prior who preceded the claustral prior in dignity and, besides assisting the abbot in the government of the monastery, had some delegated jurisdiction over external dependencies of the abbey

prior of the cloisters *see* **claustral prior**

prior provincial The regional superior of certain orders, such as the Dominicans and Carmelite friars

prioral Pertaining to a priorate

priorate; priorship The dignity, office, or government, of a prior

prioress; sister prior Depending on the order, the head of a women's religious community, or the second in in rank after an abbess; also a woman who is the second in charge of a double monastery

priorship *see* **priorate**

priory; cell; obedience A religious house presided over by a prior or prioress; sometimes an offshoot of, and subordinate to, an abbey

prisons Some monastic houses in Europe had their own prisons and even torture chambers (a common civilian criminal feature in the Middle Ages) for serious offenders in the community. Punishments varied, sometimes inmates were released for services, but others were kept shackled to a staple in the floor, and some were given solitary confinement for a year in a cell.

A detention cell at the Benedictine Durham monastery in England was called the lynghouse. Imprisonment could be sitting for a year in chains with the malefactor not permitted to speak to anyone but the abbot who let food down on a cord. A similar Benedictine monastic prison at Ely was called helle, appropriately enough. It should be noted, that monastic prisons were used in other orders besides the Benedictines.

pristrinum *see* **bakehouse**

privy *see* **rere-dorter**

probation *see* **postulancy**

procession The ordered entry of a monastic community into the church. Some communities do not process in for the Little Hours.

procuration The fee paid by a monastery to the official visitor

professed Having taken vows in a monastic order, or a person who has done so

profession The vows by which one becomes a member of a monastic or religious community. Full profession is the taking of solemn or life vows. Simple or junior profession is the taking of simple or temporary vows. Profession follows successful completion of the novitiate. In Benedictine profession, the vows are stability, obedience, and conversatio morum. In most other communities they are poverty, chastity, and obedience. • *See also* **conversatio morum**

profession ring A ring sometimes worn by monastics after they have taken solemn vows

prohegumen In the Orthodox Church, a hegumen who has resigned

pronoetes In the Eastern Orthodox Church, a guardian of monastery property

proprietary A monk or nun who had kept goods and effects for themselves despite their renunciation of all their possessions at the time of profession

proprietary church A church in private ownership, the property of a landlord or of a monastery—the condition of most rural churches in the early Middle Ages

protohegumen In the Greek Catholic Church, the head of all monasteries in a certain area

protopresbyteros In the Eastern Church, a head of the priests of a church or monastery

protos In the Eastern Church, the head of a group of monasteries and hermitages

province A geographic units of administration within a monastic order

provincial A monastic superior, who, under the general of their order, has the direction of all the religious houses of the same fraternity in a given province of the order; of, like, or relating to a province of a religious order

provisor ***see*** **cantor**

provost; praepositus (Latin) The term once used for an abbot in the *Rule of St. Augustine*; in some religious orders, especially those under the patronage of royalty or nobility, the ecclesial management of the order is placed under the jurisdiction of a provost; in Benedictine monasteries it was once applied to the immediate subordinate to the abbot, although the holder of this position is now more commonly called a prior

Pseudo-Apostles ***see*** **Apostolic Brethren**

pseudomonastic Falsely monastic

psychika In the Eastern Church, gifts made to monasteries in exchange for commemoration of the donors and/or their relatives after death

pudding house A building or chamber near at hand to the main kitchen wherein puddings and pastries were made and pudding wives could work

pudding wife A married female servant chosen by the larderer and paid to help in the kitchen with the making of puddings and pastries and other foods deemed to need a feminine touch. They worked in the pudding house as opposed to the main kitchen.

puer oblatus ***see*** **child oblate**

puja; pūjā The devotional observances that are conducted at Buddhist monasteries daily (morning and evening), on uposatha (monthly meeting) days, or on other special occasions

pulpitum A partition or screen separating the community's choir stalls from the nave of the church

Pure Rules; Cheonggyu Rules for daily life and practices to be observed by Zen Buddhist monastics in monasteries

pyloros ***see*** **porter**

~Q~

quasimonastic Similar to, but not exactly the same as traditional monasticism, as the claswyr or maechi. Semi-monastic is half monastic, such as a third order.

questarius In Western Christian mendicant orders, the monk who collected funds for the monastery

quire *see* **choir**

~R~

Rabanus Maurus Magnentius (ca. 780–856); Rhabanus; Hrabanus A Frankish Roman Catholic Benedictine abbot, theologian, teacher, writer, hymnodist, and archbishop. He wrote an encyclopedia, biblical commentaries, and treatises on education and grammar. One of the outstanding teachers and writers of his time, he was called "Praeceptor Germaniae" ("Teacher of Germany.")

As a monk in the Benedictine Abbey of Fulda in Hesse, he was ordained a deacon in 801. In 803 he was put in charge of the abbey school and made it a preeminent center of scholarship and book production. In 814 he was ordained a priest. In 822, he became the abbot at Fulda and did well but resigned in 842 to have more time for study and prayer. In 847, however, he was made Archbishop of Mainz.

Radha Charan Mahasthabir *see* **Mahastabair Nikaya**

rajoharan A broom-like object made from dense, thick thread strands carried by Jain Śvētāmbara monastics to sweep the ground ahead of them or before sitting down to avoid inadvertently crushing small insects. This replaces the ogho (a small broom made of wool) given to initiates.

rakusu The smallest style of kasaya (robe), shaped like a bib and worn around the neck by Buddhist monks, nuns, and lay persons—it is received during the jukai (receiving of certain Buddhist precepts) ceremony and is symbolic of the Buddha's patched robe.

Rama IV *see* **Mongkut**

Ramakrishna Order A Hindu reform monastic organization inspired by Sri Ramakrishna (1936–1886) and founded by his disciple Swami Vivekananda (1886–1902) in 1897. The Ramakrishna Order consists of the Ramakrishna Mission and the Ramakrishna Math monastery. There are over 166 centers located everywhere but Australia. The mission provides aid in political conflicts and natural disasters.

Candidates for monastic life are aspirants for a year, then have four years of formation before taking simple vows of celibacy, renunciation, and service. After another four years they may be solemnly professed and given ocher robes. Both monastics and missioners are known for their religious tolerance.

Rancé, Armand Jean le Bouthillier *see* **de Rancé, Armand Jean le Bouthillier**

raso *see* **outer cassock**

rasophoros *see* **rassophore**

rasso *see* **outer cassock**

rassophore; rasophoros (Church Slavonic) An Orthodox monastic ranking above a novice and below a stavrophore. When novices become rassophores they are tonsured and receive the outer cassock. In the Greek tradition they are given a kalimavkion (brimless hat), which is covered with a veil called an epanokalimavkion. In the Russian tradition these two items are stitched together and collectively called a klobuk. If they have not previously received it, a leather belt is fastened around their waist. Their habit is usually black, signifying that they are now dead to the world, and they receive a new name. Although rassophores do not make formal vows, they are still morally obligated to continue in the monastic estate for the rest of their lives. Some will remain rassophores permanently without going on to the higher degrees.

In the Coptic Church there are only two degrees of professed monks, the first corresponding to the rassophore combined with the stavrophore and the second corresponding to the great schema.

rasura *see* **shaving**

Raymond of Fitero, St. *see* **Order of Calatrava**

RB A commonly used abbreviation for the *Rule of St. Benedict*

reader in frater The monastic who reads during meals

reclinatoria Crutches used for support by ill or elderly monastics in the 11th and 12th centuries when it was forbidden to sit down in church. • *See also* **leaning staff**

recluse see anchorite

Recollects A reform branch of Franciscans (Order of Friars Minor) established at the end of the 16th century in France for devotion to prayer, penance, and spiritual reflection. They are best known for their presence as missionaries in various parts of the world, most notably in early Canada. Many were also chaplains in the French army.

The friars wore gray habits with pointed hoods, and used the post-nominal initials O.F.M. Rec. or O.M.R. The French Recollects had 11 provinces with 2,534 friars by the late 18th century, but they were suppressed during the French Revolution. The order was dissolved in 1897 by Pope Leo XIII and integrated into the general Franciscan order.

rector In medieval canon law the incumbent of a parish entitled to receive the tithe. If a parish church was appropriated to a monastery, the monastery became the corporate rector.

rector general The title given to the superior general of certain religious orders, such as the Clerics Regular of the Mother of God • *see also* **superior general**

Red Friars *see* **Order of the Most Holy Trinity**

Redemptionists *see* **Order of the Most Holy Trinity**

refectorer; refectorian; refectorias; fraterer A monastic in charge of the refectory, responsible for procuring and maintaining furniture, linens, and so forth

refectorian *see* **refectorer**

refectorias *see* **refectorer**

refectorium *see* **refectory**

refectory; refectorium; frater; fratery; trapeza (Eastern Church); aristeterion (Greek) The dining hall in monasteries or nunneries

refectory pulpit; frater pulpit A pulpit or reading desk, generally near the high table, from which the reader reads during meals

reformado A monk of a reformed order

Reformed Bernardines *see* **Feuillants**

regula *see* **rule of life**

Regula Bullata The 1223 version of the *Rule of St. Francis,* as called by Franciscan writers

Regula Canonicorum **see** ***Rule of Chrodegang***

Regula Magistri **see** ***Rule of the Master***

Regula Non Bullata The 1221 version of the *Rule of St. Francis,* so called because it was never approved by papal bull

Regula Prima The 1221 version of the *Rule of St. Francis,* so called by older Franciscan writers because it was the first one known in text

Regula Secunda The 1223 version of the *Rule of St. Francis,* as called by Franciscan writers

Regula Virginum **see** ***Rule for Virgins***

regular canon *see* **canons regular**

regular canonesses *see* **canonesses regular**

regular clergy; regulars Roman Catholic clergy who live by a rule (regula), typically in a monastic house, as opposed to secular clergy. Regular clergy take vows of poverty, chastity, and obedience; they may own no property and must give up their will to their superiors. The term was once applied to groups such as the Society of Jesus, who are not properly monastics. It has since fallen into official disuse and now only the term "canons regular" is used.

Regular Clerks of the Community *see* **Theatines**

Regular Clerks of the Divine Providence *see* **Theatines**

regular oblate *see* **conventual oblate**

Regularis Concordia The code of rules compiled for English Benedictine communities in 970 and the most important document of the English Benedictine Reform. It was compiled by Ethelwold of Winchester and others and was sanctioned by the Council of Winchester in about 973. The creation of the document was prompted by the disorder and misconduct in monasteries.

regulars *see* **regular clergy**

Relaxati *see* **Order of Friars Minor Conventual**

religious A member of a religious order or congregation

religious house Usually, a place of prayer or retreat which may or may not be administered by a religious community; also a residence for a religious community, such as a monastery, nunnery, or priory

religious institute In the Roman Catholic Church, a society in which members pronounce public vows and lead a life of brothers or sisters in common, with a degree of separation from the world. Historically, what are now called religious institutes were distinguished as either religious orders or religious congregations. The Church no longer makes that distinction and applies to all such institutes the single name "religious institute" and the same rules of canon law. While solemn vows once meant those taken in what was called a religious order, and although the distinction between solemn and simple vows is still maintained, "today, in order to know when a vow is solemn it will be necessary to refer to the proper law of the institutes of consecrated life."

Religious of the Assumption; Religious Sisters of the Assumption; Sisters of the Assumption A Roman Catholic congregation of women founded by St. Marie Eugénie Milleret in Paris in 1839. Their communities are committed to effecting change in society through prayer and education. In 2016, the congregation had over 1,300 members in 35 countries. The mother house is in Paris, France.

Religious of the Third Order Regular of St. Francis ***see*** **Third Order Regular of St. Francis**

religious order; order A monastic society of the Western Church following the same rule or under a common administrative and spiritual structure and commit themselves for life or a certain period of time. Jains, Buddhists, and Hindus also have orders, but notably, the Eastern Orthodox Church does not.

Religious Sisters of the Assumption ***see*** **Religious of the Assumption**

remoboths ***see*** **sarabaites**

Rennyo (1415–1499) Japanese, Buddhist monk, abbot, organizer of Pure Land Buddhism, 8th monshu (head-priest) of the Hongan-ji Temple of the Jōdo Shinshū sect of Buddhism, and descendant of the founder Shinran. Jōdo Shinshū Buddhists often refer to Rennyo as the restorer of the sect.

During a period of warfare, Rennyo united most of the factions of the Jōdo Shinshū sect under the Hongan-ji Temple, reformed liturgy and practices, and broadened support among different social classes.

renunciate One who renounces secular life for religious life

renunciation The renouncing of secular life for religious life, particularly in Buddhism and Hinduism

rere-dorter; necessarium; domus necessaria A privy situated at the rear of the dormitory in a religious house; the toilet block of a religious house

retro-choir; retro-quire (UK) A space between the pulpitum and rood screen which provided an assembling point for processions, a place for monastics entering too late to be seated in the choir, and a place the aged and infirm

retro-quire ***see*** **retro-choir**

reverend father ***see*** **abbot; prior**

reverend mother ***see*** **abbess prioress**

revestiarius An assistant to the sacristan in charge of the vestments, curtains, and hangings in a monastic church

Rhabanus ***see*** **Rabanus Maurus Magnentius**

riasa ***see*** **outer cassock**

Riepp, Benedicta (1825–1862) German Benedictine nun, teacher, abbess, and founder of four American convents. She was also the founder of the Roman Catholic Sisters of the Order of St. Benedict in North America.

In 1844, she entered St. Walburg Convent in Eichstätt, Bavaria and was professed in 1846. In 1852, she then volunteered to teach the children of German immigrants in Pennsylvania in 1852 and established St. Joseph Monastery, the first Benedictine nunnery in North America. She was the superior for six years but was plagued with the interference of local churchmen, notably Abbot Boniface Wimmer of St. Vincent Abbey in Latrobe, Pennsylvania. Nevertheless, she managed to establish nunneries in Erie, Pennsylvania, Newark, New Jersey, and St. Cloud, Minnesota.

In 1857, she travelled to Europe where she hoped her superiors would help resolve the controversy surrounding the independence of the new nunneries in North America. She received no help and failing in health, she returned to the U.S. in 1858 and found herself no longer welcome in the nunneries she had founded in the East and moved to the convent in St. Cloud, Minnesota where she died of tuberculosis.

rinpoche An honorific term used in the context of Tibetan Buddhism as a way of showing respect when addressing those recognized as reincarnated, older, respected, notable, learned, and/or an accomplished lamas or teachers of the Dharma. It is also used as an honorific for abbots of monasteries.

rintan In Japanese Zen Buddhism, the monk who sits next to one in the zendō (meditation hall)

RM An abbreviation of *Rule of the Master* that is commonly used in texts

Robert of Molesme, St. (ca. 1028–1111) A French Benedictine who became a monk at age 15. He was made the abbot of Saint Michel-de-Tonnerre around 1070 but the monks were disobedient and he resigned. In 1074 he became the abbot of Molesme Abbey in Burgundy. Under his leadership it became so successful and wealthy that it detracted from the community's spiritual life and Robert twice tried to leave but was ordered back by the pope. Finally, in 1098, Robert and 21 of his monks left Molesme and founded Cîteaux Abbey with Robert as abbot. In 1099, the monks of Molesme asked Robert to return and they agreed to submit entirely to his interpretation of the *Rule of St. Benedict*. He agreed and Molesme became a major center for the Benedictines under his tutelage.

rochet A white vestment generally worn by a Roman Catholic or Anglican bishop in choir dress. It is unknown in the Eastern churches. The rochet in its Roman form is similar to a surplice, except that the sleeves are narrower. In its Anglican form it is a descendent of the traditional albs worn by deacons and priests. A rochet is occasionally worn in some monastic religious orders.

rohatsu; rōhatsu In Japanese Zen Buddhist monasteries, the severest sesshin (meditation retreat) of the monastic year, commemorating the enlightenment of the Buddha. It is usually held from December 1 until the morning of December 8, during which period the monks are not allowed to lie down to rest.

Romuald, St. (ca. 950–ca. 1025–1027) An Italian monk, reformer, and founder of the Camaldolese which is considered part of the Benedictine family. He first entered the Benedictine Order at Sant'Apollinaire in Classe, which was a traditional community under the influence of the Cluniac reforms. Romuald chose to be under a spiritual master, Marinus, who followed a much harsher ascetic and solitary lifestyle that was originally of Irish eremitical origins. Some years later, Marinus and Romuald settled near the Abbey of Saint Miguel de Cuxa, where Abbot Guarinus was also beginning reforms but was building mainly upon the Iberian Christian tradition. Later drawing on his various early experiences, Romuald was able to establish his own monastic pattern, though he himself never thought of it as a separate unit, seeing it as a full part of the Benedictine tradition. • *See also* **Camaldolese Order**

roshi; rōshi A Japanese Zen Buddhist monastic master in the Sōtō organization. It is somewhat less formal than shike.

Roswitha ***see*** **Hrothswitha of Gandersheim**

rota ***see*** **tabula; turning window**

rotularius ***see*** **breviator**

rotulus ***see*** **mortuary roll**

Royal, Celestial and Military Order of Our Lady of Mercy and the Redemption of the Captives ***see*** **Order of the Blessed Virgin Mary of Mercy**

Rule for a Recluse **see** ***Ancrene Wisse***

Rule for Virgins; Regula Virginum The first western monastic rule written exclusively for women. It was written by St. Caesarius of Arles in 512, and was very strict, prescribing claustration, specified times for prayer, modesty, and plain dress.

Rule of Ceili De; Rule of Céilí Dé A brief rule used by the Culdees which may have been written either by St. Máel Ruain (d. 792) or his disciple Óengus the Culdee (fl. 9th century). The rule appears to have been modeled on the sayings of the Desert Fathers of Egypt, in particular the *Conferences* of John Cassian. Typical concerns in them include the importance of daily recitation of the Psalter, of self-restraint and forbearance from indulgences in bodily desires, and of separation from worldly concerns.

Rule of Grandmont ***see*** **Grandmontines**

rule of life; regula A set of guidelines and commitments directing one's life, especially in a religious community. Two of the most notable in the Western Church are those of St. Augustine and St. Benedict. Although not considered a rule as such, the Eastern Church is most notably influenced by St. Basil's *Asketikon*.

Rule of St. Albert The shortest of the rules of Roman Catholic spiritual tradition. It was originally composed for Carmelite hermits by St. Albert Avogadro (1149–1214), a priest of the Canons Regular and a canon lawyer between 1206 and 1214. It was revised slightly 20 years later to reflect the realities or mendicant and monastic life due to the threats of Muslim attacks in Palestine. It is composed almost exclusively of scriptural precepts.

Rule ***of St. Augustine*** A brief rule for monastic communities nominally composed of writings of St. Augustine of Hippo (354–430) put together by a follower in the 5th century, predominately using Augustine's Letter 211 to the nuns at Hippo Regius, which was governed by his sister and where his cousin and niece also lived.

Though he wrote chiefly to quiet troubles incident to the nomination of a new superior, Augustine took the opportunity to discuss some of the virtues and practices essential to religious life as he understood it. He emphasized such considerations as charity, poverty, obedience, detachment from the world, the apportionment of labor, the mutual duties of superiors and inferiors, fraternal charity, prayer in common, fasting and abstinence proportionate to the strength of the individual, care of the sick, silence, and reading during meals.

The *Rule* was revived in the 11th century and by the 12th century and is in use not only by Augustinians but by such communities as the Dominicans, Servites, Mercederians, and Norbertines.

Rule of St. Basil **see** ***Asketikon***

Rule of St. Benedict; Regula Benedicti A set of rules and guidelines for Benedictine monastic communities that was composed by Benedict of Nursia in the 6th century. It is composed of 73 short chapters and gives both administrative and spiritual guidance. The *Rule* outlines a moderate path between individual and institutional needs that has made it widely popular and influential.

The *Rule of St. Benedict* is heavily influenced by the writings of John Cassian, and shows a strong affinity with the *Rule of the Master*. But it also has a unique spirit of balance, moderation and reasonableness and this persuaded most religious communities founded throughout the Middle Ages to adopt it. As a result, Benedict's rule became one of the most influential religious rules in Western Christendom. For this reason, Benedict is often called the founder of Western Christian monasticism. Some form of the *Rule* is still the most common rule of life in the Western Church. Abbreviated as RB. • *See also* **Benedict of Nursia, St.**

Rule of St. Chrodegang; Regula Canonicorum A rule written around 755 by St. Chrodegang for the canons in his cathedral in Metz, Germany. The rule, containing 34 chapters and was based on the *Rule of St. Benedict* and also on the *Rule of St. Augustine*. The aim of Chrodegang's rule was to encourage the mutual support of a monastic while recognizing the responsibilities of canons serving the spiritual needs of the laity. In its day it gave an important boost to the spread of community life among the secular clergy. In 816, it was incorporated in part into the Institutio Canonicorum Aquisgranensis established by the Council of Aachen. By the 11th and 12th centuries, the *Rule of Chrodegang* was gradually supplanted by more popular rules based on the *Rule of St. Augustine*.

Rule of St. Clare The monastic written by St. Clare of Assisi for Second Order Franciscans (Poor Clares). It is thought be the first rule of life written by a woman for her own community. The rule was naturally influenced by the *Rule of St. Francis*, but it reflects the unique experience of enclosed women as opposed to mendicant friars. Her decision to write a rule was a radical departure from the religious norms of her time and it was a struggle to have it accepted by the pope. It was finally approved only two days before her death in 1253. The rule that was accepted relaxed the extreme poverty required of its members, but the degree of observance required of members remained a major source of conflict within the order, resulting in numerous secessions. • *See also* **Clare of Assisi, St.**

Rule of St. Columba One of the shortest of monastic rules, it contains 28 sentences. Although attributed to St.

Columba, it was set down some time after his death. • *See also* **Columba, St.**

Rule of St. Columbanus A short rule established by St. Columbanus early in the 7th century and influenced by the customs of Irish monasteries. It only has ten chapters and deals with obedience, silence, food, poverty, humility, chastity, choir offices, discretion, mortification, and perfection. It also makes a provision for perpetual prayer (laus perennis), by which choir succeeded choir, both day and night. It was largely superseded by the *Rule of St. Benedict* by the end of the 7th century. • *See also* **Columbanus, St.**

Rule of St. Francis There is, as in so many other points in the life of St. Francis, not a small amount of doubt and controversy about the *Rule of St. Francis.* Whether St. Francis wrote several rules or one rule only, with several versions, whether he received it directly from heaven through revelations or from his long experiences, whether he gave it the last touch, or whether its final form is due to the influence of others. All these are questions which find different answers. One may speak of three successive rules or of three successive versions of the same rule, but that makes little difference, since the spirit in the three cases is the same.

Rule of 1209: This is the rule St. Francis presented to Pope Innocent III for approval in the year 1209; its real text is not known but hearsay indicates that this primitive rule was little more than some passages of the Gospel heard in 1208 in the chapel of Portiuncula. It is not known from which Gospel the words were taken. The text of the primitive rule seems to have perished very early, perhaps by the middle of the 13th century. All that can be said is this, that St. Francis did not take as his model any monastic order, but simply the life of Christ, his apostles, and the Gospel itself.

Rule of 1221: It seems that the Rule of 1209 was successively improved at the annual general chapters at Portiuncula by new statutes, the fruit of ever-growing experience. During the years 1219–1220 in the absence of the St. Francis in the East, some events happened which caused him to recast his rule in order to prevent similar troubles in the future. Cardinal Ugolino was urged to use his friendship with Francis that he might introduce some organization into the Order according to the rules of St. Augustine, St. Benedict, and St. Bernard. St. Francis being questioned, answered that he was called to walk by the way of simplicity, and that he would always follow the folly of the Cross.

The *Rule of 1221* is called *Regula Prima* by all older Franciscan writers, it being the first known in its text, and also *Regula Non Bullata,* for it was never solemnly confirmed by a papal Bull. It has been preserved in many manuscripts and has been often printed, but there are some noteworthy discrepancies of text. The Rule of 1221 consists of 23 chapters, some of which are composed almost entirely of scriptural texts; in other manuscripts many admonitions are found and towards the end even prayers. It is thought that the second rule is only an enlarged version of the primitive one.

Rule of 1223: This is the Franciscan Rule properly so called, and the rule which the Friars Minor still observe. It is named by Franciscan authors *Regula Bullata* or *Regula Secunda*. The question has been put whether St. Francis was quite free in drawing up the definitive text of his rule. From what has been already said, it may be gathered that St.

Francis successively developed his rule, adapting it to the circumstances; hence if all the particulars of the former rules are not found in the last one that is no reason to say St. Francis omitted them against his own will. The rule contains many commandments, tempered by the sweet exhortations of St. Francis. It is the tender voice of a loving father that speaks to his children through the rule. This rule has been praised in the highest terms by different authorities. Despite the controversy in interpretation, its influence for over 700 years has been immeasurable.

Rule of St. Stephen ***see*** **Grandmontines**

Rule of the Knights Templar **see** ***Specific Behavior for the Templar Order***

Rule of the Master; Regula Magistri An anonymous 6th century rule of life probably written two or three decades before the *Rule of St. Benedict.* St. Benedict used some of the sections directly and modified others. The *Rule of the Master* was influenced by the writings of John Cassian and also St. Augustine's "Letter 211." The rule contains precise regulations and reflections on the reasoning behind the regulations. There is an introduction and 95 chapters, 20 of which are devoted to the Daily Office. There is no evidence that the *Rule of the Master* was ever actually used in a community. The title *Rule of the Master* is commonly abbreviated as RM.

ryasa ***see*** **outer cassock**

~S~

sa di ***see*** **samanera**

Sabaite A monk of Mar Saba • *see also* **Mar Saba**

Sabbas the Sanctified, St. (439–532) A Cappadocian-Syrian monk, priest, founder of several monasteries, and composer of the *Jerusalem Typikon,* the first monastic rule of church services. He became a monk when he was 17 and lived as a cenobite until he became a hermit in a lavra at age 30. About 473, he moved to a cave in the Kidron Valley south of Jerusalem where disciples began to gather around him causing the Great Lavra to spring up about 484. This has come to be considered the mother of all Eastern Orthodox monasteries. When some of the monks opposed his rule and demanded a priest as their abbot, he left for the New Lavra which he had built near Thekoa. Patriarch Salustius of Jerusalem ordained him in 491 and appointed him archimandrite (senior abbot) of all the monasteries in Palestina Prima in 494. • *See also* **Mar Saba**

Sacred Congregation for Consultations about Regulars ***see*** **Congregation for Institutes of Consecrated Life and Societies of Apostolic Life**

Sacred Monastery of the God-Trodden Mount Sinai ***see*** **St. Catherine's Monastery**

sacristan; ecclesiarch (Eastern church); skeuophylax (male, Eastern Orthodox Church); skeuophylakiss (females, Eastern Orthodox church) A monastic in charge of the furnishings of a monastic church, the sacristy, and all things necessary for services

sacristy; skeuophylakion (Eastern Orthodox) A place for keeping vestments and altar implements and furnishings. Usually it is a room near the altar, but in some monasteries it may be in a separate building.

sadhu, sādhu; sannyāsī; swami; vairagi A religious ascetic, mendicant, monk, or any holy man in Hinduism and Jainism who has renounced worldly life. The sādhu seeks mokṣa (liberation), through meditation and contemplation of Brahman. Hindu sādhus usually wear simple saffron-colored clothing. Jain sādhus wear white clothing or sometimes no clothes at all to symbolize their renunciation of material desires.

While all sādhus live simple lives, other practices vary by sect. Some are solitaries, some live in groups, some are homeless wanderers, and some are cenobites. Celibacy is the usual practice, but some sects condone impersonal tantric sex.

While the exact requirements for a man to become a sādhu vary by sect, it usually involves finding a guru willing to take him on as a student.

It is estimated that there are four to five million sādhus in India. It is believed that they benefit society by burning off karma.

sadhvi; sādhvī; sanyāsini; swamini; swāmini A Jain or Hindu nun, ascetic, or holy woman. Sādhvīs exist in many sects. Often the women that take to the life of renunciation are widows, and these types of sādhvīs often live secluded lives in ascetic compounds. Sādhvīs are sometimes regarded by some as manifestations or forms of Devi (Goddess) and are honored as such. There have been a number of charismatic sādhvīs that have risen to fame as religious teachers in contemporary India.

As with men, a woman who wants to become sādhvī must first find a guru willing to take them on as a student.

Saicho (767–822 CE); Dengyō Daishi Japanese Buddhist monk and author who founded the Tendai school of Buddhism based on the Chinese Tiantai school. He became a novice monk at 14, and fully professed at 20. He then retreated to Mt. Hiei near Kyoto for intensive study and practice. In time he attracted other monks both and the Enryaku-ji community formed. He went to China in 804 and studied Tiantai Buddhism. Returning to Japan, he founded the Tendai Lotus school (Tendai-hokke-shū) which won official recognition in 806. Despite opposition from the traditional Buddhist schools, the Tendai school was granted full privileges in by the emperor 822, several days after Saicho's death. Legend has it that as a result of his trip to China he also introduced tea into Japan.

St. Catherine's Monastery; Sacred Monastery of the God-Trodden Mount Sinai Located in Egypt's Sinai Peninsula at the mouth of a gorge at the foot of Mount Sinai. According to the Old Testament, Mt. Sinai is where Moses received the Ten Commandments from God. The monastery is controlled by the autonomous Church of Sinai, part of the wider Eastern Orthodox Church, and is a UNESCO World Heritage Site. Built between 548 and 565, at the order of Emperor Justinian I, the monastery is one of the oldest working Christian monasteries in the world. According to tradition, St. Catherine of Alexandria was a Christian martyr sentenced to death on the breaking wheel. When this failed to kill her, she was beheaded. According to tradition, angels took her remains to Mount Sinai. Around the year 800, monks from the monastery found her remains. The site is sacred to Christianity, Islam, and Judaism.

In addition to many works of art, the

monastery also houses the world's oldest continually operating library, possessing the second largest collection of early codices and manuscripts in the world, exceeded only by the Vatican Library.

St. Peter's Abbey, Solesmes *see* **Solesmes Abbey**

saiza Lunch, the main meal of the day in a Japanese Zen Buddhist monastery

Sakya Pandita *see* **Kunga Gyeltsen**

sakya-putta; sākya-putta Literally, "son of the Sakyan"—an epithet for Buddhist monks, the Buddha having been a native of the Sakyan Republic

Salesian Sisters *see* **Order of the Visitation of Holy Mary**

sallekhana; santhara A Jain vow practiced mostly by monks and nuns, which involves a voluntary and gradual reduction of food and liquid intake under conditions of severe famine, incurable disease, great disability, old age, or when a person is nearing his end. It is seen as spiritual detachment requiring a great deal of spiritual accomplishment and maturity and a declaration that a person is finished with this world and has chosen to leave. Jains believe this allows one to achieve death with dignity and dispassion along with a great reduction of negative karma.

salter; mustardarius Usually, a paid lay servant appointed by the kitchener, who had the responsibility for preparing and supplying mustard and other spices. In the days before refrigeration, this was an important and necessary job.

Salvatorian Fathers *see* **Basilian Order of the Most Holy Saviour**

samakaccka An undervest worn by Buddhist nuns

samakaksika A buckled belt sometimes worn with the kāṣāya (robe) by Buddhist monks and nuns

samana A junior monastic in the Jain Śvētāmbara Terapanth sect

samanen *see* **samanera**

samaner *see* **samarera**

samanera; sāmaṇera (Pali); samanen (Thai); samaner (Khmer); sa di (Vietnamese); śrāmaṇera (Sanskrit); shāmí (Chinese); getsül (Tibetan); shin thamanei (Burmese) A Buddhist novice monk. They keep the Ten Precepts as their code of behavior and devote themselves to the religious life during breaks from secular schooling, or in conjunction with it if devoted to formal ordination. They often ordain as novices at a young age, but generally no younger than seven or eight. Higher ordination, conferring the status of a full bhikkhu, is given only to men who are aged 20 or older. The novitiate is normally at least one year.

samanerapsaka In a Theravedin Buddhist monastery, the official who supervises novices

samaneri; sāmaṇerī (Pali); śrāmaṇerī (Sanskrit); śrāmaṇerikā (Sanskrit); shāmíní (Chinese); śikṣamāṇā (Sanskrit); sikkhamānā (Pali); shìchāmónà (Chinese); getsulma (Tibetan) A Buddhist novice nun. They keep the Ten Precepts as their code of behavior and devote themselves to the religious life during breaks from secular schooling, or in conjunction with it if devoted to formal ordination. The novitiate for samaneris can be from one to five years. Women usually choose to ordain as novices as adults, since there is no expectation that they do so in childhood.

Higher ordination, conferring the status of a bhikkhuni, is usually given only to those 20 or older. A woman is to be ordained, according to the traditional *Vinaya* (monastic regulations), by both a monk and a nun.

samgha ***see*** **sangha**

samghati; saṃghāti A double layered robe of fully ordained Buddhist monks and nuns, used as an outer cloak for various occasions. It comes over the middle robe (uttarasanga), and the inner robe (antarvasa). In representations of the Buddha, the saṃghāti is usually the most visible garment, with the antarvasa protruding at the bottom. It is quite similar in shape to the Greek himation. • *See also* **kasaya**

samnyasa ***see*** **sannayasa**

samu Manual labor in a Japanese Zen Buddhist monastery—a part of training equally important to zazen (meditation)

samue Working or everyday clothes for a Japanese Zen Buddhist monk

samvegi Wandering Jain monks

sanctinomiales ***see*** **nuns**

sando In a Japanese Zen Buddhist monastery, to formally enter the zendō (meditation hall) as a new member of the monastic community following the completion of niwazume (the waiting period)

sangha; saṃgha (Sanskrit); sēngjiā (Chinese) Literally, "community"—most commonly the term is used to mean the Buddhist community of monks and nuns; sometimes the term is expanded to mean all those Buddhists who have at least experienced direct emptiness (srotāpanna); in popular usage it can be used to include all Buddhist practitioners

sangha-bheda Schism in a Buddhist monastic community

sangha sammuti The head of the Shwegyin Nikaya in Burma [Myanmar]

sanghadisesa An offense which must be judged by an entire Buddhist monastic community

sangharaja In some Theravada Buddhist countries, the senior monk of a nikaya (monastic fraternity), or of the sangha (monastic community). In some cases, the sangharaja may be chosen by seniority, royal appointment, or elected by monks or laity. The authority and responsibility of a sangharaja can vary significantly. Buddhist monasticism does not impose obedience as a requirement, although in practice, seniors are given respect. Further, most monasteries are self-governing or dependent on a larger temple in the same region. • *See also* **thathanabaing**

Sangharaja Nikaya A reformist order of Theravada Buddhist monks in Bangladesh formed in 1864 by Sangharaja Saramedha Mahasthabira, a Burmese Buddhist monk invited to Bangladesh in 1856 by Radha Charan Mahasthabir, a prominent Bengali monk. Saramitra Mahasthabir stayed a few months to learn of conditions there which at the time had mixed in many Hindu practices including animal sacrifice and worship of Hindu deities such as Shiva. Further the Buddhist Vinaya was increasingly ignored and monks were commonly married, drank alcohol, and even ate meat. In 1864, Sangharaja Saramedha returned to Bangladesh at the invitation of other Bengali monks and began preaching reform. He persuaded a number of Buddhist monks to be re-ordained and follow traditional Buddhist practices, and this began the Sangharaja Nikaya order. • *See also* **Mahasthabir Nikaya**

Sangharaja Saramedha Mahasthabira ***see*** **Sangharaja Nikaya**

sanguinati ***see*** **bloodletting**

sanno ***see*** **jisha**

sannyasa; sannyāsa; saṃnyāsa A Hindu form of renunciation of material desires and pursuits that is parallel in many ways to monasticism but is not monasticism itself. An individual in Sannyāsa is known as a sannyāsi (male) or sannyāsini (female). There are no formal demands on them, but often they are celibate itinerants with no material possessions or emotional attachments, and are vegetarians.

sannyasi ***see*** **sadhu**

sannyasini ***see*** **sadhvi**

santhara ***see*** **sallekhana**

sanzen Formal meditation study with a Zen master; also the private meetings between master and disciple in a Japanese Zen Buddhist monastery in which the master instructs the disciple in meditation

sarabaites; remoboths; sylfdemas (Anglo-Saxon) Monastics who either continued to live in their own homes, or dwelt together in or near cities. They acknowledged no monastic superior and obeyed no definite rule. They were numerous in Egypt. Never highly thought of, by the time of St. Benedict the term typically was used for degenerate monks whose nonadherence to Church canons was exceeded only by the gyrovagues.

sarozium A narrow band of white cloth—a vestige of a scapular—worn over the shoulder and hanging down both front and back over a cassock for the weekday wear of the Austrian congregation of the Augustinian Canons Regular of St. Augustine

sarvabhutahita Kindness to all creatures—a basic tenet of Hindu monasticism

Savignac Order; Congregation of Savigny A Roman Catholic religious reform order originating in Savigny, France in 1105 when Vitalis of Mortain established a hermitage in the forest. A number of disciples gathered around him and they followed the *Rule of St. Benedict*. The community wore gray habits.

It grew to 33 daughter houses, but by 1147 had financial and administrative difficulties and affiliated with the Cistercians, which helped for a time, but deterioration set in once again. Commendatory abbots did not help matters. In 1509 Savigny Abbey was pillaged and partly destroyed by the Calvinists, and by 1510, only 24 monks remained. The abbey continued to exist until the French Revolution destroyed it and scattered its remaining members.

Savonarola, Girolamo (1452–1498) An Italian Dominican friar and preacher active in Renaissance Florence. In 1475 he joined the Order of Friars Preachers and was ordained a priest in 1476. Even at the time, he was critical of what he thought to be a decline in austerity, which irritated his superiors who then transferred him about to several different monasteries. For several years he was an itinerant preaching reform and repentance, and denouncing clerical corruption and exploitation of the poor. He prophesied the coming of a new biblical flood that would reform the Church, so when

France invaded Italy and threatened Florence in 1494 he helped establish a republic declaring it the New Jerusalem. When Pope Alexander summoned him to Rome in 1495, Savonarola refused and was excommunicated 1497. Public opinion turned against him and he was hanged and burned in the main square of Florence in 1498.

sayadaw Venerable teacher—an honorific title and form of address for a senior or eminent Buddhist monk in Myanmar (Burma)

sayalay ***see*** **maechi**

S.C. The post-nominal initials for members of the Sisters of Charity

scapular A monastic garment that appeared perhaps as early as the 7th century in the Order of St. Benedict. It is a somewhat large length of cloth suspended both front and back from the shoulders of the wearer, often reaching to the ankles. Monastic scapulars originated as aprons worn by medieval monks to keep the tunic clean. The cowl, or hood, was later added to provide warmth in drafty and unheated churches. The term "scapular" is frequently used to designate the scapular and cowl together.

scedula A loose leaf inserted into a monastery's register with notes of daily happenings which were reviewed at the end of the year for possible inclusion in the permanent register

scetis In modern Greek Orthodox usage, an isolated monastic cell that is not part of a religious house

Scetis; Sketis; Wadi El Natrun A valley located in the northwestern Nile delta of Egypt that was one of the three early Christian monastic centers—the other two being Nitria and Kellia (The Cells). These three centers are often easily confused and sometimes referred to as a single place—such as Nitria or the Nitrian Desert—but the locales are distinct, though geographically close together and with interrelated histories. Scetis, now called Wadi El Natrun, is best known today because some of its ancient monasteries remain in use, unlike Nitria and Kellia which have only archaeological remains.

The monastic presence in Scetis was begun by St. Macarius of Egypt around 330 where he established himself as a solitary. His presence attracted anchorites who settled nearby in individual cells centered on a communal church and facilities. Walls and watchtowers were added because of attacks by nomads. At the end of the 4th century, four distinct communities had developed there: Baramus, Macarius, Bishoi, and John Kolobos.

schema The cowl worn by an Orthodox schema monk or schema nun

schema monk ***see*** **great schema**

schema nun ***see*** **great schema**

Schenoudi ***see*** **Shenoute the Great, St.**

schima ***see*** **great schema**

Scholastica, St. (ca. 480–543) An Italian woman held to be the twin sister of St. Benedict of Nursia. She is the foundress of the women's branch of Benedictine monasticism. Because she came from a wealthy family, she was educated and literate, and able to establish a hermitage about five miles from Monte Cassino. Some say that this was the first Benedictine monastery for women.

Schutz, Roger (1915–2005) Swiss Christian leader, monastic, and writer who founded the Taizé ecumenical monastic community in Burgundy, France. He served as its prior until his murder in 2005. The Taizé Community attracted international attention and continues to welcome thousands of young pilgrims every week. Schütz avoided personal publicity and prior to his murder by a mentally ill young woman was planning to retire. • *See also* **Taize**

Scientology monasticism Scientology is a body of religious beliefs and practices launched in 1952 by American author L. Ron Hubbard (1911–1986). He first developed a program of ideas called Dianetics, which was distributed through the Dianetics Foundation. The foundation soon entered bankruptcy, and Hubbard lost the rights to his seminal publication *Dianetics: The Modern Science of Mental Health* in 1952. He then recharacterized the subject as a religion and renamed it Scientology, retaining the Dianetics terminology, doctrines, and practices. Scientology maintains a "fraternal order" called the Sea Organization, which was founded in 1967 on board ships at sea to avoid governmental control. It controls all operations of the Church of Scientology and provides services only for the church. Members sign billion year contracts and live communally with lodging, food, clothing, and medical care provided by the church. Discipline is very strict and some critics have compared it to a paramilitary or totalitarian organization.

scriptorarius The head scribe in a monastery scriptorium, who both delegated tasks and gave out books to be read by other monks

scriptorium In a monastery, the room or cloister walkway set apart for writing or copying manuscripts. They first appeared in monasteries in the 7th century.

Sea Organization ***see*** **Scientology monasticism**

Second Benedict A nickname of St. Benedict of Aniane

second order Within the Roman Catholic Church a religious institute for men

Second Order of St. Francis ***see*** **Poor Clares**

secular abbot ***see*** **abbas laicus**

Secular Carmelites ***see*** **Secular Order of Discalced Carmelites**

Secular Franciscan Order ***see*** **Third Order Secular of St. Francis**

Secular Institute A Roman Catholic semi-monastic organization of individuals who live in the world but profess the evangelical counsels of chastity, poverty, and obedience. Secular Institutes received recognition from Pope Pius XII in 1947. In 2017 there were approximately 60,000 people belonging to more than 200 Secular Institutes around the world. Most members are lay people, but diocesan priests or deacons may also join who wish to lead a consecrated life while still working in the diocesan framework. • *See also* **Christian Community**

Secular Institute of St. Angela Merici ***see*** **Company of St. Ursula**

secular oblates ***see*** **oblates**

Secular Order of Discalced Carmelites; Ordo Carmelitarum Discalceatorum Saecularis; Secular Carmelites; Secular Order of Discalced Carmelites of the Blessed Virgin Mary of Mount

Carmel and of the Holy Mother St. Teresa of Jesus A religious quasimonastic association of the Roman Catholic Church composed primarily of lay persons and secular clergy. They practice a two-fold or three-fold Daily Office, contemplative prayer, and attend daily Mass when possible. Lectio divina and spiritual retreats are also highly encouraged. They wear the brown scapular of Discalced Carmelite Order of which they are a part. Profession of the Promise of the Seculars requires several years of formation. Members use the post-nominal initials O.C.D.S. • *See also* **Carmelites; Order of Discalced Carmelites; Order of the Brothers of the Blessed Virgin Mary; Third Order of Our Lady of Mt. Carmel**

Secular Order of Discalced Carmelites of the Blessed Virgin Mary of Mount Carmel and of the Holy Mother St. Teresa of Jesus *see* **Secular Order of Discalced Carmelites**

secularization Conversion from regular or monastic to secular

secularize To convert from regular or monastic into secular, as to secularize a priest or a monk

Segarelli, Gerard *see* **Apostolic Brethren**

seichu *see* **ango**

self-immolation The sacrificing of oneself for the good of others is considered an act of charity by some Buddhists, though rejected by others. Still, it is part of a long-standing tradition in Eastern Asia. While in recent years photographs have made self-immolation by fire the only method in the popular imagination, it may be done in different ways, as a group of eight Chinese monks who fasted to death in 574 in protest of imperial persecution of Buddhists.

semandron *see* **semantron**

semantarion *see* **semantron**

semantron; semandron; semantarion; xylon; xulon; toaca (Romanian); bilo (Russian); klepalo (Bulgarian, Macedonian, Serbian) A wooden or metal percussion instrument used in Eastern Orthodox monasteries used at the start of a procession or to summons the community to prayer • *see also* **tabula**

semi-monastic Somewhat monastic, as a third order. By way of comparison, a quasimonastic community is closer to full monastic life. • *See also* **quasimonastic**

senasanagghahapaka In a Theravedin Buddhist monastery, an official in charge of assigning lodgings

senasanapannapaka In a Theravedin Buddhist monastery, an official in charge of assigning beds

sengjia *see* **sangha**

senich kaihogyo *see* **kaihogyo**

senmon dojo *see* **sodo**

sennichi kaihogyo *see* **kaihogyo**

senpectae Old and wise monastics—in the *Rule of St. Benedict,* the abbot is directed to send senpectae to speak with troubled monastics to coax them back into the fold

Senuti *see* **Shenoute the Great, St.**

septimanarian A monastic who is given a week of duties to perform

Seraphic Doctor A nickname of St. Bonaventure

Seraphim of Sarov, St. (1754 or 1759–1833) Russian Orthodox monk, priest, and ascetic considered the greatest of the 19th century startsy (elders). He became a poslushnik (novice) in 1777 and was fully professed in 1786. Shortly afterwards, he was ordained a hierodeacon (monastic deacon). In 1793, he was ordained as a hieromonk (monastic priest) and then became a hermit in a small log cabin in the woods for 25 years. Here he was attacked and beaten by robbers which left him with a hunched back. After spending five months in a monastery recovering, he spent 1,000 successive nights on a rock in continuous prayer with his arms raised to the sky.

In 1815, he began seeing hundreds of pilgrims a day as a confessor and was reputed to be able to answer his guests' questions before they could ask.

He was canonized by the Russian Orthodox Church in 1903.

Serge of Radonezh *see* **Sergius of Radonezh**

Sergey Radonezhsky *see* **Sergius of Radonezh**

Sergius of Radonezh, St. (ca. 1314–1392); Sergey Radonezhsky; Serge of Radonezh Russian Orthodox monk, priest, monastic reformer, and highly venerated saint. Upon his parents' death, he and his older brother Stefan who was a monk went to live an ascetic life in the forest at Makovets Hill. Here he built a build a small cell and a church and thus started the Trinity-St. Sergius Lavra.

In time, Stefan moved to a monastery in Moscow where he took monastic vows, then returned to the forest as a hermit. Soon, however, other monks started building their cells around him and chose him as their hegumen (abbot). He was ordained as a priest and his disciples founded about 40 monasteries and his influence spread widely. Asked to become a metropolitan, however, he declined, preferring to remain a monk. He has been called the Abbot of Russia.

He was canonized in 1452.

Servites *see* **Order of the Service of Mary**

servitors; sizars Members of the community on a weekly rota for service at meals, in the infirmary, or in the refectory

sesshin An intensive meditation retreat in a Japanese Zen Buddhist monastery, generally lasting one week

setsu ango The winter training season at a Japanese Zen Buddhist monastery

Seven Holy Founders *see* **Order of the Service of Mary**

Sext; Sixth Hour (Orthodox) A fixed time of prayer of the Daily Office of almost all the traditional Christian liturgies. Sext consists mainly of psalms and is said at noon. Its name comes from Latin and refers to the sixth hour of the day after dawn. It was widely established as a canonical Hour in the 4th century.

seynies; seyny *see* **bloodletting**

Shakers; United Society of Believers in Christ's Second Appearing A Protestant monastic order that grew out of Quakerism in 18th century England. Shakers are celibate, ascetic, live communally, and have both men and women in the same group. They are noted for treating women as equals. There was a novitiate of one year, and another four years was required before becoming a full member. At its peak in the mid–19th century, there were 6,000 Shakers, but by 1920, there were only 12 communities left. In 2017, there was only one community left and it only had two people.

shakuhachi A Japanese end-blown flute traditionally made of bamboo used by Japanese Zen Buddhist monks of the Fuke school of Japanese Zen Buddhism in the practice of suizen (blowing meditation) • *see also* **suizen**

shamarpa A lineage holder of the Karma Kagyu school of Tibetan Buddhism held to be the mind manifestation of Amida (a celestial Buddha). He is a monk traditionally associated with Yangpachen Monastery near Lhasa. The first shamarpa, Drakpa Senggé (1283–1349), was the principal disciple of Rangjung Dorje, the third karmapa lama. The fifth dalai lama saw the shamarpa as equal to the karmapa.

In 1792 the Tibetan government exiled the tenth shamarpa for inciting a war between Tibet and Nepal, and a ban was placed on future incarnations. A modern historian, however, proved that the tenth shamarpa had in fact mediated the conflict. At that time it was not practicable to have any shamarpa recognized so everything was kept secret. The incarnations appeared, but were not revealed. In 1963, following a request from the 16th karmapa, the Tibetan Government in Exile lifted the ban.

shamí *see* **samanera**

shamini *see* **samaneri**

shaucha Purity of body speech and mind—a basic tenet of Hindu monasticism

shaveling Formerly a term of contempt for a tonsured monk or cleric

shaving; rasura In the Western Church, beards came to be regarded as a sign of pride and monks were generally shaved once a month by the chamberlain or a barber. This might be more often in warm weather. Seniors were shaved first when "the razors were sharp and the towels were dry." Mendicants and lay brethren sometimes were not shaven and could be called barbati.

Shen-hsiu *see* **Shenxiu**

Shenouda *see* **Shenoute the Great**

Shenoute of Atripe *see* **Shenoute the Great**

Shenoute the Archimandrite *see* **Shenoute the Great**

Shenoute the Great, St. (ca. 350–ca. 466); Shenoute the Archimandrite; Shenoute of Atripe; Shenouda; Schenoudi; Senuti Egyptian Coptic monk, abbot, writer, and theologian. Around 385, he became the abbot of the White Monastery which had about 30 old monks. By the time of his death the monastery had 2,200 monks and 1,800 nuns, who lived in an area about 3,000 times its original size. Shenoute predated St. Benedict is using a combination of work and prayer and this helped support his lavra. He also taught all his monks to read and write which proved to be an additional draw in itself, aside from improving their spiritual lives.

Shenxiu (ca. 606–706) Influential Chinese Chan (Zen) Buddhist monk, Chan master, and a patriarch of the East Mountain Teaching of Chan Buddhism. He became a Buddhist at 13 and received the full precepts of a monk in 625. He then disappeared from records until somewhere between 665 and 668 when he was banished by the emperor for an unknown reason and did not return to public notice until sometime between 676–679. Soon thereafter the Monastery of the Six Perfections was built for him where spent the next quarter century.

In late 700 the Empress Wu invited Shenxiu to the capital at Luoyang to teach Chan Buddhism where he was welcomed with great enthusiasm. For the last 5 years of his life, he taught the Buddhist Dharma.

shichamona *see* **samaneri**

shichido garan The classical layout of the Japanese Zen Buddhist monastery with seven buildings—the sanmon (mountain gate), butsuden (Buddha hall), hatto (Dharma hall), and hojo (abbot's quarters) are aligned on a north-south axis, with the yokushitsu (bath house) and kyozo (sutra library) to the east and the sōdō (monk's hall) to the west.

shika The hostler of a Japanese Zen Buddhist monastery

shike The master of a Japanese Zen Buddhist monastery. Shike is roughly synonymous with rōshi, although considered somewhat more formal.

shikunichi In a Japanese Zen Buddhist monastery, dates containing the number 4 or the number 9, on which there is a head shaving, bath, and a general cleaning of the monastery

shin thamanei *see* **samanera**

shin'igi In Japanese Zen Buddhist monasteries, the formal wear used by unsui (postulants) during ceremonies

shinkin In a Japanese Zen Buddhist monastery, money received by the monks from the monastery

shinpyu *see* **pabbajja**

Shinran (1173–1263) Japanese Buddhist monk and advocate of Pure Land Buddhism. He was the founder of what ultimately became the Jōdo Shinshū sect in Japan.

Shinran entered the Shoren-in Temple in 1181 when he was 9 years old and his parents died. He then practiced for the next 20 years but was, as he himself confessed, a Tendai dōsō or "hall monk"—that is to say, undistinguished. In 1201, a vision directed him to become a disciple of Hōnen, who was also a disillusioned Tendai monk. Under Hōnen's guidance, Shinran attained enlightenment at age 29. During his time as a disciple of Shinran caused a great stir among society by getting married and eating meat. Both practices were strictly forbidden for monks, but Shinran took these drastic steps to show that Amida's (a celestial Buddha) salvation is for all people and not just for monks and priests.

In 1207, the Buddhist establishment in Kyoto persuaded the military to impose a nembutsu (chanting) ban, after an incident where two of Hōnen's most prominent followers were accused of using nembutsu practice as a cover-up for sexual liaisons. These two monks were subsequently executed. Hōnen and Shinran were exiled, and Shinran was defrocked. Shinran then renamed himself Gutoku (Foolish, Bald-Headed One), coming to understand himself as neither monk nor layman. While in exile, Shinran spread the doctrine of salvation through Amida Buddha's compassion, as expressed through the nembutsu practice, however in time his teachings diverged from Hōnen enough that later followers would use the term Jōdo Shinshū or "True [Essence of the]

Pure Land Sect," as opposed to Jōdo-shū or "Pure Land Sect."

In 1211, the nembutsu ban was lifted and Shinran was pardoned. In 1224 he wrote his most significant text, *Kyogyoshinsho,* which is a series of selections and commentaries on Buddhist sutras (aphorisms or teachings) supporting the new Pure Land Buddhist movement, and establishing a doctrinal lineage with Buddhist thinkers in India and China.

Shinran believed that in the age of Dharma Decline, it was no longer possible to achieve enlightenment through traditional monastic practices, and thus one could only rely on the vows of Amida, in particular the 18th or "Primal Vow" and seek rebirth in the Pure Land.

shinto A new Japanese Zen Buddhist monk, usually in his first year at the monastery

shippei A bamboo staff which curves slightly, which is used as a symbol of a master's authority in Japanese Zen Buddhism. In contrast to the keisaku, the shippei was often used as a disciplinary measure for poorly meditating monks.

shokan The first koan received by a Japanese Zen Buddhist monk

shripujya The head of an institution of Śvētāmbara yatis (stationary monks). Only a celibate yati could become a shripujya. The term of acharya is now used instead.

shukin The cord a Japanese Zen Buddhist monastic wears around their waist

shuto ***see*** **soehi**

shuya In a Japanese Zen Buddhist monastery, the evening fire-watch at the time of kaichin, when one or two monks make the rounds of the monastery buildings and properties to make sure that all fires are out

Shwegyin Nikaya; Shwekyin Nikāya The second largest order of monks in Burma [Myanmar]. It has about 50,000 members, constituting about 5% of Burmese monks. It was founded in the mid–19th century and is more orthodox and hierarchical than the Thudhamma Nikaya. The sangha sammuti is the head of the order.

Shwekyin Nikaya ***see*** **Shwegyin Nikaya**

Sibyl of the Rhine Nickname of St. Hildegard of Bingen

siesta ***see*** **nap**

Sikhism There are no Sikh monastics. Monasticism is specifically forbidden in the Sikh faith.

sikkhamana ***see*** **samaneri**

siksamana ***see*** **samaneri**

siladhara ***see*** **maechi**

sima; sīma In Buddhism and Hinduism, a boundary in which official sangha (monastic community) acts may take place; a monastic chapter house or meeting area • *see also* **chapter house**

simple priory ***see*** **obedientiary priory**

simple silence ***see*** **little silence**

simple vows; first vows Religious vows that must be renewed after a period of time. In some orders, these are all that are given. In other orders, these are given when one passes out of their novitiate and lives under them before being replaced by solemn vows when one makes their final profession. Generally, oblate vows are considered simple vows.

singnad janeu A small horn, rudraksha bead (for the protection of Lord Shiva), and a ring attached to the thread on a woolen thread worn around the neck by both Nath monks and householders. The horn is important to their religious practice and is blown during certain festivals, rituals, and before they eat.

sister prior *see* **prioress**

Sisterhood of the Holy Communion *see* **Ayres, Anne**

sisters *see* **nuns**

Sisters for Christian Community A contemporary Christian semi-monastic ecumenical community founded in 1970. Members live according to the evangelical vows. The vow of poverty is lived as serving and sharing; obedience is practiced by the individual member through a careful listening to God and the poor; and chastity is lived as celibate love. Members are self-supporting and each member determines her own ministry according to her own call and ability. There is a two-year formation program before vows are taken. As of 2015, there were 31 regions spread throughout 14 nations.

Sisters of Charity An Anglican religious order following the Rule of St. Vincent de Paul. They were founded in 1869 and do parish and mission work in and around Plymouth, England. They also run a nursing home. Their post-nominal initials are S.C. They had a convent in West Virginia serving children and dogs, but the American branch merged with the Community of St. Mary in 2008 and are now housed in their convent in Sewanee, Tennessee. • *See also* **Community of St. Mary**

Sisters of St. Joseph of Peace *see* **Cusack, Margaret Anna**

Sisters of Suffering *see* **Capuchin Poor Clares**

Sisters of the Assumption *see* **Religious of the Assumption**

sisya A person who wants to become a sādhu or sādhvī

Sixth Hour *see* **Sext**

sizars *see* **servitors**

skepe *see* **magoulikion**

skete A monastic community of the Eastern Church that has a number of small isolated cells with a centralized church. A skete is considered a bridge between strict anchoretic and cenobitic lifestyles since it is a blend of the two. A typical cell usually consists of a front room for work, sleep, and receiving visitors, and another room for prayer and contemplation. The cell of St. Macarius was rumored to have had a small tunnel dug in the back that led to a cave where he could escape from the throngs that came to visit him.

Furnishings for a cell would typically consist of a mat and sometimes a simple woven stool called an embrimia. By day the monk would do his labor in the front chamber sitting on his mat, and at night he would pray on his embrimia and perhaps later use it as a pillow. Occasionally a cell would have elaborate furnishings and even a courtyard. Monks usually stayed alone all week only gathered on the weekends for common worship.

The two most common skills in the early sketes were rope making and basket weaving. Even Macarius the Great, founder of Egyptian monasticism, was a skilled basket weaver who trained other monks how to weave. These two jobs were prevalent because there were numerous marshes around the Scetis valley that provided the raw materials. The monks would either take their finished products to the church on the weekends to be sold or sell them to camel caravans when they passed by their cells.

The skete monastic style fell out of favor with the Church at the beginning of the Middle Ages because of the need for safety from raiders. Skete monasteries still exist, however.

Sketis *see* **Scetis**

skeuophylakion *see* **sacristy**

skeuophylakissa *see* **sacristan**

skeuophylax *see* **sacristan**

skoufos *see* **skufia**

skufia; skufiya; skoufos A soft-sided brimless black cap worn by monastics in the Eastern Church. The Russian style top is pointed, the Greek style is flat and pleated, and the Romanian style is flat with raised edges. Typically, monastics receives their skufia either when they first become a novice or when they are tonsured. A monk or nun who has been tonsured to the great schema will wear a skufia that has been embroidered with prayers, crosses, and figures of seraphim. A nun will sometimes wear a skufia over her monastic veil, while monks often wear the skufia (without a veil) when the epanokalimavkion (a cloth veil, usually black, which is worn with a kamilavkion) might get in the way of work.

skufiya *see* **skufia**

slype A narrow passage between two buildings, as between the transept and chapter house of a monastery; any passage piercing a claustral complex so as to allow access to the cloister from outside

small schema *see* **stavrophore**

snaghati *see* **samghati**

soan *see* **an**

societa *see* **confraternity**

society of apostolic life In the Roman Catholic Church, a society that resembles a religious institute, but differs in that their members do not take religious vows. They pursue an apostolic while leading a life in common as brothers or sisters and striving for the perfection of charity through observing the society's constitutions. In some of these societies the members assume the evangelical counsels by a bond other than that of religious vows.

The Congregation for Institutes of Consecrated Life and Societies of Apostolic Life has ecclesial oversight of institutes of consecrated life.

Society of St. Augustine; Societas Sancti Augustini; Augustinians of Kansas A Roman Catholic Institute of Consecrated Life founded in 1981. It includes priests, brothers, and laity. It differs somewhat from other Augustinian Communities in that it places great emphasis on the inclusion and involvement of the laity in the life and ministry of the community.

Members wear a black or white mendicant tunic, black leather cincture, scapular and capuce.

The religious sisters affiliated with the Society, share in the charism of the community, but are governed separately from the men.

Society of St. John the Evangelist; Cowley Fathers An Anglican monastic order for men founded in 1866 at Cowley, England by Richard Meux Benson and Charles Chapman Benson that is considered the first stable men's monastic order founded in the Anglican Communion since Henry VIII closed the monasteries in the 16th century. In 1870, the order opened a house in Boston, Massachusetts. It became part of the Episcopal Church of the United States and is now located in Cambridge, Massachusetts. The order also had houses in Scotland, India, South Africa, Japan, and Canada, but these are all closed. Only the monastery in Massachusetts remains.

Members of the order use the post-nominal initials S.S.J.E.

socius A fellow friar elected to accompany the provincial to meetings of the general chapter

sodo; sōdō; sorin, senmon dōjō A formal Zen training monastery, at which a monk can gain qualification for priesthood. Note that in traditional monasteries there is a building called the monks' hall which is also called a sōdō, in which practitioners sleep, eat, and practice zazen (meditation) together.

sohei; sōhei; shuto Buddhist warrior monks of both medieval and feudal Japan. At certain points of history they held considerable power, obliging the imperial and military governments to collaborate, but often they were ineffective against regular armies. The prominence of the sōhei rose in parallel with the ascendancy of the Tendai school's influence between the 10th and 17th centuries. The warriors protected land and intimidated rival schools of Buddhism, becoming a significant factor in the spread of Buddhism and the development of different schools.

Many of these so-called monks made little pretense of religion other than shaving their heads, and many were little better than bullies and hooligans. The naginata, a thrusting pole arm four to eight feet long with a slightly curved iron blade of about two inches on the end was the standard weapon of the sohei from the 11th to 15th centuries and became their symbol.

Soldiers of St. Antony *see* **Antonines**

solemn vows; life vows; perpetual vows Religious vows that are considered to be permanent, although in practice they may be annulled by proper authority

Solesmes Abbey; Abbaye Saint-Pierre de Solesmes; St. Peter's Abbey, Solesmes A Benedictine abbey founded in 1010 and located in Solesmes, France. It was sacked and burned in the Hundred Years War (1337-1453) then later rebuilt. It went into decline in the first part of the 17th century under commendatory abbots, but revived was it was put under the auspices of the Maurists in 1664. It was put out of commission and partially destroyed during the French Revolution in 1790 and the monks either imprisoned or exiled to the island of Jersey. In 1825, the government put the abbey up for sale and in 1832 it was bought by Prosper Gueranger, a local priest. The Benedictines moved back in 1833. Still, it was dissolved by the French Government no fewer than four times. In 1880, 1882, and 1883 the monks managed to move back after being exiled or dispersed. Between 1901 and 1922 the monks were exiled in England before returning yet again. Besides its history of survival against all odds, the abbey is the mother house of 25 monastic foundations and is notable for its revival of Gregorian chant. • *See also* **Gueranger, Prosper Louis Pascal**

Sons of the Covenant *see* **Members of the Covenant**

sosan; sōsan Sanzen (formal meditation) held on the first, fourth, and seventh evenings of a sesshin (meditation retreat) in a Japanese Zen Buddhist monastery, during which the shika (hostler) rings the kansho (small hanging bell), and the monks meet the rōshi (monastic master) in order of rank. All monks must participate. • *See also* **dokusan**

sostikon The habit of a monk in the Orthodox Church—it is similar to a cassock

Sovereign Military Order of Malta *see* **Knights Hospitaller**

sozarei A formal sarei (tea ceremony) in a Japanese Zen Buddhist monastery that all monks are required to attend. Usually held before important affairs

spatiamentum A four hour walk that Carthusians take every Monday, in an otherwise very strict weekly regime. During the walk, the monks may talk freely in a light-hearted and simple way. The monks walk in pairs and change partners every half hour so that during the walk each has eight partners. This permits a fraternal sharing between the monks and is an important complement to what is otherwise an extremely solitary life.

Specific Behavior for the Templar Order; Latin Rule; Rule of the Knights Templar A monastic rule with 72 clauses attributed to Bernard de Clairvaux and Hugues de Payens that outlines the ideal behavior of a knight. Predominately inspired by the *Rule of St. Benedict,* it also borrows from the *Rule of St. Augustine.* Originally written in Latin in 1128, it was translated into French and modified about ten years later. Still later, it was expanded to 609 articles, notably covering hierarchy and justice within the order.

speke house *see* **parlor**

spendement *see* **bursary**

Spiritual Franciscans; Spirituals; Fraticelli; Spiritual Franciscans; Zelanti; Michaelites; Fraticelli de Paupere Vita; Brothers of the Poor Life Various Roman Catholic sects appearing chiefly in Italy during the 14th and 15th centuries that were extreme proponents of the *Rule of St. Francis,* especially with regard to poverty. They regarded the wealth of the Church as scandalous. Their history is very confused, being called different things at different times, and shifting from one group or another. Various popes tried to reconcile them but it never quite worked out. They repudiated the pope at times, were declared heretical, excommunicated, and eventually faded away.

Spirituals *see* **Spiritual Franciscans**

squint *see* **hagioscope**

sramanera *see* **samanera**

sramaneri *see* **samaneri**

sramanerika *see* **samaneri**

S.S.J.E. Post-nominal initials of the Society of St. John the Evangelist

stabilitas *see* **stability**

stability; stabilitas One of the three Benedictine vows in which a monastic promises to stay in the community in which profession was made until the time of death. Stability is also the rule among Augustinian Canons and among monastics of the Eastern Church.

stall The place assigned to a monastic in the choir

staple A district granted to an abbey

starets *see* **startsy**

staritsa *see* **startsy**

startsy; starets (men); staritsa (women) Elders of a Russian Orthodox monastery who function as venerated advisers and teachers. It is believed that through ascetic struggle, prayer, and hesychasm (quietness), the Holy Spirit bestows special gifts onto the elder including the ability to heal, prophesy, and most importantly, give effective spiritual guidance and direction. Startsy are looked upon as being an inspiration to believers and an example of saintly virtue, steadfast faith, and spiritual peace. They are not appointed by any authority; they are simply recognized by the faithful as being people "of the Spirit."

statio The place in which monastics formed up before processing into the church; also the practice of monastics lining up and composing themselves before processing into the church or oratory

stationaries Old and retired monastics for whom some of the rules have been relaxed. Often this took place after 50 years of service and they were lodged in the infirmary.

stauropegial monastery *see* **stavropegial monastery**

stauropegion In the Eastern Church, a monastic foundation charter issued by local bishop or the patriarch

stavropegial monastery; stavropegic monastery; stauropegial monastery An Eastern Orthodox or Eastern Catholic monastery subordinated directly to a patriarch or synod rather than to a local bishop

stavropegic monastery *see* **stavropegial monastery**

stavrophore; stavrophoros (Greek); little schema; lesser schema; microschema; small schema; krestonosets (Church Slavonic) An Orthodox monk ranking above a rassophore and below a schema monk. This rank is given when the superior believes the monastic has reached an appropriate level of discipline, dedication, and humility. At this stage, the monastic makes formal vows of stability of place, chastity, obedience, and poverty. At the investiture, the new stavrophore is given a wooden cross and a paramand. The outer cassock worn by a stavrophore is more ample than that worn by a rassophore.

In the Coptic Church there are only two degrees of professed monks, corresponding to the rassophore combined with the stavrophore and the great schema. • *See also* **paramand**

stavrophoros *see* **stavrophore**

Stein, Edith (1891–1942); Teresa Benedicta of the Cross; Teresa Benedicta a Cruce (Latin) Polish Discalced Carmelite nun and philosopher. Born into an observant Jewish family, she was an atheist as a teenager. In 1916 she earned a doctorate in philosophy summa cum laude from the University of Gottingen and obtained an assistantship at the University of Freiberg, but because she was a woman was unable to advance. From her studies, she became drawn to the Roman Catholic Church and was baptized in 1922. She wanted to join the Carmelites but was dissuaded by her spiritual advisors. In 1933 she lost her teaching position because she was of Jewish heritage, but in 1934 was at last admitted as a Carmelite novice. In 1938, she and her sister Rosa, an extern Carmelite tertiary sister, were sent to the Netherlands for their safety, but in 1942 they were arrested and died in a gas chamber at Auschwitz in 1942. She was canonized in 1998.

Stelliferi *see* **Knights of the Cross with the Red Star**

Stephen of Muret, St. *see* **Grandmontines**

Stephen of Perm, St. (1340–1396) Russian Orthodox monk and missionary credited with the conversion of the Komi to Christianity and the establishment of the Bishopric of Perm. Stephen took his monastic vows in Rostov. In 1376, he voyaged to lands along the Vychegda and Vym rivers and engaged in the conversion of the Zyriane (Komi peoples). Rather than imposing the Latin or Church Slavonic on the indigenous pagan populace, as his contemporary missionaries did, he learned their language and traditions. Although his destruction of pagan idols earned him the wrath of some Permians, Pimen, the Metropolitan of All Rus, created him the first bishop of Perm.

stew pond; stew A fish pond used to store live fish ready for eating. During the Middle Ages, stew ponds were often attached to monasteries to supply fish over the winter.

Stockdale, Henrietta (1847–1911) British Anglican religious sister and nursing pioneer. In 1874, she went to South Africa and was one of the founding members of the Community of St Michael and All Angels there that same year. About 1875, she took her full vows. She worked first as a nurse in the mining camps, but returned to England in 1876. Upon her return to South Africa she established the country's first training school for nurses. She strongly influenced the passage of the Cape Colony's passage of the Medical and Pharmacy Act of 1891, which was the world's first law providing for the registration of nurses and midwives. • *See also* **Community of St. Michael and All Angels**

Stoudion *see* **Studios**

Stoudios *see* **Studios**

Stoudite *see* **Studite**

Strict Observance of the Order of Grandmont *see* **Grandmontines**

Studion *see* **Studios**

Studios; Stoudios; Stoudion; Studion; Monastery of Stoudios; Monastery of St. John the Forerunner Founded in 462, and in its day the most important monastery of Constantinople. Its laws and customs were taken as models by the monks of Mount Athos and of many other monasteries of the Eastern Orthodox Church and their influence still remains. It was destroyed by Crusaders in 1204 and not fully restored until 1290. It was largely destroyed again in 1453 when the Turks conquered Constantinople. The only part to survive into the 20th century was the Cathedral of St. John Baptist, a 5th century basilica that is probably the oldest remaining church in Istanbul. In 2014, there were plans to convert it into a mosque.

Studite; Stoudite A monk of Studios; of, like, or relating to Studios

stupa A mound-like or hemispherical structure containing the remains of Buddhist monks or nuns that is used as a place of meditation

stylite Originally a form of monastic asceticism that arose in 4th century Syria in which a hermit lived in the open air exposed to the elements. Legend has it that it was invented by Maro, after whom the Maronite Church is named. Symbolically, living on a pillar suspended the stylite between heaven and earth.

In the 5th century, St. Symeon Stylites adapted this practice by living on the relatively broad top of a pillar for the last 37 years of his life. He ate and slept very little and slept standing up leaning against a balustrade. There were many other stylites that followed. One or two isolated attempts seem to have been made to introduce this form of asceticism into the West, but it met with little favor so it remained mainly a practice in the Eastern Church, where it persisted into the 14th century.

subalmoner An under almoner

subcantor ***see*** **succentor**

subcellarer; parakellarios (Eastern Church); parakellarites (Eastern Church) An assistant to the cellarer

subdean An under dean; the deputy or substitute of a dean • *subdeanery*: the office or rank of subdean • *subdecanal*: of or relating to a subdean or subdeanery

Subiaco Abbey; Abbey of St. Scholastica; Abbazia di Santa Scolastica An Italian Benedictine abbey located just outside the town of Subiaco. Founded in the 6th century by St. Benedict of Nursia, it was one of 13 monasteries that sprung up around Benedict.

It was sacked by Saracens several times in the 9th century but grew powerful in the 11th and 12th century when it boasted vast lands, a large number of monks, and elaborate, ornate liturgy. Grasping commendatory abbots sapped that strength in the 14th through to 18th centuries. Some relief came in 1753, when Pope Benedict XIV decided to remove commendatory abbots' power over the day-to-day running of affairs. At the end of the 18th century, the abbey was suppressed when the French occupied the Papal States. Pope Pius VII restored it as soon as he regained his independence. The abbey today has a little over 20 monks. • *See also* **Benedict of Nursia, St.**

Subiaco Cassinese Congregation An international congregation of Roman Catholic Benedictine houses within the Benedictine Confederation. It developed from the Subiaco Congregation that was first formed in 1867 as a reform of the Cassinese Congregation which was originally formed in 1408. In 2013, these two congregations joined together to form the Subiaco Cassinese Congregation. In 2013, it had 80 men's houses with 45 affiliated women's houses. There are 1,329 members of whom 535 are priests.

Subiaco Congregation ***see*** **Subiaco Cassinese Congregation**

subordinate prior ***see*** **subprior**

subordinate prioress ***see*** **subprior**

subprior; subprioress Among communities of friars, the second superior is called the sub-prior and his office is similar to that of the claustral prior in the Benedictine Order. In many monasteries, especially larger ones, the claustral prior is assisted by a subprior, who holds the third place of authority in the monastery. • *See also* **warden of the order**

subprioress ***see*** **subprior**

subsacrist; undersacristan; paraecclesiarch (Eastern church) An assistant to the sacristan

succentor; subcantor A monastic subordinate to the precentor—during antiphonal chants, the succentor leads the liturgical northern half of the choir, in addition to encouraging singing, maintaining attentiveness, and making sure the choir books were in place. Other duties include ringing the bell and winding the clocks.

Sudhamma Nikaya ***see*** **Thudhamma Nikaya**

Suger (ca. 1081–1151) French Benedictine monk, abbot, friend, and counsellor both of King Louis VI and King Louis VII, historian, and early patron of Gothic architecture. He began his monastic career in 1091, when he was given as an oblate to the abbey of St. Denis at the age of ten. In 1106 he became secretary to the abbot of Saint-Denis. In 1107 he became provost of Berneval in Normandy, and in 1109 of Tours. In 1118, Louis VI sent him as a representative to the court of Pope Gelasius II at Maguelonne.

On his return in 1122, he became the abbot of St-Denis and continued to serve as a statesman while undertaking the reorganization and reform of abbey.

suikai In Japanese Zen Buddhism, warnings or instructions from the master or from superior monks

suizen The Japanese Zen Buddhist practice of playing the shakuhachi bamboo flute as a means of attaining self-realization. The monks from the semi-monastic Fuke sect of who practiced suizen were called komusō (emptiness monks).

superior The head of a religious community

superior general; general superior The chief executive of a Roman Catholic religious institute. The office first appeared in the 13th century with the development of the centralized government of the mendicant orders. Because of restrictions, it wasn't until the 19th century that religious congregations of women were able to have superiors general, but the position is now common.

In Roman canon law, the generic term supreme moderator is used instead of superior general. Many orders and congregations use their own title for the person who holds this position. Some examples are abbot general, custos-general, master general, minister general, mother general, prior general, rector general, general director, general directress.

Sometimes there is a provincial superior who holds an intermediate position between a superior general and the superior of an individual community. • *See also* **master general**

supper; cena A light meal served in evening to supplement the major meal which was served at noon

supreme moderator ***see*** **superior general**

suzu A small hand bell rung through the halls of a Japanese Zen Buddhist monastery as a wakeup call

Svetambara; Śvētāmbara One of the two orders of Jain monastics. The other is Digambara.

Initiation involves a procession in which the initiate symbolically disposes of their material wealth and makes donations. This is followed (or preceded) by another ritual in which the initiate receives an ogho (a small broom made of wool) from their mentor as a symbol of welcome into the monastic order. The initiate then puts on monastic clothing and plucks out hairs by hand. Further rituals formally initiate them into the monastic order.

The Śvētāmbara Terapanth sect requests written permission from a person's parents before initiating them into the ascetic order and has a new rank of samana (junior monk). The Śvētāmbara sādhus (monks) and sādhvīs (nuns) both wear white seamless clothes. They also carry a rajoharan (a broom-like object made from dense, thick thread strands) to sweep the ground ahead of them or before sitting down to avoid inadvertently crushing small insects. The yati (stationary monks) of the Śvētāmbara sect do not wander; they usually live in temples and perform daily rituals.

swami ***see*** **sadhu**

swamini ***see*** **sadhvi**

sylfdemas ***see*** **sarabaites**

Sylvestrine Congregation A congregation of Roman Catholic Benedictine monks founded in 1231 by St. Sylvester Gozzolini. They are members of the Benedictine Confederation. The congregation does not include women and does not have abbeys. The only abbot it has is the abbot general who supervises all the houses of the congregation. Sylvestrines wear a habit of dark blue. They may use the post-nominal initials O.S.B. Silv., although since they joined the Benedictine Confederation in the mid–20th century, that is not common.

Symeon the New Theologian, St. (949–1022) Byzantine Orthodox monk, abbot, priest, mystic, and poet. By the time he was 30, he was tonsured as a monk, ordained as a priest, and abbot of the Monastery of St. Mammas, a position he held for 25 years.

Symeon's attempts to return monasticism to its original simpler form were not always popular with his monks and at one point about 30 of them rebelled and took their case to the Patriarch Sisinios. The patriarch supported Symeon, and exiled the monks. Symeon nevertheless pardoned the monks and urged them to return.

In 1005 Symeon resigned as abbot in 1005 and took up a more solitary life at the monastery. Some of his strongly held positions—especially the need to have actual experience of the Holy Spirit to speak about God—rankled church authorities and in 1009 they sent him into exile on the Asiatic shore of the Bosporus, supposedly alone, in the middle of winter, and without food. Here he found a deserted chapel and supporters donated land and money to start the monastery of St. Macrina. His supporters appealed to Sergius II, the Patriarch of Constantinople, who lifted the order of exile, and offered him a see in Constantinople. Symeon refused the bishopric and stayed at St. Macrina where his efforts and beliefs were appreciated.

synaxis In the Eastern Church, an assembly for liturgical purposes, generally through the celebration of Vespers, Matins, the Little Hours, and the Eucharist, but also for major feasts

synodikon An inventory in a Eastern church or monastery that registered items donated and the commemoration day of the donor; the room in an Orthodox monastery used for chapter meetings

~T~

Ta Tao Fa Tzu *see* **Voramai Kabilsingh**

tabula A wooden board hung in a Cistercian monastery and struck with a mallet by the prior to summon the monks to eat, wash, or attend a meeting. It was also used during the Easter period when no bells were allowed to be rung. If one of the community was about to die the tabula was sounded continually to call the brethren to gather around the dying man. The community's notice-board that hung in the east gallery of the cloister was also called a tabula, and listed the rota (weekly schedule) of hebdomarians and servitors.

T'ai-hsu *see* **Taixu**

Taixu (1890–1947); T'ai-hsu Chinese Buddhist monk and activist who advocated for the reform and renewal of Chinese Buddhism. He was ordained a monk in the Linji School of Chan (Zen) Buddhism in Xiao Jiǔhuá Temple in Suzhou at the age of 16. In 1911 he made contact with the revolutionaries plotting to overthrow the Qing dynasty and participated in some secret revolutionary activities.

After the establishment of the new Republic of China, he founded the Association for the Advancement of Buddhism, but it lasted only a short time due to resistance from conservative Buddhists. Nevertheless, until his death Taixu worked toward the revival of Buddhism in China, although because of the economic and political turmoil that China experienced through wars and revolutions, few of his projects were successful.

Taize A ecumenical New Monastic community of men with a Protestant bent founded in Switzerland in 1940 Roger Schutz-Masauche. After the war, they moved to Taizé, a small village near Cluny in France. They are dedicated to communal life, prayer, reconciliation, and service, and are particularly active in youth ministry. They pledge obedience and chastity and live according to the *Rule of Taizé,* written by Br. Roger. Although attracting about 100,000 visitors a year, the community does not plant daughter houses, although some small groups live away from the monastery performing community services. At the end of 2010, the community was composed of about 100 brothers, from Protestant and Catholic traditions, who originate from about 30 countries across the world.

taking the veil Receiving or being covered with a veil as a nun's symbol of retirement from the world; to become a nun

taku Wooden clappers, two pieces of hard wood, used in Japanese Zen Buddhist monasteries. They make a sharp clacking noise and are used to lead walking meditation and to punctuate mealtime recitations.

takuhatsu Japanese Zen Buddhist mendicancy; the monastic begging rounds

talapoin; talapoy A Buddhist monk—an obsolete term sometimes formerly used in the West

talapoy *see* **talapoin**

tan Literally, "venerable," the Thai term of address for a monk. Monks of more than ten years of service and abbots are addressed as "ajahn."

tanbuton A large cushion upon which Japanese Zen Buddhist Rinzai monks sit during zazen (meditation)

tangaryo *see* **niwazume**

tangazume *see* **niwazume**

tanto; tantō One of two officers in a Japanese Zen Buddhist monastery in charge of training monks

Taoist monasticism Quanzhen Taoism, which is present almost exclusively in the north of China, and includes all Taoist orders which have a monastic institution. The lifestyle of the monks and nuns is comparable to that of Buddhist monastics in that they are celibate, vegetarian, and live in monasteries. Taoism itself was in a long period of decline, but there has been renewed interest in it, with many temples are being restored—at least as tourist attractions—and there has been a modest growth in monastic vocations.

taphiotes A Greek Orthodox monk in charge of a cemetery

tashi-lama *see* **panchen lama**

tasooni A Coptic nun. The word literally means sister.

taylery The tailor shop of a monastery in the Western Church. It is supervised by the chamberlain and usually located in the curia (outer courtyard). In larger monasteries it may employ laymen.

Teacher of Germany A nickname of Rabanus Maurus Magnentius

Teaching Priests of the Ardèche *see* **Congregation of St. Basil**

teihatsu In a Japanese Zen Buddhist monastery, the shaving of the head

Templars *see* **Knights Templar**

temple town *see* **abbey town**

tempora minutionis *see* **bloodletting**

ten precept mother *see* **maechi**

Ten Precepts The precepts or training rules for Buddhist sramaneras (novice monks) and sramaneris (novice nuns). They are the same in most schools of Buddhism.

1. Refrain from accepting money.
2. Refrain from incorrect speech.
3. Refrain from killing living creatures.
4. Refrain from singing, dancing, playing music or attending entertainment programs (performances).
5. Refrain from sitting on high chairs and sleeping on luxurious, soft beds.
6. Refrain from stealing.
7. Refrain from taking food at inappropriate times (after noon).
8. Refrain from taking intoxicants.
9. Refrain from unchastity (sensuality, sexuality, lust).
10. Refrain from wearing perfume, cosmetics and garlands (decorative accessories).

Tendai monks *see* **kaihogyo**

tengai The straw basket hat of komuso semi-monastics

tenjin A meal served to an unsui (itinerant monk) at the home of a believer. Japanese Zen Buddhist monks often receive tenjin at the end of the morning takuhatsu (begging) rounds.

Tenzin Gyatso (1935–) A Tibetan Buddhist monk who is the 14th Dalai Lama. His birth name was Lhamo Dondrub. He was formally recognized as the dalai lama in 1939. In 1959, he escaped to India to avoid capture by the Chinese, and has lived in India ever since. He received the Nobel Peace Prize in 1989 and the American Congressional Gold Medal in 2007. He has traveled the world and has spoken about the welfare of Tibetans, environment, economics, women's rights, non-violence, interfaith dialogue, physics, astronomy, Buddhism and science, cognitive neuroscience, reproductive health, and sexuality, along with various Buddhist teachings. All attracting worldwide notice.

In a 2013 Harris Poll of 7,245 adults across the five largest European countries and the United States, the Dalai Lama was tied with President Barack Obama with the highest levels of popularity, of the world's leaders. He is currently considered the world's most popular monastic.

He has stated that he may not choose to be reincarnated at all, or to be reincarnated as a woman.

tenzo In a Japanese Zen Buddhist Sōtō monastery, the kitchen; also the head cook for a monastery

Terce; Third Hour (Orthodox) A fixed time of prayer of the Daily Office in almost all the Christian liturgies. It is considered one of the little hours, consists mainly of psalms, and is said about 9 a.m. Its name comes from Latin and refers to the third hour of the day after dawn. The origin of Terce, like that of Sext and None to which it bears a close relationship, dates back to Apostolic times.

Teresa Benedicta a Cruce *see* **Stein, Edith**

Teresa Benedicta of the Cross *see* **Stein, Edith**

Teresa of Avila, St. (1515–1582); Teresa of Jesus Prominent Spanish Carmelite nun, mystic, writer, and theologian. She was a reformer of the Carmelite Order and the movement she initiated, later joined by St. John of the Cross, eventually led to the establishment of the Discalced Carmelites. Her paternal grandfather was a marrano (Jewish convert to Christianity) and was condemned by the Spanish Inquisition for allegedly returning to the Jewish faith.

Teresa entered a Carmelite Monastery of the Incarnation in Ávila, Spain in 1535, where she was dismayed with the spiritual malaise prevailing at the monastery. This caused her to find a sponsor for a new monastery. She resolved to found a reformed Carmelite convent correcting the laxity which she had found in the Monastery of the Incarnation and others. Guimara de Ulloa, a woman of wealth and a friend, supplied the funds. In 1562 the Convent of San José was founded featuring absolute poverty, renunciation of property, flagellation, and discalceation. Local authorities thought this was scandalous and threatened suppression, but papal support saved it.

In 1567, she received a patent from the Carmelite general to establish new houses for her order, and recruited John of the Cross and Anthony of Jesus to help found the first monastery of Discalced Carmelite Brethren in 1568.

In 1576 the older observant Carmelite Order got her confined in Toledo and forbade the founding of further houses. It wasn't until 1579 that the charges were dropped and she went on to found a large number of reformed Carmelite monasteries and convents.

Her books, notably her autobiography *The Life of Teresa of Jesus* and her seminal work *The Interior Castle*, are an integral part of Spanish Renaissance literature as well as Christian mysticism and Christian meditation practices.

She was canonized in 1622, and named a Doctor of the Church in 1970.

Teresa of Calcutta, Mother (1910–1997) An Albanian Roman Catholic nun who founded the Missionaries of Charity order in 1950. Born Anjezë Gonxhe Bojaxhiu, best known as Mother Teresa. Since her canonization in 2016 she known officially in the Catholic Church as St. Teresa of Calcutta. She won the Nobel Peace Prize in 1979. A controversial figure during her life and after her death, Teresa was widely admired for her charitable work. However, she was both praised and criticized for her opposition to abortion, and criticized for poor conditions in her houses for the dying.

She joined Sisters of Loreto at Loreto Abbey in Rathfarnham, Ireland, in 1928 at the age of 18. She arrived in India in 1929 and began her novitiate in Darjeeling, where she learned Bengali and taught school near her convent. She took her first vows in 1931 and made her solemn profession 1937. She was a teacher in Calcutta for about 20 years and appointed headmistress in 1944.

She began missionary work with the poor in 1948, adopted Indian citizenship, and founded a school in Calcutta, In 1949 she was joined by other women and this was the basis for the Missionaries of Charity which was founded in 1950. By 1997 the 13-member Calcutta congregation had grown to more than 4,000 sisters who managed orphanages, AIDS hospices, and charity centers worldwide, caring for refugees, the blind, disabled, aged, alcoholics, the poor, homeless, and victims of floods, epidemics, and famine.

Teresa of Jesus ***see*** **Teresa of Avila**

Teresians ***see*** **Order of Discalced Carmelites**

terrar ***see*** **bursar**

territorial abbey; abbey nullius; abbatia nullius dioecesis An abbey outside diocesan control, and that controls territory around the abbey. They developed around the 9th century in the Western Church, to serve the spiritual needs living around the abbey, especially in mission territories. The abbey's own chapel was used as a space for public worship of the laity. Territorial abbeys were primarily established in the Western Church, and were primarily either Benedictine or Cistercian. Since the Second Vatican Council they have gradually been done away with, and in 2018, only 11 remained. There are a few territorial abbeys in the Eastern Church.

territorial abbot; abbot nullius; abbot nullius dioeceseos The head of a territorial abbey. His authority is nearly equivalent to a bishop. Within the Roman Catholic Church, he has episcopal powers, except for the ordaining of priests and deacons. Although elected by his particular community, territorial abbots can only be installed with the pope's blessing.

tertianship The last three years of simple profession for sisters in the Missionaries of Charity, during which advanced religious studies are taken in Washington, D.C., Calcutta, or Rome.

tertiary A member of the third order of any monastic order, as the Franciscans, Dominicans, or Carmelites

Tertius Ordo Regularis S. Francisci ***see*** **Third Order Regular of St. Francis**

tesho-lama ***see*** **panchen lama**

teshu-lama ***see*** **panchen lama**

Teutonic Knights ***see*** **Order of Brothers of the German House of St. Mary in Jerusalem**

Thai Forest Tradition ***see*** **Forest Tradition**

thathanabaing; thathanapaing; thathanapyu Formerly, the head of the Buddhist monks in Burma [Myanmar], the position is somewhat akin to an archbishop. He had charge of monastic hierarchy and of monastic education. Originally called sangharaja when the office was established in the latter 14th century, the term thathanabaing and its variants gradually became more common. The office was abolished under British colonial rule in 1938 and never revived.

thathanapaing ***see*** **thathanabaing**

Theatines; Congregation of Clerics Regular of the Divine Providence; Regular Clerks of the Community; Pauline Monks; Apostolic Clerks; Regular Clerks of the Divine Providence An order of Italian monks, established in 1524, expressly to oppose the Reformation, and to raise the tone of piety among Roman Catholics—they hold no property, nor do they beg, but depend on what providence sends. The order is dedicated to the Holy Cross, and was founded by St. Cajetan (Gaetano dei Conti di Thiene), Paolo Consiglieri, Bonifacio da Colle, and Giovanni Pietro Carafa (afterwards Pope Paul IV). The mission of the order was to promote high standards among the clergy and the practice of virtue by the laity. The prohibition on owning property and soliciting alms tended to limit applicants to members of the aristocracy. The order was largely confined to Italy. In 1700, the Theatines had 1,400 members, but then decline set in. In 2014, they had only 170 members, of whom 139 were priests. Members use the post-nominal initials C.R.

Theodore of Stoudios ***see*** **Theodore the Studite**

Theodore of Studium ***see*** **Theodore the Studite**

Theodore the Studite, St. (ca. 758–ca. 826); Theodorus Studit; Theodore of Stoudios; Theodore of Studium Byzantine Greek monk, priest, abbot, and writer. He became a monk in 781, and was ordained a priest. In 797 or 798, he was named abbot of the abbot of the Monastery of St. John the Forerunner (Studios). To restore the monastery's primitive vigor he drew up new constitutions which gradually spread to monasteries in the rest of the Eastern Roman Empire. The monastery became a an active center of intellectual and artistic life and a model that exerted considerable influence on monasticism in the Eastern Church. To this day the *Constitutions of Theodore* constitutes a chief part of the Eastern Orthodox monastic tradition.

Theodorus Studit ***see*** **Theodore the Studite**

Theodosius of Kiev, St. (d. 1074); Theodosius of the Caves Ukrainian monk, abbot, and spiritual director, who helped bring cenobitic monasticism to Kievan Rus. He became a monk at 23, then later joined St. Anthony of Kiev in founding the Monastery of the Kiev Caves. When Theodosius was named abbot of the monastery he introduced the *Constitutions of Theodore* to the monastery from where it spread to all the monasteries of the Russian Orthodox Church. He is also credited for introducing spiritual direction as we know it today.

thera Elder—an honorific title automatically conferred upon a Buddhist monk of at ten years' standing

Therapeutae A Jewish contemplative monastic sect which flourished in Alexandria and other parts of the diaspora of Hellenistic Judaism in the final years of the Second Temple period (530 BCE–70 CE). First mentioned in *De Vita Contemplativa,* purportedly by the Jewish philosopher Philo of Alexandria (ca. 20 BCE–50 CE), the Therapeutae were described as celibate, ascetic, living in separate cells, and not believing in owning property. Their entire day was said to have been given up to spiritual exercises. Their holy books were the Pentateuch, the Prophets, the Psalms, and arcane writings of their own tradition.

Eusebius of Caesarea (ca. 263–339 CE) identified Philo's Therapeutae as the first Christian monks, as did Epiphanius of Salamis (ca. 315–403 CE), and also Pseudo-Dionysius, in the 5th century. It has to be noted that the first Christians were Jews who both accepted Jesus and also continued Jewish religious practices.

Therese of Lisieux, St. (1873–1897) French Carmelite nun, writer, and inventor of the "Little Way." She is one of the most popular saints of the Roman Catholic Church and is nicknamed "The Little Flower of Jesus."

She became a postulant in the cloistered Carmelite community of Lisieux, Normandy in 1888 at the age of 15. She became a novice in 1889, but 1893 asked not to receive further vows but to remain a novice permanently. She was inspired by a passage from Proverbs: "Whosoever is a little one, let him come to me" (Prov 9:4).

She died of tuberculosis at age 24, was canonized in 1925, and named a Doctor of the Church in 1997.

theri Elder—an honorific title automatically conferred upon a Buddhist nun of at ten years standing

Thich Nhat Hanh (1926–); Nguyen Xuan Bao Vietnamese Buddhist monk, peace activist, and writer of over 100 books. Born as Nguyen Xuan Bao in 1926, he entered the monastery at Từ Hiếu Temple at age 16 and was ordained as a monk in 1949.

His non-violent peace efforts created many enemies in Vietnam. In 1966, he came to the U.S. where he influenced Dr. Martin Luther King, Jr., to denounce the Vietnam War. When the war was over, he was denied permission to return to Vietnam, but led efforts to rescue boat people in the Gulf of Siam until stopped by pressure from the governments of Thailand and Singapore.

In 1966, he created the Order of Interbeing a monastic and lay group, teaching Five Mindfulness Trainings and the Fourteen Precepts. Afterwards, he created a number of monasteries and groups in the U.S., Europe, and Vietnam.

thilashin *see* **maechi**

Third Hour *see* **Terce**

third order; third order secular An association of lay persons who live according to the ideals and spirit of a Roman Catholic, Anglican, or Lutheran religious order (usually Franciscan, Carmelite, or Dominican), whose members share in the spirit of the order while in secular life, lead an apostolic life, and strive for Christian perfection under the higher direction of the order, but do not fall under the strictures of the vowed brothers and sisters of the order. Within the Benedictine tradition, members of the third order are properly called oblates.

Third Order of Our Lady of Mount Carmel; Lay Carmelites A quasimonastic branch of the Order of the Brothers of the Blessed Virgin Mary established in 1476. It is an association of Roman Catholic lay people who choose to live the Gospel in the spirit of the Carmelite Order and under its guidance. At Florence in 1308 some wore the habit and observed the rule. Still others became recluses in the anchorages attached to Carmelite churches.

The term "lay Carmelite" is somewhat problematic when describing the Secular/Third Orders because there are a number of ordained ministers (deacons, priests and bishops) who, while not lay people, are professed members of the Secular/Third Orders. Apart from attending a monthly community meeting, Lay Carmelites wear the brown scapular of Our Lady of Mt. Carmel as an external sign of dedication to Mary, and of trust in her protection. They are expected to participate in the daily celebration of the Eucharist when possible, and should spend about one half-hour in meditation each day, reflecting on the Scriptures, lectio divina, or some other appropriate type of personal reflective prayer. They also pray both Morning Prayer and Evening Prayer. • *See also* **Carmelites; Order of the Brothers of the Blessed Virgin Mary**

Third Order Regular of St. Francis of Penance *see* **Third Order Regular of St. Francis**

Third Order Regular of St. Francis; Third Order Regular of St. Francis of Penance; Religious of the Third Order Regular of St. Francis; Tertius Ordo Regularis S. Francisci A Franciscan mendicant order that grew out of the Third Order Secular and was founded in 1447. Unlike the Seculars, the Regulars make religious vows and live in community, and members are considered on a par with the first order Friars Minor. A new rule was approved in 1978 and is followed by both men and women. There are 176 Third Order Regular communities with 870 members, 576 of whom are priests. Members use the post-nominal initials T.O.R.

third order secular *see* **third order**

Third Order Secular of St. Francis; Secular Franciscan Order; Ordo Franciscanus Saecularis A semi-monastic order originally founded by St. Francis in 1212 for brothers and sisters who do not live in a religious community. Members of the order continue to live secular lives, however they gather regularly for fraternal activities. Although Secular Franciscans make a public profession and are consecrated, they are not bound by public vows as are religious living in community. There are 17,000 members in the United States alone.

third prior; third prioress In some abbeys, an official who is subordinate to the subprior or subprioress. In cathedral priories, they are equivalent to a subprior in other abbeys. A third prior in this case might also be called deece, deace, or deice and may also be the prior's chaplain.

Thomas Aquinas, St. (1225–1274) Brilliant Italian Dominican friar, priest. writer, theologian, hymnodist, and philosopher. At 19 Thomas he resolved to join the recently founded Dominican Order but his family was opposed and held him prisoner for a year. His mother helped him escape in 1245 and joined the Dominicans in Paris. In 1248 went to teach in the university at Cologne and declined an offer by the pope to make him abbot of the Benedictine abbey at Monte Cassino. During his time in Cologne, he wrote numerous works. In 1265 he became the papal theologian in Rome.

His best-known works are the *Disputed Questions on Truth*, the *Summa contra Gentiles*, and the *Summa Theologiae*. In the Roman Catholic Church he is regarded as the model teacher for those studying for the priesthood.

He was proclaimed a saint in 1323, and a Doctor of the Church in 1567.

thudong *see* **tudong**

thyroros *see* **porter**

ti-khau-ni *see* **bhikkhuni**

time of lessening *see* **bloodletting**

Tironensian Order *see* **Order of Tiron**

Tironensians; Tironians Members of the Order of Tiron

Tironian Of, like, or relating to the Order of Tiron

Tironians *see* **Tironensians**

tithing A group of ten monastics under the supervision of a dean

titivil A demon or devil in monasteries said to collect fragments of words dropped, skipped, or mumbled in the recitation of divine service, and to carry them to hell, to be registered against the offender

titular abbot One who has been named the abbot of an abbey that has been either destroyed or suppressed

titulus An administrative unit of the English province of the Hospitallers, based on a region with a preceptory at its center

toaca *see* **semantron**

tokudo To be ordained as a Japanese Zen Buddhist monastic

Tolomei, Bernardo *see* **Olivetans**

tonsure The practice of cutting or shaving some or all of the hair on the scalp, as a sign of religious devotion or humility. It developed first in monasticism and by the 7th century the Western Church for clerics as well. Tonsure is still a traditional practice in some religious orders, but not nearly as widespread as it was formerly. Buddhist monks and nuns both shave their heads. In Thailand, monks also shave their eyebrows because there was once a problem with lay people shaving their heads and collecting alms. While shaven heads were not uncommon at the time, shaven eyebrows on a layman would immediately identify him as an impostor.

T.O.R. The post-nominal initials used by Third Order Regulars of St. Francis

Transcendental Meditation Movement The Transcendental Meditation Movement has been called a spiritual movement, a new religious movement, a millenarian movement, a world affirming movement, a new social movement, a guru-centered movement, a personal growth movement, a religion, and a cult. Participation in TM programs does not require a belief system and is practiced by people from a diverse group of religious affiliations. It is said to be a "world affirming" and "accommodating" movement that does not seek to interfere with its members' involvement in their various religions.

Whatever one's viewpoint, the Movement has two groups that they self-define as monastic. In 1990 the Purúsha community consisted of 200 men who conducted "administrative and promotional details" for the worldwide organization. As of 2002 there were 300 male residents whose daily routine consisted of meditation from 7 a.m. to 11:30 a.m. and another group meditation in the evening. The rest of the day is taken up by educational presentations, fundraising, and work for "non-profit entities associated with the Spiritual Center." The residents also read Vedic literature and study Sanskrit. As of 2007, there was also a Purúsha community of 59 men in Uttarkashi, India. In 2012 the USA Purúsha group moved to a newly constructed campus called the West Virginia Retreat Center, located in Three Churches, West Virginia, USA. The campus consists of ten buildings and 90 male residents plus staff.

As of 2002 the 100 residents of the Mother Divine community for women was located at the Spiritual Center in Boone, North Carolina as part of an organization called Maharishi Global Administration through Natural Law. Their daily routine is similar to the Purúsha community and in addition they operate The Heavenly Mountain Ideal Girls' School, a fully accredited North Carolina non-public school for grades 9 through 12.

trapeza *see* **refectory**

trapezarios In the Eastern Church, the monastic in charge of discipline in the refectory

trapezopoios In the Eastern Church, the monastic in charge of setting the table the monastery refectory and waiting on other members

Trappistines *see* **Order of Cistercians of the Strict Observance**

Trappists *see* **Order of Cistercians of the Strict Observance**

Traveling Saint A nickname of Ippen Shonin

treasuress The female officer (obedientiary) in charge of a monastic community's wealth and valuables. This was an important and prestigious post.

Trinitarians *see* **Order of the Most Holy Trinity**

tudong; thudong The practice of Forest Tradition monks of wandering on foot through the countryside either on pilgrimage or in search of solitary retreat places in nature. During such wanderings, the monks sleep wherever is available and eat only what is offered by lay people along the way. They inhabit remote wilderness and forest dwellings as spiritual practice training grounds. • *See also* **Forest Tradition**

tulka In the Tibetan Mahayana school of Buddhism, a high-ranking lama who can choose their own manner of rebirth

tungshag hakang; confession temple A Tibetan Buddhist hall dedicated to the recitation of the Sutra of Confession and used for the monthly confession assembly for monastics. They are found only very large monasteries.

tunic A long-sleeved ankle length garment for monastics that is similar to a cassock, over which a scapular is worn. The main difference between a cassock and a monastic tunic is that tunics do not have the symbolic 33 buttons of Roman Catholic tunics or the 39 buttons of Anglican cassocks. Instead they have just enough to hold the garment together, and also the buttons are hidden behind a placket. In modern practice, postulants wear only a tunic, and do not receive the scapular until they are accepted into the novitiate.

turn ***see*** **turning window**

turnbroach A paid servant boy that helped in a monastery kitchen doing simple jobs like turning the spit for roasting, carrying in fuel, and catching fish in the stew-pond

turning window; turn; turntable; rota; magna fenestra versatilis A small revolving compartment next to the cell door in a Carthusian charterhouse and some Gilbertine houses to allow meals and other items to be passed in and out of the cell without the hermit having to see the bearer. In Gilbertine double monasteries, it was used to pass food through from the monks' side to the nuns'.

turntable ***see*** **turning window**

typicon ***see*** **typikon**

typikon; typicon; hypotyposis A document in the Eastern Church that includes both the rule of life of the community and the rule of prayer

~U~

ubhato-sangha A Buddhist community of both monks and nuns

Ugolino's Rule A rule of life drawn up for the Poor Clares by Ugolino, the Cardinal Bishop of Ostia (the future Pope Gregory IX). It was adopted by Poor Clare monasteries at Monticello, Perugia, Siena, Gattajola, and elsewhere and allowed for property to be held in trust by the papacy for the various communities. It was not adopted by Clare herself or her monastery at San Damiano. *Ugolino's Rule*, originally based on the *Rule of St. Benedict*, was amended in 1263 by Pope Urban IV to allow for the communal ownership of property and was adopted by a growing number of monasteries across Europe. Communities adopting this less rigorous rule came to be known as the Order of St. Clare (O.S.C.) or the Urbanist Poor Clares.

Clare herself resisted the Ugolino rule, since it did not closely enough follow the ideal of complete poverty advocated by Francis. In 1253, she managed to obtain a papal bull establishing a rule of her own (the *Rule of St. Clare*), more closely following that of the friars, which forbade the possession of property either individually or as a community. Originally applying only to Clare's community at San Damiano, this rule was also adopted by many monasteries. Communities that followed this stricter rule were fewer in number than the followers of the rule formulated by Cardinal Ugolino, and became known simply as "Poor Clares" (P.C.) or Primitives.

uncloister To release from a cloister; to remove from a monastic community

uncowl, defrock, uncloister To remove from a monastic community

undaka-satika A bathing robe for Buddhist nuns

undercroft The vault beneath a large building such as a dorter

United Society of Believers in Christ's Second Appearing *see* **Shakers**

unpan A flat, cloud-shaped gong used to signal mealtimes in Japanese Zen Buddhist monasteries

unsui; kōun ryūsui Broadly, an itinerant monk. Specifically, a Japanese Zen Buddhist postulant awaiting acceptance into a monastery. Sometimes they will travel from monastery to monastery on a pilgrimage to find the appropriate Zen master to study with.

upadhyay A Jain monk who both studies and teaches

upadhyayani *see* **abbess**

upajjhaaya The senior monastic who sponsors the candidate for ordination as a Buddhist monastic and on whom the new monk or nun will always depend for instruction

upasampada; upasampadā Literally, "approaching or nearing the ascetic tradition." In more common parlance it specifically refers to the rite of ordination by which one undertakes the Buddhist monastic life. Ordination takes place during the Vassa (retreat during the period of the monsoon). According to Buddhist monastic codes, a person must be 20 years old in order to become a monk or nun.

uposatha (Sanskrit); posadha (Pali) The monthly gatherings of Buddhist monks and nuns at the new moon and full moon where they recite the *Vinaya* rules and confess any violations

uposathagara The Buddhist hall where an uposatha takes place

Ursulines The term comprises a number of religious institutes of the Roman Catholic Church whose prime mission is the education of girls and young women. • *See also* **Company of St. Ursula; Order of St. Ursula**.

Ursulines of the Roman Union *see* **Order of St. Ursula**

Usages; Usus Conversorum The modified Cistercian rule used by lay brothers. First drawn up by Stephen Harding, probably in the early 1120s, it was used until the early 13th century to establish uniformity of practice.

uttarasanga; uttarāsaṅga A robe covering the upper body of fully ordained Buddhist monks and nuns. It goes over the inner robe (antarvasa). In representations of the Buddha, the uttarasanga rarely appears as the uppermost garment, since it is often covered by the outer robe (samghati). • *See also* **kasaya**

~V~

vagabundi; vagantes *see* **apostates**

vairagi *see* **sadhu**

Valadites *see* **Lebanese Maronite Order**

Vallombrosan Congregation; Vallombrosians A Roman Catholic Benedictine congregation, founded in the 11th century by Gualberto Visdomini, a Benedictine monk.

Gualberto adopted the *Rule of St. Benedict* but made it much more severe including perpetual silence, strict enclosure, and scourging for rule breaking. In addition, they were strictly choir monks and used lay brothers for physical work. Gualberto later mitigated his rule because it attracted few postulants and by the 13th century it had over 60 monasteries in Italy.

The congregation was reformed in the middle of the 15th century by Cassinese Benedictines, and again at the beginning of the 17th century. From 1662–1680 it was united to the Sylvestrines. In 1808 Napoleon troops plundered Vallombrosa and it lay deserted until 1815. Between war and commendatory abbots the congregation had continual trouble with decline.

The habit was originally gray, then tawny, but is now black like other Benedictines. Members of the congregation use the post-nominal initials O.S.B. Vall.

Shortly after the founder's death lay sisters were attached to the monastery of Vallombrosa. They were under the charge of an aged lay brother, lived in a separate house, and performed various household duties. This institute survived for less than a century, but when they ceased to be attached to the monasteries of monks these sisters probably continued to lead a conventual life. St. Humility is usually regarded as the foundress of the Vallombrosan nuns. • *See also* **Humility, St.**

Valor Ecclesiasticus; King's Book A survey of the finances of the church in England, Wales and the parts of Ireland that England controlled. It was done in 1535 on the orders of Henry VIII after the Act of Supremacy made him supreme head of the Church in his lands in 1534. All clergymen, parish priests, heads of monasteries, colleges, hospitals, and other institutions under church auspices were commanded to give sworn testimony before their local commissioners as to their income, the lands their establishments owned, and the revenues they received from all other sources. This was a prelude to him later claiming church and monastic properties.

vandan To respect teachers and monastics, one of the six duties of all Jains

Varangghana Vanavichayen *see* **Dhammarakhita Samaneri**

vardapet A hegumen (abbot) in the Armenian Apostolic Church

Vassa The three month rainy season retreat during which monastics of some Buddhist sects stay in monasteries or temple grounds. The practice actually predates Buddhism as it was a long-standing custom for mendicant ascetics in India not to travel during the rainy season as they may unintentionally harm crops, insects, or even themselves during their travels. Vassa is not typically observed where there is no rainy season. • *See also* **Kathina**

veghar A conical cowl worn by apeghas (monastic priests) of the Armenian Apostolic Church symbolizing their renunciation of worldly things

veil A headdress worn by members of women's religious communities. It drapes over the top and back of the head to the shoulders—sometimes as far as the back, and usually identifies the status of a woman within the community by its color and/or design.

Vespers; Evening Prayer; Evensong; Hesperinon (Greek Orthodox) The evening Daily Office that takes place about 5 p.m. Vespers gives thanks for the day just past and makes an evening sacrifice of praise to God (Ps 141:1).

vestarium A room in a monastery for storing the ordinary clothes of the monastics

vestiarius *see* **chamberlain**

vestivarius the monastic who distributes personal clothing, toiletries, and linens

vicar A priest employed as a substitute for a member of a religious house which has appropriated the revenue for the position

vicarage The endowment for a vicar

Vigils; Mesonyktikon (Orthodox) The Daily Office that in early monastic practice was a single office recited at midnight. The number of psalms, which at first varied, was subsequently fixed at 12, with the addition of a lesson from the Old Testament and another from the New Testament. From this developed three of the canonical hours: Vespers, Matins, and Lauds. This was the arrangement already in the days of Hippolytus (d. 236). St. Benedict of Nursia (6th century), in his description of the liturgy of the hours, always refers to Vigils as the night office. In the later Middle Ages Matins and Lauds were collectively referred to as Vigils.

vihara (Sanskrit, Pali); biara (Malay); wihan (Thai); kyaung (Burmese); wihara (Burmese); vihear (Khmer) A Buddhist monastic dormitory with small cells. A mahavihara is a monastic complex of viharas, in the manner of Mt. Athos in Greece.

vihara-civara Robes left in a Buddhist monastery by the laity for future use

vihear *see* **vihara**

villegiatura The practice beginning in the Middle Ages in which monastics of the Western Church were able to retreat to a small house in the country where the rule was relaxed to allow spiritual, mental, or physical recuperation

Vinaya One of the three parts that make up the *Tripiṭaka* (Buddhist scriptures). Its primary subject matter is the monastic rules for monks and nuns. The dating of the *Tripiṭakas* is unclear and could have been in the 3rd century BCE and transmitted orally from until written down in the 1st century BCE. Versions differ somewhat. The Patimokkha sections contain the rules themselves. The Vibhanga sections of the *Vinaya* constitute a commentary on these rules, giving detailed explanations of them along with the origin stories for each rule. The Khandhaka/Skandhaka sections give numerous supplementary rules grouped by subject, again with origin stories.

virgins' house In a kind or precursor to cenobitic life, a house where virgins of the early Church lived together under the care of a bishop or priest, and where they prayed together and served the poor

visitation The formal inspection of a religious community by a bishop or religious superior

Visitation of Holy Mary *see* **Salesian Sisters** *see* **Order of the Visitation of Holy Mary**

Visitation Order *see* **Salesian Sisters** *see* **Order of the Visitation of Holy Mary**

Visitation Sisters *see* **Salesian Sisters** *see* **Order of the Visitation of Holy Mary**

visitor The ecclesiastical official with the right of visitation with respect to a monastic community. They may be a member of a parent house, a representative of the monastery's order, a bishop, or a papal delegate.

Vistandines *see* **Order of the Visitation of Holy Mary**

Vitalis of Mortain *see* **Savignac Order**

vocation director The monastic who receives all inquiries about membership in a community and assists enquirers in discerning their call to monastic life.

Volotsky, Joseph *see* **Joseph of Volokolamsk**

Voramai Kabilsingh (1908–2003); Ta Tao Fa Tzu Thai Theravedan Buddhist bhikkhuni (nun) who was the first modern Thai bhikkhuni. Ordination as a bhikkhuni was not possible in Thailand at the time so she was ordained in Taiwan, where it is permitted. After her ordination, she returned to Thailand where she turned the family home into the Songdhammakalyani Monastery, which remains the only nunnery in Thailand. Her daughter, Dhammananda Bhikkhuni, is now the abbess. • *See also* **Dhammananda Bhikkhuni**

vowess; avowess A woman who took up a modified form of monastic life in the Middle Ages falling somewhere between a third order and oblation. It was assumed by widows and included the vows of chastity, the wearing of a distinctive habit, and inhibited remarriage, but did not involve solemn vows.

~W~

Wadi El Natrun *see* **Scetis**

Walafrid Strabo (ca. 808–849) A Germanic Benedictine monk, abbot of Reichenau, and esteemed poet, historian, and theologian. He entered the monastery on the island of Reichenau as a young boy. Recognized for his accomplishments, he was sent to the imperial court at Fulda and as a reward for tutoring his son, Charles the Bald, Louis the Pious appointed Walafrid the abbot of Richenau in 838. His fellow monks objected, not to Walafrid himself, but because the political appointment negated their rights to freely elect their own abbot and Walafrid was exiled. In 842, through the intervention of the abbot of St. Gall, Walafrid returned to his office as abbot of Richenau and served seven years without incident until he tragically drowned in the Loire while serving Charles the Bald on a diplomatic mission.

Waldensian monasticism The Waldensians are a Christian sect founded in France by Peter Waldo about 1173. The Waldensians were very much like

Roman Catholics at first but gradually became more influenced by Protestantism and today consider themselves Protestants in the Reformed tradition. They had both monks and nuns who practiced poverty, preaching of the Gospel, and charity. Beyond that, practices varied wildly. Some communities had two or three year probation periods, others believed that embracing poverty was enough to join. Some offered sacraments once a year, some daily. Early on, nuns could offer the sacraments.

Waldo, Peter *see* **Waldensian monasticism**

walking place The passage connecting two domestic buildings and formed by the two crosswalls between the nave and the choir in friary churches. The tower was often built over the walking place.

waraji Straw rope sandals which are mostly worn by Japanese Zen Buddhist monks

warden *see* **custodian**

warden of the order An officer of a religious house responsible for discipline, keeping the rule, etc., in a manner similar to circators. However, unlike circators, the warden of the order was second in command of a house, as the prior in an abbey or the subprior in a priory. • *See also* **circator; epistemonarches**

warden of the shrine; feretrar A monastic charged with the safety of the community's shrines and relics

warming house; calefactory; calefactorium; pisalis Until the late Middle Ages, one of the few rooms in early monasteries that was heated. It was used as a sitting room and to carry out certain tasks such as greasing boots, preparing ink, and bloodletting.

warrior monks *see* **Hindu warrior monks; Knights Hospitaller; Knights Templar; Order of Calatrava; sohei**

watching loft An observation post overlooking a shrine or sanctuary for the prevention of theft or sacrilege. It was supervised by the sacristan warden of the shrine.

westensetla *see* **anchorite**

Westminster Abbey Founded in London in the 10th century as a Benedictine abbey by St. Dunstan. The abbey no longer houses monks, but is very an much active church in the Church of England. The only traces of St. Dunstan's monastery remaining are round arches and massive supporting columns of the undercroft and the pyx chamber.

White Canonesses *see* **Order of Canons Regular of Prémontré**

White Canons *see* **Order of Canons Regular of Prémontré**

White Friars *see* **Order of the Brothers of the Blessed Virgin Mary of Mount Carmel**

White Ladies *see* **Cistercians; Order of Canons Regular of Prémontré**

white martyrs *see* **martyrdom**

White Monks *see* **Cistercians**

White Nuns *see* **Cistercians**

Wilfrid, St. (634–709) English monk, abbot, and bishop. Born as a Northumbrian noble, he entered religious life as a teenager. About 660 he became the abbot of a newly founded monastery at Ripon. While he lived a rather ostentatious life for a monk, he is nevertheless seen as a champion of monasticism.

In 664 Wilfrid acted as spokesman for the Roman position at the Synod of Whitby, and became famous for his speech advocating that the Roman method for calculating the date of Easter be adopted. This prompted the king's son, Alhfrith, to appoint him Bishop of Northumbria but when Alhfrith led an unsuccessful revolt against his father, King Oswiu, Oswiu had appointed Ceadda in his place and Wilfrid retired to his monastery at Ripon. When Theodore the Archbishop of Canterbury deposed Ceadda in 668 he restored Wilfrid as the Bishop of Northumbria. He was successful until he quarreled with the both the Archbishop Theodore and King Wilfrid of Northumbria and the king imprisoned him for a time and then exiled him to Sussex where he formed a new see. Archbishop Theodore and Alhfrith the new Northumbrian king settled their differences and Wilfrid returned to Northumbria only to be expelled again in 691. This time he went to Mercia and served as a bishop.

His opponents in Northumbria excommunicated him and tried to take his property but the pope supported him and he regained possession of Ripon and Hexham, his Northumbrian monasteries.

Wilhelm von Hirschau ***see*** **William of Hirsau (ca. 1030–1091)**

William of Hirsau (ca. 1030–1091); Wilhelm von Hirschau German Roman Catholic Benedictine monk, abbot, polymath, and monastic reformer. He was born in Bavaria and entrusted to the Benedictines as a child oblate. He became a monk in St. Emmeram's Abbey.

In 1069 he was called to Hirsau Abbey as the abbot. Here he composed the *Constitutiones Hirsaugienses,* based on the uses of Cluny, and was the father of the Hirsau Reforms, which spread to over 200 Benedictine monasteries in Germany. These reforms particularly focused on discipline and obedience, continuous supervision of the monks, and tough punishments for infringements of the rules. To control the many laymen flocking to Hirsau he instituted conversi (lay monastics) in the German Benedictine monasteries.

Willibrord, St. (ca. 658–739) English Benedictine monk, bishop, and missionary to the Frisians, known as the "Apostle to the Frisians."

His father, newly converted to Christianity, entrusted Willibrord as a child oblate to the Abbey of Ripon and withdrew from the world. Willibrord joined the Benedictines and spent the years between the ages of 20 and 32 in the Abbey of Rathmelsigi, in Ireland, and from there was sent with 11 others to Christianize the pagan Frisians of the North Sea coast.

In 695, he was consecrated as the first bishop of the Frisians and established churches and the Abbey of Echternach in 698.

Wimmer, Boniface (1809–1887) A German Benedictine monk, archabbot, missionary, and priest. In 1855 Wimmer founded the American-Cassinese Congregation of the Benedictine Confederation.

Wimmer was ordained a priest in 1831. He took his solemn vows as a monk in 1833.

In 1846, he helped found St. Vincent Archabbey in Latrobe, Pennsylvania. It was the first Benedictine monastery in the United States. He became its abbot in 1855, and in 1883, was granted the title of archabbot by Pope Leo XIII. By the time of his death, Wimmer had founded ten Benedictine abbeys, 152 Roman Catholic parishes, and numerous schools.

wimple A covering of silk, linen, or other material, for the neck and chin, formerly worn by women as an outdoor protection, and still retained in the dress of some nuns

windows *see* **communion window; fenestra parvula; hagioscope; parlor window**

Wisdom of the Elders of Ethiopia **see** ***Ethiopic Collectio Monastica***

Wolter, Maurus (1825–1890) German Benedictine monk, priest, theologian, and advocate of liturgical reform. He was ordained as a priest in 1850. He was professed as a monk in 1857. In 1863 he became the first abbot of Beuron Archabbey which he founded together with his brother Placidus. In 1875 the Kulturkampf forced the monks to leave Beuron for 12 years, but in exile Maurus founded several new monasteries. Wolter implemented his vision of a liturgical life by emphasizing a return to the original sources of monastic tradition. He was also the one who originated the Benedictine Latin motto, "Ora et Labora" ("Pray and Work.")

Wolter, Placidus (1828–1908) German Benedictine monk and priest. In 1852, he entered the monastery of St. Paul-outside-the-Walls in Rome. He founded the Beuron Archabbey together with his brother Maurus in 1863. His brother appointed him as the first abbot of Beuron's first foundation in Maredsou in Belgium in 1872. On the death of his brother in 1890, Placidus was appointed archabbot of Beuron where he promoted a rigorous monastic observance and liturgical life, which affected Benedictine houses throughout the world.

Wonder Worker of Britain Nickname of St. Cuthbert

Wonhyo (617–686) Korean Buddhist monk, and a leading thinker, writer, and commentator of the Korean Buddhist tradition. He spent the earlier part of his life as a monk, but in 661 after mistakenly drinking what he thought was refreshing water from a human skull he left the priesthood and began spreading the Buddha dharma as a layman. Together with his extensive literary output, he became one of Korea's most eminent and influential scholar-monks.

~X~

xenodocheion *see* **xenodochium**

xenodochios The monastic in charge of a xenodochium

xenodochium; xenodocheion In the Middle Ages, a room in a monastery for the reception and entertainment of strangers and pilgrims, and for the relief of paupers

xulon *see* **semantron**

xylon *see* **semantron**

~Y~

yagubhajaka An official in charge of the distribution of gruel in a Theravedin Buddhist monastery

yakuseki The Japanese Zen Buddhist monastic supper. In Buddhism it was originally forbidden to eat after noon, however, in China, where Zen developed, it was cold in the winter, so the monks would put heated stones against their abdomens to assuage the pangs of hunger. Later a light meal, consisting of the day's leftovers, came to be served and this was named after the stones used to ease hunger.

yati Originally the general term for a Jain monk. In the late medieval period it came to represent a stationary monk as opposed to a wandering monk. The term was more common for the Śvētāmbara monastics than Digambaras. It has occasionally been used for ascetics from other traditions.

The heads of the institutions of Śvētāmbara yatis were often termed shripujya. Only a celibate yati could become a shripujya. They are now called acharyas.

yogism In Hinduism and Jainism, yogism is an ascetic practice, but being a yogi does not make one a monastic. However, there are a number of yogis who are also monastics.

yokuju The monk that prepares the bath in a Japanese Zen Buddhist Rinzai monastery

yokushitsu The bath house in a Japanese Zen Buddhist Sōtō monastery

yokusu The bath manager in a Japanese Zen Buddhist Sōtō monastery

Yosai ***see*** **Eisai**

yugyoso; yugyōsō Itinerant Japanese Zen Buddhist monks who lived a large part of their lives independently from religious establishments

Yuquan Shenxiu ***see*** **Shenxiu**

~Z~

zagu The rectangular piece of cloth carried by a Japanese Zen Buddhist monk on which ritual bowing is done

zanka A permitted absence from a Japanese Zen Buddhist monastery lasting longer than three days and two nights. It is often used at present to indicate the termination of a monk's sōdō (formal) training.

zazen Japanese Zen Buddhist meditation

Zelanti ***see*** **Spirituali Franciscans**

zelator; geku (Tibetan) An older monk in charge of disciplining younger monks; the novice-master's assistant

zelatrix An older nun in charge of disciplining younger nuns

zendo; zendō A Japanese Zen Buddhist meditation hall; in monasteries, the monastics live in the zendō

Zhiyi (539–597 CE); Chih-i Chinese monk, writer, and founder of the Tiantai tradition of Buddhism in China noted for being the first in Chinese Buddhism to create a complete, critical and systematic classification of Buddhist teachings. He is also credited with making a significant break from the Indian Buddhist tradition and forming an indigenous Chinese tradition.

Zhu Hong (1535–1615); Chu Hung Chinese Buddhist monk, leader, and anti–Jesuit. He became a monk at 31 despite the existence of his second wife, who later became a nun. Zhu Hong is best remembered for his persistent hostility to Roman Catholicism.

Traditional Buddhist monasticism had declined by Zhu Hong's time and he complained that "Monks are also geomancers, diviners, physiognomists, physicians, gynecologists, potion makers, spirit healers, and alchemists." The arrival of Jesuit missionaries entry into 16th century China made matters worse and provoked a strong response.

zhuchi ***see*** **abbot**

Zoroastrianism Zoroastrianism rejects all forms of asceticism and monasticism.

zostiko ***see*** **inner cassock**

Zuien ***see*** **Ippen Shōnin**

zutabukuro A bag for Japanese Zen Buddhist monastics, hung around the neck to keep personal effects in

Springer Series: FOCUS ON WOMEN

Violet Franks, Ph.D., Series Editor

Confronting the major psychological, medical, and social issues of today and tomorrow. *Focus on Women* provides a wide range of of books on the changing concerns of women.

VOLUME 1
THE SAFETY OF FERTILITY CONTROL
Editor-in-Chief: Louis G. Keith, M.D.; Associate Editors: Deryck R. Kent, M.D.; Gary S. Berger, M.D., and Janelle R. Brittain, M.B.A.

VOLUME 2
THERAPY WITH WOMEN: A Feminist Philosophy of Treatment
Susan Sturdivant, Ph.D.

VOLUME 3
SHELTERING BATTERED WOMEN
A National Study and Service Guide
Albert R. Roberts, D.S.W.

VOLUME 4
WOMEN OVER FORTY: Visions and Realities, Revised Edition
Marilyn R. Block, Ph.D., Janice I. Davidson, M.S., and Jean D. Grambs, Ed.D.

VOLUME 5
THE STEROTYPING OF WOMEN: Its Effects on Mental Health
Violet Franks, Ph.D. and Esther D. Rothblum, Ph.D.

VOLUME 6
THE BATTERED WOMEN SYNDROME
Lenore E. Walker, Ed. D.

VOLUME 7
WOMEN THERAPISTS WORKING WITH WOMEN
New Theory and Process of Feminist Therapy
Claire M. Brody, Ph.D. Editor

VOLUME 8
CAREER GUIDE FOR WOMEN SCHOLARS
Suzanne Rose, Ph.D.

VOLUME 9
A MOTE IN FREUD'S EYE: From Psychoanalysis to the Psychology of Women
Hannah Lerman, Ph.D.

VOLUME 10
WOMEN'S THERAPY GROUPS: Paradigms of Feminist Treatment
Claire M. Brody, Ph.D., Editor

VOLUME 11
WOMEN AND DEPRESSION: A Lifespan Perspective
Ruth Formanek, Ph.D., and Anita Gurian, Ph.D., Editors

VOLUME 12
TRANSITIONS IN A WOMAN'S LIFE: Major Life Events in Developmental Context
Ramona T. Mercer, Ph.D., F.A.A.N., Elizabeth G. Nichols, D.N.S., F.A.A.N., Glen C. Doyle, Ed.D., R.N.

Jean Dresden Grambs received her B.A. degree from Reed College and her M.A. and Ed.D. in educational sociology from Stanford University. Her experience includes public school teaching and administration. She taught at Stanford University and George Washington University prior to joining the faculty of the University of Maryland. She was a Fulbright Fellow in Taiwan, The Republic of China. She has published widely in the fields of education, human relations, school desegregation, educational sociology, sex differences, women's issues, and gerontology. She was instrumental in establishing the Women's Studies Program and the Center on Aging at the University of Maryland. She retired as Professor Emeritus from the Department of Human Development at the University of Maryland.

Women Over Forty

Visions and Realities

Revised Edition

Jean Dresden Grambs

SPRINGER PUBLISHING COMPANY
New York

Springer Publishing Company, Inc.
536 Broadway
New York, NY 10012

89 90 91 92 93 / 5 4 3 2 1

Library of Congress Cataloging-in-Publication Data

Grambs, Jean Dresden, 1919-
  Women over forty.

  (Springer series, focus on women ; v. 4)
  Previous ed. by Marilyn R. Block, Janice L. Davidson, Jean D. Grambs.
  Bibliography: p.
  Includes index.
  1. Middle aged women—United States. I. Block, Marilyn R. Women over forty. II. Title. III. Series.
HQ1059.5.U5G73 1989 305.24'4'082 89-10093
ISBN 0-8261-3003-8
ISBN 0-8261-3002-X (pbk.)

Printed in the United States of America

Contents

Preface

As I complete the manuscript for *Women Over Forty*, I receive notice that my university has named me Professor Emeritus. For the first time since I graduated from college I can contemplate the months ahead with no schedule, no classes to prepare for, no department meetings or committees. I am moving into another phase of life as an older woman, and like those who have preceded me, I don't know if I am glad or sorry.

When I first became involved in the field of gerontology (I was well over 40), I joked that the study of the old should be left to the young; there were too many disturbing descriptions of relationships lost, bodily processes failing, memory going astray. As more of these symptoms became part of my own aging, I found them increasingly fascinating and not nearly so distressing; in fact, I found most of the predicted changes to be grossly overated—I hardly felt a day over 40 no matter what my chronological age became.

In gathering the material for the first edition of this book, and now for the revision, I have been continually checking my own experiences against the research reports. In a sense, I am a one-person validation of much that I have reported in this book. What I have found regarding the older woman has been both reassuring and unsettling—reassuring because I have managed to cope fairly well so far with many of the expected changes that come with age, social and physical; unsettling because I realize how many women have not been so fortunate and face great difficulty in dealing with aging. Many of these difficulties stem from ignorance, stereotypes, mythologies, and social practices and policies that have worked against women in the past. By bringing these problems to the fore in this book I am hopeful that women in the future will find that growing older is another stage in development, with unique rewards, and that the problems that arise are within our power to solve.

The first edition of this book grew out of my work with the Center on Aging of the University of Maryland. My interest in the status of women led me to wonder how much was known about the older woman and to ask if this material was included in courses in gerontology. My initial inquiry led me to the conclusion that women were typically overlooked as a special category of older persons. In fact, most of the research was on men or "elders." With the encouragement of Jody K. Olsen, director of the Center on Aging, I applied for a grant from the Administration on Aging of the then Department of Health, Education and Welfare to develop a course on the older woman. I had been able to locate only one other such course in any college or university in the country at that time (1975). I received an award to produce such a course, which eventually was taught by Marilyn R. Block, graduate research assistant on the project. The course was well-received by students, and we decided that a book based on the research we had gathered for the course would be an addition to the gerontology literature. Springer Publishing Company agreed, and the first edition of *Women Over Forty*, written with Marilyn R. Block and Janice L. Davidson, was published in 1981.

In the fall of 1985 I approached Barbara Watkins, vice president and senior editor of Springer, about the possibility of a revision. She was most enthusiastic and encouraging. My two colleagues on the first edition have had career changes and felt they did not have the time to work on a revision, so I undertook the task alone—with some trepidation and concern. It has taken three years to complete the revision, an entirely new book. The first edition provided a framework, but so much has happened in the field of gerontology that I found extensive material to add to what was, as I now see it, only a beginning.

In searching for material for the first edition, we could locate relatively few research studies that focused specifically on the older woman. Now I have found the field to be almost explosively enlarged. As a result, most of the research cited in the revision has been published in 1980 or later.

Women have contributed a great deal to this increase in the attention paid to women as they age, and this in turn may be a by-product of the women's movement. However, there is increased awareness of the complexity of the aging process, of the many forces that act on an individual, and of such things as ethnic origin, socioeconomic status and family relationships, achievement patterns and work life, all of which interact with sex and gender. Individual development is influenced throughout the life span by gender. We have also learned a great deal more about the effects of aging on women's physical processes and health. In all the areas touched on in this book, however, much more research is needed.

The development of the book was aided by the advice and counsel of many people. I discussed my ideas and circulated drafts of chapters to my colleagues. I was fortunate in being able to teach a graduate seminar on the older woman twice in the last two years, after a hiatus of some time; the students in those classes gave me new insights and helped hone my focus. I gratefully acknowledge the help of my friends and colleagues: John Mayor, Jody K. Olsen, Franklin Patterson, Elizabeth Ann Robertson-Tchabo, Carol Seefeldt, Nancy Schlossberg, Mary C. Sengstock, M. Brewster Smith, and Bonnie Tyler. My seminar students: Maria Aceituno, Mildred Cannon, Rafaela Coella, Anita Kedas, Lyn Hagood, Margaret Lloyd, Suzanne Matteson, Katherine Megyeri, Norma Prosopiow, Phyllis Rumbarger, Hubert Sonnenschein, Mary Anne Sonnenschein, and Karen Thatcher. A am also very appreciative of the generous administrative support provided by George Funaro and Robert Hardy of the University of Maryland.

Perhaps I have learned the most about growing old, however, from the members of my family who have shared freely with me their observations criticisms, suggestions, and love: my husband Harold, our children, Peter, Marya, and Sarah, and our grandchildren, Jesse Schwartz and Leah Horton.

1
Introduction

The changing status of women has been one of the most dramatic of the social upheavals of the second half of the 20th century. Women are entering the labor force earlier and remaining at work for more years, even if they have young children. More women are divorced and heading their own households. More women are going to college, obtaining professional and advanced degrees, and seeking careers in law, medicine, and business. There are more women active in politics at every level of government. Women artists, writers, and musicians are gaining significant recognition, far more than achieved in any previous era. Women are even finding an increased place in the armed services. And more women are living longer than have ever done so before.

Although the data have been available for some time, the meaning of female longevity has only recently been examined. Ever since antisepsis was introduced into childbirth procedures, accompanied by better nutrition and improved general health care, women have experienced a longer life span than that of men. Women who were 65 in 1980 could expect to live, on the average, an additional 18.35 years; men only 14.02 years more. The phenomenon of women outliving men characterizes every Western country, as well as others where health care is even moderately available.

Life expectancy on the whole has increased for both men and women, which means that there is now an unprecedented number of older people living beyond age 65. Figure 1.1 shows the dramatic changes that have occurred in longevity since 1900. It also shows the change in the sex ratio that has taken place. The number of women over age 60 will be significantly greater in the year 2050 than it is today.

FIGURE 1.1 Actual and projected change in population distribution, 1900–2050.

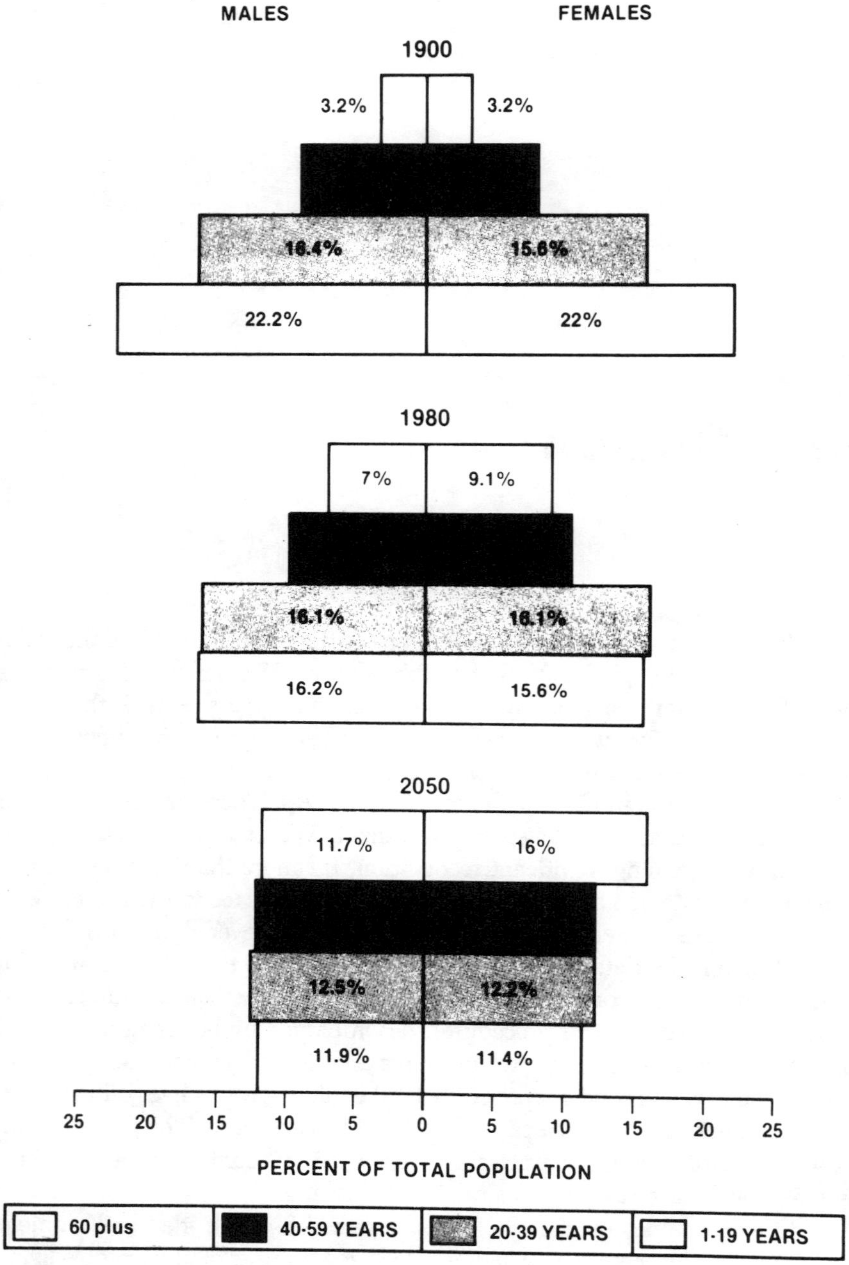

[a]Projections are middle series.

From U.S. Bureau of the Census, Decennial Censuses of Population, 1900–1980 and Projections of the Population of the United States; 1982 to 2050, Current Population Reports, Series P-25, No. 922, October, 1982.

With debate sharpening over the appropriate amount of federal support for the old, the sheer numerical presence of the elderly has had an impact on important policies. What was once mainly of interest to gerontologists is now drawing the attention of Congress, and the American Association of Retired Persons has become the numerically largest lobby in the country. Who is going to take care of all of these old people if they become too sick or too poor? Planning for one's own aging becomes difficult when it is possible that aging parents may require financial and personal help in competition with the demands of one's own spouse or children. What are the measures one has to take to ensure a healthy and active old age, how much will this cost, and who will pay for it?

Because so many women are living to a ripe old age—the fastest-growing age group in the country is women over 80—these questions and many others are of particular concern to them. In fact, the issues of old are are beginning to be recognized as women's issues. Will this mean that needed remedies will be more or less forthcoming? Given the poor showing of policymakers in recognizing such women's issues as provision of child care and equity in earnings and pensions, there is not much assurance that support for aged women will be a policy priority.

INVISIBLE WOMEN

Much of the research on older people has been based either on studies of men or of men and women lumped together with no analysis of sex differences. Older women have been "invisible." Finding data on the attitudes and behavior of older women has been difficult because "many of the theoretical constructs and measurement instruments for adult development have been standardized on samples of males" (Lachman, 1984). As Antonucci (1982) observes, "Very few large datasets have focused exclusively on women in their middle years." She also notes that "it may seem as though we have only just discovered that man continues to grow and develop through adulthood. Nevertheless, it is time to modify this statement and attend to the fact that both men and women continue to grow and develop over their life course and not necessarily in a similar fashion." Beeson (1975) makes the point that even when studies have shown significant differences, "somehow these differences do not show up in theoretical statements, nor do they often lead to generalizations by scholars about the situation of aging women."

Gerontological research reflects a general research bias that distorts perception and analysis of behavior (Bleier, 1984). The dominance of male views regarding both animal and human behavior has saddled us with some very unscientific notions, as recent feminist critics have pointed out (Fausto-

Sterling, 1985; Hardy, 1981; Shaw & Darling, 1985). The meagerness of research on women—very limited until 1970 and still modest compared to most research—has been explained by the fact that most researchers are men, and they feel "safer" doing research on males, for whom such norms have already been established. This limitation has not prevented researchers from extending generalizations to women or from discounting women's differences as deviant (Prescott, 1978). A typical expression of the view that older women are somehow different from older people in general is the following comment regarding the heterogeneity of the elderly population: "older women, older blacks, older Hispanics, aging gays, and the rural aged, to mention a few, have needs and concerns that often diverge from those of the elderly population as a whole" (Achenbaum, 1983, p. 150). Since women in fact make up a majority of the aging population, how can their interests be "divergent" from that of "most" elderly?

After examining the limited research on older women as of 1975, Beeson (1975) concludes that "when women have been included as subjects their experience of aging has frequently been compared to that of men and evaluated as less problematic, less traumatic, and their difficulties seen as more easily resolved." As we will point out in this book, this conclusion is far from accurate. Gilligan (1982) makes the point that a basic redefinition of human experience, to account for the life experience of each sex, is necessary:

> The failure to see the different reality of women's lives and to hear the differences in their voices stems in part from the assumption that there is a single mode of social experience and interpretation. By positing instead two different modes, we arrive at a more complex rendition of human experience that sees the truth of separation and attachment in the lives of women and men but recognizes as well their differential refraction in the ethical languages of responsibilities and rights. (pp. 112–113)

In a review of the status of sociology and research on women, Lopata (1976) finds that sexual identity "affects all, or almost all, social roles." She goes on to say that it is difficult to locate any sex-neutral roles because "American men and women are constantly reminded of this identity in all the roles they perform and are expected to act differently in any supposedly identical role." Sexual identity, she asserts, pervades "every niche and cranny of American life." Indeed, as we report in this book, sexual identity is as important in understanding the elderly as in understanding any other age group.

One of the important purposes of this book is to show, on the basis of research, that gender is a potent force in many significant aspects of one's life story, no matter how old one may be.

Much of what we know about the aged has come from studies of male-only samples, with the generalizations often assumed to apply equally to women. Studies in which generalizations are made to all aged persons, regardless of sex, should be treated with suspicion. Because of these limitations on the available data, there will be found throughout this book repeated references to large gaps in our information on women and aging and lack of comparative studies by gender.

Identifying the research to include in this book has often been frustrating. A survey of research practices in the *Journal of Gerontology* showed that many investigators omitted information about the age, health, and gender of their subjects (Hoyer, Raskind, & Abrahams, 1984). Even where both sexes are identified as subjects of a study, there is commonly no analysis of the findings by sex. Particularly irksome are studies of subjects over age 75, most of whom are women; if there are a few men in the sample, the results are rarely analyzed for sex differences, nor are the results reported as describing the majority of those studies—women. It is as though the older one gets, the less gendered one becomes.

Even finding the studies that do exist on older women or on sex differences and aging is not easy. For instance, recent handbooks on aging, major sources of research reviews, do not admit sex differences, judging by the indexes. In the *Handbook of Biology of Aging* (1985) there are no entries for "women," "men," "sex differences," or "gender." The same indexer must have worked on the *Handbook of Psychology of Aging*, since such entries are also missing from that volume. What is baffling is that in fact there are many significant discussions of sex differences in both volumes, which the persistent and careful reader can find, but not by trusting the index. *The Handbook on Aging and the Social Sciences* (1985), published by the same company, has an index entry for "aging and gender differences" followed by over 40 page references, none of which are identified by topic. There are, however, many more discussions of sex differences in individual chapters, which may or may not be concealed in the "gender differences" listing. A very useful summary of research, headed "Gender contrasts and sex-role identity," cannot be found in the index. The generally excellent reviews of the research on aging compiled by the American Psychological Association (Poon, 1970, 1980) are also coy about revealing coverage of sex differences or material on older women, to judge from the indexes. Only one reference to sex differences could be found (under the entry for "grandparents") in the 1980 edition, although a number of chapters have important discussions of such differences. A major exception to these findings is the *Encyclopedia of Aging* (Maddox, 1987), which provides ample coverage of women's concerns, clearly identified in the index.

A student seeking to become informed about older women will also encounter trouble. The omission of any extended discussion of sex differences or inadequate indexing of what is included haunts many of the introductory textbooks in gerontology, even the most recent (for example, see Cunningham & Brookbank, 1988; Hendricks & Hendricks, 1986; Kart, 1985; Kermis, 1984; Turner & Helms, 1986). One text devotes two chapters to gender differences in adulthood, though the material is not identified in the index (VanHoose & Worth, 1982). Only one text has a chapter on women (Barrow, 1986).

There is in fact considerable research on the midlife and older woman, and a great deal of the popular writing on aging is about and for women. Two recent specialized bibliographies are devoted to material on older women (Borenstein, 1984; Dolan & Gropp, 1984). A list of dissertations, covering the years 1983 to 1985 (Moore, 1986) reveals that, on the basis of gender-related words in the titles, research specifically focused on women or on sex differences accounted for about one-fourth of all those listed. It is probable that many of the other dissertations included analysis of data by gender.

In seeking research material for this volume a number of books were located, of recent publication date, that are specifically devoted to women's aging; they include such topics as widowhood, menopause, health, retirement, work. Other edited books on special topics in aging also give coverage to research on women's roles and behavior in areas such as ethnicity, aged parents, and elder abuse. The women's movement provided the impetus for the launching of a number of excellent scholarly journals devoted to women and sex roles. A new journal, *Women and Aging*, had its premier issue in 1989. In addition, the scholarly journals in psychology, sociology, human development, and family relations have been increasingly interested in publishing articles on the older woman and on sex differences and aging. The apparent lag in integrating much of this material into the introductory gerontology textbooks should be remedied in the next generation of publications.

WOMEN: HOW DIFFERENT?

Despite the greatly increased amount of research on older women, there are still significant problems in the way in which the elderly are studied and described. One basic assumption made by much of the gerontological literature is that "all old men and women are more alike than they are different." The purpose of this book is to challenge that assumption and to demonstrate, on the basis of research findings, that women and men at any age may differ in some significant ways; that older women as a group typically age differently, confront different personal and social problems, and have a different set of social and personal priorities from those of men.

One of the points we make repeatedly in this book, on the basis of available research, is that women experience a number of life events that are different from those men encounter, and they experience many of the same events—such as work, retirement, and family life—in different ways. These differences are as important in midlife as they are in old age.

Women, of course, are the bearers of children. Their reproductive physiology is obviously different from men's. Menstruation, childbearing, and menopause mark key physiological occurrences in women's lives; men have nothing comparable. Women continue to be and to view themselves as the principal child rearers in the family; and single heads of households with children are almost always women. The world of work continues to channel most women into jobs with lower salaries, fewer opportunities for advancement, and less adequate benefits, including retirement coverage. Although recent generations of women are getting more and better education, at least three decades will have to pass before this begins affecting the lives of most older women. For now, many women aged 40 and over can anticipate being widowed and economically disadvantaged after age 60. In midlife, women become the caretakers of older parents, and in old age women are more apt to be abused, and to be the abusers.

Feminists have attempted to alert gerontologists to be aware of sex differences. However, as Hess (1985) points out, "Neither . . . activism on the part of feminist gerontologists nor the surge of research on aging women has been completely successful in changing the level or direction of the public and professional discourse on aging." She reports as an example a study on public policy and aging in which the author ignores or overlooks the fact that "every policy failure he so carefully details has a different impact by gender and race." She continues: "not only are the real problems of aging disproportionately experienced by women, but it is women who are increasingly expected to bear the brunt of dealing with these problems."

There is a substantial body of research on older women, as this book demonstrates. These findings need to be widely disseminated and incorporated in our education about aging and life-span human development so that in the future more adequate personal planning, as well as more informed social policy, can meet the special needs of those who make up most of the elderly: women.

WHO IS THE "OLDER WOMAN"?

One vivacious 70-year-old, when asked to give her age replied, "You would say I was lying if I told you I was forty, but that is exactly how old I really feel." In a society where age grading is continuous and ubiquitous, age is both a subjective and a legal experience. The law has established certain age criteria: You couldn't go to grade school until you were 6; couldn't get a driver's license until you were 16; couldn't get liquor until you were 21, though you could vote when you were 18. Other markers, such as religious ceremonies, emphasize age: first communion, bar mitzvah, or bas mitzvah. Old age is defined by specified times for retirement and eligibility for receiving benefits such as Medicare and discounts for drugs, organization dues, and entrance fees. In some states, a driver's license renewal requires a performance test after a certain age.

There are also informal age norm expectations. Every one of us has encountered, as we were growing up, an irritated adult chiding us to "act your age." This usually meant we were getting "too big for our britches" or were acting childish when we should have known better. The same expectation of acting one's age is a potent force in the lives of older women and men (Atchley, 1988; Bastida, 1987). For example, the clothing preferences of older women showed that they were acutely aware of what was appropriate rather than stylish for someone of their age (Richards, 1981).

The legal markers of one's early years were, in a sense, a comfort. They marked limits, opportunities, and achievements. From then on, perceptions of age become largely subjective: you are as old as you think you are (Breytspraak, 1984). When does one feel "adult"? It may be when one gains full responsibility for one's own finances and is economically on one's own. For those who go to college and then to further graduate study, adulthood may not come until their 30s. Others may be on their own in their teens, with children of their own.

But the time comes when each of us begins to think not of the years one has lived but about how many are left. A "moment of truth" occurs—usually around age 40—when, often rather suddenly, one experiences a sense of one's own mortality. One is conscious in an acute and vivid fashion that life does not stretch indefinitely ahead, that in fact there are very specific and real limits to one's own life. This marks the awareness of age; one achieves a sense of generations, and there is a new interest in family history and genealogy.

About 10 or 15 years later, depending in part on one's health, there comes another epiphany, another shift in one's consciousness of aging. It is not just that one's life will end, but one thinks quite concretely about how many years one has. Now you are getting old, moving from just being a "mature adult" to being an "old adult" (Sill, 1980). This becomes a time to write wills, settle old disputes, and reminisce about the joys, adventures, and sorrows of the past. A few years later another shift takes place as friends and relatives die, as one's own health becomes more precarious, and the question becomes "What will I die of?" Now one is really "old" (Neugarten & Neugarten, 1986).

These subjective stages seem to mark the progression of many people from youth through old age. These moments of changed awareness occur at different chronological times for different people. Good health tends to push awareness of aging upward, whereas poor health, one's own or that of a spouse or friends, can make a 45-year-old feel vulnerable and aging.

What we have just described may account for how most people experience aging, but women as a group are also much more apt than men to be aware of the biological clock: beyond a certain age they can no longer have children. Thus, the life decisions of women are often couched in different terms than those of men. All women will also experience a physiological marker that signifies getting old: menopause. This physiological event produces some important related changes in appearance, which soon differentiate the older from the younger woman. If, subjectively, a woman feels as skittish at 50 as she did at 30, menopause and its accompanying changes will jolt her into a realization that she is, in fact, no longer young. Ambivalence about aging, inevitable as it may be, is a significant factor in individual well-being, and it may affect women more than men because appearance is more involved in women's self-esteem (Rossi, 1980).

ABOUT THIS BOOK

The subjective feelings about aging and the actual physiological experience of menopause occur after age 40 for most women. For the purposes of this book, then, we are interested primarily in the women of middle years (40s) and beyond, always keeping in mind that chronological age is only part of the meaning of age. Women over 40 are considered "mature" or "adult." As they move into their next decade, they experience "midlife" or begin to feel that they are now "middle-aged." Age groups have also been divided into the "young-old," aged 65 to 74, and the "old-old," 75 and over. Improved health care, better nutrition, and more active lives have produced an emerging group of older people who have the energy, outlook on life, and self-perceptions that not only make them resist being labeled "old" but also discourage others from stereotyping them as elderly. These are the young-old. The old-old are one of the fastest-growing groups of the elderly as we stretch longevity to its maximum—and most of these are women.

The second important point about this book is that generalizations, conclusions, and speculations will be based on published scholarly research and analysis. When the first edition of this book was written (1979–80), there was a much more limited number of relevant studies. Researchers were less sensitive to women's development, there were fewer women doing research, and those who were did not focus on women any more than men did. There was not much speculation in the scholarly literature about women's development in maturity and old age, although pioneering work by Neugarten and Lopata pointed to some key factors in women's aging. It is quite different today. There is now a great deal of published research that fits into our topic. We have looked for research that informs us on key issues. In particular, we have tried to avoid popular views that may feel right but are not supported by objective studies. Unpublished papers have been omitted in order to make it possible for readers to locate sources for additional information; scholarly papers presented at conferences are often difficult to locate and retrieve.

Who is the audience for the book? First, it is hoped the book will be used as a text in gerontology courses and women's studies courses since so few provide much if any coverage of the older woman. Second, other gerontologists may be stimulated to pursue further research, to confirm or extend our knowledge, or to challenge accepted generalizations. Throughout the book we have had to admit, over and over, that we did not really know what was true because "there is little research in this area." Third, policymakers, practitioners in the field of aging, and leaders in professional organizations devoted to aging may find the information and the discussion of issues helpful in giving more emphasis to the needs of older women. Finally, there may be the educated layperson who is interested in becoming more informed about her own development or that of someone she knows. Early drafts of the chapter on menopause, for instance, were tried out on graduate students in a seminar on the older woman; these students, all midlife women, were very interested in the information, much of which was new to them. Several made copies to give to friends. It is hoped that other chapters will meet similar needs.

Growing old female is to experience the changes and problems faced by all aging persons and also many that are unique to women in our society. Women are in the vanguard of revolutionary social change as they experience, for the first time in human history, the power to control fertility. No longer are their lives dominated by the roulette wheel of pregnancy. "As we face the changing social, economic, and political times, it is becoming evident that women are experiencing, affecting, and influencing these changes to a degree that is perhaps greater than any other time in history" (Antonucci, 1982). When we study and understand the problems of older women today, we can do much to develop interventions that will enable women to face the added years of life optimistically, serenely, and with a sense of accomplishment.

REFERENCES

Achenbaum, W. A. (1983). *Shades of gray: Old age, American values, and federal policies since 1920*. Boston: Little, Brown.

Antonucci, T. C. (1982). Longitudinal and cross-sectional data sources on women in the middle years. In J. Z. Giele (Ed.), *Women in the middle years* (pp. 241–276). New York: John Wiley.

Atchley, R. C. (1988). *Social forces and aging: An introduction to social gerontology*. Belmont, CA: Wadsworth.

Barrow, G. M. (1986). *Aging, the individual and society*. St. Paul, MN: West Publishing Co.

Bastida, E. (1987). Sex-typed aged norms among older Hispanics. *The Gerontologist*, *27*(1), 59–65.

Beeson, D. (1975). Women in studies of aging: A critique and suggestion. *Social Problems*, *23*, 52–59.

Birren, J. E., & Schaie, K. W. (Eds.). (1985). *Handbook of the psychology of aging* (2nd ed.). New York: Van Nostrand Reinhold.

Blier, R. (1984). *Science and gender: A critique of biology and its theories on women*. New York: Pergamon Press.

Borestein, A. (1984). *Older women in twentieth century America: A selected annotated bibliography*. New York: Garland.

Breytspraak, L. M. (1984). *The development of self in later life*. Boston: Little, Brown.

Cunningham, W. R., & Brookbank, J. H. (1988). *Gerontology: The psychology, biology, and sociology of aging*. New York: Harper and Row.

Dolan, E. F., & Gropp, D. M. (1984). *The mature woman in America: A selected annotated bibliography, 1977–1982*. Washington, DC: The National Council on the Aging.

Fausto-Sterling, A. (1985). *Myths of gender: Biological theories about women and men*. New York: Basic Books.

Gilligan, X. (1982). *In a different voice*. Cambridge, MA: Harvard University Press.

Hendricks, J., & Hendricks, C. D. (1986). *Aging in mass society: Myths and realities* (3rd ed.). Boston: Little, Brown.

Hess, B. B. (1985). Aging policies and older women. In A. S. Rossi (Ed.), *Gender and the life course* (pp. 319–331). New York: Aldine.

Hoyer, W. J., Raskind, C. L., & Abrahams, J. P. (1984). Research practices in the psychology of aging: A survey of research published in the *Journal of Gerontology*, 1975–1982. *Journal of Gerontology*, *39*(1), 44–88.

Kart, C. S. (1985). *The realities of aging* (2nd ed.). Boston: Allyn and Bacon.

Kermis, M. D. (1984). *The psychology of human aging*. Boston: Allyn & Bacon.

Lachman, M. E. (1984). Life-span developmental approach. In G. Baruch & J. Brooks-Gunn (Eds.), *Women in midlife* (pp. 31–68). New York: Pergamon Press.

Lopata, H. Z. (1976). Sociology. *Signs, 2*(1), 165–176.

Maddox, G. L. (1987). *The encyclopedia of aging*. New York: Springer Publishing Co.

Moore, J. L. (1986). A bibliography of doctoral dissertations on aging from American institutions of higher learning, 1983–1985. *Journal of Gerontology, 41*(4), 535–552.

Neugarten, B. L., & Neugarten, D. A. (1986). Age in the aging society. *Daedalus, 115*(1), 31–50.

Prescott, S. (1978). Why researchers don't study women: The response of 62 researchers. *Sex Roles, 4*(6), 899–905.

Poon, L. W. (Ed.). (1970). *Aging in the 1970's*. Washington, DC: American Psychological Association.

Poon, L. W. (Ed.). (1980). *Aging in the 1980's*. Washington, DC: American Psychological Association.

Richards, M. L. (1981). The clothing preferences and problems of elderly female consumers. *The Gerontologist, 21*(3), 263-267.

Rossi, A. S. (1980). Life-span theories and women's lives. *Signs, 6*(1), 4–32.

Shaw, E., & Darling, J. (1985). *Female strategies*. New York: Walker.

Sill, J. S. (1980). Disengagement reconsidered: Awareness of finitude. *The Gerontologist, 20*(1), 457–462.

Turner, J. S., & Helms, D. B. (1986). *Contemporary adulthood*. New York: Holt Rinehart & Winston.

Van Hoose, W. H., & Worth, M. R. (1982). *Adulthood in the life cycle*. Dubuque, IA: William C. Brown.

2

Older and Female: Myths and Realities

Is it better to be young than old? In contemporary American culture there are few compensations for growing old. Middle age, with children successfully launched, enough money, no mortgage, and good health, may be a time of general serenity, but even during these years (for the lucky ones) there are apt to be many moments of nostalgic longing for the years of young love, romance, no obligations, many choices, unlimited energy, and youthful good looks. Beyond the middle years lies old age—to be endured, maybe feared, but not anticipated with eagerness. No one chooses to grow old. The aged are pushed aside by the public. They find it hard, if not impossible, to get or change jobs; doctors have less time for them; their life experience is discounted. We now call this "ageism." The elderly experience an uncomfortable shift from mainstream to margin. And aging can be doubly burdensome if one is female.

Is it harder to grow up—and grow old—female than male? This question has been debated without any definitive conclusion (Grambs & Waetjen, 1979). Boys and girls grow up surrounded by cultural messages that imbue gender differences with complex and multiple meanings (Best, 1983; Shaver & Hendrick, 1987; Tavris & Wade, 1984). In the last 20 years we have seen a tremendous growth in studies of how we live and grow as male or female. The data are still coming in and still controversial. We do know now that in many crucial aspects of our lives gender does make a difference; the life histories of men and women are different (Harrison, 1983).

We no longer hold that biology is destiny, but it is certainly one of the key influences on development. Biology is particularly significant for women. When a woman menstruates, it is a private matter; but when menstruation ceases,

> other indicators of aging [become] important to the social self presented to others: gray hair, wrinkles, dentures, drowsiness, age spots, thickening of the waistline, sagging abdomen and breasts and bifocal glasses may touch aspects of aging that matter to social and particularly intimate interaction. (Rossi, 1980).

Men also show marks of aging—baldness, gray hair, added weight—but these changes have fewer personal and social consequences.

The signs of age in women are much more tightly bound to chronology and physiology than is true of men. After menopause, which occurs inevitably between ages 45 and 55, women begin to look their age. But women have lived ever since puberty with physiological age markers linked to the sex-specific function of women: the bearing of children. Vital as this function is to the survival of the species, it has been used in every culture to define, and often to limit and restrict, women's participation in power and leadership functions—economic, political, religious, aesthetic. The women's movement of the last several decades has advanced a strong, and to some a disturbing challenge to such definitions and limitations (Harrison, 1983). Women also assert today that the behaviors associated with good mothering, whether biologically scripted or not, establish legitimate norms for social interactions and place special obligations on the body politic. The cohorts of women who reach middle and old age after the year 2000 will have lived very different lives from those experienced by the women who are 60 and older in the 1990s.

In the following sections we will look at cohort effects on changing expectations, social definitions of the older woman, how women view themselves, and the role of mass media in influencing social perceptions. Finally, we will consider theories of aging as they do or do not help us understand how women age.

ATTITUDES AND COHORTS

What we know about women 70 and older today is based on studies of women born between 1900 and 1919; women in their 50s or 60s today were born in the 1920s or 1930s (Ryff, 1985). It is very important to keep this in mind. These are women socialized at a time when there were very different norms from the ones young adults encounter today. Can one generalize, from the data at hand, to those who will be entering the ranks of the elderly 20 or 30 years hence? We believe this question is particularly pertinent to women.

What we need to account for is the effect of one's cohort. "Cohort" is a more precise term than "generations," and it has gained currency in recent years in discussions of aging. "Cohort" refers to a group of persons born in the same year or the same decade, and "cohort effect" means those events or social changes that can be assumed to have had an impact on all of those in the same cohort. The concept makes it possible to focus on "potentially distinctive and continuing effects of the interaction between individuals of approximately the same age and environments in which they are located" (Maddox & Campbell, 1985; see also Palmore, 1976).

One's cohort provides more of an explanation of how one will respond and what beliefs one will have than does chronological age alone. That is, a 40-year-old in 1940 is not the same as a 40-year-old in 1990. For this reason it is very important to know the date of research cited and to be cautious about generalizations from conclusions reached decades apart. Many studies reported in current literature were, in fact, conducted using data gathered in the 1970s. This needs emphasis. The research on women is particularly sensitive to cohort effect since women, far more than men, have been involved in a revolution in life chances and life potential.

Cohort research requires accounting for how comparative groups differ in composition. Glenn (1977) warns that when setting up a particular sample for study,

> Even when there is no reason to suspect bias due to changes in sample design, it is wise initially to perform cohort analyses separately for males and females. Intracohort change (and other variation shown by cohort data) may vary by sex, and as a cohort grows older, the proportion of females in it becomes greater due to higher mortality among males. To correct for this compositional change in aging cohorts, the male and female data should be kept separate and interpreted separately." (p. 37)

If not, the researcher should keep a standardized sex ratio. But even the 50-50 ratio that Glenn suggests could also distort results, since one important demographic fact is that older women constitute a larger proportion of the aging population, which in itself may change attitudes, opportunities, decisions, and experiences. Findings about the elderly may have only limited generalizability unless one keeps in mind the context of the research (Green, Parham, Kleff, & Pilisuk, 1980; Matthews, 1979).

Recent social change has had a particularly dramatic effect on women. Women now reaching their 40s were the first cohort to be legally able to exert fertility control: "Its members are the first females able to plan and begin a career with high assurance that it will not be interrupted involuntarily by pregnancy" (Glenn, 1977, p. 60). Access to legal, inexpensive abortion on demand, as well as the affluence of a generation with enough money to send both daughters and sons to college, has changed the lives of women in a fundamental fashion experienced by no other group of women at any previous time in human history. The consequence of these unprecedented factors, as Glenn notes, "may result in a quite different process of social and psychological aging than that experienced by previous cohorts" (p. 60; see also Harter, 1977).

A popular examination of the "baby boom" generation (Jones, 1980) shows vividly and in detail how the children born between 1946 and 1957 constitute a cohort different from anything previously recorded. The women who were "hippies," who marched for civil rights, demonstrated against the Vietnam War, and took over the offices of college presidents may be less fortunate in old age because family support will have to be supplemented by Social Security and Medicaid."The final irony may be that the iconoclastic baby-boom women, who had so ambitiously reshaped our schools and jobs, will ultimately find that their last revolution was to make an entire generation the ward of the state" (p. 379).

The richness of insight that cohort analysis can provide is seen in the reports by Elder (1981, 1982), which trace the historical influences on women's lives over a period of 40 years in two successive birth cohorts, 1920–21 and 1928–29. Specific attention was given to the impact of the Great Depression. Some women were able to deal with the challenge of economic disaster; others succumbed. Social class turned out to be a key variable. The different coping styles then became part of the endowment these women handed on to their own daughters: women as victims or as controllers of their fate (Brooks-Gunn & Kirsh, 1984).

Significant events in women's lives have been perceived and confronted differently by different birth cohorts: divorce, for instance. For women in the 1930s divorce was a family shame and an individual disgrace; today it is so commonplace as to be almost taken for granted. The timing as well as the sequencing of life-course events is also influenced by cohort: when one gets married, completes a family, finishes one's education (Goldhaber, 1986; Long & Porter, 1984; Riley, 1978). In one's own life and family it is possible to see the great significance of birth cohort. Take any specific attitude—something as minor as women and smoking—and ask your grandmother and mother how this behavior was viewed when they were growing up. Compare this to your views and those of your peers; you will have a vivid example of how cohorts differ. Words change their meaning: "gay" means jolly or happy to an older generation; it means homosexual today (Lachman, 1984).

Differences between cohorts in terms of life events and social influences have characterized our modern technological world. One result is a gap in values and outlook that can cause friction and unhappiness if the source is not understood. The perceived conservativism of the elderly is in reality the continuation of values learned in their youth.

HOW OLDER WOMEN SEE THEMSELVES

How do women feel about getting older? Is old age a dreaded preamble to death? Or are many of the years after 40 a time of maximum power and energy? Are the years after 65 a time for personal fulfillment, freed of responsibility for work or family? Levinson (1980) points out that the "dominant generation" is always those aged 45 to 60. From this group come the leaders in politics, industry, the arts—if you are a man. Do these middle years have the same promise for women? The different meanings old age has for men and women is a major influence on self-concept (Ward, 1984).

It is a folk truism that no woman freely admits her age. Perhaps this is a response to reality. One study (Kogan, 1979) showed that women were perceived to age more quickly than men do. The elderly also consistently see themselves as younger than they really are (Linn & Hunter, 1979; Turner, 1979; see also Kastenbaum, Derbin, Sabatini, & Artt, 1972). The world of older women as they themselves perceive it was assessed by Matthews (1979). These older women suppressed information about their real age, redefined what it meant to be old, attributed being old to others but not themselves, and called on outside sources to attest to their own youthfulness.

America, as we know only too well, glorifies much that is youthful. In the terms of several observers, the normative standard of effectiveness is the white nonaged male (Williamson, Shindul, & Evans, 1985). To be young is to be intrinsically attractive. And this attractiveness can be enhanced by many expensive and elaborate aids. For at least four decades female Americans spent more on cosmetics and personal care products than on any other single category. (Freedman, 1986).

The basis for this excessive expenditure is the manipulation of self-image that the advertising industry does so well. As Freedman (1986) points out, "no matter how good she looks or smells, something is always missing" (p. 44), so the woman must continue the pursuit of the right cosmetic forever. Nor is it just her face; today's woman is concerned about making her body fit a prescribed image: "Eager to reshape their lives, some women focus excessively on reshaping their bodies" (p. 45). For older women, such preoccupations are dismaying and expensive.

A study by Berkun (1983) shows what happens when women face middle age. Sixty healthy, alert, white, suburban women, aged 40 to 50, were interviewed to see how they viewed changing appearance. On the whole, these women had positive self-images, but they all agreed with a negative stereotype of middle age. Because marriage is only for "attractive"—meaning youthful—women, they agreed that they might stay in a less than optimal marital relationship because they sensed that they could never attract another mate. Two-thirds of the women appeared to acquiesce to the inevitability of middle age, but one-third were quite negative. The women in the study had fully accepted the "social imperatives about appearance. The use of make-up was considered normal and vital. . . . Never would the women . . . be seen at work with a bare face. . . . The two women who used no make-up were notably embarrassed and considered themselves to be deviant in that respect." The women dyed their hair, a practice started earlier because they did not like their hair color, but they "had no plans to allow their hair to show up as gray." But gray hair (because it could be easily covered up) was less worrisome than wrinkles, which were not easy to deal with. Some of the women were convinced that age made them less attractive, but on the whole, most of the women were quite positive about their appearance.

The women in Berkun's study who had the most positive attitudes about appearance and aging were married women who did not work. However, if they had younger children, they might indulge in "heroic efforts" to overcome an aging appearance. The careless remarks of older children about how old they looked caused discomfort. The older women who worked were most concerned about appearance. Home and family were more important than appearance for all of the women, but concerns about how they looked remained a haunting presence.

With safer and more expert procedures there has been a tremendous increase in cosmetic surgery for women, either for correcting some facial defect, to reduce weight, or to erase obvious signs of aging. Health insurance policies often cover the costs. Thus, there is a strong commercial interest in convincing women that aging appearance is correctable. Will millions of women succumb, and admit by so doing that getting older and looking it is a terrible thing? The psychological implications are unfortunate and disturbing, not to mention that such cosmetic surgery may be dangerous, is temporary at best, and in many instances borders on consumer fraud. (See Chapter 5.)

Being attractive in youth may bring important rewards. But the winner of the beauty pageant may have the most to lose when she ages (Baker, 1984). Women who were beautiful when young were found to be less happy when middle-aged than those who did not consider themselves once beautiful (Berscheid & Walster, 1972). The depression experienced by some middle-aged women may be caused in part by the recognition of their loss of physical attractiveness (Scarf, 1980).

There are few research studies that correlate self-esteem and physical appearance in midlife or older women, but the folk wisdom is that of course self-esteem, particularly for women, must be related to how one looks. Popular books by Baker (1984) and Freedman (1986) make a strong case for this position, and it is persuasively presented in an often quoted essay, "The Double Standard of Aging" by Susan Sontag (1972).

Self-esteem also is derived from a sense of accomplishment and efficacy. Women in our culture have traditionally been permitted to acknowledge marriage and family as their primary achievement goal (Kaufman & Richardson, 1982). When women do succeed in careers—at least in the cohorts reaching age 60 and beyond in the 1990s—they often are apt to be apologetic or evasive because they were perceived and perceived themselves as being invaders in male domains. Thus, career success could only partially contribute to a sense of self-worth. We are seeing a major shift in the views of young women today, who apologize to no one for their ambitions and successes outside the family context.

Studies of self-esteem are prone to many of the definitional and methodological problems of "soft psychology." In their review of studies in this area, Bengtson, Reedy, and Gordon (1985) point out that this is even more evident in the field of aging research. Furthermore, there are few reliable studies of older women.

The factors that contribute to self-esteem differ for men and women, as Baruch (1984) points out in a review of the relevant studies. Generalizations about a "midlife crisis" need to place in perspective for example, the differential impact of life expectancy: A man at age 45 has to face the fact that he may, on the average, have only 20 more years to live; "a woman of 45, who can expect to live perhaps 35 more years, is . . . concerned about living too long, with the specter of dependency and loneliness" (p. 169). The middle-aged man, on the other hand, faces the gap between his achievements and his expectations. Though women may be concerned about the years ahead,

> Most women now in their middle years . . . did not have expectations of astounding achievements in the adult world of work; therefore few find their accomplishments falling short of expectations. Rather, many midlife women . . . are amazed and delighted at achieving more than they imagined possible.

To assume that an older woman's self-esteem depends heavily on physical appearance is to overlook other factors that are of great importance in the lives of women. Furthermore, as women obtain more education and move into careers with potential achievement available, the kind of security and self-esteem that comes with proven accomplishment may make age and age-related appearance irrelevant in a way that has not been possible for many contemporary older women.

MASS MEDIA AND MODERN MYTHS ABOUT OLDER WOMEN

How we view ourselves is derived from our perceptions of how others view us and from an idealized conception of how persons like ourselves ought to appear and behave. The most important source of information regarding how we ought to be is derived from mass media. Even the judgments of parents, teachers, and peers, their admonitions of how to act, talk, dress, think, and feel, are often interpretations of the messages conveyed by the powerful social communications of television and other media. How is the older woman treated by these media?

Images in Television and Film

The mythology of past centuries has been replaced by the mythology of contemporary mass media. Television does not have much place for the aged of either sex, and for women least of all. Though outnumbering men in the older population, women are severely underrepresented on prime-time television, and where they are most apt to be found, in soap operas, their major concerns are the complexities of romance (Cantor, 1987). On prime-time television, a "viewer would have to wait between 4 and 5 hours to view an older woman while waiting only 22 minutes to encounter an older male" (Kehl, 1985).

In contrast to prime-time television, in daytime serials older women have more on-camera time than older men, but male dominance is the norm. Older men are apt to be identified as working and older women as nurturant, traditional, family members (Elliott, 1984). These older adults do not represent the true sex ratio, and their socioeconomic status and family life bears no resemblance to reality (Cassata, Anderson, & Skill, 1980).

A study of television in the 1980s (Steenland, 1986) reported that nearly 70% of television women are widows; 16% are divorced. The true figures show that more than half of the women over 50 are married and only 6% divorced. Black older women constitute 11% of older characters on television, but there are no Hispanic or Asian older women.

One study found that when older women are portrayed on television they are presented as "lacking common sense, acting silly, or being eccentric. This male-female distinction is not salient in the other age groups"

(Gerbner, Gross, Signorielli, & Morgan, 1980). Older women, when they appear, have more passive roles than older men (Davis & Davis, 1986) and are more apt to be failures in what they attempt (Aronoff, 1974). Older women characters are also likely to be hurt or killed or to fail, but men of similar ages are effective adults with possibilities for romance (Williamson, Shindul, & Evans, 1985).

The benevolent and supportive grandmother of the popular show of the 1960s, "The Waltons," or the poignant, ambiguous role given to Edith, Archie Bunker's wife—dumb but wise—in "All in the Family" have given way to a new genre: "Dynasty" and "Falconcrest," which star scheming, malicious, manipulative, glamorous, and sexy older women. These women are very rich—more than one in four are millionaires—have slim, voluptuous bodies, wear negligees, kiss passionately, and have love affairs (Steenland, 1986). In some episodes of "Dallas" the older woman is nurturant and helpful, but she appears infrequently. In another series ("Murder, She Wrote") she is the smart but humble detective. Though she figures out who did it, she often defers to the bumbling or conniving men around her.

The effect on viewers of this biased view of the elderly is problematic and contradictory. Surveys of viewer attitudes by Louis Harris and Associates have shown that all viewers picture the old as "unalert, physically inert, narrow-minded, ineffective, sexually finished . . . rotting away in poor health, without proper medical care and without enough money to live on" (Real, Anderson, & Harrington, 1980; see also Gerbner et al., 1980). However, a recent study by Passuth and Cook (1985) strongly challenges the conclusions of Gerbner et al. (1980), using the same data set and measurements. They conclude that there are too few elderly represented on television to influence viewers and that most of the representations are more positive than negative.

An interesting light on what lies behind expressed attitudes comes from an ingenious study of attitudes toward the elderly conducted by Berman, O'Nan, and Floyd (1981). These experimenters found that older women were more apt to be viewed in a negative and stereotyped fashion if male opinions were asked for in an all-male group as against a mixed-sex group. Women's opinions varied only slightly depending on group composition. The authors conclude that with regard to the male shift, "beauty is not only in the eye of the beholder but also in the social situation in which the beholder happens to be."

As the number of middle-aged and older persons are recognized as a major segment of the television-viewing audience, programming may change. In response to criticisms leveled against the media by advocates for the aged, a report, *Television Looks at Aging* (1985), defends the record and lists several hundred special national and local programs around the country that have reported on or dramatized the place of the aged in American life; but we do not know how many included older women.

Children are another group of viewers whose attitudes can be influenced by what they see on television. Saturday morning cartoons ignore the elderly almost completely. The few times they were mentioned, "the remarks were nearly always negative and easily classified into the stereotypes so frequently found in attitudinal research on aging" (Bishop & Krause, 1984). No analysis was made for gender. A comparison of television for children in the United States and Japan found that, despite the presumed higher status of the aged in Japan, "American programs provided significantly more exposure to older characters both in frequency and time of appearance" (Holtzman & Akiyama, 1985). The gender imbalance was similar in both countries, with far fewer older women than older men.

The invisibility of the old of both sexes continues in the movies, helping to perpetuate the distortion and diminution of the older woman. Movies have been a popular form of entertainment for over half a century and as such have been a powerful force in educating the American public about their social world. Older women have been depicted in films in terms of simple stereotypes. Between 1930 and 1945 aging women were present only as "Mother" (Stoddard, 1983). "What is significant," reports Stoddard, "is the numbing intensity with which the image was reiterated (almost to the exclusion of other characterizations of older women" (p. 27). Postwar films presented another version of the older woman: "Rather than seeing older women characters who basked in the adulation of their families, audiences began to be exposed to older women who had denied themselves the traditional role and were not just unhappy about it, but in many instances actually driven insane" (p. 90; see also pp. 119–142). In the 1970s the growing awareness of aging as a personal and social phenomenon resulted in films that showed aging, particularly that of men, as a complex process that deserved our sympathetic understanding. The films with middle-aged and older women advanced beyond the homemaker-grandmother stereotype of an earlier age but fell far short of portraying the reality and the diversity of life situations of older women (Tuchman, Daniels, & Benet, 1978).

Images in Advertising

Advertising conveys a highly stereotyped picture of the older woman. Most of the time she is simply ignored (Hollenshead & Ingersoll, 1982). When she does appear, it is to sell laxatives, denture goods, or arthritis or incontinence aids or to give homey advice about soap, tomato sauce, toothpaste, or cooking. A study of seven large mass-circulation magazines showed, as one would expect, more men in the pages of *Sports Illustrated*, but there were also more elderly men than women in "women's magazines" such as *The Ladies Home Journal* and *Ms.* (Gantz, Gartenberg, & Rainbow, 1980).

The older woman who is portrayed in advertising has an expression of "surprised dismay" (Uniker-Sebeck, 1981). When she is shown as middle class, she "dispenses information of a womanly sort, for example as an Avon lady or someone selling feminine products." The lower-middle-class and middle-aged woman seen in advertisements serves others as a waitress, nurse, housekeeper. Middle-aged couples are shown traveling together, though they seem rather cool toward each other compared to the amorous positions of younger couples. In old age grandparent couples have been returned to a rural setting:

> Grandmother's dress is of natural cotton and bears a floral design. . . . Grandmother may demonstrate how to make a pie, grandfather how to whittle. . . . Grandmother and grandfather tend to look very much alike. . . . Models representing advanced old age, or senility, are rare in magazine advertisements, and gender distinctions for such persons are, as in picture of infants, unimportant.

Images in Print Media

The literature about the elderly in popular magazines sends a mixed message: some studies find mostly positive portrayals; others, mostly negative (Schuerman, Eden, & Peterson, 1977). Magazines designed primarily for women have been found to portray men and women equally. Schuerman and colleagues studied 216 stories from 108 issues of the most popular magazines in 1975. Elderly men and women were found to be equally represented as healthy, affluent, and married. The authors conclude:

> The image of aging presented through these stories is both positive and inaccurate. Older characters are present and perform essential functions, but are shown as extensions of the readers' views of themselves, rather than as realistic old people. Old age is described more through cosmetic changes in appearance, i.e., white hair and wrinkles, rather than through the characteristic changes in survival, marital status, health, financial status, and retirement that actually mark transition to old age.

The truth about old age doesn't sell.

In contemporary novels, biography, and autobiography one can find a significant number of books with older women as the subject. One analysis (Sohngren, 1977) identified a number of modern novels that depicted the actual experience of growing old (see also Heilbrun, 1984).

An interesting earlier study of the stereotype of women teachers in fiction (Foff, 1956) concluded that they

> grow older, but not happier, loving but unloved, wanting but unwanted, eternal strangers who devote their lives to the education of other women's children, graying, sharpening, harshening with the years, becoming autocrats in the classroom and recluses in the community, accepting their roles as old maids as they once accepted their roles as young school mistresses, dimly seeking some answer to all the pains and frustrations they can neither articulate nor understand. (p. 21)

Though the old maid schoolteacher may no longer appear very frequently in literature, a negative view of older women teachers persists in professional evaluations still tainted by earlier stereotypes (Grambs, 1987).

Published humor is another way in which attitudes are expressed. Jokes about the elderly are apt to be negative, especially about women (Palmore, 1971). There is "much negative humor about 'old maids' but not about 'old bachelors'" (Maddox, 1987, p. 341). A study of magazine cartoons found both elderly men and women were the negative butt of the humor (Smith, 1979). Capturing the intent of humor is difficult, as Demos and Jache (1981) found when they tried to assess humor in birthday greeting cards. Though most cards could be addressed to either sex, those that were sex-specific were more negative when addressed to women, "and women are more likely than men to be the focus of messages dealing with physical appearance and age concealment" (see also Bishop & Krause, 1984).

A review of the wit and humor in literature from ancient to modern times indicates that making fun of old people has been popular in every age and every form of writing (Kehl, 1985). Where older women are concerned, one recurring theme emerged: "Perhaps no other single incident has been so common a subject of the humor of aging in literature as female age concealment. The motif runs from Homer in the 8th century C.C. to the present." A famous quote from Oscar Wilde sums up this genre: "One should never trust a woman who tells her age: a woman who would tell that would tell anything."

Images in Children's Literature

Adult attitudes are the subject of extensive research to find out what people think and how attitudes, and thus behavior, can be influenced. But much of what adults report has its basis in impressions and instruction in childhood. Direct causality cannot be proved, but socialization is a process of receiving many messages from the environment that result in a body of beliefs, values, and behaviors, which, if established in childhood, are highly resistant to change. Children's attitudes are undoubtedly influenced by the literature and by school texts written especially for them. A study of the books young children first encounter (Ansello, 1977) shows that very few (16%) of the 656 books examined contained an "old" character; 1% of the illustrations showed an old character alone, which, in these books, is a mark of importance. Over 50% of these elderly characters were male. Female characters were "significantly more nurturant, less physically exertive, less general-verbal, less self-disclosing, more fantasy prone, and more victimized." Little description was wasted on these old characters: most of them were just "old." They were also "poor" applied to almost twice as many female characters as male characters. They also were "sad," "wise," and "dear."

A study of school readers (Robin, 1977) found that middle-aged and old men and women appeared in different proportions, depending on grade level and the date when the texts were published. Old women were more apt to be in primary-grade books and middle-aged women in middle-grade books, but males were overwhelmingly the characters in the books at all age levels except infancy. Of the total books published in 1975, 70% of the books had no female characters at all. When they appeared, the elderly were presented in a positive fashion. In concluding their analysis of 53 books with older characters, Peterson and Eden (1977) conclude that, although they found no blatantly negative descriptions, "the routinizing of the activities of older people makes them appear uninteresting, one-dimensional and boring."

The impact on children of these messages from the television they view and the books they read may play a significant role in children's attitudes. Recent research by Seefeldt, Jantz, Galper, and Serock (1977) indicates that children's views of the elderly are negative and stereotypic. Children were interviewed following their responses to a series of attitude tests: "The majority of the children stated that older people couldn't do anything but sit and rock, go to church, or be pushed in wheelchairs. The physical characteristics of age—wrinkles, white hair, false teeth—were viewed with horror by children." However, the children also made many positive comments about the elderly, referring fondly to those whom they knew in person. The research did not differentiate the elderly by gender. Evidently, children hold particularistic and positive views of those elderly—grandparents—with whom they have actual contact and retain stereotyped and negative views of all others.

Impact of Media Images

In the more complex world of adult attitudes, extensive research has focused specifically on perceptions of the elderly (McTavish, 1971). Only a few studies were found that differentiated on the basis of sex, and what was reported was contradictory: "it appears that the association with sex may be more complex than previously shown" (see also Schonfield, 1982).

Viewing a great deal of television can distort one's views of reality (Gerbner & Gross, 1976). This holds true for the elderly themselves. Older women watch more television than do older men (Schreiber & Boyd, 1980). Nearly two-thirds of the women in the sample studied watched more than 3 hours of television, while slightly more than 50% of the men did. Less educated women over 70 sometimes confused the commercials with the programs; but the young-old, with more education and more years of exposure to television, were more likely to see television advertising as very influential. People over 55 "consume more television than any other segment of the population, including children" (Real et al., 1980), and older women watch the most daytime television. The various media, as Hess (1974) points out, "keep the aged informed about what is happening to everyone else" and also about themselves. What older women learn from television is the same message that others learn: old women are unimportant, weak, undesirable.

A Harris public opinion poll showed the wide gap between public perceptions and the realities of aging—the myths about aging that gerontologists are trying hard to counter (Harris, 1975). Hess (1974) suggests that to resolve the dilemma between myth and reality two courses are open: One can assume that one's own situation or knowledge about aging is the exception that proves the rule, or one can succumb to a self-fulfilling prophecy and behave and feel as the media indicate one should; after all, who wants to be "different"? (See also Powell & Williamson, 1985.) The older women on "Golden Girls" cavorting for a half hour a week do not counter the repeated messages of the negative and marginal role of older women conveyed during the rest of the media hours.

We have devoted a large portion of this chapter to the research on how older women are presented in the mass media because it is such a powerful educator of the public. No previous culture has had a communication tool such as television—a national "curriculum" teaching all of us, rightly or wrongly, about our world and ourselves. Television viewing is the major recreation of most of the American public. This and other popular media continue to perpetuate stereotypes of the middle-aged and older woman. These media deal in stereotypes of almost every group in the culture; the difference with older women is, unfortunately, that most of the portrayals are consistently negative or demeaning (or so idealized that no one really believes them), and they show older women as marginal and forgettable when it comes to the real concerns of life.

GROWING OLD FEMALE

One task we face in dealing with the lives of older women is locating a theory of aging and/or life-span development that will provide a basis for understanding how the diverse data fall into a meaningful whole. There are four related questions:

1. Is there a life-span theory that applies to both men and women about how they grow and age?
2. Is the development of males and females different enough so that different sequences are required to explain this process for each sex?
3. Do gender differences continue in old age specifically?
4. What is the degree of stability or change in personality over the life span, and how it is affected by gender?

A number of theorists have presented formulations that identify stages or subjective sequences through which individuals pass during their life course. The best known—Erikson (1959); Ryff and Migdal, (1984), Havighurst (1979), and Maslow (1970)—give little recognition to sex differences as individuals grow and age. A major underlying assumption is that all persons experience and attempt to cope with similar sequences. Others, theorists such as Levinson (1980), Peck (1968), and Gould (1978), are more interested in midlife and aging; but these theories too are explicitly applied to men (as in the case of Levinson) or make little mention of possible sex differences.

One of the problems with task or stage theories is the assumption of a normative sequence. That is, most people expect to encounter a given developmental stage at more or less the same time: graduation from high school and college, getting married, starting a family, becoming grandparents, retiring. However, as Hogan (1985) points out, contemporary life challenges many of these "normative" experiences (see also Haan, 1981). Many women, for instance, are returning to pick up their college education a number of years after starting a family; this is "out of sequence." The meaning and impact of a college education is qualitatively different for the 18-year-old sorority sister and her 35-year-old classmate, a single mother with two babies at home. Similarly, establishing a family is one thing in the life of a 22-year-old woman, fresh out of college with one or two years of work experience, and quite another thing in the life of a 40-year-old childless divorcee marrying a man with three children. A man who remarries at age 50 or even 60 can start a new family with a younger wife. A woman over 50 will be beyond childbearing. Remarriage for her will have a very different potential. In each instance, the sequences in the woman's life are sufficiently different from the "norm" that the theories seem nonexplanatory (Rossi, 1980).

A distinction has been made between "normative-age-graded" change processes and one's individual history, in which crises produce non-normative changes (Baltes, Cornelius, & Nesselrode, 1978). However, we would argue that there are so many non-normative events in women's lives that a general theory based on normative sequences tells us very little about women's development over the life span.

Critics of these theories also point out that there is a male bias in a number of their assumptions—for instance, the centrality of career choice and work achievement, which so far has dominated men's life choices and life chances far more than women's. There is in these theories an underemphasis on childbearing and child rearing (and the physiological changes that occur, such as menopause), which are significant female concerns (Scarf, 1980; Sheey, 1976). In addition, Gilligan (1982) makes the point that the way women are socialized in our culture results in the fact that "women are more embedded in lives of relationship than men, more contextual in their perceptual and cognitive style, more oriented towards relationships of interdependence, and more concerned in their judgements with the activity of caring" (p. 106). Women's family role relationships are very complex and have a higher salience in their lives than in men's lives. The agonizing struggle women go through in balancing career and family is hardly ever experienced by men. Although the persistence of sex differences throughout the life span has been addressed by a number of social and behavioral scientists (Fausto-Sterling, 1985; Reinisch, Rosenblum, & Sanders, 1987; Richardson & Wirtenberg, 1983; Rossi, 1985a), current theories of life-span development do not take this into account.

The second question we asked—is the development of males and females different enough so that different sequences are required to explain this process for each sex—has been answered in the affirmative by a large body of research (see analyses and summaries of research in Baker, 1987; Klein, 1985; Maccoby & Jacklin, 1974; Richardson & Wirtenberg, 1983; Wilkinson & Marrett, 1985). What happens in adulthood and old age grows out of decisions and experiences early in life. If girls, for instance, do not persist in mathematics—for reasons still unclear (Fennema & Peterson, 1985)—they cannot seek careers in science, engineering, mathematics, or many of the mathematically oriented social sciences such as economics, psychology, and sociology (Stage, Kreinberg, Eccles, & Becker, 1985). Our social order asserts that sex differences are important, and the sexes *must* be different (Deaux & Kite, 1987; Linn & Petersen, 1985). Yet in the gerontological literature, gender differences are often overlooked. In fact, studies show that probably "sexism is a major component in the neglect of the elderly by mental health professionals" (Maddox, 1987, p. 551; see also Chapter 1, this volume).

Our culture equates masculinity with aggressive and assertive behaviors and personality, femininity with nurturant and expressive behaviors—strength versus weakness. It is in reaction to this that feminists have, on the one hand, challenged the biases in research and interpretation that exist in male-dominated psychology, psychiatry, history, and social science and have pointed out forcefully that there may be more human similarities than differences between the sexes, that a rigid sex dichotomy is harmful to both men and women. On the other hand, some feminists would assert that female values are so different from male values, and so much more life-affirming, that women should not only celebrate but publicize their differences and separateness from men.

The emerging body of research on sex differences and the debate on how sex role learning influences all of later development have enormous implications for our study and understanding of older women, and they are particularly important as we look to how future cohorts age. What is called for is a new, more comprehensive theoretical construct that will take into account how we grow and develop as sexually different persons and how we move through midlife and into old age as male and female (Ryff, 1985, 1986; Sherif, 1982).

Our third question asks: do gender differences continue as significant influences of behavior in old age? Throughout this book we examine research that points to ways in which aging for women is a distinctive and different experience from that of men. Our society, like every other, places heavy emphasis throughout one's life on sex-appropriate behaviors. Every deviance from the stereotypical male or female is evaluated against what society perceives to be the norm. Also, we have documentation regarding the major and subtle physiological differences, which are sex-linked and over which we have no control. It is difficult to accept a view that after living 50 years in a gender-labeled world one would discard one's sex identity. The persistence of that identity as a particular, unique man or woman, aged 40 or aged 80, is one that we cherish (Kohli, 1986). We reminisce and review our past almost wholly in the context of expectations of fulfilling our role as a man or woman; without that the past lacks integration and meaning (Dowd, 1986). Although we may accept the fact that gender is an enduring influence throughout the life span, we may also wonder if either sex has an advantage in the journey from birth to death (Wershow, 1981).

Our fourth question asks to what extent there is change or stability in personality and how this may be influenced by gender. The debate on persistence of personality over the life span has particular interest for women. In pioneering research, Neugarten (1968) presented a new picture of the older woman as someone who, with age, became more expressive, managerial, and assertive, while at the same time men seem to become more nurturant, passive, and dependent. These findings have become a staple of gerontology texts and most discussions of personality in old age.

To what extent the findings of Neugarten (1968) are an accurate portrayal of basic personality change has been tested by other researchers. Ryff (1986) found that "women gave greater priority to instrumental values during middle age than old age, and they perceived themselves changing subjectively in the same fashion." Livson (1976) accounts for the more assertive change found in some older women as the result of increased options in a changing society: "Middle age can loosen the boundaries of one's life style and call forth suppressed parts of the self." Many women, she found, had not so much changed as found a way to fulfill earlier but unexpressed potential. In a review of developmental theory, Livson (1981) points out that the research supports "an intrinsic or developmental shift in the quality of maleness and femaleness as the individual moves through successive stages of the life cycle." She points out studies of preindustrial societies in which postmenopausal women enjoy freedoms and powers not available earlier. It is possible that a culture that forbids married and childbearing women to enter public life may perceive a change in personality in the older women freed from such restraints. Such a change, however, could be in behavior rather than some fundamental personality change (Livson, 1981).

Another problem with the Neugarten (1968) data, Rossi (1980) suggests, is the limitation imposed by the experiences of the cohort of women studies in 1968, particularly in respect to the impact of the "increased variance in both the timing and sequencing of life events." The longitudinal study of Maas and Kuypers (1974) found that as they became older there was more variability in life-styles among women than among men, and their life-style differences in old age were predictable from the attitudes and behaviors of these women when they were 30. In other words, women who showed the kind of assertive competence that Neugarten talks about as emerging only in midlife or later were, in fact, always competent. They may, however, have had difficulty perceiving themselves as such. Women in the Maas–Kuypers study who found child rearing and family life trying and difficult at 30 found coping difficult when they were 70. Those who coped well as young mothers were also active and positive in old age. A similar finding emerges from the study of women in the mining area of West Virginia. Geisen and Datan (1980) found that there was a perception of "executive competence" in such older women. It was not a personality trait that suddenly emerged in middle age. The conditions of survival in their lives had required them to be good managers from early years. A study of middle-aged women before and after their children left home supported the view that feminine women did not become masculine as they grew older but rather were able to express aspects of personality repressed by family expectations (Cooper & Gutmann, 1987).

The studies of change over the life span are further confounded by cohort effects, as discussed earlier. Riley (1978) points out that, unlike men, women growing up in postwar America have had many varied options available to them, which also differentiates them from previous cohorts of women. As she points out, "*different cohorts age in different ways.*" She notes, for example, that the age of menarche has shifted downward from age 17 to ages 12–13 in a century. These added years of fertility have, as we know to our distress, produced an epidemic of teenage pregnancy in the last decade. As they reach middle age, these young women will be a different group from their comparison group—women who are 50 in the 1990s. It is possible that the cohort of women studied in 1968 did demonstrate a significant personality change; we may still be cautious about asserting that the same influences will be operating on women coming of age in the future.

The widespread acceptance of the Neugarten (1968) findings may be an artifact of women's life patterns, particularly of generations growing old in the 1960s or earlier. Most women with families have always had to be competent managers, but it is typically underreported, understudied, and underestimated. Earlier cohorts of women accepted the norm of male dominance. Outwardly, they exhibited a passive role in decision making so that they could present image of the "good mother," who nurtures and obeys. In fact, most women with several children (particularly those who worked outside their homes) are or soon learn to be competent managers, or they and their families cannot survive. But how can they tell anyone about this kind of competence? What their world views as competence has to do with activities in the public sphere—careers, political activity, and freedom of action to visit or travel, seek more education, use their own money, express their own views. Thus, the family competence of women is invisible and comes to light only in old age.

We tend to be persuaded by the findings of the Maas–Kuypers study: competent and assertive women have been there all along and do not suddenly spring forth in middle age. Those who felt defeated or overwhelmed by personal and family cares in early and middle age will feel the same way when they are older. Retrospective reports of older women, particularly those of eminence who have written autobiographies, typically show a woman of independence and assertive vitality throughout her life (Eichorn, Clausen, Haan, Honzik, & Mussen, 1981).

Perhaps another reason for the folk view of a personality change in older women is derived from the discomfiture that a newly retired husband feels when he finds that his wife is now the "bossy woman" who is not all that gentle about his interest in her home. The typical retired husband won't know how to run the washing machine or negotiate with the plumber, or what floor polish to buy. Retirement presents potential role threats for both husband and wife, but the fact is that the older woman, newly perceived as assertive by her aggrieved husband, has not necessarily undergone a personality change; she always has been a manager. There is also the fact that, as Turner (1982) points out, the emerging dominance of the wives vis-à-vis their husbands may be due in large measure to "their physical vigor relative to that of their husbands" who may be a number of years older; the "old battle-ax" is apt to be "viewed with alarm by the younger generation—and her husband." The energies a woman gave to child rearing and housework can now, in old age, be devoted to "doing her own thing."

We do not have enough data about women's lives to postulate a women-only theory of life-span development. What seems somewhat more substantial is the accumulation of research that points out the stability of personality of women from one decade to the next within the same cohort. The old battle-ax of 65 was probably no shrinking violet at age 16; few shy wallflowers become senators. There is, in fact, so little longitudinal research about women that much of what we know about women's development must remain speculative until another generation of researchers can report.

SUMMARY

Older women have an image problem. In order to escape the negative stereotypes conveyed through every media, women are vulnerable to all kinds of commercial efforts to keep them from "looking their age."

The vast social changes that have occurred in women's roles in recent years underline the importance of reexamining the data we have on hand, which describes cohorts who grew up under quite different circumstances. It is highly probable that most of what we think we know about older women, based on research now available, will be wrong if generalized to women entering their 40s and 50s in a few more years.

Not only must we restudy older women and correct current information, we also need to examine theories of life-span development to see if they help us understand women's aging. Currently, no adequate theory is available since the age-stage sequences no longer fit the non-normative lives women lead. There is also reason to question whether women's personalities change significantly in their later years or if the changes are more in the eye of the beholder.

While young women will find that they do not replicate the lives of their mothers, there is still much to be done to revise the image that persists in mass media. The dangerous difference between myth and reality has had a negative and distorting impact on how older women view themselves. Perhaps as women move into more positions of influence in the production of such media messages, they can see to it that a more adequate image of older women—in all of their complexity, variety, and vigor—is conveyed.

REFERENCES

Ansello, E. F. (1977). Age and ageism in children's first literature. *Educational Gerontology, 2*, 255–274.

Ansello, E. F. (1978, January). Ageism: The subtle stereotype. *Childhood Education*, pp. 118–122.

Aronoff, C. (1974). Old age in prime time. *Journal of Communication, 24*(4), 86–87.

Baker, M. A. (Ed.). (1987). *Sex differences in human performance*. New York: John Wiley.

Baker, N. C. (1984). *The beauty trap: Exploring woman's greatest obsession*. New York: Franklin Watts.

Baltes, P. B., Cornelius, S. W., & Nesselrode, J. R. (1978). Cohort effects in behavioral development: Theoretical and methodological perspectives. In A. Collis (Ed.), *Minnesota Symposium on Child Psychology* (Vol. 11, pp. 149–170). Hillsdale, NJ: Erlbaum.

Baruch, G. K. (1984). The psychological well-being of women in the middle years. In G. Baruch & J. Brooks-Gunn (Eds.), *Women in midlife* (pp. 161–180). New York: Plenum.

Bengtson, V., Reedy, M. M., & Gordon, C. (1985). Aging and self-conceptions: Personality processes and social contexts. In J. E. Birren & K. W. Schaie (Eds.), *Handbook of the psychology of aging* (pp. 544–593). New York: Van Nostrand Reinhold.

Berkun, C. S. (1983). Changing appearance for women in the middle years of life: Trauma? In E. W. Markson (Ed.), *Older women* (pp. 11–35). Lexington, MA: Lexington Books.

Berman, P. W., O'Nan, B. A., & Floyd, W. F. (1981). The double-standard of aging and the social situation: Judgments of attractiveness of the middle aged woman. *Sex Roles, 7*(2), 87–96.

Berscheid, E., & Walster, E. (1972, March). Beauty and the beast. *Psychology Today*, pp. 27–31.

Best, R. (1983). *We've all got scars: What boys and girls learn in elementary school.* Bloomington, IN: Indiana University Press.

Bishop, J. M., & Krause, D. R. (1984). Depictions of aging and old age on Saturday morning TV. *The Gerontologist, 24*(1), 91–94.

Botwinnick, J. (1984). *Aging and behavior* (3rd. ed.). New York: Springer Publishing Co.

Briller, B. R. (Ed.). (1985). *Television looks at aging.* New York: Television Information Office.

Brooks-Gunn, J., & Kirsh, B. (1984). Life events and the boundaries of midlife for women. In G. Baruch & J. Brooks-Gunnn (Eds.), *Women in midlife* (pp. 11–30). New York: Plenum.

Cantor, M. G. (1987). Popular culture and the portrayal of women: Content and control. In B. B. Hess & M. M. Ferree (Eds.), *Analyzing gender: A handbook of social science research* (pp. 190–215). Newbury Park, CA: Sage.

Cassata, M. B., Anderson, P. A., & Skill, T. D. (1980). The older adult in daytime serial drama. *Journal of Communication, 30*(1), 48–49.

Cooper, K. L., & Gutmann, D. L. (1987). Gender identity and ego mastery style in middle-aged, pre- and post-empty nest women. *The Gerontologist, 27*(3), 347–352.

Datan, N. (1983). Star-crossed love: The developmental phenomenologies of the life cycle. In G. D. Rowles & R. J. Ohta (Eds.), *Aging and milieu* (pp. 29–40). New York: Academic Press.

Davis, R., & Davis, J. A. (1986). *TV's image of the elderly.* Lexington, MA: D. C. Heath.

Deaux, K., & Kite, M. S. (1987). Thinking about gender. In B. B. Hess & M. M. Ferres (Eds.), *Analyzing gender* (pp. 92–117). Beverly Hills, CA: Sage.

Demos, V., & Jacke, A. (1981). When you care enough: An analysis of attitudes toward aging in humorous birthday cards. *The Gerontologist, 21*, 121–124.

Dowd, J. J. (1986). The old person as stranger. In V. W. Marshall (Ed.), *Later life* (pp. 147–190). Beverly Hills, CA: Sage.

Eichorn, D. H., Clausen, J. A., Haan, N., Honzik, M. P., and Mussen, P. H. (Eds.). (1981). *Present and past in middle life.* New York: Academic Press.

Elder, G. H. (1981). Social history and life experience. In D. H. Eichorn, J. A. Clausen, N. Haan, M. P. Honzik, & P. H. Mussen (Eds.), *Present and past in middle life* (pp. 3–32). New York: Academic Press.

Elder, G. H., Jr. (1982). Historical experience in the later years. In T. K. Hareven & K. J. Adams (Eds.), *Aging and life course transitions: An interdisciplinary perspective* (pp. 75–108). New York: Guilford Press.

Elliot, J. (1984). The daytime television drama portrayal of older adults. *The Gerontologist, 24*(6), 628–633.

Erikson, E. H. (1959). Identity and the life cycle. *Selected Papers, Psychological Issue Monograph Series,* 1 (No. 1). New York: International Universities Press.

Erikson, E. H. (1963). *Childhood and society* (2nd ed.). New York: Norton.

Fausto-Sterling, A. (1985). *Myths of gender.* New York: Basic Books.

Fennema, E., & Peterson, P. (1985). Autonomous learning behavior: A possible explanation of gender-related differences in mathematics. In C. B. Marrett & L. C. Wilkinson (Eds.), *Gender influences in classroom interaction* (pp. 17–36). Orlando, FL: Academic Press.

Foff, A. (1956). The teacher as hero. In A. Foff & J. D. Grambs (Eds.), *Readings in education* (pp. 19–21). New York: Harper.

Freedman, R. (1986). *Beauty bound.* Lexington, MA: Lexington Books.

Gantz, W., Gartenberg, H. M., & Rainbow, C. K. (1980). Approaching invisibility: The portrayal of the elderly in magazine advertisements. *Journal of Communication, 30*(1), 56–60.

Geisen, C. B., & Datan, N. (1980). The competent older woman. In N. Datan, & N. Lohmann (Eds.), *Transitions of aging* (pp. 57–82). New York: Academic Press.

Gerbner, G., & Gross, L. (1976). The scary world of TV's heavy viewers. *Psychology Today,* 9, 41–45, 89.

Gerbner, G., Gross, L., Signorielli, N., & Morgan, M. (1980). Aging with television: Images on television drama and conceptions of social reality. *Journal of Communication, 30*(1), 37–47.

Giele, J. Z. (1980). Adulthood as transcendence of age and sex. In N. J. Smelser & E. H. Erikson (Eds.), *Themes of work and love in adulthood* (pp. 151–173). Cambridge, MA: Harvard University Press.

Gilligan, C. (1982). *In a different voice: Psychological theory and women's development.* Cambridge, MA: Harvard University Press.

Glenn, N. D. (1977). *Cohort analysis.* Beverly Hills, CA: Sage.

Goldhaber, D. (1986). *Life span human development.* New York: Harcourt Brace Jovanovich.

Gould, R. (1978). *Transformations.* New York: Simon and Schuster.

Grambs, J. D. (1987). Are older women teachers different? *Journal of Education, 169*(1), 47–64.

Grambs, J. D., & Waetjen, W. B. (1979). *Sex: Does it make a difference?* Belmont, CA: Wadsworth.

Green, B. Parham, I. A., Kleff, R., & Pilisuk, M. (1980). Introduction: Old age: Environmental complexity and interventions. *Journal of Social Issues, 36*(2), 1–7.

Haan, N. (1981). Common dimensions of personality development. In D. H. Eichorn, J. A. Clausen, N. Haan, M. P. Honzik, & P. H. Mussen (Eds.), *Present and past in middle life* (pp. 117–151). New York: Academic Press.

Harris, L., & Associates. (1975). *The myth and reality of aging in America.* Washington, DC: National Council on Aging.

Harrison, J. (1983). Women and aging: Experience and implications. *Aging and Society,* 3, 209–235.

Harter, C. L. (1977). The "good times" cohort of the 1930's: Sometimes less means more (and more means less). *PBS Reports* (Population Reference Bureau), *3*(3), 1–4.

Havighurst, R. J. (1979). *Developmental tasks and education* (4th ed.). New York: David McKay.

Heilburn, C. (1984). Middle-aged women in literature. In G. Baruch & J. Brooks-Gunn (Eds.), *Women in midlife* (pp. 69–79). New York: Plenum.

Hess, R. R. (1974). Stereotypes of the aged. *Journal of Communication, 24*(4), 76–85.

Hochschild, A. R. (1978). *The unexpected community: Portrait of an old age subculture*. Berkeley, CA: University of California Press.

Hogan, D. P. (1985). The demography of life-span transitions: Temporal and gender comparisons. In A. S. Rossi (Ed.), *Gender and the life span*. New York: Aldine.

Hollenshead, C., & Ingersoll, B. (1982). Middle-aged and older women in print advertisements. *Educational Gerontologist, 8*(1), 23–41.

Holtzman, J. M., & Akiyama, H. (1985). What children see: The aged on television in Japan and the United States. *The Gerontologist, 25*(13), 62–68.

Jones, L. Y. (1980). *Great expectations: American and the baby boom generation*. New York: Ballantine.

Kastenbaum, R., Derbin, V., Sabatini, P., & Artt, S. (1972). "The ages of me": Toward personal and interpersonal definitions of functional aging. *International Journal of Aging and Human Development, 3*, 197–211.

Kaufman, D. R., & Richardson, B. L. (1982). *Achievement and women: Challenging the assumptions*. New York: The Free Press.

Kehl, D. G. (1985). Thalia meets Tithonus: Gerontological wit and humor in literature. *The Gerontologist, 25*(5), 539–544.

Klein, S. S. (Ed.). (1985). *Handbook for achieving sex equity through education*. Baltimore: Johns Hopkins University Press.

Kogan, N. (1979). A study of age categorization. *Journal of Gerontology, 34*, 358–367.

Kohli, M. (1986). The world we forgot: A historical review of the life course. In V. W. Marshall (Ed.), *Later life* (pp. 233–270). Beverly Hills, CA: Sage.

Lachman, M. E. (1984). Life-span developmental approach. In G. Baruch & J. Brooks-Gunn (Eds.), *Women in midlife* (pp. 31–68). New York: Plenum.

Levinson, D. J. (1978). *The season's of a man's life*. New York: Alfred A. Knopf.

Levinson, D. J. (1980). Toward a conception of the adult life course. In N. J. Smelser & E. H. Erikson (Eds.), *Themes of work and love in adulthood* (pp. 265–290). Cambridge, MA: Harvard University Press.

Linn, M. C., & Petersen, A. C. (1985). Facts and assumptions about the nature of sex differences. In S. S. Klein (Ed.), *Handbook for achieving sex equity through education* (pp. 53–76). Baltimore: Johns Hopkins University Press.

Linn, M. W., & Hunter, K. (1979). Perception of age in the elderly. *Journal of Gerontology, 34*(1), 46–52.

Livson, B. F. (1976). Patterns of personality development in middle-aged women: A longitudinal study. *International Journal of Aging and Human Development, 7*, 107–115.

Livson, B. F. (1981). Paths to psychological health in the middle years: Sex differences. In D. H. Eichorn, J. A. Clausen, N. Haan, M. P. Honzik, & P. H. Mussen (Eds.), *Present and past in middle life* (pp. 195–221). New York: Academic Press.

Long, J., & Porter, K. L. (1984). Multiple roles of midlife women. In G. Baruch & J. Brooks-Gunn (Eds.), *Women in midlife* (pp. 109–159). New York: Plenum.

Lopata, H. (1987). *Women's family roles in life course perspective*. In B. B. Hess & M. M. Ferree (Eds.), *Analyzing gender: A handbook of social science research* (pp. 381–407). Newbury Park, CA: Sage.

Maas, H. S., & Kuypers, J. A. (1974). *From thirty to seventy: A forty-year longitudinal study of adult life styles and personality*. San Francisco: Jossey-Bass.

Maccoby, E. E., & Jacklin, C. M. (1974). *The psychology of sex differences*. Stanford, CA: Stanford University Press.

Maddox, G. L. (1987). *Encyclopedia of aging*. New York: Springer Publishing Co.

Marshall, V. W. (1986). Dominant and emerging paradigms in the social psychology of aging. In V. W. Marshall (Ed.), *Later life: The social psychology of aging* (pp. 5–25). Beverly Hills, CA: Sage.

Maslow, A. H. (1970). *Motivation and personality*. Evanston, IL: Harper and Row.

Matthews, S. H. (1979). *The social world of old women: Management of self and identity*. Beverly Hills, CA: Sage.

McTavish, D. G. (1971). Perceptions of old people: A review of research methodologies and findings. Part 2. *The Gerontologist, 11*, 90–101.

Neugarten, L. (1964). *Personality in middle and late life*. New York: Lieber-Atherton.

Neugarten, B. (Ed.). (1968). *Middle age and aging: A reader in social psychology*. Chicago: University of Chicago Press.

Neugarten, B., & Gutman, D. L. (1968). Age-sex roles and personality in middle age. In B. Neugarten (Ed.), *Middle age and aging*. Chicago: University of Chicago Press.

Palmore, E. (1971). Attitudes toward aging as shown by humour. *The Gerontologist, 11*, 181–186.

Palmore, E. (1978). When can age, period, and cohort be separated. *Social Forces, 57*(1), 282–295.

Passuth, P. M., & Cook, F. L. (1985). Effects of television viewing on knowledge and attitudes about older adults: A critical reexamination. *The Gerontologist, 25*(1), 69–77.

Peck, R. C. (1968). Psychological developments in the second half of life. In B. L. Neugarten (Ed.), *Middle age and aging*, pp. 51–75. Chicago: University of Chicago Press.

Peterson, D. A., & Eden, D. Z. (1977). Teenagers and aging: Adolescent literature as an attitude source. *Educational Gerontology, 2*, 311–325.

Powell, L. A., & Williamson, J. B. (1985, Summer). The mass media and the aged. *Social Policy*, pp. 38–49.

Real, M., Anderson, H. L., & Harrington, M. H. (1980). Television access for older adults. *Journal of Communication, 30*(1), 81–88.

Reinisch, J. M., Rosenblum, L. A., & Sanders, S. A. (Eds.). (1987). *Masculinity/Femininity*. New York: Oxford University Press.

Richardson, B. L., & Wirtenberger, J. (1983). *Sex role research*. New York: Praeger.

Riley, M. W. (1978). Aging, social change and the power of ideas. *Daedalus, 107*(4), 39–52.

Riley, M. W. (1985). Women, men and lengthening life course. In A. S. Rossi (Ed.), *Gender and the life course* (pp. 33–34). New York: Aldine.

Robin, E. P. (1977). Old age in elementary school readers. *Educational Gerontology, 2*, 275–292.

Rossi, A. S. (1980). Life-span theories and women's lives. *Signs, 6*(1), 4–21.

Rossi, A. S. (Ed.). (1985a). *Gender and the life course.* New York: Aldine.

Rossi, A. S. (1985b). Gender and parenthood. In A. S. Rossi (Ed.), *Gender and the life course* (pp. 161–191). New York: Aldine.

Ryff, C. D. (1985). The subjective experience of life-span transitions. In A. S. Rossi (Ed.), *Gender and the life course* (pp. 97–114). New York: Aldine.

Ryff, C. D. (1986). The subjective construction of self and society: An agenda for life-span research. In V. W. Marshall (Ed.), *Later life* (pp. 233–270). Beverly Hills, CA: Sage.

Ryff, C. D., & Migdal, S. (1984). Intimacy and generativity: Self-perceived transitions. *Signs, 9*(3), 470–481.

Scarf, M. (1980). *Unfinished business: Pressure points in the lives of women.* New York: Doubleday.

Schuerman, L. E., Eden, D. Z., & Peterson, D. A. (1977). Older people in women's periodical fiction. *Educational Gerontologist, 2*, 211–218.

Schreiber, E. S., & Boyd, D. A. (1980). How the elderly perceive television commercials. *Journal of Communication, 30*(1), 61–70.

Seefeldt, C., Jantz, R. K., Galper, A., & Serock, K. (1981). Healthy, happy and old: Children learn about the elderly. *Educational Gerontology, 7*(1), 37–45.

Shaver, P., & Hendrick, C. (Eds.). (1987). *Sex and gender.* Newbury Park, CA: Sage.

Sheey, G. (1976). *Passages: Predictable crises of adult life.* New York: Dutton.

Sherif, C. W. (1982). Needed concepts in the study of gender identity. *Psychology of Women Quarterly, 6*(4), 375–398.

Smith, M. D. (1979). The portrayal of elders in magazine cartoons. *The Gerontologist, 19*(4), 408–412.

Sohngren, N. (1977). The experience of old age as depicted in contemporary novels. *The Gerontologist, 17*(1), 70–78.

Sontag, S. (1972). The double standard of aging. *Saturday Review, 55*(39), 29–38.

Schonfeld, D. (1985). Stereotyping whom and why. *The Gerontologist, 25*(4), 431–434.

Stage, E. K., Kreinberger, M., Eccles, J., & Becker, J. R. (1985). Increasing the participation of girls and women in mathematics, science and engineering. In S. Klein (Ed.), *Handbook for achieving sex equity through education.* Baltimore: Johns Hopkins University Press.

Steenland, S. (1986). *Prime time women.* Washington, DC: National Commission on Working Women.

Stoddard, K. M. (1983). *Saints and shrews: Women and aging in American popular film*. Westport, CT: Greenwood Press.

Tavris, C., & Wade, C. (1984). *The longest war: Sex differences in perspective* (2nd ed.). New York: Harcourt Brace Jovanovich.

Tuchman, G., Daniels, A. K., & Benet, J. (1978). *Hearth and home: Images of women in the mass media*. New York: Oxford University Press.

Turner, B. (1979). The self-concepts of older women. *Research on Aging, 1*, 464–480.

Turner, B. F. (1982). Sex-related differences in aging. In B. B. Woman (Ed.), *Handbook of developmental psychology* (pp. 912–936). Englewood Cliffs, NJ: Prentice-Hall.

Uniker-Sebeck, J. (1981). The seven ages of women: A view from American magazine advertising. In C. Mayo & N. M. Henley (Eds.), *Gender and nonverbal behavior* (pp. 209–251). New York: Springer-Verlag.

Ward, R. A. (1984). The marginality and salience of being old: When is age relevant. *The Gerontologist, 24*(3), 227–232.

Wershow, H. J. (Ed.). (1981). *Controversial issues in gerontology*. New York: Springer Publishing Co.

Wilkinson, L. C., & Marrett, C. B. (Eds.). (1985). *Gender influences in classroom interaction*. Orlando, FL: Academic Press.

Williamson, J. B., Shindul, J. A., & Evans, L. (1985). *Aging and public policy: Social control or social justice*. Springfield, IL: Charles C. Thomas.

3
Is There Life after Menopause?

In a culture in which female sexual appeal and motherhood have been considered the main factors in feminine valuation, menopause has been considered the end of life rather than a change of life. Along with other influences the women's movement has had on the quality of life for women, a major contribution is the affirmation that even if reproductive life is over after menopause, sexual life can continue as long as one is willing and the opportunity is there.

Understanding what goes on at menopause is not easy. Like menstruation, menopause has been encircled by a miasma of myth and misinformation. Research is limited and still inconclusive. The relationship between physical changes and discomfort associated with menopause is not easily ascertained. The interventions to ease or ameliorate problems associated with menopause have been surrounded by controversy.

In this chapter we will look at the physiology and mythology of menopause, the related physiological changes and symptoms, and what can be done to ease the transition into postmenopausal status. We will examine the claims and counterclaims for medications to ease "hot flashes" and other menopausal symptoms. We will also look at the impact of menopause on other physiological processes, such as osteoporosis, and what can be done to alleviate or prevent such problems. Then we will see what research says about the sexual life of older women and the psychological response of women to their changing and changed physiology.

MENOPAUSE AND AGING

Menopause is a uniquely human female experience. There is some evidence that animal models might be available and could be studied to obtain more information about physiological changes, but they have not yet been located. Locating such models is difficult because "no mammals except humans continue to live a significant period after menopause" (Rosenmayer, 1982; see also Finch & Gosden, 1986). It can be argued that having a large percentage of postreproductive individuals available "confers a survival advantage to younger . . . human individuals" (Rosenmayer, 1982, p. 34). Until recent improvements in living conditions relatively few women lived past menopause (Lancaster & King, 1985).

Unfortunately, the accepted view of women after menopause has been, until recently, one of redundant, unattractive, and unhappy persons. Fausto-Sterling (1985) quotes a book popular in the 1970s that pointed out that after menopause

> The vagina begins to shrivel, the breasts to atrophy, sexual desire disappears. . . . Increased facial hair, deepening voice, obesity . . . coarsened features, enlargement of the clitoris, the gradual baldness complete the tragic picture. Not really a man but no longer a functional woman, these individuals live in the world of intersex. (pp. 110–11)

Thousands of readers and probably many in the current cohort of older women, have been misled by this unpleasant and damning picture. A woman facing menopause would have been truly devastated.

Improved nutrition, better health practice, more options for one's own life, and more information result in women's experiencing menopause today in a manner very different from the miserable creatures portrayed in the literature of earlier generations. But as we shall discuss below, many of the myths of menopause still persist.

One of the key problems making the assessment of menopausal effects difficult is that there is controversy over what is "normal" aging, and this seems to be particularly difficult when it comes to the reproductive systems of men and women (Minaker & Rowe, 1986). Sex differences in normal aging need to be accounted for. For a time researchers came up with a solution they found eminently satisfying. Since men as they age do not experience a clearly marked physiological episode similar to menopause, then it was only a short step to conclude that women's different experience was due to physiological defects. This conclusion does not satisfy us today, but unfortunately, most of the research on "normal" aging has been conducted on males, who do not experience the major physiological event of menopause.

The lack of adequate research becomes particularly critical when we examine menopause because we lack a baseline of "normal" aging in women.

The way in which men and women age differs in terms of endocrine performance. This difference is substantial and involves many aspects of bodily functioning, which in turn influences susceptibility to physical disabilities, perceptions, emotions, and life decisions: "men and women have *different* reproductive cycles, *both* of which are normal" (Fausto-Sterling, 1985, p. 121).

WHAT IS MENOPAUSE?

Normal physiological aging for women includes menopause. It is inevitable and inescapable for any woman who lives past age 50, when menopause usually occurs. The age range for menopause is 40 to 60, but 50 is usually given as the modal age. The age given for menopause has been so consistent throughout history that it is thought to be genetically programmed and not subject to environmental factors (Maddox, 1987, p. 433).

There is nothing simple about this event, including its definitions. There has been a lack of clarity in the use of the terms "menopause" and "climacteric." According to Posner (1979), who reviewed the way gynecological texts and popular books for women used the terms,

> "climacteric" should properly refer to the widespread changes that affect the whole body during middle and old age in both men *and* women, while "menopause" should refer specifically to the cessation of menses and concomitant changes in ovulation and hormone secretion in women.

She comments further that it is undoubtedly due to the double standard of aging that "our culture has chosen to ignore the climacteric for men and to hang women's more general aging ills on menopause."

The 1981 World Health Organization's technical report on menopause recommended the following definitions:

Menopause: Permanent cessation of menstruation resulting from loss of ovarian, follicular activity

Perimenopause (also referred to as the climacteric): The period immediately prior to menopause when endocoronological, biological, and clinical features of approaching menopause commence, continuing for at least the first year after the menopause

Postmenopause: A period dating from the menopause, although it cannot be determined until after 12 months of spontaneous ammenorrhea (no menstruation)

Premenopause: The whole of the reproductive period prior to the menopause. (Voda & George, 1986)

Most women are not so precise about nomenclature, referring to menopause as being whatever time period it is that covers symptomatology related to this biological process. "Change of life" is used as a common euphemism. Medically, the distinctions implicit in the WHO definitions above are useful and, if they became more widespread, could help in the communication between women and their doctors.

These medical distinctions may solve only part of the communication problem, however. For decades the textbooks that doctors used presented a sexist and archaic view of menopause and its effects on women (Posner, 1979). That many doctors still adhere to this view is the reported experience of many women (Corbett, 1984). The research about, and medical practice in regard to, menopause is what Koeske (1982) uses as a prime example of "bad science." This kind of science discredits women's subjective experience and does not admit that women's social reality is different from men's. On the one hand, science does not accept the subjective world of women, and on the other hand, the behavioral sciences discount biological factors. As a result, what women have been told about menopause is that it is either a disease needing medical treatment or that their symptoms are all in their heads. The newer feminist science calls for the study of menopause based on "just what features distinguish menopausal experience from other life experiences" (Fausto-Sterling, 1985, p. 211).

CULTURE, PSYCHOLOGY, AND MENOPAUSE

Few events in women's lives have been more surrounded by myth and irrational beliefs than menopause has. Of course, it also was only recently that there has been an accurate scientific accounting for menstruation, so it is not unexpected that the cessation of menses should also be clouded by misinformation. The first appearance of the word *menopause* and the identification of the symptoms appeared in France around the time of the French Revolution; it did not exist as a word in the English language until late in the 19th century (Voda & George, 1986).

Menopause has been traditionally and widely viewed as an event that *must* be psychologically traumatic for women. After all, since women's main function is to reproduce, to lose that ability must be devastating. In Japan the many negative responses to menopause are the cause of a great deal of acute distress and denial (Rosenberger, 1986). Many older women today undoubtedly experienced these forces when they went through menopause some 20 years ago. However, the horror with which some women now in their 40s anticipate menopause has much more to do with its symbolism as indicating aging rather than with loss of fertility. The irony, as Posner (1979) puts it, is that

> if menstruation is a "curse" as the literature and everyday talk indicate, then menopause should be a blessing! We know however that this is not the case. In classic Catch-22 fashion women are damned if they do (menstruate) and damned if they don't (menopause).

For the modern woman who has had her 1.2 children, being no longer fertile does not threaten her self-esteem; being old does. The enlightened woman of today, who does not find turning 50 and passing through menopause as the end of meaningful life, may define the years after menopause as a time when she is freed of biological restraints and can be more rather than less sexual and female.

A number of cultures described in the anthropological literature have defined the postmenopausal period in very positive terms. In the Ibibio of Nigeria the postmenopausal woman is a "senior wife" with important powers and opportunities to enter the male world. In other cultures she is recognized as the source of teachings about women's rituals, the trainer of young wives, and the repository of knowledge about healing herbs. "For an older woman there are many more freedoms. She may sit in on councils of men from which she was once excluded" (Hotvedt, 1983). Posner (1979) points out that "in many traditional societies postmenopausal women are permitted to go freely, use obscene language and handle food and other ceremonial objects which were previously prohibited from their contact due to the contamination of menstruation." (See Chapter 8 for more extended discussion.)

When menopause has positive personal and status outcomes in a given society it is assumed, therefore, that women would have few if any symptoms. There is little information on whether this is in fact the case. Most of the anthropologists who have collected the original field data on other cultures were men, and they did not or could not ask the women.

There has been a folk view in our culture, on the basis of no data, that women who viewed menopause in a positive light would have few if any symptoms, just as there is often a suspicion that women who suffer from acute morning sickness early in pregnancy do not want to be pregnant. In the literature on menopause there have been consistent implications that women who have the worst symptoms are psychologically at risk. The research to support this assumption is conflicting. Bart (1971) interviewed

20 women hospitalized for depression. She reported that the women who were overprotective and overinvolved with their children were more likely to have menopausal depression; also, housewives had more depression than working women. Unfortunately, like the male doctors, Bart dismissed physiological state as a contributing factor. Other researchers see the differences in psychological distress as a function of quality of self-esteem rather than a function of the physiological changes of menopause (Gannon, 1985; see also Notman, 1982). Adapting to menopause without major personal disruption is seen by Moaz and Landau (1983) as a function of a woman's holding traditional or modern views regarding sex roles, but such an interpretation discounts the reality of physical symptoms (Kaufert, 1985).

The gynecological textbooks reviewed by Posner (1979) invariably related menopausal symptoms to psychological problems, with some "authorities" insisting that the physiology of menopause has nothing to do with women's symptoms—it is all in their heads. As Posner comments, "A social psychological model of menopause merely exacerbates the problem by encouraging women to feel guilty about unjustifiable menopause symptoms." The myth of women's psychological invention of menopausal symptoms is nicely summarized by Gannon (1986):

> Psychological symptoms seem to be unrelated to hormonal levels but do seem to covary with premenopausal personality characteristics, levels of stress, and cultural factors, while physical symptoms tend to covary somewhat with hormonal levels and seem unrelated to personality, stress, or cultural factors. (p. 169; see also Notman, 1982)

What appears to be established is that if an individual has a prior history of psychological problems, has many other stressors to cope with, is part of an ethnic group that values fertility in women above all else, then one can predict emotional trouble during the menopausal years.

For at least the last 20 years increased psychiatric symptoms were felt to be caused by menopause. Now we are not so sure (Kerzner, 1983). Menopause may be less the cause of the assumed increased emotionality of women during their midlife years than other life circumstances occurring at the same time (Fausto-Sterling, 1985; Weg, 1983).

It is still the case that most of the emotional and physical ailments that women complain of in middle age tend to be attributed to menopause, but there is a reverse trend that discounts all such complaints as having no relationship at all. The confounding of physical and psychological symptoms continues in the popular press, however, as evidenced by a 1987 poll sponsored by the *Saturday Evening Post* (SerVaas, 1987). Women were asked to indicate which of a list of nonphysical symptoms they experienced during menopause, such as irritability, anxiety, difficulty concentrating. Naturally, one would draw the conclusion that there were caused by menopause. The evidence of more scientific research is that women may feel this way in midlife, but it is unlikely that physiological changes caused these psychological symptoms unless, of course, the physiological symptoms were particularly severe.

Women who visit a doctor with rather nonspecific physical or psychological complaints any time between the ages of 45 and 55 suffer the danger of misdiagnosis. According to Delorey (1984), "gynecologists attribute women's reasons for office calls to menopausal reasons at a 64% higher rate than women themselves do." Women who do not consult a doctor about some symptoms that occur along with menopause may, however, be in danger of other problems. As Kaufert (1986) points out, if there is pain, spotting between menses, or heavy menstrual flooding, pathological conditions needing medical attention may exist.

A rational view of menopause that informed middle-aged women can accept will include the fact that there are important biological changes occurring and that they will, in many instances, produce symptoms of varying degrees of physical discomfort. But one should not assume that any other woman's experiences with menopause will necessarily be one's own; individual variations are extensive, and the causes have not been established (Sherman, Wallace, Bean, Chang, & Schlabaugh, 1982). However, the most uncomfortable symptoms, as we will discuss below, can be ameliorated with appropriate medication.

It is also true that for some women the onset of menopausal symptoms can be psychologically threatening because it is a clear marker of age. Other women may be coping with the stress of job, adolescent children, an insensitive husband or one who is facing his own midlife crisis, and/or the demands of an ailing parent. If at the same time a woman is going through menopause, she may well become depressed or distraught. Other women will feel a major psychological lift from finally being freed of "the curse." All of these varieties of response are legitimate. It is as unwise to discount the biological basis for physical symptoms as it is to dismiss the psychologically distressing behavior without seeking a possible physiological cause.

PHYSIOLOGY OF MENOPAUSE

What happens during menopause can be briefly summarized:

> With the aging of the ovary the number of primordial follicles decreases and the production of estrogen falls off. Failure of good corpus luteum formation occurs, accompanied by reduced progesterone secretion, disrupting formerly

> smooth workings of the menstrual cycle. When estrogen levels eventually fall below those needed to induce endometrial shedding, menstruation ceases. These events may occur rapidly, leading to an abrupt cessation of menses, or, more commonly, take place over several months or years of greater and greater menstrual irregularity until menstruation finally terminates. (Goodman, 1980, p. 740; see also Harman & Talbert, 1985)

A woman is born with all of the ova she will have during her life span; some undeveloped ova may remain after menopause, though they are no longer released. Other physiological changes also occur. The uterus begins to atrophy and become very small since it will no longer be needed. The vaginal and urogenital lining becomes thin, vaginal secretions diminish, and vaginal muscles shorten and become less flexible.

Despite the reports in medical and popular literature that there are numerous menopause "symptoms,"

> only three signs can be directly attributed to changes in estrogen production: 1. changes in menstrual cycle, 2. hot flashes and sweats ("vasomotor instability") and 3. vaginal changes (decrease of moisture and elasticity in the vagina, sometimes called "atrophy") (Corbett, 1984, p. 445)

Gannon (1985) has a much more extensive list:

> a variety of clearly unpleasant symptoms and changes including hot flashes, profuse sweating, headaches, increased weight, dryness and thinning of the vaginal walls, increased incidence of vaginal infections, depression, insomnia, loss of breast firmness, dizziness, sensations of cold in the hands and feet, irritability, pruritus of the sexual organs, constipation, artherosclerosis, and osteoporosis. (p. 160)

Lest this list terrify anyone not yet in the throes of menopause, Gannon goes on to state that in fact most women do not experience all of these symptoms.

Additional symptoms, only recently recognized as part of the menopausal experience, include gaining of weight and thinning of the skin, with resulting wrinkles and appearance of aging. There is some evidence that the added weight due to fat accumulation that many women experience, to their dismay, after menopause is actually a beneficial response. Women who have more fat (but are not obese) are far less likely to have osteoporosis in old age than their thinner sisters (Siiteri, 1986).

The considerable doubt about the extent of symptomatology results from the fact that most of the research on menopause "has suffered from either design or methodological flaws" (Voda & George, 1986). Gannon

(1985) points out that there is a "lack of a reliable and valid measure of menopausal symptoms" (p. 161). McKinlay and McKinlay (1986) claim that the predominant medical view is based on "biased clinical encounters and is actually without epidemiological foundation." From their own research, the McKinlays conclude that the erroneous views of how women suffer during menopause are due to reports of the many problems faced by those who have had artificial menopause (hysterectomies with or without removal of ovaries) and to a lack of accurate epidemiological studies of healthy women experiencing aging.

What can most women expect in terms of menopausal symptoms? The first, menstrual irregularity, can also be accompanied by occasional massive and unexpected menstrual bleeding. This can be embarrassing and sometimes alarming. How extensive this symptom is we do not know. All women experiencing natural menopause will notice decreasing menstrual flow accompanied by irregular occurrence until all menstruation ceases.

As estrogen production declines, mammary glands in the breast are replaced by fat tissue, and breasts may become less firm. The skin begins to thin and become dry.

The most uncomfortable symptom is "hot flashes" (sometimes referred to as "hot flushes"). These are due to the temporary disruption of the mechanism that controls body temperature, with the result that one feels extremely hot—as though swept by a sudden fever—for a few moments; then it passes. These incidents may occur many times during the day or may be infrequent. Women may also experience cold sweats at night. How many women have these symptoms is not known for sure, but some research suggests that between 30 and 50% have some discomfort (Gannon, 1985). Most of the cited studies reporting how many women experience hot flashes are several decades old (Judd, 1986), and their methodology may be questioned (McKinlay & McKinlay, 1986). In a review of studies of menopause, the McKinlays (1973) point out the limitations of these medical reports:

> First, clinical observation is frequently reported without presenting even limited data referred to, and descriptions of the clinic population(s) are vague or nonexistent. Second, there is a consistent omission of any judgment as to the objectivity and generalizability of these observations. Third, menopausal symptomatology, its origin and treatment, is repeatedly described with no empirical basis other than "experience."

Why the vasomotor system is out of balance for a time during menopause is not understood (Gannon, 1985), but studies do support the conclusion that the central nervous system, not just surface changes, is involved (Kerzner, 1983). According to Judd (1986), who summarized the scientific evidence, "menopausal hot flushes apparently represent normal thermoregulatory events triggered centrally by altered hypothalmic activity." A recent study of the mechanism of the hot flash was reported by the National Institute on Aging (1986), but *why* this occurs is still unknown.

It is this symptom, hot flashes, that most women find difficult to deal with at the onset of menopause and for which estrogen replacement therapy, which we will discuss below, has been most widely used. The duration and severity of hot flashes varies; some women report few or none at all, and others experience them for as much as 5 years. In one study of a large number of women who reported hot flashes with menopause there appeared to be few "antecedent menstrual, reproductive, or health related factors" that could have caused some women and not others to have this symptom (Sherman et al., 1981). The cause of the individual variations does not seem to be known.

The decrease in estrogen also affects the vaginal area. A common symptom, it can be easily treated with appropriate creams and rarely leads to major discomfort (Corbett, 1984). There are other important physiological effects of menopause, such as osteoporosis, which we will discuss at greater length below.

The above descriptions are, of course, simplifications. There are many more changes that occur, both subtle and complex. Nor are all of the changes understood or their interrelationships established. A great deal more research is needed for a better understanding of this natural event that affects all women who reach midlife. For more detailed and scientific discussions of what is known to date about the physiological changes related to menopause, see Nicosia (1986), Gannon (1985, pp. 153–159), and Siiteri (1986).

One of the major problems with menopause, other than the discomfort of hot flashes and night sweats, is the burden of psychological distress that occurs in many women coincident with the hormonal changes during this period, as we have discussed above. Gannon (1985) points out that the symptoms of menopause should "be separated into two distinct types: one category for physical symptoms ..; a second category for psychological symptoms, consisting of fatigue, depression, tension, insomnia, irritability, headaches and weight gain" (p. 160). Most current authors agree that much of the popular and even some of the scientific literature up to now has confused physiological with psychological symptoms. Although the former are inevitable, the latter are more problematic as being directly the result of menopause. Finally, it is imperative to remove menopause from classification as a "disease" since it is a naturally occurring physiological change (Downing, 1987).

THE ESTROGEN DEBATE

In 1966 Dr. Robert A. Wilson published *Feminine Forever* (1966), in which he identified estrogen loss as responsible for the "disease" of menopause. As Fausto-Sterling (1985) comments, thousands of copies of the book were sold, and physicians prescribed estrogen to "millions of women, many of whom had no clinical 'symptoms' other than cessation of the menses" (p. 112). Today we would say that Wilson had a severe case of conflict of interest: he was head of a research foundation supported by the makers of Premarin®, which, after Wilson's boost, became the fourth or fifth most popular prescription drug. In 1975 came the first warnings that estrogen treatment appeared to be associated with uterine cancer.

A detailed review of the medical controversy over estrogen for menopausal women is depressing (Kaufert & McKinley, 1985). The profitability of the medication was undeniable. However, after researchers associated unacceptable cancer risk levels with the use of estrogens, the Federal Drug Administration in 1976 issued a regulation requiring a drug insert for patients informing them of the risk. As a result, the prescription of estrogens dropped markedly. However, individual doctors (and pharmaceutical companies) were outraged at this interference with medical practice. Those doctors who saw comparatively few patients did not notice the increases in endometrial cancer. However, epidemiologists, looking at a large number of cases, implicated estrogen therapy. Later research with modified estrogen replacement therapy appears to have no effect on increased incidence of endometrial cancer (Harman & Talbert, 1985).

Interestingly enough, the persons for whom the newfound miracle drug was prescribed were most likely to be white middle-class women who already were high users of medical services. Kanfert and McKinley, (1985) point out that what had occurred was the "medicalization of the menopause" and the creation of the "medical stereotype of the menopausal patient—white, middle class, neurotic, physician dependent."

When women received estrogen treatment, they were not informed about what was prescribed. To quote Kanfert and McKinley (1985): "Estrogen was another item in a well publicized series (the pill, DES, medicalized childbirth, and the high rate of hysterectomies) in which medical care appeared to have acted in ways injurious to women's health." They go on to warn of a "currently . . . carefully orchestrated campaign [that] is advocating estrogen as a barrier against osteoporosis." Others strongly support estrogen as a bone-loss preventive, as we will discuss at greater length in the next section.

Estrogen replacement therapy, however, has been shown to ameliorate "atrophic vaginitis" (Gannon, 1985), the postmenopausal condition in which "the walls of the vagina become smooth and dry and produce less lubrication, and it has been assumed that this condition is due to the lack of estrogen" (p. 192).

Some other claims for estrogen have not been clinically established. According to Gannon (1985), "the research has not been supportive of [estrogen replacement therapy] as an effective mode of treatment for symptoms commonly attributed to menopause, such as depression, nervousness, insomnia, fatigue, and headaches" (p. 193). Unfortunately, popular advice to women, as in a regular medical column in the *Washington Post* (Siwek, 1986) suggests that "possibly memory problems and anxiety" could be helped by estrogen. However, estrogen may be helpful in reducing risk of coronary disease due to artherosclerosis in women. In their review of the research on estrogen replacement therapy in the *Handbook of the Biology of Aging*, Harman and Talbert (1985) conclude that

> current evidence favors the position that benefits of estrogen replacement after the menopause probably outweigh the risks especially when the protective effect against osteoporotic fractures is considered. Adverse effects can probably be minimized by using low doses of estrogen, cyclic therapy, and regular opposition with 10 to 12 days of a progestin. (p. 477)

These assurances may not be sufficient. The Boston Women's Health Book Collective is apprehensive about estrogen medications (Corbett, 1984). They discuss other ways women can cope with menopausal discomforts: proper diet, exercise, herbal teas, and relaxation exercises. Women should be wary about simply trusting their doctors to know what medication is going to be helpful, no matter what their complaints, if they are in their menopausal years.

OSTEOPOROSIS

We have argued in the earlier sections of this chapter that menopause is a normal part of the aging process for women. However, the endocrine changes that result may produce some unwanted side effects. One of these is osteoporosis, or loss of bone mass.

The picture of the little old lady, bent nearly double, hobbling along with her cane is a familiar stereotype. We now know a great deal more about why she looks that way; she has osteoporosis.

Osteoporosis is "characterized by a decrease in skeletal mass or quantity of bone, without a change in the quality of the existing bone. . . . This reduction in bone mass is regarded as the major factor in osteoporotic fractures, which typically occur in the vertebra, distal radious, and the hips" (Gannon, 1985, p. 180; see also Coralli, Raisz, & Wood, 1986). It is particularly common among older women. Menopause is generally believed to be a contributing and possibly primary factor in women with this problem, but there are few reliable statistics about the incidence of the disease (Gannon, 1985). Other factors, such as obesity, lack of exercise, and limited calcium intake, are also implicated in the development of osteoporosis.

Women start off with a disadvantage, having 25% less bone mass than men have. Some bone loss occurs gradually after age 30, but women's bone loss is accelerated 5 to 10 years after menopause, adding to the bone loss that can be attributed to other aging processes (Coralli et al., 1986). By age 65, about 25% of white women have have one or more fractures, and 70% of those are caused by osteoporosis. Spinal fractures can cause intense pain, deformity, and even death. Hip fractures, which cost $3.8 billion in health care in 1984, have a death rate of from 12 to 20%. Many hip fracture patients enter nursing homes, where 70% die within a year; and even if patients return to their homes, 40% die within 2 years (Kaplan, 1985; Kolata, 1986).

Osteoporosis is not readily diagnosed; some women find out that they have the disease only when they suffer a fracture. Repeated fractures are common once the process has started (Corbett, 1984). As Kaplan (1985) puts it, "If hypertension is a silent killer, osteoporosis is a silent thief. It insidiously robs the skeleton of its banked resources, often for decades, before the bond is weak enough to sustain a spontaneous fracture." When the spine is involved, vertebrae suffer a collapse, height decreases, and the body shows the bowed look called "dowager's hump" or "widow's hump."

The clue to whether osteoporosis is involved can be "an episode of acute pain in the middle to low thoracic or high lumbar regions while at rest or during routine daily activity such as standing, bending, or lifting" (Kaplan, 1985, p. 103). This may be the first indicator of the problem. Pain is sudden, often following an activity that would not normally cause a fracture. Bed rest is the only relief.

Osteoporosis came to widespread public attention following a conference sponsored by the National Institutes of Health (Napoli, 1986). It was declared a preventable disease if it could be identified early. Almost immediately detection centers sprouted across the country. By 1986 there were more than 500. "Hospitals seeking new customers are now opening women's health clinics with osteoporosis screening as a major draw" (Napoli, 1986).

It is now clear, however, that the several kinds of expensive tests available can detect normal bone loss at age 50 but cannot predict those individuals whose bone loss will increase by age 65 due to osteoporosis. Medicare and some insurance companies reimburse for these dubious procedures. According to Napoli (1986), manufacturers of radiological screening equipment provide only minimal training for the operators.

At the conference noted above it was recommended that calcium intake by Americans should be increased immediately. Almost at once women were bombarded by ads touting the benefits of patented over-the-counter calcium products. In 1983 calcium supplement sales totaled $47 million; in 1987 it was close to $200 million. Calcium is being added to everything from bread to diet colas. But there is serious question as to whether all of this calcium can even be absorbed by the system (Culliton, 1987).

Like other simple—and profitable—remedies, adding calcium to one's diet to prevent bone loss cannot be expected to cure or even prevent osteoporosis in older women. The only medication that has shown effectiveness is low-dose (0.3 mg) estrogen in conjunction with 1500 mg of calcium daily. Dairy products are the best source of bioavailable calcium (Culliton, 1987; see also Cassel, 1987, Kase, 1986). The most likely candidates for this prescription are thin white women immediately after menopause. Research reported in mid-1987 suggests that estrogen given 8 to 10 years after menopause will not be effective (*Science*, 1987).

Load-bearing exercise was promoted as a preventive measure for young women. However, a study of 6,000 women compared athletes with nonathletes and found no difference in risk of bone fractures or osteoporosis after menopause. Increased calcium and vitamin D in the diet was helpful before age 35; after menopause, calcium, vitamin D, and in some cases estrogen therapy were found to retard bone loss (*Washington Post Health*, Jan. 27, 1987).

Millions of dollars have been made from selling dubious medications for osteoporosis. Before taking any, on the advice of friends or advertising, women need to be informed. Though the fear of fractures in old age from osteoporosis is real, the disease actually affects relatively few. However, hip fractures are a threat from other causes. In a controlled study of over 6,000 patients, the use of psychotropic drugs that produced unsteadiness of gait and confusion was identified as the cause of falls resulting in hip fractures (Cassell, 1987).

MENOPAUSE AND CANCER

Cancer is the ghost that haunts older women. Will it strike me? When? Is there anything I can do to prevent it? Am I more at risk after menopause?

Definitive answers to these questions cannot be found in the existing research. Most cancers in women are age-related; the peak years for all forms are 25 to 30 for women, 55 to 60 for men (Maddox, 1987). Cancers that occur after midlife are considered late-developing tumors. However, cancer is the fourth or fifth leading cause of death for older women, depending on what statistics you use (Verbugge, 1985). Breast cancer will strike 1 of 11 women at some time in their lives; it is more common in postmenopausal women, but their chance of survival appears to be better than that of younger women (Gee & Kimball, 1987). The major risk factors are having a mother or sister who had breast cancer before the age of 40, being exposed to large doses of radiation or exogenous estrogens, or a previous personal history of cancer. Women's reproductive organs are also the site of cancers, but although many may manifest themselves in old age, or be discovered only after death in autopsy, age is coincidental rather than causative. That is, if we live long enough, the cancers that are lurking somewhere in our bodies will manifest themselves. Many cancers are due to environmental factors, such as smoking or exposure to asbestos. Menopause does not seem to be implicated in any increase in risk of cancer.

The use of estrogen replacement therapy to counter the symptoms of menopause was challenged, as we noted earlier, because of a presumed increase in breast cancer. After the first scare, and some additional research, authorities decided that a more carefully modulated medication at lower doses, plus the addition of small amounts of progesterone, would remove the cancer threat (Gannon, 1985).

There have also been fears that estrogen therapy could increase the danger of breast cancer. Kase (1986) asserts that there is "no significant association between estrogen use and breast cancer risk" (p. 274). A recent report from the Centers for Disease Control ("Estrogens Exonerated," 1987) should be reassuring: The largest study to date of women with breast cancer showed that "the rate of breast cancer was the same overall in women who had used estrogens as in those who had not. Women who went through natural menopause and subsequently used estrogen were at 80 percent of the risk of women who had not used estrogen."

Another kind of cancer was also identified as increasing when estrogen replacement therapy was prescribed. In his review of the research on this medication, Kase (1986) makes the point that endometrial cancer is also caused by obesity, hypertension, and diabetes, making it difficult to establish clearly the risk factor of estrogen replacement therapy. He also points out that endometrial cancer, though increasing in incidence, is still very rare and there is a high cure rate. He exonerates estrogen replacement therapy, if properly prescribed and monitored, as a factor in the increase in cancer, and he is very positive in supporting the value of this medication for relieving the uncomfortable symptoms of menopause.

SEX AND THE OLDER WOMAN

The mythology of the sexless older woman, shorn of her femininity and sexual interest after surviving the devastations of menopause, has influenced the thinking of men, women, and the medical profession until very recently. When few women in fact lived beyond menopause, they were too small a group to garner much attention. Now, however, most women who reach age 50 can expect to live 20 to 25 years after menopause. Do they also give up their sexual lives? The evidence appears to be overwhelmingly no (Linderman, 1981; Luria & Meade, 1984).

The work of Masters and Johnson in 1966 (McKenzie, 1980) showed that sexual interest does not decline in women as they age any more than it declines in men. The only difference in amount of sexual activity for most women was related to the presence or absence of a sexually competent partner. Sexual responsiveness, according to the observations of Masters and Johnson, is independent of estrogen; orgasm can still be achieved up to a very old age. These findings of Masters and Johnson are very reassuring, but, as Starr (1985) points out, their conclusions are based on 11 women over age 60.

It is very important to be aware of the effect of medications on sexuality. A drug that has been shown to inhibit ejaculation in a man may also be suspected of suppressing orgasm in a woman, although often there are no data on the latter (Simonson, 1984). Many drugs, particularly those taken for hypertension or depression, have been shown to greatly reduce sexual interest, and they are more apt to be prescribed for older women than for men.

The sexuality of older women has been traditionally viewed as a function of the sexual capacity and availability of older men rather than of the women themselves (Turner & Adams, 1983). Cohort effects are probably more pronounced in this area than in most others; sexual activity is as much a matter of attitude as of opportunity. However, it is not easy to get accurate data on sexuality of persons who are 60 or older in part because they are rarely included in such studies and also because they may be offended by such intimate questions or be nonresponsive (Dressel & Avant, 1983). When they were growing up and growing old, sex was not something one discussed—with anyone. A study of the sexual attitudes of mothers toward the sexual activity of their college-age daughters showed that the mothers were far more liberated in their views of what they would accept and what they would do than their own mothers had been with them (Yalom, Brewster, & Estler, 1981). This changed view of appropriate sexual behavior, which the older generation extends to the young, has been one of the most evident social changes of recent decades, and it is certain to have a distinct effect on how women (and men) view sexuality as they age. It is likely that the sexual freedom so avidly explored by today's young women will have a marked influence on the role of sex in their lives when they are postmenopausal.

Older people have been given very inadequate guidance regarding sexual behavior in old age, as evidenced by a review of advice books (Arluke, Levin, & Suchwalko, 1984). Books offering advice published prior to 1970 were most apt to view sexual activity of the elderly with aversion. One book "claimed that sexuality among the elderly would probably be forced, unpleasant, and undesirable, if not harmful psychologically and maritally." After 1970 the books were more supportive of the actuality of marital sex for the elderly but were not in favor of remarriage and dating for elderly individuals. Some of the advice books did accept the idea that women were more likely than men to continue to have unimpaired sexual ability into old age. Women now in their 60s and 70s were undoubtedly influenced by such popular guides to living. The result was a diminished subjective capacity to maintain sexuality as they aged.

A limited definition of sexuality may also interfere with how the sexual behavior of the aged is viewed. As Weg (1983) points out: "What may be most critical, and most absent, are research and comment on sexuality in the elderly that refer to affection, tenderness, love and relationships" (p. 47). Another limitation on understanding how sexual needs may be met among the elderly is the presumption that sexuality can be expressed only in heterosexual relationships and legally acceptable couples. That is, if one wants sex, the only person one can have this experience with is a legal spouse. For older women, 60% of whom are widows, this means an effective end of sexuality. Such beliefs are being challenged by the evolution of new social norms and new research into the sexual behavior of older women.

Another inhibiting factor may be the view of gerontologists themselves. If the prestigious *Handbook of the Biology of Aging* (Finch & Schneider, 1985) is any indicator, sexuality in older women is nonexistent. In the chapter on reproductive aging (Harman & Talbert, 1985) two pages are devoted to the sexual activity of the male but no comment is made on the female. Sexuality does not appear as an index entry in other source books (Binstock & Shanas, 1985; Birren & Schaie, 1985). There is a lack of research on physiologically caused sexual dysfunction in women, although there is considerable research on men (Fordney, 1986). There are also, as Starr (1985) reports, many problems with previous research on sexuality in the aging, particularly women.

Although there is continued ambivalence about the expression of sexuality by the older person, human needs are in fact not easily ignored or circumscribed, particularly in an era in which sexual liaisons outside marriage are the norm for young people and increasingly part of adult experience for both sexes. Furthermore, the taboo against masturbation has receded, and it is spoken of approvingly as a valid sexual expression for both elderly men and women (Butler & Lewis, 1976; Starr, 1985). The research by Starr and Weiner (1981), based on a group of 518 women and 282 men, provides insight into the complexity of the sexual dimension for the elderly. These authors also concluded that older women were more likely to find some new solutions to meet their sexual needs than to resign themselves to frustration, denial, or sublimation. Women who were sexually active earlier are apt to remain sexually active in old age (Gee & Kimball, 1987).

After menopause women may have a wider range of alternatives than previously appreciated for meeting their sexual needs (Corby & Zarit, 1983). One of the alternatives that older single women may choose is the development of homosexual relationships. In a collection of first-person accounts of older lesbian women, many report that they arrived at this relationship as older widows or divorcees (Adelman, 1986). (See Chapter 6 for further discussion of lesbian life-style and aging.)

Older persons who have to be institutionalized because of chronic ailments, poverty, or disability face the added prejudices of their caretakers. "Nursing home personnel generally come from social classes in which attitudes towards sex are far from enlightened" (Kassel, 1983; see also Simonson, 1984). Masturbation as a form of sexual release for older men and women is viewed by these caretakers as "dirty" and reprehensible.

Although there is some discussion of how nursing homes or other residences for the elderly should treat the sexuality of their clients, the taboos surrounding this topic make it difficult to conduct definitive research. Kassel concludes:

> Within all of the limitations, sex is an opportunity for good, clean entertainment that provides laughter and joy in the heart and the intimate giving of one person to the other. Unfortunately, it is in the long-term care institution that the American aged remain most deprived of human intimacy. (p. 182)

The double standard that up to now has determined the effective social roles of men and women continues to restrict many women to a sterile sexuality after menopause. The concept of desirability as a function of youth and young adulthood has led too many women to believe that they do not need—and do not deserve—a sex life after 50. Such a view is certainly widespread among older women in the 1980s. That this view will change in line with society's generally revised view of what is sexually appropriate is the promise of the future (Luria & Mead, 1984).

SUMMARY

The related topics of menopause and sexuality continue to be poorly understood by women experiencing physiological change and by the practitioners to whom women turn for professional advice. Menopause is the result of hormonal change, the external sign of which is a slow cessation of the menstrual flow until 12 months have passed without a menstrual period. At that point menopause has occurred. The whole of the physiological process involved is not yet fully described, nor the mechanisms at work that produce unpleasant side effects, such as hot flashes and vaginal dryness.

Dealing with these symptoms through the recently discovered estrogen replacement therapy, while effective, has produced a whole new range of controversies. It is now agreed that such therapy, if carefully modulated and monitored, can control the most unpleasant side effects of menopause, and fears of increased cancer rates are not supported by careful longitudinal research. In addition, estrogen has been shown to be a valuable agent in reducing the incidence of osteoporosis.

Changed views of sexually appropriate behavior for the aged are expected to make life a good deal more pleasant and interesting for cohorts yet to come. Meanwhile, older women, by becoming more informed and by seeking the help of educated professionals, can seek sexual intimacy and joy.

REFERENCES

Adelman, M. (Ed.). (1986). *Long time passing: Lives of older lesbians*. Boston: Alyson.

Arluke, A., Levin, J., & Suchwalko, J. (1984). Sexuality and romance in advice books for the elderly. *The Gerontologist, 24*(4), 415–419.

Bart, P. B. (1971). Depression in middle-aged women. In V. Gornick & B. K. Moran (Eds.), *Women in sexist society* (pp. 99–117). New York: New American Library.

Binstock, R. H., & Shanas, E. (1985). *Handbook of aging and the social sciences*. New York: Van Nostrand Reinhold.

Birren, J. E., & Schaie, K. W. (1985). *Handbook of the psychology of aging*. New York: Van Nostrand Reinhold.

Butler, R. N., & Lewis, M. J. (1976). *Love and sex after sixty*. New York: Harper & Row.

Cassel, C. K. (1987). Geriatrics. *JAMA, 258*(16), 2248–2250.

Coralli, C. H., Raisz, L. G., & Wood, C. L. (1986). Osteoporosis: Significance, risk factors and treatments. *The Nurse Practitioner, 11*(9), (5–35).

Corbett, L. (1984). Menopause. In Boston Women's Health Book Collective. (Eds.), *The new our bodies ourselves* (pp. 442–450). New York: Simon and Schuster.

Corby, N., & Zarit, J. M. (1983). Old and alone: The unmarried in later life. In R. B. Weg (Ed.), *Sexuality in the later years* (pp. 139–147). New York: Academic Press.

Culliton, B. J. (1987). Osteoporosis reexamined: Complexity of bone biology is a challenge. *Science, 235*, 833–834.

DeLorey, C. (1984). Health care and midlife women. In G. Baruch & J. Brooks-Gunn (Eds.), *Women in midlife* (pp. 277–313). New York: Plenum.

Dowing, C. (1987). *Journey through menopause*. New York: Crossroad.

Dressel, P. L., & Avant, W. R. (1983). Range of alternatives. In R. R. Weg (Ed.), *Sexuality in the later years* (pp. 183–210). New York: Academic Press.

Estrogens exonerated in breast cancer. (1987, January 24). *Science News*, p. 57.

Fausto-Sterling, A. (1985). *Myths of gender: Biological theories about women and men*. New York: Basic Books.

Finch, C. E., & Gosden, R. G. (1986). Animal models for the human menopause. In L. Mastroianni & A. Paulsen (Eds.), *Aging, reproduction, and the climacteric* (pp. 3–34). New York: Plenum.

Finch, C. E., & Schneider, E. L. (1985). *Handbook of the biology of aging*. New York: Van Nostrand Reinhold.

Fordney, D. S. (1986). Female sexuality during and following menopause. In L. Mastroianni & C. A. Paulsen (Eds.), *Aging, reproduction and the climacteric* (pp. 229–240). New York: Plenum.

Gannon, L. R. (1986). *Menstrual disorders and menopause*. New York: Praeger.

Gee, E. M., & Kimball, M. M. (1987). *Women and aging*. Toronto: Butterworths.

Glowacki, G. (1985). Geriatric gynecology. *The Female Patient, 10*, 99–108.

Goodman, M. (1980). Review essay: Toward a biology of menopause. *Signs*, 5(4), 739–753.

Harman, S. M., & Talbert, G. B. (1985). Reproductive aging. In C. E. Finch & E. L. Schneider (Eds.), *Handbook of the biology of aging* (2nd ed.; pp. 457–510). New York: Van Nostrand Reinhold.

Hotvedt, M. (1983). The cross-cultural and historical context. In R. B. Weg (Ed.), *Sexuality in the later years* (pp. 13–39). New York: Academic Press.

Judd, H. L. (1986). The basis of menopausal vasometer symptoms. In L. Mastroianni & A. Paulsen (Eds.), *Aging, reproduction and the climacteric* (pp. 215–240). New York: Plenum.

Kase, N. (1986). Estrogen deprivation: The physiology, pathophysiology, and informed management of female menopause or castration. In L. Mastrioanni & A. Paulsen (Eds.), *Aging, reproduction, and the climacteric* (pp. 263–286). New York: Plenum.

Kassel, V. (1983). Long-term care institutions. In R. B. Weg (Ed.), *Sexuality in the later years* (pp. 167–184). New York: Academic Press.

Kaufert, P. A., & McKinley, S. M. (1985). Estrogen replacement therapy: The production of medical knowledge and the emergence of policy. In E. Lewin (Ed.), *Women, health and healing: Toward a new perspective.* Tavistock, England: Metheun.

Kaufert, P. A. (1986). Menstruation and menstrual change in midlife. In V. L. Olesen & N. F. Woods (Eds.), *Culture, society and menstruation* (pp. 63–76). Washington, DC: Hemisphere.

Kaufert, P. A. (1985). Midlife in the Midwest: Canadian women in Manitoba. In J. K. Brown & V. Kerns (Eds.), *In her prime* (pp. 181–197). South Hadley, MA: Bergin and Garvey.

Kerzner, L. J. (1983). Physical changes after menopause. In E. W. Markson (Ed.), *Older women* (pp. 99–314). Lexington, MA: Lexington Books.

Koeske, R. D. (1982). Toward a biosocial paradigm for menopause research: Lessons and contributions from the behavioral sciences. In A. Voda, M. Dinnerstein, & S. O'Donnell (Eds), *Changing perspectives on menopause* Austin, TX: University of Texas Press.

Kolata, G. (1986, August 6). Calcium for bones: Second thoughts. *Washington Post, Health*, p. 10.

Lancaster, J. B., & King, B. J. (1985). An evolutionary perspective on menopause. In J. K. Brown & V. Kerns (Eds.), *In her prime* (pp. 13–20). South Hadley, MA: Bergin and Garvey.

Linderman, K. (1981). The sexuality of the older person: Review of the literature. *The Gerontologist, 21*(2), 203–208.

Luria, Z., & Meade, R. G. (1984). Sexuality and the middle-aged woman. In G. Baruch & J. Brooks-Gunn (Eds.), *Women in midlife* (pp. 271–397). New York: Plenum.

Maddox, G. L. (1987). *Encyclopedia of aging*. New York: Springer Publishing Co.

McKenzie, S. (1980). *Aging and old age*. Glenview, IL: Scott-Foresman.

McKinlay, S. M., & McKinlay, J. B. (1973). Selected studies of the menopause: Annotated bibliography. *Journal of Biosocial Science, 5*, 533–555.

McKinlay, S. M., & McKinlay, J. B. (1986). Health status and health care utilization by menopausal women. In L. Mastroianni & A. Paulsen (Ed.), *Aging, reproduction, and the climacteric* (pp. 243–262). New York: Plenum.

Minaker, K. L., & Rowe, J. W. (1986). Methodological issues in clinical research on the aging reproductive system. In L. Mastroianni & C. A. Paulsen (Eds.), *Aging, reproduction and the climacteric* (pp. 35–57). New York: Plenum.

Moaz, B., & Landau, E. (1983). Continuity of self-actualization: Womanhood in the climacterium and old age. In R. B. Weg (Ed.), *Sexuality in the later years* (pp. 251–269). New York: Academic Press.

Napoli, M. (1986, December 1). Disease of the week: The latest in getting sick. *The New Republic*, pp. 17–18.

National Institute on Aging (1986). *Research advances in aging, 1984–85*. Bethesda, MD: Author.

Nicosia, S. V. (1986). Ovarian changes during the climacteric. In L. Mastroianni & A. Paulsen (Eds.), *Aging, reproduction, and the climacteric* (pp. 179–200). New York: Plenum.

Notman, M. (1982). Midlife concerns of women: Implications of the menopause. In C. C. Nadelson & M. T. Notman (Eds.), *The woman patient, Vol. 2, Concepts of femininity and the life cycle* (pp. 135–144). New York: Plenum.

Parlee, M. B. (1984). Reproductive issues including menopause. In G. Baruch & J. Brooks-Gunn (Eds.), *Women in midlife* (pp. 303–314). New York: Plenum.

Posner, J. (1979). It's all in your head: Feminist and medical models of menopause (strange bedfellows). *Sex Roles*, *5*(2), 179–190.

Rosenberger, N. (1986). Menopause as a symbol of anomaly, the case of the Japanese woman. In V. L. Olesen & N. F. Woods (Eds.), *Culture, society and menstruation* (pp. 15–24). Washington, DC: Hemisphere.

Rosenmayer, L. (1982). Discontinuities in the study of aging. In T. K. Hareven & K. J. Adams (Eds.), *Aging and life course transitions: An interdisciplinary perspective* (pp. 27–54). New York: Guilford Press.

SerVaas, C. (1987, January/February). More about estrogen skin patches. *Saturday Evening Post*, pp. 52–54, 100–104.

Sherman, B. M., Wallace, R. D., Bean, J. A., Chang, Y., & Schlabaugh, L. (1982). The relationship of menopausal hot flushes to medical and reproductive experience. *Journal of Gerontology*, *36*(3), 306–309.

Siiteri, P. (1986). Nongonadal estrogen and endocrine function during the menopause. In L. Mastroianni & A. Paulsen (Eds.), *Aging, reproduction, and the climacteric* (pp. 210–215). New York: Plenum.

Simonson, W. (1984). *Medications and the elderly*. Rockville, MD: Aspen Systems.

Siwek, J. (1986, October 15). Consultation. *Washington Post Health*.

Staff. (1986, March). Osteoporosis: The silent disease. *GHA News*, Group Health Association of Washington, DC.

Starr, B. D. (1985). Sexuality and aging. In C. Eisdorfer (Ed.), *Annual review of gerontology and geriatrics* (pp. 97–126). New York: Springer Publishing Co.

Starr, B. D., & Weiner, M. B. (1981). *The Starr-Weiner report on sex and sexuality in the mature years*. New York: McGraw-Hill.

Turner, B. F., & Adams, C. (1983). The sexuality of older women. In E. W. Markson (Ed.), *Older women* (pp. 55–72). Lexington, MA: Lexington Books.

Verbugger, L. M. (1985). An epidemiological profile of older women. In M. R. Haug, A. B. Ford, & M. Sheafor (Eds.), *The physical and mental health of aged women* (pp. 41–64). New York: Springer Publishing Co.

Voda, A. M., & George, T. (1986). Menopause. In H. H. Werley, J. J. Fitzpatrick, & R. Taunton (Eds.), *Annual review of nursing research* (pp. 55–75). New York: Springer Publishing Co.

Weg, R. W. (1983). The physiological perspective. In R. W. Weg (Ed.), *Sexuality in the later years* (pp. 40–81). New York: Academic Press.

Wilson, R. A. (1966). *Feminine forever.* New York: M. Evans.

Yalom, M., Brewster, W., & Estler, S. (1981). Women of the fifties: Their past sexual experiences and current sexual attitudes in the context of mother/daughter relationships. *Sex Roles,* 7(9), 877–887.

4
Health and the Older Woman

Slowly but surely the myth of women as the weaker sex is giving way to the reality: on the average, women outlive men by a substantial margin and are less prone than men to succumb to many significant devastating and life-threatening events. But women have their own health problems as they age. What is "normal aging" and what is specific to each sex is one of the challenges of current research into the health of the elderly. On the basis of what we now know there are a number of differences that favor women.

In this chapter we will look at why women outlive men. Then we will examine the process of gender differences in normal aging, how this is reflected in health and disease patterns, and the gender differences in mortality. We will look into the data on mental health in older women and how the health delivery system serves older women.

WOMEN LIVE LONGER THAN MEN

Every discussion of the demographics of aging reveals a constant phenomenon: there are more older women than older men in every age bracket. However, the ratio of males to females favors males in the earliest years; then the sex ratio is balanced until about age 50. The demographic "pyramid" in Figure 4.1 shows this change.

FIGURE 4.1 U.S. Population by age and sex: 1986.

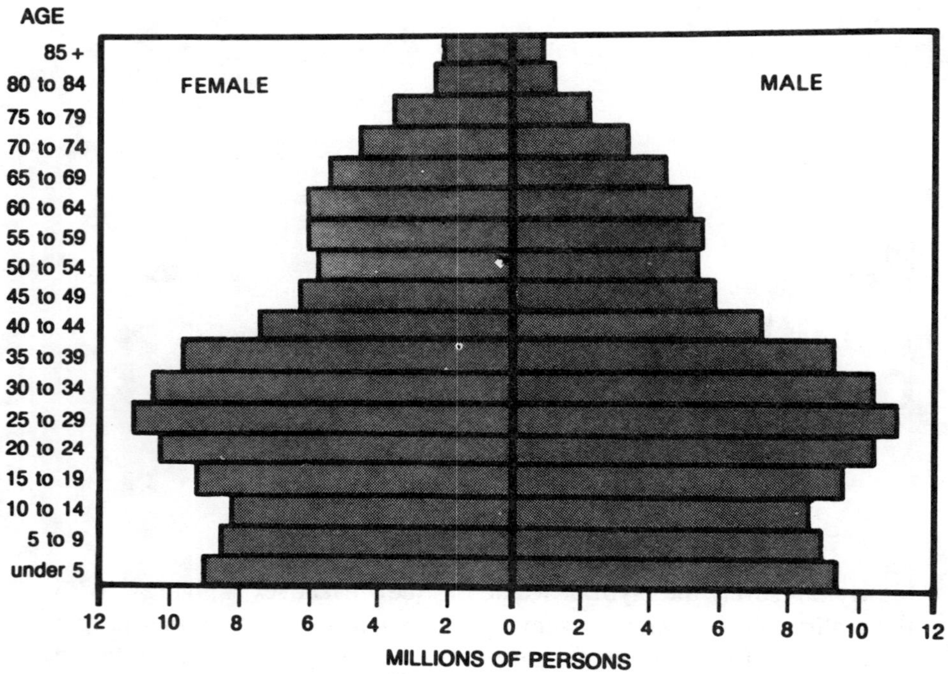

From U.S. Bureau of the Census, "Estimates of the Population of the United States by Age, Sex, and Race: 1980 to 1986." *Current Population Reports* Series P-25, No. 1000 (February 1987).

The differences in numbers of males and females in the years after age 65 are significant. Figure 4.2 shows the ratios. As of 1987, the Bureau of the Census data show that there were 83 men for every 100 women aged 65 to 69; by age 85 and over, there were only 40 men for every 100 women. If all age categories are lumped together, there are 3 women over age 65 for every 2 men.

When stated in terms of life expectancy—how many years one can expect to live as of date of birth—the data show a continuing trend for women to outlive men. Table 4.1 shows the trend in life expectancy by cohort. The changes that have occurred since 1900 are striking. At birth, in 1900, a male could expect to live to age 46.3 years and a female 2 years longer. By 1985 the life span has increased dramatically: a male can anticipate living, on the average, to age 71.2 years and a female to age 78.2.

FIGURE 4.2 Number of men per 100 women by elderly age group: 1986.

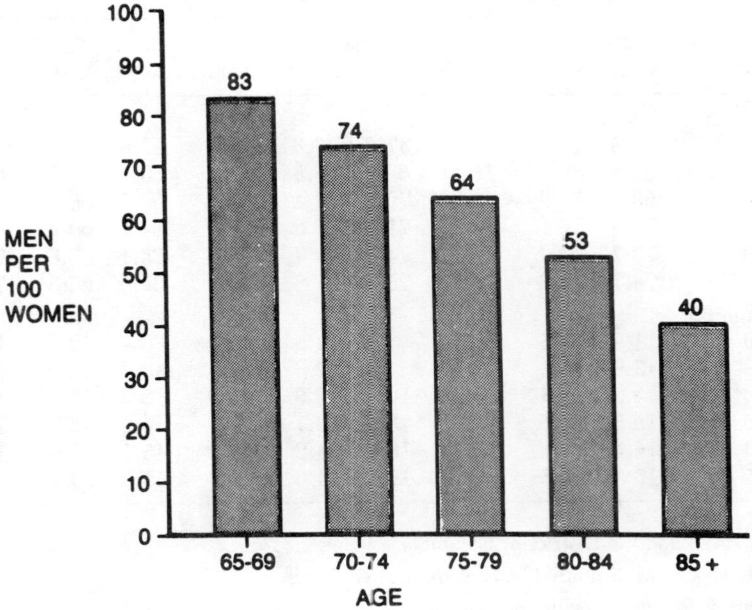

From U.S. Bureau of the Census, "Estimates of the Population of the United States by Age, Sex, and Race: 1980 to 1986." *Current Population Reports* Series P-25, No. 1000 (February 1987).

The difference in longevity has risen from 2 years for those born in 1900 to 7 years projected for those born in 1985. The projections for Blacks in 1900 were much less than for whites, and females had only a 1-year advantage in longevity. By 1985 the data are more promising, but Blacks of both sexes have a 5-year disadvantage compared to whites. Black females born in 1985 will have an 8.4-year advantage over Black males. Table 4.1 also shows what happens at age 65: in 1900 white males who reached age 65 could anticipate living only another 11.5 years; white females, not quite a year longer. By 1985 when all groups are combined, a male reaching age 65 could anticipate another 16.8 years—to age 79.6—whereas when all females are combined a woman could anticipate living to age 83.6

The data on longevity have been calculated into the middle of the next century. Table 4.2 shows both the actual and projected life expectancies at birth and at age 65 by sex by birth cohort decades. Differences in longevity between men and women are predicted to hold true into the middle of the 21st century. Although elderly men can expect to gain 2.8 years by

TABLE 4.1 Life Expectancy at Birth and Age 65 by Race and Sex: 1900–1985

	All races			White			Black		
Year	Both sexes	Male	Female	Both sexes	Male	Female	Both sexes	Male	Female
At birth:									
1900[a,b]	47.3	46.3	48.3	47.6	46.6	48.7	33.0[c]	32.5[c]	33.5[c]
1950[b]	62.8	65.6	71.1	69.1	66.5	72.2	60.7	58.9	62.7
1960[b]	69.7	66.6	73.1	70.6	67.4	74.1	63.2	60.7	65.9
1970	70.9	67.1	74.8	71.7	68.0	75.6	64.1	60.0	68.3
1980	73.7	70.0	77.4	74.4	70.7	78.1	68.1	63.8	72.5
1985[b,d]	74.7	71.2	78.2	75.3	71.8	78.7	69.5	65.3	73.7
At age 65:									
1900–02[a,b]	11.9	11.5	12.2	—	11.5	12.2	—	10.4[c]	11.4[c]
1950[b]	13.9	12.8	15.0	—	12.8	15.1	13.9	12.9	14.9
1960[b]	14.3	12.8	15.8	14.4	12.9	15.9	13.9	12.7	15.1
1970	15.2	13.1	17.0	15.2	13.1	17.1	14.2	12.5	15.7
1980	16.4	14.1	18.3	16.5	14.2	18.4	15.1	13.0	16.8
1985[b,d]	16.8	14.6	18.6	16.8	14.6	18.7	15.5	13.3	17.2

[a]Ten states and the District of Columbia.

[b]Includes deaths of nonresidents of the United States.

[c]Figure is for the nonwhite population.

[d]Provisional data.

From National Center for Health Statistics, *Health, United States, 1986*. DHHS Pub. No. (PHS)87-1232, Washington: Department of Health and Human Services, December 1986.

the year 2050, elderly women will gain an additional 4.5 years. The Census Bureau has charted the trends since 1950, and Figure 4.3 shows what their estimates and expectations reveal about the gap between men and women. Note that the use of different data bases accounts for the slight difference in the curve between 1985 and 1990.

The trend for women to outlive men since the turn of the century is expected to continue for another half-century at least. Nor is the United States alone in this population profile. Almost all of the other countries of the world that can provide such data show that women outlive men anywhere from 2.8 years in Indonesia to 8 years in Poland and France. In two countries, India and Bangladesh, where health care is minimal for most of the population, women die sooner than men. Figure 4.4 gives the data by countries that provided information to the U.S. Census Bureau. These longevity statistics are translated into how many more women one can find in the population of a given country. The comparative data in Figure 4.5 show clear national differences. Some of these ratios reflect the impact of

TABLE 4.2 Life Expectancy at Birth and Age 65 by Sex and Calendar Year

	Male		Female	
Calendar Year	At birth	At age 65	At birth	At age 65
1900	46.56	11.35	49.07	12.01
1910	50.20	11.38	53.67	12.10
1920	54.59	11.81	56.33	12.34
1930	58.01	11.38	61.36	12.91
1940	60.89	11.92	65.34	13.42
1950	65.33	12.81	70.90	15.07
1960	66.58	12.91	73.19	15.89
1970	67.05	13.14	74.80	17.12
1980	69.85	14.02	77.53	18.35
1990	72.29	15.11	70.85	19.92
2000	73.42	15.71	81.05	20.81
2010	73.93	16.08	81.62	21.27
2020	74.42	16.45	82.18	21.73
2030	74.90	16.81	82.74	22.18
2040	75.37	17.18	83.29	22.64
2050	75.84	17.55	83.84	23.11

From Social Security Administration, Office of the Actuary, September 1982.

wars on the proportion of older women to older men. In India the ratio is reversed until age 80, when women have a very slight advantage.

The increase in the number of elderly is a worldwide phenomenon; less well known is the fact that such a large proportion of those living beyond age 65 will be women (Van Hoose & Worth, 1982). In many countries there are important variations in the sex-difference ratio between rural and urban areas, due to patterns of internal migration, access to health facilities, and other local factors. There appears to be little agreement as to why this sex difference persists worldwide and has apparently increased since the turn of the century (Brody & Brock, 1985; Pelletier, 1982). Better statistics may in part account for the increased number of the very old (Rosenwaike & Dolinsky, 1987). Also, the very old are more likely to report their true age.

The increase in longevity of women also produces a great increase in the actual numbers of women. There were 45% more women aged 65 to 85 in 1980 than in 1940 (Rosenwaike & Dolinsky, 1987). There are far more women over age 100. These exceptionally long-lived women have outlived family and friends, are apt to be institutionalized, have less income than those 85 to 100 years old, and find their care to be very costly (Spencer, Goldstein, & Taeuber, 1987; see also Olson, 1986). Later in this chapter we will look at the consequences of women's longevity. But first we need to consider why women have this advantage.

FIGURE 4.3 Gap between female and male life expectancy: 1950–2050 (female life expectancy minus male life expectancy).

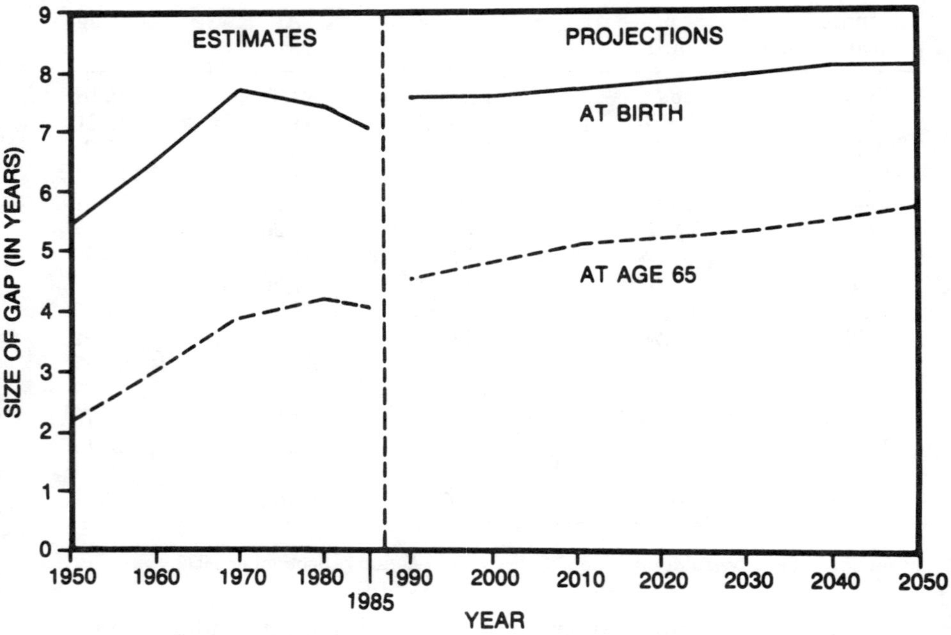

Life expectancy estimates (1950–1985) are taken from National Center for Health Statistics data while life expectancy projections (1990–2050) are drawn from Census Bureau data. The use of two different data bases accounts for the slight jump in the life expectancy differential between males and females from 1985 to 1990.

From National Center for Health Statistics. *Health, United States, 1986* DHHS Pub. No. (PHS)87-1232, Washington: Department of Health and Human Services, December 1986. Spencer, Gregory, U.S. Bureau of the Census, "Projections of the Population of the United States by Age, Sex, and Race: 1983 to 2080." *Current Population Reports* Series P-25, No. 952 (May 1984).

WHY DO WOMEN LIVE LONGER?

Since women are traditionally considered the weaker sex, it comes as something of a surprise to learn that, on the average, women outlive men. Why this is so puzzles gerontologists, who advance several hypotheses to account for the phenomenon. One focuses on life-style differences and another on innate physiological advantages; a third suggests that it is a result of natural selection.

Men do not live as long as women, according to one hypothesis, because of their high mortality at younger ages. Men engage in much more destruc-

FIGURE 4.4 Female advantage in life expectancy at birth: 1985 (difference in years between females and males).

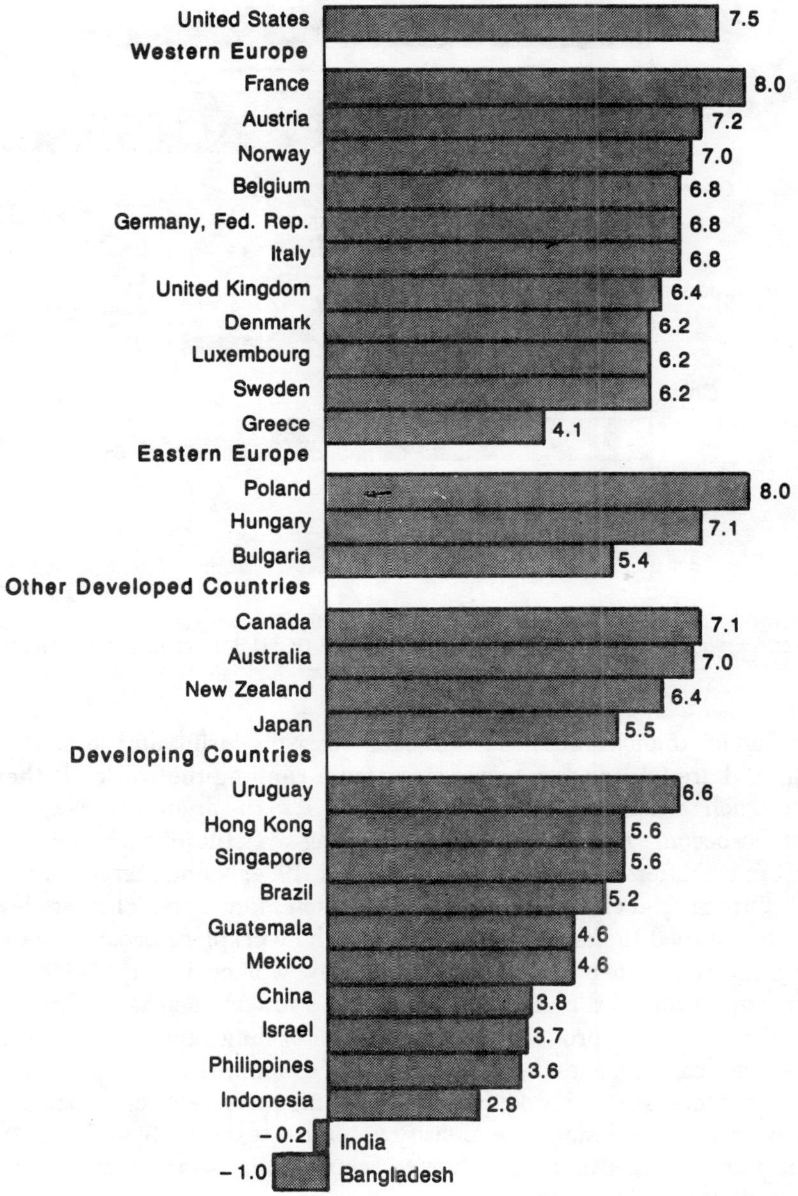

From Torrey, B. B., Kinsella, K., & Taeuber, C. M. (1987). *An aging world: International population reports*. Series P-95, No. 78. Washington, DC: U.S. Bureau of the Census.

FIGURE 4.5 Percent female, by age: 1985.

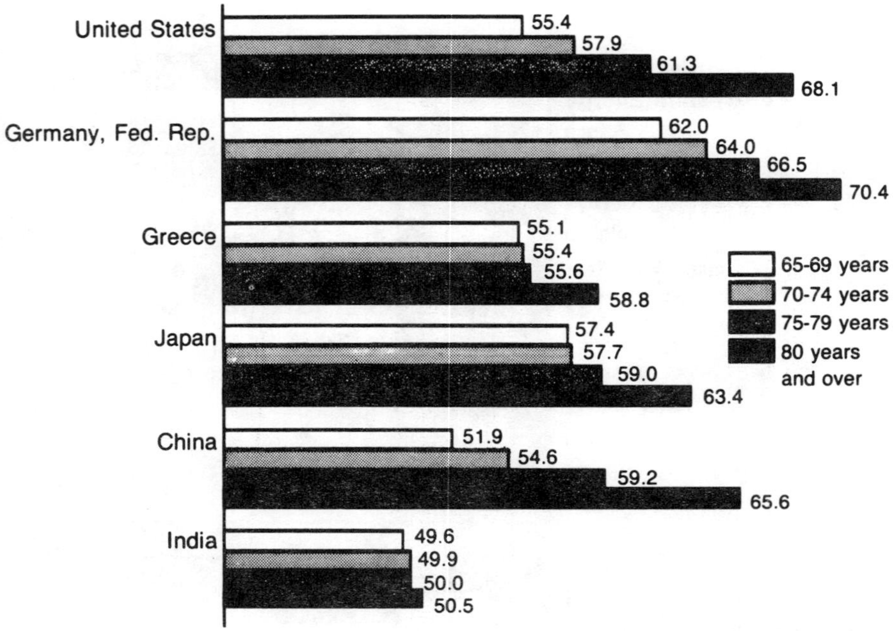

From Torrey, B. B., Kinsella, K., & Taeuber, C. M. (1987). *An aging world: International population reports*. Series P-95, No. 78. Washington, DC: U.S. Bureau of the Census.

tive behavior than women: they kill each other off, drink and smoke too much, and are under more severe stress from running the world. If they gave up such stressful and destructive behaviors, so the argument goes, and if women become more like men in occupying stressful jobs, there won't be that much difference in longevity (Botwinick, 1984; Nathanson & Lorenz, 1982). Other social causes may influence women's longevity. They are less apt to be exposed to destructive elements in the workplace because of the sex-segregated nature of work; for example, few women are exposed to the dangers of mining and black-lung disease, and few women work directly with asbestos, which produces a virulent form of lung cancer. Women, it is believed, deal with stress better because they can more easily express emotions that otherwise could produce life-threatening pressure. Women's health practices are better designed to identify chronic diseases early and to treat it, and they also pay more attention to their ailments—all of which add up to a lifelong advantage for women.

A commonly held belief is that if men could only change their behavior they would live as long as women. That men can improve their life expectancy by more healthful life-styles has been shown through studies of Mormon elders (male) and the Amish (Pelletier, 1982). Men can also increase their longevity if they marry women considerably younger than themselves, according to one analysis (Foster, Klinger-Vartabedian, & Wispe, 1984), but we do not know how this affects women's longevity.

One study conducted to test the hypothesis regarding the impact of life-style on sex differences and longevity used the mortality statistics of male and female Catholic teaching orders. Since both groups were assumed to live essentially similar lives (the males did not engage in the self-destructive activities of their lay peers), any sex differences in longevity could be assumed to be innate. The findings support this view: nuns outlived priests in the expected direction (Siegel & Taeuber, 1986).

The news is not encouraging for men: the longevity gap probably cannot be entirely closed by merely changing the way one lives.

> With the virtual elimination of infective and parasitic disease, the great reduction in material mortality, and the emergence of chronic degenerative diseases (heart disease, cancer, stroke, etc.) as the principal causes of death, the biological superiority of women has evidenced itself more strongly. (Siegel & Tauber, 1986, p. 95)

There may be some basic personality restructuring taking place as both men and women become more androgynous in life-styles, but Siegel and Tauber doubt if even these changes will erase women's biological advantage.

Other hypotheses explain women's longevity as a result of the innate biological superiority of women. According to one researcher, longevity has to do with the genetic makeup of humans. A new human receives half of his or her genes from the mother and half from the father. It is the sperm that determines which sex a child will be: If the sperm carries two X chromosomes, the child will be female; if one Y and one X, then a male will be conceived. The X, or female chromosome, bears a gene, according to Katz ("Hormone Conversion," 1986), that is specific for female longevity. Having two such genes, the XX female is doubly ensured of survival. The male, with only one such gene on his X chromosome, is not so endowed. Another version is that the X chromosome is larger than the Y chromosome, and this extra genetic material provides protection for the female. Estrogen, for example, may protect against heart disease. There may be an "immunity factor activated prenatally [that] is directed against the Y chromosome, which is foreign to the mother's makeup" (Kermis, 1984, p. 25), thus making the male more vulnerable to later stressors.

Another theory regarding women's longevity has to do with natural selection and the survival of the species. "The longer a woman lives the more children she can produce. Selection constantly favors increased longevity in women" (DeVore & Lovejoy, 1985, p. 36). Although modern women live many years beyond menopause, these authors contend that

> for the greater part of [the] time that our species has existed, so few women have survived to this age, that selection has been powerless to extend the length of the reproductive period. . . . A male who fathers a large number of children early in his life will have a high fitness, even if he fails to achieve longevity. On the other hand, the female's reproductive rate is linear with age, and she must survive in order to achieve her full reproductive potential. . . . Women are always more reproductively valuable than men, will always constitute the primary gender, and will always direct (via natural selection) the adoption of mating and reproductive strategies. (p. 37)

It is also believed that women "may have greater biological resistance to most cardiovascular diseases and possibly to malignant neoplasms" Verbugge, 1985, p. 61).

While the exact cause of longevity remains unknown, a physiological advantage for the female of the species seems reasonable. After all, she has to be able to withstand the massive physiological demands made on her body by childbirth and breast-feeding. Prior to the very recent age of modern medicine, childbirth posed the greatest danger to women. Widowers with two, three, or four wives in succession were common up to the 20th century. Queen Elizabeth I purportedly did not marry in part because she rightly feared dying in childbirth. Though maternal mortality is still high in some developing countries, most women survive childbirth with health intact. The physiological endowment that supports women through childbirth and infant feeding (Lancaster, 1985) serves to give women a physiological advantage through the life span. Furthermore, "the reproductive period plays a protective role in the health of women with respect to the clotting factor, hormonal balance, cholesterol metabolism, and the elasticity of the vascular system" (Siegel & Taeuber, 1986).

Women are built to be survivors so that the species may survive. This applies not only to humans: "for virtually every species as far down the phylogenetic tree as can be studied . . . it has been documented that there is a female survival advantage" (Brody & Brock, 1985, p. 5). If we knew why females lived longer than males, we would have basic insight into the dynamics of longevity (Dawkins, 1976; Nathanson & Lorenz, 1982; Shaw & Darling, 1985).

CONSEQUENCES OF WOMEN'S LONGEVITY

The fact that women live longer than men do has important societal consequences. Since the advent of modern medical practice and with an abundance of nutritious food, most people can expect to live far longer than their ancestors. But at the same time fewer children are being born, particularly in those countries that are most affluent. Thus, the proportion of the population that is in the older age brackets is growing in an unprecedented way. In 1900 those under age 19 made up 44% of the population; in 1980 they were only 6.4% of the population. In 1980 those over 60 made up 6.4% of the population; in 1980 they made up 16.1% of the population. Because of the maturation of the baby-boom generation, by the year 2010 more than one-quarter of the total U.S. population will be over 55; 1 in 7 persons will be at least 65. By 2030 1 person in 3 will be at least 55 (U.S. Senate Special Committee on Aging, 1988). As we pointed out earlier in this chapter, (see Figure 4.1), males and females are balanced in the younger age brackets, but each decade after age 50, women become an increasingly large majority.

One area in which women's longevity is of particular importance is health care; women are both the victims and the beneficiaries of improved health knowledge and services. Although the aged are increasingly more healthy, the over-75 group "consumes the greatest amount of medical care per capita" (Avron, 1986). The aged, who are no longer needed to raise their children, "have become a biologically surplus and financially burdensome group" (Callahan, 1986). Much of this financial burden comes from the high cost of their medical care. In England, for instance, expensive health care interventions, such as renal transplants, are rationed: persons over age 60 are not provided with this option (Welch, 1984). Older women are more likely to be affected by such rationing of health care as costs rise unless there is a societal consensus that any available health service should be provided to all in need.

The insurance industry has resisted the development of unisex tables for insurance purposes because of this longevity/gender gap. If women are charged the same amount as men for insurance premiums, they may not get similar benefits because the benefits have to be stretched out over more years. To obtain similar benefits, women would have to pay higher premiums (Lengerman & Wallace, 1986). Recent federal pension policies have mandated, over the protests of business, unisex coverage for employees; but private life insurance companies are not required to comply.

The implications of women's longevity for all aspects of later life have not been sufficiently understood or appreciated: "Lives have been extended, but role structures and opportunities for men as well as for women have been slow to catch up," Riley (1985) points out. The real task ahead, she continues, is to "make increasing use of what we already know about social change, aging, and health and to postpone disability and dependency to the very last years of the extended life course." The greater longevity of women has implications for almost every aspect of the lives of older women. The issues that will engage gerontologists in the decades ahead, particularly those concerning persons over 65, will be women's issues (Callahan, 1987; Dychtwald, 1986).

AGING AND HEALTH CONCERNS

What kinds of changes in health are part of normal aging and what changes are abnormal? Are the symptoms of "normal" aging different in men and women? These are very difficult questions to answer since so much is still unknown about how aging affects the human organism. It is additionally difficult to identify aging patterns by sex since most of the basic physiological information has been gathered on males or on "elders." The causes of aging itself are a source of controversy among gerontologists (Edinburg, 1982; Fry, 1986; Whitbourne, 1985).

Some health differences between men and women are well known. Older men, for instance, are more likely to experience acute illnesses that are life-threatening, while elderly women are more apt to be physically disabled by chronic illnesses. Arthritis is much more common among older women, while coronary heart disease incapacitates older men (U.S. Senate Special Committee on Aging, 1988).

Men and women also respond differently to some of the normal consequences of aging that are not health-related. Women are apt to be distressed by age changes in appearance. Wrinkling and sagging of skin, breasts, and upper arm muscles occurs because subcutaneous fat tissue loses flexibility with age and firmness is lost. Lean muscle tissue is replaced by fat tissue, and we have middle-age spread. Women gain 25 to 35% in girth in the middle years; men gain 5 to 16% (Whitbourne, 1985). Both men and women lose hair color as they age, and hair generally becomes thinner. Gray hair on a woman connotes aging, but on a man it may be considered a mark of distinction. However, the pattern baldness so typical of men, and often a source of great discomfort, rarely occurs with women (Whitbourne, 1985). Men are more apt to be upset by changes in strength and agility than women are. Such physiological changes have no direct effect on one's physical health, but they can be very threatening to one's self-esteem and even emotional stability.

Health becomes an ever-increasing preoccupation as one ages. Despite this, since there is also an expectation of physical deficits with aging, there is apt to be underreporting of symptoms by older persons. When you get older, you expect to have aches and pains, so why waste the time of a doctor to complain (Rowe, 1985).

Subjective feelings about age and health are important indicators of quality of life. Interestingly enough, despite their seemingly greater concern over how aging affects their appearance, older women in general report feeling healthier than older men do as shown in Figure 4.6. Because more younger women than men report concern about health, it has been an accepted folk view that older women also feel more sickly; the data do not support this.

Another reason that it is generally assumed that women are, or feel, less healthy than men is the often-cited fact that women go to the doctor more than men do. The irony is that one reason women think they are

FIGURE 4.6 Self-assessment of health by sex and age: 1981.

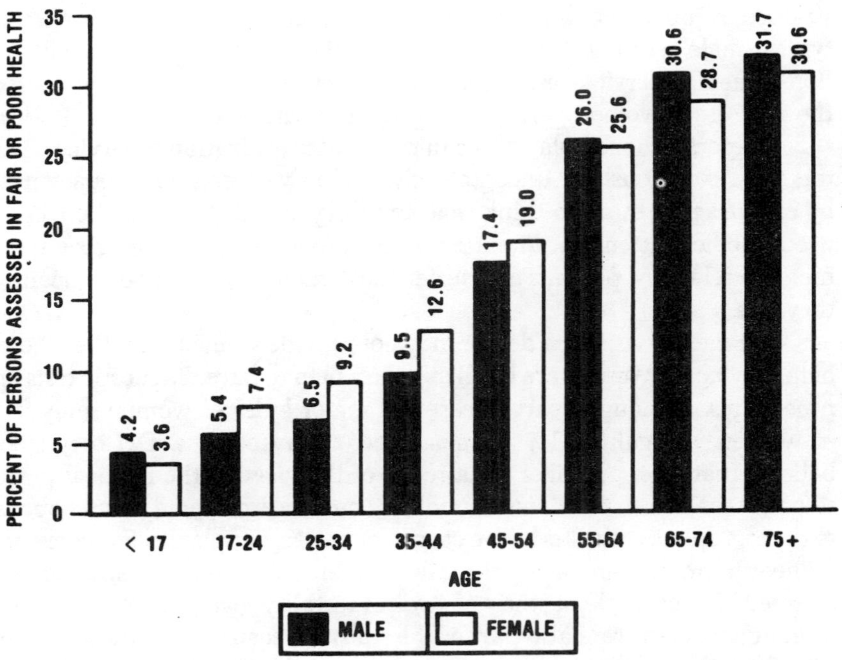

From Aging America (1984), p. 102.

healthier may be that they ask for more help in order to stay that way. Older women have more colds, infections, and stomach upsets than older men do, but they also are more apt to take curative actions when ill (Verbugge, 1985). Women worry more about illness, are more sensitive to symptoms of ill health, believe they are susceptible to illness, have greater knowledge about health, and are more apt to seek medical help on a voluntary basis than men are (Nathanson & Lorenz, 1982).

Women have more hospitalizations than men do, but much of this is related to obstetric or gynecological problems; women have more internal organs that can go wrong than men do. As Nathanson and Lorenz (1982) point out, "In American society, bodily processes are defined as requiring medical management. Women's biology, therefore, may indeed play a role, even if an indirect one, in their relatively greater reported illness and health service use."

Women may also find it easier to take the sick role because they are socialized to be dependent. Such socialization was part of the life experience of women now in their 60s or older, but it may be much less of a factor in the cohorts of women coming of age in the year 2000. Women who did not have demanding jobs or careers and were primarily homemakers could make use of health services because they had the time and were not constrained by job demands to go to work no matter how bad they felt—a more typical male response (Marcus & Siegel, 1982). Such a pattern of utilization of medical services, established early, continues in later years and affects the way older women perceive and utilize health care.

Doctors also may play a role in the greater utilization of services. Doctors may, consciously or unconsciously, exploit women's dependency needs by encouraging them to think that anything that happens to their bodies needs medical attention. Men do not seem to get this message. As a result, men are reluctant patients and suffer the consequences in poorer health as they age.

But merely visiting a doctor may not provide women with the medical help they need. Women are less likely than men to have diagnostic tests and procedures. Although heart disease is a major killer of women, only 27% of women, as against 41% of men, receive cardiograms. DeLorey (1984) believes that such practices are a result of the view by the medical profession that the health problems of midlife women are centered on menopause, so doctors do not seek alternative causes for health complaints. Some research on health problems focuses primarily on men even though women are also affected. For example, a study of stroke mortality gives data only on men, although women were also part of the study; "because the data were quite complex," they were presented only for white males (Baum & Manton, 1987).

Another problem that women encounter with the medical profession is the overuse of drugs. Elderly persons were reported taking, on the average, 3.8 different drugs; 83% were taking at least two, and only 8% reported taking no drugs (LaRue, Dessonville, & Jarvik, 1985). These data were gathered in 1978; one suspects that the rates would be higher today (see also Simonson, 1984).

Since body fat differs in men and women, drug reactions can be very different. A higher proportion of fat cells permits the accumulation of some drugs. Such accumulation can be dangerous since "drug intoxication is frequently mistaken for senility" (Edinburg, 1982). Using over-the-counter drugs mixed with prescription drugs can be damaging. Some of these drugs can be addicting, and the interactions of the drugs can be disabling or even lethal (Finlayson, 1984; Kofoed, 1984).

Older women are high consumers of both over-the-counter drugs and prescription drugs, so doctors need to be especially alert to the need for greatly increased drug monitoring with older women patients. "Despite the observation that the elderly are often the beneficiaries (or victims) of new pharmacologic agents, drug studies seldom have included subjects over 65 years of age. Even less common are subjects over 75 years of age" (Pepper & Robbins, 1987; see also Simonson, 1984). Particularly alarming is the fact that a large class of drugs, known as anticholinergic drugs (antihistamines, antispasmodics, antidepressants, and antipsychotic agents), which are widely prescribed for elderly women, can have memory loss as a side effect (Edinburg, 1982). The great fear of so many elderly of losing cognitive functioning may be aggravated by some common over-the-counter self-medications or by interactions with prescribed drugs (Pepper & Robbins, 1987). Better monitoring of drug use by older patients is vital.

The older we get, the more concerned we are about our health, but for older people today it may be too late to do much to reverse the effects of earlier poor health practices. It must be remembered that those who are now over 65 grew up when health care was sought only for dire emergencies, most people did not have access to regular medical care, good nutrition was either unavailable or unknown, and many health practices we take for granted today were not common. The great interest that Americans of all ages now show in their health will be reflected in improved health status and health practices in old age.

HEALTH PROBLEMS OF OLDER WOMEN

Our bodies tell us that we are getting older. After age 40 most of us will need glasses. When the weather turns cold, joints we never knew we had start to ache. People seem to mumble more when they talk. We find ourselves puffing when going upstairs, and we are more tired than we used to be after a day's work. Are these markers of age the same for men and women?

The leading causes of chronic conditions for women are, in rank order, arthritis, hypertension, heart conditions, chronic sinusitis, varicose veins, arteriosclerosis, visual impairment, back and spine impairment, and diabetes. The rank order of these conditions differs for men, as does the prevalence (Maddox, 1987). However, although some health problems may be reported by both men and women, women have higher rates; for example, twice as many women as men reported the presence of arthritis (Verbugge, 1985). Men, on the other hand, are more prone to heart trouble. More older men than women say they are limited in their primary activities by chronic health problems. Women find their secondary activities, such as running errands, mobility, and personal care, to be more affected by chronic health conditions. Men are more likely to suffer from hearing impairments and skin cancer, but women are more apt to have vision problems (Verbugge, 1985).

Some diseases may be linked to differences in reproductive physiology—diabetes, for instance: women develop late-onset diabetes between the ages of 45 and 54 at twice the rate of men. Studies indicate that women are more prone to develop diabetes if they have had many children, higher birth weight children, and/or are postmenopausal (Dolger & Seeman, 1985). However, the physiological mechanism at work here is not understood. In Chapter 3 we discussed osteoporosis, which is directly related to bone mineral loss after menopause and can result in fractures from falls; 1 in 4 women over 65 will have some fracture due to osteoporosis, and by age 80, 1 of 4 will have had a hip fracture. For very old women a hip fracture leads to institutionalization in a hospital or nursing home and often death.

Arthritis affects about 50% of all persons over 65, and most of those limited by this affliction are women, though it is unclear why women are more apt to be earlier victims than men and at a greater rate. Many women complain about their joints aching, take some aspirin, and go about their business, and they probably will not seek any medical attention. However, since the disease is progressive and control of pain is inadequate, an older woman may find that her life and social activities have become limited by the time she finds out she has a serious health problem. It is believed that many elderly persons in nursing homes who have restricted mobility are the victims of "missed and easily treatable" arthritic conditions (Moskowitz & Haug, 1986).

Some arthritic symptoms may be misdiagnosed. For instance, "dry mouth" is a common symptom accompanying menopause, but it is also a symptom of Sjögren's, a rare but severe form of rheumatoid arthritis. Another relatively rare arthritis, systemic lupus erythematosus, occurs mostly in women but can be misdiagnosed because early symptoms include joint swelling and pain. The back pain that older women report may be caused by arthritis affecting the spine (Kushner, 1985). Dry eyes is another overlooked or untreated symptom that may be related to rheumatoid arthritis (Bajart, 1985).

Cancer is one of the most feared diseases of old age. Of the ten leading causes of death in women, cancer is the first for ages 35 to 54, second for ages 55 to 74, and third for those over 75 (Mann, 1985). Women report more current and past cancers, but men are more likely to be hospitalized for cancer and are more apt to die of cancer. Women's cancers, such as those of the breast and reproductive system, are now diagnosed and treated earlier (Verbugge, 1985).

The increased use of mammograms for early detection of breast cancer and education in breast self-examination have greatly increased early detection and treatment and have improved the overall survival rates of women. Less intrusive surgery means that breast cancer is not as disabling as it once was, and the public acknowledgment of their cancer by people such as Betty Ford and Nancy Reagan has improved public awareness. Survival rates have consistently improved, although follow-up studies of women who have had breast cancer indicate that eventually 80% of them will die from it; it can be controlled but not cured (Boston Women's Health Book Collective, 1987). Cancer of the cervix can be detected by the Pap smear; surgery and treatment in early stages has resulted in a cure rate of 85% (Mann, 1985). In older cohorts women's lower rate of smoking was reflected in much lower rates of lung cancer, but increasingly their rates are approaching those of men as more women have taken up smoking.

Hypertension occurs with age in both men and women, but the consequences are different. It occurs at a lower rate in women, and they have fewer fatal outcomes as a result (Krakoff, 1985). Women are more apt to have strokes as a result of arteriosclerosis; and when they do have a heart attack as a result of heart impairment, they are more likely to die.

One of the secret horrors of old age is incontinence. It is such an embarrassing problem that accurate data on incidence is hard to obtain (Mitteness, 1987). It can be a major and devastating experience: "social consequences of urinary incontinence range from embarrassment, depression, and confusion to extreme social isolation and an unwarranted vulnerability to institutionalization." Stress incontinence is considered common in women over 70. Older women consider this a normal part of aging, and few of them report their symptoms to a doctor. A majority of older people in nursing homes are reported to be incontinent, but in only 15% of cases is this considered a medical problem. When patients told physicians about their incontinence, nearly half of the doctors were reported to have responded "either by ignoring the statements of symptoms, or by providing a dismissive explanation." Mitteness comments that most elderly people did not expect any help but believed that it is a "normal, irreversible part of the aging process which must be accepted and managed rather than reversed and cured." Women who suffered incontinence were obliged to do "massive amounts of laundry because of soiling and to prevent gossip or ostracism." Inability of caretakers to cope with incontinence has been one of the key factors in determining whether an individual can maintain an independent life in the community (Mitteness, 1987).

There are several effective ways of managing incontinence. Infection, drug side effects, or other medical problems need to be treated or ruled out (Mitteness & Wood, 1986). At a recent conference on women's health, one doctor was quoted as saying that there "continues to be a conspiracy of silence about a common disorder that is devastating millions of lives for which, in fact, there are adequate treatment procedures in most cases" (Randall, 1986). It is encouraging to observe the ads on television for various kinds of adult "diapers" to help with the problem. These started appearing in the late 1980s; the taboo of mentioning this in public has evidently been overcome.

One area of women's health status that has been relatively ignored in the literature is that of occupational health. Only a minority of the women in the oldest age cohorts today spent a significant proportion of their lives in the work force. Increasingly, however, women will work outside their homes and thus be exposed to the health hazards of the workplace. Although they are not engaged in the same kinds of hazardous work as men are, there is accumulating evidence that some of the industrial and manufacturing jobs that women routinely are hired for have special risks that may produce disability in later life. The fine work of the electronics industry and the acids, fumes, and dust of the textile factory may result in higher incidence of vision problems, lung damage, and cancer for a heavily female work force (U.S. Senate Special Committee on Aging, 1984).

It is known that the "economic consequences of poor health appear to be more severe for women than for men of the same age" (Chirikos & Nestel, 1983). Poor health in women results in reduced working hours and job loss greater than that experienced by men. Older and less well educated women in lower-paying jobs are more apt to suffer the greatest economic losses (see, for example, Burkhauser, Butler, Mitchell, & Pincus, 1986; Stellman, 1987). It must also be pointed out that older women face many health hazards at home, and these are not covered by any workmen's compensation (Wilson & Sapiro, 1985).

The health problems of women that we have reviewed above show that there are important gender differences in both incidence and outcome of the physical changes and diseases of old age. While the litany of problems may appear depressing, in fact one of the most remarkable changes of recent years is the emergence of the vigorous and healthy older individual. Although modern medicine does not have all of the answers to our health problems, and we have some questions about how older women fare in the hands of today's doctors, many of the devastating infections and illnesses that brought early death to our forebears have been conquered. Future cohorts of elderly will benefit greatly from what gerontologists call "the compression of morbidity" (Fries, 1980; Maddox, 1987). With improved health practices and preventive medicine it is possible that in the future chronic illness and the need for care by others can be postponed until later in the life span, and a relatively shorter percentage of one's life will be spent at the end in illness or infirmity.

MENTAL HEALTH AND OLDER WOMEN

Good mental health means that we feel pretty good about ourselves and confident in our ability to manage our lives; poor mental health means being ridden with anxiety, feeling unhappy much of the time, and fearing that we cannot cope with whatever happens in the future. As one gets older, there are many changed conditions that can affect one's mental health. Mental ill health can become mental illness needing therapeutic or psychiatric help. It is important to note also that it is estimated that only "10% of those over 65 have emotional or cognitive problems severe enough to warrant professional attention" (LaRue et al., 1985).

The difficulties encountered in diagnosing mental illness are compounded when dealing with older people because many physical conditions also can result in emotional and cognitive impairment. Some symptoms are the result of medication, as we noted above. Relatively little psychiatric research has been done on the elderly, so there is much debate, confusion, and reinterpretation. Many physicians fail to recognize psychiatric symptoms in their elderly patients or may treat patients for psychiatric disorders they do not have (Waxman & Carner, 1984).

There is a folk belief that women are more prone to mental health problems because they are more emotional. Perhaps this is not the whole explanation.

> We know that women report more emotional problems than men. In addition, women seek psychiatric help at a higher rate than do men with comparable emotional problems. Evidence suggests that this difference is largely due to the fact that women more readily translate nonspecific feelings of distress into conscious recognition that they have an emotional problem. (Russo, 1984, p. 34)

Women who have experienced emotional difficulties in growing up that have not been adequately resolved will have difficulty in old age. Furthermore, there is evidence that there are gender differences in the mental health problems that arise with aging.

Community surveys show that depressive symptoms are found in 30 to 65% of persons over 60. Both mild and severe depression is generally reported to be higher for women than for men (LaRue et al., 1985). The true incidence for women is difficult to ascertain because many elderly, including aged women, are excluded from community psychiatric surveys (Holzer, Leaf, & Weissman, 1985).

Depression in the elderly is very tricky to diagnose. In an extensive review of the literature on depression in the elderly, Fry (1986) makes it clear that there are many physiological as well as psychological factors at work that interact with the normal processes of aging, so diagnosing and treating depression in the elderly is difficult. Also, "the clinician would do well to explore those potentially age-related somatic problems prior to attributing them to a depressive disorder, especially in older women" (Berry, Storandt, & Coyne, 1984). Older women may be physically sick, but doctors may diagnose them as depressed; they may also be clinically depressed, and doctors may treat them for physical ailments (Frangley, 1987). However, recent studies conclusively show that there is an excess of depression in females, and this is not an artifact of help-seeking behavior (Holzer et al., 1985).

Why is depression more of a mental health problem for older women than for older men? Krause (1986) studied a large sample of elderly, of whom two-thirds were women over 65. The financial difficulties and economic problems they faced appeared to account for the greater incidence of depression in the women. One commentator asserts that "women will continue to be overrepresented among the depressed as long as they are overrepresented among the poor" (Belle, 1984). Another explanation is offered by Bernard (1976), who feels that depression among women is inevitable because "the feminine role . . . prescribes for women crippling attitudes, beliefs, and behaviors which in and of themselves tend to generate depression," beliefs that women are helpless, powerless, and vulnerable. Critical to the midlife woman, as Bernard interprets it, are the community barriers and limitations that have deprived women of the support of the traditional "world of women" and do not substitute other sources of emotional support. The negative impact of these conditions peak as women experience menopause or see children leave home and husbands become absorbed in work or careers. Such factors could be at work in the psychological stress felt in earlier cohorts of women. The women's movement, which has legitimized women's achievement orientation and reinstated the female support network, may be a factor in the future in reducing the incidence of late-onset depression in women. Such changes do seem to be taking place. Porcino (1985) cites research showing that "the decline in an aging woman's self-esteem found in the early 1950s did not show up in the 1970s and 1980s" (see also Barnett, 1984; Bernard, 1984; Maiden, 1987; Notman, 1984).

New roles and options may spell improved mental health for many older women; for others it may create new stress, as options and expectations multiply but support is fragile and the community may be hostile. A study of depression among older women in Switzerland (d'Epinay, 1985) showed the impact of social change as basically a cohort effect. These older women, raised in one tradition, found it difficult to deal with the modernization they encountered: "Criticizing the social structure of which they were a part would have involved renunciation of their deepest beliefs, and that is out of the question. Thus the only outlet is depression."

As we pointed out in Capter 3, the medical profession tends to view midlife depression in women as a reaction to menopause. By prescribing estrogen some doctors assume they are also curing depression, which does not seem to be warranted by the data (Notman, 1984). The actual losses or changes that occur with age—retirement, physical disabilities, death of spouse, financial insecurity—are realistic sources of depression (House & Robbins, 1983). Menopause has not been identified as a primary source of depression in women. An older woman may appear generally not as upbeat and optimistic as a more youthful person, but few are clinically depressed. Many elderly who retain a generally serene demeanor may be more skillful in adapting to stress and less overwhelmed by events than are younger persons, who do not have a lifetime perspective. Also, persons with a history of fighting depression will continue to do so when old.

Suicide is a response to unbearable stress, but it is far less likely to be a choice for older women than for older men. Suicide by males exceeds that of females at all age levels, but the peak for females is between the ages of 45 and 54, after which rates continue to decline. Male rates rise steeply between ages 16 and 24 and continue to climb into old age. (Manton, Blazer, & Woodbury, 1987). Precipitating events for suicide in older women seem to be fear of probable institutionalization, fear of mental illness, and severe physical illness. Stressful events, such as death of a spouse, retirement, disturbed personal relationships, and alcoholism or drug abuse are implicated in suicide of the elderly (Osgood & McIntosh, 1986).

Mental impairment and loss of cognitive ability with aging are probably more feared by the elderly than any other kind of disability. It is estimated that in the United States approximately 5 to 7% of the over-65 group will be afflicted with severe senile dementias, and possibly as many as 10 to 50% may have borderline symptoms of some kind of mental impairment. More women will suffer from these because there are more of them in the elderly population. When previous cohorts of elderly evidenced symptoms of mental disorientation, they would be placed in a mental hospital; the nursing home has taken the place of these institutions. As a result, as Table 4.3 shows, nearly two-thirds of elderly nursing home patients have some kind of cognitive impairment.

There are more women than men in each of the categories of impairment, and there are more individuals having the problems at each age level. Many individuals with senile dementias are not institutionalized but are cared for at home, and it is women who are the majority of the caretakers (see Chapter 6).

The most dreaded pronouncement a family can receive is that an elderly family member is suffering from Alzheimer's disease. There has been a surge of publicity for this condition in recent years. It affects relatively few before age 65; after this age 5% have been diagnosed as Alzheimer's disease victims and 20% of those over 80 (Shanas & Maddox, 1985). Fifty percent of all cases are accounted for by those over 80 (Mader & Ford, 1987). Of those affected there are 2½ times more women than men (Edinburg, 1982).

TABLE 4.3 Percentage of Elderly Nursing Home Residents with Cognitive Impairment by Age, Sex, and Race: 1985

Age, sex, and race	% Disorientation or memory impairment	% Senile dementia or chronic organic brain syndrome
Total (65 years and over)	62.6	47.0
Age		
65–74 years	55.7	34.0
75–84 years	60.8	45.4
85 years and over	66.6	52.9
Sex		
Male	58.8	42.1
Female	63.9	48.6
Race		
White	62.2	46.8
Black	69.5	51.4[a]
Other	56.2	35.2

[a]Figure does not meet standard of reliability or precision.

From Hing, Esther. "Use of Nursing Homes by the Elderly: Preliminary Data from the National Nursing Home Survey." *Advance Data* No. 135, National Center for Health Statistics (May 14, 1987).

Although there are more women than men who are diagnosed with Alzheimer's disease, this is probably not a true sex difference but a function of age. G. D. Cohen (cited in Maddox, 1987) questions whether the greater longevity of women is the whole explanation, but he offers no further data. Some family heredity may be involved since research has shown that if a close relative has the disorder the chances are four times greater for an individual to become a victim than for the general population. The causes of Alzheimer's disease have so far eluded researchers, nor is there any known cure. Greatly increased federal funding for research into this mysterious disease holds promise for new insights and interventions in the future. Because women suffer more from Alzheimer's disease than men do and because the burden of care for these persons falls mainly on women, this is truly a woman's issue.

HEALTH CARE DELIVERY: WHAT DO OLDER WOMEN GET?

Obtaining adequate health care is one of the major problems that older women confront. Despite advances in medical services and financing there are still continuing difficulties with the system that have an impact on women in their later years.

Those who are over 60 today can remember when health care was the total responsibility of the individual. If you could afford it, you could see a doctor; if you could not afford it, you had to rely on charitable groups or public clinics, which were few and far between. Health care is, of course, far more available to more people than ever before in our history, but the burden of paying for it rests on the elderly because they have more need of it. Persons over 65 spend 3.4 times as much for health care as do those who are younger (Olson, 1985).

The entry of the federal government with Medicaid support for the destitute and Medicare for the elderly was assumed to care for those most in need. Neither program has proved sufficient. Current and proposed legislation may provide minimal state support for health care for every citizen. The United States and South Africa are the only developed countries that do not provide such service.

The limitations of current medical coverage have a differential impact on older women. Furthermore, "for older women with substantial mobility limitations and inadequate public transportation, medical care has become increasingly inaccessible" (Olson, 1985, p. 171). An analysis of Medicare by Lewis (1985) leads her to conclude that "the illness and disability patterns of older women are not adequately reflected in the nation's major health reimbursement plan for the old." In addition, many widows have already had to "spend down" to Medicaid levels to pay for their husband's last illness, so they have few resources for their own possible disability. Some elderly women find it difficult to seek health services. In a study by Keith (1987) a group who were widowed, divorced, or never married had not sought aid when it was needed initially because they could not afford it, but over time other subjective factors also inhibited seeking needed health care. Education and outreach are important factors in providing needed services, and many impoverished women living alone find themselves outside the system.

Nevertheless, one study of the use of health services shows that "women use more health services than men, the widowed use more health services than the nonwidowed, and those who work use fewer health services than those not gainfully employed" (Homan, Haddock, Winner, Coe, & Wolinsky, 1986). Living alone is the major precipitating factor in the greater use of health services by women.

Under Medicaid reimbursement policies many elderly women have had to be placed in nursing homes rather than in alternative care settings. As a result, 70% of nursing home patients are female, and they are 80% of those over age 75 (Shanas & Maddox, 1985).

As we point out in Chapter 5, the nursing home is only one of the housing options available to the elderly, but it is unfortunately the one many elderly dependent single women are destined to enter. How good is the care they get? Life in a nursing home is as good as the quality of the residence and the staff. Unfortunately, many of the nursing homes that provide the bulk of care for Medicaid-reimbursed patients—most of them older women—have been considered minimally adequate. Many of them are for-profit institutions, and weak regulation by state or federal authorities results in less than optimal conditions. (See also Chapter 5.)

Even in the best-run nursing homes there may be lack of recognition of the need the elderly have to retain their autonomy and control over their environment. Helplessness, as Langer (1983) points out, can "contribute to psychological withdrawal, physical disease, and death" (p. 230). Studies of nursing home patients, most of them women, clearly demonstrated that those who were "encouraged to make decisions for themselves, given decisions to make, and given responsibility for something outside themselves" showed improved health (p. 238). Those who were merely told that everything was done to provide adequate care became more debilitated over time. Current debates in Congress suggest that future legislation will support more extensive use of Medicare and Medicaid funds for alternatives to nursing home care for elderly patients (Barthydt-Wezenaar, 1986).

SUMMARY

Women are blessed with a remarkable physiology. They are endowed with physical attributes that allow them to bear children and nurse them, and with due attention to proper care they survive to a ripe old age. This advantage, allowing women to enjoy more years of life than men do and postponing death by a significant number of years, is also a hazard. Women will outlive their spouses and possibly face years of impoverished widowhood. The older one is, the more apt one is to fall prey to chronic ailments that are debilitating, limiting, and even destructive of cognitive and physical competence. There will be more women living to advanced ages in the decades ahead, to experience both the good and the bad, than ever before in any society.

To prepare for what lies ahead for succeeding cohorts, women need to be alert to the ways in which health care and delivery of health services are biased, resulting in misdiagnosis and mistakes in medication, surgery, and institutionalization.

The generalizations we make about the health of older women must be tempered by the realization that the data we depend on now have been derived from cohorts of older women who enjoyed less adequate health care and were the victims of inadequate research and stereotyped perceptions. The unprecedented extension of life presents an opportunity to identify ways to conquer debilitating disease so that more of us will, truly, die of old age.

REFERENCES

Atkinson, R. M. (1984). Substance use and abuse in late life. In R. M. Atkinson (Ed.), *Alcohol and drug abuse in old age* (pp. 1–22). Washington, DC: American Psychiatric Press.

Avron, J. L. (1986). Medicine, health, and the geriatric transformation. *Daedalus, 114*, 211–226.

Bajart, A. M. (1985). Common eye problems of older women. In S. Golub & R. J. Freedman (Eds.), *Health needs of women as they age* (pp. 85–94). New York: Haworth Press.

Barnett, R. C. (1984). The anxiety of the unknown—choice, risk, responsibility. In G. Baruch & J. Brooks-Gunn (Eds.), *Women in midlife* (pp. 341–357). New York: Plenum.

Barthydt-Wezenaar, N. (1986). Home care and hospice. In S. Jonas (Ed.), *Health care delivery in the United States* (3rd ed.). New York: Springer Publishing Co.

Barum, H. M., & Manton, K. A. (1987). National trends in stroke-related mortality: A comparison of multiple cause mortality data with survey and other health data. *The Gerontologist, 27*(3), 293–301.

Belle, D. (1984). Inequality and mental health: Low income and minority women. In L. E. Walker (Ed.), *Women and mental health policy* (pp. 135–150). Beverly Hills, CA: Sage.

Bernard, J. (1976). Homosociality and female depression. *Journal of Social Issues, 32*(4), 213–238.

Bernard, J. (1984). Women's mental health in times of transition. In L. E. Walker (Ed.), *Women and mental health policy* (pp. 181–196). Beverly Hills, CA: Sage.

Berry, J. M., Storandt, M., & Coyne, A. (1984). Age and sex differences in somatic complaints associated with depression. *Journal of Gerontology, 39*(4), 466–467.

Boston Women's Health Book Collective. (1987). *Ourselves, growing older: Women aging with knowledge and power.* New York: Simon & Schuster.

Botwinick, J. (1984). *Aging and behavior* (rev. ed.). New York: Springer Publishing Co.

Brody, J. A. & Brock, D. B. (1985). Epidemiologic and statistical characteristics of the U.S. elderly population. In C. E. Finch & E. L. Schneider (Eds.), *Handbook of the biology of aging* (pp. 3–20). New York: Van Nostrand Reinhold.

Burkhauser, R. V., Butler, J. S., Mitchell, J. M., & Pincus, R. (1986). Effects of arthritis on wage earnings. *Journal of Gerontology, 41*(2), 277–281.

Callahan, D. (1986). Adequate health care and an aging society: Are they morally compatible? *Daedalus, 115*, 247–267.

Callahan, D. (1987). *Setting limits: Medical goals in an aging society.* New York: Simon and Schuster.

Chirikos, T. N., & Nestel, G. (1983). Economic consequences of poor health in mature women. In L. B. Shaw (Ed.), *Unplanned careers: The working lives of middleaged women* (pp. 93–108). Lexington, MA: Lexington Books.

Chu, J., Diehr, P., Feigl, P., Glaefke, G., Begg, C., Gliksman, A., & Ford, L. (1987). The effect of age on the care of women with breast cancer in community hospitals. *Journal of Gerontology, 42*(2), 185–190.

Cook, F. L., Kramek, L. M. (1986). Measuring economic hardship among older Americans. *The Gerontologist, 26*(1), 38–47.

Dawkins, R. (1976). *The selfish gene.* New York: Oxford University Press.

DeLorey, C. (1984). Health care and midlife women. In G. Baruch & J. Brooks-Gunn (Eds.), *Women in midlife.* New York: Plenum.

d'Epinay, C. J. L. (1985). Depressed elderly women in Switzerland: An example of testing and of generating theories. *The Gerontologist, 25*(6), 597–604.

DeVore, I., & Lovejoy, C. O. (1985). The natural superiority of women. In M. R. Haug, A. B. Ford, & J. Sheafor (Eds.), *The physical and mental health of aged women* (pp. 27–37). New York: Springer Publishing Co.

Dolger, H. & Seeman, B. (1985). *How to live with diabetes* (5th ed.). New York: W. W. Norton.

Dychtwald, K. (Ed.). (1986). *Wellness and health promotion for the elderly.* Rockville, MD: Aspen.

Edinburg, G. (1982). Women and aging. In C. C. Nadelson & M. T. Notman (Eds.),

The woman patient, Vol. 2, Concepts of femininity and the life cycle (pp. 164–194). New York: Plenum.

Feltin, M. (1987). *A woman's guide to good health after 50.* Washington, DC: American Association of Retired Persons.

Finlayson, R. W. (1984). Prescription drug abuse in older persons. In R. M. Atkinson (Ed.), *Alcohol and drug abuse in old age* (pp. 62–70). Washington, DC: American Psychiatric Press.

Fisher, A. (1986). *In the patient's best interest: Women and the politics of medical decisions.* New Brunswick, NJ: Rutgers University Press.

Foster, D. L., Klinger-Vartabedian, L., & Wispe, L. (1984). Male longevity and age differences between spouses. *Journal of Gerontology, 39*(1), 117–120.

Frangley, J. D. (1987). Depression. *Generations, 12*(1), 29–33.

Fries, J. F. (1980). Aging, natural death, and the compression of morbidity. *New England Journal of Medicine, 303*, 130–135.

Fry, P. S. (1986). *Depression, stress, and adaptations in the elderly.* Rockville, MD: Aspen.

Hailes, J. (1981). Questions women want to ask about menopause. In B. Musgrove & Z. Mennell (Eds.), *Change and choice: Women and middle age* (pp. 35–53). London: Peter Owen.

Holzer, C. E., III, Leaf, P. J., & Weissman, M. M. (1985). Living with depression. In M. R. Haug, A. B. Ford, & M. Sheafor (Eds.), *The physical and mental health of aged women* (pp. 101–116). New York: Springer Publishing Co.

Homan, S. M., Haddock, C. C., Winner, E., Coe, R. M., & Wolinsky, F. D. (1986). Widowhood, sex, labor force participation, and the use of physician services by elderly adults. *Journal of Gerontology, 41*(6), 793–796.

Hoppel, C. L. (1985). The uses and misuses of pharmacology. In M. R. Haug, A. B. Ford, & M. Sheafor (Eds.), *The physical and mental health of aged women* (pp. 27–37). New York: Springer Publishing Co.

Hormone conversion key to long life? *Science News*, (1986) p. 129, 375.

House, J. S. & Robbins, C. (1983). Age, psychological stress, and health. In M. W. Riley, B. B. Hess, & K. Bond (Eds.), *Aging in society: Selected review of recent research* (pp. 175–197). Hillsdale, NJ: Erlbaum.

Keith, P. M. (1987). Postponement of health care by unmarried older women. *Women and Health, 12*(1), 47–60.

Kermis, M. D. (1984). *The psychology of human aging.* Boston: Allyn and Bacon.

Kofoed, L. L. (1984). Abuse and misuse of over-the-counter drugs by the elderly. In R. M. Atkinson (Ed.), *Alcohol and drug abuse in old age* (pp. 50–59). Washington, DC: American Psychiatric Press.

Krakoff, L. R. (1985). Hypertension in women: Progress and unsolved problems. In S. Golub & R. J. Freedman (Eds.), *Health needs of women as they age* (pp. 75–83). New York: Haworth Press.

Krause, N. (1986). Stress and sex differences in depressive symptoms among older adults. *Journal of Gerontology, 41*(6), 727–731.

Kusher, I. (1984). *Understanding arthritis.* Mt. Vernon, NY: Consumers Union.
Lancaster, J. B. (1985). Evolutionary perspectives on sex differences in the higher primates. In A. S. Rossi (Ed.), *Gender and the life course* (pp. 3–27). Hawthorn, NY: Aldine.
Langer, E. (1983). *The psychology of control.* Beverly Hills, CA: Sage Publications.
LaRue, A., Dessonville, C., & Jarvik, L. F. (1985). Aging and mental disorders. In J. E. Birren & K. W. Shaie (Eds.), *Handbook of the psychology of aging* (pp. 664–702). New York: Van Nostrand Reinhold.
Lengerman, P. M., & Wallace, R. A. (1985). *Gender in America: Social control and social change.* Englewood Cliffs, NJ: Prentice-Hall.
Lewis, M. (1985). Older women and health: An overview. *Women & Health, 10*(1), 1–16.
Maddox, G. L. (Ed.). (1987). *Encyclopedia of aging.* New York: Springer Publishing Co.
Mader, S. L., & Ford, A. B. (1987). Morbidity and mortality trends among the aged. *Generations, 12*(1), 5–7.
Maiden, R. (1987). Learned helplessness and depression: A test of the reformulated hypothesis. *Journal of Gerontology, 42*(1), 60–64.
Mann, W. J. (1985). Reproductive cancer. In S. Golub & R. J. Freedman (Eds.), *Health needs of women as they age* (pp. 63–73). New York: Haworth Press.
Manton, K. G. (1980). Sex and race specific mortality differentials in multiple cause of death data. *The Gerontologist, 20*(4), 480–493.
Manton, K. G., Blazer, D. G., & Woodbury, M. A. (1987). Suicide in middle age and later life: Sex and race specific life table and cohort analysis. *Journal of Gerontology, 42*(2), 219–227.
Marcus, A. C., & Siegel, J. M. (1982). Sex differences in the use of physician services: A preliminary test of the fixed role hypothesis. *Journal of Health and Social Behavior, 23,* 186–196.
Meyer, T. J. (1987). Cancer in the elderly. *Generations, 12*(1), 20–24.
Mitteness, L. S. (1987). The treatment of urinary incontinence by community living elderly. *The Gerontologist, 27*(2), 185–193.
Mitteness, L. S., & Wood, S. J. (1986). Social workers' responses to incontinence confusion and mobility impairment in frail clients. *Journal of Gerontological Social Work, 9*(3), 63–78.
Moser, P. W. (1987). An anti-aging cream with a new wrinkle; it may work. *Discover, 8*(8), 72–79.
Moskowitz, R. W., & Haug, M. R. (1986). *Arthritis and the elderly.* New York: Springer Publishing Co.
Nathanson, C., & Lorenz, G. (1982). Women and health: The social dimensions of biomedical data. In J. Z. Giele (Ed.), *Women and the middle years* (pp. 37–87). New York: Wiley.
Notman, M. T. (1984). Reflections and perspectives on therapeutic issues for today's

adult women. In G. Baruch & J. Brooks-Gunn (Eds.), *Women in midlife* (pp. 357–369). New York: Plenum.

Olson, L. K. (1986). Older women: longevity, dependency and public policy. In V. Sapiro (Ed.), Women, biology, and public policy, 85–92, 94, 118. Newbury Park, CA: Sage.

Osgood, N. J., & McIntosh, J. L. (1986). *Suicide in the elderly: An annotated bibliography and review*. Westport, CT: Greenwood Press.

Pelletier, K. R. (1982). *Longevity: Fulfilling our biological potential*. New York: Delta.

Pepper, G. A., & Robbins, L. I. (1987). Improving geriatric drug therapy. *Generations, XXii*(1), 57–60.

Porcino, J. (1985). Psychological aspects of aging. In S. Golub & R. J. Freedman (Eds.), *Health needs of women as they age* (pp. 115–122). New York: Haworth Press.

Porcino, J. (1987). The health concerns of older women: Osteoporosis, hysterectomy, breast cancer. *Perspective on Aging*, xvi, 7–8.

Randall, R. (1986, December 2). Controlling the bladder: Until recently, even medical texts shunning the problem. *Washington Post Health*.

Riley, M. W. (1985). The changing older woman: A cohort perspective. In M. R. Haug, A. B. Ford, & M. Sheafor (Eds.), *The physical and mental health of aged women* (pp. 3–15). New York: Springer Publishing Co.

Rowe, J. W. (1985). Health care of the elderly. *New England Journal of Medicine*, VI, *312*(13), 827–835.

Rosenwalker, I., & Dalinsky, A. (1987). The changing determinants of the growth of the extreme aged. *The Gerontologist*, *27*(3), 275–280.

Russo, N. F. (1984). Women in the mental health delivery system: Implications for research and public policy. In L. E. Walker (Ed.), *Women and mental health policy* (pp. 21–42). Beverly Hills, CA: Sage.

Scarf, M. (1980). *Unfinished business*. New York: Doubleday.

Shanas, E., & Maddox, G. L. (1985). Health, health resources and the utilization of care. In R. H. Binstock & E. Shanas (Eds.), *Handbook of aging and the social sciences* (pp. 696–726). New York: Van Nostrand Reinhold.

Shaw, E., & Darling, J. (1985). *Female strategies*. New York: Walker.

Sheehy, G. (1980). *Passages*. New York: Doubleday.

Siegel, J. S., & Taeuber, C. M. (1986). Demographic perspectives on the long-lived society. *Daedalus, 115*, 77–118.

Simonson, W. (1984). *Medication and the elderly: A guide for promoting proper use*. Rockville, MD: Aspen Systems.

Spencer, G., Goldstein, A. A., & Jacuber, C. M. (1987). *Americans centenarians*, p. 94. Washington, DC: Bureau of the Census and National Institute on Aging.

Stellman, J. M. (1987). The working environment of the working poor: An analysis based on workers' compensation claims, census data, and known risk factors. *Women and Health*, *12*(3/4), 83–102.

Torrey, B. B., Kinsella, K., & Taeuber, C. M. (1987). *An aging world: International population reports.* Series P-95, No. 78. Washington, DC: Bureau of the Census.

U.S. Senate Special Committee on Aging. (1984). *Aging America.* Washington, DC: U.S. Dept. of Health and Human Services.

U.S. Senate Special Committee on Aging. (1988). *Aging America* (1987–88 edition). Washington, DC: U.S. Dept. of Health and Human Services.

Van Hoose, W. H., & Worth, M. R. (1982). *Adulthood in the life cycle.* Dubuque, IA: William C. Brown.

Verbugge, L. M. (1985). An epidemiological profile of older women. In M. R. Haug, A. B. Ford, & M. Sheafor (Eds.), *The physical and mental health of aged women* (pp. 41–64). New York: Springer Publishing Co.

Waxman, H. M., & Carner, E. A. (1984). Physicians' recognition, diagnosis, and treatment of mental disorders in elderly medicaid patients. *The Gerontologist, 24*(6), 593–597.

Welch, C. E. (1984). Surgery and aged women: Indications and contraindications. In M. R. Haug, A. B. Ford, & M. Sheafor (Eds.), *The physical and mental health of older women* (pp. 194–206). New York: Springer Publishing Co.

Whitbourne, S. K. (1985). *The aging body: Physiological and psychological consequences.* New York: Springer-Verlag.

Wilson, G. K., & Sapiro, V. (1985). Occupational safety and health as a women's policy issue. In V. Sapiro (Ed.), *Women, biology, and public policy* (pp. 137–156). Beverly Hills, CA: Sage.

5 Life Patterns and Social Networks

The physical changes that occur with age are accompanied by psychological and social changes. Social situations shift as society's expectations alter over time as a woman ages. Friends and relatives also grow older and change, neighborhoods and communities decay or prosper, and the climate of existence may shift from benign to menacing. Although each woman's life pattern is unique, the members of generations move together through the decades experiencing the same national and world events. How do these societal and personal happenings affect the older woman and how does she respond?

In this chapter we will look at some of the recurring situations with which women must deal as they age. We will look at the crucial relationships that women develop with friends and colleagues outside the family. What housing and living options are open to older women: remaining independently in their homes and familiar communities or being placed voluntarily or involuntarily in some other custodial arrangement? How do older women fare in the urban centers of our country? What kinds of community activity, volunteer work, religious and political interests involve older women?

FRIENDSHIPS AND NETWORKS

Friends sustain us. Loneliness is one of the most feared aspects of old age. Relatives move and die; the younger generation is not interested in the wisdom of old age and is impatient with the trials and ailments that seem to increase with every decade after 50. What is left is the companionship of friends.

Women have always known the significance of having intimate friendships with other women. Since the male world was off limits except for one's marital partner, women sought out their female peers. The separate community of women appears in the memoirs and letters of women of all eras (Smith-Rosenberg, 1975). The importance of friends and the significant roles they play in the lives of older women are reported widely in the research literature (Gouldner & Strong, 1987).

Friendship among older women is an ambiguous concept and difficult to define. Matthews (1986a) uses specific case material to illustrate how friendships and what they mean change over time with changed circumstances. The friends a married couple make may not last into widowhood, or retirement from work may cut connections with workplace friends (Matthews, 1986b).

Friendship, as Heinemann (1985) points out, is a term that covers a great deal of territory. "Friendships vary with regard to level of affection, openness, trust, sharing, and the length of commitment" (p. 168). The conclusions drawn from her study of elderly urban widows was that "women tend to find friendships more meaningful and are more dependent upon it in comparison to men; elderly women are more likely than their male counterparts to have confidant relationships among their friends." A study conducted in Philadelphia (*Aging*, 1977) of over 1,000 elderly men and women found that when men needed someone to confide in they chose their wives, whereas women chose a relative or a friend. Also, many more women than men had someone to confide in.

Similar findings were obtained in a study of elderly in Iowa (Powers & Bultena, 1976). Women were found to be much more likely than men to have relationships with a wide variety of people. Men were much less likely than women to have an intimate friend. The homogeneity of men's friends, versus the variety of women's friends, is also reported in a study by Usui (1984), and it held true for both the blacks and whites in his sample. The longitudinal study by Maas and Kuypers (1974) identifies varying friendship patterns on the part of older mothers, but for all of the women, friends were an important element in their lives.

The functions friends serve and their relationships to oneself are qualitatively different from that of family. Heinemann (1985) points out that

> friends tend to be homogeneous age peers who value one another as unique individuals or for the relationship itself. Friendships require considerable assertiveness and reciprocity for development and maintenance and are less stable than family relationships. Exchanges are immediate and equal in value. (pp. 175–176)

The changes in women's friendships were charted over a 3-year period by Adams (1987). As the author points out,

> Most current gerontological literature emphasizes the restrictions on choice imposed by physical decline and social losses such as retirement and widowhood. The elimination of social role obligations can, however, be a liberating experience. Not only are there fewer obligations, but there are fewer sets of normative expectations. Although members of the status groups [in the study] experienced different changes in their friendship networks, they all tended to be liberated from their previous patterns.

Merely counting numbers of friends may miss entirely the quality of the friendships. For the older women in Adams's study, friendships played important roles in their lives; but the roles changed and became more diverse over time, and so did the number and kinds of friendship. Friendships may also be critical in helping women deal with stress. Although the elderly women studied by Arling (1987) were more likely than men to be subject to life strain and to live alone, they had "larger social networks, more contact, and greater support." Despite their greater stress, women's support networks served to counter their greater vulnerability.

When there are limits on mobility, the circle of visiting friends will shrink. The telephone provides a vital link with friends and kin. Hochschild (1978), who studied elderly residents in a retirement home, found that the women received an average of one phone call an hour and made many themselves (p. 6). For some of the women in Hochchild's study these non-kin relationships maintained by telephone contact were more involving than those with relatives who were only intermittent visitors. The residential friendships were highly influenced by propinquity: those on the same floor tended to find their friends there.

As would be expected, the need for friends and interaction with them increases upon widowhood, a finding supported by the research of Roberto and Scott (1984/85). The researchers report that over 84% of the widows studied name a woman who was not a relative as their closest friend. When family ties are weak or are lost, women are more apt to rely on their friends for support than are men (Blau, 1973). Livson (1983) makes the point that "traditional feminine qualities—sociability, emotional expressiveness, intimacy—may gain value as women age." According to Livson, women also have sex role flexibility, which allows them to become more "masculine" with age—assertive, independent, and achievement-oriented. These qualities combined not only reinforce women's utilization of friendships for support in their old age but also provide the impetus to seek out and maintain such relationships.

An interesting speculation about the role of intimate female friendships in women's lives suggests that these may allow women to remain in unsatisfying marriages, since the friends provide the emotional support needed. And after widowhood or divorce such friendships may act as an inhibitor to remarriage. In fact, in most non-Western societies untouched by our romanticism, women do not even expect friendship from their husbands but rely on female kin and friends for their social support (Adams, 1985).

The affiliative needs of women are nowhere more positively seen than in the establishing and maintaining of intimate friends. This capacity serves elderly women remarkably well. As women age and encounter personal and family stress, friendships provide a source of support that complements or replaces that provided by kin (Roberto & Scott, 1984).

SOCIAL NETWORKS

The concept of social networks is a valuable social science term used to describe the ways in which persons use their environments (Antonucci & Akiyama, 1987). Applying the concept of networks to neighborhoods provides added insight into how elderly people live in their communities. The intensive study of such networks and neighborhoods made by Golant (1984) showed that elderly women obtain more satisfaction from the community in which they lived than did elderly men. He hypothesized that these women were dependent on walking and had utilized local community services for an extended period of time; since the men worked at a distance, their utilization of local resources was of much shorter duration, occurring only with retirement. Thus, elderly women would feel more at home in their local community. Widows were more satisfied with their neighborhoods than were married elderly, finding the local scene a source of familiar, albeit impersonal, contacts. But this very dependency on the local community can become a negative force if the community undergoes changes such as the kind of inner-city gentrification that replaces familiar groups with upwardly mobile young professionals. Other changes—a store closing, relocation of transportation, moving a health clinic—can be devastating to elderly residents (Silverman, 1987).

Informal helping relationships are complex when closely scrutinized. In her study of neighbors' help to widows living alone O'Bryant (1985) found that when neighbors knew that widows had kin nearby, they appeared more willing to provide help also. However, there was a lower level of such support for childless widows.

> Perhaps neighbors are more reticent about being supportive of older women who have no close families. As widows age and their needs become greater,

neighbors may feel obligated to extend and expand their care of them beyond reasonable limits and, rather than opening the door to such possibilities, neighbors may shy away from becoming too heavily involved in the first place."

One study of a group of elderly women in a low-income area produced interesting findings. Although "relatives were described as providing companionship, they were not utilized for emotional support or for problem solving. Neighbors, but not relatives, were said to provide problem-solving help" (Heller & Mansbach, 1984). For those with relatively few confidant-friends, church attendance was important, particularly if there had been a loss of persons in their friendship network. Heller and Mansbach observed the older men and women at a nutrition site. The seating arrangements were significant: "While the women tended to congregate in small groups to eat together and linger after the meal, the men almost without exception ate alone."

Women stay in touch, and they seek and provide social support in a variety of ways and settings. Elderly women who are physically and financially able to do so can maintain independent living because they are able to take advantage of informal support systems in their community (Soldo, Sharma, & Campbell, 1984). The older women who were most satisfied with their lives in the study of Maas and Kuypers (1974) were those who had developed a range of activities during their years as mothers and homemakers—work, community, or recreation—that continued and even expanded when their parental responsibilities waned. If such activities were not developed in midlife, older women could not develop them when they were needed and consequently were apt to be dissatisfied with their postparental years.

The pattern of sex differences in the activities of the elderly were described in a study in which women were much more socially engaged than men (Berghorn, Schafer, Steere, & Wiseman, 1978). The authors believe that "this is not an indication that women are more gregarious than men, but that earlier social 'conditioning' was different for this cohort of women." The data they gathered showed that there was "a marked decline in the rewards of family interaction for women, as well as for men, and a corresponding increase in women's involvement in church work and neighboring."

Older women also found intergenerational contacts with other women a source of support and satisfaction. In one water-based aerobics program in which women of all ages participated, the age integration was liked by over 96% of the participants because it provided satisfying reciprocal support (Heller & Mansbach, 1984). Research by Bretyspraak, Halpert, and Olson (1985) in rural areas shows the significant function performed by homemakers clubs sponsored by agricultural extension service. When the age structure of the group changed, the kinds of support provided to members also shifted. But for the older women members the club participation functioned to "maximize the overlap of family, friends, and neighbors." The intergenerational sharing was considered an important asset (Weiss & Jamieson, 1987).

It is even possible that this kind of relationship, both giving and receiving confidences and services, may also contribute to women's longevity. That women thrive when they can socialize with others is an important attribute that needs to be taken into account when housing and other social arrangements are planned for older women.

VOLUNTEERS AND ACTIVISTS

For many generations the unpaid work of women has been needed to keep many of the nonprofit social services of a community going. Women are the volunteers who taught Sunday School and led Cub Scout and Girl Scout troops, brought books to patients, served on boards of libraries and hospitals, organized charity bazaars, and solicited funds for all kinds of worthy causes. When most middle-class married women were full-time homemakers, this kind of community activity was expected and was essential to keep many such services alive. With the growing professionalization of charity activity, as an example, the scope of women's voluntary activity has been reduced; Lady Bountiful has been replaced by a woman with a master's degree in social work. At the same time increasing numbers of women have become part- or full-time members of the labor force and unavailable for traditional community service. Now it is the older woman, released from home commitments to children, possibly widowed, and retired from work, who is being recruited for community service and who also seeks community activity (Maas & Kuypers, 1974). A 1982 study by Gallup Associates found that older persons, aged 50 to 64, had the highest proportion of involvement in voluntary (40%) or charitable (38%) organizations. The percentage over 65 who are involved is still impressive, equal to that of the 30–49-year-old group (U.S. Senate Special Committee on Aging, 1984). These data do not tell us how many women are among those engaged in such activities, but since women are the majority of those over 65, it is probable that they are well represented in community activities.

Community service in voluntary organizations is attractive because it allows free entry and exit—unlike family relationships—and also provides for reciprocity in giving and receiving (Payne & Bull, 1985). Many of the intergenerational activities that are actively promoted by local and federal programs are of this nature. In some programs young people provide a needed service for the elderly, such as shopping, companionship, health care, or household help; other programs emphasize elderly volunteers who assist in children's centers, provide tutoring, or sponsor and counsel youngsters in trouble with the law (*Synergist*, 1981). Foster Grandparents, RSVP, and ACTION provide opportunities for the elderly to participate in community service (Buckley, 1985; Hilgendorf, 1985; Riley, 1985; Schmidt, 1985; Tice, 1985). Programs of the American Association of Retired Persons (AARP) and AART encourage local chapters to support voluntary programs. The Peace Corps actively recruits retired men and women for their international programs. There are many opportunities for older women to remain active, but the actual number who are involved is unknown (Chambre, 1987).

The organizations in which men and women participate have traditionally differed, and this remains the case for the elderly. Although the number of organizations to which they belong is about the same, there are qualitative differences in size and type. The women's organizations were often auxiliaries of men's groups, or, as in the case of labor unions, women's were far smaller than men's. Women were apt to be members of neighborhood, youth, and community organizations, while men belonged to business, professional, or national service organizations. Men's organizations provided "contacts" leading to jobs or other economically advantageous connections; women's organizations were locally service-oriented. Men's participation dropped drastically with retirement, whereas retirement had much less effect on women's participation (McPherson & Smith-Lovin, 1982).

Participation in organizations is thought to be a key component in "successful" aging (Payne & Bull, 1985). Most programs appeal, however, to the white middle class, who are already most able to deal with the problems and stresses of aging. Creative programming and energetic leadership are needed to reach minority and impoverished elderly women, who could gain significantly from community involvement.

POLITICAL ACTIVITY

Significant social movements have emerged in the second half of the 20th century that have forever changed the ways in which Americans define and resolve political issues: the civil rights movement, the women's movement, the antinuclear/peace movement, and the movement to conserve and protect the environment and natural resources. Although not often recognized as such, the emergence of the elderly and their advocates has in many respects had a similar impact on the national debate regarding allocation of resources, specifically in the area of medical and social programs. One reason, of course, for a new perception of the elderly as a political force is their sheer numbers. This is the first time in human history that the percentage of the elderly in the population has been so large—and growing at a faster rate than younger age groups. Inevitably, social policies are reviewed in terms of which part of the population will benefit or suffer (Hoskins, 1987). As it became clear in the 1970s that the elderly needed more social support than was forthcoming under existing policies, extensive public debates ensued regarding their "fair share" of the public purse (Preston, 1984; see also Kingson, Hirshorn, & Cornman, 1986).

The political significance of being elderly is a recent phenomenon. In the elections of 1972 and 1976, for instance, those who identified themselves as elderly were less active politically and less apt to vote than those elderly who did not identify themselves as such (Miller, Gurin, & Gurin, 1980). But this has changed. The percentage of voters in different age brackets is noteworthy: only 40% of those under 25 voted in 1980, whereas 58% of those over 75 voted. The peak of voter participation is at ages 55 to 64; 71% of this age group voted (U.S. Senate Special Committee on Aging, 1984; see also Preston, 1984). The latest census figures projected that in 1988 women over 65 would comprise nearly 60% of the voters in that age group. The power of the vote by the elderly is evident in Florida, where the median age is 45 and one-fourth of all voters are over 65. These voters have returned Representative Claude Pepper to office (who is himself over 80) because he is known as the advocate of the elderly. Other states have significant blocs of elderly voters: one-fifth of the voters in Iowa, Pennsylvania, and Arkansas are over 65 (U.S. Census Bureau, 1988). These voters in the 1980s are voting as elders. The "new demography" is going to have a major impact on the political agenda of the future, particularly as more affluent, physically able, and better-educated aged assess the policy implications of leaders and legislation (Hudson, 1987).

Voting rates of the elderly show the traditional patterns of voter participation influenced by sex, race, and ethnicity as shown in Table 5.1. All groups declined in voter participation between 1984 and 1986; 1984 was a presidential election, and 1986 a congressional election. The former always produces higher voter turnouts. Women vote at lower rates than men in all age brackets, with the sharpest differences over age 75 for all but Hispanic groups. The rates for blacks and Hispanics are much lower than for whites, and the rates for Hispanic women are the lowest. Tradition, plus language problems, may account for much of this.

There are some strong efforts being made to turn around the traditional disinclinations of women to participate in politics. The leadership of women in advocacy groups for the aged has been a visible sign of their current political awareness. Maggie Kuhn, founder and moving spirit of the Gray Panthers, which enlists both men and women, inspired many older women to join because of her own visibility (Barrow, 1986, pp. 460–461). Under the auspices of the National Organization of Women and the leadership of the late Tish Sommers, the needs of older women were articulated

TABLE 5.1 Percent of Older People Who Reported Voting in Elections by Age, Sex, Race, and Hispanic Origin: 1984 and 1986 (excludes people in institutions)

	65–74 years		75 years or older	
Race and Hispanic origin	Male	Female	Male	Female
1984 Election				
Total	73.9	70.2	68.3	57.2
White	75.0	71.2	69.6	57.8
Black	65.9	57.9	64.0	55.0
Hispanic origin	49.7	44.6	30.3	29.2
1986 Election				
Total	68.7	62.2	63.1	48.8
White	70.1	63.3	64.2	49.5
Black	58.9	55.8	52.1	43.9
Hispanic origin[a]	43.7	35.8	32.6	30.9

[a]People of Hispanic origin may be of any race.

From U.S. Bureau of the Census. "Voting and Registration in the Election of November 1984." *Current Population Reports* Series P-20, No. 405 (March 1986) and unpublished data from the November 1986 Current Population Survey.

to the most active national women's political group. One organization, the Older Women's League (OWL), directs its activities to policy issues as they relate to older women and to active lobbying on their behalf. The AARP, considered one of the most powerful lobbies, has a special "women's initiative" program designed to address women's concerns. Another organization, the Displaced Homemakers Network, coordinates and provides technical assistance to the hundreds of local programs helping these women, most of whom are in midlife or older.

In the last few years the older Americans lobby has been vociferous and visible. Data are not available to show how many women have actually participated in these activities. As women become more sensitive to their vulnerability in old age and more educated in public affairs, we can expect both more participation and more leadership from older women (Rossi, 1986), and we can hope for increased awareness on the part of policy developers of the particular needs of the woman over 40.

RELIGIOUS INVOLVEMENT

Americans report a high rate of religious affiliation; only 8% of all Americans say they have no such affiliation. Of Americans aged 50 to 69 (as of 1981) fully 96% claim a religious affiliation, as do 97% over age 70 (U.S.

Senate Special Committee on Aging, 1984). Religion is important to the elderly: 82% of respondents over age 65 said that religion was the most important influence in their lives, 89% said they tried hard to put their religious beliefs into practice, and 87% derived personal comfort and support from religion (U.S. Senate Special Committee on Aging, 1984). Unfortunately, the data give no breakdown by sex. Those under 30 reported themselves to be significantly less involved with religion, but we do not know if this is an age or cohort effect.

A review of the literature on aging and religiosity showed that there was "no consensus in the literature regarding the relationship between aging and religion" (Hansberger, 1985). To gain some data in this area, Hansberger interviewed a nonrandom sample of elderly Canadians, of whom 61.2% were women. The data, while inconclusive and limited, seem to point to an increase in religiosity with age among those who held the most highly orthodox Christian beliefs but no increase on the part of those who were less orthodox; the data were not analyzed by sex. A group of AARP members in El Paso, Texas, 78% of whom were women, were asked about their religious activity. The findings showed that young-old people participated more in formal religious activities, whereas old-old people were more apt to participate in private devotions. More involvement with kin and friends means more involvement with private religious practices (Young & Dowling, 1987). The authors stress the importance of social networks as a factor in religious observance; decline in activity might be due to lack of such supports rather than to age-related disability. As we note in Chapter 6, black elderly women turn to religion and religious institutions for solace in times of stress.

Church attendance was related to life satisfaction in one study of elderly women (Heller & Mansbach, 1984). The relationship of religiosity and morale, particularly the ways in which religious elements contribute to mental health, was investigated by Koenig, Kvale, and Ferrel (1988). They found that "religion was highly associated with morale in women [whereas] financial status was, after health, the predominant correlate of morale among men." They also reported that "women were significantly more likely than men to engage in church and related activities, private activities such as prayer and Bible reading, and more likely to score higher on intrinsic religiosity." With the decrease in other obligations, such as work and children, elderly women would have more time for religious participation. The general belief that women, particularly elderly women, are the mainstay of organized religion results from observing congregations in attendance at services. Research has repeatedly demonstrated major sex differences in the "prevalence and salience of religious attitudes and activities" (see also Montero, 1979).

One of the ways in which religion can be practiced in contemporary America is through watching religious broadcasting and participating via mailed donations to television ministries. The scandals surrounding such activity in 1987–88 focused public attention on the supporters of television ministers. One report stated that there were

> five-million hard-core donors, most of them women from fifty to seventy-five, with seventy-one as the peak age for giving. Many live alone on social security, some in nursing homes. Many are too disabled for church going. Lonely, neglected, they see the electronic evangelist as their pastor. A widow's mite dropped in an offering is anonymous, but the smallest donation to a TV preacher brings a warm letter of thanks that makes the giver feel he or she is a true partner in a great soul-winning enterprise. (Gardner, 1987)

As more older women swell the population, there may be a new tension between local building-based churches and television ministries as each compete for the affiliation and financial support of this group, who may not be well armed to detect the difference between the authentic and the charlatan.

HOUSING

Older women face their most soul-wrenching decision after retirement or the death of a spouse, the departure of all of the children, and the advent of one or more chronic ailments: whether to stay in the old familiar house or apartment or move—someplace. The accumulation of possessions of a lifetime will have to be discarded. Friends will be left behind. As Figure 5.1 shows, the percentage of older women living alone increases dramatically with each decade after age 55. The contrast with men is striking: at ages 55 to 64, only 9% of men live alone; 11% at ages 65 to 74, and 19% over age 75 (U.S. Senate Special Committee on Aging, 1984). The decision to move or to remain rests heavily on women living by themselves.

Living alone does not necessarily mean being lonely. As Rubenstein (1985) points out in his review of the research, elderly individuals often choose to live alone because they value an independent life-style. Living alone mixes both negative and positive features, which are significant to each individual in the context of his or her own needs and values. The key component is choice. To live alone on the basis of one's own choice is one thing; to have to live alone because of finances or lack of relatives or friends is another.

Some people are self-identified "loners." Many single older men and a few elderly women live in single room occupancy hotels, typically found in run-down parts of cities, through even in these settings women create different social networks (Sokolovsky & Cohen, 1983).

FIGURE 5.1 Living arrangements of older women, March 1982.

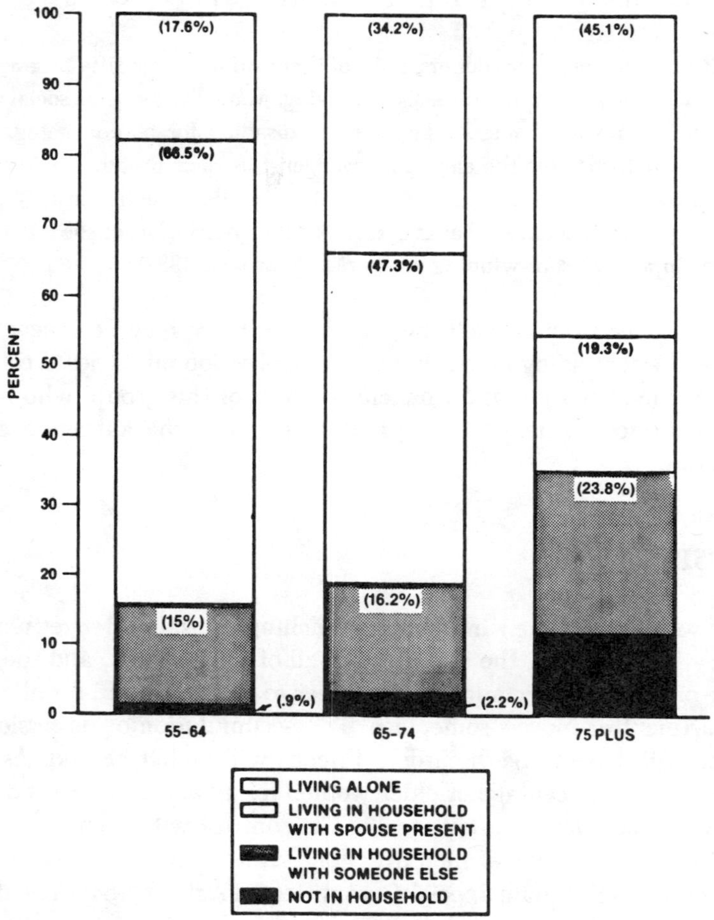

From U.S. Bureau of the Census, Current Population Reports, Series P-20, unpublished.

Women will continue to constitute the largest group either choosing or being forced to live alone. It is important to base programs on individual preference and situation, rather than on unfounded assumptions about what is "good for dear old Mom" (Berg, Mellstrom, Persson, & Svanborg, 1981).

There are in fact many housing alternatives available, even given the typical limited resources of older women. However, many women are not able to assess adequately the personal or financial consequences of moving or remaining in place. Many widows, for instance, own their own homes, free of mortgages. Relatives or real estate agents may have an ulterior interest in urging them to sell, and their advice may not be the best. Other considerations are important in making the decision to move from a beloved residence. Individuals may not be able to negotiate several flights of stairs with the groceries, walk five blocks to public transportation, or be certain they can reach a phone in case of an emergency. Housing is of critical importance to the elderly when problems of maintenance, affordability, access to needed services, and safety can no longer be taken for granted.

Relocating is an option that a significant number of elderly take every year. There are age-specific rates of moving, with local or short-distance moves declining as individuals age; but after age 75 longer moves are made, especially by widowed women. Interstate migration jumps after age 65, and the migrants are likely to be more affluent; persons who moved little in adulthood are unlikely to move when they get older (Silverman, 1987). Many who move seek the assumed better life to be found in the sunbelt states, while others flee the stress of big cities and return to smaller cities and towns. Most of those who move are couples. Interestingly, a small but statistically significant number of persons over 60 who moved to sunbelt states early in their retirement move back as they get older to be near their children (U.S. Senate Special Committee on Aging, 1986, 1988). Many of those returning are below the poverty line, disabled, or living in institutions for the elderly, and probably many of them are widows.

Are there some housing needs that are specific for older women? In one study widows and divorced/separated women, who were economically the worst off, also were found to have paid an excessive amount of their income for housing, whether they were owners or renters (Lawton, 1981). However, finding that the quality of the women's housing was much better than that of elderly men, Lawton comments:

> This finding is the most paradoxical of the results, particularly in light of the great income advantage that widowers and divorced/separated men have over their female counterparts. The conclusion is inescapable that despite their low incomes and social role proscribing home-maintenance work, women alone succeed better than men in a similar condition in achieving housing quality.

When older women have to move, they take greater care than men in searching for higher-quality housing, are more motivated to keep a "good house," are more likely to get more help from friends, and are more likely to do household maintenance chores if they have to. It is somewhat surprising that Lawton feels these differences in favor of women to be "paradoxical."

Studies of housing quality have often cited the congregation of the elderly in run-down neighborhoods and dilapidate housing and have assumed that this must result in less satisfying lives. After studying the housing satisfaction of the elderly, Golant (1982) concluded that this could be very misleading: "dwelling satisfaction was unrelated to sex, widowhood and never married status, separated/divorced status, race, education or income." An observer would have seen the housing to be objectively undesirable, but the study indicated that subjective factors were more important to elderly individuals. What "place" means to an individual is more important than what the objective assessment of the quality of that place may be. What forces many elderly to leave their homes may be lack of appropriate adaptation to disabilities. Modifications to enhance safety and other devices to help an individual manage living along could be a significant factor in helping many elderly single women stay in their own homes as they prefer to do (Maddox, 1987).

There has been considerable discussion in gerontological literature as to the desirability of age-segregated or age-integrated housing (Silverman, 1987). Most older people appear to be more satisfied with their living arrangements if they have age peers close by. In a study of urban elderly (Berghorn et al., 1978) it was found that those neighborhoods with concentrations of elderly had more female residents who were less dependent on family members. Another study of older residents found that they tended to interact more with other older residents even if they did not express a preference for this kind of association; we do not know if there are any sex differences in the preferences expressed (Sherman, Ward, & LeGory, 1985). Older persons who seek out retirement communities may well be expressing a preference for the "amenities and services" provided rather than for the exclusive company of other oldsters. A study of one group of older women who moved to Phoenix, Arizona, after the death of their husbands, shows that the move to an age-segregated community had many positive outcomes, in part because of the women's above-average financial status and also because they were able to successfully "re-establish emotional bonds with their new homes, each mixing some of the past with the present" (Hartwigsen, 1987).

Federally subsidized apartment buildings for the elderly was one program intended to meet the housing needs of elderly poor, but this program has been cut in recent years. However, many localities have recycled old schools into residences for the elderly, and some developers have considered this a potentially lucrative market given generous tax breaks. Such housing will inevitably have a high proportion of elderly single women; we do not have data on how women feel about such programs in terms of housing preference (Maddox, 1987).

Living in a segregated community of elderly produces a different kind of world. About 6% of elderly now live in age-segregated housing. Within these residences the elderly create their own special world or as Hochschild (1978) called it, an "accidental community." The ethnography of a retirement hotel, reported by Teski (1981), provides a wealth of vignettes that illuminate the life of the elderly in such a setting. The women were much more active in socializing, participating in committees, and assisting in planned activities, and they showed more "chatty behavior at the dining room tables. The effect is that the men seem much more passive and often, in fact, have less to do than the women" (p. 18). Hochschild (1978) summarized the impact on the women living in the home she studied:

> . . . communal solidarity can renew the social contact the old have with life. For old roles that are gone, new ones are available. If the world watches them less for being old, they watch one another more. Lacking responsibilities to the young, the old take on responsibilities toward one another. Moreover, in a society that raises an eyebrow at those who do not "act their age," the subculture encourages the old to dance, to sing, to flirt, and to joke. They talk frankly about death in a way less common between the old and the young. They show one another how to be, and trade solutions to problems they have not faced before. (p. 140)

Planned retirement communities, which require very large investments for initial entry and large monthly payments for housing and services, are an alternative for the well endowed. Many of the original tenants are couples, and the arrangements provide for a scaled progression of housing including, in some instances, a nursing home when the individual becomes completely disabled. Most of those living in such retirement villages are happy with their surroundings, while others find them limited and restrictive (Silverman, 1987).

Another housing alternative that has attracted considerable interest is the apartment or house in which three to five elderly unrelated persons live, sharing facilities, usually with a housekeeper to take care of meals and with supervision from local social service agencies. Procuring expanded federal support for such facilities would greatly increase the number available. In the view of many gerontologists this kind of congregate housing provides the services needed for competent ambulatory elderly and is far preferable to, as well as less expensive than, nursing home care. Older women will be the beneficiaries of housing policies that provide more alternatives.

There may be unanticipated social consequences to any deliberate housing arrangement, resulting in age segregation. When the majority of the rest of the community do not have frequent occasions to interact with the elderly, it can be understandably unsympathetic to their needs, particularly as those needs become translated into costly public programs. A whole literature has grown up around the presumed or potential conflict between generations vying for the public dollar (Preston, 1984). There is even an organization, supported by a number of congressional leaders, that is dedicated to examining the policy implications of different generational expectations and competing entitlements: Americans for Generational Equity. Programs that help bring together the old and the young, as discussed in Chapter 5, can help to overcome the possible social consequences of housing segregation of the elderly.

Policies for publicly supported housing for the elderly will have a major impact on the quality of life of millions of older women. One factor that needs to be recitified is the lack of fit among perceptions of the needs of the elderly by social planners, actual needs as reported by the elderly themselves, and omission of the elderly in the development of housing policies affecting them. Much also needs to be done in understanding better the design problems of housing planned for the elderly (Howell, 1980; Windley & Scheidt, 1980). There is little in the literature that tells us about the housing preferences of older women. What we can infer from the affiliative needs of women, their capacity and need for friendships, would support a public policy that encourages the development of congregate housing, apartment clusters that include common living areas, "Granny flats," and apartments in the homes of relatives. Expansion of adult day care facilities that provide many kinds of needed care for ambulatory as well as impaired adults, thus allowing them to stay in their home community, is another alternative to rehousing the elderly. However, the impact of current federal policy has been to make custodial institutions more attractive to the financial community, even if uniformly less preferred by the elderly (AARP, 1984; Pollack, 1987).

NURSING HOMES

The housing least preferred by the elderly is the nursing home. No one wants to be placed in one if there is any kind of feasible alternative. However, about 5% of the elderly are in nursing homes at any one time (about 1.2 million individuals), but the probability of such institutionalization over a *lifetime* is estimated to be 48%. For those over 65 the risk is 65% (Wingard, Jones, & Kaplan, 1987; see also Manton, Woodbury, & Lui, 1984). These probabilities have important implications for women:

> In 1980, seven out of ten residents of nursing homes, and almost four out of five older-aged residents of nursing homes, were women. The increase in the number of elderly women in institutions has been more marked than that of elderly men. Between 1970 and 1980, the elderly female population of institutions increased by 48 percent, as compared with 19 percent for males. (Siegel & Taeuber, 1986.)

The typical resident in 1985 was found to be a white, widowed female, aged 79, who had been in the facility 2.6 years. She came to the institution from a hospital, had multiple physical and mental problems, and needed help dressing, bathing, and eating (Barrow, 1986). The population of nursing homes is predicted to increase by 47% between 1985 and 2000, and by 2040 it will more than double, to 4.4 million (U.S. Senate Committee on Aging, 1986). Table 5.2 shows the important factors that enter into nursing home placement: being female, white, single. Furthermore, 63.1% have living children, compared to 81.3% in the community. The low percentage of Blacks in nursing homes suggests strongly that they have greater difficulty in obtaining financial support for nursing home placement despite the large numbers who would actually qualify for Medicaid.

Women are at higher risk than men of being admitted to a nursing home (Wingard et al., 1987). Women outlive their husbands and thus have no spouses to care for them when they are disabled. Never-married women are highly likely to have to move to a nursing home in old age. Most of those admitted to nursing homes have severe physical problems that make it impossible to live independently. It is not that individuals are needlessly placed in nursing homes but that the situation of women makes them so likely to be residents (Johnson, 1987). If nursing homes were not available to care for the disabled elderly, "many children and other relatives would have to make drastic changes in their lives in order to care for the dependent elderly" (Johnson, 1987). An Alzheimer's disease patient can wreak havoc on a household; with so many women living past 75 their chances of suffering from this disease rises dramatically. Nursing homes are thus a necessary institution.

Most elderly dread having to go to a nursing home and would prefer to be in their own homes, with the help of kin or paid helpers, or in adult day care. But many would choose a nursing home over moving in with a relative (McAuley & Blieszner, 1985). Most residents who enter do not expect to leave (Johnson, 1987). Far more women than men are likely to die in a nursing home (Kastenbaum & Candy, 1973).

The facilities provided for the indigent and/or sick elderly were demeaning and inadequate in the 19th and early 20th centuries (Cole, 1987). A series of reforms since 1935 has resulted in the development and growth of the privately owned, for-profit nursing home as the dominant type of facility. The deinstitutionalization of the mentally ill elderly resulted in a 36% decline in the number in mental institutions between 1940 and 1970, with a 105% increase in other types of institutions for the impaired aged, such as nursing homes, during the same period (Johnson, 1987). As of 1973, 77% of the nearly 22,000 nursing homes were for profit, and in 1979 nearly one-third of all homes and 35% of the beds were part of multistate chains. The powerful nursing home lobby "has promoted favorable reimbursement rates and weak regulation" (Cole, 1987, p. 14). However, because of a changed

TABLE 5.2 Selected Characteristics of Nursing Home and Community Residents 65 Years and Older: 1985 and 1984

Subject	Living in nursing homes, 1985	Living in community, 1984
Total 65 +		
Number (thousands)	1,316	26,343
Percent	100.0	100.0
Age		
65–74 years	16.1	61.7
75–84 years	38.7	30.7
85 +	45.2	7.6
Sex		
Male	25.4	40.8
Female	74.6	59.2
Race		
White	93.1	90.4
Black	6.2	8.3
Other	0.7	1.3
Marital status[a]		
Widowed	64.2	34.1
Married	16.4	54.7
Never married	13.5	4.4
Divorced or separated	5.9	6.3
With living children	63.1	81.3
Requires assistance in		
Bathing	91.2	6.0
Dressing	77.7	4.3
Using toilet room	63.3	2.2
Transferring[b]	62.7	2.8
Eating	40.4	1.1
Difficulty with bowel and/or bladder control	54.5	(NA)[c]
Disorientation or memory impairment	62.6	(NA)
Senile dementia or chronic organic brain syndrome	47.0	(NA)

[a]For nursing home residents, martial status at time of admission.

[b]Getting in or out of bed or chair.

[c]Although comparable data are not available, the 1984 SOA (see source) found that 6% of the community-resident older population had difficulty with urinary control or had urinary catheters.

(NA) Not available.

From National Center for Health Statistics. Data from the National Health Interview Survey, Supplement on Aging, 1984, and 1985 National Nursing Home Survey, *Advance Data* Nos. 115, 121, 133, and 135; and unpublished data.

climate in Congress, plus some notorious nursing home scandals, stronger controls were legislated in 1987.

What are some of the problems associated with life in a nursing home that might be particularly burdensome for older women? One element identified by researchers is that of patient autonomy: being able to make decisions about one's environment and care (Langer, 1983). One study (Moos, 1980) compared skilled nursing facilities, residential care facilities, and apartments for housing the elderly. In the first two environments there were few areas of choice. Residents could not choose when to eat dinner, could not have a hotplate or coffee maker in their room, could not keep a fish or bird in their room, and participated very little in any kind of planning. The least amount of choice was in the skilled nursing facility. Some facilities allowed the residents to have their own furniture, but only in the residential care facility were they allowed to move it around. Only 30% of facilities allowed the use of alcohol in rooms. One conclusion reached by Moos was that "a combination of high choice and control, in a setting with more women residents, and residents with greater functional resources, led to increased cohesion, organization, and observer-rated pleasantness." Moos also reports:

> Surprisingly, the lack of such choices as when to get up, go to bed, bathe, and eat, and whether to do their own personal laundry, affected women more than men. This was probably because most of the elderly women in group settings did not spend much of their lives working outside their homes and were used to organizing their own pattern of daily activities.

Although we may argue that the reason for women's greater need for autonomy in the details of daily living is that they had not worked outside their homes, we would agree with the conclusion reached by Moos that "the impact of one set of environmental resources needs to be studied in relation to the types of residents for which it is provided as well as the general context in which these residents function."

The importance of participating in decision making is also revealed in other studies of elderly women in nursing homes. They responded positively to such things as having coffee and orange juice in a common room (Blackmore, Howe, & Pinkston, 1976), making instant pudding together (Derx, 1972), and being given a weekly beauty treatment (Ernst, 1974; see also Aizenberg & Treas, 1985; Stafford & Bringle, 1980). In an excellent summary of the research to date on health and the sense of control by Rodin (1986) only one study mentioned any sex differences. A recent issue of *The Gerontologist* (Vol. 28, Supplementary Issue, June 1988) was devoted to reports and discussion of autonomy and long-term care; however, there was no comment as to differences in gender and the needs of elderly.

It is clear from the above that a crucial aspect of how patients fare in nursing homes has to do with often overlooked aspects of care. For example, a provocative study by Kayser-Jones (1986) challenges our perception that patients prefer private or semiprivate rooms, when in fact many, if given a choice, might prefer the socialization and interaction available in an open ward. In such a ward patients can monitor the type of care given, look after those needing help, and be supported when requesting help for themselves. The study reports how "elders" feel, so we do not know if gender enters into the preference. The complexity of one-to-one interactions between caretakers and patients, as well as the serious problems inherent in such institutions, is presented by Vespri (1983); see also (Tisdale, 1987; Retsinas, 1986).

The problems surrounding long-term care are, of course, critically important to women, since most of the elderly patients receiving such care are women (Crystal, 1982). A dismal scenario is provided by Williamson, Shindul, and Evans (1985), who predict:

> If such discrimination against women prevails in terms of employment and Social Security, then nursing homes will continue to be filled disproportionately with very old and very poor white women who outlive their spouses or peers. This segment of the population will continue to be controlled by state-funded facilities and caretakers and will represent an acutely disenfranchised group or what one gerontologist refers to as the "drop-out aged." (p. 235)

When women must depend on Medicaid, they face discriminatory treatment practiced by for-profit nursing homes. A number of legally dubious practices can keep eligible patients out of well-run homes, and even within the homes there is documented evidence that Medicaid patients may receive less care than private-pay patients, even though this is against the law (Edelman, 1987).

The housing problems of the elderly are numerous and complicated. Being able to live in the place of one's choice, with family or friends nearby, having access to needed services and adequate personal care, and if long-term care is required, receiving it from caring and competent providers—these are the hopes of all elderly. The particular needs of women, as a group or as individuals, have been overlooked by most researchers; there is reason to believe that what women want from their home environments might not be the same as what men want.

CRIME AND OLDER WOMEN

Elderly people in our cities are concentrated in those areas that are marked by "deteriorating and filthy neighborhoods . . . and must survive on streets considered dangerous even for the hardiest of souls" (Silverman, 1987, p. 243). Elderly women are very concerned about being the victims of crime. They may be less likely than younger women to be raped, assaulted, or murdered; but if they live in inner city areas, they experience a higher rate of "larceny with contact"—purse snatching and wallet stealing—than other age groups (Lawton, 1985, p. 469). Elderly women express the greatest fear of crime, but in fact it is elderly men who are more at risk: they are 70% more likely to be victims than older females (U.S. Senate Special Committee on Aging, 1984).

In old age women who live alone—and a majority of them do—identify crime as one of their top concerns. If the elderly woman is poor and black and lives in an inner city slum, the rate of victimization is terrifyingly high, although white victims get the most media attention (Markson & Hess, 1980).

Fear often restricts the elderly's activities to daylight hours; efforts to provide escort services, more police protection, and relocation to safer apartments have not reached the majority of elderly. The fear of crime is a major negative influence on the quality of life of many elderly women (Dowd, Sisson, & Kim, 1981). It is predicted that crime against the elderly will decrease in absolute terms in the future because there will be a decline in the numbers of youth, who commit the crimes, while the numbers of aged will increase (U.S. Senate Special Committee on Aging, 1984). Meanwhile, protective programs are needed in communities and neighborhoods with a high density of elderly men and women so that they may live out their lives in tranquility and safety.

The elderly are also victims of another kind of crime, that of consumer fraud. Slick salespeople can sell them overpriced or shoddy "bargains" or play on their sympathies for nonexistent or deceptive "causes." The prevalence of this kind of crime is regularly reported, yet it is hard to prosecute. Particularly easy targets are older uneducated women whose dependency and ignorance is exploited by authoritative others. "Financial abuse can be difficult to detect, investigate and prove" (Quinn & Tomita, 1986, p. 48). Because there are more older women, this kind of fraud finds many of the victims among them. However, even the young-old woman falls prey to advertisers who promise that a grossly overpriced cosmetic product will bring back her youthful skin. Unscrupulous doctors can persuade her to have an unneeded operation or expensive surgery that will permanently erase the age lines from her face (Barrow, 1986).

Wealthy widows are a favorite target of fund raisers for dubious causes or fortune hunters who can prey on their suspicions and their loneliness. Older women are also the targets for deceptive long-term care policies that in fact do not provide the promised protection from high medical bills. After hearing about such deceptive practices, a report by a congressional committee concluded: "At present, the consumer's odds of collecting off these policies are better at the track, at the lottery, or with Los Vegas slot machines" (Quinan, 1987).

Increased efforts at consumer education may help protect the older woman against such fraud, though much of it may still remain unreported; many are reluctant to being charges, which will only reveal their own gullibility (Block, 1983). These kinds of crimes, however, may be less prevalent in the future because of higher educational levels of succeeding cohorts and the increased sophistication of older women that comes from having worked and handled their own finances.

SUMMARY

The lives of older women are defined not only by their physical state and appearance but the personal and community relationships they develop. Gender plays a powerful role in defining how the older person will interact with non-kin and with others in the neighborhood or community.

Friendship with other women plays a major role in the lives of older women. Since so many are or will be alone in their later years, the ability to develop and establish close and mutually helpful relationships with other women often is more important than the help and support provided by relatives. Social support networks are developed by women in many of the settings in which they live.

Older women in the community are active in organizational and volunteer work. With the increasing level of good health enjoyed by the young-old, it is possible that such activities will be an important part of the lives of older women, and they will become more influential in local and national politics.

The living arrangements of older women depend heavily on financial resources, local housing and service programs for the elderly, and their physical well-being. However, we have little information regarding the role of gender in determining preferences. Elderly women who live alone in high-crime areas of cities are fearful of being victims. Many women are easy targets for consumer fraud of all kinds.

Women constitute the majority of residents in nursing homes, which is increasingly the only option for the very old, the frail, and the never-married. Nursing home care providers and researchers have so far been insensitive to possible gender differences in organizing and providing care and to countering the debilitating feelings of helplessness that can contribute to the physical decline of nursing home patients.

REFERENCES

Across the ages. (1981). Journal of ACTION, *Synergist, 10*(2), 19–38.

Adams, R. G. (1985). People would talk: Normative barriers to cross-sex friendships for elderly women. *The Gerontologist, 25*, 605–611.

Adams, R. G. (1987). Patterns of network change: A longitudinal study of friendships of elderly women. *The Gerontologist, 27*, 222–227.

Aging, 1977, –268-269, Feb.-Mar.

Aizenberg, R., & Treas, J. (1985). The family in late life: Psychosocial and demographic considerations. In J. E. Birren & K. W. Shaie (Eds.), *The psychology of aging* (pp. 201–214). New York: Van Nostrand Reinhold.

American Association of Retired Persons (AARP). (1984). *Housing options for older Americans.* Washington, DC: Author.

Antonucci, T. C. (1985). Personal characteristics, social support, and social behavior. In R. H. Binstock & E. Shanas (Eds.), *Handbook of aging and the social sciences* (pp. 94–128). New York: Ban Nostrand Reinhold.

Antonucci, T. C., & Akiyawa, H. (1987). Social networks in adult life and a preliminary examination of the convoy model. *Journal of Gerontology, 42*(5), 107–113.

Arling, G. (1987). Strain, social support, and distress in old age. *Journal of Gerontology, 42*(1), 107–113.

Barrow, G. (1986). *Aging, the individual, and society.* St. Paul, MN: West Publishing Co.

Berg, S. D., Mallstrom, D., Persson, G., & Svanbog, A. (1981). Loneliness in the Swedish aged. *Journal of Gerontology, 36*(3), 342–349.

Berghorn, F. J., Schafer, D. E., Steere, G. H., & Wiseman, R. F. (1978). *The urban elderly: A study of life satisfaction.* New York: Universe Books.

Blackman, D., Howe, M., & Pinkston, W. M. (1976). Increasing participation in social interaction of the institutionalized elderly. Part 2. *The Gerontologist, 16*, 125–128.

Blau, Z. S. (1973). *Old age in a changing society.* New York: New Viewpoints, Franklin Watts.

Block, M. (1983). Special problems and vulnerability of elderly women. In J. I. Kosberg (Ed.), *Abuse and maltreatment of the elderly: Causes and interventions* (pp. 220–233). Boston: John Wright/PSG Inc.

Bretyspraak, L. M., Halpert, B. P., & Olson, R. G. (1985). The voluntary organization as a supportive system in the aging process. In M. S. Peterson & J. Quadango (Eds.), *Social bonds in later life* (pp. 273–286). Beverly Hills, CA: Sage.

Buckley, S. (1985). Parent aides provide support to high risk families. *Children Today, 14*, 16–19.

Chambre, S. M. (1987). *Good deeds in old age: Volunteering by the new leisure class.* Lexington, MA: Lexington Books.

Coercive placement of elders: Protection or choice? (1987, Summer). *Generations: Quarterly Journal of the American Society on Aging*, pp. 3–75.

Cole, T. R. (1987). Class, culture, and coercion: A historical perspective on long-term care. *Generations, 11*, 9–15.

Crystal, S. (1982). *America's old age crisis: Public policy and the two worlds of aging.* New York: Basic Books.

Datan, N. (1983). Star-crossed love: The developmental phenomenologies of the life cycle. In G. D. Rowles & R. J. Ohta (Eds.), *Aging and milieu* (pp. 29–40). New York: Academic Press.

Derx, E. I. (1972). Recreational activity for institutionalized children or adults. *Journal of Psychiatric Nursing and Mental Health, 10*(6), 12–14.

Dowd, J. J., Sisson, R. P., & Kim, D. M. (1981). Socialization to violence among the aged. *Journal of Gerontology, 35*(3), 350–361.

Edelman, T. S. (1987). Nursing homes that shun medicaid. *Perspectives on Aging, 16*(4), 13–15.

Ernst, M. (1974). *Self-esteem among older institutionalized females.* Dallas, TX: Dallas Geriatric Research Institute.

Fitzgerald, F. (1983, April 25). A reporter at large: Interlude. *The New Yorker*, pp. 54–109.

Gardner, M. (1987) Giving God a hand. *New York Review of Books, 34*(13), 17–23.

Golant, S. M. (1982). Individual differences underlying the dwelling satisfaction of the elderly. *Journal of Social Issues, 38*, 121–134.

Golant, S. M. (1984). *A place to grow old: The meaning of environment in old age.* New York: Columbia University Press.

Gouldner, H., & Strong, M. S. (1987). *Speaking of friendships: Middle-class women and their friends.* Westport, CT: Greenwood Press.

Hansberger, B. (1985). Religion, age, life satisfaction, and perceived source of religiousness: A study of older persons. *Journal of Gerontology, 40*, 615–620.

Hartwigsen, G. (1987). Older widows and the transference of home. *International Journal of Gerontology and Human Development, 25*(3),

Heinemann, G. D. (1985). Interdependence in informal support systems: The case of elderly, urban widows. In W. A. Peterson & J. Quadagno (Eds.), *Social bonds in later life: Aging and interdependence* (pp. 165–186). Beverly Hills, CA: Sage.

Heller, K., & Mansbach, W. E. (1984). The multifaceted nature of social support in a community sample of elderly women. *Journal of Social Issues, 40*(4), 99–112.

Hilgendorf, L. (1985). Transmitting tribal traditions. *Children Today, 14*, 30–32.

Hochschild, A. R. (1978). *The unexpected community: Portrait of an old age subculture.* Berkeley, CA: University of California Press.

Hoskins, I. (1985). International equity: An overview of a public policy debate in the United States. *Aging International, 14*(1), 5–8, 13.

Howell, S. C. (1980). Environments as hypotheses in human aging research. In L. W. Poon (Ed.), *Aging in the 1980's* (pp. 424–434). Washington, DC: American Psychological Association.

Hudson, R. B. (1987). Tomorrow's able elders: Implications for the state. *The Gerontologist, 27*(4), 405–409.

Johnson, C. L. (1987). The institutional segregation of the elderly. In P. Silverman (Ed.), *The elderly as modern pioneers* (pp. 375–388). Bloomington, IN: Indiana University Press.

Kastenbaum, R., & Candy, S. E. (1973). The 4% fallacy: A methodological and empirical critique of extended care facility population statistics. *Aging and Human Development*, 15–21.

Kayser-Jones, J. S. (1986). Open-ward accommodations in a long-term care facility: The elderly's point of view. *The Gerontologist, 26*(3), 63–69.

Kingson, E. R., Hirshorn, B. A., & Cornman, J. M. (1986). *Ties that bind: The interdependence of generations*. Washington, DC: Seven Locks Press.

Koenig, H. G., Kvaler, J. N., & Ferrel, C. (1988). Religion and well-being in later life. *The Gerontologist, 28*(1), 18–28.

Langer, E. (1983). *The psychology of control*. Beverly Hills, CA: Sage Publishing.

Lawton, M. P. (1981). An ecological view of living arrangements. *The Gerontologist, 21*, 59–66.

Lawton, M. P. (1985). Housing and living environments of older people. In R. J. Binstock & E. Shanas (Eds.), *Handbook of aging and the social sciences* (pp. 450–478). New York: Van Nostrand Reinhold.

Livson, F. B. (1983). Changing sex roles in the social environment of later life. In G. D. Rowles & R. J. Ohta (Eds.), *Aging and milieu* (pp. 131–152). New York: Academic Press.

Maas, H. S., & Kuypers, J. A. (1974). *From thirty to seventy: A forty-year longitudinal study of adult life styles and personality*. San Francisco: Jossey-Bass.

Maddox, G. L. (1987). *The encyclopedia of aging*. New York: Springer Publishing Co.

Manton, K. G., Woodbury, M. A., & Lui, K. (1984). Life table methods for assessing the dynamics of a U.S. nursing home utilization. *Journal of Gerontology, 39*(4), 79–87.

Markson, E. W., & Hess, B. B. (1980). Older women in the city. *Signs, 5*(3) (Suppl.), S127–S141.

Matthews, S. H. (1986a). Friendships in old age. In V. W. Marshall (Ed.), *Later life: The social psychology of aging* (pp. 233–269). Beverly Hills, CA: Sage.

Matthews, S. H. (1979). *The social world of old women*. Beverly Hills, CA: Sage.

Matthews, S. H. (1986b). *Friendships through the life span: Oral biographies in old age*. Beverly Hills, CA: Sage.

McAuley, W., & Blieszner, R. (1985). Selection of long-term care arrangements. *The Gerontologist, 25*, 188–193.

McPherson, J. M., & Smith-Lovin, L. (1982). Women and weak ties: Differences by sex in the size of voluntary organizations. *American Journal of Sociology, 87*, 883–904.

Miller, A. H., Gurin, P., & Gurin, G. (1980). Age consciousness and political mobilization of older Americans. *The Gerontologist, 20*, 691–700.

Montero, D. (1979). Disengagement and aging among the Issei. In D. E. Gelfand &

A. J. Kutzik (Eds.), *Ethnicity and aging* (pp. 193–205). New York: Springer Publishing Co.
Moos, R. H. (1980). Specialized living environments for older people. *Journal of Social Issues, 36*, 75–94.
Neugarten, L. (1964). *Personality in middle and late life*. New York: Lieber-Atherton.
O'Bryant, S. L. (1985). Neighbors' support of older widows who live alone in their own homes. *The Gerontologist, 25*(3), 305–310.
Payne, B., & Bull, C. N. (1985). The older volunteer: The case for interdependence. In W. S. Peterson & J. Quadango (Eds.), *Social bonds in later life* (pp. 251–272). Beverly Hills, CA: Sage.
Pilisuk, M., & Minkler, M. (1980). Supportive networks: Life ties for the elderly. *Journal of Social Issues, 36*, 95–116.
Pollak, P. B. (1987). Housing options for seniors today. *Aging, 356*, 2–5.
Powers, E. A., & Bultena, G. L. (1976, November). Sex differences in intimate friendships of old age. *Journal of Marriage and the Family*, pp. 147–149.
Preston, S. H. (1984). Children and the elderly in the United States. *Scientific American, 251*(6), 44–49.
Quinan, A. (1987). The D. C. scene: Nursing home insurance: Caveat emptor. *OWL Observer, 6*(5), 2.
Quinn, M. J., & Tomita, S. K. (1986). *Elder abuse and neglect*. New York: Springer Publishing Co.
Retsinas, J. (1986). *It's OK, Mom: The nursing home from a sociological perspective.* New York: Tiresias Press.
Riley, P. (1985, September/October). Teens and older adults: Partners in teaching children. *Children Today*, pp. 27–29.
Roberto, K., & Scott, J. P. (1984–85). Friendship patterns among older women. *International Journal of Aging and Human Development, 19*(1), 1–9.
Rodin, J. (1986). Health, control and aging. In M. M. Baltes and P. B. Baltes (Eds.), *The psychology of control and aging*, pp. 157–167. New York: Erlbaum Publishing.
Rossi, A. S. (1986). Sex and gender in an aging society. *Daedalus, 115*(1), 141–170.
Rowe, J. W., & Kahn, R. L. (1989). Human aging: Usual and successful. *Science, 237*, 143–149.
Rubenstein, R. L. (1985). The elderly who live alone and their social support systems. In C. Eisdorfer (Ed.), *Annual review of gerontology and geriatrics* (Vol. 5, pp. 165–193). New York: Springer Publishing Co.
Schmidt, A. V. (1985). Family friends. *Children Today, 14*, 13–15.
Sherman, S., Ward, R. A., LaGory, M. (1985). *Journal of Gerontology, 40*(1), 102–109.
Siegel, J. S., & Taeuber, C. M. (1986). Demographic perspectives on the long lived society. *Daedalus, 115*(1), 77–118.
Silverman, P. (1987). Community settings. In P. Silverman (Ed.), *The elderly as modern pioneers* (pp. 234–262). Bloomington, IN: Indiana University Press.
Sjaldo, B., Sharma, M., & Campbell, R. T. (1984). Determinants of the living arrangements of older unmarried women. *Journal of Gerontology, 39*, 492–498.

Slivinske, L. R., & Fitch, V. L. (1987). The effect of control enhancing interventions on the well-being of elderly individuals living in retirement communities. *The Gerontologist, 27*, 176–181.

Smith-Rosenberg, C. (1975). The female world of love and ritual: Relations between women in 19th century America. *Signs, 1*(1), 1–30.

Sokolovsky, J., & Cohen, C. (1983). Networks as adaptation: The cultural meaning of being a "loner" among the inner-city elderly. In J. Sokolovsky (Ed.), *Growing old in different societies* (pp. 189–201). Belmont, CA: Wadsworth.

Stafford, J. L., & Bringle, R. G. (1980). The influence of task success on elderly women's interest in new activities. *The Gerontologist, 20*, 642–648.

Teski, M. (1981). *Living together: An ethnography of a retirement hotel*. Washington, DC: University Press of America.

Tice, C. H. (1985). T-LC: Developing friendships between teens and adults. *Children Today, 14*, 20–22.

Tisdale, S. (1987). *Harvest home: Portrait of a nursing home*. New York: Henry Holt.

U.S. Bureau of the Census. (1988). *Projections of the population of voting age for states*. Series P-25, No. 1019. Washington, DC: U.S. Government Printing Office.

U.S. Senate Special Committee on Aging. (1984). *Aging America: Trends and projections*. Washington, DC: U.S. Dept. of Health and Human Services.

U.S. Senate Special Committee on Aging. (1986). *Aging America*. Washington, DC: U.S. Dept. of Health and Human Services.

U.S. Senate Special Committee on Aging. (1988). *Aging America*. Washington, DC: U.S. Dept. of Health and Human Services.

Usui, W. M. (1984). Homogeneity of friendship networks of elderly blacks and whites. *Journal of Gerontology, 39*(3), 350–356.

Vespri, M. (1983) The reluctant consumer: Nursing home residents in the post-Bergman era. In J. Sokolovsky (Ed.), *Growing old in different societies* (pp. 225–237). Belmont, CA: Wadsworth.

Weiss, C. R., & Jamieson, N. B. (1987). Affective aspects of an age-integrated water exercise program. *The Gerontologist, 27*, 430–433.

Williamson, J. B., Shindul, J. A., & Evans, L. (1985). *Aging and public policy: Social control and social justice*. Springfield, IL: Charles C. Thomas.

Windley, P. C., & Scheidt, R. J. (1980). Person-environment dialectics: Implications for competent functioning in old age. In L. W. Poon, *Aging in the 1980's* (pp. 407–423). Washington, DC: American Psychological Association.

Wingard, D. L., Jones, D. W., & Kaplan, R. M. (1987). Institutional care utilization by the elderly: A critical review. *The Gerontologist, 27*, 156–163.

Young, G., & Dowling, W. (1987). Dimensions of religiosity in old age: Accounting for variety of participation. *Journal of Gerontology, 42*(4), 376–380.

6

Home Sweet Home: Family Relations of the Older Woman

Families are not what they use to be. The changes that have occurred in the marketplace are as drastic as those that have taken place at home. And as is the case in many other aspects of life, it is women who have experienced these changes most intimately. The cohorts born in the 1920s, who are in their 60s now, are probably the last group in which the "traditional" family—the wage-earner father and homemaker mother with two to five children—describes the adult life experiences of a majority of women. Succeeding cohorts have experienced changes in marital and societal patterns that in turn will mark the way they age, with each generation moving farther and farther from the traditional family norm.

In this chapter we will look at what the research says about the family relationships of the older woman. We will look at the overall trends in family life that will have an impact on the quality of a woman's later years. What are the adjustments of the mother when all of the children have grown and left home? And, conversely, how does the middle-aged woman cope with rearing her adolescent children, caring for a husband, holding down a job, and responding to a call to care for an aging parent or parents? The particular relationships between adult daughters and aging mothers will be examined. Marital satisfaction, divorce, and widowhood are also concerns. What it means to be a grandmother and the older woman's relationships with other kin will be discussed. We will see how those who have chosen not to marry fare in contemporary America. Finally, we discuss a topic newly emerged from the family closet: abuse of the elderly.

FAMILY PATTERNS: NEW AND OLD

Changes in family patterns are associated with differences in life expectancy. "Reduced mortality and greater longevity have been far more pronounced for women, and altered fertility patterns have reshaped women's adulthood more than men's" (Hagestad, 1986, p. 134). In 1970 the average length of marriage until one spouse died was 43 years. But in 1974, for the first time, more marriages were terminated by divorce than by death. Older women now can expect that their children will be part of such divorce statistics, with all of the painful complexities of relationships that family dissolution involves (Hagestad, 1986). Since divorce was a disgrace when these women were growing up, and relatively few of them had independent incomes, the breakup of a marriage at any age was experienced as a devastating personal disaster.

Women now in their 50s and 60s were the producers of the baby-boom generation after World War II. Many of these women had three, four, or five children, spurred by the affluence and optimism of the postwar years and the glorification of the homemaker. But the family norm for succeeding cohorts has dropped quickly to one or two children, or none. Women with many fewer children than their mothers had may feel more vulnerable in old age, particularly if divorced or widowed. If any of these women outlives her children, and she may well outlive her sons and her male siblings, she must look to her daughters (if she has any) for family support.

Only dire financial circumstances would have forced today's older woman into the workplace when she was married. Professions were pursued only by spinsters; a proper wife and mother stayed home, tending her family and doing good works for free in the community. All of this has changed: women today expect to work a good part of their adult lives. As they watch the divorce statistics rise, they know they need skills and work experience to fall back on if their supporting husbands defect. The middle-aged woman today, facing the years ahead, is likely to be juggling family and work, often with diminished satisfaction in both.

These trends that are changing family life present a tremendous difference between the life experiences of the older woman of the 1980s and 1990s and those who are contemporaneously in their 20s and 30s. There may be a greater gap between the values and beliefs of today's older women and those of the younger generation than at any time previously (Gee & Kimball, 1987). Such value and life-style differences may account for some of the strain between mothers and their adult daughters. There may be additional problems when parents who are older than the norm have children (Morris, 1988).

These trends are not necessarily indicators of any decline in family relatedness. Generations are still tightly enmeshed in each other's lives (Alpert & Richardson, 1980). On the basis of a study of three-generation families, Cohler and Grunebaum (1981) say:

> Persons in contemporary families are much more a part of closely knit social groups than has traditionally been understood either by social scientists or by those, particularly mental health professionals, who read what social scientists write. Throughout life, people continue to remain attached to or dependent both on their own parents and on their offspring to a far greater extent than has been considered "ideal" by many [male] psychological theorists. (p. 334)

Most older women are in close touch with family members, and in turn relatives look to them for advice and provide them with care and support; in fact, this occurs far more today than seems to be true for past generations (Haber, 1983).

All families create their own histories. They share rituals, ceremonies, and celebrations. They have family stories about birth, marriage, death, migrations, honors, and failures. Children increasingly inherit few material things from their parents, but they will inherit, whether they want to or not, those nonmaterial things that bind family members: names, etiquettes, politics, expectancies. These connect family members across generations. Central to this family system are the women who are the keepers of the family stories, the persons who "stay in touch" and know the intricacies of family genealogy. It is this family role that mothers pass on to daughters.

EMPTY NEST OR NEW BEGINNINGS

Do women shut the door after their last child leaves home with a sigh of relief or with a pang of despair? "The mother-child relationship may well be the most salient and enduring in human experience, and its importance does not stop when the child reaches adulthood" (Wood, Traupmann, & Hay, 1984). One is always a child to one's mother until her death. Separation from the mother is an individual's major developmental task on the way to independent ego status and eventual adulthood. Some persons negotiate this easily; some do not. As children have to separate, so do mothers have to let go. Yet the emotional content and interdependence of the relationship endures. As longevity increases, so does the mother-child dyad continue over a major portion of the life span of both. In 1890 the average woman was widowed before her last child left home; her last child would marry when the mother was 55, and she would live to about age 68 (Neugarten & Datan, 1973). In 1966 a woman in her middle to late 30s could expect to be 48 when her last child left home to marry and to be 64 when her husband died; and she could expect to live to age 74. Today a woman who marries at age 22 will be 45 when her last child leaves home, will be widowed at about age 65, and will live to age 83.

The impact of children's departure from home depends to a large extent on the fit between a woman's life-style, resources, and personality. According to Livson (1976), some traditional family-centered women who did not want to change themselves or their situations and appeared happy with their life-styles continued to feel of value in the role of wife and mother even after their children left home, and they found satisfaction in their relationships with others. There was minimal conflict between their personalities, their life-styles, and changed circumstances. But another group of women appeared to have identity crises when their children reached adolescence: "Having suppressed their intellectual competence and grown away from child-care skills, they seem unable for a time to connect with a workable identity." The departure of their children, however, stimulated them to revive their intellectual skills, to develop intimacy with others, and to become more goal-oriented.

Home-oriented women, who are probably the majority of today's women over 60, clearly faced a more critical period after their children grew up than men did at a similar point (Lowanthal, Thurnher, & Chiriboga, 1975). Passage through the postparental transition is complex and tied to the expectations mothers have for their children. For some mothers it is as important for their children to be "on time" in their developmental tasks as it is to be "on time" themselves (Spence & Lonner, 1971). For example, a daughter's refusal or failure to marry right after finishing her education may interfere with a mother's expectations of her role as a grandmother. Literature is full of anecdotes about the married daughter fending off her mother's continued query: "Well, isn't it time you started a family? You know, you aren't getting any younger!" A mother may be afraid about her children's abilities to lead successful lives so that they can feel free to pursue goals for themselves. As Spence and Lonner found, when these older mothers whose children had departed "spoke of alternative goals toward which they could restructure their lives, they sounded very tentative, vague, and even pessimistic." A mother may bask in her children's success, but it is the children's failure that can be cruelly laid at her doorstep. Unfortunately, some mothers seem to accept the psychologically destructive burden of blame when children do not realize their expectations. As Faver (1984) points out, "Women's socialization to be vicarious achievers makes them dependent for a sense of accomplishment on the behavior of husbands and children over whom they have only limited control" (p. 119).

The "overprotective mothers, whose identities were centered on motherhood, and who had not been gradually expanding their interests over the years often felt lost, aimless, or even severely depressed when their last child left home" (Long & Porter, 1984). Women with only one or two children may be at particular risk: "The focus of attention on one or two children may lead to overcommitment, risky for both parents and child. The overconcerned and overprotective mother of the reproductive years finds it difficult or impossible to relinquish control over them" (Whiting, 1984).

The departure of adult children from home is rarely as sudden as the "empty nest" concept implies. Several conditioning situations provide an opportunity to anticipate postparental roles (Deutscher, 1968). Children's lives in the modern high school are often beyond parental control or knowledge. Adolescents move with a vengeance from the world of parents to the world of peers. Children depart for college, service in the armed forces, or even full-time employment and return home periodically.

With several children, the nest is not emptied all at once. A mother prepares for the final departure of all of her children as she lets one go at a time. A study of women aged 40 to 59 in Manitoba, Canada, found that fewer than one-third lived in a home without children, and 52% of the households included children below the age of 18 (Kaufert, 1985). It was not until 5 or 10 years beyond menopause that even half of these women lived in a household without children.

In an increasing number of families the postparental period may be delayed considerably by the fact that more unmarried young people continue to live at home with their parents. In 1984, 54% of Americans between 18 and 24, or 15.5 million, were living at home (U.S. Census Bureau, 1984). Or the postparental period may be interrupted temporarily or even indefinitely, with adult children leaving home but then returning because of financial or personal problems. After divorce some adult children return home with children of their own.

When all of the children have finally gone, the mother is prepared for it (Cooper & Gutmann, 1987). That women's midlife depression is due to the "empty nest" is an enduring piece of popular mythology, but in only a minority of instances does this appear to be true. In fact, the postparental parents interviewed by Deutscher (1968) saw this as a time of freedom. "No longer do the parents need to live the self-consciously restricted existence of models for their own children" (p. 264). If the mother wants to lie abed till noon, leave clothes tossed around and beds unmade, eat TV dinners all week, spend the weekend in frivolity, or buy herself a new dress, she doesn't have to consider what the children will think or need, nor stir herself for special efforts she must make on their behalf.

Marriages may improve after the children leave home (Glenn, 1975). Postparental women report greater marital happiness on the whole than women in the same age range who are still in the parental role (Cooper & Gutmann, 1987). In many families children are a source of marital conflict. Such items as how the children dress; whom they date; what they do with their money; potentially dangerous behavior involving drugs, alcohol, or dubious friends; and their future goals are often the subject of intense parental disagreement. Once the troubling adolescent has departed, peace descends. There may be a revival of self-esteem, too, when the vibrant sexuality of the young is no longer a constant reminder of one's own fading attraction; adolescents are notorious for pointing out to vulnerable parents all of their shortcomings. However, women who may be relieved that their children are no longer underfoot may find that their husbands are so engrossed in their midlife career peak (or lack of it) that they are unavailable as companions. But if they are lucky, husband and wife can find again the shared interests that brought them together in the first place.

The relief women may feel when their last child leaves home may also be a result of the triple burden many of them bear: marriage, work, and family (Long & Porter, 1984). The midlife depression reported for women (see Chapter 4) has been seen as the response to the tremendous difficulty of juggling these competing demands. For those mothers who have never worked but who seek employment as their children get older or leave home, venturing into the world of work can be an extremely unsettling and even psychologically devastating experience (see Chapter 7). A marriage held together by shared concern for children may collapse once the children have departed. The husband may feel deserted if, after they have gone, his wife feels a new freedom to go back to school, become more active in community affairs, or find employment. He may leave, find another woman, or become depressed or abusive.

Long and Porter (2984) point out, further, that "retiring from active motherhood can potentially detract from a woman's economic well-being as well." If she is a single-mother head of household, she loses eligibility for Aid to Dependent Children when her children turn 18. If her children have received survivor's benefits (as a widow with minor children), these are terminated at age 18 as well. Being forced to enter the job market at middle age, for whatever reason, is not easy, and the skills gained as a mother and home manager have no currency in the marketplace. Women who were widowed while children were still minors or who have never been married also face the particular loneliness of having no spouse to share the empty home. But as the research by Faver (1984) shows, such women are better off than the childless never-married older woman or widow. As we will discuss below, adult children are an important source of support for older widows or single mothers.

Though children are a critical source of support for an older woman without a spouse, it might also be assumed that "the morale of parents would be directly and positively associated with the frequency of contact with their children" (Weishaus, 1979). Research cited by Weishaus indicates the contrary. To be too involved with children suggests dependency or may cause tensions due to different value systems. Achieving appropriate reciprocity in relationships with adult children, typically the responsibility of the mother, requires delicate balancing of needs and expectations (Steinman, 1979).

Although many women are dissatisfied in midlife, there are other forces than children leaving home that may be the cause (Grambs, 1987; see also Rubin, 1979). A study by Radloff (1980) provided clear evidence that for her sample " 'empty nest' parents were not more depressed than those living with children. If anything, they were less depressed. Furthermore, this was as true for women who were 'only' housewives as it was for wives (and husbands) employed outside the home."

Powell (1977) looked at the relationship of employment to the adjustment of older college-educated mothers. He found significantly higher psychiatric symptom scores exhibited by women not employed outside the home than by women employed full-time. In contrast, family-oriented women in Lowenthal's (1975) study were depressed and anxious, and a majority of them worked outside the home. Outside employment did not compensate for the satisfactions of the mothering role (Higgins, 1975), and being employed was apt to produce conflicts with family-related demands (Grambs, 1987).

Like many other simplistic generalizations, the concept of the empty nest syndrome as a time of trauma and despair for mothers overstates the case. Some mothers are devastated; others are delighted. For almost all there is a period of reorganization of relationships as sons and daughters move into a more or less successful adulthood (Aldous, Klaus, & Klein, 1985), and parents reshape their lives around being a couple once more. The impact on the single mother may be more problematic. Individual reactions to these events depend on circumstance, personality, life-styles, support systems, and expectations of a benign or uncertain future. Certainly the options for succeeding generations of older women may make the postparental period far less traumatic for many than has been documented for those in their late years today.

MARRIAGE: IS OLDER BETTER?

Most women over 60 in the 1980s are or have been married. They have been married a long time: an average of 43 years (Goldman & Lord, 1983). Sixty-seven percent of women aged 55 to 64 are married with spouse present, and this is also true of 49.3% of women aged 65 to 74. The figures for men are much higher: 83.5% and 81.5%, respectively (Brubaker, 1985).

Married life for the elderly is not the same as married life for younger adults, but most research and theory development on family life relates to the young family—how families are started and how partners adjust to each other and to children. The older family is different, as Kuypers and Bengston (1983) remind us.

Marriage is "especially important" for older women, as Faver (1984) found from her research comparing three cohorts of women. She comments: "Most of these women were socialized to expect marriage, and they had fewer objective career and job opportunities as viable alternatives to marriage" (p. 128). In one of the few longitudinal studies of marital attitudes, Holahan (1984) found that over a 40-year period women reported no decline in marital satisfaction, but they did change their attitudes toward expecting a more egalitarian role in family decisions.

Atchley and Miller (1983) report on a study of 208 elderly, white, middle-class couples. On nearly all measures these couples reported positively. They enjoyed life, they enjoyed each other, and they were close to their grown children. The survey results were supported by in-depth interviews. The researchers comment:

> It was a genuine pleasure to be around these couples. They accepted one another fully, were often obviously devoted to one another, and were very much enjoying their lives together. They were very pleased that their marriages had endured. For these people, aging together was indeed a pleasure. (p. 90)

The satisfaction that elderly couples express may be the result of their shared history. "Over the course of the relationship, partners learn how best to comfort, advise, and support one another. In addition, the longevity of relationships seems to be linked to greater tolerance and acceptance—but also to less lofty expectations" (Depner & Ingersoll-Dayton, 1985). This same study of older couples found that conjugal support declined even when the need was perceived to increase. More women than men said they provided and received less support, whereas husbands perceived that more support was exchanged than wives did. As the authors point out, it is the subjective perceptions of relationships that is being reported rather than actual behavior. They conclude that "with age, adults provide their spouses less support. . . . Furthermore, husbands and wives have discrepant views about the level of support exchanged in the marital relationship."

A review of literature on the quality of life of long-term marriages provides mixed results. Some studies report increased satisfaction; others, a decrease (Ade-Ridder & Brubaker, 1983). One study (Pineo, 1968) found disenchantment taking its toll, with a drop in marital satisfaction as couples age. Sexual intercourse diminished, there were fewer shared activities, and "confiding, kissing and reciprocal settlement of disagreements became less frequent; more individuals report loneliness." One theory of the changes over time in marital satisfaction "suggests that the more one invests in a relationship, the higher it will be valued, since not to do so would imply that one has wasted one's life" (Ade-Ridder & Brubaker). Studying the perception of marital satisfaction of long-term marriages is "complicated by the likelihood of obtaining socially desirable responses," so the reality of older marriages may be difficult for researchers to catch (Ade-Ridder & Brubaker, 1983; see also Maddox, 1987).

That all may not be satisfying in older marriages was found indirectly by Caine (1978), who studied the adjustment of widows. She found a surprising number of older married women attending her discussions on the topic "Women Alone—How to Make Your Life Meaningful." These women considered themselves as alone as the widowed, divorced, or single women in the group. "They are lonely women, without a secure identity of their own, women who—deprived of love and recognition—are dying spiritually" (p. 51).

Do men and women adjust their sex-role expectations as they age? Some research suggests that there is a shift toward androgyny on the part of both husband and wife, particularly after retirement, when both come to share household tasks and men become more dependent on their wives for support and nurturance (Sinnott, 1982). However, Brubaker (1985) suggests that although attitudes may reflect some shift in sex role definitions, actual behaviors are still "gender specific" (p. 36; see also Chapter 2, this volume).

The marital satisfaction of women is also influenced by the effect of the husband's retirement on the couple's relationship. Wives who were unhappy about the retirement tended to be older, in poorer physical health, less active, and more unhappy in their marriages in general and to have husbands in manual occupations. The health of the husband also affected how the wife felt. After 10 or more years of living with a retired husband the wives reported feeling more sorry than glad about their lives (Heyman & Jeffers, 1968).

Retirement planning for a man rarely includes consideration of how this may affect his wife (Sengstock, 1987). A study by Fengler (1975) revealed that wives who were pessimistic about their husbands' retirement were concerned about how the men would deal with the excess free time and afraid that they might meddle with the wives' domestic sphere. Those who were optimistic about retirement, about 40% of the group studied, looked forward to retirement as a time when they could do things together again. The ones who expected no difference were mostly working-class women. Much of the research on retirement adjustment seems to indicate that patterns of interaction established earlier in marriage will continue in later life. However, as we point out earlier in this book, some of the resentment that men feel toward their wives upon retirement is the result of finding a wife they really did not know—an energetic and efficient manager with a range of friends and community activities that the husband does not share.

Husbands' retirement can also precipitate a new range of economic problems. Pension and/or Social Security may be inadequate, and the couple could plunge into or near poverty. Many now in their late 60s and 70s, who had been dependent on the income of only one wage earner, dwell at the margin of survival. Young women today are becoming more aware of how fragile their economic future in old age may be if they have not, as a couple, made careful plans, including contributions by the wife through her own wage earnings, pensions, and Social Security benefits.

Older married women face another unanticipated change: caring for an ailing spouse. As of 1982 over one-third of elderly men living at home and needing care were cared for by their wives; only 1 in 10 elderly disabled women were cared for by their husbands (U.S. Senate Special Committee on Aging, 1988). It has been noted with some chagrin that when they have ailing husbands "many wives are drawn back into a repetition of the mother–nurse role they experienced while raising children" (Turner, 1982). Furthermore, "the end result for women of the sex-related differential in health can be a paradoxically continued servitude and caring function instead of new freedom and individuation."

A recent study (Miller, 1987) suggests that there is a significant gender difference in the behavior and attitudes of a spouse responsible for care. Men, used to being authoritative, are able to feel adequate in taking charge of another person. "For the women, this is not the case. The control associated with raising children provides little preparation or anticipatory socialization for assumption of authority and responsibility over an adult, especially an adult male." The husbands were more concerned with aspects of the environment of care, while the wives expressed concern over the nuances of relationships and the comfort of the one being cared for. Wives more often than husbands are caregivers for their spouses, and in a number of instances these women are themselves elderly and in poor health (Brubaker, 1985). Twenty-three percent of older wives find themselves caring for a frail spouse (Stone, Cafferata, & Sange, 1987). The burden this places on wives may have a positive side. As Doty (1986) points out, the great investment made in providing this care may offset loss of other roles and give a renewed sense of usefulness to the wife.

Being part of a family is the normative expectation for most of us; yet as we grow older, roles, relationships, satisfactions, and disappointments may present us with unanticipated contingencies. For a few women the family system may completely collapse, as in the case of "shopping bag women" (Hand, 1983). Women's psychological development makes them more involved in all aspects of relationships so that the emotional and psychological burdens and rewards of family life in old age are particularly salient. (Brubaker, 1986). And it is unlikely that this will change at any time in the future.

WHEN MARRIAGE ENDS: DIVORCE

Women who are over 60 today grew up when divorce was considered a shameful admission that one had failed at marriage or had been unwise in selecting a mate. Divorce could mean social ostracism and inevitably meant loss of status and drastic reduction in income. Most women remained married no matter how dissatisfied and unhappy. Even so, 1984 statistics gathered by the Bureau of the Census show that 9% of women aged 55 to 64 have been divorced, as well as 5% of those aged 65 to 74 and 3% of those over age 75 (U.S. Senate Special Committee on Aging, 1986). Of women born between 1910 and 1939 who married, 80.77% married once and never divorced. The percentage of never-divorced declines with each decade (Norton, 1983; Weitzman, 1985). The annual divorce rate of persons 65 and older nearly doubled between 1970 and 1975, but the rate is still low compared to that of younger individuals (Uhlenberg & Meyers, 1981).

The divorce figures for older women usually do not tell us when they were divorced; divorce at age 25 without children is far different from divorce at age 40 with young children or at 55 or 60 when all children are gone. DeShane and Brown-Wilson (1982) agree that more older persons will be divorced than in the past but expect that this may be due largely to middle-aged persons divorcing and remaining unmarried while moving into old age.

How many older couples actually divorce after midlife? According to government statistics as of 1982, about 100,000 people over 55 years of age get divorced each year. An analysis of divorce statistics for the elderly by Uhlenberg and Meyers (1981) indicates how complicated it is to obtain accurate data on the lifetime divorce histories of the aged.

Most late-life divorce is initiated by husbands. Women married for 25, 30, 35, or 40 years, or even longer, who had assumed that marriage would be a lifelong commitment and had spent most or all of those years as housewives and mothers, find themselves suddenly faced with divorce (Cain, 1982). New divorce laws allowing for no-fault divorce, while reducing the amount of litigation and subterfuge, have worked to the disadvantage of women of all ages (McLinden, 1987; Weitzman, 1985). Older women may be particularly victimized by unfair divisions of property, refusal of alimony if deemed able to work—even if they have no recent or any employment history—and denial of rights to their husbands' pensions by outright fraud (Older Women's League, 1980).

Wife-initiated, late-life divorce, though still rare, can be expected to increase in the future due to the changing work habits and value systems of women. Cain (1982) reports on a University of Michigan support group for older divorced women. She found that the relatively few older women who chose divorce over the somewhat more favorable economic advantage of staying married did so because the marriage environment presented excessive stress. Divorce for them was a "court of last resort" after years of increasing dissatisfaction, of which their husbands were often unaware.

Divorce after many years of marriage, whoever initiates it, is much more difficult to deal with psychologically than divorce as a young adult when there are still many years ahead in which to develop a new relationship. Men were more depressed and unhappy, women were more apt to be emotionally upset, and older women were more apt to report health problems (Chiriboga, 1982). Unlike widowhood, there are no established social norms and self-expectations (Hennon, 1983). Less social support may be extended to the divorcee than to the widow. In his study of a sample of divorced and widowed older women, Hennon found few adjustment differences, but he points out that the group he studied might be atypical. Overall, there are few definitive studies of the impact of divorce on the elderly (Brubaker, 1985).

Many of this cohort of older women, though themselves not experiencing divorce, are likely to see their own children through the throes of marital breakup. What they do not suffer firsthand they are likely to have to deal with as a concerned and involved relative. According to Bastida (1984), in 1980 relatively few women aged 66 to 70 had been divorced, but 47.4% of women aged 26 to 30 had been divorced, which means that for many of the younger people their middle-aged or older parents could be involved. So far little attention has been paid to the impact of children's divorce on their older parents (Hennon, 1983). Though the statistics are against long-lasting marriages in contemporary America, at least the first time around, the young adult women who experience this upheaval today are better able to cope with it than preceding generations were, in large part because of the drastically changed social climate. Divorce is too common for it to result in social disapproval; it certainly made no difference in the popular vote for America's first divorced president, Ronald Reagan.

WHEN MARRIAGE ENDS: WIDOWHOOD

Two-thirds of all women over 75 who have ever married will be widows. If they are Black, then 77.9% of those over age 75 will be widowed (U.S. Senate Special Committee on Aging, 1984).

The statistics on widowhood as the normative condition for women over 65 have been available for the last several decades, but only recently has the impact of this trend been recognized by policymakers. Because women live significantly longer than men, these years of widowhood can affect the quality of life for them and their relatives, who are apt to be charged with their care as they become old and disabled during their remaining years.

As life expectancy has increased, so has the age of widowhood. In 1900 the median age for widows was 51, and it moved up to 59 in 1964. By contrast, the median age for widowers was 45 in 1900 and 65 in 1964. (Stub, 1982). In 1979 the median age for widows was 68, and for men it was 71 (Heinemann, 1983). Because most women marry older men, they will be widowed earlier, with a large proportion of their life span following the death of a spouse. The possibility of widowhood is a fact that every married woman should face, yet most widows had never considered this possibility; their husbands' deaths found them unprepared psychologically and financially (Peterson & Briley, 1977).

The general antipathy to recognize death as ever present in life characterizes our culture (Marshall, 1986) and conspires to make widowhood even more of a shock. Younger widows are particularly vulnerable since the death of a spouse is less expected. But even for older wives there may be active resistance to thinking about death, their own or that of their spouse. Only when death occurs after a long illness may there be serenity in the acceptance of the inevitable.

The circumstances that precipitated widowhood will affect how the role transition occurs or, as one widow is quoted as saying, "going from 'us' to 'me'" (Brubaker, 1985, p. 88). Brubaker identifies three different death experiences: the sudden death, due to accident or heart attack; the unexpected death, occurring during an illness that was not considered life-threatening; and the expected death, as the result of an illness such as cancer. One study (Willis, Thomas, Garry, & Goodwin, 1987) found that an unexpected event, such as the sudden illness of a loved one, was more stressful than the death of that person if the death was anticipated. Although death after a long illness might be welcomed as a relief of suffering, the wife, who in most instances is the primary caregiver and may have invested months or years in that task, is now without either husband or nursing role (Willis et al., 1987). Suicide rates for men peak in early adulthood and again in old age, but the impact of suicide on a surviving elderly spouse is not reported in the literature.

When widowhood occurs, there is a painful transition period to be negotiated: the grief and mourning that accompany bereavement. Modern America does not provide the kind of ritual community support for bereavement that serves other cultures, cushioning the impact of the event, giving the survivor visible evidence of caring, and providing legitimate expressions of grief and loss (Silverman, 1986). The Irish wake, the Jewish shiva, the extensive and heavily symbolic ceremonies of traditional cultures—for example Chinese, Japanese, Hindu—are dramatic contrasts to the sterile practices of mainstream America. Death usually occurs in a hospital, the corpse is hurried out of sight, and a brief mortuary or church and graveyard service is carried out as expeditiously as possible (Marshall, 1986). Public lamentations are considered poor taste in middle-class America.

There is no doubt that for many elderly women the passage from marriage to widowhood is their most psychologically painful experience. During this transition the widow must mourn the loss of a loved one and create a different life for herself. Some women can move into the new role rather quickly, while others may continue to grieve for many years (Parkes, 1972).

Whether loss of spouse is more difficult for one sex than for the other has long been debated. The fact that men die within a few years of the death of their wives has sometimes been causally related; more probable is the fact that men are older than women when they are widowed and thus more likely to die fairly soon in any event. A study by Scott and Kivett (1985) of 257 rural widows and widowers found that the sex of the respondent did not affect morale. If there were financial or health problems, morale was significantly affected regardless of gender. It was concluded that "although differing social role performance creates difficult and differing social adjustments for men and women, on the whole, neither sex is more adversely affected on social-psychological dimensions than the other." And "it is the availability of resources, not gender, that influences the morale of older widows and widowers." Research on bereavement goes a long way in supporting the view that the loss of a spouse is experienced by men and women as similarly devastating (Lund, Caserta, & Dimond, 1986). However, at least one study found that men considered the loss a "dismemberment," whereas women viewed it as an "abandonment" (Rando, 1984, p. 145; see also Schuchter, 1986).

Widowhood thrusts some women suddenly into a whole range of new responsibilities and decisions. In traditional couples the wife may never have handled any of the finances and may be at the mercy of unscrupulous advisors or relatives. She may be pressured to sell her home and move to a different residence or to move in with a member of her family. Some elderly couples have planned ahead for the death of a spouse, but many have not; so, compounding her grief, a widow may be confronted by many critical decisions (Brubaker, 1985). The extensive research by Lopata (1973, 1979, 1980), on which many researchers have built, provides some of the basic data about how widows in an American city adjust. Silverman (1986) provides a sensitive and comprehensive report on how different women react to widowhood, the great complexity of the relationships and problems encountered, and the kinds of help and support that may be offered.

It is expected that family members will rally around the newly widowed, and in most instances this is true. Children especially, as reported by Heinemann (1983), become involved in providing support (see also Matthews, 1979). The widows' siblings may also assist. In the stress of bereavement the widow may fail to take into account the feelings of her children at loss of their father; other unresolved issues of family relationships may become aggravated under the stress of bereavement and widowhood (Brubaker, 1985; Matthews, 1979).

The financial situation of many widows is precarious (Atchley, 1975). Inheritance and property laws, which fall within the purview of states rather than the federal government, are not uniform. The inheritance and property rights of widows depend primarily on whether legal residence is established in a community-property state or a common-law state. Depending on the laws of the state a widow may automatically inherit all or only half of the couple's property. The death of a husband may remove the wife's main source of income. Inadequate income can create social isolation; a car may be beyond the widow's means, or she may not be able to afford the clothes or fees involved in social and community groups and activities. The resulting isolation may be misunderstood as part of mourning, when in fact it may be due to lack of money.

In 1984 the median income for men over 64 was $10,450; the median income for women the same age was $6,020 (Older Women's League, 1986). In one study of elderly couples only 10% were impoverished, but after the death of the husband, 40% of the widows fell below the poverty level (Burkhauser, Holden, & Feaster, 1988; Colburn, 1987).

Reforms in retirement benefits legislated in 1984 protected women for the first time against complete loss of survivors' benefits. Before these changes went into effect a widow could find herself without any benefits. Recent reforms reduce some of the financial impact of widowhood; unfortunately, the meager amount available under most pensions, as well as Social Security, has resulted in older women being the poorest of any other segment of the population (Older Women's League, 1986). Elderly poverty in America will be widows' poverty for some time to come. Lopata and Brehm (1986) point out that the Chicago widows studied by Lopata (1973) are not typical of cohorts to come. These widows were either foreign-born or married to foreign-born mates; they had minimal education, and their work life was in low-paying jobs usually not covered by any benefits. Widows in the future are expected to be much more financially secure.

Why don't widows go to work to supplement their income? Many, of course, are too old and may be in poor health. Those who were employable and positively oriented toward working were already in the work force (Morgan, 1979, 1984). Like divorcees, older widows may lack the credentials, work experience, and skills needed to take a job, as well as having to face age and sex discrimination (Thompson, 1980; see also Chapter 7, this volume).

Loss of spouse may be the most difficult to deal with, but older women face the additional stress of loss of friends and relatives. The older a woman is, the more apt she is to find herself a lonely survivor. In the group of widows studied by Lopata (1973) one-fourth had no living relatives. Having friends in old age is associated with good adjustment and improved mental health, but the friends may die before oneself. Deaths of friends may, in fact, be more disturbing than deaths of relatives among women whose families have drifted away or died. It is also a hazard in the age-segregated housing arrangements often recommended for older people, which places women "in direct contact with deaths of numerous peers" (O'Laughlin, 1983).

Despite the fact that most elderly women who have married will find themselves widows, our culture provides few formal supports. As Silverman (1986) points out:

> The widow in our society suffers not only from the pain associated with her loss, but also from the lack of rituals that guide her mourning, help her understand what is happening, facilitate the comfort offered by others, and help her reorganize her life in light of the many changes caused by her husband's death. (p. 19)

And at the same time she is apt to be impoverished.

Dismal as the picture may be, particularly for those at the bottom of the heap, widowhood, like divorce, frees many women to do things they did not or could not do when their husbands were living. It is common to see tour groups composed mostly of single elderly women at Trafalger Square, at the Great Wall of China, at St. Peter's in Rome. Many become enthusiastic volunteers (see Chapter 5), and some even join the Peace Corps as President Jimmy Carter's mother did. Others return to school or become active in politics and in such organizations as the Older Women's League. And widows adjust better than divorcees or widowers over time (Hyman, 1983).

REMARRIAGE IN OLD AGE

Remarriage after divorce or widowhood is typical for young adults. But most women who find themselves single after age 50 are likely to remain so for the rest of their lives.

The probability of remarriage declines with age, and this decline is faster for women than for men. In 1977 the Census Bureau reported that "over three-quarters of women who lose their spouses prior to age 30 remarry, but only 6.4 percent of those aged 50–75 do so" (Morgan, 1979). Even so, widowed persons have less chance to remarry than divorced persons of the same age have. There may be a psychological barrier; widowed persons may not want to go through the same experience of death and bereavement again (a concern of women), whereas a divorced person may want to replace an unsatisfying earlier marriage with a new and promising relationship. People who remarry seem to prefer a spouse who has a marital history like their own, so among the widowed there are numerically more widowed women than widowed men available (Balkwell, 1981). This in turn may account in part for the much higher rate of remarriage by widowed older men, which is about seven times higher than the rate for widowed women (U.S. Senate Special Committee on Aging, 1984). Social stigma prevents younger men from marrying women significantly older than themselves. The future for most women who are single after age 50 is that entering another marriage is unlikely.

Data and anecdotal material indicate that in some instances adult children oppose an older parent finding another spouse, especially if the parent is widowed. They do not like to see an older parent, particularly a mother, as part of a sexual couple. The sudden role change may be difficult to accept (McKain, 1972). If there is any kind of substantial estate, children may also fear that their inheritance may be jeopardized. The changing norms of the 1980s may find children more tolerant of, if not actually encouraging parents' remarriage, not only for the sake of the widowed parent but also because they recognize that remarriage decreases their own responsibility for an aging parent. The study by Jacobs and Vinick (1979) of 24 remarried older couples found that adult children were more supportive of the remarriage than were friends of either partner.

Another factor inhibiting remarriage for older women is attitudes formed in their youth (Pifer, 1986). A study by Adams (1985) of nonmarried senior citizens in a middle-class suburb illustrates the dilemma. None of the women had close friendships with men: "These women viewed cross-sex friendships with similar age peers as synonymous with romance." They were discouraged from forming such friendships, not only because of lack of eligible males of their own age but because of perceptions that their children would object and that they would be the object of unfriendly gossip.

Financially, remarriage may be undesirable. If each partner receives Social Security benefits, upon marriage only one can be the main recipient, the other becoming the dependent spouse, which could result in a sharply decreased income. Yet for many older persons, "living in sin" is an unacceptable alternative (Jacobs & Vinick, 1979).

The ambivalence about sexuality in old age also becomes an inhibiting force. Although the sexually active old man may be derided as an "old goat" or "old lecher" if he remarries, there is acknowledgment that he can still be sexually effective. Not so in the case of the older woman, who is typically defined as sexually finished and may so view herself. This is certainly true for today's older women. Only recently has there been recognition that women's sexuality may not be impaired in old age if there is a sexually adequate partner available. It is hoped that the good word will reach women in succeeding cohorts.

THE NEVER-MARRIED

Although marriage is the expectation of most women, an increasing number of women are not getting married at all. One group is composed of mothers who did not marry, most of whom are in poverty. A second group are women who chose to remain single and without children.

There are relatively few never-married mothers—those who had children out of wedlock and did not marry—among those 50 and older today. However, the epidemic of out-of-wedlock teenage pregnancies may lead to a significant rise in the number of never-married mothers in adulthood and old age 30 years from now. If welfare policies that now penalize a family with an able-bodied but unemployed male present are changed, as is currently being discussed, these changes will be too late for several cohorts of unmarried mothers, who may well continue into adulthood and old age without a marriage partner.

Another group of never-married older women are those who have chosen not to marry. Prior to World War II a married woman faced a career dilemma: if she married, she risked instant dismissal. If she did not marry, she could pursue a career, but her achievement would be limited by persistent prejudice against women in all professions. And no matter how successful the single woman might be, she was stigmatized by society as an old maid or spinster. There was continued suspicion, too, that such women pursued careers only because no one wanted to marry them.

Following the recruitment of married women to work in war industries during World War II and the relaxation in the 1950s of prohibitions against married women working, some of those who sought careers felt able both to have families and to achieve career recognition. But most women left the workplace when they married and had children, and relatively few returned (see Chapter 7). A small group of career women persisted and chose not to marry. These women are now in their 60s and 70s. Their life stories shed an interesting and often painful light on the situations faced by single women who are now elderly (Simon, 1987). Estimates are that about 6% of elderly women (4% of elderly men) have never married (U.S. Senate Special Committee on Aging, 1984). Actually, the statistics show a 21% decline in numbers of never-married women between 1970 and 1982 (Brubaker, 1985). This decline may be due to the fact that more women can combine careers and marriage today than earlier generations could.

Research on the never-married older woman is scarce. In a review of what is available, Braito and Anderson (1983) report that single older women are better educated and have higher incomes than do single older men. The main motive given for those who remain unmarried is "freedom," particularly in the pursuit of a career. Although some regret not having had children, most are proud of their achievements. They report better physical and mental health than do those who are single because of divorce or widowhood.

Although they are better educated than single males and are more committed to their work, single women are also more vulnerable. In the words of Braito and Anderson (1983), the ever-single "are still the relatively unseen elderly and may be the ones falling through society's safety net because of lack of family assistance, death of confidants, and marching into the frail-elderly category." Even if they worked all of their lives, these single women earned significantly less than men overall even if they were in comparable jobs. Never-married women are also more apt to be institutionalized, placed in nursing homes as they became less able to care for themselves, than older single women with adult children.

In a recent study of never-married older men and women Rubenstein (1987) shows how varied the life-styles and living patterns of these individuals are. Some have lived all of their lives with their parents; and when the last parent dies, they find themselves all alone. Although the term may suggest social isolates, Rubenstein found this not to be true. In fact, a lower percentage of never-marrieds live alone than do those who are widowed, separated, or divorced. "Because more than 49% of nevermarried elderly live with others, these numbers are a good indication that for many, social isolation in the form of living alone is not a current characteristic" (p. 111).

Another group of never-married women are lesbians. The shift in public awareness of homosexuality among men and women has been a phenomenon of the late 1970s. Although difficulties still surround many who have "come out of the closet," the climate of social acceptance has dramatically improved. Lesbian women are apt to be much less visible than gay men, in part because single women living alone or with a close female friend has long been an acceptable life-style and such arrangements have not automatically labeled them as lesbian. Of course, many of them are not.

Older lesbian women have been less aggressive and less public than men about their sexual preference, more apt to create networks of friends and colleagues, and unlikely to frequent gay bars. Some once-married women may develop lesbian relationships as they reach old age and experience decision points in work and home as dissatisfied and unhappy married women or lonely single women. There is little information about this group; what exists is mostly anecdotal and individual (Adelman, 1986; see also Maddox, 1987; Simon, 1987).

The women's movement has opened up new options and new careers for women; significant numbers have flocked to previously male-dominated professions. More women, it is predicted, will seek lifelong careers, and many of these may find it difficult or undesirable to combine marriage, children, and career achievement. It is thus possible that the trend toward fewer never-married women in old age could be reversed for succeeding cohorts.

WHERE IS GRANDMOTHER?

One of the leading social markers of old age has been becoming a grandparent. This may no longer be true. Earlier marriages and more closely spaced child rearing has meant that many a 45-year-old woman discovers (possibly to her distress) that she is now a grandmother and she certainly does not consider herself "old" (Wood & Robertson, 1976). In a group of Black families studied by Burton and Bengston (1985) there were some women who had become grandmothers between the ages of 25 and 40, with a median age of 32! At the other extreme, there is a pronounced trend emerging in the 1980s for later first marriages and postponed childbearing until the last biologically safe age, between 35 and 40. If the children of these women follow their mother's model and in turn have children relatively late, the grandmothers could be in their 70s before the first grandchild is born.

There is not much research on grandparenting. The recently published *Encyclopedia of Aging* (Maddox, 1987) does not even have a separate entry for this topic. Sex of grandchild and of grandparent are assumed to be important, but the research is very scattered and incomplete (Troll, 1980).

Whenever grandmotherhood occurs, it initiates a whole new set of relationships. An extensive study of three-generation families of Italian Americans found that older immigrant Italian women are ambivalent about their role as grandmothers. The older women sought a more independent and less family-oriented role, whereas their daughters wanted to retain greater mother-daughter relatedness and more grandmotherly behavior. As a result, there was continued tension between the two generations (Cohler & Grunebaum, 1981).

Despite the stereotypes, grandmothers are neither a bountiful source of gifts nor interfering nags. Neugarten and Weinstein's (1968) study of grandparents identified five groupings: some were involved in providing "fun" for their grandchildren—the indulgent grandmother of the stereotypes. A second group were interested but remained "formal" and psychologically remote, maintaining only intermittent contact; these were primarily older grandmothers. A third group became "surrogate parents" and were almost entirely composed of grandmothers. A fourth group were "reservoirs of wisdom" and were mostly grandfathers. A fifth group were distant and almost invisible, more likely to be composed of grandfathers than grandmothers.

Grandchildren's contact with grandparents follows mothers' relationships; bonds with maternal grandmothers were reported to be closer than those with paternal grandparents (Matthews & Sprey, 1985). Adult grandchildren also were more apt to be significantly closer to maternal than to paternal grandparents, and the maternal grandmother was the person with the closest emotional ties (Hoffman, 1979-80).

Older women can also anticipate becoming great-grandmothers. Fully one-half of all persons 65 and over with living children are members of four-generation families (Wentowski, 1985). Women were both happy and ambivalent about becoming great-grandmothers. Most of those studied by Wentowski felt less responsibility for great-grandchildren than they had for grandchildren. For these women, "relationships with adult children were the most important emotionally and socially, and the women depended on the middle generations to link them to their great-grandchildren."

The complexity of generational relationships increases with the divorce of adult children (Hagestad, 1986). Which grandparents can claim the allegiance of these children? If a bond has been created prior to divorce and remarriage, will the new partner accept visits by grandchildren to the parents of a former partner? Or if custody is given to the in-law, will grandparents be able to retain attachments to the grandchildren? The kinds of problems that emerge depend on previous family interaction patterns, tensions developing from different dependency expectations, the age of the grandmothers, and the timing of the children's divorce (Johnson, 1985). In a study of 50 parent-grandparent dyads (Johnson & Barer, 1987), it was found that divorce had occurred not only for adult children but also for grandparents. Some at both generational levels had remarried, adding new stepchildren or step-grandchildren. It was found that paternal grandmothers were far more likely to retain contact with former daughters-in-law than were maternal grandmothers to keep contact with former sons-in-law. For some, divorce meant a shrinking of the kin network; for others, it meant expansion.

Although divorce is becoming more common at every stage in family life, until recently there was little research regarding the role of grandparents (DeShane & Brown-Wilson, 1982; Uhlenberg & Meyers, 1981). What research there is indicates that the role of grandmother is marginal whether the family is intact or not; she lives on the fringe of the family group in most instances. An exception is the active role of the black grandmother, who is often seen as the force maintaining family stability (Lesnoff-Caravaglia, 1982). On the whole, though they may assume an active role in cases of family disruption or emergency, "grandparents do not seem to expect tangible commitments from their grandchildren; they appear to be content if their grandchildren give them a modicum of interest and concern however ritualistic and superficial this may be" (Wood & Robertson, 1976, p. 302; see also Bengston & Robertson, 1985; Cherlin & Furstenberg, 1986).

MOTHERS AND DAUGHTERS: THE ENDURING BOND

A son is a son till he takes him a wife;
A daughter's a daughter for the rest of her life

There has been a myth subscribed to by both Americans and foreigners that this generation of Americans does not provide as much care for elderly parents as do other cultures. In fact, as Brody (1985) points out, in modern America most elderly are cared for at home and placed in nursing homes only when their disabilities can no longer be handled by relatives or when single elderly women are without close family members. Recent extensive research into who cares for the elderly has now established that, yes, old people are cared for by their families, and those who do most of the actual caring are adult daughters or daughters-in-law. The statistics are impressive: According to a report prepared for the House Select Committee on Aging (1987), "Women can expect to spend more years caring for an aging parent than for a dependent child. . . . Today, the average woman will spend 17 years of her adult life caring for a dependent child and 18 years helping her elderly parent" (p. 9).

As Figure 6.1 indicates, men provide 28% of the care that the elderly receive, and women account for the remaining 72% of care. If one leaves out the professional caregivers (nurses and aides), "caregivers tend to be female, about 57 years of age, and live in the same household as the care recipient" (House Select Committee on Aging, 1987, p. 17). They are themselves apt to be in poor or frail health, less likely to be employed, and poor or near poor (House Select Committee on Aging, 1987). The older woman can expect, on the one hand, to require assistance from her daughter or to be the giver of such care in late middle age to her mother. Older mothers are cared for more than older fathers because there are, in fact, more mothers living to old age.

Daughters may also feel more of a filial obligation toward mothers than they do toward fathers, who presumably are better able to care for themselves (Finley, Roberts, & Banahan, 1988). Also, more older men have spouses to care for them. At ages 65 to 74, 81.5% of men and only 49.3% of women had spouses at home. At age 75, 22.4% of women were still married; 70.2% of men over 75 had spouses. (U.S. Senate Special Committee on Aging, 1984).

The above data reflect the higher rate of remarriage of men after divorce or widowerhood and also the disparity in death rates: women are the survivors. Since women must look to younger generations for help, this may be "one reason why women, throughout their adulthood, invest more time and energy in intergenerational ties than men do" (Hagestad, 1986). Though this may suggest a more deliberate motivation in the ways women relate to their children, we know that women place a high priority on retaining kin relationships. Proximity, of course, helps: daughters who live nearby are the ones most apt to be identified as sympathetic and helpful (Aldous et al., 1985).

Whatever their age, women are involved in intergenerational caring. An intensive study of women in three-generation families found that not only do most daughters believe that they have an obligation to provide support for their older mothers, they also believe that their own daughters

FIGURE 6.1 Distribution of informal caregivers by relationship to elderly care recipient: 1982.

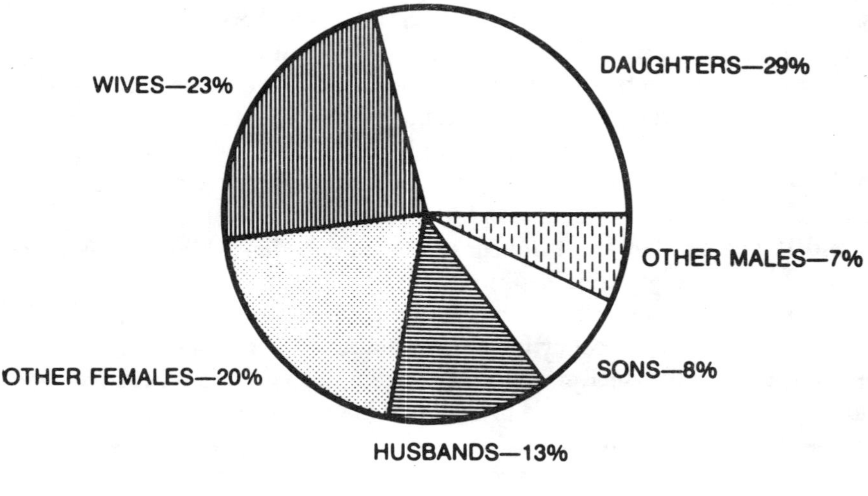

From Select Committee on Aging, U.S. House of Representatives. *Exploding the Myth: Caregiving in America*, January 1987.

Caregiver population includes primary and secondary caregivers.

should share this belief (Brody, Johnson, Fulcomer, & Lang, 1983; Brody, Johnson, & Fulcomer, 1984). A study of 75 Jewish widows, aged 65 to 84, showed that they maintained positive and mutually valuable relationships with their daughters, which, although fluctuating in terms of satisfaction, did not resemble the neurotic clinging or tension between the generations that has often been assumed (Bromberg, 1983a, 1983b). Hochschild (1978), who studied a housing project with mostly elderly women, reported: "Women have traditionally bound the generations together, and in Merrill Court it is the daughters who most often visit and call" (Bromberg, 1983a, p. 90).

Why are daughters the caregivers of their mothers? Cohler and Grunebaum (1981) locate the source in the family.

> The biosocial fact of the parental imperative acts as the background against which the child's own sex-role socialization takes place . . . . [The result is] the encouragement of a kind of closeness and lack of separateness between young women and their mothers that is not present in the relationship between young men and their fathers (p. 23; see also Finley et al., 1988)

The relationship is not based solely on bonds of affection, however, but has strong elements of lineage loyalty and the concept of filial responsibility, which we in the West have so admired in Asian cultures yet have overlooked behind our own doors.

The strength of this "female axis" may have been underestimated.

> Mothers and daughters can now expect more than a half-century of joint survival. The first part of the next century may witness generations of mothers and daughters who not only share the experiences of growing old, but whose adult lives have shared more similarities than was the case in the latter part of this century. (Hagestad, 1986)

The difference between the caregiving provided by sons and daughters was studied by Horowitz (1985b). Only if a female sibling is unavailable will a son take over primary responsibility, and "when they do serve as caregivers, they tend to provide less extensive support to their older parent as compared to adult daughters and to have less stressful caregiving experiences"(see also Ungerson, 1987).

Adult daughters who provide care may face unanticipated personal conflicts (Marshall, Rosenthal, & Synge, 1983; Matthews, 1979; Scharlach, 1987a, b). It is now popular to call those women who must manage a balancing act between the competing expectations of their children and parents the "sandwich generation." When the daughters are dealing with the tensions and demands of their own adolescent children, their aging mothers are also asking for personal as well as material support. The emotional pull between these two kinds of dependents (often including a nonsupportive husband) can be excruciating (Steuve & O'Donnell, 1984). Recognition of the difficulties that these women face has produced new interest in support groups for them (Fischer, 1986; Scharlach, 1987; Wasserman, 1983).

There is indeed a high level of psychological stress experienced by those who must care for impaired elderly (Gallagher, 1985). Whatever problems and tensions may exist between adult daughters and older mothers are exacerbated if the mother is physically frail or demented (Deimling & Bass, 1986; Zarit, Reever, & Bach-Peterson, 1980). Many popular books have been published giving advice on all levels of care (Cicirelli, 1981; McNulty & Dann, 1985; Sommers & Shields, 1987). The title of one such book is revealing: *Caring for an Aging Parent: Have I Done All I Can?* (Ball, 1987). A leading advocate group for the aging, the National Council on Aging, has established a separate division, Family Caregivers of the Aging.

Brody (1985) has pointed out that care for elderly parents has become so common due to the longevity of the older generation that it can be considered a "normative family stress." Although the need for older parents to require economic support from their adult children has dropped significantly—from about 50% in 1950 to 1.5% in 1979—other kinds of care and attention make heavy demands. There is every indication that the bonds of caring that tie mothers and daughters together today will be as strong for succeeding generations as they are today; although Hess and Waring (1983) warn that changes in federal policies of financial versus service support for the elderly may further complicate family decisions (see Horowitz, 1985a, for a comprehensive review).

"GRANNY BASHING"

The positive outcomes of family caregiving are evident in much of the literature we have reviewed above. But there is another side to the coin. One of the less savory outcomes of the increase in the number of dependent elders, most of them women, has been the concomitant increase in our knowledge of the abuse they suffer at the hands of their caretakers.

Abuse of the elderly is far from new although it went unacknowledged for generations. Prior to our own century, when sufficient national affluence permitted assignment of some resources to the care of the nonproductive old and disabled, such persons were at the mercy of relatives and meager private charitable institutions. History shows that there was not much real charity available from either source (Haber, 1983).

Once a highly taboo topic, since it went against all of our vaunted notions of filial devotion, elder abuse—like child abuse and wife battering—has come out of the closet. Until very recently only anecdotal data suggested the existence of this social pathology (Davidson, 1979). Elder abuse is also difficult to document. The frail elderly may be completely invisible because their disabilities keep them at home, and even potential friends who might have visited are themselves too frail to venture out.

Many older women are extremely reluctant to admit to abuse, which in their view would be an admission of their failure as mothers. The daughters who provide the most solace to their elderly mothers are also the ones most often implicated in abuse (Gelles & Cornell, 1985; Horowitz, 1985b).

One study, cited by Gelles and Cornell (1985), found that in only one out of four cases of abuse had the victim been the complainant. The dependence of the woman on her abusers serves as a major restraint. The difficulty a young woman has when trying to leave a husband who batters her is well documented; how much more difficult it is for the frail and dependent older woman. The alternative to the abusive home—a nursing home or being frightened and alone in a room or apartment—may be feared more. Persons who might suspect abuse—friends, social workers, doctors, emergency room staff, financial advisors—must be aware not only of the symptoms of abuse but the tendency of many elderly women to deny that it has occurred (Quinn & Tomita, 1986). The problem is compounded by the fact that professionals may also have different, sometimes contradictory, views of what elder abuse is (Hickey & Douglass, 1981).

Elder abuse has been defined by the AARP (1987) as falling into five categories: passive neglect, psychological abuse, material/financial abuse, active neglect, and physical abuse. Sengstock and Barrett (1986) add violation of rights (see also Quinn & Tomita, 1986; Valentine & Cash, 1986).

When all forms of neglect and abuse are considered, the best estimate is that 5% of the elderly are affected (Poertner, 1986). Of this group, estimates are that 70% are women, which is to be expected since the largest group of frail elderly are older single women. The typical victim is female, average age 75 years (Winter, 1986). In another study based on a stratified random sample (Pillemer & Finkelhor, 1988), there were contradictory findings. Those living with a spouse were particularly liable to abuse, which in this group meant that more husbands than wives were abused, as well as those in poor heath, and males in general. This discrepancy—other studies report women as most apt to be abused—is based on the fact that the women were more seriously hurt and more apt to be very upset; therefore, they reported the incident to protective agencies. Overall, however, the authors conclude that the incidence of abuse is no more than 1.8 per 1000 reported, but that many more, as high as 26 per 1000, may actually be the case.

Why does abuse occur? In a number of studies the abuser is dependent on the victim for housing and financial support and may be dissatisfied or angered by the older person's behavior or how she uses her economic power (Atchley, 1988). Unresolved tensions from earlier parent-child relationships may precipitate abuse when the parent is no longer powerful. Children who were abused by parents may, when the parents are dependent on them for care, become the abusers. Where there is actual violence, this may be related to characteristics of the abuser rather than those of the victim. A study by Sengstock, Barrett, and Graham (1984) found that in many instances the abusing family members had been subject to many kinds of stress in addition to having the care of an elderly mother. The disability of the victim may impose an intolerable burden on the caretaker who is not equipped to provide round-the-clock nursing care or deal with incontinence or the irrationality of those suffering from senile dementias (Poertner, 1986; see also Anetzberger, 1987; Deimling & Bass, 1986; Langley, 1981; Stone, Cafferata, & Dange, 1987; Zarit, Reever, & Bach-Peterson, 1980).

The lack of programs and resources to care for the disabled elderly has brought the dilemmas of the caretakers to public attention. Support groups for relatives of those with Alzheimer's disease have sprung up in many communities. Books of advice have proliferated (Anetzberger, 1987; Ball, 1987; Cicirelli, 1981; Pillmar & Wolf, 1986). The first step in dealing with elderly abuse is the recognition of the problem; the next step is programs to deal with policies and procedures to aid both abusers and their victim. Like many other problems of the elderly, this is a women's problem.

SUMMARY

The family is the most salient context in which women grow old. The generation now in their 60s and above became adult when the focus of their energy and the source of their sense of self and self-esteem came from their family roles. They are women who knew that family concerns always overrode career or personal interests. Then, as they aged, things changed. They experienced divorce, death of a spouse, financial insecurity, physical ailments and disability, and new dependency on those who were once dependent on them—their children. They retained close ties with adult daughters and often relished being grandmothers.

The coming generations of older women may be different in some significant ways. "One of the most dramatic contrasts between the elderly of today and the cohorts who will constitute the elderly of tomorrow is the portion of their life span in which they and the society in which they live have been age conscious" (Cutler, 1981). Women make up the majority of the elderly and also of those who care for them. The quality of family relationships influences our growing up and our growing old.

REFERENCES

Adams, R. (1985). People would talk: Normative barriers to cross-sex friendships for elderly women. *The Gerontologist, 25*(6), 605–611.

Adelman, M. (Ed.). (1986). *Long time passing: Lives of older lesbians.* Bostom: Alyson.

Ade-Ridder, L., & Brubaker, T. H. (1983). Quality of long-term marriages. In T. H. Brubaker (Ed.), *Family relationships in later life* (pp. 21–30). Beverly Hills, CA: Sage.

Aldous, J., Klaus, E., & Klein, D. M. (1985). The understanding heart: Aging parents and their favorite children. *Child Development, 56*, 303–316.

Alpert, J. L., & Richardson, M. S. (1980). Parenting. In L. W. Poon (Ed.), *Aging in the 1980's* (pp. 441–454). Washington, DC: American Psychological Association.

American Association of Retired Persons. (1987). *Domestic mistreatment of the elderly*. Washington, DC: Author.

Anetzberger, G. J. (1987). *The etiology of elder abuse by adult offspring*. Springfield, IL: Charles C. Thomas.

Atchley, R. C. (1975). Dimensions of widowhood in later life. *The Gerontologist, 15*(2), 176–178.

Atchley, R. C. (1988). *Social forces and aging: An introduction to social gerontology* (5th ed.). Belmont, CA: Wadsworth.

Atchley, R. C., & Miller, S. J. (1983). Types of elderly couples. In T. H. Brubaker (Ed.), *Family relationships in later life* (pp. 77–99). Beverly Hills, CA: Sage.

Balkwell, C. (1971, January). Transition to widowhood: A review of the literature. Family Relations, pp. 117–127.

Ball, J. A. (1987). *Caring for an aging parent: Have I done all I can?* New York: Prometheus Books.

Bastida, E. (1984, March). Introduction: Demographic profile of today's older women. *Older Women, Current Issues and Problems*. pp. 5–14.

Bengston, V. L., & Robertson, J. (Eds.). (1985). *Grandparenthood*. Beverly Hills, CA: Sage.

Braito, R., & Anderson, D. (1983). The ever-single elderly woman. In E. W. Markson (Ed.), *Older women* (pp. 195–226). Lexington, MA: Lexington Books.

Brody, E. M. (1981). Women in the middle and family help to older people. *The Gerontologist, 21*(5), 471–478.

Brody, E. M. (1985). Parent care as a normative family stress. *The Gerontologist, 25*(1), 19–29.

Brody, E., Johnson, P. T., & Fulcomer, M. C. (1984). What should adult children do for elderly parents? Opinions and preferences of three generations of women. *Journal of Gerontology, 6*, 736–746.

Brody, E. M., Johnson, P. T., Fulcomer, M., & Lang, A. M. (1983). Women's changing roles and help to elderly parents: Attitudes of three generations of women. *Journal of Gerontology, 38*(5), 597–607.

Bromberg, E. M. (1983a). Mother-daughter relationships in later life: The effect of quality of relationship upon mutual aid. *Journal of Gerontological Social Work, 6*(1), 75–92.

Bromberg, E. M. (1983b). Mother-daughter relationships in later life: Negating the myths. *Aging, 340*, 14–20.

Brown, D. S. (1986). *Handle with care: A question of Alzheimer's*. Buffalo, NY: Prometheus Books.

Brubaker, T. H. (1985). *Later life families*. Beverly Hills, CA: Sage.

Brubaker, T. (1986). *Married for fifty years*. Boston: D. C. Heath.

Burkhauser, R. V., Holden, K. C., & Feaster, D. (1988). Incidence, timing, and events associated with poverty: A dynamic view of poverty in retirement. *Journal of Gerontology, 43*(2), S46–52.

Burr, W. R. (1970). Satisfaction with various aspects of marriage over the life cycle: A random middle-class sample. *Journal of Marriage and Family, 32*, 29–37.

Burton, L. M., & Bengston, V. L. (1985). Black grandmothers: Issues of timing and continuity of roles. In V. L. Bengston & J. Robertson (Eds.), *Grandparenthood* (pp. 61–78). Beverly Hills, CA: Sage.

Cain, B. S. (1982, December 12). Divorce at late life. *New York Times Magazine*, pp. 88–96.

Caine, L. (1978). *Lifelines*. New York: William Morrow.

Cherlin, A. J., & Furstenberg, F. F. (1986). *The new American grandparent: A place in the family, a life apart*. New York: Basic Books.

Chiriboga, D. A. (1982). Adaptation to marital separation in later and earlier life. *Journal of Gerontology, 37*(1), 235–250.

Cicirelli, V. G. (1981). *Helping elderly parents: The role of adult children*. Dover, MA: House Publishers.

Cohler, B. J., & Grunebaum, H. U. (1981). *Mothers, grandmothers and daughters*. New York: Wiley.

Colburn, D. (1987, April 28). The woes of widows in America. *The Washington Post Health*, pp. 8–9.

Cooper, K. L., & Gutman, D. L. (1987). Gender, identity, and ego-mastery style in middle-aged, pre- and post-empty nest women. *The Gerontologist, 27*(3), 347–352.

Cutler, N. E. (1981). Political characteristics of elderly cohorts of the twenty-first century. In S. B. Kiesler, J. M. Morgan, & V. K. Oppenheimer (Eds.), *Aging social issues*. 151–159. New York: Academic Books.

Davidson, J. L. (1979). Elder abuse. In Marilyn Block & Jan D. Sinnott (Eds.), *The battered elder syndrome: An exploratory study*. 57–66. College Park, MD: University of Maryland, Center on Aging.

Deimling, G. T., & Bass, D. M. (1986). Symptoms of mental impairment among elderly and their effects on family caregivers. *Journal of Gerontology, 41*(6), 778–784.

Depner, C. E., & Ingersoll-Dayton, B. (1985). Conjugal social support patterns in later life. *Journal of Gerontology, 40*(6), 761–766.

DeShane, M. R., & Brown-Wilson, K. (1982). Divorce in late life: A call for research. Journal of Divorce, 4(4), 81–91.

Deutscher, I. (1968). The quality of postparental life. In B. L. Neugarten (Ed.), *Middle age and aging*. Chicago: University of Chicago Press.

Doty, P. (1986). Family care of the elderly: The role of public policy. *Milbank Memorial Fund, 64*, 34–75.

Dressler, D. M. (1973). Life adjustment of retired couples. *International Journal of Aging and Human Development, 4*(4), 335–349.

Faver, C. A. (1984). *Women in transition: Career, family and life satisfaction in three cohorts*. New York: Praeger.

Fengler, A. P. (1975). Attitudinal orientations of wives toward their husband's retirement. *International Journal of Aging and Human Development, 6*, 139–152.

Finley, D. J., Roberts, M. D., & Banahan, B. F. (1988). Motivators and inhibitors of attitudes of filial obligation toward aging parents. *The Gerontologist, 28*(1), 73–78.

Fischer, L. R. (1986). *Linked lives: Adult daughters and their mothers*. New York: Harper and Row.

Gallagher, D. E. (1985). Intervention strategies to assist caregivers of frail elders: Current research status and future research directions. In C. Eisdorfer (Ed.), *Annual review of gerontology and geriatrics* (Vol. 5, 249–282. New York: Springer Publishing Co.

Geer, E. M., & Kimball, M. M. (1987). *Women and aging*. Toronto, Canada: Butterworths.

Gelles, R. J., & Cornell, C. P. (1985). *Intimate violence in families*. Beverly Hills, CA: Sage.

Glenn, N. D. (1975). Psychological well-being in the postparental stage: Some evidence from national surveys. *Journal of Marriage and the Family, 37*(1), 105–110.

Goldman, N., & Lord, G. (1983, May). Sex differences in life cycle measures of widowhood. *Demography*, pp. 177–195.

Grambs, J. D. (1987). Are older women teachers different? *Journal of Education, 169*(1), 47–64.

Haber, C. (1983). *Beyond sixty-five: The dilemma of old age in America's past*. Cambridge, England: Cambridge University Press.

Hagestad, G. O. (1986). The aging society as a context for family life. *Daedalus, 115*(1), 119–140.

Hand, J. (1983). Shopping-bag women: Aging deviates in the city. In E. W. Markson (Ed.), *Older women* (pp. 155–177). Lexington, MA: Lexington Books.

Heinemann, G. D. (1983). Family involvement and support for widowed persons. In T. H. Brubaker (Ed.), *Family relationships in later life*, 127–148.

Hennon, C. B. Divorce and the elderly: A neglected area of research. In T. H. Brubaker (Ed.) *Family Relationships in Later Life* (pp. 149–172). Beverly Hills, CA: Sage.

Hess, B. B., & Waring, J. (1983). Family relationships of older women: A women's issue. In E. W. Markson (Ed.), *Older women* (pp. 227–252). Lexington, MA: Lexington Books.

Heyman, D., & Jeffers, F. (1968). Wives and retirement: A pilot study. *Journal of Gerontology, 23*(5), 488–496.

Hickey, T., & Douglass, R. L. (1981). Neglect and abuse of older family members: Professionals' perspectives and case experiences. *The Gerontologist, 21*(2), 171–176.

Higgins, D. H. (1975, October). *Female "nestitis": Self-concept, role flexibility, and achievement.* Paper presented at the 28th annual meeting of the Gerontological Society, Louisville, KY.

Hochschild, A. R. (1978). *The unexpected community: Portrait of an old age subculture.* Berkeley, CA: University of California Press.

Hoffman, E. (1979). Young adults' relations with their grandparents: An exploratory study. *International Journal of Aging and Human Development, 10*(3), 299–309.

Holahan, C. K. (1984). Marital attitudes over 40 years: A longitudinal and cohort analysis. *Journal of Gerontology, 38*(1), 49–57.

Horowitz, A. (1985a). Family caregiving of the frail elderly. In C. Eisdorfer (Ed.), *Annual review of gerontology and geriatrics* (Vol. 5, 194–246. New York: Springer Publishing Co.

Horowitz, A. (1985b). Sons and daughters as caregivers of older parents: Differences in role performance and consequences. *The Gerontologist, 25*(6), 612–617.

Hyman, H. H. (1983). *Of time and widowhood.* Durham, NC: Duke University Press.

Jacobs, R. H., & Vinick, B. H. (1979) *Re-engagement in later life: Re-employment and remarriage.* Stamford, CT: Greylock Publications.

Johnson, C. L. (1985). Grandparenting options in divorcing families: An anthropological perspective. In V. L. Bengston & J. F. Robertson (Eds.), *Grandparenthood* (pp. 85–96). Beverly Hills, CA: Sage.

Johnson, C. L., & Barerm B. M. (1987), Marital instability and the changing kinship networks of grandparents. *The Gerontologist, 27*(3), 330–335.

Kaufert, P. A. (1985). Midlife in the Midwest: Canadian women in Manitoba. In J. K. Brown & V. Kerns (Eds.), *In her prime: A new view of middle-aged women* (pp. 181–197). South Hadley, MA: Bergin and Garvey.

Kerckhoff, A. C. (1966). Family patterns and morale in retirement. In I. H. Simpson & J. C. McKinney (Eds.), *Social aspects of aging.* Durham, NC: Duke University Press.

Kuypers, J. A., & Bengston, V. L. (1983). Toward competence in the older family.

In T. H. Brubaker (Ed.), *Family relationships in later life* (pp. 77–90). Beverly Hills, CA: Sage.

Langley, A. (1981). Abuse of the elderly. *Human Services, 27,* 19–27.

Lesnoff-Caravaglia, G. (1982). The black "Granny" and the Soviet "Babushka": Commonalities and contrasts. In R. C. Manuel (Ed.), *Minority aging* (pp. 109–114). Westport, CT: Greenwood Press.

Livson, F. B. (1976). Patterns of personality development in middle-aged women: A longitudinal study. *International Journal of Aging and Human Development, 7*(2), 107–115.

Long, J., & Porter, K. L. (1984). Multiple roles of midlife women. In A. Baruch & J. Brooks-Gunn (Eds.), *Women in midlife* (pp. 109–159). New York: Plenum Press.

Lopata, H. Z. (1973). *Widowhood in an American city.* Cambridge, MA: Scheckman.

Lopata, H. Z. (1979). *Women as widows.* New York: Elsevier.

Lopata, H. Z. (1980). The widowed family member. In N. Dattan & N. Lohman (Eds.), *Transitions of aging* (pp. 93–115). New York: Academic Press.

Lopata, H. Z., & Brehm, H. P. (1986). *Widows and dependent wives: From social program to federal program.* New York: Praeger.

Lowenthal, M. F. (1975). Psychosocial variations across the adult life course: Frontiers for research and policy. Part 1. *The Gerontologist, 15*(1), 6–12.

Lowenthal, M. F., Thurnher, M., & Chiriboga, D. (1975). *Four stages of life: A comparative study of women and men facing transition.* San Francisco: Jossey-Bass.

Lund, D. A., Caserta, M. S., & Diamond, M. F. (1986). Gender differences through two years of bereavement among the elderly. *The Gerontologist, 26*(3), 314–320.

Maddox, G. (Ed.). (1987). *The encyclopedia of aging.* New York: Springer Publishing Co.

Marikides, K., Boldt, J. S., & Ray, L. A. (1986). Sources of helping and intergenerational solidarity: A three generation study of Mexican Americans. *Journal of Gerontology, 41,* 506–511.

Marshall, V. W. (1986). A sociological perspective on aging and dying. In V. W. Marshall (Ed.), *Later life* (pp. 125–146). Beverly Hills, CA: Sage.

Marshall, V., Rosenthal, C. J., Synge, J. (1983). Concerns about parental health. In E. J. Markson (Ed.), *Older women* (pp. 253–273). Lexington, MA: Lexington Books.

Matthews, S. H. (1979). *The social world of older women: Management of self-identity.* Beverly Hills, CA: Sage.

Matthews, S. H., & Sprey, J. (1984). The impact of divorce on grandparenthood: An exploratory study. *The Gerontologist, 24*(1), 41–47.

Matthews, S. H., & Sprey, J. (1985). Adolescent's relationships with grandparents: An empirical contribution to conceptual clarification. *Journal of Gerontology, 40*(5), 621–626.

McKain, W. (1972). A new look at old marriages. *Family Coordinator, 21,* 60–61.

McLinden, J. B. (1987). Separate but unequal: The economic disaster of divorce for women and children. *Family Law Quarterly, 21*(3), 351–409.

McNulty, E. G., & Dann, M. S. (1985). *The dilemma of caring for your loved one.* Springfield, IL: Charles C. Thomas.

Miller, B. (1987). Gender and control among spouses of the cognitively impaired: A research note. *The Gerontologist, 27*(4), 447–453.

Morgan, L. A. (1979). Problems of widowhood. In P. K. Ragan (Ed.), *Aging parents* (pp. 66–82). Los Angeles, CA: University of Southern California Press.

Morgan, L. A. (1984). Continuity and change in the labor force activity of recently widowed women. *The Gerontologist, 24*(5), 530–535.

Morris, J. (1988). *The buzz of autumn: Children of older parents.* New York: Columbia University Press.

Neugarten, B. L., & Datan, N. (1973). Sociological perspectives on the life cycle. In P. Baltes & K. W. Schaie (Eds.), *Life-span developmental psychology.* New York: Academic Press.

Neugarten, B. L., & Weinstein, K. K. (1968). The changing American grandparent. In B. L. Neugarten (Ed.), *Middle age and aging.* Chicago: University of Chicago Press.

Norton, A. J. (1980). Family life cycle: 1980. *Journal of Marriage and the Family, 45*(2), 267–275.

O'Laughlin, K. (1983). The final challenge: Facing death. In E. W. Markson (Ed.), *Older women* (pp. 275–296). Lexington, MA: Lexington Books.

Older Women's League. (1980, August). The disillusionment of divorce for older women. *Gray Paper*, p. 6.

Parkes, C. M. (1972). *Bereavement: Studies of grief in adult life.* New York: International Universities Press.

Pearlin, L. I. (1975). Sex roles and depression. In N. Datan & L. H. Ginsberg (Eds.), *Life-span developmental psychology: Normative life crisis.* New York: Academic Press.

Peterson, J. A., & Briley, M. P. (1977). *Widows and widowhood.* New York: Association Press.

Pifer, A. (1986). The public policy response to population aging. *Daedalus, 115*(1), 373–393.

Pillemer, J., & Finkelhor, D. (1988). The prevalence of elder abuse: A random sample survey. *The Gerontologist, 28*(1), 51–57.

Pillmar, K., & Wolf, R. S. (Eds.). (1986). *Elder abuse: Conflict in the family.* Dover, MA: Auburn House.

Pineo, P. C. (1968). Disenchantment in the later years of marriage. In M. Sussman (Ed.), *Sourcebook in marriage and family.* New York: Houghton Mifflin.

Poertner, J. (1986). Estimating the incidence of abused older persons. *Journal of Gerontological Social Work*, 9(3), 3–15.

Powell, B. (1977). The empty nest, employment, and psychiatric symptoms in college-educated women. *Psychology of Women Quarterly, 2*, 35–43.

Quinn, M. J., & Tomita, S. K. (1986). *Elder abuse and neglect: Causes, diagnosis, and intervention strategies*. New York: Springer Publishing Co.

Radloff, L. L. (1980). Depression and the empty nest. *Sex Roles, 6*(6), 775–781.

Rando, T. A. (1984). *Grief, dying and death: Clinical intervention for care givers*. Champaign, IL: Research Press.

Reiss, S., & O'Neil, M. (1987). Adults perceptions of their mothers: A life span analysis. *Psychological Record, 34*, 333–342.

Rubenstein, R. L. (1987). Never married elderly as a social type: Re-evaluating some images. *The Gerontologist, 27*(1), 108–113.

Rubin, L. B. (1979). *Women of a certain age: The midlife search for self*. New York: Harper.

Scharlach, A. E. (1987a). Relieving feelings of strain among women with elderly mothers. *Psychology and Aging, 2*(1), 9–13.

Scharlach, A. E. (1987b). Role strain in mother–daughter relationships in later life. *The Gerontologist, 27*(5), 627–631.

Schecter, J. H. (1985). The retirement equity act: Meeting women's pension needs. *Compensation Review, 17*, 13–21.

Schuchter, W. R. (1986). *Dimensions of grief: Adjustments to death of a spouse*. San Francisco: Jossey-Bass.

Scott, J. P., & Kivett, V. R. (1985). Differences in the morale of older, rural widows and widowers. *International Journal of Aging and Human Development, 21*(2), 121–135.

Select Committee on Aging, House of Representatives. (1987). *Exploding the myths: Caregiving in America*. Committee Publication #99-611. Washington, DC: U.S. Government Printing Office.

Sengstock, M. C. (1987, April). *Retirement planning—a feminist view*. Paper presented to the North Central Sociological Association, Cincinnati, OH.

Sengstock, M. C., & Barrett, S. (1986). Elderly victims of family abuse, neglect and maltreatment: Can legal assistance help? *Journal of Gerontological Social Work, 9*(3), 43–61.

Sengstock, M. C., Barrett, S., & Graham, R. (1984). Abused elders: Victims of villains or of circumstances? *Journal of Gerontological Social Work, 8*(1/2), 101–111.

Silverman, P. R. (1986). *Widow-to-widow*. New York: Springer Publishing Co.

Simon, B. L. (1987). *Never married women*. Philadelphia: Temple University Press.

Sinnott, J. D. (1982). Correlates of sex roles of older adults. *Journal of Gerontology, 37*, 587–594.

Sommers, T., & Shields, L. (1987). *Women take care*. Gainesville, TX: Triad.

Spanier, G., Lewis, R., & Cole, C. (1975). Marital adjustment over the life cycle: The issue of curvilinearity. *Journal of Marriage and Family, 37*, 263–275.

Spence, D., & Lonner, T. (1971). The "empty nest": A transition within motherhood. *Family Coordinator, 20*(4), 369–376.

Steinman, L. A. (1979). Reactivated conflicts with aging parents. In P. K. Ragan (Ed.), *Aging parents* (pp. 126–148). Los Angeles: University of California Press.

Steuve, A., & O'Donnell, L. (1984). The daughter of aging parents. In G. Baruch & J. Brooks-Gunn (Eds.), *Women in mid-life* (pp. 203–225). New York: Plenum.

Stone, R., Cafferata, G. L., & Sange, J. (1987). Caregivers of the frail elderly: A national profile. *The Gerontologist, 27*(5), 617–626.

Stub, H. R. (1982). *The social consequences of long life*. Springfield, IL: Charles C. Thomas.

Thompson, C. B. (1980). Economic status of late middle-aged widows. In N. Datan & N. Lohman (Eds.), *Transitions of aging* (pp. 134–152). New York: Academic Press.

Treas, J. (1977). Family support systems for the aged: Some social and demographic considerations. *The Gerontologist, 17*, 486–491.

Troll, L. E. (1980). Grandparenting. In L. W. Poon (Ed.), *Aging in the 1980's* (pp. 474–484). Washington, DC: American Psychological Association.

Turner, B. F. (1982). Sex related differences in aging. In B. B. Wolman (Ed.), *Handbook of developmental psychology* (pp. 912–936). Englewood-Cliffs, NJ: Prentice-Hall.

Uhlenberg, P., & Meyers, M. A. (1981). Divorce and the elderly. *The Gerontologist, 21*(3), 276–282.

Ungerson, C. (1987). *Policy is personal: Sex, gender and informal care*. New York: Tavistock.

U.S. Bureau of the Census. (1977). *Social indicators 1976*. Washington, DC: U.S. Government Printing Office.

U.S. Department of Health, Education and Welfare, Administration on Aging. (1976). *Elderly widows*. Statistical Memo No. 33. Washington, DC: U.S. Government Printing Office.

U.S. House Select Committee on Aging. (1987). Women in our aging society: Hearings. Washington, DC: Government Printing Office.

U.S. Senate Special Committee on Aging. (1984). *Aging America*. Washington, DC: U.S. Dept. of Health and Human Services.

U.S. Senate Special Committee on Aging. (1986). *Aging America*. Washington, DC: U.S. Dept. of Health and Human Services.

U.S. Senate Special Committee on Aging. (1988). *Aging America*. Washington, DC: U.S. Dept. of Health and Human Services.

Valentine, D., & Cash, T. (1986). A definitional discussion of elder mistreatment. *Journal of Gerontological Social Work*, 9(3), 17–28.

Wasserman, A. (1983). A support group for the sandwich generation. *Aging, 340*, 2–4.

Weishaus, S. (1979). Aging is a family affair. In P. K. Japan (Ed.), *Aging Parents*. (pp. 155–174). Los Angeles: University of Southern California Press.

Weitzman, L. J. (1985). *The divorce revolution, the unexpected social and economic consequences for women and children in America*. New York: Free Press.

Wentowski, G. J. (1985). Older women's perceptions of great-grandmotherhood: A research note. *The Gerontologist*, *25*(6), 593–596.

Whiting, B. B. (1984). Problems of American middle-class women in their middle years. In G. Baruch & J. Brooks-Gunn (Eds.), *Women in midlife* (pp. 261–273). New York: Plenum.

Willis, L., Thomas, P., Garry, P. J., & Goodwin, J. (1987). A prospective study of response to stressful life events in initially healthy elders. *Journal of Gerontology*, *42*(6), 627–630.

Winter, A. (1986). The shame of elder abuse. *Modern Maturity*, *29*, 51–57.

Wood, V., & Robertson, J. F. (1976). The satisfaction of grandparenthood. In J. F. Gubrium (Ed.), *Time, roles, and self in old age*. New York: Behavioral Publications.

Wood, V., Traupmann, J., & Hay, J. (1984). Motherhood in the middle years: Women and their adult children. In G. Baruch & J. Brooks-Gunn (Eds.), *Women in midlife* (pp. 227–244). New York: Plenum.

Zarit, S. H., Reever, K. E., & Bach-Peterson, J. (1980). Relatives of the impaired elderly: Coorelates of feelings of burden. *The Gerontologist*, *20*(6), 649–655.

7

Education, Work, Retirement, and Survival

Women's lives have changed more in the world of work in the past dozen years than perhaps in almost any other aspect of living. More women are in the labor force in the 1980s, remaining in or returning to work after child-bearing, and more of their total life span will be spent in the world of paid labor than we have known. These changes have an enormous impact on every aspect of women's lives. However, older women today—those over 40 and particularly those in their 60s and beyond—do not, on the whole, show these patterns of labor force participation.

In this chapter we will look at what the current generation of older women are experiencing and the findings on previous cohorts. But what we find and the generalizations we draw probably will not be true for the rising generations.

Because the kind of work women can get depends to a great extent on their educational level, we will first examine how women have fared in the schools and colleges. We will look next at employment patterns, salaries, and related issues. After work comes retirement; how well do older women fare when they are no longer in the work force, are widowed or divorced? Retirement can be satisfying or terrifying, particularly for those only marginally surviving. The policies of Social Security and private and public pension plans are crucial for older women, as we shall see.

The proportion of their life span that individuals devote to education, work, and retirement have changed over time but far more dramatically for women than for men. Figure 7.1 shows these changes. In the following sections of this chapter we will examine the implications of these changes in the lives of older women.

EDUCATION

Although education was not always linked to income and status, the 20th century has seen it increase in importance as the pathway to financial and social mobility. Harry Truman will probably be the last President who did not go to college.

The link between education and achievement has been established for men, but until recent years this was less significant for women because so few achieved high financial levels or social status through work. This has all changed. Families at one time were reluctant to invest in a daughter's education; it was considered a waste since she only got married. Increased affluence, growth of accessible and inexpensive higher education, and the perceived advantages accruing to women who attained more education have resulted in sharply increased college attendance rates for women since World War II. High school completion and some college attendance is increasingly the norm for young women in the last quarter of the 20th century. In 1985, 85.6% of American women aged 25 to 44 had completed secondary school. By comparison, only 48.9% of those aged 65 or over have 12 years of schooling (U.S. Senate Special Committee on Aging, 1988).

Women who are in their 60s and older in the 1980s do not have high levels of education. Although the majority of them may have completed high school, there are large numbers with only a grade school education or less. Many of these older women arrived as non-English-speaking immigrants and never became full literate in English even if they were literate in their own language. Efforts to cope with this illiteracy were part of the Adult Education Act of 1980, P.L. 91-230, as amended and incorporated into the Adult Literacy Initiative. As of 1985, 2.9 million adults were served, of whom 185,642 were over 60, compared to 128,650 in 1980 (Haigler, 1987). This was doubtless due to increased efforts to reach this group plus the actual increased numbers of those over 60.

The relationship between education and survival has been keenly felt by one group of adult women: those divorced in midlife or widowed and left with minimal support. Colleges and universities became conscious of a new group of students in the 1970s—returning older women. As a group they were fearful and uneasy in a climate geared to 18–20-year-olds. Many institutions responded by putting into place special counseling and support programs for the returning woman student and now offer a wide range of

FIGURE 7.1 Life-cycle distribution of education, labor force participation, retirement and work in the home: 1900–1980.

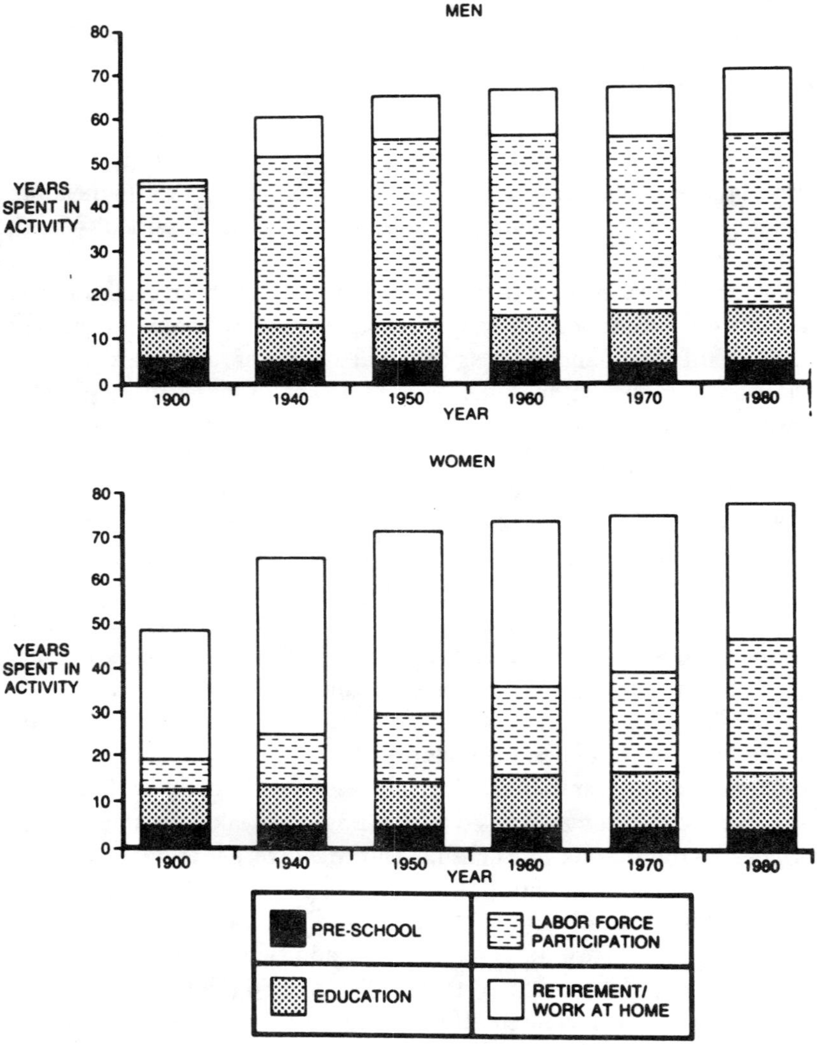

From U.S. Bureau of the Census. "Education Attainment in the United States: March 1981 and 1980." *Current Population Reports* Series P-20, No. 390 (August 1984) (median years of school for persons 25 years or older, 1940–80). Best, Fred. "Work Sharing: Issues, Policy Options, and Prospects." Upjohn Institute for Employment Research, 1981, page 8 (1900 estimates of median years of school for persons 25 years or older). National Center for Health Statistics. *Vital Statistics of the United States, 1984*. Vol. 2, Section 6, March 1987 (life expectancy data). Smith, Shirley J. "Revised Worklife Tables Reflect 1979–1980 Experience." *Monthly Labor Review* Vol. 108, No. 8 (August 1985) (worklife estimates).

services. These programs are no longer identified as merely for the returning older woman, but most of those served are women, although there are significant numbers of returning men as well. At the University of Maryland, for instance, the 1986 data are indicative: those over 40 constituted 5.4% of all students. Of 1,318 students aged 40 to 49, 844 are women. Of those aged 50 to 59, 228 of 319 are women. Only after age 60, at which age students are eligible for a Golden ID card that entitles them to attend without paying any tuition or other fees—and there are very few such students—do men outnumber women. At the undergraduate level there were twice as many women as men aged 40 to 49. Of the students over 70, however, there were 69 men to 49 women. (University of Maryland, 1986). This latter figure is interesting, since we know there are many more women than men in that age group. One could hypothesize that they represent a cohort that did not consider higher education an option for women, or they were more intimidated at the thought of a university setting.

Adult education programs, which typically offer skills training and retraining and recreational and hobby classes, present a different picture of involvement. A survey of adult education programs reported that about 25% more men aged 55 to 64 enrolled in courses for job-related reasons. (U.S. Senate Special Committee on Aging, 1984). The difference in sex patterns between college-based and adult education job-related courses is interesting. Perhaps women find it more acceptable, or receive more support from spouses and family, to return to college than to take courses in community-based programs. Or the offerings in the latter setting may be geared, for whatever reason, to the kinds of skills and informational needs of traditionally male occupations rather than female ones.

The particular problems of the older student in the classrooms has been the focus of considerable interest. As Malcolm Knowles (1987) has pointed out, the adult learner is qualitatively different from the younger learner. Is the college classroom really suitable for older students? In one study both younger and older students were favorably disposed toward an intergenerational classroom, and the experience changed the attitudes of a majority of the younger students toward more favorable appreciation of the elderly. The data were not analyzed by sex and, as the authors note, are severely restricted as to generalizability (Kay, Jensen-Osinski, Beidler, & Aronson, 1983).

That returning older women students are different was the personally shocking discovery of a college instructor who had presented her course for such students in the same way as for the traditional young woman undergraduate. Her older students were unhappy with this and complained bitterly, prompting the professor to look at the data on such students. She realized that this was indeed a different kind of student, which meant that she had to relate to them more as mature peers than as naive undergraduates (Yudkin, 1987). An interesting study of older women graduate students studying gerontology found that these students had educational qualifications comparable to younger students and had the advantage of work histories in relevant social service settings. The researchers point out that a very high proportion of these older students were not married (widowed, divorced, or separated) and suggest that faculty in gerontology programs could assist these students if there were more women with similar personal-experiential backgrounds as faculty members (Garcia & Kosberg, 1985).

Now that colleges and universities have had a decade of dealing with older students, it has been found that they are typically more serious, conscientious, motivated, and in fact a pool of future students for institutions fearing enrollment declines. Even the old barriers to admitting students over 35 or 40 to doctoral programs, which were in place prior to 1970, have been dropped by most disciplines. Doctorates have been earned by persons in their 70s and 80s.

The need to catch up by returning to school in order to obtain better jobs may not be a necessity for younger women, but for the woman over 40 this is an important option if she can afford the time and money. Unfortunately, many an older woman lacks both; displaced homemakers may have to settle for low-paying dead-end jobs because they cannot find or take advantage of training programs to improve their qualifications.

Not all learning activities pursued by older women are for career and job purposes. An enthusiastic report by Weinstock (1978) enumerates the rich variety of noncredit, nondegree offerings in colleges and universities. Much of the programming in community-based adult education is recreational or for personal enhancement. Publicly supported programs offered by schools and recreation departments are active in developing courses and group programs that appeal to a wide clientele. Since so many of the elderly are women, many programs offer activities of presumed interest to women: sewing, cooking, flower arrangement, financial planning, shopping excursions to discount centers. Data for 1981 show that between ages 55 and 64, nearly three times as many women as men take non-job-related adult education courses, and after age 65 women account for over 50% of those taking such courses (U.S. Senate Special Committee on Aging, 1984).

How older adults learn and what their capacity is for learning new skills, information, and abstract concepts has been the subject of extensive study. The research does not tell us whether there are any differences between men and women in those characteristics most closely tied to physiological age. The highly significant roles played by motivation and self-concept suggest that these factors would clearly differentiate between the aims of men and women as to further learning in old age; the data do not tell us about this nor is it a question that anyone seems to raise, to judge by the summary in the *Handbook of the Psychology of Aging* (Willis, 1986).

In another context, Robertson-Tchabo (1987) points out the lack of evidence thus far as to whether women will show the same decline in cognitive performance that longitudinal studies of men have shown. She states: "The literature on sex-related differences in cognitive performance of the elderly is extremely limited and the findings are not consistent."

The pattern of very few women obtaining advanced degrees in earlier decades results in few women over 60 enjoying the personal and financial benefits that result from higher educational attainment. These few women in the various professions could hardly exert any influence on their career areas or their academic disciplines. There are, of course, notable exceptions, such as the work of Jessie Bernard (1964) and Alice Rossi in sociology (1980), Margaret Mead (1949) in anthropology, Karen Horney (1973; see also Westkott, 1986) in psychoanalysis, Eleanor Maccoby (1966) in psychology, and Mary Beard in history (1946). The explosive emergence of a vast amount of feminist scholarship in almost every area of work or study is very recent and in most instances is the work of younger scholars.

The kind, quality, and level of educational achievement are intricately involved with all other aspects of a woman's life. If she is better educated, she can expect a more rewarding and better-paying job, she can perform her family tasks and participate in her community with more effectiveness, she can make more informed decisions about her own health and health practices, she can live a personally richer life, and she can experience a more comfortable old age. This has not always been the case; in the past, educational rewards for women were more limited, particularly in regard to work and careers. Changed educational achievement patterns promise a qualitatively different life for older women in future decades.

WHEN OLDER WOMEN WORK

When the first-grader was asked what her mother did, she replied, "My mother doesn't work. She stays home all day." What this child defined as work has been the cultural definition since industrialization transformed men's work. Technology required that men leave home and engage in paid employment. This was "work." The tremendous toil required of women to feed, clothe, and maintain a home for a family—for no pay—was thus not "work." Social norms defined this view of work, and though some early feminists strongly objected, they were solitary and unheard voices. It is this definition that has created continuing problems for women who have been or who remain housewives, as well as for those who have had paid employment outside their homes.

A study by Shaw (1983) presents a most revealing picture of the complexity of the work experience of women in their mid-20s to mid-50s during the years 1964 to 1977, women who are in their 40s to 70s today. Many of these are the mothers of the baby-boom generation; they had large families and experienced the economic expansion and recession that characterized those years. As a group they worked more than any previous generation of women; only one-fourth of the white women in the sample had a mother who had worked. Most of these women were not prepared to go to work in midlife, but 80% of them were propelled to do so by a variety of forces, primarily economic necessity. But their work careers were not very rewarding. Only 30% had continuous employment, another third were employed intermittently, and 20% worked part of the time. They needed to work because they found themselves impoverished by being widowed or divorced in midlife, many with children to support. But work was threatened by a high incidence of health problems, as well as the vicissitudes of an economically unstable labor market. The work they did was low-paying; even a prior work record did not result in higher reentry pay. Very few of the sample studied were in nontraditional jobs; there were only three doctors and one lawyer, three had doctorates, and only 1% held reasonably high paying jobs in private industry. As Shaw observes, "Clearly the much-publicized movement of women into high-level jobs has scarcely touched [this] generation of women" (p. 133).

Many older women are working, but the pattern of work has changed over the decades. In 1960, nearly 50% of women aged 45 to 54 were in the labor force. In 1980, 61.9% were employed. In the age bracket 55 to 64 the percentages are not as different: in 1960 37.2% versus 41.5% of women were at work. Women over 65 are rarely in the work force, but in 1960, 10.8% had to work. By 1980, probably due to improved Social Security and pension benefits, only 7.8% of these elderly women were still working (Blau & Ferber, 1985). More women are working in midlife, but fewer will stay after they are eligible for Social Security. The greatest shift is occurring at younger age levels, with significant implications for these women's lives when they approach retirement: nearly 70% of women aged 20 to 44 were working in 1980, and the percentages are expected to rise in succeeding decades.

The increased rate of labor force participation is due not only to more women entering the work force but also to fewer departing, as was the pattern found by Shaw (1983) for the midlife women studied in 1964 to 1977. The amount of time a woman spends in the work force has also changed dramatically:

> In 1940, a 20-year-old woman had an expected work life of about 12 years. This was about 30 percent of the estimated male work-life expectancy of about

> 40 years. In 1977, . . the estimated work-life expectancy of a 20-year-old woman had risen to 26 years or 71 percent of the male figure of 37 years. (Blau & Ferber, 1985, p. 27)

Extrapolations of these Labor Department figures indicate that as of 1980 women will spend nearly 30 years at paid employment (U.S. Senate Special Committee on Aging, 1986).

Amount of education has always been a predictor of work force participation, but for women the social climate needed to be positive. With four years of high school in 1964, 44.6% of the women worked. The changed climate in 1982 saw a 57.6% participation rate. Four years of college propelled 50% into the labor force in 1964, but in 1982, 70.2% of women with a college education were working. In both time periods, women who had invested a great deal of time in education—5 or more years of college—were most likely to be working (Blau & Ferber, 1985).

The changed work pattern of women is clear from the data: more women are getting more education, are working more, and will spend more years of their life in the work force. All of these changes are unprecedented. In addition to the sheer numbers of women at work, the jobs they hold also are changing. For example, in 1959 "over 47 percent of women bachelor's degree recipients received their degrees in teaching; by 1980 the proportion had declined to 19 percent" (Jacobs, 1985). The women who shifted out of teaching found they could successfully enter previously all-male domains. Between 1979 and 1986 the percentage of women among full-time workers in a number of occupations has changed markedly, for example:

> Accountants and auditors, up from 34% to 45%
> Computer programmers, up from 28% to 40%
> Lawyers, up from 10% to 15%
> Electrical and electronic engineers, from 4% to 9% (U.S. Bureau of the Census, 1987)

Another report shows that women were 12.2% of physicians in 1973 and 15.8% in 1984; women made up 18.4% of managers and administrators in 1973 and had increased their representation to 32.4% in 1984 (Kahn & Crosby, 1985). This certainly suggests a very different perception of self for women with work experience in such occupations when they reach midlife and later retire, as well as differences in other aspects of their lives. But the women who are in their middle years or older in the 1980s did not experience this workplace revolution and must deal now with serious problems of survival.

The women studied by Shaw (1983) could obtain only jobs that were typically low-paying, low-skill, and subject to layoffs and industrial recession. The jobs were those traditionally filled by women in factories and service occupations.

The pattern of sex segregation in occupations paralleled women's entry into the marketplace. In fact, technology increased the amount of segregation: in 1900 "60 percent of working women were in occupations in which at least half of their coworkers were also female; in 1980, the percentage increased to 75 percent" (Kahn & Crosby, 1985). Gender inequality in occupations is also affected by racial and ethnic factors (Almquist, 1987). The historical roots and social dynamics underlying sex segregation are complex, and despite the obvious problems it poses for women, such segregation will undoubtedly be difficult to alter (Bergmann, 1986; Boulding, 1976; Hartmann, 1976; Lipman-Blumen, 1976).

Sex segregation at work has several important consequences for women, which become particularly apparent as they age. First, the jobs open to women pay, on the average, about half of what men are paid. This gives women less economic security and reduces their commitment to work, which in turn justifies keeping women's wages low and limiting their advancement into better-paying jobs. Second, channeling women into low-paying "women's jobs" makes it difficult, if not impossible, for women to invest and save for their old age, resulting in continued economic marginality and dependency (Olson, 1985). It is this picture of the old age poverty of women that we will examine more fully below. For women who worked a substantial part of their lives, such poverty clearly derives from the market conditions that have been in place over the years.

The struggle for job equity continues, but the barriers that prevent entry by women into better-paying men's jobs are still socially supported by many women and most men. Efforts to achieve equal pay are thwarted by job classifications—jobs defined as appropriate for women just pay less. In 1984 women who worked without interruption averaged $7.44 an hour, compared to $10.76 for men. In terms of all female work, women earned $.69 for every $1.00 earned by men. This ratio did not change with comparable years on the job. Younger women, however, aged 21 to 29, have an earnings rate of .82, which shows promise for their future (U.S. Bureau of the Census, 1987). An analysis of the impact of policies enacted during the Reagan years reveals that, overall, the elderly benefited, but those who started with more also gained more. The total impact was to increase the income differential between older men and women (Moon, 1986).

In an effort to reduce this invidious ratio, feminists have argued for the concept of "comparable worth" (Feldberg, 1984). The heavy concentration of women in a few job categories need not be a justification for lower pay when men in jobs with similar qualifications and responsibility are paid more. One group based in Washington, the National Committee on Pay Equity, believes there is promise on this front. They report that, as of 1986,

13 states had adjusted employees' salaries, 36 had set up task forces to study the problem, and 32 were conducting studies to evaluate the existence of pay inequities (New Directions for Women, 1987). Although comparable worth presents some difficulties, "nonetheless, comparable worth does question the ideology of the marketplace in the setting of wages, it reveals the systematic devaluation of the work women do, and it does promote collective action by working-class women" (Blum, 1987). And it can basically improve women's life chances.

The outcome of these several trends—more women qualifying for an entering nontraditional jobs, pressure for pay equity for women, and salaries based on similar qualifications—may make the survival picture for midlife and older women more secure in the future. But, as Bergmann (1986) points out, active pressure in the public and private sector is required for women to gain these needed rewards for their work. Today's older woman is the victim of traditional policies that have restricted women to low-paying jobs not covered by Social Security or other benefits, highly prone to business cycle unemployment, and poorly protected if at all by private pensions.

The midlife women in Shaw's (1983) study moved in and out of the work force for a variety of reasons. Family responsibilities and health reasons accounted for intermittent employment and long absences from work. Family mobility resulted in job interruption. Unemployment for periods of time was also due to business problems. "Women who were new labor-market entrants left the labor force again in areas of high unemployment, and wages of reentrants were found to have worsened in recent years" (Shaw, 1985, p. 57). Keating and Jeffery (1983) also suggest:

> Most women who are now in their sixties had little socialization toward the acquisition of a long-term work role. . . . most women reached marriageable age with few specific job skills and with the attitude that work was of importance primarily to bridge the gap between exit from one's family and entry into one's family of procreation.

In their study of a sample of retired women in central Alberta, Canada, it was found that none of the married women had a continuous work career, whereas 55% of the never-married women had worked without interruption. Married women were apt to delay entry into the work force and nearly one-third reported that their work patterns were unstable (Keating & Jeffery, 1983). The perception of women as not committed to careers and putting family concerns above job concerns has justified discriminatory treatment of women (Grambs, 1987). The persistent view of women as undependable employees provides ample ammunition to employers to defend putting women into the lowest-paying job categories and denying them promotions. The low pay and lack of potential reward results, of course, in low work commitment in women, an unbroken and vicious cycle.

Is this likely to change and so affect the life chances of future cohorts of older women? When more women remain in the work force throughout their working life, one would assume they would benefit from occupational mobility, much as one sees in male work patterns, with resultant improved pay and retirement benefits. As Treiman (1985) points out, such women now constitute a small minority of the work force. He also makes the telling point that in Communist Eastern European countries with full lifelong employment for both men and women, occupations are still sex-segregated, and the earnings gap is as large as in the United States. In summarizing the institutional barriers against women's achieving gender equality in the work force, Baron and Bielby (1985) perceive little hope for substantive institutional change.

Another reason to be pessimistic about how well older women in succeeding generations will fare in their work careers is the fact that employment policies and assessments are based on a male work model—a continuous work career with upward job mobility (except in times of unemployment). For women to approach this model there are, as we are now seeing with the young women in the work force, serious consequences for family life. A recent case in Virginia highlights problems women face. A woman sued for unemployment benefits when she had to quit work to join her husband who had relocated to another part of the state. A Virginia law denied such benefits, but on appeal the law was declared unconstitutional. Many states bar such compensation, claiming that this is a voluntary act and not entitled to benefits (*Washington Post*, Sept. 26, 1987).

To succeed in getting the market share accorded women in the workplace it would appear that women must devote only a minimal amount of time to child rearing and forgo any but marginal assistance to aging parents. Although there is growing pressure on private firms to provide adequate maternal leave, only a minority of companies have implemented such a policy. In one or two noteworthy cases, firms have instituted a family-leave care policy, which allows an individual to be given protected leave not only for childbirth but to care for a sick relative or an aging parent (Chapman, 1987). The academic world does not seem any more supportive of maternal leave policies than does industry, and the American Association of University Professors is opposed to such policies (Mangan, 1988). Considering the glacial rate at which child care and maternity legislation is enacted and the resistance of private industry to governmental intervention, one cannot expect much to change unless there is more pressure from women at the grass roots.

DISPLACED HOMEMAKERS

One particular group of women has been hurt by these attitudes and market forces: displaced homemakers. As Sommers and Shields (1978) point out, older women today had "bought the social contract of man the breadwinner and woman the homemaker. They assumed that their retirement benefits, health insurance, and economic security flowed from their marriage" (p. 91). The displaced homemaker is typically a middle-aged woman who provided unpaid household service for family members. She has not had regular outside employment. Now she is displaced from her homemaking role through separation, divorce, or widowhood.

Women who are in the category of displaced homemaker often find themselves destitute, without any financial security. If under 65, they are too young for Social Security benefits, assuming they qualify. Until very recently, the Social Security survivor benefits of a male employee went to his most recent wife and left penniless a previous spouse who might have his children and no livelihood. Recent legislation has now provided that a spouse can make a claim on survivor's benefits if married for at least 10 years. In 1979 Congress recognized the acute problems faced by the displaced homemaker and added these women to the categories of the hard-to-employ under Titles II, III, and VII of the newly authorized Comprehensive Employment and Training Act (CETA). In 1982 the Reagan administration replaced CETA with the Job Partnership Training Program. Unfortunately, that administration also reduced funding for efforts under CETA, so any benefits for displaced homemakers have been reduced. Harlan (1985) presents a critical review of the federal program, showing that current policies permitting great local leeway for defining their own programs have benefited men far more than women.

If a woman is really desperate and unable to find work, she may not even be eligible for welfare unless she is totally disabled or has children under 18, which is not true for most displaced homemakers. As of 1983, 25% of all women aged 35 to 64 were single, widowed, or divorced (Barrow, 1986), and women in the last two categories accounted for a disproportionate number of women in poverty. The federally funded efforts to help the displaced homemaker, laudable as these efforts may be, reach only a minority of the women affected. We have all known a woman who shockingly finds herself divorced at age 40 or 50 and faces a traumatic personal adjustment, made worse by financial desperation. As Bergmann (1986) points out, the painful situation of the displaced homemaker can affect the life of one whose marriage is intact:

> She and her husband both know that if he were to decide on a divorce, her economic and social situation would seriously deteriorate. This realization gives the husband power to get his way when there is a disagreement between them. If he wants to use that power in a harsh and dictatorial way, the housewife's situation can be made very difficult. (p. 218)

The knowledge of this possible bleak future if marriage goes sour is undoubtedly a force in the determination of young women today to obtain job skills and persist in careers despite often heavy burdens of home and child care; they don't intend to be left high, dry, and poor in middle and old age.

WHEN AGEISM AND SEXISM MEET AT THE WORKPLACE

The older woman at work, or the older woman seeking work, may find herself facing a pervasive prejudice against older workers. There is a persistent belief that

> older workers cost more to keep, get sick and are absent more, and are more prone to accidents. These notions, in addition to those about poorer productivity and teachability, have never been supported by important evidence comparing them with younger workers. Yet, in a remarkable way, such notions became the basis of personnel policies in the workplace and at the hiring door, and, for all practical purposes, still are. (Kieffer, 1984)

The Age Discrimination in Employment Act of 1967 was supposed to prevent the kind of actions that have made older people so vulnerable in the job market. A former Secretary of Labor wrote:

> The government's experience in enforcing the Age Discrimination Employment Act has shown beyond a doubt that many older workers lose their jobs, get demoted or otherwise are treated unfairly solely because of their age, rather than their work performance. . . . once older workers lose their jobs they are likely to stay unemployed longer than younger workers [due to] the mistaken idea that this age group is less productive, less capable or less energetic than younger workers. (Donovan, 1984; see also AARP, 1986)

An analysis of the work histories of women show that they suffer age discrimination "earlier, at different stages of employment, and for different reasons" from men (Leonard, 1982). Age discrimination is very hard to document, and even the victim may not be aware of what has happened. As Leonard points out, there are code words that are used to deny women employment: "overqualified," or "lack of paid work experience" even when one presents a résumé full of experience as a volunteer. The displaced homemaker finds this particularly discouraging; there is no protection in the law under either sex or age discrimination. Women have benefited from successful suits that forced private concerns to cease firing women from such jobs as airline attendant because they were "too old," but they still face strong resistance when they attempt to enter or reenter such jobs in midlife or later.

Unions could provide assistance to women, though many are less than energetic in encouraging women, old or young, within their particular area. Relatively few women are in unions, and their representation as officers at local and national levels is small to nonexistent. Most women are employed in occupations that have low rates of unionization. Although a few unions are actively seeking pay equity for their women members, many do not show much interest. The unions are also insensitive to or unaware of the problems of the reentry older woman worker (Leonard, 1982).

Although trends indicate that increasingly women will remain in the work force without significant interruption for most of their working years, it is also probable that many will continue to move in and out of jobs because of family demands. Unless they have built up significant work histories, their reentry problems will be similar to those faced by midlife and older women today. The only optimistic note is the possibility that because of the shrinking proportion of the labor pool of younger workers, there will be more interest in recruiting older persons (Robinson, Coberly, & Paul, 1985). A new category of worker, the so-called fast-food Granny is to be found at McDonald's and Burger King outlets because of a shortage of traditional teenage workers. The teacher shortage that alarmed school systems in the 1980s has been challenged as not as bad as it might seem because of the availability of women who left teaching after a few years and could be enticed back with good salaries (Feistritzer, 1986). Demographics may indeed be a boon to the older woman a few decades hence, but meanwhile the job discrimination that now exists places a heavy burden on the older woman who seeks work in vain.

Another critical area of discrimination linked to age is women's lack of representation at the upper echelons of government or business. Why this is so has been a topic of heated debate by feminists ever since the publication of Friedan's *The Feminine Mystique* (1962). In the federal civil service nearly 80% of the women employed are in the lowest job classifications, and only a minuscule number are among senior top-level bureaucrats. In colleges and universities most women are at the instructor or assistant professor level; very few are full professors. As a woman ages, she cannot anticipate much upward mobility at work, where barriers long in place allow only a few women to rise. Recent appointments of women to top jobs appear to favor younger women with recent and superior training, rather than providing in-service training for advancement of the older women already in place.

Does women's own socialization prevent such upward mobility? An interesting study of women teachers found that many were very uncomfortable if they had to vie with others for power and even more uncomfortable when they achieved such power. "Many in the group found psychological separation and alienation from the rest of the group too much to bear" (Woo, 1985). This group of women represent a cohort who grew up feeling that women should not be bosses and who derived great support from their peer groups of women at work and in the community. If such women want or need to improve their situation, they may need special help, such as that provided by one program designed to assist women to move into school principalships (Metzger, 1985). The very real knowledge of rebuff if one applies for higher-status jobs is, of course, not be be underestimated. Coming generations of women may not be so restrained, and they may be more comfortable with power and success, particularly if there are more women at the top. It is women in midlife who will confront these nontraditional life chances.

RETIREMENT: WOMEN DO IT DIFFERENTLY

Retirement is a major age marker. Before retirement, one is considered able-bodied and competent, and age can be pushed aside as a subjective concern. But once one has crossed the line from work to retirement, the age label is inescapable. Even if one is classified as an "older worker," one can subjectively maintain a sense of being in the mainstream of life. But after retirement one is outside and old. The role of worker no longer applies. The literature and mythology are full of dire predictions for men upon retirement, though there are countermyths of the carefree liberation that also can come from retirement. How do women fare? What shocks, surprises, or satisfactions does retirement bring?

"Literature addressing gender differences in the retirement transition is scant in volume and ambiguous in results" (Palmore, Burchett, Fillenbaum, George, & Wallman, 1985, p. 105). Research on women's retirement is quite recent. A survey of the literature showed that such studies were practically unheard of before 1975 (Sziniovacz, 1982a). Previous research that did look at gender differences in reaction to retirement supported the view that there were few to be found, particularly as to overall life satisfaction. However, there are more specific variables—income, health, activities, community and family relationships, self-concept—that, according to the literature, do differ by gender.

Women are less apt to prepare for retirement than men are, but the relationship between such planning and retirement adjustment has not been shown (Palmore et al., 1985). Women who work without interruption will have higher income at retirement, but otherwise work history does not predict adjustment to retirement. The research that Palmore and his associates conducted on a large sample of women retirees showed that retirement did not bring as many changes in the life-style of women as it did for men. Prediction of retirement behavior was found to be less successful for women than for men; individual patterns were more varied. Marital status was highly important for both men and women in predicting satisfaction and behavior. A study by Keith (1985) of never-married workers and those who were single due to widowhood, divorce, or separation identified the latter group of women as most vulnerable to stress at retirement and most in need of planning ahead.

The history of women's retirement is embedded in the story of retirement in general. One gets only a glimpse of some of the problems when one looks at the struggles of teachers, almost all women, to obtain and protect pension rights and benefits. In one famous incident, 68 older teachers were dismissed by the Chicago schools in 1916 on the pretext that they were incompetent, when in fact the pension fund was bankrupt. Eliminating the older women teachers before they could claim a pension was intended to prevent the revelation that the fund could not pay for the pension obligation (Graebner, 1980).

Current debates about retirement policy present a very complex picture, confounded by economic and demographic trends, the changing views of individuals toward work and leisure, and legislation making arbitrary retirement ages illegal (Forman, 1984). In an excellent review of retirement Morrison (1986) identifies the issues that must be addressed in order to develop adequate policies. But missing from Morrison's review is any recognition of gender differences as adding another level of complexity.

Despite the fact that we know little about gender differences in retirement, men and women have almost always been *treated* differently. For example, women could draw early retirement benefits from Social Security as of 1956, men not until 1961. The United Nations compiled a list of retirement ages for 29 countries. In some countries these tended to be the same for men and women when the retirement age was 65 to 70. However, "when the normal retirement age for males is lower than 65, a still lower age is listed for females" (Cowgill, 1986, p. 125). Cowgill knew of no particular reason for this and found it "difficult to ascertain the rationale for such a differentiation at any age level." In countries such as the USSR, Japan, Italy, and Hungary women retire at age 55 and men at age 60. In

Israel, the United Kingdom, and East and West Germany men retire at age 65 and women at age 60. Considering the data we have on women's longevity, it seems ironic that women are expected—if not required—to leave the work force before men are.

One possible reason for women's earlier retirement ages is to make it attractive for women to retire around the same time their older husbands do; but if the woman lacks a husband, her lesser retirement income—because of fewer years worked—could be a real problem. We do not have data on how many older women, thus forced out of full-time employment, consequently find it necessary to find part-time jobs or employment outside governmental protection or face a dependent and impoverished existence. One study of married women's retirement plans (Shaw, 1984) showed that a married woman would retire early if she had pension coverage and if her husband was retiring and was in good health (see also Campione, 1987).

In the volume edited by Maximiliane Sziniovacz (1982b) are some of the most pertinent reviews of research and reports of original research dealing with women's retirement. The studies show that women's retirement planning and experiences are complex and do not parallel men's. The whole work pattern of women has a bearing on retirement. Women who saw their role as housewives first and workers second retired to a familiar role. Women retiring from professional careers or who spent their adult lives in uninterrupted work anticipated retirement differently and had different adjustments to make. In dual-career families women expected more sharing of household tasks than actually occurred, though housewives who retired did not have such expectations. Most preretirement programs are accused of neglecting the impact of retirement on marital adjustment. As expected, income level affected retirement satisfaction. A women who previously had a high income was more pleased with retirement than a woman with a low income. A study of women in rural areas showed that considerable community support was widely available for retired married or widowed women (Dorfman & Moffett, 1987).

Though there is considerable discussion about offering retirement planning in industry, little appears to focus specifically on women. However, when such planning is provided in academic settings, women are found to utilize the service more than men do (Kaye & Monk, 1984).

Finally, what women do after retirement does not follow male patterns. For example, Kaye and Monk (1984) found that there are quite different patterns of retirement behavior among academics. While both men and women enjoyed retirement, "male retirees were most likely to continue to occupy themselves with work-oriented pursuits whereas female educators spent more time participating in social or recreational activities." Szinovacz (1982b) summarizes the material in the volume she edited:

> Retirement entails significant changes in a woman's life circumstances and routines, and her life experience as an employee results in situational and personal characteristics that diverge from those of the older homemaker. The widely held assumption that women retirees just become full-time homemakers once they quit work outside the home is clearly not warranted, and it is important to note that major differences exist within the group of women retirees. (p. 233)

Both more research and more appropriate programs for women are necessary (Szinovacz, 1982a). Finally, as Palmore and associates (1985) concluded from their research, what is really needed is a "different theoretical foundation for understanding men's and women's retirement" (p. 121), since retirement theory has evolved from studies of male-only samples.

SURVIVAL

Ah, those golden years! To while away the time in comfortable surroundings untroubled by financial cares! The dream is possible—if you are married to a man who has invested wisely or was smart enough to spend a lifetime in a job that paid well and provided substantial retirement and survivors' benefits for him and his dependent spouse. Like many other dreams, the reality is that proportionately more older people can enjoy that dream, and proportionately more will be destitute (Schulz, 1988). It is the middle group that has shrunk, those between poverty and comfort. And those who are impoverished are most likely to be poor white, black, and Hispanic women.

The data on poverty among elderly women are depressing, as Table 7.1 shows. When the "near poor" are added to the category, 82% of Black elderly women were officially impoverished, as calculated from the 1980 census (Minkler & Stone, 1985). The statistics on income by age group, sex, race, and Hispanic origin (Table 7.2) reveal the dramatic differences among these groups, with women being the worst off in every comparison.

Most of the income of those over 65 derives from Social Security and pensions, and here again one notes the handicaps that reduce the economic status of women. As we have seen, women work at jobs that consistently pay less than men, and they are in and out of the work force. Lower-paying jobs provide less in pensions; 40% of women, as compared to 55% of male full-time employees, are employed by companies that provide pensions. Moving from job to job means loss of pension rights. A number of private pension plans are structured with such stringent qualifications that many employees receive no benefits on retirement. Few provide even a stipend

TABLE 7.1 Percentage of Elderly below Poverty by Race, Hispanic Origin, Sex, and Living Arrangement: 1986

	Living arrangement of persons below poverty line		
Race and Hispanic origin	% In families	% Unrelated individuals	Total
White			
Male	4.9	16.7	6.9
Female	5.3	23.7	13.3
Total	5.1	22.1	10.7
Black			
Male	18.7	39.8	24.2
Female	17.8	59.8	35.5
Total	18.2	53.9	31.0
Hispanic[a]			
Male	15.1	[b]	18.8
Female	12.2	55.1	25.2
Total	13.6	50.2	22.5
All races			
Male	6.0	19.6	8.5
Female	6.4	26.8	15.2
Total	6.2	25.2	12.4

[a]Hispanic persons may be of any race.

[b]Percentage not shown if base population is less than 75,000.

From U.S. Bureau of the Census. "Money Income and Poverty Status of Families and Persons in the United States: 1986." *Current Population Reports*, Series P-60, No. 157 (July 1987). Unpublished data from the March 1987 Current Population Survey.

for surviving spouses. If an employee dies before retirement, all pension benefits are lost to the surviving spouse. As Olson (1985) comments, "most working women, although subject to mandatory and informal retirement policies, are not protected economically by the private sector during their older years," and a husband's efforts to provide for himself and his wife are apt to be frustrated by the way the system works. The most significant event that precipitates a woman into poverty is widowhood, according to research carried out at the University of Wisconsin's Institute for Research on Poverty (Burkhauser, Holden, & Myers, 1986).

When women are dependent on their own earned pensions for retirement income, they also do not fare very well. In 1984 it was reported that only 20% of women over 65 had pensions, compared to 43% of men; and the median pension for women was $233 a month, compared to a man's

TABLE 7.2 Median Income of Persons Age 65 and Older by Age, Race Hispanic Origin, and Sex: 1986

Race and Hispanic origin	Both sexes			Male			Female		
	65 plus	65–69	70 plus	65 plus	65–69	70 plus	65 plus	65–69	70 plus
All races	$8,154	$ 9,407	$7,729	$11,544	$13,304	$10,581	$6,425	$6,671	$6,346
White	8,544	10,032	8,083	12,131	14,041	11,130	6,738	7,045	6,639
Black	5,030	5,455	4,901	6,757	7,078	6,577	4,508	4,625	4,464
Hispanic	5,510	5,655	5,400	7,369	8,083	7,060	4,583	4,466	4,622

[a]Hispanic persons may be of any race.

From U.S. Bureau of the Census. "Money Income and Poverty Status of Families and Persons in the United States: 1986." *Current Population Reports* Series P-60, No. 157 (July 1987). Unpublished data from the March 1987 Current Population Survey.

$484 per month (*Washington Post*, July 4, 1986). Current problems regarding pension protection when companies go bankrupt have prompted some new legislative initiatives to see to it that reserve pension funds are not tapped to pay off creditors and stockholders. But for some that intervention is far too late; millions of workers find themselves left to the mercies of the Social Security system for all retirement coverage.

Social Security is not much better than the private pension system as far as a woman is concerned, unless she has worked without interruption for a lifetime—which is true of only a minority of older women today. To obtain adequate retirement income a woman needs to stay employed into the late 60s and 70s, and as Rix (1987) comments, these jobs are "those that are undesirable and demanding and also not conducive to a longer work life." Another and not easily understood policy is to allow companies to "integrate" Social Security benefits with private pensions, with the disastrous result that all benefits are drastically reduced. This grossly unfair system led, not to the reform of the private pension system, but to the initiation of the IRA, or Individual Retirement Account. Only those with an extra $2,000 a year to forgo out of current income could afford this new device, and it was made less attractive by the tax reform act of 1986, all of which adds up to trouble for women.

Are unisex pensions the answer? The usual pattern for figuring pension payments and benefits is for women either to pay more into the system in order to receive equal benefits (because they live longer) or pay equal amounts into the system but receive reduced monthly benefits (because they live longer). Is there any way to have a system that requires men and women to pay the same amounts and receive the same benefits? This is, of course, wholly possible, but it requires subsidizing the woman's pension because she will, on the average, receive more than the man. After an examination of how a unisex system would work, Gohmann and McClure (1987) state that

> the change from a sex-based plan to a unisex plan reduces pension wealth for men and increases pension wealth for women, on average. Second, the movement from a sex-based plan to a unisex plan results in an increase in women's net wage and a decrease in men's net wage. Finally, as the proportion of women in the cohort changes, the size of these two effects changes."

And, as the authors conclude, these effects, which benefit women overall, are likely to create "tension" as such plans are debated.

The sex bias of pension plans and the reluctance of the courts to intervene is highlighted by the Norris case (Heen, 1986). The Supreme Court ordered employers to convert to sex-neutral retirement systems. However, insurance bought outside of employment, and the use of age- and sex-based mortality tables persists "despite the fact that eighty-four percent of women as a group will not live longer than their male counterparts." Interestingly enough, as Heen reports, sex-based tables for group life insurance penalize women through higher premiums; in group annuities men benefit from sex-based mortality tables, so women again have lower payouts.

If the retiree is a dependent of a husband covered by Social Security, in most instances her income is greater under his benefits than if she were to forgo that coverage and claim only her own pension; she cannot have both. Social Security was designed in the 1930s and based on the traditional family with only one (male) breadwinner. Benefits were devised accordingly. It has been a struggle since then to achieve some kind of equity when both spouses work. One recent major change has made it possible for a divorced wife who was married to the beneficiary for at least 10 years to claim some part of the retirement income. Also, the husband cannot sign away dependent benefits without the signature of his spouse. But so far a solution to the imbalance between own entitlement and that of a dependent spouse remains unsolved. The result is a pained realization on the part of millions of women that upon retirement they are better off not getting anything from the system into which they were required to invest.

Another governmental program designed to meet the problems of the impoverished elderly is SSI, Supplementary Security Income. Though it sounds like Social Security, this program includes a stringent means test: you have to prove eligibility or you don't get it. This smacks so much of welfare that some elderly refuse to apply, or face humiliation if they do. They must "spend down" their assets to meet SSI criteria, cannot have an unrelated man in the house, must be over 65, can have only minimal outside earnings, and lose benefits if living with kin (Pearldaughter, Deam, Leonard, & Sommers, 1980).

The "femininization of poverty" was identified as a significant national problem in the mid-1980s (Ehrenreich & Piven, 1984; see also Holden, Burkhauser, & Myers, 1986). A close look at what was happening showed that it was not only the woman head of household with small children who was a victim; elderly women are also an economically deprived class (Minkler & Stone, 1985). Table 7.2 shows the details of elderly female poverty. Studies of income changes show that women experience a "significant drop in income with entrance into old age, and this drop was larger in the 1970's than in the 1960's" (Uhlenberg & Salmon, 1986). Furthermore, "the drop in income associated with entering old age has increased for women more recently making the transition." Uhlenberg and Salmon predict that there will not be much improvement in the future, with the drop in income made worse by heightened expectations. "Taken together, these trends suggest that large increases in federal expenditures will be required to maintain the economic status quo for the older population," but even now there are rumblings that the old are getting too much of the social pie. A great deal of political attention is now being paid to what some perceive as a trend toward making the younger generation bear too much of a burden for the well-being of their elders, a claim strongly refuted by Kingson, Hirshorn, and Cornman (1987). Midlife women need to be vigilant lest when they reach old age they will be no better off than their mothers and grandmothers before them.

Not all is dismal for elderly women. A woman fortunate enough to have been married to a spouse with a good income, who took out adequate life insurance and made prudent investments, or who herself worked at a well-paying job with good retirement benefits may find widowhood or even divorce a time to enjoy life without encumbrances. Many still-married couples are seen to have more discretionary income than a goodly proportion of the rest of the population. The conspicuousness of some of these upper-middle-class older couples may be deceiving, however. Senator John Heinz (R., PA) pointed out that in fact a smaller proportion of the elderly than any other age group has such discretionary income after paying for necessities, and one should be careful about how the statistics on income are interpreted (*Washington Post*, Dec. 21, 1985). Certainly, for many older women old age can be financially secure, but the unfortunate facts are that most women over 65 are not faring very well.

SUMMARY

The world of education, work, pensions, and retirement is a complicated one. The older woman today is disadvantaged on almost all counts: she has had less access to education when young, was channeled into dead-end, low-paying jobs if she worked, often lacked retirement benefits, and, when she did retire, might find her benefits much less than those of men. If she was a displaced homemaker and needed to find work in midlife, she faced sex and age discrimination.

In few areas of the life of the older woman has persistent and consistent bias been so evident as in the economic area. Contemporary social policies, derived from an era when men were the chief breadwinners and divorce was unheard of, persist in the face of changed social realities. Publicity by women's groups has focused on many of these discriminatory practices, and redress is slowly being achieved against massive opposition by industry and labor. The fact that a very large proportion of women today are obtaining more education and acquiring adequate work records, that they are alerted to some of the more egregious sex-biased practices in the workplace and are actively working for substantive change, makes us optimistic about a more financially secure future for older women—at least by the next century.

REFERENCES

Almquist, E. M. (1987). Labor market gender inequality in minority groups. *Gender and Society, 1*(4), 400–414.

American Association of Retired Persons (AARP). (1986). *Workers over 50: Old myths, new realities.* Washington, DC: Author.

Baron, J. M., & W. T. Bielby. (1985). Organizational barriers to gender equality: Sex segregation and job opportunities. In A. S. Rossi (Ed.), *Gender and the life course* (pp. 233–251). New York: Aldine.

Barrow, G. M. (1986). *Aging, the individual, and society.* St. Paul, MN: West.

Beard, M. (1946). *Women as force in history.* New York: Macmillan.

Bergmann, B. (1986). *The economic emergence of women.* New York: Basic Books.

Bernard, I. (1964). *Academic women.* University Park, PA: University of Pennsylvania Press.

Blau, F., & Ferber, M. A. (1985). Women in the labor market: The last 20 years. In L. Larwood, A. H. Stromberg, & B. Gutek (Eds.), *Women and work: Annual review* (Vol. 1 (pp. 19–45). Beverly Hills, CA: Sage.

Blum, L. M. (1987). Possibilities and limits of the comparable worth movement. *Gender and Society, 1*(34), 380–399.

Boulding, E. (1976). Familial constraints on women's work roles. Part 2. *Signs, 3,* 95–117.

Burkhauser, R. V., Holden, K. C., & Myers, D. A. (1986). Measuring the well-being of older women: The transition from wife to widow. *Focus Newsletter* (University of Wisconsin-Madison, Institute of Research on Poverty) 9, 21–24.

Campione, W. A. (1987). The married women's retirement decision: A methodological comparison. *Journal of Gerontology, 42*(4), 381–386.

Chapman, F. S. (1987, September 22). Taking time out to have a baby. *Washington Post,* pp. 13–15.

Cowgill, D. O. (1986). *Aging around the world.* Columbia, MO: University of Missouri Press.

Donovan, R. J. (1984, February–March). Planning for an aging work force. *Aging,* pp. 4–7.

Dorfman, L. T., & Moffett, M. M. (1987). Retirement satisfaction in married and widowed rural women. *The Gerontologist, 27*(2), 215–221.

Ehrenreich, B., & Piven, F. F. (1984). The femininization of poverty. *Dissent,* 2, 162–170.

Feistritzer, C. E. (1986). Teacher crisis: Myth or reality? *Teacher Education Reports,* Washington, DC: National Center for Education Information.

Feldberg, R. L. (1984). Comparable worth: Toward theory and practice in the United States. *Signs, 10*(2), 311–328.

Forman, B. I. (1984). Reconsidering retirement: Understanding emerging trends, *The Futurist,* 43–47.

Friedan, B. (1962). *The feminine mystique.* New York: Dell.

Garcia, J., & Kosberg, J. I. (1985). The older female graduate student in gerontology: An analysis of the University of Florida's fifteen year experience. *Gerontology and Geriatrics Education, 5,* 69–79.

Gohmann, S. F., & Mclure, J. E. (1987). Supreme Court rulings on pension plans: The effects on retirement age and wealth of single people. *The Gerontologist, 27,* 471–477.

Graebner, W. (1980). *A history of retirement.* New Haven, CT: Yale University Press.

Grambs, J. D. (1987). Are older women teachers different? *Journal of Education, 169*(1), 47–64.

Haigler, K. O. (1987). Volunteers are the key to literacy strategy. *Perspectives on Aging, 16,* 6–9.

Harlan, S. L. (1985). Federal job training policy and economically disadvantaged women. In L. Larwood, A. H. Stromberg, & B. Gutek (Eds.), *Women and work: Annual review* (Vol. 1), 282–310. Beverly Hills, CA: Sage.

Hartman, J. (1976). Capitalism, patriarchy, and job segregation by sex. Part 2. *Signs, 3*(1), 137–170.

Heen, M. L. (1986). Sex distribution, mortality tables, and pensions: Improving the economic status of older women. *Women and Health, 11*(1), 119–131.

Holden, K. C., Burkhauser, R. V., & Myers, D. A. (1986). Income transitions at older stages of life: The dynamics of poverty. *The Gerontologist, 26,* 292–297.

Horney, K. (1973). *Feminine psychology,* New York: Norton.

Jacobs, J. A. (1985). Sex segregation in American higher education. In L. Larwood, A. H. Stromberg, and B. Gutek (Eds.), *Women and Work: Annual review* (Vol. 1, pp. 191–215). Beverly Hills, CA: Sage.

Kahn, W. A., & Crosby, F. (1985). Discrimination between attitudes and discriminating behavior. In L. Larwood, A. H. Stromberg, and B. Gutek (Eds.), *Women and work: Annual review* (Vol. 1, 215–238). Beverly Hills, CA: Sage.

Kay, E. J., Jensen-Osinski, B. H., Beidler, P. G., & Aronson, J. L. (1983). The graying of the college classroom. *The Gerontologist, 23,* 196–199.

Kaye, L. W., & Monk, A. (1984). Sex role traditions and retirement from academe. *The Gerontologist, 24*(4), 420–426.

Keating, N., & Jeffery, B. (1983). Work careers of ever married and never married retired women. *The Gerontologist, 23,* 416–421.

Keith, P. M. (1985). Work, retirement, and well-being among unmarried men and women. *The Gerontologist, 25,* 410–416.

Kieffer, J. (1984). New roles for older workers. *Aging, 47,* 11–16.

Kingson, E. R., Hirshorn, B. A., & Cornman, J. M. (1987). *Ties that bind: The interdependence of generations.* Bethesda, MD: Seven Locks Press.

Knowles, M. (1987, January–February). Older adults as learners. *Perspectives on Aging,* pp. 4–5.

Leonard, F. (1982). Not even for dogcatcher: Employment discrimination and older women. *Gray paper #8* Washington, DC: Older Women's League.

Maccoby, E. (Ed.). (1966). *The development of sex differences.* Stanford, CA: Stanford University Press.

Mangan, K. S. (1988). Women seek time off to bear children without jeopardizing academic careers. *Chronicle of Higher Education.* *24*(21), A1, A16.

Mead, M. (1949). *Male and female.* New York: William Morrow.

Metzger, S. (1985). Helping women prepare for principalships. *Phi Delta Kappan, 67,* 292–296.

Minkler, M., & Stone, R. (1985). The feminization of poverty and older women. *The Gerontologist, 25,* 351–357.

Moon, M. (1986). Impact of the Reagan years on the distribution of income of the elderly. *The Gerontologist, 26*(1), 32–37.

Morrison, M. H. (1986). Work and retirement in an aging society. *Daedalus, 115,* 269–294.

New Directions for Women, 16(2), 3.

Olson, L. K. (1985). Older women: Longevity, dependency and public policy. In V. Sapiro (Ed.), *Women, biology and public policy* (pp. 151–175). Beverly Hills, CA: Sage.

Palmore, E. B., Burchett, B. M., Fillenbaum, G. G., George, L. K., & Wallman, L. M. (1985). *Retirement, causes and consequences.* New York: Springer Publishing Co.

Pearldaughter, A., Dean, V., Leonard, F., & Sommers, T. (1980). Welfare: End of the line for women. Gray Paper #5. Washington, DC: Older Women's League.

Rix, S. E. (1987). Pensions, Social Security gain from longer worklife. *Perspectives on Aging, 16,* 3–6.

Robertson-Tchabo, E. (1987). Psychological changes with aging. In L. Jacobs-Condit (Ed.), *Gerontology and communication disorders* (pp. 73–130). Rockville, MD: American Speech–Language–Hearing Association.

Robinson, P. K., Coberly, S., & Paul, C. E. (1985). Work and retirement. In R. H. Binstock & E. Shanas (Eds.), *Handbook of aging and the social sciences* (pp. 503–527). New York: Van Nostrand Reinhold.

Rossi, A. A. (1980). Life span theories and women's lives. *Signs, 6,* 4–32.

Schulz, J. H. (1988). The economics of aging (4th ed.). Dover, MA: Auburn House.

Shaw, L. B. (1983). *Unplanned careers: The working lives of middle-aged women.* Lexington, MA: Lexington Books.

Shaw, L. B. (1984). Retirement plans of middle-aged married women. *The Gerontologist, 24*(2), 154–159.

Sommers, T., & Shields, L. (1987). *Women take care.* Gainesville, FL: Triad Publishing.

Sziniovacz, M. (1982a). Introduction: Research on women's retirement. In M. Szinovacz (Ed.), *Women's retirement: Policy implications of recent research* (pp. 13–21). Beverly Hills, CA: Sage.

Sziniovacz, M. (Ed.). (1982b). *Women's retirement: Policy implications of recent research.* Beverly Hills, CA: Sage.

Treiman, D. J. (1985). Work histories of women and men. What we need to know and what we need to find out. In A. Rossi (Ed.), *Gender and the life course* (pp. 213–231) New York: Aldine.

Uhlenberger, P., & Salmon, M. A. P. (1986). *The Gerontologist, 26*(2), 164–170.

University of Maryland, Office of Institutional Studies (1986). *Institutional Studies* (Vol. 12, No. 2). College Park, MD: Author.

U.S. Bureau of the Census. (1987). *Male-female differences in work experience, occupations, and earnings* Series P-70, No. 10. Washington, DC: U.S. Government Printing Office.

U.S. Senate Special Committee on Aging. (1984). *Aging America.* Washington, DC: U.S. Dept. of Health and Human Services.

U.S. Senate Special Committee on Aging. (1986). *Aging America.* Washington, DC: U.S. Dept. of Health and Human Services.

U.S. Senate Special Committee on Aging. (1988). *Aging America.* Washington, DC: U.S. Dept. of Health and Human Services.

Weinstock, R. (1978). *The graying of the campus.* New York: Educational Facilities Laboratories.

Weskott, M. (1986). The feminist legacy of Karen Horney. New Haven, CT: Yale University Press.

Willis, S. (1986). Towards an educational psychology of the older adult learner: Intellectual and cognitive bases. In J. E. Birren & K. W. Shaie (Eds.), *Handbook of psychology of aging* (pp. 818–847). New York: Van Nostrand Reinhold.

Woo, L. C. (1985). Women as administrators: Profiles of success. *Phi Beta Kappa, 6*(4), 285–291.

Yudkin, M. (1987). I thought I was a terrific teacher until the day . . . *Ms., 16*(4), 66–67.

8

The Older Woman in Historical and Cross-Cultural Perspective

We cannot fully understand the role and status of older women today unless we take a backward glance at the historical record. Many of the perceptions and beliefs we have about aging and about older women in particular are part of our historical heritage, derived primarily from Western European traditions.

It is valuable, too, in order to gain some perspective on our own culture, to examine how other cultural groups respond to older women. The reports that anthropologists bring back from field studies in primarily nonindustrialized settings, relatively untouched by westernizing influences, give us some insight into the variety of ways that culture can define both women and aging.

As we struggle to develop appropriate policies for our elderly so that they are enabled to live out their life span in tranquility with optimum personal and social support, it is helpful to see how other technologically advanced cultures deal with similar situations. We can learn a great deal from their experiences. Older women in every corner of the globe will be the majority group of an increasingly large population of elderly; it is important to gain an international perspective on a phenomenon that will affect us all.

OLD WOMAN AS WITCH

Culture has not been kind to old women. Whenever a culture has believed in witches, the majority have been women, and this is true in cultures as different as African, Burmese, or 17th-century European (Garrett, 1977).

The persecution of women as witches is a dark chapter in Christian history (Walker, 1985): "The charge of witchcraft was to prove a convenient way to get rid of poor widows and other indigent women, too ill or enfeebled to do productive work, therefore a drain on parish funds" (p. 132). In the Middle Ages "the old woman was an ideal scapegoat: too expendable to be missed, too weak to fight back, too poor to matter" (p. 137). A sad example of this view of old women is the Bideford witches: "three crazed old women who were put to death in the West Country [of England] in 1682 . . . provide tragic examples of persons who were probably guilty of little except advancing age, destitution, and wandering wits" (Fraser, 1984, p. 113).

Most of the witches who were actually tried were old widows. Society at that time "connected witchcraft with the menopause," which was itself thought of as a time of the 'stopping of their monthly melancholic flux'" (Fraser, 1984, p. 112). Ugly and poor old women were the most apt to be suspect: "suspicion fell on 'every old woman with a wrinkled face, a furred brow, a hairy lip, a squint eye, a squeaking voice, or a scolding tongue, a skull cap on her head, a spindle in her hand, a Dog or Cat by her side'" (p. 113). Read Macbeth; Shakespeare has provided a memorable contemporary description. Haber (1983, pp. 129-135) hypothesizes that the persecution of women as witches during the Middle Ages and later was men's revenge against the perceived debasing power of women (see also Rogers, 1966).

It has been estimated that between 300,000 and 2 million witches, mostly women, were executed in Europe during the height of the witchcraft mania, which lasted for 300 hundred years (*Encyclopedia Americana*, 1967). Seventy-five percent of the witches persecuted in Massachusetts were women (Chafetz & Dworkin, 1986). The Salem witch trials have fascinated historians and were the subject of a memorable play by Arthur Miller, *The Crucible*, (1971). Garrett (1977) discusses the many sources for selecting old women for this socially suspect role and points out the variety of pathways whereby different cultures arrived at similar views of the evil, demonic, possessed old woman.

Today we gleefully revive the old witch every Halloween, with her black hat and broomstick and sharp, bony profile. A popular comic strip, "Broom Hilda," features such an old woman, so ugly that she drives the objects of her passion to desperate actions; but she is also clever and powerful. The myth of old woman as witch is far from dead; the form it takes may be just as insidious and, fortunately for us, less deadly. Still, there is just something about old women . . . .

Old women have not always personified evil. Walker (1985) presents a wealth of material from history, pointing out the role of the wise, benevolent, powerful, and nurturing old woman, a source of profound spiritual comfort. In Greek mythology a woman, Circe, was the goddess of fertility. (See Walker [1985] for sources on women in mythology.)

The negative term used for an old woman, *hag*, appeared earlier in the English language than any such term for old men (Covey, 1988). Though deriving from an earlier Greek form meaning "holy one," the term evolved into one that personified evil and vice. "By 1337, *hag* meant an ugly, repulsive woman. . . . During the mid-fifteen hundreds, the word was used to represent a female demon." This negative "tone has carried over to the way older women have been perceived and treated in succeeding eras." Covey discusses additional words such as "crone," "anile" (referring to female senility), and other slang terms used in earlier periods to refer negatively to old women. Some, like "harridan" and "old bag," are still in use. These negative words "have generally reflected the perceived lower status of old women. There has also been a long tradition of associating old women with evil and with spiritual forces." By contrast, old men were apt to be "targeted for sexual incompetence, physical decline, and conservative financial practices."

In his overview of the aged in history and society, Achenbaum (1985) points out the negative as well as positive views of the elderly through the ages. Most of the record refers to older men; older women have rarely been the subject of historical writing. Future social historians may find a richer role for older women in preindustrial Europe than we now know about. The negative residue in language, as Covey (1988) discusses, may not be the whole story.

The history of old age in America is slim because it has rarely been the object of study. When old women are mentioned in historical documents, they do not fare very well. A widow in colonial America typically found that control of her property passed to her son, and unless her husband's will specified that she be taken care of, she might very well be left without resources and become a burden on the community. Cotton Mather, the great religious leader of the time, wrote that "the State of Widowhood is a state of affliction," and he admonished the populace to see that these poor women were cared for. To ensure this, some localities in Massachusetts would not allow a son to inherit his father's property unless he promised to take care of his mother (Haber, 1983).

The first homes for the indigent poor established by private charitable groups were for old women. The directors of the first old age home in Philadelphia, the Indigent Widows' and Single Women's Society, wrote in

1842: "With the aged [women] we have few sympathies. . . . They belong to a generation that has passed away; they can promise us neither reciprocation nor reward" (Haber, 1983, p. 97). Prior to the Civil War a number of homes were established, under the auspices of various religious groups, to care for impoverished elderly women. Not until after the war were any homes established to care for old men.

As can be seem from the brief review above, the status of older women in modern times rests on a dubious legacy. Not only have women been accused of witchcraft, they have been treated as redundant and useless in widowhood and old age down through the centuries.

ANTHROPOLOGICAL FINDINGS

All societies assign specific roles, behaviors, responsibilities and opportunities on the basis of sex and age. As van den Berghe (1983) puts it, "age is put to social use in creating differentiated social structures." After reviewing cross-cultural data on older women, Cool and McCable (1983) conclude: "(1) Women in many disparate societies become increasingly dominant and powerful as they age, and (2) with such a transition in female power and status, there may be a concomitant decline in the power and dominance of the older men in these societies" (p. 62).

The dominance and power that older women may exercise in many cultures comes from their traditional roles in their own homes. "A woman's power in the domestic group tends to increase with age, so that by the time she is old she often has considerable control over, and commands respect from, a large number of people" (Foner, 1984, p. 75). An older woman's "dominance can range from a rather awesome authority to gentle role of advisor and guide" (p. 77). When cultural norms demanded subservience of younger women, old age could be a very positive goal; a woman with adult sons and grandchildren could at last command help, respect, and deference. But conflict with modern, educated, independent-minded daughters-in-law, with co-wives, or, in a matrilineal society, with their own adult daughters, could produce a tension-filled old age.

The power achieved by older women in some cultures may be due to attributions of witchcraft or evil power (Foner, 1984) reminiscent of our own history of seeing old women as witches. Cool and McCable (1983) report that in some societies the ambiguous role of older women results in their being endowed with evil potential. In other societies, because women have been relatively powerless, men fear that in old age they may use witchcraft to get even for the years of subjugation (Keith, 1982).

Some traditional societies hold that "the death of a man is caused by the wife; widows are therefore labelled as sorceresses. One of the most unpleasant rites that a widow must go through in one tribal society is having her head shaved when she loses her husband" ("A Little Courage," 1985). The widow is vulnerable to tribal or social practices that may make her life intolerable, though in some cultures she is protected and supported (Lopata, 1987).

In cultures where women have relatively high status in adulthood they will continue to do so in old age (Cool & McCable, 1983), as in traditional ! Kung society in sub-Saharan Africa (Lee, 1985). Where men's status may be tied to the ability to do heavy work, physical decline in old age will mean a drop in status and power; whereas women's work in the home is not affected by physical changes for many years (Foner, 1984). Taiwanese older women, for example, are able to assert more power in the household when the older man no longer can do the heavy labor in the fields and has to cede control to a son (Wolf, 1972).

A significant source of power for older women is knowing the rituals and practices attendant on childbirth, familiarity with healing herbs and potions, and other aspects of the arcane knowledge of a folk society passed on from one women's generation to the next (Silverman & Maxwell, 1983). Traditional Samoan society did not have any age segregation, but certain tasks were reserved for each sex and age group. "One job completely reserved for aged women has been the burning of candlenut and collecting the soot which is used for pigment in tattooing" (Holmes & Rhoads, 1983). Although their role as midwives has given way to Western medical practitioners, the old Samoan women are the "repositories of knowledge concerning the medicinal properties of herbs . . . and many of the specialists in traditional therapeutic massage belong to the senior age group." It is these women, too, who prepare bodies for burial and take care of the gravesite.

A study of grandparenthood in traditional Baganda culture showed that children perceived them to be kind and gentle but were "almost four times as likely to do things for their grandmothers as with or for their grandfathers" (Nahemow, 1983) The respect shown was in greater obedience and service to grandmothers, and grandmothers were more likely to be teachers of their grandchildren. These relationships are an extension of existing sex role expectations.

Older women may exert considerable pressure behind the scenes even though they may have little public power. In Taiwan, for instance, although the older women cannot directly control their male kinfolk, they utilize their women's network to voice criticism of the men: "When a man behaves in a way they consider wrong, they talk about it—not only among themselves but to their sons and husbands" (Wolf, 1972, p. 40). This gossip network exerts a powerful influence in small rural communities. Harrell (1981) points out that in Taiwan traditional society "old women are freer than almost anybody but small children and village idiots" (p. 207).

Few societies establish specific markers for entry into old age for men, but women bear their own physiological age marker: cessation of menses. As Keith (1986) observes, some societies establish "age sets" for men, but few have any for women. This may be because women lead home-centered as against public-centered lives and do not need such age-power identities. However, Keith also suggests that since women have physiological markers that define age, men, who have no such markers, have to erect them. In some cultures the status of a postmenopausal woman becomes that of a "nonwoman," in the view of anthropologists, and allows her to leave the homebound constrictions of those still fecund (Cowgill, 1986; Foner, 1984). The agricultural culture of Somalia allows a husband to divorce a wife who is past menopause so that he can marry a younger, fertile woman (Gibson, 1985).

In traditional Taiwan, in order for a dead woman's spirit to be released, it is necessary to break the pollution bond created by women's menstrual blood:

> Hence, one of a son's deepest filial obligations to his mother is to perform the ceremony of the "blood bowl" at her funeral. At this ceremony, a son symbolically drinks his mother's menstrual blood and breaks the blood bowl, thereby freeing his mother from her polluted state and opening her way to heaven. (Sangren, 1983)

In some of the sectarian cults in rural Taiwan "revelations that postmenopausal women have attained male divinity status are common" (Sangren, 1983).

The main themes that run through the material cited is that aging is, as we would expect, treated and perceived differently by gender in traditional cultures. In some societies age provides positive changes in the woman's status. In others, even if not accorded more power, she at least is freer to move into the public arena and in many cultures acquires or achieves positions of influence not available when she was younger (Cowgill, 1986). There are also societies where the elderly are discarded and abandoned when they can no longer serve a useful economic function and have no economic power regardless of sex. Foner (1984) cites a study that found instances of abandoning or killing the aged in 42 societies. Where resources are scarce, elderly persons are at great risk, particularly if they are childless or sonless (Foner, 1984; see also Gibson, 1985).

Westernization is rapidly eroding traditional agrarian cultures. In some ways the changes in women's lives may be for the better. In Nepal, for example, an 80-year-old woman commented about the crowd of young women at the new village water pump:

> Ha! When I was a young girl I could not even look upon the face of my husband's brother. You see these girls today? They talk to anyone, even to strangers.

> They even walk out in the night. This was not permitted when I was a girl. These young women today, they have ideas. You listen to them. . . . And shall I tell you what we think? I am the oldest mother of this village and I say it is good. We all do. Why should a woman spend her life hiding in the house? (Cameron, 1985)

By contrast, adhering to old customs in a changed economy can be devastating to an older woman. In Zimbabwe a widow's brother-in-law would take back the things that by tradition belonged to the husband's family of origin. He would also acquire the custody and care of his brother's widow and children,

> a sound, practical, and universally acceptable solution to the problems of widows. But now, with the financial pressures of modern urban society, the brother cannot afford to care for an extended family. He puts into practice just half of the customary law tradition: he takes back all the belongings of his late brother and leaves the widow with her four children and an empty house. (Slapgard, 1985)

When families move to urban areas, where housing is typically scarce and minimal, there may no longer be a place for the older parent. The modernization occurring in developing countries can have extremely adverse effects on the uneducated older woman, though her daughters can benefit (Gibson, 1985).

Old women, representing traditional society, may oppose new ways that offer different benefits to women (Foner, 1984). One of the most distressing examples of this is the insistence that young girls in some traditional societies be subjected to female circumcision, which "surgically excises the clitoris, labia minor and inner walls of the labia majora and sutures up the two sides of the vulva." (Hardin, 1985) This practice occurs in some traditional Muslim countries and in others in sub-Sahara Africa, including Egypt, Kenya, and Ethiopia. A map where these practices occur can be found in Seager and Olson (1986). The grandmother of one girl insisted she be operated on: "If she does not have this done, she will become a harlot" (Hardin, 1985). Only very recently has this barbarous practice been given any publicity, with a few brave younger women speaking out against it.

Old women may derive significant benefits from maintaining the sex inequality that enforces the subordination of young women. "Old women . . . have been known to support and even resist change in such customs as feminine modesty standards and menstrual restrictions that keep young women in an inferior position not only in relation to old women but also in relation to men" (Foner, 1984, p. 252). It is the middle-aged and older women who enforce the sexual norms for younger women in a tribal group in Belize (Kerns, 1985).

New ways may bring some important changes in women's lives, but unintended consequences, particularly the conflict with traditional practices, may leave older women in jeopardy and younger women unprotected when they reach old age. A brilliant collection of statistics on women's status around the world can be found in *Women in the World: An International Atlas*, compiled by Seager and Olson (1986). What these data tell us about the conditions of women's lives now becomes a good predictor of how older women will fare in a few decades in many cultures, and much of it is alarming. (For further material, see Broan & Kerns, 1986; Gibson, 1985; Murguia, Schultz, Markides, & Janson, 1984; Torrey, Kinsella, & Taeuber, 1987).

OLDER WOMEN IN CONTEMPORARY TECHNOLOGICAL SOCIETY

It is often difficult for the average insular American to realize how profoundly many of our accepted social norms differ from those of contemporary industrialized cultures in large portions of the rest of the world. One shared similarity, however, is the fact that in "developed" countries, such as the United States, France, Britain, and West Germany, life expectancy of women averages 8 years more than that of men. In less industrialized countries, such as India, Pakistan, China, where health practices lag or are not universally available, women have only a 2-year advantage (U.S. Senate Special Committee on Aging, 1984). In the less developed countries the sex ratio over age 60 is 93 males to every 100 females; in the more developed countries the ratio is 66 to 100. The percentage of older people is greater in the more developed regions, at 15% as against 6% in the rest of the world (Hoover & Siegel, 1986). The authors comment that the sex imbalance in old age "is typically associated with the following characteristics: widowhood, one-parent (female-headed) or one-person (female) households, reduced income and increased poverty of older women, and greater risks of ill health and institutionalization of women."

The developed countries are those dominated by Western technology, with a generally adequate standard of living. The elderly poor in the less developed countries fare very badly; if most of the population lives on the edge of disaster, the elderly are apt to be pushed over the brink. When food is scarce, those who are no longer able to contribute economically may go unfed. Older women who are widowed or divorced may have few resources for survival (Seager & Olson, 1986).

Although the traditional societies we described in the preceding section did not always treat their elderly with respect, and women's status was often more problematic than men's, as long as women performed valued functions as repositories of tribal history, folk medicine, rituals, and the rules of etiquette, there was a place for them. Most traditional tribal societies valued and supported their aged. In industrialized societies the value of the elderly is equated primarily with economic contributions and only secondarily with family support. They are not needed in the work force, and their families do not depend on them for much of anything. As a result, Western industrial nations must find other sources than the family to care for the elderly.

One response has been provided in some countries by all-inclusive social welfare programs. In Scandinavia, governments have been especially noted for extensive, publicly funded programs that provide basic social services from birth to death. Adult children are not expected to have to care for the economic needs of their elderly parents. Family connections may then more likely be voluntary and mutually rewarding or remote and uninvolved (Barrow, 1986). An attitude study by Skogland (1980) showed that young women had a favorable view of the elderly, perhaps a function of the fact that they did not have to anticipate the future burden of aging parents.

Some of the elderly in Great Britain are fortunate enough to live in the "New Towns," which are planned intergenerational communities. New Town elders are embedded in supportive community systems, according to Hornum (1983), who studied these communities, and they are able to avoid the isolation and loneliness that the elderly in America anticipate. The arrangements provide for the development of helpful networks: "some of the housewives . . . pool the cab fare and taxi into and out of the town center on a weekly basis to do their marketing." The day centers provided for the elderly help to offset potential intergenerational conflicts. As one adult daughter put it, "'Mum going to the day center means she doesn't expect to have me pop in every day. She is making new friends, and they can grouse about the way things ought to be.'"

Older parents are encouraged to move into the same New Town community as their adult children live in as one way of meeting another need created by new life-styles. A physically agile grandmother "may act as child minder" for a working daughter. There are obvious advantages for older women from this kind of planned intergenerational community for those of modest means. Another description of an indigenous community in Great Britain is provided by Francis (1984), who studied the elderly in a neighborhood in Leeds. The pattern of living close to family and friends, together with social services designed to facilitate and support the Jewish life-style of this particular group of inhabitants, provides a satisfying existence for the mostly elderly widows in the community. Unfortunately, only a minority of British aged benefit from the New Town policy (Pinker, 1980).

The contrast between the Scandinavian programs and British programs for the elderly and the situation of the rural Irish is depressing and desperate:

> The combined effects of increased longevity due to medical technology, urbanization pressures and values, and higher education for the younger generation everywhere contribute to decline in gerontocratic authority. The old ones of rural Ireland are, ironically enough, suffering from their own demographic gains. (Scheper-Hughes, 1983)

Without land or other financial resources, isolated from family or lacking any family, they become depressed, often developing highly eccentric behavior. The county mental hospital "has become the largest recipient of the unwanted elderly. Throughout Ireland, 30 percent of the psychiatric population is elderly—65 and older" and mostly female. Some widows and mothers are able to maintain "some influence and command respect in spheres of life from which village males are generally excluded." These include religious observance and influence over adult children as a result of affectional bonds developed over the years with both sons and daughters. The modernization of this rural society has, on the whole, left many of the aged without family or community support, and the only public provision for them is the mental hospital.

In Yugoslavia the inroads of modernization have not yet destroyed a family system in which kinship is a central focus of individual life. According to Simic (1983), "there are few transcendental values which can vie with those associated with the family." Parents have priority over spouses in terms of affectional ties. Even urbanization has not appeared to weaken such relationships. An older mother or widow would face old age without the fear of loneliness and abandonment experienced by the Irish.

Japan provides some of the most interesting data on the changing role of the elderly and on the challenge that an aging population presents to a technologically advanced society. Americans have long had a highly idealized view of the place of the elderly in Japanese culture, one that is not fully supported on closer examination (Tobin, 1987). Ancestor worship is central to religious observance among traditional Japanese. "Since reverence and devotion to dead ancestors are of supreme importance, respect and duty toward living parents and grandparents (who will soon become dead ancestors) become the second most important things in life" (Palmore & Maeda, 1985, p. 20). An elaborate etiquette defines the ways in which younger persons address and treat the elderly. There is even a national holiday, "Respect for the Elders Day."

However, an unfamiliar side of this filial ethic is a recognition that when the elderly become burdensome "they had an obligation to leave this world" (Plath, 1983) and younger family members might even assist them in doing so. This concept is embodied in the image of *obasute* ("discarding granny"). A mountain 90 miles from Tokyo still bears this name, though such abandonment is not practiced in fact in modern Japan. There is, however, leniency toward kinfolk who have hastened the death of an aging and ailing relative. Older people pray for a quick and painless death, and large numbers of the elderly visit a temple said to respond to such prayers at stated times during the year.

The devout wish not to be a burden in old age is reflected in suicide statistics. In the United States suicide by women decreases sharply in old age, while the rate for men continues to rise; in Japan the curve rises steadily for women to age 80, with even higher rates than for old men (Plath, 1983).

The typical outcome of Japanese filial responsibility in practical terms is that three-generational families will share the same home, usually that of the oldest son, a living arrangement that accounts for 7 of 10 elderly Japanese. This compares with 13% living with an adult child in the United States, 8% in Great Britain, and 21% in France (Palmore & Maeda, 1985). An even higher percentage of widowed elderly Japanese live with an adult child.

The grandmother is particularly important: "Typically she prepares or supervises preparation of meals, supervises younger children, does small gardening, and helps with the laundry" (Palmore & Maeda, 1985). She is also the one who perpetuates religious observances, and when the mother is needed in the fields, she will represent her at school affairs. In a study comparing the attitudes of American women and Japanese women living in Tokyo regarding care of the elderly, it was daughters who felt that they were responsible in the former group and daughters-in-law in the latter. Both samples agreed that the family has a responsibility for such care, but there appeared to be evidence that the crowded multigenerational families in Tokyo caused "negative feelings and a potential for domestic conflict" (Campbell & Brody, 1986) The Tokyo women "tended to agree that old people are too powerful and that they are unlikely to become wiser with age." If the older woman lives alone, as many do, she may receive "even more visits, support, allowance, help and gifts from [her] children than those living in joint households" (Palmore & Maeda, 1985, p. 43), which may be a way of keeping her from moving in.

Unlike older women in the United States, Japanese elderly may remain in the labor force after age 65. In 1965, 18% of older Japanese women were working, compared to 9% in the United States; in 1980 the numbers declined to 16% and 8%, respectively (Palmore & Maeda, 1985). Although "the status and integration of the elderly in Japan has declined substantially from a peak when Japan was an agricultural society" (p. xvi), their status is still considerably higher than in other cultures, and women appear to benefit also; as elderly women their status is considerably higher than it was at earlier ages.

China, which shares with Japan many of the Confucian beliefs in filial piety, also has a deeply imbedded tradition of oldest sons caring for aging parents. The policy adopted by the Communist leadership of the People's Republic of China reducing population growth through restricting families to only one child has been viewed with great concern by the parent generation. At least one son is needed to care for parents in old age, and with a restriction to only one child, many become frantic if that child is a girl. The government has tried to reassure the people that women have the same filial obligations and responsibilities, and it is pursuing an active policy to support female aspirations in the work force, but it has become increasingly difficult to resist demands to allow daughter-only families to have a second child (Hong, 1987).

Grandparents are very important in China. It is probably the only country that has legislated their obligations and the responsibilities of others for them. Article 22 of *The Marriage Law of the People's Republic of China* (1982) states:

> Grandparents or maternal grandparents who have the capacity to bear the relevant costs have the duty to rear their grandchildren or maternal grandchildren who are minors and whose parents are deceased. Grandchildren or maternal grandchildren who have the capacity to bear the relevant costs have the duty to support and assist their grandparents or maternal grandparents whose children are deceased."

This law also stipulates that "after a marriage has been registered, the woman may become a member of the man's family, or the man may become a member of the woman's family, according to the agreed wishes of the two parties." The latter provision is designed to ease the concern that, lacking a son, old parents would be without supporting children or descendants to perform ritual lineage observations.

All Chinese are expected to be gainfully employed. Retirement age is 60 for men and 55 or 50 for women, depending on the employing unit. Pensions, based on time worked, range from 60 to 75% of the standard wage, and there is a supplement if the total amount is too low (Tao, 1986). Since women's wages lag behind men's, their retirement wage is less. However, the majority of the population, the peasants, are not covered by pension plans.

In 1982, 70.6% of China's elderly were widows (Lin, 1987). In traditional China it was a disgrace for a widow to remarry. As one woman reported, "After my first husband died, my eldest daughter had very strict views on what I should do. 'For the honor of our family and our late father's name,' she said, 'you must never marry again' " (Lin, 1986). Luckily for Mrs. Lin, her daughter realized the injustice of traditional ways when she was abandoned by her husband, and she relented toward her mother's remarriage. In 1980s Shanghai, 20% of the elderly were without spouses. "Although many widows would like to take on a new partner, feudal notions still have a hold, not only among the widows themselves but among their children and other relatives as well" so the media stepped in to dispel these old myths. Matchmaking agencies exclusively for the elderly were established, and three weddings soon resulted. "The amorous couples have already turned out to be trendsetters, giving other widowed seniors the courage to remarry" (Lin, 1986). An addition to the basic marriage law regarding the interests of the aged is expected soon.

Since all women in modern China are expected to work outside the home, finding child care is imperative. Grandmothers, particularly the wife's mother, are overwhelmingly preferred; bringing in the son's mother "runs the risk of setting up the old explosive confrontation between husband's mother and wife. Maternal grandmother taking over the child care appears to be relatively commonplace" (Barlow & Lowe, 1985, p. 146). But even if this solves one problem, it may produce another: "having grandma around constantly means she will meddle more in the couple's intimate life." Young women felt "the effect of having been raised by grandmothers. Such a great gap separated the very old-fashioned expectations bred into them by the older women, from the modern ideas about women's social roles taught in school, later" (p. 147).

A recent study by Ikels (1983) compares the life and adaptations of Chinese elderly in Hong Kong and Boston. Though family care for elderly women in both situations was forthcoming, modernization and urbanization in both sites forced significant changes in the family roles of the elderly, who usually represent traditional ways.

We have been able to give only a cursory overview of a few of the social patterns existing in other industrialized countries that affect the lives of older women. What is apparent is that each culture evolves a pattern consistent with other cultural values. Most of the countries of the world are facing rapid social change including unprecedented increases in the proportion of elderly—and elderly women—in the population. Many of the practices and attitudes reported now may be drastically altered for future cohorts.

SUMMARY

We do not know much about the ordinary lives of older women from the historical record; historians have not looked for them in a sustained and scholarly fashion. However, one aspect of old women has been noted: the myth of old woman as witch. Thousands of unfortunate individuals were put to death during the height of witch mania in the 17th and early 18 centuries. It is a heritage that has not wholly disappeared.

The variety of ways that cultures choose to define the role and status of the older woman is staggering. In some societies older women achieve freedom and power; they are respected for their knowledge of rituals and herbal lore. In other cultures they oppose any modernization because they rightly fear that even though the lives of younger women may improve, it will relegate them, as upholders of tradition, to a useless and vulnerable old age; other older women recognize that modernization can only improve their lot and are supporters of change.

The need for extensive social programs to care for dependent elderly, most of them women, has been met by technologically advanced countries in a variety of ways. In some, such as Scandinavia, older people are fully cared for by government programs, relieving families of the obligation. In countries such as Japan tradition is still a strong determinant of how the elderly survive, whereas in China, which is attempting to mandate modernization, there are strains between tradition and government goals; often older women feel uneasy about their future.

REFERENCES

Achenbaum, W. A. (1985). Societal perceptions of aging and the aged. In R. H. Binstock & E. Shanas (Eds.), *Handbook of aging and the social sciences* (pp. 129–148). New York: Van Nostrand Reinhold.

Barlow, T. E., & Lowe, D. M. (1985). *Chinese reflections: Americans teaching in the People's Republic*. New York: Praeger.

Barrow, G. M. (1986). *Aging, the individual and society* (3rd ed.). St. Paul, MN: West Publishing.

Broan, J. K., & Kerns, V. (Eds.). (1986). In her prime: A new view of middle-aged women. So. Hadley, MA: Bergin & Garvey, Publishing.

Campbell, R., & Brody, E. M. (1986). Women's changing roles and help to the elderly: Attitudes of women in the United States and Japan. *The Gerontologist, 26*(6), 584–592.

Cameron, S. (1985). Give us more credit, *UNICEF News*, Issue 122, 20-23.

Chafetz, J. A., & Dworkin, A. G. (1986). *Female revolt: Women's movements in world historical perspective*. Totawa, NJ: Roman and Allenheld Publishing.

Cool, L., & McCabe, J. (1983). The "scheming hag" and the "dear old thing": The anthropology of aging women. In J. Sokolovsky (Ed.), *Growing old in different societies* (pp. 56–68). Belmont, CA: Wadsworth.

Covey, H. C. (1988). Historical terminology used to represent old people. *The Gerontologist, 28*(3), 29–297.

Cowgill, D. O. (1986). *Aging around the world*. Belmont, CA: Wadsworth.

Foner, N. (1984). *Ages in conflict: A cross cultural perspective on inequality between old and young*. New York: Columbia University Press.

Francis, D. (1984). *Will you still need me, will you still feed me when I'm 84?* Bloomington, IN: Indiana University Press.

Fraser, A. (1984). *The weaker vessel*. New York: Knopf.

Garrett, C. (1977). Women and witches, *Signs*, *3*(2), 461–470.

Gibson, Rose C. Blacks in an aging society. *Daedalus*, 1986, 115, *1*, 349-371.

Haber, C. (1983). *Beyond sixty-five: The dilemma of old age in America's past*. New York: Cambridge University Press.

Hardin, B. (1985, July 13). Africans keep rite of girls' circumcision. *Washington Post*, pp. A12-13.

Harrell, S. (1981). Growing old in rural Taiwan. In P. T. Amoss & S. Harrell (Eds.), *Other ways of growing old: Anthropological perspectives* (pp. 193–210). Stanford, CA: Stanford University Press.

Holmes, L., & Rhoads, E. (1983). Aging and change in Samoa. In J. Sokolovsky (Ed.), *Growing old in different societies* (pp. 119–129). Belmont, CA: Wadsworth.

Hong, L. K. (1987). Potential effects of the one-child policy on gender equality in the People's Republic of China. *Gender and Society*, *1*(3), 317–326.

Hoover, S. L., & Siegel, J. S. (1986). International demographic trends and perspectives on aging. *Journal of Cross-Cultural Gerontology*, *1*, 5–30.

Hornum, B. (1983). The elderly in British New Towns: New roles, new networks. In J. Sokolovsky (Ed.), *Growing old in different societies* (pp. 211–224). Belmont, CA: Wadsworth.

Ikels, C. (1983): *Aging and adaptation: Chinese in Hong Kong and the United States*. Hamden, CT: Shoe String Press.

Keith, J. (1982). *Old people as people: Social and cultural influences on aging and old age*. Boston: Little Brown.

Kerns, S. (1985). Sexuality and social control among the Garifuma (Belize). In J. K. Brown & V. Kerns (Eds.), *In her prime: A new view of middle-aged women* (pp. 87–98). South Hadley, MA: Bergin & Garvey.

Lee, R. B. (1985). Work, sexuality, and aging among the Kung women. In J. K. Brown & V. Kerns (Eds.), *In her prime: A new view of middle-aged women* (pp. 23–36). South Hadley, MA: Bergin & Garvey.

Lin, Y. (1987). When a widow remarries. *China Reconstructs*, *35*, 13–14.

A little courage and imagination go a long way. (1985). *UNICEF News*, No. 122, 13–14.

Lopata, H. Z. (1987). *Widows: The Middle East, Asia, and the Pacific*. Durham, NC: Duke University Press.

Murguia, E., Schultz, T. M., Markides, K. J., & Janson, P. (1984). *Ethnicity and aging: A bibliography*. San Antonio, TX: Trinity University Press.

Nahemow, N. (1983). Grandparenthood among the Baganda: Role options in old age. In J. Sokolovsky (Ed.), *Growing old in different societies* (pp. 104–115). Belmont, CA: Wadsworth.

Palmore, E. B., & Maeda, D. (1985). *The honorable elders revisited: A revised cross-cultural analysis of aging in Japan*. Durham, NC: Duke University Press.

Pinker, R. A. (1980). Facing up to the eighties: Health and welfare needs of British elderly (Great Britain). Part 1. *The Gerontologist, 20*(3), 273–283.

Plath, D. (1983). "Ecstasy years"—old age in Japan. In J. Sokolovsky (Ed.), *Growing old in different societies* (pp. 147–153). Belmont, CA: Wadsworth.

Rogers, K. M. (1966). *The troublesome helpmate: A history of misogyny in literature*. Seattle, WA: University of Washington Press.

Sangren, P. S. (1983). Female gender in Chinese religious symbols: Kuan Y, MaTsu and the "Eternal Mother." *Signs, 9*(11), 4–25.

Scheper-Hughes, N. (1983). Deposed kings: The demise of the rural Irish gerontocracy. In J. Sokolovsky (Ed.), *Growing old in different societies* (pp. 130–146). Belmont, CA: Wadsworth.

Seager, J., & Olson, A. (1986). *Women in the world: An international atlas*. New York: Simon and Schuster.

Silverman, P., & Maxwell, R. J. (1983). The significance of information and power in the comparative study of the aged. In J. Sokolovsky (Ed.), *Growing old in different societies* (pp. 43–55). Belmont, CA: Wadsworth.

Skogland, J. (1980). Attitudes towards the elderly in Sweden: Correlates of age group comparisons. In J. Hendricks (Ed.), *In the country of the old* (pp. 77–92). Farmingdale, NY: Baywood.

Slapgard, S. (1985). Tradition against the law. *UNICEF News*, No. 122, 26–27.

Tao, L. (1986). A new future for the old, *Women of China, 11*, 1.

Tobin, J. J. (1987). The American idealization of old age in Japan. *The Gerontologist, 27*(1), 53–58.

Torrey, B. B., Kinsella, K., & Taeuber, C. M. (1987). *An aging world*. International Population Reports, Series P-95, No. 78. Washington, DC: Bureau of the Census.

van den Berghe, P. (1983). Age differentiation in human societies. In J. Sokolovsky (Ed.), *Growing old in different societies* (pp. 72–81). Belmont, CA: Wadsworth.

Walker, B. G. (1985). *The crone: Woman of age, wisdom and power*. New York: Harper and Row.

Wolf, M. (1972). *Women and family in rural Taiwan*. Stanford, CA: Stanford University Press.

9
Being Female, Ethnic, and Old

Having grown up female, women enter the decades after age 40 facing personal and social expectations that increasingly differ from those in their youth. The situations encountered by older women who are members of ethnic minority groups are more difficult to negotiate. So far in this book we have addressed the gender issues that apply to the dominant Caucasian group in a Western and technologically sophisticated society. Now we have to ask how women fare when they grow old in cultural settings far from their ethnic roots and as members of a minority/ethnic group in a white majority community.

It is part of the unfortunate history of minority groups in the United States that their status is marginal. Members of such groups can encounter the barriers of social prejudice against members of their groups, typically including a whole array of stereotypes, mostly negative. Many have been hampered by their immigrant origins; they may not be fluent or literate in English, may not know the norms and mores of American social interaction, and may have life-styles that differ from mainstream America. Often included among these differences is the place of women in the family and the roles women are expected to play in society. Many but not all immigrant ethnic groups traditionally relegate women to a subservient role, whose main functions are those related to family maintenance. Many crucial decisions may be made by a woman's husband or parents, and she is typically not expected to seek an independent career or enter the work force except for dire financial need.

In this chapter we will look at how older women fare when they are members of an ethnic or racial group. We will examine in particular the situation of older Hispanic and Black women.

FEMALE, OLDER, MINORITY

The theories that have been developed to gain insight into the aging experience have not included consideration of aging in America's ethnic groups (Markides & Mindel, 1987). Because of this omission, applications of such theories to explain minority aging often do not "fit" the data. In trying to account for ways in which minority status affects aging, analysts of the problems faced by Black aged in the United States advanced the concept of "double jeopardy." This hypothesis "which was originally applied to older Blacks, states that in addition to suffering from the prejudices, stereotypes, and discrimination associated with old age, ethnic minority aged also bear the burden of being Black, Chicano, Native American, or of being a member of another minority group." Such a hypothesis rests on a deficit theory of aging and of minority group status, which in turn makes assumptions about relative social and economic deprivation. But minority status is not necessarily all negative. Ethnicity may in fact be "a significant resource in dealing with problems of aging" (Bengtson, 1979).

Discussions of minority aging have overlooked or underestimated sex differences. Sokolovsky (1983) states:

> No analysis of aging is really complete without dealing with the differential impact of this process on men and women. The sexual dichotomy in aging seems universal. . . . Yet despite the fact that in the vast majority of societies, persons over 60 are more likely to be women than men, until recently many anthropological studies have tended to describe only one response to aging in a given sociocultural context or to portray males as the exclusive holders of significant roles in old age. (p. 12)

Foner (1984) comments, "Like women generally, old women have been given short shrift in most ethnographic accounts, and much less material is available on them than on old men, particularly concerning tensions with younger people" (p. 68). Some researchers ignore sex as a variable or assume that generalizations about men's aging is all that we need to know (Hendricks, 1980; Maxwell & Silverman, 1980).

When one reviews reports on aging and minority/ethnic groups, it becomes quite clear that women in these groups often face a more complex and more problematic aging than men. There is a triple burden for those who are older, minority, and female. Our largest minority/ethnic groups—Black and Hispanic—are also among the poorest.

While contemporary America is struggling to deal with changes in women's traditional role, minority women are more typically apt to be enmeshed in subcultures that resist new definitions of that role. In some groups, such as Black Americans, traditional views of women become highly positive in old age; it is a time when the woman can express her own needs and can be accorded power and status in the community. Others define the older woman as redundant and useless, particularly if she is no longer able to contribute financially. Some traditional cultures, such as the Italian-American, have built-in patterns of relationships that often create intergenerational conflict. The older woman is sometimes the winner and sometimes the loser.

The status of older women, as many biographies and autobiographies of immigrant women reveal, became tenuous when these societies and groups encountered the New World and the social and economic changes resulting from industrialization (Kramer & Masur, 1976). The younger generation of women may or may not be benefited by modernization when they in turn become old.

Ethnic differences are woven into the fabric of American life. All of those who have populated our country, except for Native Americans, have come here bringing their culture with them. Over the centuries these groups have adapted to settings different from those they left; they have in most instances learned a new language and in later generations married outside their ethnic group.

The transition from immigrant to American has rarely been easy. To help both the newcomer and family members, particularly the elderly, many ethnic groups, prior to the enactment of Social Security, built up mutual-aid societies. Although these societies could not meet all of the needs of their group, in many instances there were the only ones to help the old and destitute (Kutzik, 1979). Such societies, built on a common ethnic bond, would be responsive to the particular cultural norms in terms of life-style, etiquette, and attitudes toward the elderly. It was not shameful to admit one's ethnicity; in fact, it was just this ethnicity that made the support of the group possible. With the advent of Social Security, following the economic devastations of the Depression, these mutual-aid societies were no longer needed. Those that survive can be found in ethnic enclaves in urban centers and primarily act as social clubs for the male elderly, with perhaps a women's auxiliary. The ethnic revival of the 1960s and 1970s and the search for one's roots revitalized such groups and gave new value to the elderly, often the family matriarch, as repositories of tradition (Novak, 1971).

Today we have another, very different immigrant group, most of whom are young adults and their children. The largest is Hispanic, composed of a very diverse population from Mexico, Puerto Rico, Cuba, and every country in Central and South America. Another new and growing group comprises Asian-pacific immigrants from China, Taiwan, Japan, the Philippines, and Korea and those from Southeast Asia: Laos, Cambodia, Vietnam, and Thailand. There are relatively few elderly in these groups, but for those who have migrated recently the problem of adapting to a new and often drastically different culture and lacking literacy in English can be overwhelming.

For some ethnic groups the culture of their country of origin remains very potent in determining how the aged will fare. Generational adaptations also are affected by ethnic identity. First-, second-, and third-generation effects have been an important part of the studies of cultural assimilation in America. The place of women in mainstream America is often very different from that of traditional cultures. The American-born second- or third-generation woman is restive under family constraints regarding whom she should marry, how much education she should seek, and what kind of work she should accept. Sons have been expected to make their way in the new world, but daughters have often been expected to stay within family-prescribed limits. The immigrant mother can be caught between the pressure to uphold tradition and the hope for a better life for her daughter and grandchildren. There is continued ambivalence in the American story regarding how much an ethnic group should retain of its Old World background, how much should be discarded, and to what degree it is desirable that ethnic differentiation be merged into an American identity. (See, for example, Handlin, 1951; Mindel & Habenstein, 1976; Novak, 1971; Patterson, 1977; Sowell, 1978).

Though foreign labor was actively recruited during the growing years of America, the individuals themselves were not necessarily treated well. The history of most immigrant groups is one of initial hostility and disdain. The result is that we have achieved a kind of "cultural pluralism in which an immigrant group, while showing some degree of assimilation and accommodation to a host culture in secondary relations, still shows marked cultural differences in face-to-face or primary group relations" (Cohler & Grunebaum, 1981, p. 279). The immigrants' pattern of settlement in ethnic ghettos in big cities or in farming communities in the Midwest provided a familiar context in an alien environment. But growing affluence, expanded economic opportunities, the influence of the common school, and easily accessible higher education, plus the Americanizing influence of television, has eroded many such enclaves, with particularly unsettling impact on the first generation—now very elderly, the remnants of the great migrations. The recent immigrants from Asia and Latin America have also established ethnic enclaves, but these immigrants appear to have a greater interest in moving into mainstream America than did those millions who immigrated at the turn of the century. It is important to understand the real differences between the old and the new immigrants, as well as changes in the country of origin—modernization, war, revolution—if social policy in general or interaction with an individual in particular is to be successful, as Sengstock (1977) points out.

Ethnicity can be positively associated with a valued immigrant culture by aging individuals and their families, or it can be negatively viewed "as a determinant of social inequality" supporting continued social class separation and conflict (Rosenthal, 1986). Ignoring this factor or being insensitive to the way it affects behavior can result in personal distress at the end of life. The Hmong, refugees from Laos, have had great difficulty in utilizing available social support, and the elderly have suffered the most (Hayes, 1987). Hirayama (1983) shows the ways ethnic differences emerged when social workers attempted to organize groups within the ethnic community. Unless appropriate cultural norms were observed, the elderly individuals would resist assistance even when it was desperately needed (Cox, 1987; Markides & Mindel, 1987).

IMMIGRANTS FROM WESTERN EUROPE:SOME EXAMPLES

The three-generation case study of Italian-American women by Cohler and Grunebaum (1981) shows the adaptations in family life resulting from immigration and the generational differences that mark the relationships of mothers and adult daughters. The Italian family in the American setting is not the same as "back home." The authors found that "the extended family structure of the Italian-American is of far greater importance in daily life than was true in Southern Italy" (p. 280). The tensions between mothers and adult daughters that the study reveals are in part due to personality differences; but they also result from the clash between ethnic family values strongly upheld by the daughters—when the older mothers became more concerned with their own self-fulfillment, a typical age-related phenomenon—less than with family concerns.

The Cohler and Grunebaum (1981) data are surprising because the daughters were more ethnically conservative than the mothers. The older women wanted to exercise more freedom and autonomy than they had experienced earlier, while the adult daughters wanted a closer, more intrusive relationship. It is noteworthy that "there is little of the second-generation rebellion against long-standing Old World traditions described in the literature. Ethnic traditions are important because they reinforce family solidarity and maintain the primacy of the family over other institutions" (p. 315).

It is apparent that for Italian-American women ethnic identity and ethnic life-styles are valued by women but have different consequences for the old and the young and may be a cause of tensions as well as satisfactions.

Another study (Johnson, 1985) of the strength of this ethnic attachment in Italian-American families also reported the ambivalent closeness between mothers and adult daughters noted by Cohler and Grunebaum (1981). Johnson identified a "gender-linked generational bond. The close ties between mothers and daughters can be traced to a continuity in domestic roles, the content of which does not change greatly over time. In contrast, changing economic conditions exert greater changes in the work roles of fathers and sons" (p. 174). Three-generation families are not uncommon. The major potential conflict between mothers and adult daughters is in the kitchen: "Many daughters and daughters-in-law resent the women of the older generation who refuse to retire from cooking." The contents and recipes for the ubiquitous tomato sauce may be the flash point for conflict:

> Tomato sauce holds a very special place in each family's diet, and each has special recipes for preparing it. . . . For the older generation, the major requirement for the sauce . . . is that no part of it should come from cans. But for second-generation respondents, the ease in the use of commercially prepared food over home canning in the summer, or searching for fresh tomatoes, is far preferable. We heard several reports of open ruptures developing over the tomato sauce. (p. 167)

The family-centered life-styles of these Italian-American families is so strong that even the childless elderly "do not tend to band together after their retirement to form age-based social units. Few respondents used senior citizen groups available in their neighborhoods" (Johnson, 1985, p. 151).

The strong family support that provides a secure home for the elderly in this group, though present in contemporary family units in the 1980s, may not survive in its present form much beyond the next generation. Changing economic conditions, smaller families, high rates of intermarriage, entry of women into the labor force, and migration from ethnic neighborhoods to integrated suburbs will weaken ethnic solidarity. The needs of spouse and children may, under these circumstances, have priority over the needs of aging parents (Johnson, 1983, 1985; Femminella & Quadagno, 1976).

In a study by Cohler and Leiberman (1979) of the personality changes occurring in three ethnic groups—Italian, Irish, and Polish—men were found to become more introverted, more preoccupied with self, and passive. However, "among women this transition from middle to old age is characterized by greater egocentrism and assertiveness, which is reflected in increased concern with active mastery, although primarily in order to provide for one's own needs rather than those of others" (p. 241). The authors see these changes as strongly influenced by the ethnic culture of the older women.

The preservation of ethnic symbols is important to many ethnic groups. An interesting study by Krause (1978; cited in Gelfand, 1983) showed that among three generations of Italian, Jewish, and Slavic women, most indexes of ethnic identity decreased from one generation to another; but one factor, preserving ethnic holidays, was considered important by 73.2% of granddaughters. Grandmothers are valued as a resource for information about the food and etiquette of such rituals. As these mothers and daughters move into old age, the ethnic factor will be muted among "old" immigrants. But even when there is agreement on some minimal ethnic celebrations, generational tensions will persist. Cohler (1982) summarizes a number of studies of ethnic groups that suggest that family ties may be a source of stress for older women rather than of support and that the preference was for "intimacy at a distance."

There are valuable studies of other European immigrant groups showing the varying patterns for gender-related experiences of the elderly. The examples given here show how complicated these are. Also, cultural subgroups based on religious practices show marked differences in their treatment of women (Brubaker & Michael, 1987; Gelfand & Olsen, 1979; Kart, 1987; see also Strange & Teitelbaum, 1987, for an annotated bibliography.)

IMMIGRANTS FROM ASIA

Another large cultural subgroup with significant ethnic differences includes those from Asian countries. The demographic patterns within Asian-American groups are quite different from those of immigrants from Western and Eastern Europe. The first Chinese and Japanese immigrants were men, recruited for hard labor building the railroads and developing agriculture. Discriminatory exclusion laws made immigration by women almost impossible for many decades. As a result, only 44% of Chinese Americans aged 45 to 64 were women, and they were 43.2% of the over-65 group, as reported in the 1970 census (Jackson, 1980). There were very few aged Japanese-American women enumerated in the 1900 and 1930 censuses, but when all states were included in 1970 (with the addition of the large population of Japanese in Hawaii), older women were 51.4% of the 45 to 64 age group and 56.6% of the over-65 group. Filipinos showed a reverse sex ratio, with women making up only 18.8% of the over-65 group in 1970, again reflecting the earlier discriminatory immigration pattern.

Koreans, a relatively recent immigrant group, have a demographic pattern similar to that of the Japanese in 1970; they have benefited by recent immigration reform that permitted the entry of whole family groups from Asia (Gelfand, 1983). The enactment of the Refugee Act of 1980 has allowed groups to enter who never before were resident in the United States: Vietnamese, Cambodian, Laotian, Thai, Iranian, Afghanistan, Hindu, Nigerian, and others. These groups differ radically from previous immigrants: most of them came not because they chose to but because they were forced to, fleeing war or revolution. Many suffered severe difficulties as they sought a safe haven. The toll on the elderly in these groups is particularly heavy. Some elderly Hmong from Laos committed suicide when they realized they could not return to their homeland to die (Hayes, 1987).

The situation of the Japanese-American aged has been the subject of special study because of their unique history in the United States. They were the only identifiable *group* singled out for incarceration, without trial of any sort, only because of their ethnicity—a shameful response to the war hysteria following the attack on Pearl Harbor in 1941.

In a study of first-generation Japanese, the Issei, Montero (1979) found that although community and neighborhood participation declined, particularly for the older Japanese woman, the old parent retained a strong presence within the family. The traditional emphasis on filial piety influences intergenerational relationships, but there is also the immigrant pattern of parental sacrifice so that children may succeed. But aged parents are cared for, as noted by Kitano and Kiumura (1976); ads for an "in-law" apartment "are a popular feature of want ads aimed at the Japanese American." The loss of hard-won economic security due to the wartime internment dislodged the Issei generation and weakened their control over Nisei and Sensei (second- and third-generation American-born Japanese). One result is that this group has one of the highest rates of intermarriage of any of the racially distinctive ethnic groups.

The Chinese constitute one of the oldest Asian immigrant groups, having been brought over to help build the transcontinental railroad. The original laborers were mostly men, and restrictive immigration policy prevented them from bringing their wives or eligible young women. The resulting imbalance in the sexes persisted for decades. However, there were 68.4% Chinese elderly women and only 31.7% elderly men in a random sample population study in California conducted in 1982–83 (Lubben & Becerra, 1987). Many of these foreign-born elderly indicate that they feel uncertain about their status here, as reflected in their preference for returning to mainland China in old age (Huang, 1976). Although there is considerable show of concern for the older parents, the gap in attitudes and values between foreign-born and American-born offspring is immense. Nearly half of the group studied by Lubben and Becerra lived with their children, but many were very bitter about what they perceived to be a lack of filial respect. Foreign-born Chinese elderly, who are often deficient in English, will utilize support services if they are located in their neighborhood and staffed with bilingual workers; otherwise services may not be utilized even when there is great need (Lum, 1983). Older Chinese women rarely venture beyond the confines of Chinatown and relatively little is known about how they fare.

NATIVE AMERICANS

A minority group whose problems are unique and often overwhelming is Native Americans. The story of the tribal groups, relocated and mishandled by decades of federal management, is a sad record of the influence on policy of prejudice, stereotypes, and greed. The damaging impact of reservation living is clearly seen in the mortality and life expectancy rates of Native Americans. A study of the Navajo calculated the life expectancy of men at birth as 58.8 years, and 71.8 years for women, "a sex gap considerably higher than that observed in the general American population" (Markides & Mindel, 1987, p. 88). Every index of social status shows the American Indian to be among those who are worst off (Block, 1979; National Indian Council on Aging, 1979). The lack of available and affordable health care is especially acute for the large numbers of widowed female elderly, who also suffer from "loneliness, inadequate transportation, and lack of resources for home maintenance and family support systems" (Edwards, 1983). Mainstream white models of caregiving are typically not applicable to the traditional norms of Native Americans (Strong, 1984).

The recent interest in cultural artifacts, the resurgence of efforts to maintain traditional tribal ways, and the importance of recording tribal history before all the elders die have given a new status to the very old among Native Americans. Older women skillful in traditional crafts find themselves sought out.

HISPANIC ELDERLY

One of the largest ethnic groups in America, Hispanics, are among both the oldest immigrant groups and the newest. The term *Hispanics* includes many subgroups: Mexicans, Puerto Ricans, Cubans, South Americans, Central Americans, and others from Spanish- or Portuguese-speaking countries (Manuel & Berk, 1983). There is a shared Latin culture among these heavily Catholic groups, but there are also significant differences in level of education, income, ethnic solidarity, and status in the United States.

In the Southwest many Mexican Americans can trace their residence back 10 generations; in Los Angeles most of the Mexican population has arrived very recently, and they make up many of the illegal and undocumented immigrants now subject to new Immigration and Naturalization Service regulations. Nor can one compare the large, relatively well-to-do, and politically powerful Cuban population of Miami with the largely impoverished and powerless Puerto Ricans of New York and New Jersey. As Torres-Gil (1986b) points out,

> despite the continuing influx of young Latin-American immigrants, Hispanics will not always be a young population. They are aging too; already, 5 percent of their number is over sixty-five. In fact, Hispanics are aging at a faster rate than whites; a greater percentage become sixty years old every year than in the white population."

While there are many published studies of the Mexican Americans, there are few that discuss the problems of other groups of Hispanic elderly.

Hispanic culture is robust and powerful, even in today's rapidly changing climate. The Mexican-American family, as Alvirez and Bean (1976) point out, is characterized by machismo: although popularly identified with demonstrations of aggressive sexual virility, it also includes "courage, honor, respect for others, as well as the notion of providing fully for one's family and maintaining close ties with the extended family." Women are expected to be submissive and homebound (Markides & Vernon, 1984). Of those 65 and over, 16.9% of males and 15% of females completed high school; the median for all Hispanic elderly is 5.7 years of school completed (Torres-Gil, 1986a). Only recently has school attendance of females equaled that of males, and far fewer women than men have any college education.

The older Mexican-American woman expects to live out her life in the family circle, either with her own children or within the extended family. A larger percentage (54.6) of Hispanic women over age 75 were living with their families, compared to the 46.8% of white elderly women who were in family settings (Manuel & Reid, 1982). However, a recent report suggests that the figure for Mexican Americans may be exaggerated. Carmela Lacayo, president of an advocacy group for Hispanic elderly, is cited as saying that "fewer than 10 percent of Hispanic elderly live with their families. 'The extended family is a myth,' she says" (Wood, 1987). Though these elderly might not live with their children, they do have a higher rate of interaction with them than do white or Black elderly according to a study conducted in New York City in the late 1970s (Cantor, 1979).

Comparisons of white, Black, and Mexican-American elderly and their satisfaction with family relationships shows that, of the three groups, Mexican-American elderly women have high levels of family contact, but they also have very high expectations that are not always realized. "These culturally defined expectations for contact differ for this group, and when they are unmet, result in lower life satisfaction" (Bengston & Morgan, 1983). Thus, a culturally positive norm—a high rate of intergenerational contact—can also be a source of low morale.

Traditional sex roles were found to be a source of depression and low satisfaction for older males, but for elderly Mexican-American women traditional sex roles provided a source of satisfaction (Markides & Vernon, 1984). A further study of three-generation Mexican Americans showed a strong interaction of women across generations (Markides, Boldt, & Ray, 1986). Women are depended on exclusively in the Mexican-American family for advice and help in health matters, with older Mexican-American women relying heavily on their daughters.

Cultural norms are alive and well among the elderly, according to a study by Bastida (1987). Interviews were conducted with participants at senior citizen centers who were of Puerto Rican, Mexican, or Cuban origin. When asked what was appropriate behavior for older persons, women were strong upholders of culturally sanctioned norms, particularly with reference to sexual behavior and sexual talk. "Findings indicated that stronger sanctions are applied to women than to males who transgress against established age-appropriate norms."

Hispanic elderly are one of the poorest groups in America. The elderly women are more impoverished than Black women ages 65 to 69 and marginally better off after age 70. Both groups are worse off than female white elderly, though all are at or below the poverty level. White males are the only group with adequate incomes after age 65.

Part of the explanation of the high rate of poverty for Hispanic women is their traditionally low rate of labor force participation. This was certainly true until quite recently for Mexican-American women, in large part because of traditional constraints and large families. Few of the oldest age group are covered by Social Security or private pension plans, and later cohorts also have low coverage (Torres-Gil, 1986a, and 1986b; Manuel & Reid, 1982). The increased urbanization of Hispanic groups, particularly those already impoverished, is likely to make for even more stress for the elderly (Markides & Levin, 1987). The ratio of older Hispanic men to older women is higher than for the population as a whole, probably because of the larger number of males in the original immigrant group (Manuel & Reid, 1982), but this ratio does not seem to alleviate the persistent and acute economic problems of the older women.

Hispanics are becoming the largest minority group in the United States, with many new immigrants swelling the ranks and a much higher birth rate adding to their numbers. The documented high rate of poverty of older Hispanic women is thus cause for concern. There may be a strong cultural norm of family interdependence, but this cannot substitute for more effective social supports, which are in woefully short supply for these groups (Hassell, 1981).

BLACK AMERICANS

Black women over 70 are the poorest group in the United States. Their median annual income in 1984 was $4,304. Those between ages 65 and 69 had a median income of $4,446. In 1984 the poverty level was defined as $4,744, which means that half of all older Black women were at least $400 below this level. Subsistence at this level is extremely precarious.

Three of every five elderly Black women were also living alone (U.S. Senate Special Committee on Aging, 1986). These women are mostly widows; Black elderly have a higher rate of widowhood than any other subgroup in our society. At ages 55 to 64, 27% are widowed, compared to only 16% of white women in that category. Over half of Black women aged 65 to 74 are widows, against 38% of whites. And 66.6% of white elderly over 75 are widowed, compared to 72% of Black women, as of 1983. The burden of widowhood is much heavier for Blacks than for whites.

The life-span predictions for Blacks and whites also show the impact of different social conditions. The survival rates shown in Figure 9.1 dramatically underline the burden of minority racial status in America. White women outlive all groups. Figure 9.1 also shows the difference between cohorts. Between 1900 and 1984 Black women nearly tripled their survival rate to age 65 but have not gained as much from 65 to 85. At birth white women have a life expectancy of 5.5 more years than Black women have; white women, on average, will live to be 78.3, whereas Black women will live to be only 73.8 (U.S. Senate Special Committee on Aging, 1986).

Over age 75 the racial difference decreases sharply, with white women having only a 1.2-year advantage in 1983 (U.S. Senate Special Committee on Aging, 1984; see also Gibson, 1986). The narrowing of the gap between Black women and white women (and men) after age 75 is striking. This phenomenon is called the white/nonwhite mortality crossover (Manton, 1982). Demographers have a hard time explaining why: "though both nonwhite males and females start out with a considerable mortality disadvantage . . . at advanced ages they become advantaged: that is, their age-specific probabilities of death are lower, while their life expectancy and the proportion surviving is greater" (p. 64); and Black women are more advantaged than men. How can this be explained? Manton speculates that those Blacks surviving to age 75 are more robust, not having succumbed to the diseases that produced a higher mortality rate for Blacks versus whites

FIGURE 9.1 Percent surviving from birth to age 65 and 85, by sex and race: 1900-02 and 1984.

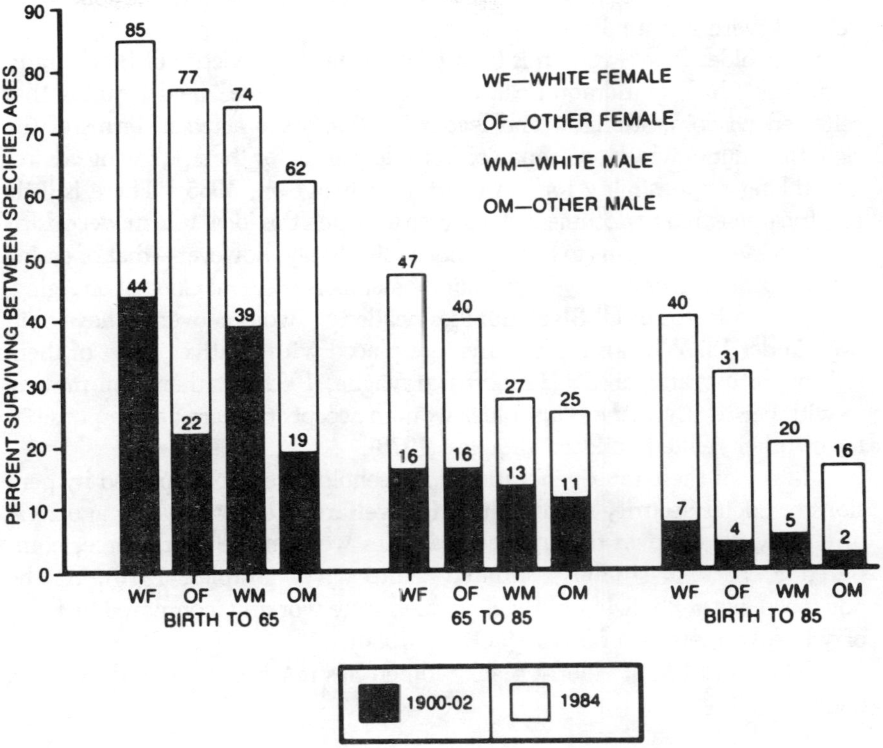

From National Center for Health Statistics. *Vital Statistics of the United States, 1984.* Vol. II, Section 6 (Lifetables), March 1987.

in earlier years. However, Manton suggests that there may be different aging mechanisms at work, with particular reference to late-onset diseases, that have an earlier mortality impact on whites than on Blacks. Another effect of this differential longevity is that the sex ratio of Blacks is 50 males to 100 females at age 85 and over, as against a ratio of 43 to 100 for whites (Manuel & Reid, 1982).

The lower overall life expectancy is directly attributable to poverty. Lack of financial resources means less adequate health care for minorities, which in turn is linked to consistently lower income and levels of education (Jackson, Kolody, & Woods, 1982). There is some indication, however, that Blacks have a higher level of life satisfaction in old age than whites have, despite greater poverty. This may be accounted for by having successfully coped with diversity, being more religious, being able to "sustain personal control and self-esteem" and enjoying the support of the extended family (Watson, 1982). The data from which these generalizations were derived were not analyzed by gender.

The older Black woman is both a beneficiary and victim of Black tradition. The Black grandmother has a noble history. She "held a status that reflected wisdom, strength, and leadership," and she acted in terms of the rights and duties which accompanied her role, caring for the sick, giving advice, and taking responsibility for kin (Burton & Bengtson, 1985). There is little empirical research to document the degree to which this ideal role model existed in fact. One aspect seems to be very much alive today, however—that of caring for grandchildren or other younger family members (Federal Council on Aging, 1979). Two-thirds of all Black families headed by women over 65 have children under 18. When Black children are placed with relatives, most of them will be with grandparents (Lesnoff-Caravaglia, 1982). Rather than moving in with her relatives, the Black older woman accepts the care and responsibility of other related children (Staples, 1976).

Many of these multigenerational households are not supported by pensions or Social Security nor qualified for welfare. Nearly 20 years ago 26% of elderly wives (over 65) in Black families were in the work force, compared to 15% of similarly situated white wives (Staples, 1976). At the advanced age of 85, 8.1% of Black women were working, compared to 4.3% of white women, as of 1970 (Jackson, 1980).

The work life of elderly Black women has not been reported in much detail:

> Most of the disadvantaged Blacks in old age are women. Their financial situation is considerably poorer than that of older men and the jobs they hold are typically lower in wages as well as in prestige. Despite the stereotype of Black women on welfare, many must earn their living (and that of dependents) by working into advanced ages. (Markides & Mindel, 1987, p. 185)

Most women become grandmothers when their daughters are in their 20s and they themselves are in their late 40s or early 50s. Becoming a grandmother is a gratifying event for many women (see Chapter 5). Recent changes in sexual activity on the part of adolescents has produced a new phenomenon: women who become grandmothers between the ages of 25 and 40 (Burton & Bengtson, 1985). The study by Burton and Bengtson identified three groups of Black grandmothers: early, on-time, and late:

> Early grandmothers (median age 32 years) and the on-time grandmothers (median age 46) indicated quite different reactions to the role of grandpar-

> ent. . . . The off-time accession to the lineage role created, for many of these young grandmothers, tensions and conflict, not only in their view of themselves, but also in the family system of cohesion and support.

The authors suggest that there is considerable discomfort on the part of the early, nontraditional grandmother, who resents the view of "elder" that being a grandmother implies. "Such tensions are not reported in portrayals of the 'traditional' Black grandmother's role, which themselves may be stereotypic or romanticized; or it may be that the social context has changed in ways that have made social time clocks more important."

Gibson (1986) observes that the rapid increase in the numbers of older Black women and the growth of Black families without men "may mean that a modal black family of the future . . . will be composed of several generations of women." She continues: "Publicly funded programs and services could encourage these roles of older black women as surrogate parents in families without fathers present," and she points to the historical precedent for these roles of Black women.

The relationship between the generations is affected when role changes, such as becoming a grandmother, occur at a nontraditional time. Expectations of intergenerational caregiving, which have been particularly strong in the Black family, may be disturbed. Unlike the white family system, in which adult children expect to care for elderly parents, in the extended Black family the younger generations look to the elderly matriarch for family cohesion and support. Not only does the grandmother—or great-grandmother in some cases—provide housing and child care, she manages an extended support system that makes up for some of the lacks inherent in subsistence living. Through this network she learns about social service entitlements—how to "work the system" (Taylor, 1982).

Although there is much evidence that many Blacks do not utilize social service programs they are entitled to because of ignorance of the service, transportation problems, and perception of discriminatory treatment, other findings have pointed out how adept many are in asserting their rights. Several reports show that Black elderly who "tended to receive aid from family and kin groups were also the ones who used the greatest number of formally supplied social services as well" (Markides & Mindel, 1987, p. 101). A cohort effect may be at work, however, with those elderly who resist using public support belonging to an older generation with strong belief in a work ethic and the "basic values of self-help and independence" (Taylor, 1982; see also Cantor, 1979). Black women may also rely on extensive "helper networks" over and above reliance on kin for support (Chatters, Taylor, & Jackson, 1985).

A picture of older Black women in the city shows some of their survival strategies. An ethnographic study by Taylor (1982), conducted in a metropolitan community in New England from 1976 to 1977, is important because of the distinctive life-styles of this group of women. The coping strategies found by Taylor "reflect both the strengths and the stresses of Black women. These include the actual or perceived strength of the family as recognized through a system of mutual support and aid; religion as a source of strength and the acceptance of Jesus as liberator; and an adherence to the American work ethic." Noteworthy as especially valued was the network of kin and friends. Money, food, companionship, and advice were exchanged. In a senior housing project the creation of a network of new friends made life less lonely, but it also supported a sense of independence for these single women.

The use of religion as a way of coping with stress has a long history in Black culture, with roots in the slave experience, as the "black church came to fulfill in many instances the needs and functions that were once met by the religion-based tribal and community organization" that Blacks brought with them from Africa (McAdoo, 1979). Contemporary studies seem to indicate that older Black women value church organizations more than men do, not because of a difference in church attendance but in the view of what they can do within the church organization (Taylor, 1986).

Substantially lower incomes for elderly Black women have to do with the kinds of jobs they held, which either were not covered by Social Security or, in the case of domestic service, were not reported even when legally required. At a time when the elderly as a whole were experiencing net gains in disposable income, between 1980 and 1984, "the only elderly group to experience losses over the period were black families" (Moon, 1986). A study of economic hardship of the elderly was conducted by Cook and Kramek (1986). The data are not alayzed by sex, but the authors report that "somewhat more women than men participated in the survey." (The term "somewhat" translates into 71.9% of respondents being women.) This study reported that Black respondents over age 65 spent $4 less per person per week than whites did; 6% of Blacks spent less than the USDA minimum; nearly 14% said their grocery spending was not adequate; and 5% needed food but couldn't afford it. Many more Black elderly than whites had housing problems: could not pay rent, were evicted, or had utilities cut off. The difference in reported medical care was very large, particularly among those aged 50 to 64. Twice as many Blacks as whites reported being sick and needing help; 14% more Blacks were without dental care because of lack of money, and 8% more lacked medical care. Both white and Black elderly in the survey do not name social service agencies as a source of support except in regard to food. The economic picture of the Black elderly female whether she is still married or living alone is bleak indeed (Manuel & Berk, 1983).

Despite the fact that "older black women are the most likely to be poor [they were] the least likely to end their own lives" (Gibson, 1986). Their reliance on prayer as a coping resource may be a partial explanation of these data.

The older Black female is apt to be the most disadvantaged of any group of elderly in the country. In spite of this, she is also apt to be part of an active support network and to have an important role to play in caring for family members, particularly grandchildren. Black women are obtaining more education than ever before and becoming qualified for middle-class jobs and careers. The gap between the more mobile Blacks and the large underclass will continue to present serious social problems for some time to come.

SUMMARY

Every culture and every society must deal with its elders. Sex-role-appropriate behaviors are not only established for children, youth, and young adults but extend into old age.

The American dilemma has always been how to deal with subgroups and subcultures, ethnic or racial, that are perceived to be "different" from mainstream culture. Some immigrant groups have fared well, but the tensions arising between immigrant mothers and their American-born daughters make the later years of these older women difficult. Particularly vulnerable are older women in the most recent refugee groups, as well as Hispanic and Black women, who today are among the poorest groups in the United States. Yet it is these women who struggle for the survival of their families.

REFERENCES

Alvirez, D., & Bean, F. D. (1976). The Mexican-American family. In C. H. Mindel & R. H. Habenstein (Eds.), *Ethnic families in America* (pp. 271–292). New York: Elsevier.

Bastida, E. (1987). Sex-typed old age norms among older Hispanics. *The Gerontologist, 27*(1), 59–63.

Bengtson, V. L. (1979). Ethnicity and aging: Problems and issues in current social science inquiry. In D. E. Gelfand & A. J. Kutzik (Eds.), *Ethnicity and aging: Theory, research, and policy* (pp. 9–31). New York: Springer Publishing Co.

Bengtson, V. L., & Morgan, L. A. (1983). Ethnicity and aging: A comparison of three ethnic groups. In J. Sokolovsky (Ed.), *Growing old in different societies* (pp. 157–167). Belmont, CA: Wadsworth.

Block, M. (1979). Exiled Americans: The plight of the Indian aged in the United

States. In D. E. Gelfand & A. J. Kutzik (Eds.), *Ethnicity and aging* (pp. 184–192). New York: Springer Publishing Co.

Brubaker, T. H., & Michael, C. M. (1987). Amish families in later life. In D. E. Gelfand & C. M. Barresi, (Eds.), *Ethnic dimensions of aging* (pp. 106–117). New York: Springer Publishing Co.

Burton, L. M., & Bengston, V. L. (1985). Black grandmothers: Issues of timing and continuity of roles. In V. L. Bengston & J. F. Robertson (Eds.), *Grandparenthood* (pp. 61–78). Beverly Hills, CA: Sage.

Cantor, M. (1979). The informal support system of New York's inner city elderly: Is ethnicity a factor? In D. E. Gelfand (Ed.), *Ethnicity and aging* (pp. 153–174). New York: Springer Publishing Co.

Chatters, L. M., Taylor, R. J., & Jackson, J. S. (1985). Size and composition of the informal networks of elderly blacks. *Journal of Gerontology, 40*(5), 605–611.

Cohler, B. J., & Grunebaum, H. U. (1981). *Mothers, grandmothers and daughters: Personality and childcare in three generation families*. New York: John Wiley.

Cohler, B., & Leiberman, M. A. (1979). Personality changes across the second half of life: Findings from a study of Irish, Italian and Polish American men and women. In D. E. Gelfand & A. J. Kutzik (Eds.), *Ethnicity and aging* (pp. 227–245). New York: Springer Publishing Co.

Cook, F. L., & Kranek, L. M. (1986). Measuring economic hardship among older Americans. *The Gerontologist, 26*(1), 38–47.

Cox, C. (1987). Overcoming access problems in ethnic communities. In D. E. Gelfand & C. M. Barresi (Eds)., *Ethnic dimensions of aging* (pp. 165–178). New York: Springer Publishing Co.

Edwards, E. D. (1983). Native-American elders: Current issues and policy implications. In L. L. McNeely & J. L. Cohen (Eds.), *Aging in minority groups* (pp. 74–82). Beverly Hills, CA: Sage.

Femminella, F. X., & Quadagno, J. S. (1976). The Italian-American family. In C. H. Mindel & R. H. Habenstein (Eds.), *Ethnic families in America* (pp. 61–87). New York: Elsevier.

Foner, N. (1984). *Ages in conflict*. New York: Columbia University Press.

Gelfand, D. E. (1983). *Aging: The ethnic factor*. Boston: Little, Brown.

Gelfand, D. E., & Olsen, J. K. (1979). Aging in the Jewish family and the Mormon family. In D. F. Gelfand & A. J. Kutzik (Eds.), *Ethnicity and aging* (pp. 206–222). New York: Springer Publishing Co.

Gibson, R. C. (1986). Blacks in an aging society. *Daedalus, 115*(1), 349–371.

Handlin, O. (1951). *The uprooted*. New York: Grosset and Dunlap.

Hassell, S. S. (1981, April). Mexican-American elderly: Are their service needs understood and addressed? *IDRA Newsletter*, pp. 4–8.

Hayes, C. L. (1987). Two worlds in conflict: The elderly Hmong in the United States. In D. E. Gelfand & C. M. Barresi (Eds.), *Ethnic dimensions of aging* (pp. 79–95). New York: Springer Publishing Co.

Hendricks, J. (Ed.). (1980). *In the country of the old*. Farmingdale, NY: Baywood.

Hirayama, H. (1983). Group services for the minority aged. In R. L. McNeely & J. L. Cohen (Eds.), *Aging in minority groups* (pp. 270–279). Beverly Hills, CA: Sage.

Huang, L. J. (1976). The Chinese-American family. In C. H. Mindel & R. H. Habenstein (Eds.), *Ethnic families in America* (pp. 124–148). New York: Elsevier.

Jackson, J. J. (1980). Minorities and aging. Belmont, CA: Wadsworth.

Jackson, M., Kolody, B., & Wood, J. L. (1982). To be old and Black: The case for double jeopardy in income and health. In R. C. Manuel (Ed.), *Minority aging* (pp. 77–82). Westport, CT: Greenwood Press.

Johnson, C. L. (1985). *Growing up and growing old in Italian families. In J. Sokolovsky (Ed.), Growing old in different societies* (pp. 92–103). Belmont, CA: Wadsworth.

Kart, C. S. (1987). Age and religious commitment in the American-Jewish community. In D. E. Gelfand & C. M. Barresi (Eds.), *Ethnic dimensions of aging* (pp. 95–105). New York: Springer Publishing Co.

Kitano, H. H. L., & Kikumura, A. (1976). The Japanese-American family. In C. H. Mindel & R. H. Habenstein (Eds.), *Ethnic families in America* (pp. 41–59). New York: Elsevier.

Kramer, S. & Masur, J. (Eds.). (1976). *Jewish grandmothers*. Boston: Beacon Press.

Krause, C. (1978). *Grandmothers, mothers and daughters*. New York: Institute on Pluralism and Group Identity. Cited in D. E. Gelfand (1983). *Aging: The Ethnic Factor*. Boston: Little Brown.

Kutzik, A. J. (1979). American social provision for the aged: An historical perspective. In D. E. Gelfand & A. J. Kutzik (Eds.), *Ethnicity and aging* (pp. 32–65). New York: Springer Publishing Co.

Lesnoff-Caravaglia, G. (1982). The black "granny" and the Soviet "babushka": Commonalities and contrasts. In R. C. Manuel (Ed.), *Minority aging*, pp. 109–114. Westport, CT: Greenwood Press.

Lubben, J. E., & Becerra, R. M. (1987). Social support among Black, Mexican and Chinese elderly. In D. E. Gelfand & C. M. Barresi (Eds.), *Ethnic dimensions of aging* (pp. 130–144). New York: Springer Publishing Co.

Lum, D. (1983). Asian-Americans and their aged. In L. L. McNeely & J. L. Colen (Eds.), *Aging in minority groups* (pp. 85–94). Beverly Hills, CA: Sage Publishers.

Manton, K. G. (1982). Differential life expectancy: Possible explanations during the later ages. In R. C. Manuel (Ed.), *Minority aging* (pp. 63–74). Westport, CT: Greenwood Press.

Manuel, R. C., & Berk, M. L. (1983). A look at similarities and differences in older minority populations. *Aging, 339*, 21–29.

Manuel, R. C., & Reid, J. (1982). A comparative demographic profile of the minority and non-minority aged. In R. C. Manuel (Ed.), *Minority aging* (pp. 31–52). Westport, CT: Greenwood Press.

Markides, K. S., Boldt, S. S., & Ray, L. A. (1986). Sources of helping and intergenerational solidarity: A three generation study of Mexican-Americans. *Journal of Gerontology, 41*(5), 506–511.

Markides, K. S., & Vernon, S. W. (1984). Aging, sex-role orientation and adjustment: A three generation study of Mexican-Americans. *Journal of Gerontology, 39*(5), 586–591.

Markides, K. S., & Levin, J. S. (1987). The changing economy and the future of the minority aged. *The Gerontologist, 27*(3), 273–274.

Markides, K. S., & Mindel, C. J. (1987). *Aging and ethnicity*. Beverly Hills, CA: Sage.

Markides, K. S., & Vernon, S. W. (1984). Aging, sex-role orientation and adjustment: A three generation study of Mexican-Americans. *Journal of Gerontology, 39*(5), 586–591.

Maxwell, R. J., & Silverman, P. (1980). Information and esteem: Cultural considerations in the treatment of the aged. In J. Hendricks (Ed.), *In the country of the old* (pp. 3–34). Farmingdale, NY: Baywood.

McAdoo, J. L. (1979). Well-being and fear of crime among the black elderly. In D. E. Gelfand & A. J. Kuztik (Eds.), *Ethnicity and aging*, pp. 277–290. New York: Springer Publishing Co.

Mindel, C. H., & Habenstein, R. W. (1976). *Ethnic families in America: Patterns and variations*. New York: Elsevier.

Montero, D. (1979). Disengagement and aging among the Issei. In D. E. Gelfand & A. J. Kutzik (Eds.), *Ethnicity and aging* (pp. 193–205). New York: Springer Publishing Co.

Moon, M. (1986). Impact of the Reagan years on the distribution of income of the elderly. *The Gerontologist, 26*(1), 32–37.

National Indian Council on Aging. (1979). *The continuum of life: Health concerns of the Indian elderly*. Albuquerque, NM: Author.

Novak, M. (1971). *The rise of the unmeltable ethnics: Politics and culture in the seventies*. New York: Macmillan.

Patterson, O. (1977). *Ethnic chauvinism: The reactionary impulse*. New York: Stein and Day.

Rosenthal, C. J. (1986). Family supports in later life: Does ethnicity make a difference? *The Gerontologist, 26*(1), 19–24.

Sengstock, M. S. (1977). Social change in the country of origin as a factor in immigrant conceptions of nationality. *Ethnicity, 4*, 54–70.

Sokolovsky, J. (Ed.). (1983). *Growing old in different societies: Cross cultural perspectives*. Belmont, CA: Wadsworth.

Sowell, T. (Ed.). (1978). *Essays and data on American ethnic groups*. New York: The Urban Institute.

Staples, R. (1976). The Black family. In C. H. Mindel & R. W. Habenstein (Eds.), *Ethnic families in America* (pp. 221–247). New York: Elsevier.

Strange, H. & Teitelbaum, M. (Eds.). (1987). *Aging and cultural diversity: New directions and annotated bibliography*. South Hadley, MA: Bergin and Garvey.

Strong, C. (1984). Stress and caring for elderly relations: Interpretations and coping strategies in an American Indian and White sample. *The Gerontologist, 24*(3), 251–256.

Taylor, S. P. (1982). Mental health and successful coping among aged Black women. In R. C. Manuel (Ed.), *Minority aging* (pp. 95–102). Westport, CT: Greenwood Press.

Torres-Gil, F. (1986a). An examination of factors affecting future cohorts of elderly Hispanics. *The Gerontologist, 26*(2), 140–146.

Torres-Gil, F. (1986b). The latinization of a multigenerational population: Hispanics in an aging society. *Daedalus, 115*(1), 325–348.

U.S. Senate Special Committee on Aging. (1984). *Aging America*. Washington, DC: U.S. Dept. of Health and Human Services.

U.S. Senate Special Committee on Aging. (1986). *Aging America*. Washington, DC: U.S. Dept. of Health and Human Services.

Watson, W. H. (1982). Mental health of the minority aged: Selected correlates. In R. C. Manuel (Ed.), *Minority aging* (pp. 83–87). Westport, CT: Greenwood Press.

Wood, J. (1987). Labors of love: What will you do when it's your turn to take care of a loved one? *Modern Maturity, 30*(4), 29–34, 90–94.

10
The Older Woman in the Year 2000

Older women in the year 2000 and beyond will experience their later years in a far different fashion than the older women we have been describing in this book. Social forces are at work that will create a very different world in which to grow old. Will this future be a better one? Will some of the problems older women face today be resolved only to be replaced by new difficulties? Do we know enough about how women age to help us predict what the future may be like? These are questions we will address in this chapter.

Research on women, which is scattered and incomplete, is of necessity on cohorts whose lives have been affected by social forces operational in earlier decades. For example, when women can get only low-paying jobs with limited opportunity for advancement, often without any pension benefits, their retirement years are financially marginal, and old age is a perilous passage to death. Currently, women can enter many professions formerly reserved for men, career ladders are more available, and they can anticipate that the earnings gap between men and women will continue to lessen. As a result, their old age will be a very different experience from that of their mothers or grandmothers. Key changes in women's lives in the last few decades and continuing into the future mean that what we currently know about older women may be of only limited predictive value for informing us about how women will age in the next half-century.

But even what we know about the older woman today is scattered and incomplete. For the woman of the year 2000 to be best served by social programs and in her own best interests, research must be drastically improved and extended. Gerontologists need to recognize that in many significant ways men and women age differently. This difference should be studied and analyzed and the findings applied to public policy. In this final chapter we will look at some predictions of the future for older women and at the areas needing greatly increased research efforts on how women age and how gender differences influence aging.

GETTING BETTER ALL THE TIME—MOST OF THE TIME

By the year 2000 the baby-boom generation will be reaching its 40s and 50s. And a remarkable generation it is indeed (Jones, 1980). There are gloomy predictions that the number of elderly will break the Social Security bank and launch a vicious intergenerational fight for federal and state funds (*Washington Post*, March 6, 1987). Since older women will comprise 60 to 75% of these elderly, the policy decisions made to meet the needs of both young and old in the next century should be the special concern of women now in their middle years.

The picture is fairly rosy for women who reach 40 in the year 2000. Health, which is the prime concern of the elderly, may be greatly improved. Older women can expect that the quality of the years after 50 may be physically much better than that experienced by older women today or in previous decades. Women's life expectancy will grow by at least two more years of continued vigor and good health. The goal of health maintenance—to be able to live out one's life span without crippling physical illness—appears within reach. Preventive health care, with adequate nutrition and exercise, based on a much better understanding of the aging body—and the aging woman's body—can help to realize this goal. Older women, too, will constitute most of the old-old, whose health care is especially costly.

Longevity, which favors women, may, however, prove to be a mixed blessing. Unless major medical breakthroughs occur in the understanding and prevention of Alzheimer's disease, for instance, many women living into their 80s may be victims. While the quality of life of the young-old may be greatly improved, that of the old-old may continue to be stressful and unrewarding (Mader & Ford, 1987; Riley & Riley, 1986; Stub, 1982; Warshow, 1981).

Because women of future cohorts will be far better educated than today's older women, they will have obtained and used health information that will prevent or reduce the impact of some of the degenerative diseases of old age. There will be wider dissemination of health information than ever before, much of it directed toward women. Women have always been more conscientious than men in health practices; in the future they will also have better data. More doctors will be trained in geriatrics and may understand how older men's and women's health needs differ and how they are the same. Doctors will have more accurate information about the differences in medication required by persons according to age and sex. Medical stereotypes and prejudices about older women may be a thing of the past (Lewis & Butler, 1972). Better health means that age 65 in the year 2000 may not have the same meaning it has today or has had in the past (Neugarten & Neugarten, 1986).

Greater understanding of menopause will result in better response to this normal phenomenon. Instead of being classified as a disease (McKinlay & McKinlay, 1986; National Advisory Council on Aging, 1980), as it so often is today, menopause will be understood as a normal part of female aging. In addition, undesirable physiological outcomes of menopause may be ameliorated with appropriate interventions when the full process of menopause is more adequately described (Nicosia, 1986).

As the very large numbers of individuals of the baby-boom generation move into the ranks of the elderly, it is probable that social evaluation of what it means to grow old will change. The media will discover that mature and older individuals are a relatively unexploited market, which may be a mixed blessing. Advertising may attract new customers but not always for desirable products. The youth orientation of our culture may shift to one in which maturity—over 40 and under 60—will be seen as desirable. it is the mature individual who will dominate the mass media, rather than the anorexic nymphets who were so ubiquitous in the 60s and 70s. There will be a general recognition that female sexuality not only does not decrease with age, it often improves. The shift in emphasis has already been observed in the 1980s.

The three-generation family of today has become the norm. With increased longevity, four or even five generations of many families may be alive at the same time in the foreseeable future (Riley, 1985). As Riley points out, "Because women are the more longevitous, they are most likely to stand alone at the top of the ladder—expected to develop new relationships that can earn, not demand, from their descendant kin the companionship, advice, and emotional support needed as death approaches" (p. 337).

Older women tomorrow, similar to older women today, will face the loneliness of widowhood and divorce. If women were to shift their marriage choices to men younger than themselves—an unlikely change—widowhood could be less typical. However, women will continue and perhaps increase their network of close friends, with whom they will establish shared or nearby living arrangements. The importance of such friends will grow because women will have fewer children to depend on for support in old age (Treas, 1981). The small families typical of the generations since the 1960s may present problems for the older woman. Although she may have cared for an ailing mother when she was in her middle years, as she herself gets older and needs such care, her one or two children may be less available. Because she will live so long, she may well outlive her resources (Hess, 1986). Though, as Riley (1985) points out, there is the potential for a greatly expanded kin network structure that can provide new options for older persons "to select and activate those relationships they deem most significant. Deep and diverse shared experiences now accrue to kindred over their long lives. The family structure is not what it used to be, nor is the process of growing old within the family."

Where there are gaps in social support, social services may be expected to intervene in those instances where neither friends nor family can help. Social policies will have to be reexamined to be sure they meet the needs of the "new old" women of the 21st century and are not continuations of outmoded policies developed earlier.

The able but lonely older woman in the future will find better and more varied alternatives in housing than she can find today. The choice between a nursing home or loneliness in a substandard room or apartment, trapped by fear of street crime, will be supplanted by affordable or subsidized eldercare hostels and residences, providing both independence and support from skilled professionals as needed. Such housing will recognize the affiliative needs of older women by more sensitive space planning and extensive opportunities for shared governance, allowing older women to exercise their skills and stay in charge of their own lives. New legislation in the 1980s promises to provide expanded Medicare and Medicaid support for alternative care so that nursing homes no longer will be the only option for many older women.

There will also be a very large number of the old-old group of women who cannot exist independently. Because so many women will need nursing home care, reforms in the delivery of such care and more active monitoring of those institutions will be necessary.

Older women in the next century will be better educated. A significant number will have completed four years of college, and many more will have advanced professional degrees. Today's older women are among the last of the huge immigrant generation of the 1900s, many of whom were uneducated and barely literate. Their work experience, if they had any, was intermittent and in the least skilled and the lowest-paying job categories. Relatively few were covered by pensions. By contrast, the older woman of two or three decades hence will have had a substantial work life, and many will have been well paid professionals and managers. There will be greatly decreased sex segregation on the job, allowing many women to ascend career ladders (Hess, 1986). Some women will not benefit as much from these overall trends, the same ones who are the least likely to benefit today: Blacks, Hispanics, and recent Asian immigrants and refugees. As they age, the women in these groups will resemble the first-generation older women of the 1980s. For such women, improved social services will continue to be absolutely essential as they reach middle and old age.

Unlike older women today, many women in the next century will be able to retire with adequate pensions because more firms will provide adequate retirement benefits protected by federal legislation, and sex inequities in coverage will be eliminated. The work patterns of women are expected to change. Higher rates of labor force participation and higher rates of persistence at work mean increased entitlement to retirement benefits (O'Rand, 1984). With good pensions older women will be able to enjoy a rich, active, and secure old age. However, as O'Rand points out,

> Public programs have been shaped by assumptions based on the life experience of men. In fact, the whole debate on aging is still often framed in what can only be considered masculinist terms: The need to work, the trauma of retirement, finding something like "work" to keep the old folk happy, or activity of any kind—as befits a society founded on the Protestant Ethic. Yet not only are the real problems of old age disproportionately experienced by women, but it is women who are increasingly expected to bear the brunt of dealing with these problems.

Older women may find that they can work as long as they wish. Their skills will be more valued and needed as the number of younger workers available declines. Bird (1987) provides an optimistic picture of the possibilities for older workers in the decades ahead. Part-time work may also be more available and attractive for older women.

The women's movement will have benefited older women even though many would disavow any feminist alliance and, except for a few strong voices, the women's movement has ignored older women (Lewis & Butler, 1972). But during their working lives women will have received equal pay for equal work or comparable work, and they will expect—and in most cases receive—equal treatment as they seek career advancement. Probably the single most important influence on the quality of the lives of older women will be this change in the world of work, since the benefits will be evident long after retirement from active employment (Hess, 1986).

It may be that the sheer numbers of women employed in formerly all-male enterprises will have a recognizable effect on how such activities are performed. More humane workplace policies will have a major impact on working women, as will the greater sensitivity on the part of women managers to the occupational hazards of the job site. More women in management could well mean that "women's issues" (more rightly named "parent issues"), such as subsidized child care in the workplace, maternity leave without jeopardizing job futures, and support for caring for an ailing parent, will be accepted as social policy in both the public and private sectors. Career patterns based on male norms, which have penalized women, will give way to career expectations that take into account women as grandmothers, mothers, and daughters as well as workers.

This will also be the first full generation to enjoy open access to birth control and legal abortion. Freedom from the fear of unwanted pregnancy, which so limited the options of women until this generation, will have many consequences, not the least of which is the increased sense of autonomy and self-esteem that women will experience when they are in control of their own destiny. Future cohorts of older women will undoubtedly be more assertive in demands for equal treatment at home and abroad. Women, unlike men, will experience significantly new patterns of work and family life. Liberating as these new forms may be, they will not be accomplished without much stress and tension (Hagestad, 1986; Riley & Riley, 1986).

Older women in the year 2000, energetic and physically more healthy than any previous cohorts, will put their energies into political activism for all kinds of causes. As Riley (1985) points out,

> Longevity will give women a new capacity for self-hood—for independence, personal mastery, assurance. Women can use this capacity to give new character to outmoded structures: To bulwark humane standards in political life in face of reaction and militarism; to teach employers to expect what older workers have long since come to know about their own competence . . . ; to infuse leisure with their special expressive and artistic talents and their accumulated experience.

The male establishment will not be able to ignore or ridicule these women advocates into silence because there will be so many of them. In fact, the next century may see a mature woman inaugurated President; and when the great powers gather in summit meetings, Margaret Thatcher's successor will be joined by a number of other women heads of state (Rossi, 1986).

Westernization will force tremendous changes in the social fabric of developing countries, much of it disruptive of traditional values. In many such societies the revered status of elderly women or their access to power when they pass menopause may give way before a market economy, and their situation will be far worse than today. In other instances tribal cultural restrictions on women will be broken to free women from powerlessness and male exploitation. The cruel and life-threatening practice of clitorectomy may be replaced by modern concepts of propriety, and the negative prejudices against females will be softened if not wholly eradicated. It will be many generations, however, before older women in traditional cultures will be adequately protected and nurtured if these groups continue to experience social revolutions, economic upheaval, and mass poverty and starvation. Meanwhile, older women in many developing countries will continue to be at risk as marginal persons.

Ethnic minorities in the United States, particularly Hispanics and Blacks, will dominate social and political life in a number of areas of the country because they produce far more children per family than majority whites. Older women in these groups may not be as well off as their peers among whites, but they will benefit from more enlightened policies of social services and medical assistance. It will take several generations more before minority women in old age achieve the educational levels and financial stability of their white peers and enjoy comparable years of life expectancy (Torres-Gil, 1986; Watson, 1986).

It has been noted by some gerontologists that since women constitute the majority of the aged, and this ratio will not change in the foreseeable future, issues of old age are increasingly apt to be considered women's issues. There is danger here because issues so labeled tend to be ignored or given only token treatment. The millions of women affected by poverty, who are desperately in need of adequate health and child care so that they can move out of dependency, have a hard time being heard because they are powerless and politically naive. Older women, however, in the generations to come, will be neither. In the next century most older women can expect to enjoy a more challenging and satisfying time of life than did their mothers or grandmothers.

RESEARCH: UNANSWERED QUESTIONS

For research to help guide programs for women in the next century, gerontologists must first admit that sex differences make a difference. As we have noted time and again in this volume, much research on older people lumps them into a neutered category: elders. Studies that have taken age into account have been done "mainly on men, despite major, well-known sex differences in many physiological functions" (Bierman & Brody, 1976, p. 15). In some instances the processes may be the same, but unless we test our data for sex differences, we will not know for sure. One of the greatest medical mysteries of all—why women outlive men—is worthy of sustained research study; it is certainly in the interests of men that this research be undertaken (Bierman & Brody, 1978).

In such a crucial area as prescribing appropriate medication, research is needed to see if prescribed drugs act the same way in a female as in a male body; we know that many basic physiological processes differ by sex in old age [Pepper & Robinson, 1987; Simonson, 1984 (especially chap. 2 and 6)]. There is still a great deal that is not known about why women suffer more than men do from a greater number of chronic diseases in old age. Arthritis, for example, is a great crippler of women as they age, but why men succumb at a later age is not known. We don't know why women get far fewer heart attacks after age 50 than men do. Typically, more drugs are prescribed for older women than for men, but it is not clear if this is based on medical need only or, as some observers suspect, on stereotypes regarding women's health complaints; or it may be for the convenience of doctors. Differential medical treatment of men and women for the same diseases in old age needs scrutiny.

The basic physiology of aging in women is less well known than that of men because much more medical research has been done on men than on women. Conspicuously missing are extensive longitudinal studies of women as they age comparable to those conducted on men. A few are underway today, but many more are needed on all aspects of women's lives. It is particularly hard to reconcile the neglect of research on older women with the fact that most older people are women, but traditional practices die hard. Men have designed and conducted most of the research in gerontology, and men study men or are oblivious to sex differences. As more women move into medical and gerontological research, we can be hopeful that this neglect will no longer be the norm.

Menopause, the unique female biological event, is still far from fully understood, but it is relatively little studied. The complicated effects of estrogen replacement therapy need considerable study if women are not to be put at risk by careless medical practices (Mastroianni & Paulsen, 1986). Medical exploitation of older women, such as cosmetic surgery and unneeded hysterectomies, needs to be more carefully monitored (Simonson, 1984). A recent report (Payer, 1988) comparing medical practices in the United States with other Western countries revealed there were far fewer hysterectomies performed in France than in our country. Are the subsequent cancer rates sufficient to defend United States practices?

Women are far less likely to commit suicide in old age than men are. Of those women who do give way to despair, we know little about its causation in old age (Kastenbaum & Mishra, 1981). The greater incidence of alcohol and illegal drug abuse and criminality among older men than among older women could be better understood if the mechanisms that work to inhibit women from these activities were known.

The mass media can have a tremendous impact on attitudes, but we have only partial understanding of how the perception of aging—that of others and of our own—is formed. Research is needed to understand better how the quality of women's lives is influenced by media representations. When all generations share television as their basic source of information about their world, we suspect that something culturally significant occurs. How similar or different will the basic values and moral attitudes of older and younger women be when both are equally avid viewers of "Dynasty," "Miami Vice," and "The Golden Girls" or whatever the current popular fantasy television world? Will the generation gap disappear in the future? How will the new awareness of the elderly as a potentially rich consumer market in turn influence how the older woman feels about herself? Will advertising continue to stress new skin treatments to erase the appearance of age, or will the emphasis be on the beauty of the mature woman, wrinkles and all?

In recent years women's studies and women's scholarship have increased tremendously, but the impact on women students—how women view themselves in culture and society—will not be felt until the next century. There are some key research questions that should be raised: How will changed views of women's roles in history and culture affect how older women will feel and act? The women who have been the pioneers in these endeavors, now young or middle-aged adults, may continue to be intellectual pioneers in old age as well; what will be the consequences?

We know relatively little about marriage and family relations in old age. The erosion of norm-driven decision making has resulted in more freedom for women to pursue nontraditional goals, such as returning to college in midlife or obtaining skills for a career change. Negatively, such a lack of a normative base for life-event sequences may leave many women feeling uneasy. When is the "right time" to be a grandmother, for example? We noted one study of very young grandmothers, but what happens when there is an entire cohort with many 40-year-old grandmothers, while at the same time there is a large clustering of much older grandmothers, those who postponed having children till there late 30s or 40s? How does the role of grandmother change? What does it mean to an older woman when her children, and their children, draw on her resources of time and money? Grandmotherhood is a greatly understudied family role. It seems obvious to assume that divorce or widowhood occurring at age 40 or at age 60 will have different effects on a woman, but we have few studies that help us understand what may happen because of age effects. As O'Rand (1984) points out, "the lifetime effects on women of pursuing different roles on different schedules are yet to be ascertained."

How do women feel about remarriage at age 50? Age 65? How can this option become more available if women want it? What is the impact on old age when having children is postponed until the middle or late 30s? And the never-married: are they different from those in previous generations, and how will this growing number of women deal with aging?

We have little information about how retirement affects marital relations and how women feel about and cope with their husbands' retirement as well as their own. Since relatively few women in previous generations worked long enough for retirement to be a significant social event, little research has been done on the meaning of retirement in the lives of women. How has aging affected the work opportunities of older women if they choose to remain in or reenter the work force? What is the extent of ageist (and sexist) prejudice against older women? (Hess, 1986).

The housing preferences of older women have been little studied. What kind of planning is needed for housing those older women who no longer can or want to live alone? How does living in a retirement community affect women? How can nursing home care be geared toward women's needs, interests, and life-styles—if in fact they are different from men's (Levenson, 1987)?

There are tremendous gaps in our knowledge about how older women fare in minority and ethnic groups in our own country. Particularly missing are studies of Hispanics who are the fastest-growing subgroup in our culture and will soon be the majority group in many areas. We lack basic data on family life, child rearing, the place of the elders in these families, and the changing role of women. Blacks have been studied more, but we need insight into what conditions help individuals escape the poverty ghetto and the role of older women in this process.

All of the needed research would be greatly assisted if we had an adequate theory about women's aging. Theories about life-span development that have wide acceptance are based on male experience and provide limited explanations of the how and why of women's lives. We need far better research and analysis of women's personality development and change in maturity and later.

As Neugarten (1985) points out, there is considerable research on how society influences how people age; but seldom is the question asked: How does the presence of increasing numbers of older people affect society? Will the fact that the majority of older persons are women make a significant societal difference as well?

Finally, current and future research about older women needs to be incorporated into the texts on gerontology and human development and into the major references that are the authoritative sources for many students of gerontology. The stereotypes, misconceptions, and misinformation, and casual omission of the available data about older women is disturbing. Scholarly journal literature needs to be monitored in the future to assure analysis of findings for gender differences wherever appropriate. Researchers need to be aware of the particular nature of the group they are studying; unlike other general population groups this is one where women predominate increasingly with every added year of life. When these changes in analyzing and disseminating research are accomplished, we may well be on the road to a fuller description and understanding of the promises and perils of growing old female.

SUMMARY

There are many reasons to predict that the world of older women in the next century will be better than may women experience today—assuming no great economic or nuclear catastrophe. Older women will be healthier, wealthier, and wiser. And there will be so many of them that they can have a major influence on public policy.

Much of this optimistic prediction and dissemination depends on the expanded production of better research on every aspect of women's lives and throughout the life span. What we know about older persons in general is too little compared to what we know about infancy, for instance. Women must be aggressive and vigilant in their insistence that research in every discipline include women and, when the subjects of study are both male and female, that the results are analyzed by gender.

The human life span has a finite limit as far as we now know, but with adequate understanding of the aging process in both women and men and of the social context in which this takes place we can do far more than we now do to vastly improve the quality of life of the final decades.

REFERENCES

Bierman, E. L., & Brody, H. (Eds.). (1976). *Report of the Panel on Biomedical Research*. NIH Publication No. 78-1445. Washington, DC: Government Printing Office.

Bird, C. (1987). The shape of work to come. *Modern Maturity, 30*(3), 33–45.

Hagestad, G. O. (1986). The aging society and family life. *Daedalus, 115*(1), 119–140.

Hess, B. B. (1986). Antidiscrimination policies today and the life chances of older women tomorrow. *The Gerontologist, 26*(2), 132–135.

Jones, L. Y. (1980). *Great expectations: America and the baby boom generation*. New York: Ballantine.

Kastenbaum, R., & Mishra, B. L. (1981). Premature death and self-injurious behavior. In R. Kastenbaum (Ed.), *Old age in the new scene* (pp. 269–282). New York: Springer Publishing Co.

Levenson, S. (1987). Innovations in nursing home care. *Generations, 22*(1), 74–79.

Lewis, M. I., & Butler, R. N. (1972). Why is women's lib ignoring old women? *Aging and Human Development, 3*, 223–231.

Mader, S. L. & Ford, A. B. (1987). Morbidity and mortality trends among the aged: Effects on clinical practice. *Generations, 22*(1), 5–7.

Mastroianni, L., & Paulsen, C. A. (Eds.). (1986). *Aging, reproduction and the climacteric*. New York: Plenum.

McKinlay, S. M., & McKinlay, J. B. (1986). Health status and health care in menopausal women. In L. Mastroianni & C. A. Paulsen (Eds.), *Aging, reproduction and the climacteric* (pp. 243–262). New York: Plenum.

National Advisory Council on Aging. (1980). *Our future selves: A research plan toward understanding aging. Summary reports*. NIH Publication No. 80-1446. Washington, DC: Government Printing Office.

Neugarten, B. L. (1985). Interpretive social science and research on aging. In A. S. Rossi (Ed.), *Gender and the life course* (pp. 291–300). New York: Aldine.

Neugarten, B. L. & Neugarten, D. A. (1966). Age in the aging society. *Daedalus, 115*(1), 31–50.

Nicosia, S. V. (1986). Ovarian changes during the climacteric. In L. Mastroianni & C. A. Paulsen (Eds.), *Aging, reproduction and the climacteric* (pp. 179–200). New York: Plenum.

O'Rand, A. (1984). Women. In E. B. Palmore (Ed.), *Handbook on aging in the United States* (pp. 125–142). Westport, CT: Greenwood Press.

Payer, L. (1988). *Medicine and culture: Varieties of treatment in the United States, England, West Germany, and France*. New York: Hentry Holt.

Pepper, G. A., & Robbins, L. J. (1987). Improving geriatric drug therapy. *Generations, 22*(1), 57–60.

Riley, M. W. (1985). Women, men, and the lengthening life course. In A. S. Rossi (Ed.), *Gender and the life course* (pp. 333–347). New York: Aldine.

Riley, M. A. & Riley, J. W. (1986). Longevity and social structure: The added years. *Daedalus, 115*(1), 31–50.

Rossi, A. S. (1986). Sex and gender in an aging society. *Daedalus, 115*(1), 141–170.

Simonson, W. (1984). *Medications and the elderly*. Rockville, MD: Aspen Systems.

Stub, H. R. (1982). *The social consequences of long life*. Springfield, IL: Charles C. Thomas.

Torres-Gil, F. (1986). An examination of factors affecting future cohorts of elderly Hispanics. *The Gerontologist, 26*(2), 140–146.

Treas, J. (1981). The great American fertility debate: Generational balance and support of the aged. *The Gerontologist, 21*(1) 98–103.

Warshow, H. J. (Ed.). (1981). *Controversial issues in gerontology*. New York: Springer Publishing Co.

Watson, W. H. (1986). Crystal ball gazing: Notes on today's middle aged Blacks with implications for their aging in the 21st century. *The Gerontologist, 26*(2), 136–139.

Bibliography

BIOGRAPHIES AND MEMOIRS OF OLDER WOMEN

Ball, A. J. *Caring for an Aging Parent: Have I Done All I Can?* Buffalo, NY: Prometheus Books, 1987. Based on author's experiences with her aging father.

Barresi, C. M. (1987). Ethnic aging and the life course. In D. E. Gelfand & C. M. Barresi (Eds.), *Ethnic dimensions of aging* (pp. 18–34). New York: Springer Publishing Co.

Bell, M. J. (Ed.). *Women as Elders: Images, Visions, and Issues.* New York: Haworth Press, 1987.

Boyle, S-P. *The Desert Blooms.* Nashville, TN: Abingdon Press, 1983. A 60-year-old woman considers her own aging.

Brown, D. S. *Handle with Care: A Question of Alzheimer's.* Buffalo, NY: Prometheus Books, 1984. The author's experiences with her mother's illness.

Bryn Mawr College. Between the generations: Thoughts on aging from the young, the old, and those in the middle. *Alumnae Bulletin*, Spring, 1986, 2–31.

Carpenter, L. *Getting Better All the Time.* Simon and Schuster, 1987. Life after a life in politics.

Cohler, B. J. (1982). Stress or support: Relations between older women from three European ethnic groups and their relatives. In R. C. Manuel (Ed.), *Minority aging* (pp. 115–120). Westport, CT: Greenwood Press.

Danforth, A. *Living with Alzheimer's: Ruth's Story*. Falls Church, VA: Prestige Press, 1987.

deBeauvoir, S. *The Coming of Age*. New York: Putnam, 1972.

Federal Council on Aging. (1979). *Policy issues concerning elderly minorities: A staff report*. Washington, DC: Department of Health and Human Services.

Francis, D. *Will You Still Need Me, Will You Still Feed Me, When I'm 84?* Bloomington, IN: Indiana University Press, 1984. Narratives of 20 elderly Jewish women in Cleveland and Leeds, England.

Hemmings, S. *A Wealth of Experience: The Lives of Older Women*. Boston: Routledge & Kegan Paul, 1985. Eight women aged 45 to 60 recount memories of their world from World War II on.

Hubbell, S. *A Country Year*. New York: Harper and Row, 1986. Thoughts of a 50-year-old divorcee.

Kates, B. *Murder of a Shopping Bag Lady*. New York: Harcourt Brace Jovanovich, 1985. A reporter investigates the lives of homeless old women.

Keith, J. (1986). Aging in anthropological research. In R. H. Binstock & E. Shanas (Eds.), *Handbook of aging and the social sciences* (pp. 231–263). New York: Van Rostrand Reinhold.

Kramer, S. and Masur, J. (Eds.). *Jewish Grandmothers*. Boston: Beacon Press, 1976.

Laird, C. *Limbo*. Novato, CA: Chandler and Sharp, 1979. Memoir of life in a nursing home.

LeShan, E. *Oh, to Be 50 Again! On Being Too Old for a Mid-Life Crisis*. New York: New York Times Books, 1986. Author at age 63.

Levin, R. F. *Heartmates: A Survival Guide for the Cardiac Spouse*. Englewood Cliffs, NJ: Prentice Hall, 1987. Author's experiences with her husband's illness.

Marriott, A. *The Ten Grandmothers*. Norman, OK: University of Oklahoma Press, 1983. Older women of the Kiowas, a tribe of Plains Indians.

McNeely, R. L. (1983). Race, sex and victimization of the elderly. In R. L. McNeely & J. L. Colen (Eds.), *Aging in minority groups (pp. 137*–152). Beverly Hills, CA: Sage.

Miller, A. (1971). *The portable Arthur Miller*. New York: Viking.

Painter, C. *Gifts of Age: Portraits and Essays of 32 Remarkable Women*. San Francisco: Chronicle Books, 1985. With photographs: women aged 61 to 103.

Paullin, E. (1986). *Ted's Stroke: The Caregiver's Story*, Bethesda, MD: Seven Locks Press.

Policy Issues Concerning Elderly Minorities: A Staff Report. (1979). Federal Council on the Aging, Washington, DC: Department of Health and Human Services.

Roach, M. (1975). *Another Name for Madness*. New York: Houghton Mifflin. A 50-year-old woman with Alzheimer's disease.

Rollin, B. *First, You Cry*. New York: Simon and Schuster, 1976. The author's bout with breast cancer.

———. *Last Wish*. New York: Simon and Schuster, 1985. On her mother's self-induced death at the last stages of cancer.

Rosenwaike, I., & Dolinsky, A. (1987). The changing demographic determinants of the growth of the extreme aged. *The Gerontologist, 27*(3), 275–280.

Sarton, M. *Journal of Solitude*, 1973; *A House by the Sea: A Journal*, 1977; *Recovering: A Journal*, 1980; *At Seventy: A Journal*, 1984. New York: W. W. Norton. Journals of a novelist and poet as she considers aging.

Scott-Maxwell, F. *The Measure of My Days*. New York: Penguin, 1968. Passionate journal of an 80-year-old.

Sheehan, S. *Kate Quinton's Days*. New York: Houghton Mifflin, 1984. A year in the life of a poverty-stricken disabled 80-year-old.

Simic, A. (1983). Aging in the United States and Yugoslavia: Contrasting models of intergenerational relationships. In J. Sokolovsky (Ed.), *Growing old in different societies* (pp. 82–91). Belmont, CA: Wadsworth.

Slaughter, O. W., & Batey, M. O. (1982). Service delivery and the Black aged: Identifying barriers to utilization of mental health services. In R. C. Manuel (Ed.), *Minority aging* (pp. 171–177). Westport, CT: Greenwood Press.

Strong, M. *Mainstay: For the Well Spouse of the Chronically Ill*. Boston: Little Brown, 1985. The author's experience.

Taylor, R. J. (1986). Religious participation among elderly blacks. *The Gerontologist, 26*(6), 630–636.

Truitt, A. *Turn: The Journal of an Artist*. New York: Viking Press, 1986.

Vining, E. G. *Being Seventy*. New York: Viking/Penguin, 1978.

Walker, B. G. (1985). *The crone: Women of age, wisdom and power*. New York: Harper and Row.

Weinberg, S. S. *The World of Our Mothers: The Lives of Jewish Immigrant Women*. Chapel Hill, NC: University of North Carolina Press, 1988.

Wing, S., Manton, K. G., Stallard, E., Mannes, C. G., & Tryolar, H. A. (1985). The Black/White mortality crossover investigation in a community based study. *Journal of Gerontology, 40*(1), 78–84.

Wolf, B. H. *The Ways of My Grandmothers*. New York: Morrow, 1981. Traditions and wisdom of older Blackfoot Indian women.

POPULAR BOOKS ON OLDER WOMEN'S LIVES AND HEALTH

Bryan, J. (Ed.). *Love Is Ageless: Stories about Alzheimer's Disease*. Oakland, CA: Serala Press, 1987.

Butler, R. N., and Lewis, M. L. *Love and Sex after 40: A Guide for Men and Women in Their Mid and Later Years*. New York: Harper and Row, 1986.

Carlin, V., and Mansberg, R. *Where Can Mom Live? A Family Guide to Living Arrangements for Elderly Parents*. Lexington, MA: Lexington Books, 1987.

Egginton, M., Kungonis, J., Mint, J., and Roser, D. *An Older Woman's Health Guide*. New York: McGraw-Hill, 1984.

Fiske, M. *Middle Age: The Prime of Life?* New York: Harper and Row, 1979.

Fonda, J. *Women Coming of Age*, New York: Simon and Schuster, 1985.

Hammond, D. B. *My Parents Never Had Sex: Myths and Facts on Sexual Aging*. Buffalo, NY: Prometheus Books, 1987.

Henig, R. M., and the Editors of *Esquire* Magazine. *How a Woman Ages: Growing Older—What to Expect and What You Can Do About It*. New York: Balantine Books, 1985.

Jacobs, R. H. *Life after Youth: Female, Forty, What Next?* Boston: Beacon Press, 1980.

———. *Older Women: Surviving and Thriving: A Manual for Group Leaders*. Milwaukee, WI: Family Service America, 1987.

Loewinsohn, R. J. *Survival Handbook for Widows (and for Relatives and Friends Who Want to Understand)*. Glenview, IL: AARP and Scott, Foresman, 1984.

Melmed, E. *Mirror, Mirror: The Terror of Not Being Young*. New York: Simon and Schuster, 1983.

Oberleder, M. *Avoiding the Aging Trap*. Washington, DC: Acropolis Books, 1982.

Tomb, D. A. *Growing Old: A Handbook for You and Your Aging Parents*. New York: Viking, 1984.

Veith, I. *Can You Hear the Clapping of One Hand? Learning to Live with a Stroke*. Berkeley, CA: University of California Press, 1988.

Indices

Author Index

Subject Index